MOON

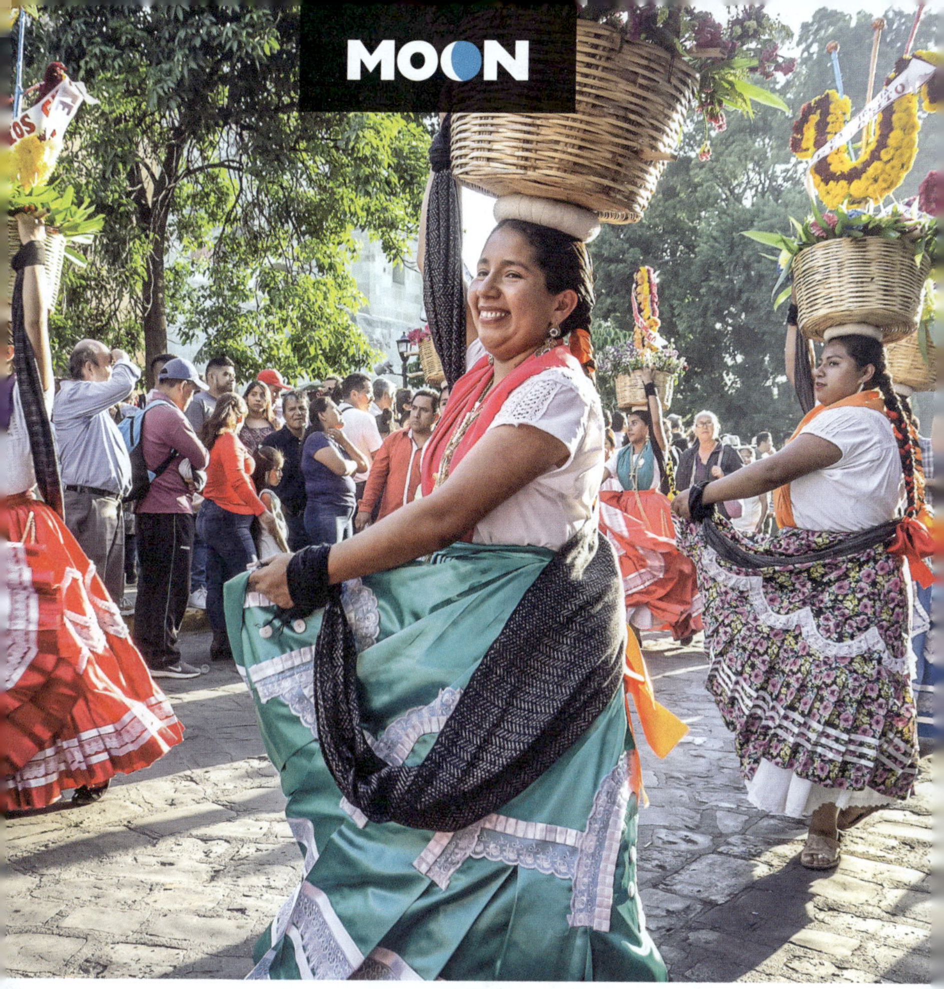

Oaxaca

ASHLEY C. ROBERTS

PUEBLA
GUERRERO
Izúcar
Tepanco de López
Cosolapa
Vicente Camalote
L. Miguel Alemán
María Isabel
Temascal
Huautla de Jiménez
Teotitlán de Flores Magón
San Felipe Jalapa de Díaz
Santa María Tecomavaca
San Juan Bautista Cuicatlán
Tomellín
Valle Nacional
SIERRA MADR
Huajuapan
San Juan Bautista Coixtlahuaca
Tamazulapan
Santo Domingo Tonalá
SAN PEDRO
Teposcolula
Santo Domingo Yanhuitlán
Nochixtlan
San Miguel Tlacotepec
Santiago Juxtlahuaca
San Martín Huamelúlpam
Tlaxiaco
MONTE NEGRO
San Pablo Huitzo
Ixtlan de Juárez
Villa de Etla
Poblado Morelos
Cuajimoloy
MONTE ALBÁN
OAXACA
Santa María del Tule
OAXACA INT'L AIRPORT
Vicente Guerrero
Tlacolula
Santiago Matatlán
San Pablo Huixtepec
Ocotlán de Morelos
Llano de las Flores
Putla Villa de Guerrero
SIERRA MADRE DEL SUR
San Sebastián de las Grutas
San Juan Cacahuatepec
Santa Catarina
Cuajinicuilapa
Ejutla
Pinotepa Nacional
Miahuatlán
Santiago Jamiltepec
Santa Catarina Juquila
San José del Pacífi
Laguna de Corralero
San José del Progreso
Río Grande
Parque Nacional Lagunas de Chacahua
Puerto Escondido
Pluma Hidalg
Santa María Huatulco
Pochutla
Mazunte
Puerto Ángel
PACIFIC OCEAN
Atoyac
Mixteco
Salado
Grande
Usila
Colorado
Verde
150
190
125
135D
93
135
175
182
131
200
OAXACA

Gulf of Mexico
Santiago Tuxtla
San Andrés Tuxtla
Catemaco
Laguna Catemaco
Cosamaloapan
Papaloapan
Sánchez Magallanes
Laguna de la Machona
Campo Magallanes
Juan Díaz Covarrubias
San Juan
Coatzacoalcos
Tuxtepec
Tesechoacan
Isla
Ixhuatlán del Sureste
Cosoleacaque
Minatitlán
Acayucan
Jáltipan
Bethania
Sayula de Alemán
VERACRUZ
Playa Vicente
Coatzacoalcos
San Juan
Trinidad
DE OAXACA
Palomares
Sarabia
Piedra Blanca
El Corte
SIERRA ATRAVESADA
San Sebastián
Tehuantepec
Los Perros
La Venta
Niltepec
Ixtepec
Presa Benito Juárez
Jalapa del Marqués
Juchitán
Niltepec
CHIAPAS
Tequisistlán
San Pedro Tapanatepec
Laguna Superior
Laguna Inferior
Tehuantepec
Arriaga
Salina Cruz
Mar Muerto
Gulf of Tehuantepec
Bahías de Huatulco
0
25 mi
0
25 km
180
145D
175
185
180D
145
179
147
145D
147
185
185D
190
190
185
200
200
© MOON.COM

Contents

Jalatlaco neighborhood decorated with papel picado

WELCOME TO

Oaxaca

To visit Oaxaca is to be caught up in a melody you didn't know your heart was yearning for. Oaxaca is filled with vibrant cultures, ancient traditions, enchanting landscapes, and world-renowned cuisine that will make you hum with delight. The whole state is bursting with rhythms waiting to be explored.

Just spend one morning in the jewel-colored capital Oaxaca City, awakening to the spirited cries of street vendors tempting your palate with warm atole and tropical fruits. As you wind through colorful markets, voices croon in friendly competition, serenading you to sample their wares. Nights are filled with laughter over clinking glasses of mezcal.

Travel outside the capital to pick up on the softer choruses of Oaxaca's natural and human-made marvels: the gentle lapping of the turquoise waves, the mighty crescendo of the ocean's surf, the call of flocks of green macaws gliding through the northern canyons. Soaring arches of Dominican architecture seem filled with echoes of heavenly hymns. Even the clouds imbued with the last golden and vermillion rays of the setting sun as seen from pine-filled mountain peaks seem to breathe out a lovely sigh.

Underneath it all, you'll find the steady beat of pride. The streets are filled with colorful festivals, parades, and parties all year long celebrating its rich heritage. The people and their diverse histories and traditions are what make Oaxaca the grand symphony it is.

Oaxaca is music, and once its song enters your heart, you'll be hard pressed to forget it. You'll find yourself agreeing wholeheartedly with the local saying "Como Oaxaca, no hay dos"—*Oaxaca, there is no one like you.*

Hierve El Agua

10 TOP EXPERIENCES

1 Exploring the structures, learning the history, and taking in the impressive views at **Monte Albán,** the ancient, pre-Hispanic capital of the Zapotecs (page 102).

2 Eating grilled meats, tlayudas, mole, and chapulines at Oaxaca City's **Mercado 20 de Noviembre** (pictured; page 76), then shopping for clothing, textiles, toys, herbs, produce, mezcal, and more for great prices at neighboring **Mercado Benito Juárez** (page 69).

3 Joining a **mezcal tour** to see how maguey plants are grown, harvested, traditionally distilled—and, best of all, how it tastes (page 64).

4 Taking in the colorful explosion of music and dance during the **Guelaguetza** festival, the largest and most joyful celebration of Oaxaca's ethnic and cultural diversity (page 65).

5 Admiring the colonial architecture of centuries-old cathedrals among the red dusted hills on the **Dominican Route** (page 215).

6 Snorkeling, yachting, fishing, or simply enjoying fresh seafood and a cerveza on the magical beaches of **Bahías de Huatulco** (page 178).

7 Honoring the dearly departed on **Día de Muertos** in Oaxaca City as the capital is bedecked with marigold-covered ofrendas and calaveras (page 66).

8 Hiking the **Pueblos Mancomunados,** a group of Zapotec villages connected by a network of trails in the beautiful Sierra Norte mountains (page 240).

9 Catching a break in **Puerto Escondido,** Mexico's surf capital, with wild waves to ride by day and oceanside party vibes at night (page 146).

10 Refreshing your spirit at a **temazcal,** where you enter a small, dark hut representing the womb of the earth, are cleansed with steam, herbs, and prayers, and emerge reborn into the world (page 36).

Planning Your Trip

WHERE TO GO

Oaxaca City

The lively capital city of Oaxaca de Juárez centers around the shady arcades of the **Zócalo,** or central plaza, from which everything the city has to offer is within walking distance. Just to the southwest are the bustling hives of the **Benito Juárez** and **20 de Noviembre markets.** The cobblestone streets to the north teem with art galleries, print shops, hip cafés and bars, Oaxacan and international restaurants, and much more of the green limestone colonial architecture that give this town its timeless character.

Valles Centrales

Sprawling desert vistas, ancient Zapotec ruins, and quaint artisan villages abound in this region that is often referred to as the Valley of Oaxaca. Spend a day shopping for local craftwork in **San Bartolo Coyotepec, Teotitlán del Valle,** or **Arrazola,** stuffing yourself with barbacoa along the way. Or admire handiwork dating back millennia at **Monte Albán** and **Mitla.** The otherworldly calcified stone "waterfalls" at **Hierve El Agua** will make you double-check what planet you're on.

La Costa and Istmo de Tehuantepec

Oaxaca's Pacific coast has beaches to suit all tastes, from surfing and nightlife in **Puerto Escondido,** to the luxury hotels and vacation homes of **Bahías de Huatulco,** to the quiet hippie hideaway of **Mazunte.** Also running along the coast are the verdant and vertiginous slopes of the Sierra Madre

Día de Muertos celebration

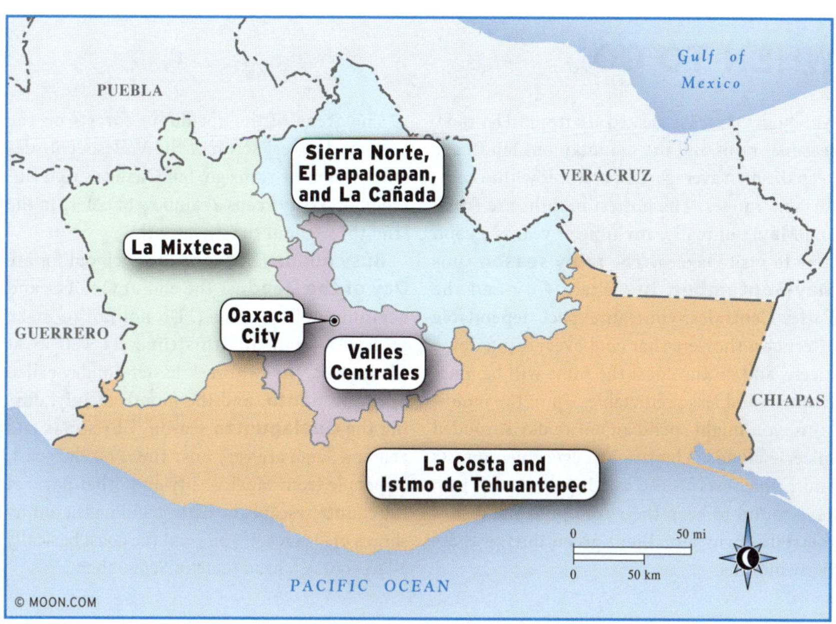

del Sur, home to **San José del Pacífico,** famous for its magic mushrooms, and **Pluma Hidalgo,** Oaxaca's prize coffee-producing village, as well as the highest peaks in the state.

The eastern terminus of the Sierra Madre del Sur is the **Istmo de Tehuantepec,** whose inhabitants really know how to party. No matter the time of year, there's a good chance a trip to the Isthmus will coincide with at least one of over a hundred velas, local festivals to celebrate patron saints and social cohorts. Puerto Escondido may boast the famed "Mexican Pipeline," but the waves off the shores of **Salina Cruz** are also of world-class quality, and the town boasts a number of surf camps and board shops.

La Mixteca

This lesser-visited region is the heartland of the Mixtecs, one of Oaxaca's most prominent indigenous cultures, and home to some of the finest examples of Dominican architecture in the state, as well as more archaeological zones, such as **Cerro de las Minas.** Visit the bustling weekly market of **Tlaxiaco** or get away from it all camping beneath the soaring cliffs of **Apoala.**

Sierra Norte, El Papaloapan, and La Cañada

The dense cloud forests, crystal-clear natural springs, and tropical rivers of the northern regions of Oaxaca offer a hearty buffet of rich experiences for nature lovers. Hike over 100 km (62 mi) of interconnected mountain paths of the **Pueblos Mancomunados,** sail to **La Isla del Viejo Soyaltepec,** and cool off in the mists of **Las Regaderas.**

WHEN TO GO

Although Oaxaca is located at a tropical latitude, seasonal rains and the mountainous landscape keep the high average temperatures within comfortable ranges. The hottest months are **April** and **May,** but really, any time of year is a good time to visit Oaxaca. The **rainy season** runs **May-September.** In Oaxaca City and the Valles Centrales, you can expect dependable afternoon showers that cool everything down nicely, and on the coast the rains will be more frequent and less predictable. Up in the mountains, you might spend an entire day shrouded in eerie clouds. The tropical evergreen forests and rainforests in the north get enough rain year-round to keep their color, but the rest of the state turns a brilliant green during these rainy months.

The green of the deciduous forests on the coast and desert scrub of the Valles Centrales fades when the rains go, but Oaxaca's rich floral biodiversity keeps a rainbow of colors in the land throughout the dry months.

Busy holiday seasons to watch out for are **Day of the Dead,** at the end of October and beginning of November. Do not fail to make reservations during this time, as well as at **Christmas,** the two-week Easter holiday called **Semana Santa,** and the month of July, during the **Guelaguetza** season. Christmas and Semana Santa are very busy times on the coast, as people from Mexico City and other parts of the country escape the daily grind on the sunny shores of Oaxaca. If you want the coast basically all to yourself, head there in September.

BEFORE YOU GO

Passports, Tourist Cards, and Visas

Make sure your **passport** has at least six months of validity left on it before you come to Mexico. It's not a guarantee that you won't be allowed in, but it's better not to risk it. You will not need to apply for a tourist visa before traveling.

If you fly to Oaxaca, the immigration fee will be included in your plane ticket, and you'll be given either a stamp in your passport, a receipt with a QR code, or a **tourist card** (known in Spanish as the **FMM,** Forma Migrátoria Múltiple) at the airport. While tourist cards are slowly being phased out, if given a tourist card, do not lose this, as you'll waste precious time and money replacing it. Make copies of everything once you arrive, and take the copies around when you leave your hotel. Stow the originals in a safe place in your accommodations.

If you cross at the border, you will have to stop in the immigration office upon entry and ask for a tourist card/FMM. You will be given the card and an invoice for the fee, which you will have to pay at a bank in Mexico before you leave. Don't forget to pay for it, and again, don't lose the card!

Vaccinations

Make sure all your basic vaccinations are up-to-date, and get vaccinated for **Hepatitis A** and **B.** If you're planning on doing some bushwhacking in the jungle, seriously consider vaccinations for nasty tropical bugs like **dengue, typhoid,** and **rabies,** just in case. Places like Apoala, in La Mixteca, are home to vampire bats that, although rarely, are known to sometimes bite people. Don't forget bug spray in these areas, either. I've been lucky with mosquito bites in Oaxaca, but you never want to find out what they carry by being their petri dish.

Reservations

For most of the year, you don't really need reservations for regular hotels just about anywhere in Oaxaca. However, always reserve ahead of time

If You Have...

- **FOUR DAYS:** If you've only got four days, spend them based in **Oaxaca City,** enjoying the city the first couple of days, and making trips out to towns in the **Valles Centrales.** For something different, spend your last day or two exploring the valleys from a base in **Mitla, Tlacolula,** or whichever town catches your fancy.
- **ONE WEEK:** A full week gives you enough time to do the aforementioned plan, with a few extra days for some adventuring. For those extra three days, you could go camping or stay in a cabaña in the **Pueblos Mancomunados** (in the **Sierra Norte**) or **Apoala** (in **La Mixteca**). Of course, the beach is also an option for those last few days.
- **TWO WEEKS:** This is the perfect amount of time for experiencing the incredible cultural, gastronomical, and natural gems of **central Oaxaca,** and then heading to the **coast** for a week of sand and surf. You won't find as many ecotourism opportunities in the **Sierra Sur** as you will in the north, but there are great hikes around **San José del Pacífico** and **Pluma Hidalgo.** For that week on the coast, you can bounce from beach to beach, or pick what suits your fancy from **Puerto Escondido, Bahías de Huatulco,** or the hippie beaches around **Puerto Ángel,** and just sit back and relax.

for ecotourism options that include stays in cabañas or at campsites.

Mountain biking in Oaxaca is very popular, and during high season, you most likely won't be able to walk into any agency and plan a mountain biking tour the next day. Make reservations well ahead of time with operators in Oaxaca City and even in lesser-visited areas like the Sierra Norte.

Transportation

The quickest way to get to Oaxaca is by **air,** and with the state's popularity rising, flights are easier to find. International airports in **Oaxaca City, Puerto Escondido,** and **Bahías de Huatulco** connect Oaxaca to the world at large. You can also travel within the state via these airports, but it will be more expensive, and you'll miss all the fun stuff on the ground along the way.

The great thing about Mexico is there is always a bus going your way. The majority of **long-distance buses** in Mexico are comfortable, have bathrooms, and play movies (or random dubbed '90s sitcoms). They are also freezing, so make sure to travel with a sweater or blanket. **Oaxaca City, Puerto Escondido,** and **Tehuantepec** are major hubs on the bus routes that go to and from Oaxaca.

Once in Oaxaca, you've got a ton of options for getting around, from **renting a car** to piling into a tiny **taxi** with five other people and their cargo for next to nothing. For longer distances in Oaxaca, take a 12-15-passenger van called a **suburban.** The companies usually have names like **Transportes Turísticos** or **Autotransportes.** For shorter distances, use the even more local **camionetas** (covered pickups) and **taxis colectivos** (shared taxis). On just about any highway in Oaxaca, you can flag down one of these types of transports, but make sure you're in a safe place for the vehicle to pull over, or they won't stop. Also, don't do it at night, anywhere. Within towns, and to get to towns close to highway intersections, a **mototaxi** will take you around for a few pesos.

La Punta, Puerto Escondido

BEST OF Oaxaca

Oaxaca is like its own country in terms of its geographic and cultural diversity. Each region has its own unique treasures to discover, so you could spend ages in each region without fear of running out of things to do. More good news for us explorers: It's a pretty easy state to navigate, and you can hit several of Oaxaca's highlights on this 10-day tour. Start your journey with a couple of days in the capital city, soaking in the best of the state's cultural, architectural, and gastronomic offerings. After a day of exploring the artisan villages of the Valles Centrales, wind your way through the southern mountains, stopping for a refreshing change of pace in San José del Pacífico. Finish your travels with a few days of relaxing on Oaxaca's gorgeous coast.

This itinerary can be done by rental car, but I recommend a mix of using private drivers and taking advantage of Oaxaca's excellent public transportation options. Taxis, colectivos, suburbans, and camionetas can take you everywhere you need to go on this 10-day trip.

Day 1: Oaxaca City

Start your day in the heart of the city—the **Zócalo.** After enjoying the people-watching and admiring the architecture, head a couple of blocks southwest to the neighboring mercados of **20 de Noviembre** (for eating—grab some mole) and **Benito Juárez** (for shopping). Refresh yourself with a tejate from **Flor de Huayapam.** After the morning mercado run, spend an hour or two exploring **Museo de Arte Prehispánico de México Rufino Tamayo.** Stop by the beautiful **Basilica de Nuestra Señora de Soledad** and enjoy the flavorful nieves at **Jardín Socrates.** Have dinner at **Tr3s 3istro** in Zócalo and enjoy the sights and sounds of a Oaxacan evening.

Day 2: Oaxaca City

Greet the morning with a walk in the garden—the **Jardín Etnobotanico de Oaxaca,** that is. Admire the ornate golden interior of **Templo Santo Domingo** and then explore the expansive **Centro Cultural Santo Domingo.** After lunch at **Los Pacos,** meander through the iconic narrow streets of **Jalatlaco.** For the evening, stroll down the pedestrian walkway **Andador Macedonio Alcala.** Top off the night with a mezcal tasting at **In Situ.**

Day 3: Valles Centrales

One of Oaxaca's most iconic attractions, **Monte Albán,** is just minutes outside the city and makes the perfect day trip. Hire a private driver or negotiate a taxi for the day, and plan to arrive at Monte Alban by 9am to avoid the worst of the crowds and sun. Spend a couple of hours exploring the mountaintop ruins of this ancient Zapotec capital. Have lunch at the on-site café before exploring the nearby artisan villages of **Arrazola** and **San Bartolo Coyotepec,** which specialize in alebrijes (brightly painted carved wooden figures) and barro negro (black clay pottery), respectively. Return to Oaxaca City and enjoy dinner at **Las Quince Letras.**

Day 4: San José del Pacífico

This small mountain village known for its mind-altering mushrooms has a lot of magic to offer, even without the psychedelic trips. Steaming cups of coffee and chocolate are especially delicious in the crisp, pine-kissed mountain air. Leave Oaxaca City by 8am or 9am so you can spend your day enjoying the views and hearty cooking at restaurants like **Cafetería Punto Sur** and **La Casa del Arbol,** hiking up to breathtaking miradores (lookout points), and delighting in the spectacular sunset. Spend the night at the natural respite **Refugio Terraza de la Tierra** or the cozy **Cabañas La Cumbre.**

Day 5: Bahías de Huatulco

Leave San José del Pacífico by 9am, so that by noon you can be splashing in the clear waters of **Playa La Entrega.** Go snorkeling and get a bite to eat at any of the many palapas (this is a great place for fresh raw oysters, with lime and chile). Take pics at **Mirador El Faro** on your way to **Playa Maguey,** where you can snorkel, kayak, float on giant inflatables, and swim—or

1: alebrijes **2:** Templo de Santo Domingo, Oaxaca City
3: Bahías de Huatulco

Choose Your Beach

With world-class surfing, primary global sea turtle nesting sites, nudist beaches, and accommodations options from hammocks to camping to rustic cabañas to five-star resorts, the Oaxacan coast has a beach for everyone. Here is a list of the best beaches organized by the primary activity (or lack thereof) on them.

SWIMMING

- **Playas Manzanillo and Puerto Angelito,** Puerto Escondido (page 144)
- **Playa Panteón,** Puerto Ángel (page 164)
- **Playa Santa Cruz,** Huatulco (page 185)
- **Playa La Entrega,** Huatulco (page 185)

SURFING

- **Playa Zicatela,** Puerto Escondido (page 144)
- **Punta Zicatela (La Punta),** Puerto Escondido (page 144)
- **Barra de la Cruz** (page 190)

SNORKELING

- **Playas Manzanillo and Puerto Angelito,** Puerto Escondido (page 144)
- **Playa La Entrega,** Huatulco (page 185)
- **Playa Maguey,** Huatulco (page 186)

SEA TURTLE OBSERVATION AND RELEASE

- **Playa Bacocho,** Puerto Escondido (page 146)
- **Mazunte** (page 170)
- **Playa La Ventanilla,** Mazunte (page 173)

CROCODILE CONSERVATION

- **Playa La Ventanilla,** Mazunte (page 173)

CAMPING

- **Chacahua,** Lagunas de Chacahua (page 158)
- **Playa Tangolunda,** Huatulco (page 188)
- **Barra de la Cruz** (page 190)

LETTING IT ALL HANG OUT (NUDISM)

- **Zipolite** (page 167)

PARTYING

- **Playa Zicatela,** Puerto Escondido (page 144)
- **Zipolite** (page 167)

SUNSETS

- **Punta Zicatela (La Punta),** Puerto Escondido (page 144)
- **Playa Bacocho,** Puerto Escondido (page 146)
- **La Punta Cometa,** Mazunte (page 170)

IN THE LAP OF LUXURY

- **Playa Carrizalillo,** Puerto Escondido (page 146)
- **Playas Chahué and Tangolunda,** Huatulco (page 188)

Oaxaca's Pueblos Mágicos

The Pueblos Mágicos are towns designated by the Mexican government as being noteworthy for their beauty, gastronomy, traditions, and history. There are over 170 magical towns (as of this writing) throughout Mexico, and Oaxaca is currently home to 6. Experience the magic for yourself.

VALLES CENTRALES

- **Mitla:** The "land of the dead," Oaxaca's second most significant archaeological ruins (page 117)

LA COSTA AND ISTMO DE TEHUANTEPEC

- **Mazunte:** Oaxaca's popular "hippie beach" with its gorgeous coastline and chill vibes (page 170)
- **Santa Catarina Juquila:** The seat of devotion to the diminutive Virgen de Juquila who draws thousands of devotees each December (page 161)

LA MIXTECA

- **San Pedro y San Pablo Teposcolula:** Home to the largest capilla abierta (open-air chapel) of its kind in Latin America (page 220)

SIERRA NORTE, EL PAPALOAPAN, AND LA CAÑADA

- **Capulálpam de Méndez:** Darling village in the Sierra Norte with many ecotourism opportunities (page 261)
- **Huautla de Jiménez:** Birthplace of the world-famous Mazatec curandera María Sabina, located in La Cañada (page 270)

just relax on the golden sand. Have dinner in **La Crucecita** at **Terra-Cotta** and enjoy an evening in the town's tiny but lively zócalo.

Day 6: Bahías de Huatulco

After a traditional and tasty breakfast at **Campestre Santa Clara,** take a day trip (booked in advance) to the **Cascadas Mágicas.** Spend a few hours soaking in the lush jungle views and cooling off in the crystal-clear pools of the waterfalls. Back in town, relax on **Playa Santa Cruz** before enjoying a fresh seafood dinner at **Doña Celia Lobster House.**

sunset from Terra Tipi bar in Chacahua

Day 7: Mazunte

Just when you thought you couldn't get more relaxed... After your 1.5-hour drive from Bahías de Huatulco, start off by checking out the **Centro Mexicano de la Tortuga** and learning about sea turtle conservation. Then it's off to **Playa Rinconcito** to swim and relax beachside. If you feel up to it and want to experience the freedom of swimming au naturel, catch a taxi or camioneta to **Zipolite.** Just be sure to make it back to Mazunte before sunset to hike up to **La Punta Cometa** to see the sun slip below the horizon. End the night with dinner and drinks at **La Tertulia.**

Day 8: Puerto Escondido

Catch a camioneta early to Pochutla and take a bus from there to Mexico's surfing capital. Enjoy the morning at **Playa Zicatela** if you surf, **La Punta** if you'd rather chill, or **Playa Carrizalillo** if you want to swim. Have lunch at **Fish Shack** if you're around La Punta, or **El Sultán** around Playa Carrizalillo. Book a tour of **Laguna de Manialtepec** for the evening, or if you like to party, begin the night in **La Punta** and end it in Zicatela at **Cactus Bar and Restaurant.**

Day 9: Lagunas de Chacahua

In the morning, head to **Parque Nacional Lagunas de Chacahua,** one of the most unique beaches Oaxaca has to offer. Tour the lagoons and spend your afternoon blissfully lounging on the shore (or surfing and swimming). Be sure to try a **tamale de tichinda** (mussel tamale). At **Terra Tipi,** spend the night in a hammock (or in one of their rooms, if it suits you), being lulled by the waves.

Day 10: Coast or Capital?

After you make your way back to **Puerto Escondido,** you have a choice. Will you spend your last day lounging about on the **beach,** or busing it back up to the city to grab some last-minute **souvenirs?** Whatever you choose, to beautiful Oaxaca you'll be saying, "Nos vemos pronto!" (See you soon!)

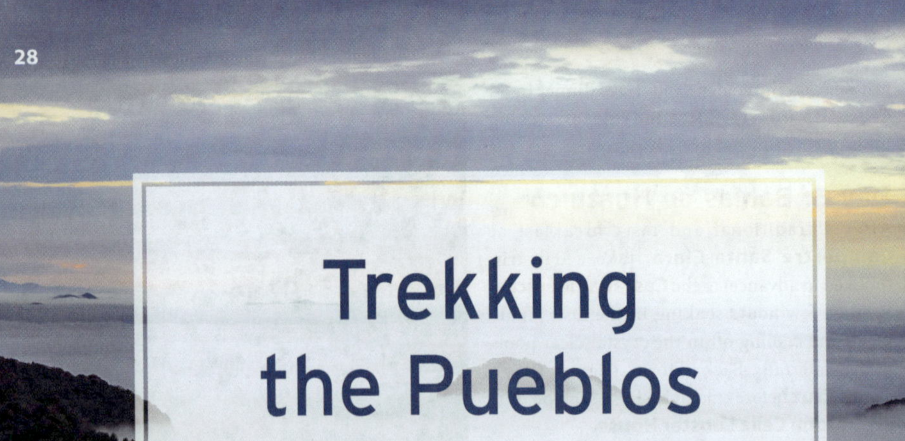

Trekking the Pueblos Mancomunados

Just 1.5 hours from Oaxaca City by car (and not much longer by bus or taxi colectivo), and 1,500 m (4,900 ft) higher, the Pueblos Mancomunados are a world away from the desert below. Translating to "United Villages," this group of eight mountain towns (though only seven were open to tourism at the time of writing) in the Sierra Norte have organized to create and sustain a paragon of **ecotourism** in Mexico. Over 100 km (62 mi) of mountain roads and footpaths connect the Pueblos Mancomunados, serving as both hiking trails for visitors and daily commutes for locals.

The citizens of these communities understand how vital their natural environment is to their livelihood, both in terms of economy and quality of life, and they share the beauty of their land and culture with love and pride. **Camp out** among the pines, or rent a **cabaña ecoturística** (ecotourism cabin) if you want to get cozy next to the fire when the temperature drops at night. Enjoy hearty, home-style meals in the local comedores, dining halls that serve traditional dishes from morning until early evening. Plan on spending three days or so in the Pueblos Mancomunados.

In each town you visit, check in with the local **ecotourism office.** If you're not spending the night, you'll need to pay an access fee (US$5.50).

Day 1: Cuajimoloyas

Start out in the gateway town of Cuajimoloyas, the highest of the communities, at 3,000-3,200 m (9,800-10,500 ft) above sea level. Often shrouded in clouds, it can get chilly, sometimes freezing, so pack appropriately, but when the sun comes out, the slopes heat up nicely and offer **breathtaking views** of the surrounding landscape. You'll find zip lines, suspension bridges, waterfalls, and more to explore.

Day 2: Benito Juárez

In the morning, take a two-hour hike on the nature trail **Ruta Needa-Yaa-Lagashxi** that leads west from Cuajimoloyas to Benito Juárez, a small village nestled in beautiful pine and oak forests. There's an impressive suspension bridge and mirador you can take a short hike out to, and zip lines as well. Make sure to organize a trip to visit the farm of **Señor Eli,** who invites visitors to spend the day with him and his family to see what daily Oaxacan mountain life is like.

Day 3: La Neveria

The **Ruta Needa-Queta-Miru** trail takes you on a pleasant hike through fields to La Neveria. Once renowned for its ice, it is now an idyllic town ideal for learning more about the local plants and herbs used in **traditional medicine** in the Sierra Norte. Hikes can also be taken out to picturesque waterfalls. For those interested in agriculture, there are opportunities to tour the town's greenhouses and learn more about the crops grown there.

suspension bridge at Benito Juárez

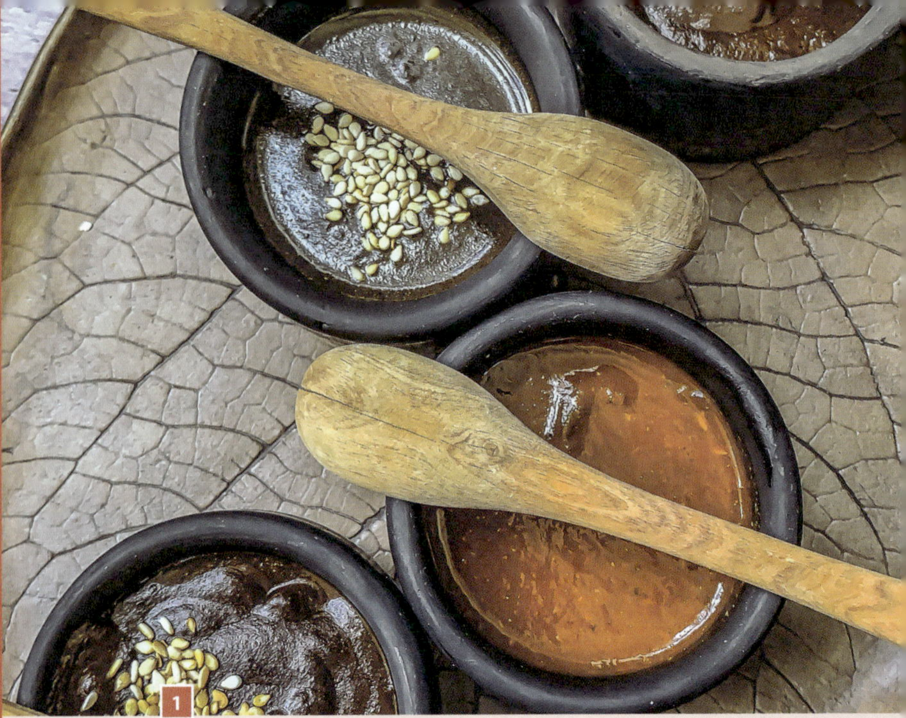
1

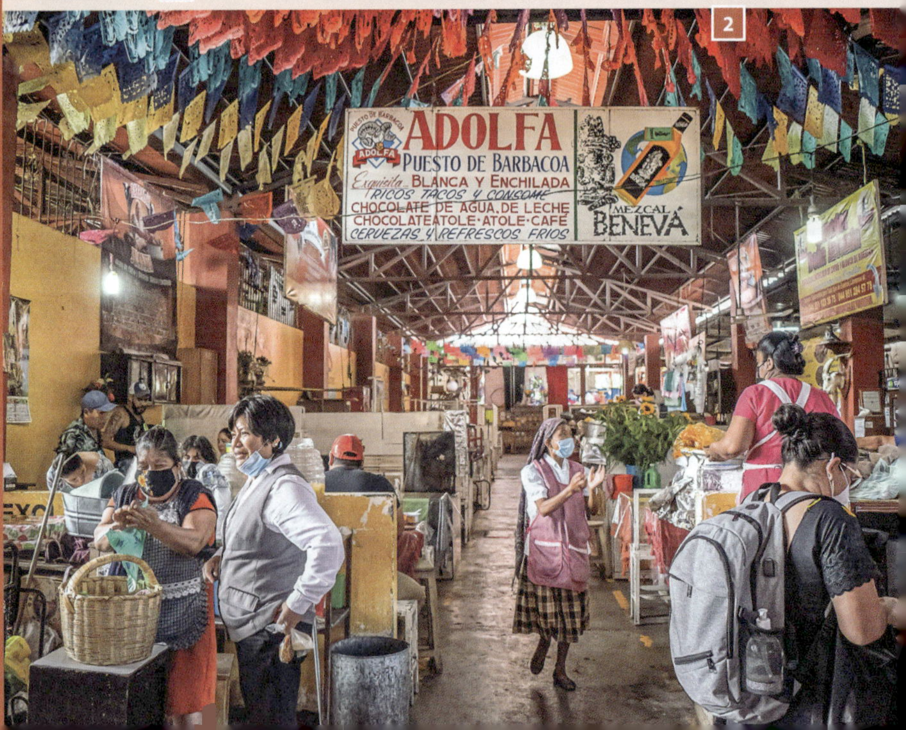
2
PUESTO DE BARBACOA
ADOLFA
ADOLFA
PUESTO DE BARBACOA
Exquisita BLANCA Y ENCHILADA
RICOS TACOS Y CONSOME
CHOCOLATE DE AGUA, DE LECHE
CHOCOLATEATOLE · ATOLE · CAFE
CERVEZAS Y REFRESCOS FRIOS
MEZCAL
BENEVÁ

IN THE SPOTLIGHT

New Frontiers of Flavor

Oaxaca boasts enough sights, stories, and activities to keep travelers of all types occupied and happy, but for us flavor fiends, it's paradise. To eat here is to venture into landscapes of flavor so different, your tongue will never be bored. What's more, Oaxacan gastronomy is colorful, storied, and spicy enough to satisfy all those other reasons for leaving home.

Mole Negro (Black Mole)

Mole negro simply means "black sauce," but it is oh so much more than that. A creation carefully crafted from a plethora of ingredients including chiles, herbs, fruits, nuts, and most famous of all, chocolate, this rich dish is emblematic of Oaxaca, and you can't leave without trying it. You can find mole negro all over the state, but it's best in the heart of Oaxaca, in the city and surrounding valleys.

Where to Try It

OAXACA CITY

- **Mercado 20 de Noviembre** (page 76)
- **Los Pacos** (page 81)

VALLES CENTRALES

- **Dulízùn Café, Teotitlán del Valle** (page 111)

LA COSTA AND ISTMO DE TEHUANTEPEC

- **Campestre Santa Clara, Huatulco** (page 181)
- **Terra-Cotta, Huatulco** (page 181)

Mole de Caderas (Goat-Meat Mole)

Mid-October to mid-November is the time to visit Huajuapan if you're coming to eat. This is the season for the regional delicacy mole de caderas, a spicy goat-meat stew made with guajillo, serrano, and costeño chiles, tomatoes, avocado tree leaves, onions, cilantro, and a type of corn endemic to the region.

Where to Try It

OAXACA CITY

- **Tierra del Sol** (page 78)

LA MIXTECA

- **Restaurante García Peral, Huajuapan de León** (page 231)

Goat and Lamb Barbacoa (Slow-Roasted Barbecue)

If meat that practically melts in your mouth is your thing, you'll have to try barbacoa, best in the markets of the Valles Centrales. Still made in the traditional way, the meat is covered in maguey leaves and slow cooked for hours in a pit. The result? Insanely tender meat served up in a delicious red consommé that will leave you licking your fingers clean.

Where to Try It

VALLES CENTRALES

- **Tlacolula Sunday Market** (page 113)
- **Zaachila's Mercado Gastronómico** (page 125)

1: tasting moles 2: barbacoa stalls at the Tlacolula market

Barbacoa en Rollo (Rolled Beef Barbacoa)

A regional variation of barbacoa, this equally succulent version swaps beef for lamb and goat. The beef is rolled up in avocado leaves (giving it its signature look) before being cooked in a pit, buried in maguey and banana leaves.

Where to Try It

VALLES CENTRALES

- **Zaachila's Mercado Municipal Alarii** (page 125)

Tlayuda (Overgrown Quesadilla/Tostada)

Though it's often referred to as a "Mexican pizza," tlayuda is more like a grilled, plate-sized tostada. A favorite Oaxacan street food staple, the giant tortilla is covered in asiento (lard), black bean paste, quesillo (Oaxacan cheese), lettuce, tomato, avocado, cabbage and, if desired, a meat of choice.

Where to Try It

OAXACA CITY

- **Mercado 20 de Noviembre** (page 76)
- **La Olla** (page 78)

VALLES CENTRALES

- **Dulízùn Café, Teotitlán del Valle** (page 111)

Garnacha (Deep-Fried Tostada)

Just when you thought you had every tasty configuration masa (corn flour) could birth, the region of El Istmo comes to blow your mind. Deep fried and topped with a tangy slaw, garnachas are a specialty of the Istmo region and a finger-lickingly delicious snack.

Where to Try It

LA COSTA AND ISTMO DE TEHUANTEPEC

- **Bladu'Yu, Huatulco** (page 189)
- **The markets of Tehuantepec and Juchitán** (pages 194 and 198)

Tejate (Foam-Topped Nutty/Chocolatey Drink)

I was initially put off by the mysterious foam that floats atop this pre-Hispanic drink, but I'm glad I got over my misgivings—this drink is delicious! Originally from the village of San Andrés Huayapam, the "drink of the gods" is made from a variety of ingredients, including mamey seeds, fermented cacao beans, toasted corn flour, and flor de cacao blossoms. It's delicate, sweet, and the foam for me became oddly addicting.

Where to Try It

OAXACA CITY

- **La Flor de Huayapam** (page 69)
- **Mercado Orgánico La Cosecha** (page 79)
- **Feria del Tejate y el Tamal (July)** (page 66)

VALLES CENTRALES

- **Tlacolula Sunday Market** (page 113)

Espuma (Foamy Chocolate-Based Drink)

Another frothy drink hailing from the Valles Centrales is espuma, a foaming chocolate beverage made from toasted rice, two kinds of cocoa, and other ingredients. The bubbly foam makes this a fun drink to try, and its only made in Zaachila.

Where to Try It

VALLES CENTRALES

- **Zaachila's Mercado Gastronómico** (page 125)

Mezcal

In Oaxaca they say, "Para todo mal, mezcal. Y para todo bien tambien" (For everything bad, mezcal… and for everything good, too.) Mezcal accompanies all of life's circumstances, and it flows in abundance throughout Oaxaca. Distilled from agave hearts cooked in pits, tequila's smokier cousin goes down smooth but sure packs a punch. It's available statewide, but the best places to taste and learn about it are in Oaxaca and the Valles Centrales.

Where to Try It

OAXACA CITY

- **Mezcalogia** (page 81)
- **In Situ** (page 83)

VALLES CENTRALES

- **El Rey Zapoteco, Santiago Matatlán** (page 117)

Coffee

Originally from East Africa, the worldwide phenomenon that is coffee took came to Mexico in the late 1700s, with Oaxaca being one of the foremost producers. While a delicious cup of café is available statewide, most of it is sourced from the coffee plantations of Pluma Hidalgo in Oaxaca's Sierra Sur. The high altitudes and wet tropical air make the perfect environment for the beloved bean to flourish.

Where to Try It

OAXACA CITY

- **Café Brújula** (page 80)

LA COSTA AND ISTMO DE TEHUANTEPEC

- **Cafetería Punto Sur, San José del Pacífico** (page 175)
- **Café Cerro de la Pluma, Pluma Hidalgo** (page 177)
- **Café Origen Mágico, Pluma Hidalgo** (page 177)

1: tlayuda 2: garnachas from El Istmo 3: tejate

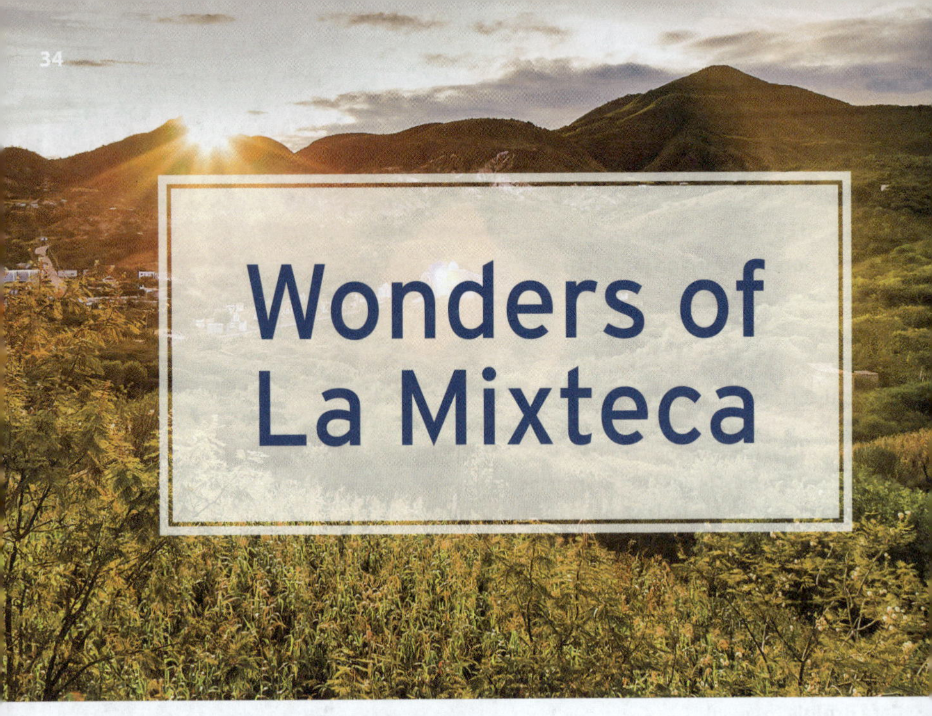

Wonders of La Mixteca

Home to the Ñuu Savi, or People of the Rain, as the Mixtecs call themselves, the landscapes of La Mixteca are simply mesmerizing. The terrain here ranges from cloudy peaks to lower scrublands with all the colors of the rainbow in the soil and stone. Mixtec legend tells that this land was conquered when a warrior called El Flechador del Sol (The One Who Wounded the Sun with Arrows) shot the setting sun with his arrow, causing it to bleed red over the hills and winning the land for the Mixtec people. Watch the sun set here, and you might start to question whether it's really a myth.

Day 1: Apoala

Begin your exploration of La Mixteca in **Santiago Apoala,** just 2.5 hours northwest of Oaxaca City. This tiny town perched on a flat shelf is used as a base for exploring the stunning valley of Apoala. Towering cliff walls good for climbing (or simply causing your jaw to drop), waterfalls and caves named after snakes and horse tails, ghostly moss-strewn oak forests, and cave paintings dating back thousands of years will keep you busy. Spend the night camping or in one of the comfortable cabañas (cabins).

Day 2: Teposcolula and the Dominican Route

After a day immersed in the marvels of Mother Nature, it's time to admire some human-made wonders. First, stop by the **Templo y Ex-Convento de Santo Domingo Yanhuitlán** en route to Teposcolula, where the capilla abierta (open-air chapel) of the **Templo y Ex-Convento de San Pedro y San Pablo** is the largest of its kind in Latin America. Next, head to **Yucunama** to visit the archaeological museum there. Back in Teposcolula, make sure to stop by **La Casa de la**

Templo y Ex-Convento de San Pedro y San Pablo

Cacica and relax in the shady zócalo. Spend the night at **Hotel Casa Franco.**

Day 3: Huajuapan de León

On your way to Huajuapan, stop by Tamazulapan to see the distinctive **Parroquia de Santa María de la Natividad.** If it's between mid-October and mid-November, you're in for a treat in Huajuapan de León, where the seasonal dish mole de caderas is served in the **Restaurante García Peral** at the hotel of the same name. This spicy, soupy mole made with goat meat has the always delicious and distinctive hoja de aguacate (avocado tree leaf), which makes everything better. But even if you're not in town during mole de caderas season, there is still plenty to enjoy. Visit the **Museo Regional de Huajuapan** and learn of the town's rich Mixtec heritage and traditions before heading to **Cerro de las Minas Archaeological Zone** for a guided tour.

TOP EXPERIENCE

Temazcal: Indigenous Sweat Lodge

When the Spanish arrived in Mesoamerica, they found the little adobe huts used for temazcal, a pre-Hispanic spiritual and medicinal sweat bath, just about everywhere they went. The Aztecs called it temazcalli, which in Nahuatl means "house of heat" or "bath house." Despite the conquistadors' attempts to quash the practice, it has thankfully survived to this day under the name temazcal.

WHAT IS TEMAZCAL?

Traditionally, a temazcal ceremony involved elements of ancient Aztec cosmology, and the process is more or less the same today. The fire for heating the stones is lit on the east side of the hut, representing the sun, and the small south-facing opening in the hut is known as "the pathway of the dead." As the ancient doctrine states, to enter a temazcal is to return to the womb, and to exit afterward is a form of spiritual rebirth.

Whether or not one is spiritually inclined, temazcal definitely has a physical effect on the body, and this medicinal aspect has always been as important as the metaphysical (in Indigenous healing systems, there is no separation between the physical, mental, and spiritual). Every temazcal is a little different, but all follow the same basic outline. A healer called a temazcalera (usually a woman) selects herbs used in the vapor according to what ails the patient and controls the heat during the sweat bath. Participants are often also rubbed down with an array of herbs, fruits, and even coffee or chocolate for their symbolic and healing properties. After the steam bath, the patient is wrapped in a blanket and told to lie on the floor, usually in a separate room, to cool down. This is also when traditional massages are usually given, or a splash in a cold water. This cooldown is essential to the process, allowing the bather to recoup the energy lost in the process. Temazcal is said to relieve conditions such as rheumatism, arthritis, muscle and nerve pain, and even assuage the pain of childbirth.

For me, there is something to the spiritual "rebirth" aspect of it. After my first temazcal, I felt joyful, lighter, clean. I like to think the glow to my skin was not just because I had rubbed guava and honey on it. After being in Mama Earth's sweltering womb and emerging in Oaxaca's mountain air, you'll feel renewed and ready to continue your journey.

WHERE TO TRY TEMAZCAL

Experience it and judge for yourself. Below are recommended temazcals listed in order of proximity to Oaxaca City.

Ceviarem Temazcal

Tlalixtac de Cabrera; tel. 951/544-9096; US$25-95

At Ceviarem Temazcal, every step of the healing process is carefully explained so participants can understand the symbolism and meaning behind what is happening. Participants are gently eased into each step. In addition to the traditional temazcal, there are also herbal baths, massages, and other traditional spiritual cleanings.

Temazcal Oaxaca

Santa María Coyotepec; tel.951/547-8850; www.temazcaloaxaca.com; US$50 pp, US$35 pp for groups of 4+

Just outside Oaxaca's city limits, Temazcal Oaxaca offers a friendly and welcoming experience to its guests. All the herbs used in the ceremony are grown right in the beautiful garden that's available to relax in before and after the session. Participants have the option of a water plunge and massage afterward.

Agua Miel

Guadalupe Etla; tel. 555/501-2017; www.aguamieloaxaca.com; aguamieloax@gmail.com; US$45-80

Every temazcal at Agua Miel includes the option to enjoy a "land-to-table" meal made with organic, local, and seasonal ingredients. In addition to private temazcal ceremonies, they offer gatherings and workshops that are open to the public, including a communal full moon temazcal each month.

Ya^a Temazcal Zapoteca

Teotitlán del Valle; tel. 951/123-2336; www.nativospa.com; US$35-65

A unique feature of Ya^a Temazcal Zapoteca is the inclusion of a cacao ritual. In a lovely and relaxing setting, the ceremony itself here is very aesthetically pleasing, and the staff clearly love what they do. This traditional spa not only has a location in the Valles Centrales, but also in the heart of Oaxaca City (Flores Magon 227; tel. 951/123-2661).

Holistik Temazcal and Masaje

Santiago Matatlán; tel. 951/409-6719; guillermoroveragg@gmail.com; US$50-95

On a tranquil hill overlooking the town of Matatlán, Holistik Temazcal and Masaje is surrounded by plenty of natural beauty and the perfect place for spiritual renewal. This thorough temazcal includes a copal smoke cleansing, pulque ceremony, herbal tea, and exfoliation. There are options that include massage and meals.

1

2

IN THE SPOTLIGHT

Oaxacan Folk Art

The work of Oaxacan hands is imbued with history, both ancient and recent, as well as boundless imagination. Some crafts, like ceramics, have been produced here for millennia. Others were created when the Indigenous peoples of Oaxaca combined native materials and techniques to the goods and practices introduced by the Spanish. What is truly incredible about these craft traditions—besides how long they have been handed down from generation to generation here in Oaxaca—is how they are constantly changing to this day. All over Oaxaca live expert and creative chefs, basket weavers, embroiderers, jewelry makers, silversmiths, leatherworkers, knife makers, and more, all with unique imaginative styles that add their own voices to the greater communal art form. This wealth of artisanal traditions fills the mercados of the state with gorgeous artifacts that make shopping in Oaxaca unique, personal, and full of fun, exploration, and learning.

Rugs, Tapestries, and Other Woven Items

Combine natural dyes sourced directly from the earth with wool and looms first introduced from Europe, and add a few centuries of Oaxacan humor and fancy, and you've got the hallucinatory tapetes (wool rugs) of Teotitlán del Valle and other communities. With 500 years of tradition supporting them, weavers in Teotitlán have recently begun experimenting with their craft by twisting three-dimensional images into their rugs.

Where to Find Them

- **Teotitlán del Valle** (page 109)

Alebrijes

The fantastic alebrijes (brightly painted carved wooden figures) of Arrazola and San Martín Tilcajete are the youngsters of Oaxacan crafts, but they have roots in pre-Hispanic spiritual traditions. The expertly carved creatures are a medley of fins, feathers, horns, hooves, tails, and tentacles, and are intricately painted in bold, vibrant colors. No two are alike, and they are one of Oaxaca's major cultural symbols.

Where to Find Them

- **Arrazola** (page 122)
- **San Martín Tilcajete** (page 127)

Barro Negro

As in other parts of Mexico, people here have been baking clay since they figured out how to do it over 4,000 years ago. However, the technique that produces the glossy barro negro (black clay pottery) of San Bartolo Coyotepec was invented by a woman named Doña Rosa relatively recently, in the 1950s. The town is filled with an assortment of stunning silky black pieces all made with this special technique, from vases and figurines to wall hangings and jewelry.

Where to Find Them

- **San Bartolo Coyotepec** (page 125)

Barro Rojo

The earthy hues of barro rojo (red clay pottery) are the perfect medium to sculpt the human form. In San Antonino Castillo Velasco, you can find sculptures of men, women, and even mermaids in sizes that could fit in the palm of your hand to ones you can look at eye to eye. Visit the workshop Taller Manos Que Ven to peruse these earthen works of art.

Where to Find Them

- **San Antonino Castillo Velasco** (page 128)

1: alebrijes in San Martín Tilcajete 2: barro negro from San Bartolo Coyotepec

1 Green-Glazed and Matte-White Pottery

Santa María Atzompa is famous for its green-glazed, matte-white, and intricate filigree pottery styles. Recent archaeological investigations on a hilltop just south of the current ceramics market here uncovered a 2,000-year-old kiln, tangible evidence that this art has been produced in the Valles Centrales continually for millennia.

Where to Find Them

- **Santa María Atzompa** (page 107)

2 Huipiles

Hand-embroidered huipiles (embroidered blouses) take a painstaking amount of not just technical skill but creativity and pride, born of tradition. Embroidered blouses are like signatures in Oaxaca—you can tell from the particular style what region it originates from. Bold, colorful giant flowers are the signature style of the Istmo region. Delicate floral and birds decorate the huipils hailing from San Antonino Castillo Velasco.

Where to Find Them

- **San Antonino Castillo Velasco** (page 128)
- **Tehuantepec and Juchitán** (pages 192 and 197)

3 Belts and Other Embroidered Items

Elaborate patterns are skillfully woven to create one-of-a-kind belts, wallets, table runners, backpacks, headbands, and more using the telar de cintura, or backstrap loom. The backstrap loom is a portable, pre-Hispanic weaving tool that is tied to the artisan's back and attached to a post.

Where to Find Them

- **Santo Tomás Jalieza** (page 128)

1: green-glazed pottery **2:** embroidered huipiles
3: belts from Santo Tomás Jalieza

Best Festivals

If there's one thing Oaxacans love more than their culture, it's celebrating it. Visit just about any time of year, and you'll be able to dance and drink and eat to celebrate a patron saint, recipe, Indigenous culture, and other things Oaxacans hold dear to their hearts. Here is a list of the state's best festivals, but there are many, many more, so if you see a calenda (street parade) coming down the street, don't hesitate to join the party.

Día de Muertos

- **Where:** Oaxaca City, San Agustín Etla, and elsewhere
- **When:** end of October, beginning of November

Oaxaca is renowned for its Día de Muertos (Day of the Dead) celebrations. The Day of the Dead is a syncretism of an ancient Mesoamerican holiday with the Catholic days of observance All Souls' Day and All Saints' Day. November 1 and 2 are the official holidays, but celebrations more or less span the months of October and November.

In Oaxaca City, the day passes in a haze of parades, costumes, and dancing in the streets. After nightfall, Oaxaca City is tinged with an eerie orange glow from burning copal incense. Visitors may be invited into the homes of strangers to view altars made to their deceased loved ones. Fireworks are everywhere.

The citizens of San Agustín Etla observe the holiday in their own unique way, with a ghoulish parade called **La Muerteada** on November 1. It's a raucous, alcohol-fueled all-nighter that fills the town's streets with music, fireworks, costumed dancers, and locals and visitors alike.

Guelaguetza

- **Where:** Oaxaca City, Zaachila, and elsewhere
- **When:** last two Mondays in July; various dates in other towns

Also called **Lunes del Cerro** (Mondays on the Hill), the Guelaguetza is a celebration of the diverse customs and creations of the various cultures tucked away in the eight regions of the state. The official Guelaguetza is held in Oaxaca City on the last two Mondays of July, but communities all over the state have their own Guelaguetza or Los Lunes del Cerro at other times of the year. One of the most popular is in Zaachila, which is also held in July.

Zipolite Nudist Festival

- **Where:** Zipolite
- **When:** first weekend in February

The Zipolite Nudist Festival is a three-day, stitch-free celebration of what your momma gave you that includes traditional dances, music, yoga, theater, calendas, and more.

Feria Anual de Teposcolula

- **Where:** Teposcolula
- **When:** end of February, beginning of March

At Teposcolula's nearly three-week-long Feria Anual (Annual Fair), experience riotous calendas, live music, regional foods, and two traditional games: pelota Mixteca, a Mixtec ball game played with a heavy rubber glove, and the juego de batalla, a game similar to hockey but played with a ball that is on fire.

Fiestas de Mayo

- **Where:** Istmo de Tehuantepec
- **When:** end of April through May

The people of El Istmo know how to party. They even have their own word for it: *vela*. The main vela season is in May, during the Fiestas de Mayo, with the first velas beginning at the end of April. A vela is typically three nonstop days and nights of drinking, eating, and dancing to the regional musical style known as el son istmeño. Even the preparations are turned into celebrations.

Danza de la Pluma (Dance of the Feather) at the Guelaguetza

Christmas decorations in Oaxaca

Feria Regional de Hongos Silvestres

- **Where:** Cuajimoloyas
- **When:** penultimate weekend in July

The Feria Regional de Hongos Silvestres (Regional Wild Mushroom Fair) is a two-day festival of workshops, classes, and hikes focused on identifying, preparing, and consuming edible wild mushrooms. This is not a magic mushroom festival—some species that grow here have medicinal properties, but the majority are for plain old cooking and enjoying.

Mazunte Jazz Festival

- **Where:** Mazunte
- **When:** mid-November

The biggest festival on this stretch of coastline is the International Jazz Festival of Mazunte. Not strictly a jazz event, this three-evening festival usually includes genres such as rock, reggae, Afrobeat, trova, and more.

Christmas and Noche de Rábanos

- **Where:** Oaxaca City
- **When:** December 23

During the colonial period, farmers would carve religious images into giant radishes to catch the eyes of shoppers in the Christmas market on December 23. The Noche de Rábanos (Night of the Radishes) was formalized into an official competition in 1897, and farmers have been carving like crazy to one-up each other ever since. Farmers from the surrounding valleys proudly display their large arrangements of vegetal nativity scenes and aspects of Oaxacan life and culture in the Zócalo in the late afternoon; judging begins around 9pm.

Oaxaca City

Oaxaca City, the delightful capital of the state, is one of the smallest major cities in Mexico—but don't let its size fool you. It more than makes up for it in a larger-than-life historical, cultural, and artistic presence. Just taking a casual stroll down any of the picturesque streets throws you into sensory overload in the best possible way. Everywhere you look, there is color—dazzlingly embroidered clothing, psychedelic alebrijes sold on the street, buildings painted in cotton-candy shades. Once your eyes have adjusted to the kaleidoscope, the next thing you notice is Oaxaca is never quiet—something is always being celebrated, and loudly so, with firecrackers, impromptu bands, and songs. Vendors singsong their wares morning and evening, mariachi bands play in the squares, church bells ring, even the gas truck has

Highlights

Look for ★ to find recommended sights, activities, dining, and lodging.

★ **The Zócalo:** The lively heart of the city, surrounded by bustling cafés and restaurants, offers a quintessential setting to feel the pulse of Oaxaca (page 51).

★ **Teatro Macedonio Alcalá:** Inspired by theaters of turn-of-the-20th-century France, this intimate theater is worth a visit for the architecture alone, not to mention its world-class cultural offerings (page 52).

★ **Basílica de Nuestra Señora de la Soledad:** A double treat—this cathedral is one of Oaxaca's most beautiful, and the neighboring Jardín Sócrates offers a plethora of nieve (ice cream) choices to enjoy (page 53).

★ **Andador Macedonio Alcalá:** Enjoy a charming taste of the city on a stroll down this cobblestone pedestrian walkway, lined with shops, restaurants, and galleries (page 54).

★ **Museo de Arte Prehispánico de México Rufino Tamayo:** One of Mexico's most famous artists, Oaxaca-born Rufino Tamayo donated his personal collection of pre-Hispanic art, which became one of Oaxaca's most impressive galleries (page 54).

★ **Templo de Santo Domingo:** This ornate temple complex includes the gold-gilded cathedral, the enchanting Jardín Etnobotánico, and the world-class Centro Cultural Santo Domingo showcasing Oaxaca's ancient treasures (page 54).

★ **Mercado Benito Juárez and Mercado 20 de Noviembre:** Work up an appetite shopping and perusing wares (page 69), and then try chapulines—roasted grasshoppers—if you're feeling adventurous (page 76).

Oaxaca City

Estatal Cerro Del Fortín Park
To Xochimilco
LOS ARQUITOS DE XOCHIMILCO
LA JICARA LIBRESPACIO CULTURAL
ZAPOTREK
To Hipico la Golondrina
MUSEO INFANTIL DE OAXACA
EX-MARQUESADO
CARR. INTERNACIONAL
PANORÁMICA DEL FORTÍN
190
PORFIRIO DÍAZ
HUMBOLDT
QUETZALCOATL
See "North of the Zócalo" Map
DIVISIÓN ORIENTE
FRANCISCO I. MADERO
ALLENDE
TINOCO Y PALACIOS
GARCÍA VIGIL
ALCALÁ
LA UNION
SABINO CRESPO
MANUEL BRAVO
ANDADOR MACEDONIO ALCALÁ
PLAZA DE LA DANZA
SPANISH IMMERSION SCHOOL
MATAMOROS
GUADALUPE VICTORIA
BASÍLICA DE NUESTRA SEÑORA DE LA SOLEDAD
MUSEO DE ARTE PREHISPÁNICO DE MÉXICO RUFINO TAMAYO
JARDÍN SOCRATES
AUTOTRANSPORTES TURISTICOS TEOAX/ FLECHADOR DEL SOL
MIGUEL HIDALGO
J.P. GARCIA
20 DE NOVIEMBRE
TEATRO MACEDONIO ALCALÁ
SERVICIOS TURÍSTICOS DE HUAJUAPAN
TERMINAL PERIFÉRICO
VALERIO TRUJANO
AUTOTRANSPORTES DE TLAXIACO
ARMENTA Y LÓPEZ
THE ZÓCALO
LAS CASAS
See "The Zócalo" Map
LA VICTORIA
PERIFÉRICO
JUÁREZ MAZA
GALEANA
MERCADO BENITO JUÁREZ
BUSTAMANTE
IGNACIO ALDAMA
CENTRAL DE ABASTOS
MERCADO 20 DE NOVIEMBRE
FRANCISCO JAVIER MINA
ZARAGOZA
DÍAZ ORDAZ
MERCADO DE ARTESANÍAS
CHOCOLATE Y MOLE GUELAGUETZA
IGLESIA DE LA DEFENSA
CONSTITUYENTES
FLORES MAGÓN
HOTEL VILLA ALTA
IGLESIA DE SAN FRANCISCO ASIS
MEZCALERÍA CUISH
AUTOTRANSPORTES ATLÁNTIDA
NUÑO DEL MERCADO
FERNÁNDEZ FIALLO
RIVERAS DEL ATOYAC
Atoyac
AUTOMORSA BUS STATION
XÓCHITL
LINEAS UNIDAS STATION
© MOON.COM
To La Soley

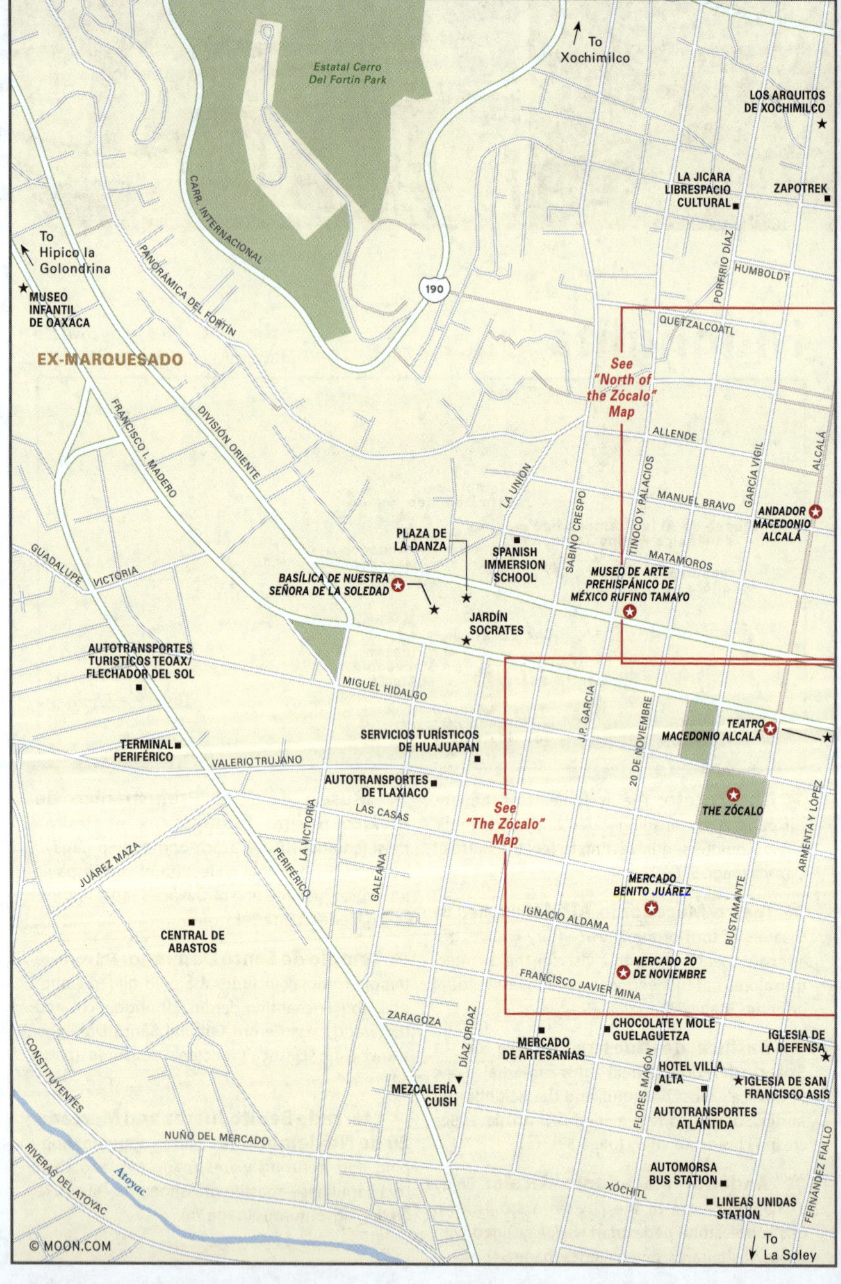

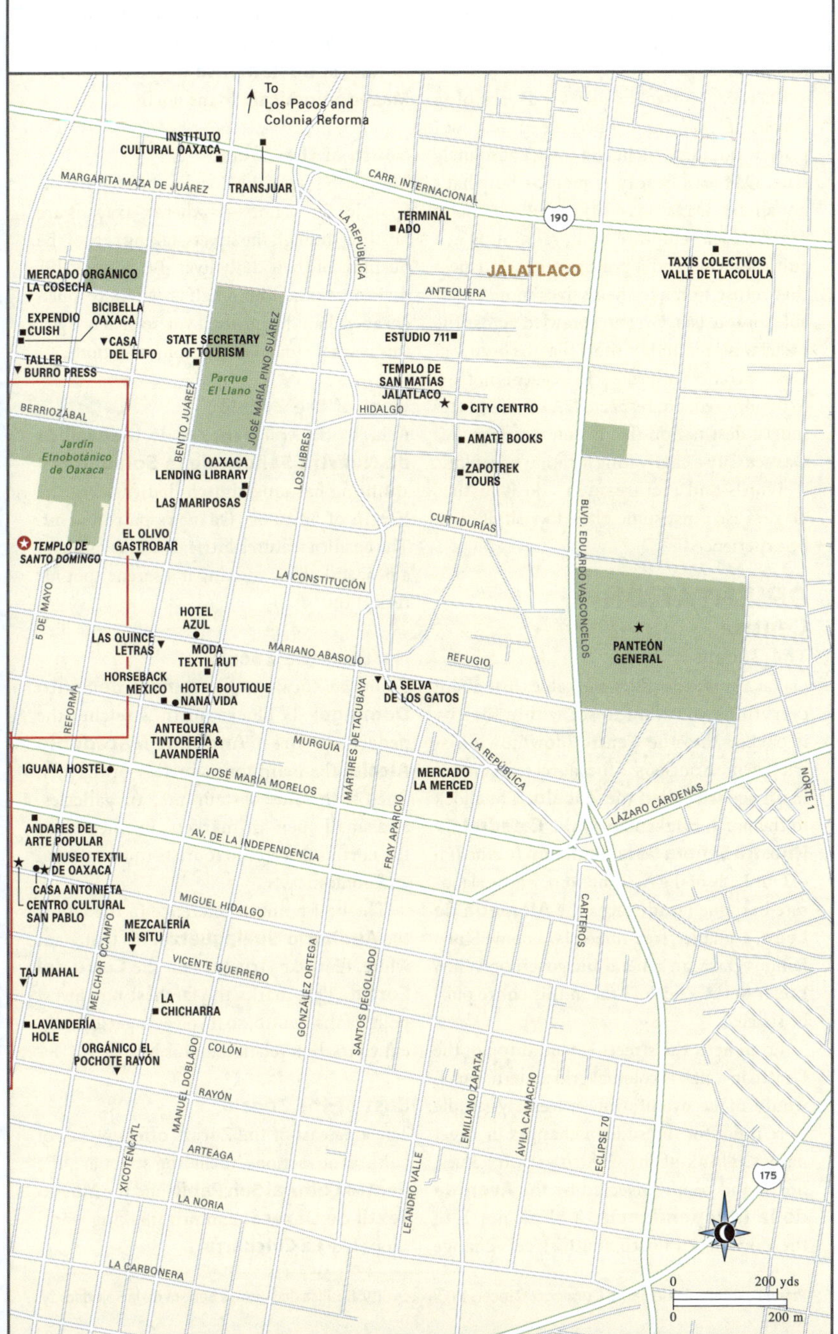
To
Los Pacos and
Colonia Reforma
INSTITUTO
CULTURAL OAXACA
TRANSJUAR
MARGARITA MAZA DE JUÁREZ
CARR. INTERNACIONAL
190
TERMINAL
ADO
LA REPÚBLICA
TAXIS COLECTIVOS
VALLE DE TLACOLULA
JALATLACO
ANTEQUERA
MERCADO ORGÁNICO
LA COSECHA
BICIBELLA
OAXACA
EXPENDIO
CUISH
CASA
DEL ELFO
STATE SECRETARY
OF TOURISM
TALLER
BURRO PRESS
ESTUDIO 711
TEMPLO DE
SAN MATÍAS
JALATLACO
HIDALGO
CITY CENTRO
AMATE BOOKS
ZAPOTREK
TOURS
Parque
El Llano
JOSÉ MARÍA PINO SUÁREZ
BENITO JUÁREZ
BERRIOZÁBAL
Jardín
Etnobotánico
de Oaxaca
OAXACA
LENDING LIBRARY
LAS MARIPOSAS
LOS LIBRES
CURTIDURÍAS
BLVD. EDUARDO VASCONCELOS
TEMPLO DE
SANTO DOMINGO
EL OLIVO
GASTROBAR
LA CONSTITUCIÓN
5 DE MAYO
HOTEL
AZUL
LAS QUINCE
LETRAS
MODA
TEXTIL RUT
MARIANO ABASOLO
REFUGIO
PANTEÓN
GENERAL
HORSEBACK
MEXICO
HOTEL BOUTIQUE
NANA VIDA
LA SELVA
DE LOS GATOS
ANTEQUERA
TINTORERÍA &
LAVANDERÍA
REFORMA
MURGUÍA
MÁRTIRES DE TACUBAYA
LA REPÚBLICA
IGUANA HOSTEL
JOSÉ MARÍA MORELOS
MERCADO
LA MERCED
NORTE 1
LÁZARO CÁRDENAS
FRAY APARICIO
ANDARES DEL
ARTE POPULAR
MUSEO TEXTIL
DE OAXACA
AV. DE LA INDEPENDENCIA
CASA ANTONIETA
CENTRO CULTURAL
SAN PABLO
MIGUEL HIDALGO
CARTEROS
MEZCALERÍA
IN SITU
VICENTE GUERRERO
TAJ MAHAL
MELCHOR OCAMPO
GONZÁLEZ ORTEGA
SANTOS DEGOLLADO
LA
CHICHARRA
LAVANDERÍA
HOLE
ORGÁNICO EL
POCHOTE RAYÓN
COLÓN
MANUEL DOBLADO
RAYÓN
EMILIANO ZAPATA
ÁVILA CAMACHO
ECLIPSE 70
XICOTÉNCATL
ARTEAGA
LEANDRO VALLE
175
LA NORIA
LA CARBONERA
0
200 yds
0
200 m

a little ditty that'll get stuck in your head... The sounds of Oaxaca become a comforting cacophony.

Oaxaca is also beautiful. Describing Oaxaca as "magical" has become so commonplace it would be cliché if it wasn't absolutely true. Oaxaca's beauty is magic—but that's not all it is. Oaxaca is a city of the arts and of protest, each sculpture or mural hinting at a cultural pride and a political consciousness that refuse to make themselves more palatable for tourists. Graffiti sprawled across the pastel walls reminds visitors that the beauty of Oaxaca comes with edges; its beauty is not just to be admired, but respected. A cookie-cutter tourist destination this is not, which makes Oaxaca City a captivating location to explore.

Words and pictures don't do it justice. Oaxaca isn't just some place to visit; it must be experienced.

ORIENTATION

Centro

The Zócalo

Oaxaca is wonderfully walkable. Just about everything you want to see within the city is packed into the Centro (downtown district), whose nucleus is the laurel tree-shaded main square called the **Zócalo.** The block to the north is taken up by the **Catedral de Nuestra Señora de la Asunción** (Cathedral of Our Lady of the Assumption), whose elaborate baroque facade faces the **Alameda de León,** a smaller, tree-lined plaza named for a famous Oaxacan general and governor. When I refer to the Zócalo, I mean this entire public space.

From here, the streets extend through the Centro in a classic colonial grid pattern, which would make orientation extremely simple were it not for the sudden changes in street names. Think of the Centro as two halves, north and south, bisected by the **Avenida de la Independencia,** a block north of the Zócalo. All north-south streets change names here, and many east-west streets (but not all) change names at the longitude of the Zócalo, at **Bustamante** to the south, and **Macedonio Alcalá** to the north.

South of the Zócalo

The south side of the Zócalo—although it offers a lot for visitors—is where Oaxacans are hustling through the streets, taking care of the business of their daily lives. Because of this division, the southern half is generally much cheaper than the north; if you're on a budget, this is where to look for accommodations.

West of the Zócalo

A few blocks west of the Zócalo, the **Basílica de Nuestra Señora de la Soledad** is a stunning baroque church dedicated to the Virgin of Solitude, Oaxaca's patron saint. The basilica features intricate stonework and a peaceful plaza, making it a serene spot for reflection.

North of the Zócalo

From the Zócalo to the **Templo de Santo Domingo,** six blocks north, stretches the pedestrian street **Andador Macedonio Alcalá,** the main tourist artery of the city, lined with cafés, restaurants, art galleries, and small open-air markets. Businesses on the north side cater to tourists (international and domestic).

The best point of reference in the city is the **Auditorio Guelaguetza.** It's that giant white, tent-like structure on the **Cerro del Fortín.** This marks the farthest northwest point of the Centro, so if you ever get lost, orient yourself in relation to this hill.

East of the Zócalo

The area east of the Zócalo offers plenty of cultural attractions, including street art, the **Centro Cultural San Pablo** and the **Museo Textil de Oaxaca,** and printmaking workshops like **La Chicharra.**

Previous: Templo de Santo Domingo; dancers in Oaxaca City; Basílica de Nuestra Señora de la Soledad.

Outside of Centro

While visiting Oaxaca, you may find yourself wandering into different barrios or colonias (neighborhoods) outside the historic center. Just north of the Centro, across Highway 190, is **Xochimilco,** Oaxaca's oldest neighborhood. Gently sloping cobblestone streets lined with eye-catching murals, the occasional weaver shops, and restaurants hidden behind stone walls and ivy make this a charming neighborhood to stroll. Xochimilco's neighbor to the east is the middle-class **Colonia Reforma,** known for upscale shopping plazas, trendy bars, and eateries. Northeast of Centro is **Jalatlaco.** Like Xochimilco, Jalatlaco is a delightfully colorful neighborhood filled with cafés, narrow streets adorned with papel picado (the colorful and intricately designed banners made of perforated tissue paper), and some of the city's best street art.

If you're planning a visit to **Museo Infantil de Oaxaca,** you'll find yourself in the local barrio of **Ex-Marquesado** (sometimes spelled Ex-Marquezado), about a 10-minute drive northwest from Centro on Calle Francisco L. Madero.

PLANNING YOUR TIME

Three or four unhurried days in Oaxaca City should give you enough time to fully experience the city. If it's your first time here, I imagine you'll be floating about in a fog of enchantment as my family did when we first arrived.

High season in Oaxaca City corresponds to the major festivals. From **mid-October to mid-November,** the streets throng with visitors for **Día de Muertos** (Day of the Dead). They fill back up again at the end of December for **Christmas** celebrations. The two-week **Semana Santa** (Holy Week) vacation around **Easter** is a popular travel period for Mexican people, and Oaxaca City is a major destination during this time. The month of **July** is also very busy, as people from all over the world come to experience the **Guelaguetza** festival, a celebration of the region's cultures.

Outside these periods, you should have no problem reserving rooms or just showing up and finding a great place to stay. If your trip coincides with the festivals, especially Día de Muertos, you'll need to book at least three to four months in advance to get the room of your choice (or anything at all).

Itinerary Ideas

DAY 1

1 Wake up and rejoice—you're in Oaxaca! Begin the day with an authentic Oaxacan breakfast at **Mercado 20 de Noviembre.**

2 Avoid mal de puerco (food coma) by hopping across the street to **Mercado Benito Juárez** to wander the aisles filled with everything you can imagine. If you get thirsty, stop by **La Flor de Huayapam** to try tejate. Ask to drink it in a jicara (gourd) for the full experience.

3 Take a 10-minute stroll to **Museo de Arte Prehispánico de México Rufino Tamayo** to enjoy one of Mexico's most impressive collections of Indigenous art.

4 Since you're only a couple of blocks away, stop by the **Basílica de Nuestra Señora de la Soledad** to enjoy a nieve (ice cream) or two at **Jardín Sócrates.**

5 Have lunch at **Restaurante Coronita.** Try one of Oaxaca's moles here—or all seven, if you're daring.

6 Spend the afternoon collecting stamps on the **Pasaporte Gráfico** as you visit some of Oaxaca's best printmaking studios.

7 Enjoy the sunset at **Templo de Santo Domingo,** then take a leisurely stroll down the **Andador Macedonio Alcalá,** popping in wherever catches your fancy.

8 End the night taking in the festivities at the Zócalo as you eat dinner at **Tr3s 3istro.**

DAY 2

1 Begin your morning the traditional way with chocolate and pan (bread) at **Pan con Madre.**

2 Time to explore the complex at **Templo de Santo Domingo.** Start with a guided tour of the Jardín Etnobotánico. Take a peek at the gold-gilded interior of the church, then see Oaxaca's most important archeological discoveries at Centro Cultural Santo Domingo.

3 Have lunch at **Los Pacos.** Try the agua de nieve de tuna (cactus fruit float).

4 Rest and relax in the shade at **Parque El Llano.** Get a raspado (flavored shaved ice) to cool off and have fun people-watching.

5 For dinner, have a tamal oaxaqueño (a mole-filled tamale) at **La Olla** (leave room for the decadent desserts!) and soak in the beautiful sunset views on the rooftop terrace.

6 End the night with a mezcal tasting at **In Situ.**

DAY 3

1 Get breakfast at **Mercado La Merced.** Afterward, shop to your heart's content, grabbing some seasonal fruit like mangoes, rambutans, or mamey.

2 Meander over to Jalatlaco. Spend the rest of the morning admiring **Templo de San Matías,** funky murals, and adorable cobblestone streets.

3 Enjoy the trilogia de moles indígena (trilogy of Indigenous moles) for lunch at **Las Quince Letras.**

4 Visit some of the smaller but well-curated museums, like **Museo Textil de Oaxaca** or **Museo de Filatelia.**

5 Grab a late-night empananda de mole amarillo from **Empanadas del Carmen Alto.**

Sights

CENTRO

★ The Zócalo

The central square of any colonial Mexican city or town is most commonly referred to as the Zócalo, but you might hear it called the Plaza de la Constitución or Plaza Central (Plaza Municipal in smaller towns). Oaxaca's Zócalo is a large plaza with a gazebo at its center and winding walkways through raised gardens, all shaded by gargantuan laurel trees.

The streets of the Zócalo are named "portales" for the broad arcades that face the square; most are full of cafés and restaurants. They are Portal de Clavería to the north, Portal de Flores to the west, Portal de Gobierno to the south, and Portal Benito Juárez to the east.

Palacio de Gobierno

Valerio Trujano, s/n; tel. 951/501-8100; 9am-5pm Mon.-Fri.

The building on the south side of the Zócalo is the Palacio de Gobierno (Governor's Palace). For years, it did not house the state government administrative offices, functioning instead as a museum showcasing the murals of Mexican painter and printmaker Arturo Bustos (1926-2017). Painted in 1980, the three murals represent three stages of Oaxacan history and development: pre-Hispanic Oaxaca, the colonial period, and independence and statehood. In 2018, however, the state government once again took up residence in the limestone building, which dates to 1783. The museum no longer exists, but you can still view the murals in the central stairwell free of charge.

Catedral de Nuestra Señora de la Asunción

Independencia 700; 10am-2pm and 4pm-6pm daily; free

The church on the north side of the Zócalo is the Catedral de Nuestra Señora de la Asunción (Cathedral of Our Lady of the Assumption), an impressive baroque building that was built stout and heavy because of the earthquakes that are so common in the region. Dating to 1535, it's also simply called the Catedral de Oaxaca. Take a stroll around inside, where

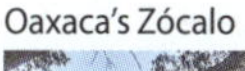

Oaxaca's Zócalo

you'll find high, vaulted ceilings, elaborate stained-glass windows of Saints Paul and Peter, and part of the legendary Santa Cruz de Huatulco (Holy Cross of Huatulco).

★ Teatro Macedonio Alcalá

Independencia 900; tel. 951/516-8312; teatro_alcala@hotmail.com

Walking inside one of Oaxaca's most beautiful buildings is sure to elicit soft gasps and murmurs of appreciation—or maybe that's just me. But this French-style theater is simply gorgeous, inside and out. Built in the early 20th century, the theater went through a couple of name changes before its current name was picked. Its namesake, violinist and pianist Macedonio Alcalá (1831-1869), composed the waltz "Dios Nunca Muere," now considered to be the de facto anthem of Oaxaca.

The theater is a dream of creams, golds, and plush crimsons with an opulent stage, high vaulted dome, white marble staircase, elegant arches, and portraits of famous artists. However, you'll only be able to admire the gorgeous interior if you attend a show. But that's no bother, because everything

Historic Churches Near the Zócalo

The vast majority of the city's tourist attractions are concentrated in the north side of the Centro, but around the Zócalo, a number of old churches will interest architecture buffs: the **Templo de la Compañia de Jesús** (on the block just southwest of the Zócalo), the **Templo de San Agustín** (at the corner of Guerrero and Armenta y López), and the **Iglesia de San Francisco Asís** (five blocks south of the Zócalo on Bustamante); all were built in the 16th century.

The 18th-century **Iglesia de la Defensa** sits quietly tucked away behind laurel trees on the corner of Arteaga and Fiallo. The most historically significant of all the churches is **Templo de San Juan de Dios** (Aldama 217), where the first Catholic mass in Oaxaca was said in 1521. Located at the northwest corner of the Mercado 20 de Noviembre, what's left of the Templo de San Juan de Dios sits quietly among the daily hustle and bustle of economic activity. Inside, you'll find paintings of said first mass, the baptism of Cocijoeza, king of Zaachila, and the miraculous Cross of Huatulco.

from symphonies, ballets, concerts, plays, and even livestreams of New York's Metropolitan Opera are offered here. Due to its beauty and the variety and caliber of events it hosts, it has earned its place as one of the most important theaters in all of Mexico.

West of the Zócalo

★ Basílica de Nuestra Señora de la Soledad

Independencia 107; 7am-6pm daily; free

Constructed in the 1680s, the Basílica de Nuestra Señora de la Soledad (Basilica of Our Lady of Solitude) has one of the most impressive baroque facades in town. Inside, you'll find a treasure trove of gilded filigrees and flourishes covering the walls and towering vaulted ceilings, as well as a central statue of the Virgin Mary, for whom the church is named.

As the story goes, in 1617 a mule driver from Veracruz on his way to Guatemala noticed an extra mule in his train when he got to Oaxaca. When he passed a small chapel dedicated to Saint Sebastian, the mule collapsed. The driver could not get the stubborn thing to stand up and move, so he alerted the authorities of the situation, so as not to arouse suspicion that he was stealing anything. The police arrived and removed the mule's load, and the animal died instantly. When they opened the box, they found an image of the Virgin Mary, prompting Bishop Bartolomé Bohórquez to order the basilica to be built in honor of the miraculous event.

Plaza de la Danza

Calle 2 de Abril; 8am-9pm daily

The limestone saints in the basilica's facade look down upon the Plaza de la Danza (Plaza of the Dance), a broad public space that is the site of many festivals, as well as tapetes (large sand paintings) during Día de Muertos. The bleacher-like stone steps on the plaza's north side are the second-best place to catch the sunset in the Centro (tops is the Templo de Santo Domingo). On the west side of the plaza is the Ex-Convento de San José.

Jardín Sócrates

Independencia 105; 10am-9pm daily

Need a midafternoon break to cool off in the shade? The steps on the southern side of the plaza lead down to the Jardín Sócrates, where a half-dozen ice cream stands sell nieves, artisanal ice cream made with ingredients you'd never think to use. Popular flavors include tropical fruits such as guanabana (soursop) and the traditional mix of tuna (cactus fruit, not the fish) with leche quemada (burnt milk). One of my favorite combinations is known as a beso oaxaqueño (Oaxacan kiss), made with chunky bits of coconut, apples, raisins, and (sounds weird, but it's delicious) carrots.

North of the Zòcalo

★ Andador Macedonio Alcalá

The Andador Macedonio Alcalá is the main tourist artery of the city, leading north from the Zócalo to the Santo Domingo church via six picturesque, car-free blocks paved with iconic Oaxacan green limestone. This winsome pedestrian walkway is constantly alive with music, art, and festivities. Four blocks north of Zócalo, **Parque Labastida** sits kitty-corner to the **Iglesia Sangre de Cristo,** the 17th-century baroque masterpiece on the corner with Calle M. Bravo. Parque Labastida is a thin, shady public space, usually alive with loquacious students, artists, and vendors.

It's easy to pass hours popping in and out of the art galleries, artisan co-ops, cafés, restaurants, and mezcalerías that line the Andador and neighboring blocks. The north end of the Andador is the best place in town to catch a sunset, where the brilliant tones of the day's end on the green limestone facade of the Templo de Santo Domingo will show you the true meaning of the photographer's term "magic hour."

★ Museo de Arte Prehispánico de México Rufino Tamayo

Morelos 503; tel. 951/688-9728; www.rufinotamayo.org.mx; 10am-5pm and 4pm-7pm Wed.-Sat. and Mon., 10am-3pm Sun.; free

This museum has one of the country's most impressive collections displaying the exceptional artistic talent of Mexico's pre-Hispanic peoples, but it is not an anthropology museum. Oaxacan-born painter Rufino Tamayo (1899-1991) and his wife, Olga, curated the collection over two decades, selecting works according to their aesthetic value. In addition to personal interest, their goal was to keep the art safe from illegal exportation, as has happened with other priceless Mexican artifacts. The 1,059 pieces are arranged thematically according to their subject and artistic style.

You'll find Olmec vases in the shape of crab-walking human figures, the grinning face of Tlaloc, the Aztec god of rain, etched into dark, porous volcanic stone, life-size Mayan stone carvings, sections of murals from Teotihuacán, and much more. The collection is in immaculate condition. Such well-preserved detail offers insight into the rich imaginations, deep spiritual lives, and, perhaps most surprisingly, fun senses of humor of the ancient peoples of Mexico.

Museo de Arte Contemporáneo de Oaxaca (MACO)

Alcalá 202; tel. 951/514-2228; www.macooaxaca.com; 11am-6pm Wed.-Mon.; US$3

Two blocks north of the Zócalo, MACO (Museum of Contemporary Art of Oaxaca) is a gorgeous venue for contemporary art exhibitions. Dating back to the early 1700s, this diligently restored colonial limestone house is called the Casa de Cortés (House of Cortés), although it was never actually owned by the conquistador. The museum's expert curators have two floors of exhibition rooms and two large patios to work with, as well as the Cubo Abierto (Open Cube), a roofless patio reserved for large exhibits. Curators balance the exhibitions between artists from Oaxaca and elsewhere in Mexico and from all over the world. The doors to the Andador are left open during museum hours, allowing passersby a peek that might tempt them into checking out the rest of the rooms.

Centro Fotográfico Manuel Álvarez Bravo

M. Bravo 116; tel. 951/516-9800; actividades.cfmab@gmail.com; 9:30am-8pm Wed.-Mon.; free

From Parque Labastida on the Andador, walk one block west on M. Bravo to find the Manuel Álvarez Bravo Photographic Center. Founded by noted Oaxacan artist Francisco Toledo (1940-2019) and named in honor of Mexico's first leading artistic photographer, who passed away in 2002, the museum hosts temporary exhibits by photographers from all over the globe.

★ Templo de Santo Domingo

Alcalá s/n; tel. 951/516-3720; 9am-7pm Mon.-Fri.; free

The local government donated the land

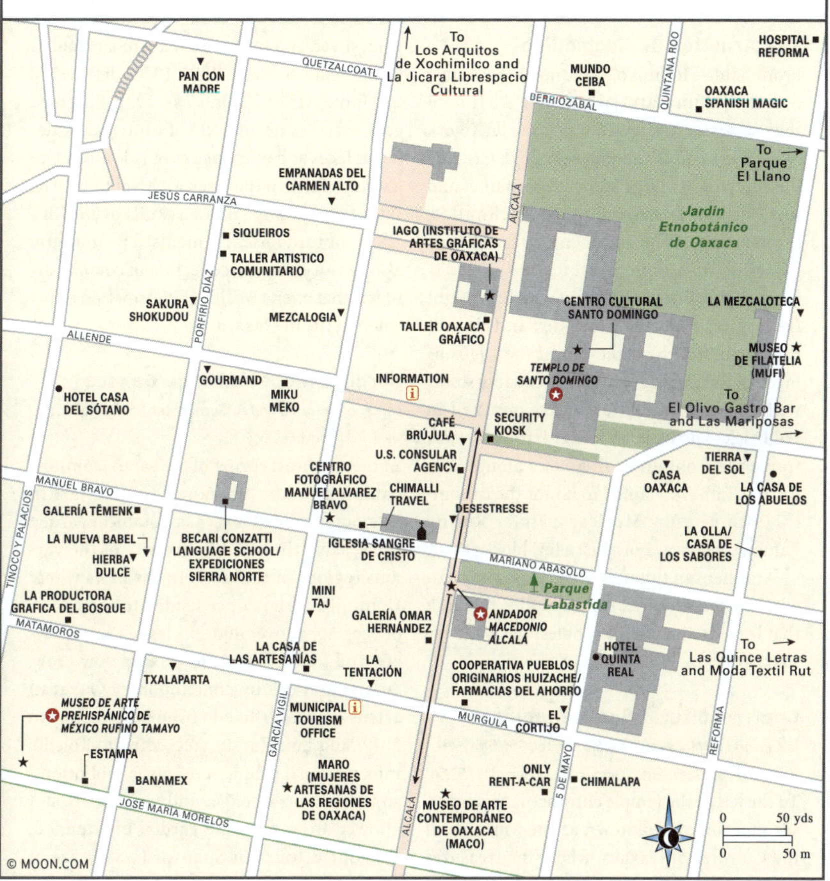

for the lavishly decorated Templo de Santo Domingo to the Dominicans in 1551, and construction on the temple and convent began immediately. The details in the molded saints and checkerboard-patterned domes of the facade alone serve to justify the fact that builders took 10 years longer than the scheduled 20 to complete construction. Gold-plated saints, cherubs, and artistic flourishes cover nearly every inch of the interior's walls and vaulted ceiling. The family tree overhead in the antechamber traces the lineage of Santo Domingo de Guzmán, founder of the Dominican Order at the turn of the 13th century, back to Mother Mary. Its breathtaking baroque architecture makes it stand out as an iconic Oaxacan landmark, and the temple is arguably the most beautiful church in the state. It's a popular place for weddings (you may catch a wedding calenda outside the church on Saturdays), and Sunday Mass is held at 7am, 11am, 1pm, 5:30pm, and 7:30pm. It's free to go inside to admire the church's beauty, during Mass or in between services, but be mindful of worshippers—if you go during Mass, you'll be expected to sit down. You'll also have to save photos and videos for when services aren't in session.

Los Arquitos de Xochimilco

From Santo Domingo, walk north on Alcalá past the Jardín Carbajal and take a left onto the short pedestrian walkway Calle de Xólotl. At its west end is the Plazuela de la Cruz de Piedra, with its large stone cross statue, and just beyond, Los Arquitos de Xochimilco, the remains of the 18th-century San Felipe Aqueduct. This picturesque 300-m (984-ft) stretch of the waterway, which brought fresh water from the Cerro de San Felipe to the north into the capital until the 1940s, is made of the iconic green cantera quarry stone, with its semicircular archways outlined in red brick. The little archways (arquitos) now frame the front doors of houses along Calle Rufino Tamayo, named to honor the canonical 20th-century Mexican painter Rufino Tamayo, who was born just a few blocks away.

Another fun tidbit: A scene from the comedy *Nacho Libre* was filmed under the arch that leads to the quaint cobblestone walkway Marcos Pérez.

Centro Cultural Santo Domingo

1a Cerrada de Macedonio Alcalá s/n; tel. 951/516-2991; 10am-5:30pm Tues.-Sat., 10am-3:30pm Sun.; US$5.25

To the left of the temple entrance is this must-see museum, also known as the Museum of the Cultures of Oaxaca, where the treasures of Monte Albán and other pre-Hispanic Oaxacan sites reside. Housed in the former Santo Domingo convent, the building is a shining masterpiece of 16th-century Dominican architecture. Two rooms around the beautifully restored cloister host temporary exhibitions. You can also peruse the shelves in the **Biblioteca de Fray Francisco de Burgoa,** a collection of over 23,000 volumes from various religious orders around the state. The oldest book, printed in 1484, is a study of the works of Aristotle by French philosopher Juan Versor.

The gold is upstairs. A handful of large rooms house a great number of well-preserved ceramic funeral urns, vases, and figurines. The first room to your right after climbing the ornate stairwell is the treasure trove of gold, silver, and turquoise that archaeologists led by Alfonso Caso (1896-1970) discovered in Monte Albán's Tomb 7 in 1931. Filigreed gold earrings decorated with intricately detailed faces and other pieces of jade and silver jewelry glitter in the weak archival light. The star of the show is a human skull covered in a "skin" of turquoise fragments. The museum also has an extensive collection of colonial artifacts that offer a wealth of information about colonial life in Oaxaca.

Jardín Etnobotánico de Oaxaca

corner of Reforma and A. Gurrión; tel. 951/516-5325; www.jardinoaxaca.mx

At the southeast corner of the Santo Domingo complex is the entrance to the Jardín Etnobotánico de Oaxaca, a botanical garden showcasing the rich biodiversity of the various regions of the state. In the plots where Dominican friars once tended to their rows of vegetables, over 800 species of cacti, flowers, and trees endemic to Oaxaca now grow, among artwork by contemporary Oaxacan artists Francisco Toledo (who passed away in 2019) and Luis Zárate. According to Toledo, informational plaques are "visual pollution," so there is no signage, and visitors are not allowed to wander the garden unattended. Scheduled tours in Spanish (US$3) are at 10am, 11am, noon, and 5pm Monday-Friday, and 10am, 11am, and noon on Saturday. English tours (US$6) are only offered at 11 am Monday-Saturday and fill up fast, so get there early to secure a spot. Children 12 and under get in free.

Museo de Filatelia (MUFI)

Reforma 504; tel. 951/514-2375; www.mufi.org.mx; 10:30am-6:30pm daily; free

The small but very well-curated MUFI (Stamp Museum), one the block to the east of the

1: Templo de Santo Domingo **2:** vendors at Parque Labastida **3:** courtyard of Museo de Filatelia (MUFI) **4:** Jardín Etnobotánico de Oaxaca

1
2
3
4

Jardín Etnobotánico, is a lot more fun than philately, or stamp collecting, sounds. In addition to an extensive collection of postage from all over the world dating back centuries, the museum also has a permanent exhibition of handwritten letters by painter Frida Kahlo, most of which were written to her doctor Leo Eloesser. There's ample courtyard space and a café to enjoy on-site, as well.

Parque El Llano

corner of Calle Berriozabal and Avenida Benito Juárez

As one of the only wooded areas in the city, Parque El Llano acts as part of Oaxaca's lungs, breathing a bit of natural refreshment in a sea of (albeit beautiful) concrete. Golden lions guard the entrances at each of its corners; located at the center is a statue of Benito Juárez, Mexico's only Zapotec president. This is an ideal place to come see a slice of Oaxacan life. There are open-air Zumba classes, joggers, roller skating classes, and folks out enjoying time with their families. Children play at the park's two playgrounds, enjoying paletas and raspados (popsicles and shaved ice). Weekends in the late afternoon provide more kiddie entertainment in the form of bouncy houses, electric cars to ride, paper canvases and ceramics set up to be painted, and more. There's some yummy food carts to try, too. I recommend the marquesitas if you have a sweet tooth.

East of the Zócalo

Centro Cultural San Pablo

Hidalgo 907; tel. 951/501-8800; www.fahho.mx/filiales-fahho/centro-cultural-san-pablo; 10am-8pm Mon.-Sat., 10am-6pm Sun.; free

Two blocks east of Zócalo, the Centro Cultural San Pablo has room after gorgeous room of exhibits that change out regularly, showcasing the work of contemporary Oaxacan artists. Originally built in the 16th century, the first Dominican convent in Oaxaca would unfortunately became the Ex-Convento de San Pablo after a pair of earthquakes in the early 17th century brought the convent crumbling to the ground; friars moved to Santo Domingo Convent.

The brick-paved courtyard spans the block and gives access to both Hidalgo and Independencia. On the Hidalgo side are an exhibition space and a café, and on the north side is the elegant SP Restaurante. Cacti grow up the west wall of the courtyard. Facing Independencia, on your right you'll see the lovely chapel Retablo de la Virgen del Rosario (Altarpiece of the Virgin of the Rosary). The entrance to the left leads to the center's main exhibition space.

The Biblioteca de Investigación Juan de Córdova (Juan de Córdova Research Library) boasts an extensive collection of texts about Zapotec, Mixtec, Mixe, and other Indigenous Oaxacan languages.

Museo Textil de Oaxaca

Hidalgo 917; tel. 951/501-1104; www.museotextildeoaxaca.org; 10am-8pm Mon.-Sat., 8am-6pm Sun.; free

Two blocks east of the northeast corner of the Zócalo, the Museo Textil de Oaxaca (Textile Museum of Oaxaca) is a shining example of curatorial talent. Given the level of skill of Oaxacan textile workers, it's no wonder people from all over the world want to put their work in the hands of curator Alejandro de Ávila Blomberg (also the director of the Jardín Etnobotánico). The lighting is ingenious: elegantly dim in a darkened room to bring out the rich tones in the pieces and nothing more, and all-white blouses lit from the inside to put the intricate needlework into relief. The museum shows these shirts, shawls, and table runners for what they truly are: fine art. This lovely museum also offers workshops for all ages.

OUTSIDE OF CENTRO

Jalatlaco

Templo de San Matías Jalatlaco

Hidalgo 211, Barrio de Jalatlaco

The colorful barrio (neighborhood) of Jalatlaco, at the far northeast corner of the Centro, is home to the quirky Templo de San Matías Jalatlaco, three blocks east of Parque El Llano. The small church stands out among

Oaxaca City for Kids

When I asked my kids what they love about Oaxaca, they said, "Everything!" Indeed, Oaxaca is very kid friendly. In a city known for its chocolate, chapulines, nieves, parades, and alebrijes, is that really a surprise? But here are a few special spots that kiddos will particularly enjoy.

playing "mercado" at Museo Infantil de Oaxaca (MIO)

SIGHTS

- **Museo Infantil de Oaxaca (MIO):** Your train aficionados will love this old train station turned children's museum. On weekends, kids can admire the model train set in the entry hall and the big train cars outside (one even outfitted with a slide). After a romp around the natural playground, there's the museum full of art activities and appreciation to explore (page 60).
- **Parque El Llano:** Weekends are when this shady park comes alive, with bouncy houses, electric cars, and art stations. But even on a weekday, two playgrounds and a paleta or two are sure to please (page 58).

RECREATION AND ACTIVITIES

- **Becari Conzatti Language School:** I know, I know, who wants to go to school on vacation? But when half the class is spent playing games, singing songs, creating piñatas, painting alebrijes, and going on excursions with other mini language learners, they'll forget that they're taking a class (page 62).
- **Chimalapa:** Get ready for chocolate overload at this delicious and educational workshop where you and your children can learn about the chocolate-making process from bean to bar. Expect to eat and drink copious amount of this Oaxacan specialty (page 64).

FOOD AND DRINKS

- **Ice cream at Jardín Sócrates:** The ice cream stands at the Jardín Sócrates will broaden your intrepid kids' horizons from vanilla, chocolate, and strawberry to new flavor heights of passion fruit, rose petal, mango, bubblegum, peanut butter, lime, gooseberry, pineapple… Need I go on (page 53)?
- **La Selva de Los Gatos:** If your kiddo is a kitty lover, then I have the *purrfect* spot for them. This outdoor cat café is filled with lounging felines who are ready to be petted and played with. The café serves up vegan snacks, desserts, and tasty drinks (page 80).

others in Oaxaca for the geometrical designs, rather than statues of saints, in its facade. Diamonds, rectangles, crosses, and a few floral flourishes adorn the church front, and zigzag designs embellish the tritostyle columns (a baroque architectural feature with decorations only on the pillar's bottom third).

Ex-Marquesado

Museo Infantil de Oaxaca (MIO)

Antigua Estacion del Av. Ferrocarril 511, Barrio del Ex-Marquesado; tel. 951/516-9388; www.mio.org.mx; info@mio.org.mx; 11am-6pm daily; free

An old railway station serves as the perfect setting for this delightful children's museum. Walking through the stone entrance and alongside the tracks feels like traveling through time. The museum makes excellent use of the space, with a few old train cars to admire, a playground/obstacle course made of natural materials in the shade of stately trees, and a carousel (3pm-6pm Thurs.-Sun.). The museum itself sparks a child's creativity, love of the arts, and cultural appreciation through expositions on Rufino Tamayo, printmaking, celebrations, market life, and more. Children will have an opportunity to create art, play Mercado, attend classes and workshops, and even catch a movie on weekends, all while learning about the beauty of Oaxacan culture.

Recreation and Activities

BIKING

Many hotels north of the Zócalo (**Hotel Azul** and **City Centro,** among others) have bikes for guests, either included in the price or to rent. Ask reception about this service. If you're not an experienced rider in urban settings, it's best to limit your pedaling to the northern half of the Centro, as the streets south of the Zócalo are congested, making it more challenging for bikers.

Bicibella Oaxaca

Alcalá 802; tel. 951/109-9727; 8:45am-7pm Mon.-Sat., 9am-3pm Sun.

Get around town on one of the refurbished vintage bikes from Bicibella Oaxaca. At just US$10 for 5 hours, it's the cheapest way to get around the Centro aside from walking, and the hours only get cheaper the longer you rent the bike. Make sure you bring an ID to leave as collateral.

Mundo Ceiba

Berriozabal 109; tel. 951/192-0419; 9am-11pm Mon.-Sat., 6pm-11pm Sun.

On the block to the north of Santo Domingo, you'll recognize this bici café (bicycle café) by the racks full of bikes in the back. It's a great place to fuel up on tacos and tlayudas, or pasta and salad, before you join them for their paseos nocturnos en bicicleta—nighttime social bike rides that the friendly, English-speaking staff organize with local bikers. They gallivant around the Centro every Wednesday, Friday, Saturday, and Sunday night 9pm-10:30pm. If you don't have a bike, you can rent one for US$12. Not very experienced in urban biking? No problem. The point of the rides is to foster safe biking practices and culture in the city, and the staff at Mundo Ceiba is here to educate as well as have fun. You'll probably see the group roaming the streets, blaring music and generally having a ball.

MOUNTAIN BIKING

If you plan on exploring on your own, the website **Oaxaca MTB** (www.oaxacamtb.org) is a detailed resource for riding Oaxaca. It has information, including maps, on dozens of routes around Oaxaca City, as well as in the Valles Centrales, La Mixteca, and the Sierra Norte.

Zapotrek Tours

Aldama 304 A, Barrio de Jalatlaco; tel. 951/257-7712; www.zapotrek.mx; 9am-5pm and 6pm-8pm Mon.-Sat.

Zapotrek Tours runs full-day cycling tours through owner Eric Ramírez's birthplace, the Valle de Tlacolula. Their **La Gente de las Nubes** (People of the Clouds) tour (US$170) descends from Cuajimoloyas, in the Sierra Norte, down the mountains into the valley. In addition to having spectacular panoramic views, you'll eat in smoky mountain comedores (family-run restaurants) and interact with farmers, business owners, and other residents along the way. Eric and the team practice responsible tourism, which focuses on spreading knowledge of a culture while minimizing negative economic, social, and environmental impacts. A Zapotrek tour will show you a side of Oaxaca you wouldn't see otherwise, and includes food, safety gear, and hotel pickup and drop-off.

Bicicletas Pedro Martínez

Aldama 418 Interior; tel. 951/514-5935 or 951/184-4506; www.bicicletaspedromartinez.com; 9:30am-8pm Mon.-Sat., 10am-3pm Sun.

When ecotourists began coming to Oaxaca in the 1980s in search of bicycles for rent, people pointed them in the direction of the bike shop of Pedro Martínez, one of Mexico's top bike racers at the time. Pedro responded to the demand by opening Bicicletas Pedro Martínez, and he has been taking visitors on exciting bike adventures ever since. One of the most popular trips visits Monte Albán, and then rides down the hill to visit San Antonio Arrazola, of alebrije-making fame, en route to Zaachila in a half day (US$145). Another goes all the way to Puerto Escondido, on the coast, in four days (US$800). They also rent bikes (US$23 per day; return by 8pm) with all the necessary safety gear.

HORSEBACK RIDING

Hipico La Golondrina

Riveras el Rio Atoyac 800, San Jacinto Amilpas, Col. Cuauhtémoc Cárdenas; tel. 951/512-7570

Sisika Annon, originally from Santa Fe, New Mexico, fell in love with horses at the tender age of seven. The love affair never ended, and she's been sharing her skill, experience, and expertise with students of all ages since 1987. Her teaching is based on a foundation of mutual respect and understanding between rider and horse, using classic techniques and exercises, modern pedagogy, and a touch of equine therapy. Hour-long classes are US$25 and include helmet and individual teachers for beginners. Intensive courses are offered over the Easter, summer, and winter school holidays, from one day (US$25) to three weeks (US$340).

Horseback Mexico

Murguía 403; tel. 951/199-7026; www.horsebackmexico.com; horsebackmexico@me.com

Native Canadian and naturalized Mexican Mary Jane Gagnier has explored Oaxaca on horseback since she moved here in 1987. She has ridden her horses clear across the state of Oaxaca, from the Pacific coast to the Puebla. Through her company Horseback Mexico, she leads fun half-day, overnight, and weeklong rides through various regions of Oaxaca. No experience required for the day rides or overnight trips; helmets and half chaps are available. Prices start at US$117 for half-day rides, US$250 for full-day rides, and US$587 for overnight trips. Reservations required. Groups are small. Book as soon as you can.

YOGA AND MEDITATION

Estudio 711

Aldama 711-A, Barrio de Jalatlaco; tel. 951/287-4288 or 951/158-9853; alosjayoga@gmail.com; US$7.50

Yogi Alosja has been sharing her yoga practice in Oaxaca for more than 15 years, and in 2021, along with fellow Yogi Tanya, they opened Estudio 711. Here you can find gentle hatha, acro, vinyasa, and restorative alignment classes, as well as workshops, massage, and reiki. Their bilingual classes are generally in the morning (8am-11am) and evening (4pm-7pm).

LANGUAGE SCHOOLS AND CLASSES

Spanish Immersion School

Matamoros 502; tel. 951/196-4567; www.spanishschoolinmexico.com; oaxacaimmersion@gmail.com; US$315-840/week

Lázaro Rojas and his faculty of experienced teachers at Spanish Immersion School utilize their greatest resource—the amazing city in which they live—to teach practical, usable Spanish effectively and quickly. Lesson plans include shopping trips to the market in which the student does all the talking (teachers help out, if necessary), or fast-paced afternoons catching rides on local buses, where students learn about the city as well as the language.

The school only offers one-on-one lessons (3-8 hours/day) and will also organize excursions, transportation, and accommodation in apartments or a local's home. They'll organize your whole trip for you, if you need it.

Oaxaca Spanish Magic

Berriozábal 200; tel. 951/195-8877; www.oaxacaspanishmagic.com; oaxacaspanishmagic@gmail.com; US$161-218/week, US$15/class

This school believes learning is magical, and they want every student's experience to be just that. The school is warm and friendly, with intensive, hands-on instruction, fluidly combining grammar with vocabulary. They also offer online classes via video call, so students can start learning before a trip in order to understand and learn more once they arrive.

Instituto Cultural Oaxaca

Juárez 909; tel. 951/515-3404; www.icomexico.com; US$250-280/week

One of the most experienced schools in town is the Instituto Cultural Oaxaca. Since 1984, ICO has offered tailor-made instruction in a gorgeous 19th-century home at the northernmost end of Calle Benito Juárez, where students lounge on the courtyard's lawns under towering palm trees. The school offers both classroom and one-on-one courses.

ICO is a proud sponsor of the **Fundación En Via** (tel. 951/515-2424; www.envia.org), a microfinance organization that supports women in Oaxaca by helping them finance businesses. Part of En Via's mission is to educate travelers about the benefits of microfinance, so they work with the school to organize tours to villages to get a unique glimpse of Oaxaca and learn about the positive impact of their program. Every Thursday and Saturday, a tour visits a village or two and meets with women who explain their projects and how they've used the loans—and provide a hearty meal at their home or business.

Becari Conzatti Language School

M. Bravo 210; tel. 951/135-6182; www.becarimb.com.mx; from US$210/week

There's no rote memorization going on here. Language learning is a social affair, and Becari Conzatti Language School gives students opportunities to learn in community. The school offers workshops from salsa dancing to weaving, as well as tours to the Valles Centrales, and even an immersive Dia del Muerto package (starting at US$718-757). Students can also choose to live with a local family during their studies.

The school has a **second location** (Gómez Farías 118) providing double the learning and volunteer opportunities. Becari partners with the **Centro de Esperanza Infantil** (Children's Hope Center) and four other local organizations to offer discounted Spanish courses in exchange for volunteer hours.

Oaxaca Lending Library

Pino Suárez 519; tel. 951/518-7077; www.oaxlibrary.org; 10am-7pm Mon.-Fri. (10am-6pm summer), 10am-1pm Sat.

If you just need a bit of practice and help, the Oaxaca Lending Library hosts free weekly intercambio (language exchange) on Saturday (10am-noon) that welcome locals, residents, and tourists alike.

1: bike tour in the Oaxacan countryside with Bicicletas Pedro Martínez **2:** on a ride with Horseback Mexico **3:** dish at Casa de los Sabores **4:** Ervit Hernández Hernández toasting cacao seeds at Chimalapa

1
2
3
4

COOKING COURSES

Many hotels and Spanish schools in Oaxaca offer cooking classes as cultural activities or as part of the curriculum. Aside from the satisfaction you'll get from creating something delicious, this is a fun and effective method for practicing your Spanish.

Casa de los Sabores

Reforma 402; tel. 951/51516-6668; www.casadelossabores.com; casadelossaboresoax@gmail.com; 9am-2pm Wed. and Fri.; group classes US$105

If you have a meal at La Olla, you'll understand why chef Pilar Cabrera is the person you want teaching you to cook Oaxacan cuisine. In addition to crafting the restaurant's toothsome menu, Pilar shares her extensive knowledge of Oaxacan ingredients, recipes, and cooking methods through her school, Casa de los Sabores. Classes (in both English and Spanish) include a shopping trip through the market, cooking class at Pilar's house, mezcal tasting, and, of course, lunch. Private classes (US$145) can be arranged for Tuesdays and Thursdays with at least two weeks' notice. Those who want to eat without attending the class can join in on the meal (US$60 pp).

Chimalapa

5 de Mayo 210; tel. 951/287-3407; www.chimalapa.com; chimalapa.cacao@gmail.com; US$26-90

Chimalapa means "golden gourd" in Zoque, an Indigenous language from the Istmo region where owner Ervit Hernández Hernández was born. The memories of the women of his Zoque village, handling cacao with sacred skill and honor, is what drives this independent project's philosophy. This is no mere chocolate workshop. This is an opportunity to take a deep dive into the culture, history, and tradition of Oaxacan cacao. Passion, love, and joy for chocolate and the people who cultivate it are evident in every class, and there is a quite a variety to choose from, including making your own chocolate bar from scratch. All the ingredients come from small farming families throughout the state, ensuring the freshest and most eco-friendly products.

TOP EXPERIENCE

MEZCAL TOURS

Zapotrek

Aldama 301-A, Barrio de Jalatlaco, Oaxaca City; tel. 951/257-7712; www.zapotrek.mx; US$110-150 pp

For a truly unique experience, call Eric Ramírez at Zapotrek. After spending 15 years in the United States, Eric returned to his native Tlacolula and realized he wanted to share the traditions, culture, and natural beauty of his homeland with others. Zapotrek tours will have you cycling through maguey fields to visit mezcal palenques (distilleries), rappelling down caves to underground rivers, and eating in local comedores in towns that aren't on anyone else's itineraries. The prices are notably higher than other agencies, but Eric makes sure that the local guides and others who provide services in the destinations get paid fairly.

Mezcal Educational Tours

Sierra Nevada 164, Colonia Loma Linda, Oaxaca City; tel. 951/505-7793 or 951/132-8203; www.mezcaleducationaltours.com; US$7-26/hr

If you want to learn about mezcal culture and production, call Alvin Starkman at Mezcal Educational Tours. A social anthropologist from Canada, Alvin has been living in Oaxaca since 2004, getting to know mezcal producers all over the state. He donates 10 percent of tour fees to the Fondo Guadalupe Musalem, a scholarship organization for Indigenous women, and he also uses the funds to pay for medical school for one of the program's graduates. (The tour's hourly rate per person depends on the number of participants.)

Festivals and Events

FESTIVALS

In his canonical essay collection on Mexican culture titled *The Labyrinth of Solitude*, poet Octavio Paz described his people's party mode with phrases like "nos desgarramos" (we tear ourselves open) and "nos disparamos" (we fire off like a gun). Oaxacan festivals are a perfect embodiment of this sentiment. As soon as the smoke of one party clears, another fuse is lit, and it's only a matter of time before the next joyous explosion. Everyone's invited. Come dance.

High season in Oaxaca City doesn't correspond to the weather—it follows the festivities. These are grand public affairs where riotous brass bands lead groups of dancing, drinking revelers through the cobblestone streets. Costumes burst with color, and the sparks and smoke of fireworks follow the boisterous processions like thunderstorms sweeping through the desert. Visit www.viveoaxaca.org for more information.

Spring

Semana Santa

March-April

The festivities surrounding Semana Santa (Holy Week), the seven days before Easter, take a much more somber tone than Oaxaca's other celebrations, but they are no less rich in culture, color, and tradition.

Before the actual Holy Week begins, one of the sweetest traditions happens the fourth Friday of Lent—the festival of La Samaritana (the Samaritan Woman), an event unique to Oaxaca. The day commemorates the biblical story of an outcast Samaritan woman who gave Jesus a drink of water. Churches, schools, and businesses set up colorfully decorated stands and give away refreshing cups of agua fresca to passersby.

For all of the Lenten season, you'll find the city draped in penitential purples and woven palm ornaments decorating doorways. During Holy Week, concerts of sacred music fill the cathedrals. Statues of Mary and Jesus are paraded through the streets by the faithful throughout the week in various neighborhoods. On Holy Thursday, Oaxacans visit seven of the city's churches for prayer and contemplation.

The only moment that quiets boisterous Oaxaca is the Procession of Silence on Good Friday. Starting at the Templo of La Preciosa Sangre de Cristo (Precious Blood of Christ) in the evening, the archbishop heads a procession of banners, images, and statues depicting Christ's passion and burial from various churches in the city. All is done in complete silence, save a solemn drum and the scrape of wooden crosses on cobblestone. (Note: Some of the men carrying the statues and crosses have their heads completely covered with pointed white or purple hoods. Don't be alarmed; this is a tradition rooted in medieval Catholic Europe, not racist domestic terrorism.)

Easter Sunday is a day of joy, with processions of the risen Christ at various churches.

Summer

TOP EXPERIENCE

Guelaguetza

July

The Guelaguetza, aka Los Lunes del Cerro (Mondays on the Hill), is a celebration of the diverse cultures tucked away in the eight regions of the state. The Zapotec name Guelaguetza means "reciprocal offering."

The official dates are the last two Mondays in July, but the city is ablaze with festivities all month. Uproarious calendas (parades) regularly fill the streets with squealing clarinets and the low bass of tubas. The leader of the revelers spins a marmota, a large white globe on a pole, and others dance inside monos, gigantic puppet figures.

The official events are held in the Auditorio Guelaguetza, the large, tent-like structure on the Cerro del Fortín. There are two shows each Monday, wherein delegations from all of Oaxaca perform their unique dances and toss their hometown treats into the cheering crowd. Tickets are sold online and at the **Secretary of Tourism of the State of Oaxaca** (Juárez 703; tel. 951/502-1200; www.oaxaca.gob.mx/sectu; 9am-5pm; US$75-85). Tickets can be notoriously hard to snag, but don't despair. The Desfile de Delagaciones (Parade of Delegations) occurs the two Saturdays before the Monday events, and it's free to attend. At this parade, each delegation performing on Monday also dances in all their splendor and shares goodies as they march down the streets of Centro, starting in Colonia Reforma, going past El Llano, heading to Zócalo. This was how my family first experienced Guelaguetza, and it was priceless.

Festival de los Moles

July

As if you needed another excuse to eat mole in Oaxaca, head to the **Centro Gastronómico de Oaxaca** (García Vigil 610) during the Festival de los Moles (Mole Festival) in July, where you can indulge all day, devouring a variety of both traditional moles and daring fusions with flavors that will have your taste buds singing for joy. In addition to the abundance of mole, traditional regional desserts, mezcal, and more are available to enjoy.

Feria Internacional de Mezcal

July

The mezcal flows freely at the Feria Internacional de Mezcal (International Mezcal Fair), a celebration of Oaxaca's favored spirit. Located at the beautiful **Centro Cultural de Convenciones de Oaxaca** (Lázaro Cárdenas 1001, Santa Lucia del Camino) just outside Oaxaca City, hundreds of mezcal companies offer up their wares for purchase, giving demonstrations and, of course, handing out abundant samples and tastings. Cultural exhibitions and performances make the fair a true celebration.

Feria del Tejate y el Tamal

July

At the Plaza de la Danza, you can stuff yourself silly during the Feria del Tejate y El Tamal (Tejate and Tamale Fair). Wrapped in banana leaves, flavored with hierba santa ("holy leaf," a ubiquitous herb in Oaxacan cuisine), and often filled with mole, Oaxacan-style tamales are delicious and satisfying. You can wash it all down with tejate, the "Drink of the Gods," once reserved for royalty, but now readily available for us commoners to enjoy.

Fall

TOP EXPERIENCE

Día de Muertos

October-November

Octavio Paz wrote that "our death illuminates our life," and nowhere in Mexico is this more apparent than in Oaxaca, renowned for its Día de Muertos (Day of the Dead) celebrations. For pre-Hispanic Mesoamerican cultures, death was more like walking through a door to another room, rather than a one-way trip to bliss or torment. They honored the dead in a month-long summer observance. The colonizers syncretized the ancient customs with their own, moving the holiday to coincide with the Catholic All Souls' Day and All Saints' Day in November.

However, Indigenous Mexicans didn't renounce all their former customs. It was common practice to display the skulls of the dead as reminders of death and rebirth. Real skulls were swapped with decorated ceramic ones, the holiday's skeletal icons.

Another example of syncretism is La Catrina, a skeletal representation of a svelte

1: Templo de San Matías Jalatlaco decorated for Semana Santa **2:** marmotas during a Guelaguetza parade **3:** Desfile de Delagaciones (Parade of Delegations) **4:** streets decorated with skulls and cempasúchil (marigolds)

1

2

3

4

woman, lavishly adorned. The image was created by printmaker José Guadalupe Posada as political satire in 1913 and subsequently popularized by muralist Diego Rivera in his "A Dream of a Sunday Afternoon in the Alameda Park." She has since become the holiday's modern connection to the Aztec "Lady of Death" Mictecacihuatl, who reigned over Mictlán, the land of the dead.

Leading up to the holiday, Oaxacans decorate ofrendas (altars) with sugar skulls, pan de muerto, cempasuchil (marigolds), cockscombs, and the favorite foods and drinks of their ancestors. The dead return to the land of the living for their ethereal family reunion. Restaurants, art galleries, and other businesses also make ofrendas. The city is filled with the smoky, sweet scent of copal incense and golden marigolds. In the evening on November 1, head to the **Panteón General** (Main Cemetery) on Calle del Refugio, just west of the Centro, to experience the cemetery decorations and rituals in Oaxaca City.

Winter

Christmas

December

In true Oaxacan celebratory fashion, Christmas Day is only the culmination of a month of festivities.

After Dominican friars introduced radishes to the region, farmers would carve religious images into giant radishes to catch shoppers' eyes in the Christmas market on December 23. The practice became so popular that in 1897 Oaxaca City's mayor formalized the **Noche de Rábanos** (Night of the Radishes) into an official event, and competitors have been carving like crazy ever since. Farmers from the surrounding valleys proudly display their vegetal masterpieces in the Zócalo in the late afternoon; judging begins around 9pm.

The magic continues into **Nochebuena** (Christmas Eve) and **Navidad** (Christmas). Verdant dioramas of the nativity are set up in Zócalo, with the Holy Family surrounded by dark-green mosses from the mountains, flor de nochebuena (poinsettias), bromeliads, and other regional flowers.

Christmastime parades, called **posadas,** represent Mary and Joseph's journey and the troubles they had finding accommodations in Bethlehem (no Moon guides back then). Children dressed as biblical characters roam the streets and are welcomed into homes and

Christmas in Oaxaca

churches, where they are given seasonal food and drinks, like ponche and tamales.

For the posadas, artisans create special piñatas made of clay jars. They're seven-pointed stars adorned with tassels, meant to represent the seven deadly sins; their bright decorations symbolize Satan's fraudulent temptations. But his wiles are no match for Virtue, represented by the stick that eventually breaks the jar open and frees the treats inside.

The Holy Mother gets her share of celebrations, too. Oaxacans celebrate the Virgin of Juquila on December 8. Mexico's patron saint, La Virgen de Guadalupe, is celebrated from the beginning of December until her official saint day, December 12. Oaxaca's patron saint, La Virgen de la Soledad, is celebrated on December 18. Even if you can't be in the city on Christmas Day, you'll find a calenda somewhere in town all month long.

The festive season continues all the way to January 6, **Dia de Los Reyes** (Three Kings Day), celebrated with Rosca de Reyes (think of a circular king cake) and gifts for children.

ART EVENTS

Posters in cafés and on the street advertise many events. The best places to find out about art events in Oaxaca are the galleries themselves. They usually have inaugural events for new exhibitions, so these depend on each gallery's schedule. The best online resource is **Qué Pasa Oaxaca** (www.quepasaoaxaca.com), which has a detailed schedule of art events in the city.

Movie buffs will love the volume of film events in Oaxaca City. The mobile cinema club **Cinema Cuervo** (tel. 951/414-7083) hosts showings all over town. Check their social media accounts or look for their posters around town for information.

Shopping

SOUTH OF THE ZÓCALO

Traditional Markets

TOP EXPERIENCE

★ Mercado Benito Juárez

Las Casas s/n; tel. 951/516-2352; 8am-7pm daily

Your first shopping stop should be the Mercado Benito Juárez, a block south of the southwest corner of the Zócalo. This is both a tourists' and locals' market, selling everything from souvenir T-shirts to traditional clothing and folk art to tortillas, vegetables, meat, and chapulines. It's also one of the best places to try the pre-Hispanic Oaxacan drink tejate. The trendy-looking puesto (vendor booth) **La Flor de Huayapam** is run by women from San Andrés Huayapam, the birthplace of the beverage. They have the classic cacao-flavored tejate, as well as a drink made with coconuts and one made with chilacayote (figleaf gourd) and sweetened with honey.

Mercado de Artesanías

corner of Zaragoza and J. P. García; no tel.; 9am-7pm daily

The selection at Mercado de Artesanías (Artisan Market) is not as ample as at other places in town—vendors here focus on the most popular textiles and pottery styles—but prices are generally very good. It's a great place to pick up a rug made in Teotitlán del Valle or barro negro ceramics from San Bartolo Coyotepec.

NORTH OF THE ZÓCALO

Art Galleries

Try turning a corner in Oaxaca City and not finding an art gallery. This is not an extensive list of the galleries but rather a selection of places that really stand out.

Galería Omar Hernández

Alcalá 303; tel. 951/516-7302; galeriaoh@gmail.com; 10am-2pm and 3pm-9pm Mon.-Fri.

You'll see some of the most interesting modern ceramic fine art being made in Oaxaca at Galería Omar Hernández. Omar finds inspiration in some of Oaxaca's most valuable cultural symbols, such as skulls, corncobs, and most notably, his representations of the plastic jugs people use to dole out mezcal during calendas and other festivities. Like other impactful Oaxacan artists, he has found that magical way to use conventionally dark themes and hair-raising motifs to celebrate the lively cultural heritage of his native land.

T.A.C. (Taller Artistico Comunitario)

Independencia 1306; tel. 951/685-3784; urtarte2017@gmail.com; 11am-5pm Mon.-Sat.

Art is the pulse of a people, and when viewing the art created by the folks at T.A.C. you can see their heart beating with a desire to empower the community. T.A.C. is responsible for a lot of the stickers, stencils, and poster street art you'll see around town and believes art to be a community affair, not just for a privileged few. In addition to doing plenty of work in local and rural neighborhoods, they provide workshops and prints for sale.

IAGO (Instituto de Artes Gráficas de Oaxaca)

Alcalá 507; tel. 951/516-6980; www.iago.com.mx; 9am-8pm daily

Fans of world-renowned Oaxacan visual artist Francisco Toledo (www.franciscotoledo.net) must visit IAGO (Graphic Arts Institute of Oaxaca), in a gorgeous 18th-century house right across from Santo Domingo. The center has rooms for temporary exhibitions, a printmaking workshop, an extensive art library, a café, and a gift shop full of items emblazoned with his haunting aesthetic.

Toledo, who was born in Juchitán (in the Istmo de Tehuantepec) in 1940, founded the center in 1988. The artist, who died in 2019, is best known for his unique mosaics of animals usually not associated with beauty, such as monkeys, alligators, and insects. Among his most popular pieces are his decorative kites, but there are also cool notebooks printed with eerie spiders, shrimps, and pelicans, and framed prints of monkeys, skeletons, and anthropomorphic scorpions made of laser-cut X-ray film. Toledo also made jewelry with this innovative technique. His ability to find beauty in what conventionally arouses disgust and fear is exemplified by these stylish and wearable crocodiles, grasshoppers, crabs, spiders, and scorpions with human legs. He added sparkle to some of the necklaces, bracelets, and earrings with coarsely applied gold film.

Artisans Cooperatives

Artisans cooperatives are some of the best places to find gifts and souvenirs in Oaxaca. The selections are wide and the prices reasonable, and, best of all, you can be sure that your money is directly supporting the artists in the co-ops.

Cooperativa Pueblos Originarios Huizache

Murguía 101; tel. 951/415-4652; 9am-9pm Mon.-Sat., 10am-8pm Sun.

The artisans at Cooperativa Pueblos Originarios Huizache created this ample and beautiful store on their own, without the help of government grants. Hailing from artisan towns such as San Bartolo Coyotepec, Atzompa, Arrazola, and beyond, they handcraft each creation with pride. Every craft comes from the families who make up this cooperative.

La Casa de las Artesanías

Matamoros 105; tel. 951/516-5062; www.lacasadelasartesaniasdeoaxaca.com; 9am-9pm daily

One block to the west of Huizache (note that Murguía changes to Matamoros at Alcalá), La Casa de las Artesanías also showcases a large selection of folk art from all eight regions of Oaxaca.

Oaxaca City's Thriving Printmaking Scene

The violence that erupted in May and June of 2006, when police opened fire on nonviolent protesters demanding higher pay for teachers, sparked an artistic conflagration that still burns bright. Lithography, xylography, and other types of printmaking existed here before this tragic event, but the art form has definitely gained popularity, and many talleres de grabado (printmaking workshops) have sprouted up around town, mostly in the blocks west of the Andador.

street art

PASAPORTE GRÁFICO

A dozen of these workshops have collaborated to support each other and printmaking in general. At the workshops listed here, you can pick up a Pasaporte Gráfico (Graphic Passport), a free brochure and map to all 12 shops. As you visit shops, ask them to stamp your passport with their unique print, which ends up becoming a cool souvenir on its own. Once you've filled it up, you get a discount at all of them.

PRINTMAKING WORKSHOPS

Each shop has its own unique style and focus, some choosing to concentrate on images of maguey, maize, skulls, and other cultural symbols of Oaxaca, others of resistance and politics. Often, the two are merged.

- **Espacio Zapata** (Porfirio Díaz 509; tel. 951/126-7110; espaciozapatagaleria@gmail.com; 11am-7pm Mon.-Sat.)
- **Casa Subterránea** (Morelos 403; tel. 951/591-1203, 951/508-0432; subterraneosoaxaca@gmail.com; 10am-8pm Mon.-Sat.)
- **La Productora Grafica del Bosque** (Matamoros 305; tel. 951/569-6460; laproductoragraficadelbosque@gmail.com; 9am-8pm Mon.-Sat.)
- **Gabinete Gráfico** (M. Bravo 216 & 219; tel. 951/203-5245; gabinetexilografico@gmail.com; 10am-8pm daily)
- **Estampa** (5 de Mayo 210; tel. 951/672-9225, 951/872-9244; estampa_galeria_oax@hotmail.com; 10am-8pm daily)
- **Oaxaca Gráfico** (Macedonio Alcalá 503; tel. 951/516-7236; oaxgrafico@gmail.com; 11am-9pm daily)
- **La Chicharra** (Xicotencatl 317; tel. 951/165-1911; lachicharra14@hotmail.com; 11am-8pm Mon.-Sat.)
- **Tëmenk** (M. Bravo 301; tel. 951/124-5705; tallertemenk@gmail.com; 10am-6pm daily)
- **Burro Press** (Humboldt 100-A; no tel.; burropress@gmail.com; 10:30am-7pm Mon.-Sat.)
- **Mini Print** (Porfirio Díaz 400-C; no tel.; miniprintoaxaca@gmail.com; 10:30am-6pm Mon.-Sat.)
- **La Santísima** (Hidalgo 1019; tel. 951/606-6191, 951/332-1208; lasantisimacolectivo@gmail.com; 11am-8pm Mon.-Sat.)
- **Taller Siqueiros** (Porfirio Díaz 510; tel. 951/361-9217; espaciosiqueiros@gmail.com; 11am-7pm Mon.-Sat.)

MARO (Mujeres Artesanas de las Regiones de Oaxaca)

García Vigil 204; tel. 951/516-0670; maroaxaca.blogspot.com; 9:30am-7:30pm Mon.-Sat., 10:30am-7:30pm Sun.

The all-female co-op MARO (Craftswomen of the Regions of Oaxaca) is made up of over 400 women artisans who have organized to provide visitors with what is probably the widest variety of artisanal products in the Centro, all at prices that are fair for both shopper and merchant. When you shop here, not only will you spot harder-to-find items, but you can be sure your money is going directly to bettering the lives of hardworking Oaxacans.

Clothing and Textiles

Aside from the co-ops, the daily open-air markets in the **Alameda de León** and on **Calle Aldama,** on the north side of the Mercado 20 de Noviembre, sell traditional huipiles (embroidered blouses) and other garments from all regions of Oaxaca. But traditional artisans aren't the only folks selling vivid vestments in the city. A number of designers purchase embroidered fabrics and other artisanal textiles to create fashionable pieces that range in style from casual to formal wear.

Moda Textil Rut

Pino Suárez 311; tel. 951/103-3235; 10am-8pm Mon.-Sat.

Moda Textil Rut incorporates textiles from the eight regions of Oaxaca into modern casual and formal designs for both men and women. They make it a point to work with artisans from all over the state in order to provide clients with a selection that represents the full range of colors, designs, and talent that Oaxaca has to offer.

Miku Meko

Porfirio Díaz 1007; tel. 951/255-2457; mikumeko.oax@gmail.com; 10:30am-7pm Mon.-Fri., noon-6pm Sat.

Two blocks west of Santo Domingo, the design and production team led by Alelí Hernandez is creating magic at Miku Meko. The majority of their work in this earthy boutique is custom-tailored clothing. You can choose both the design and the fabric of the pieces. Each is made with an artisanal techniques, such as cloths woven from backstrap looms and colored with natural dyes, creating truly unique pieces for each individual.

Bookstores

La Jicara Librespacio Cultural

Porfirio Diaz 1105; tel. 951/205-1450; librelajicara@gmail.com; 1pm-11pm Mon.-Sat.

Oaxacan doorways are as colorful as they are mysterious; you never know what lies beyond the facade. From the outside looking in, you'd never guess that this old house has been transformed into a lovely "cultural freespace," made up of a bookstore, vegetarian restaurant, and a small shop stocked with organic goodies, connected by a lush canopy of leafy vines and bougainvillea. The independent bookstore is well stocked with a variety of titles, full of local artists and poets who cover topics from feminism to neo-colonialism. There's also a children's reading room with imaginative toys, La Jicarita. Literary and artistic events are often hosted here too. After shopping, stop by Calabacitas Tiernas, the on-site vegetarian restaurant, for a tasty bite to eat.

EAST OF THE ZÓCALO

Artisans Cooperatives

Andares del Arte Popular

Independencia 1003; tel. 951/688-7593; www.andaresdelarte.com; 10am-7pm daily

On the block northwest of the Centro Cultural San Pablo, Andares del Arte Popular (Journeys in Folk Art) curates its products like artifacts in a museum. The beautifully arranged displays treat Oaxaca's rich communal art traditions like the fine art they truly are.

1: decorations outside an artisans co-op **2:** T.A.C. (Taller Artistico Comunitario) **3:** rugs from Teotitlán del Valle

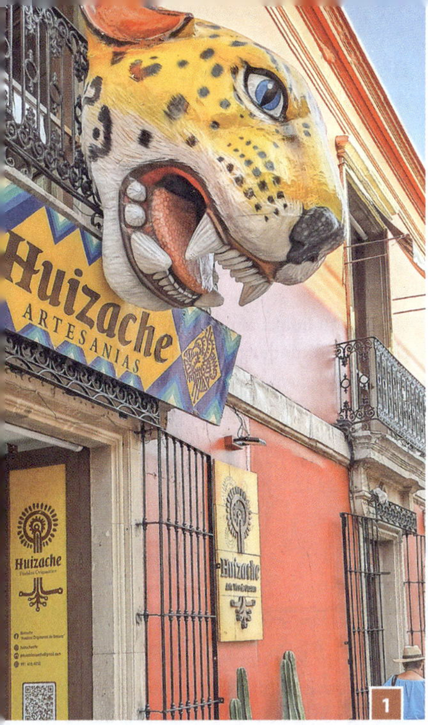
Huizache
ARTESANIAS
Huizache
Huizache

1

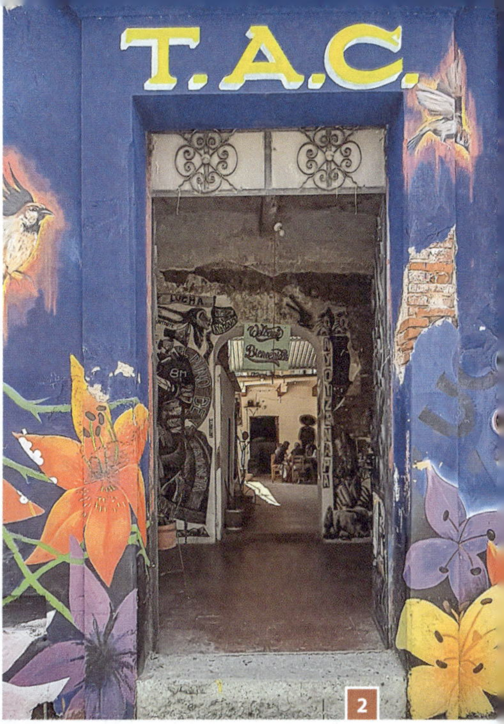
T.A.C.

2

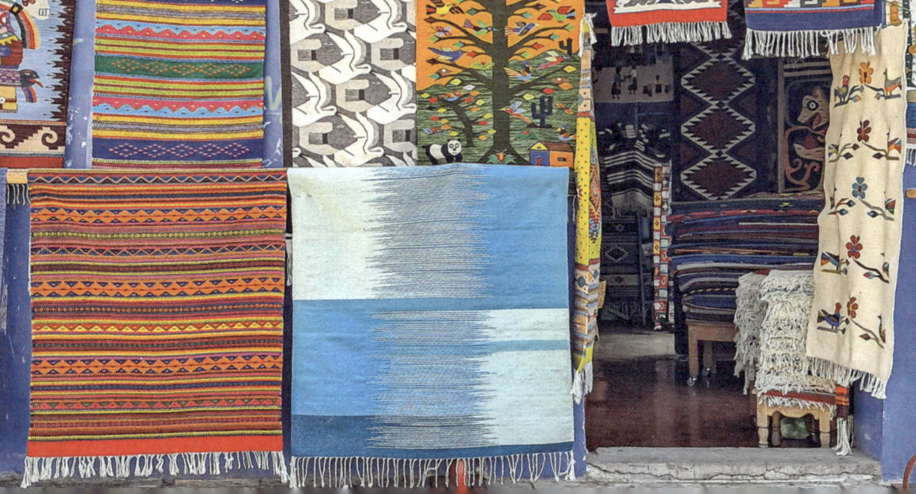

3

OUTSIDE OF CENTRO

Traditional Markets

Mercado La Merced

Morelos 1522A; tel. 951/321-7244; 6am-6pm daily

For a more local shopping experience, try Mercado La Merced just east of Centro. A number of food stalls, or fondas, serve up delicious Oaxacan fare, such as flavorful moles, delicious tasajo, and tasty memelitas. After your meal, waddle over to the shopping side, where you can find fresh fruits and veggies, knickknacks (I may have bought a mini tortilla press or two), anything really. There is even an ATM conveniently located in an air-conditioned booth outside if you run out of efectivo (cash).

Bookstores

Amate Books

Aldama 318, Barrio de Jalatlaco; tel. 951/672-3377; amateoaxaca@gmail.com; 10:30am-7:30pm Mon.-Tues. and Thurs.-Sat., 1pm-7pm Sun.

I just love a good bookstore, and one of the best English-language bookstores in Mexico is Amate Books, nestled in the Jalatlaco neighborhood. The selection runs both deep and wide, with books about Oaxaca plus lots of classic and modern literature and translations of Mexican authors, for both children and adults. There is also a small but splendid selection of folk art for purchase.

Food

Well, Oaxaca isn't called the gastronomic capital of Mexico for nothing. From street tacos to tlayudas (think overgrown quesadillas) to organic health food to the original culinary inventions of the new vanguard of Oaxacan chefs riding high on the wave of the mezcal boom, the extensive range of ingredients, flavors, and prices here offers something for everyone, no matter your tastes or budget.

THE ZÓCALO

Most of the restaurants around the Zócalo have large menus featuring both traditional Oaxacan cuisine and international meals like club sandwiches and cheeseburgers. Aside from the couple of gems mentioned, you won't find the best of what Oaxacan kitchens have to offer here, but that's not really the point. Eat here for the lively ambience beneath the shade of the towering laurel trees.

Mexican

Restaurante Coronita

Diaz Ordaz 208; tel. 951/205-8907; www.restaurantecoronita.com; 8am-6pm daily; US$6-15

Born of the love story of a girl from Etla and a boy from Zaachila, this restaurant has been serving up the best of all the cuisine the Valles Centrales has to offer since 1948. They have great breakfast options such as enfrijoladas and chilaquiles (made with mole amarillo for a Oaxacan twist), traditional eats like memelas and chapulines, and most excitingly, all seven of Oaxaca's traditional moles, including the rare mole chichilo. If you tend to be indecisive, no worries—the mole sampler plate serves two for US$40.

★ Tr3s 3istro

Portal de Flores 3; tel. 951/501-0407; 9am-11pm daily; US$10 25

The best combination of flavor, ambience, and price is the understatedly swanky Tr3s 3istro, above Cafetería Del Jardín. The service is impeccable, and the ample menu of traditional moles (including the harder-to-find mole manchamanteles) and house specialties does not disappoint. The seafood is always fresh, and oysters are flown in from Baja California daily to stock the oyster bar.

The Seven Moles of Oaxaca

degustación de moles

The truth is, there are not just seven moles to be found in Oaxaca. There are dozens, perhaps hundreds. Derived from the Nahuatl word *molli*, meaning "mixture" or "sauce," moles vary from region to region and even town to town. You'll find the sour mole estofado down in Istmo, and spicy, red-hot moles paired with seafood, like mole de tichinda (mussels), in the Afro-Mexican villages of Costa Chica, and a special mole de cadras (goat) in La Mixteca—but only in the fall.

But for the sake of simplicity, let's go with the seven "classic" moles (a list that still varies depending on who you ask). Because we have to start somewhere, right?

- **Mole Negro (Black Mole):** The king of the moles, the classic black mole is made of over 30 ingredients, including a variety of toasted chiles and chocolate. It's a labor-intensive sauce to make—a labor of love—which you can taste in its rich and robust flavor.
- **Mole Coloradito (Little Red Mole):** My personal favorite, a derivative of mole colorado. Made with ancho and gualillo chiles, dried fruit, nuts, and cinnamon, it has a delectably sweet kind of heat.
- **Mole Amarillo (Yellow Mole):** This golden mole is one of the only moles you'll eat as a street food. You will find these served with shredded chicken in empanada form.
- **Mole Verde (Green Mole):** Fresh and verdant, this is the lightest of all the moles. Herbs favored in Oaxaca such as epazote and hoja santa (also known as hierba santa), as well as the more common cilantro and parsley, give this mole its color and brightness.
- **Mole Almendrado (Almond Mole):** This sweet almond-based mole has a mild but no less rich flavor. If you find other moles a bit too spicy, this is a good option.
- **Mole Manchamanteles (Tablecloth-Staining Mole):** You'll want to leave your crisp vacation whites at home for this one. With fruity notes from pineapples, plantains, and pears balancing out the spicy chiles, it almost tastes like dessert.
- **Mole Chichilo:** The least known among travelers of all the moles, this rare dish is made with the ash of charred tortillas and chile seeds, and often made for funerals.

WHERE TO TRY THEM

- If you want to turn a mole sampler into a platter, head to **Restaurante Coronita** (page 74).
- If you want to experience all seven moles, **Los Pacos** does a complimentary degustación de moles (mole tasting), where you can sample each mole as a staff member explains the ingredients and what the mole is usually paired with (page 81).

Basque

El Asador Vasco

Portal de Flores 10-A; tel. 951/514-4755; www.asadorvasco.com; 1:30pm-11:30pm daily; US$11-20

Just above Café Del Jardín is the award-winning El Asador Vasco (The Basque Grill), with a large menu of the hearty surf and turf of Basque country. Decorated like a medieval inn where Don Quixote would have regaled diners with outrageous tall tales, El Asador Vasco serves classic Basque fondues and seafood, as well as its namesake, grilled meats like filet mignon and veal au gratin. The restaurant consistently earns the Achievement of Distinction from DiRoNA (Distinguished Restaurants of North America). It also gets extra points for having a small playspace for children up to age 4 to play while the big folks enjoy their meal.

SOUTH OF THE ZÓCALO

You'll notice a marked difference between the streets north of the Zócalo and those to the south. Here the streets teem with people, carts, cars, buses, and the best-priced food in the Centro. There are fantastic restaurants north of the Zócalo, but they are admittedly cooking for tourists. The south is where you'll find delicious everyday Oaxacan food—from tiny nooks selling fresh juice and tortas (Mexican sandwiches) to affordable terrace bars for buckets of beer and plates of botanas (finger foods) to family-run comedores—for a fraction of the price. This is not the best area for people with serious personal space issues. It's much more crowded down here, yes, but don't let that deter you. Elbow in and wish those around you "¡Buen provecho!" (Enjoy your meal!).

Markets

TOP EXPERIENCE

★ Mercado 20 de Noviembre

20 de Noviembre 512; tel. 951/516-2352; 7am-7pm daily; US$2-3

If you leave Oaxaca City without having a meal at the Mercado 20 de Noviembre, you're doing it wrong. This crowded, hectic, and delicious collection of food stalls is the best introduction to Oaxacan food you can find.

Sandwiched in between the bakers' counters on the north side and the mole vendors on the south side, the small diner-style counters serve up fresh hot Oaxacan chocolate with pan de yema (egg yolk bread) and other comida típica (traditional food) from the region, like mole negro, enmoladas (enchiladas made with mole coloradito), enfrijolados (same, but with a bean sauce), tlayudas, chiles rellenos, and more. Just find an empty spot at one of the dozen or so counters, and you're set. Every chef in this market building knows exactly what he or she is doing, and you will not be disappointed. On the market's east side, the butchers of **El Pasillo de las Carnes Asadas** (The Hall of Grilled Meats) grill fresh tasajo (thin-cut beef), cecina (thin-cut pork), and chorizo (spicy sausage) for hungry carnivores all day long.

Musicians often stroll the aisles, livening up the atmosphere with melodies and rhythm. Support them. They are part of what makes this place a unique eating experience.

Mexican

La Red

Las Casas 101; tel. 951/514-6853; noon-8pm daily; US$5-8

Locals are so fond of seafood restaurant La Red that waiters sometimes control the regular line out front with a chain pulled across the door. I tend to trust lines for food like this in Mexico, and it is indeed worth the wait. La Red serves seafood specialties from all over Mexico, like camarones a la diabla (devilishly spicy shrimp) and huauchinango a la veracruzana (red snapper baked in a spicy, Veracruz-style tomato sauce).

Orgánico El Pochote Rayón

Rayón 411; no tel.; 8am-6pm daily

For something healthier, head to the Mercado Orgánico El Pochote Rayón, where a cluster of booths serve up salubrious, veggie-heavy

The Hall of Grilled Meats

That frenetic hallway on the east side of the Mercado 20 de Noviembre is **El Pasillo de las Carnes Asadas,** or The Hall of Grilled Meats. Also called El Pasillo del Humo (The Hall of Smoke), for obvious reasons, this is a unique dining experience for carnivores.

If it looks confusing, that's because it is, at first. Smoke rises from meat sizzling on grills while people squeeze by carrying trays of condiments, gripping multiple bottles of Coca-Cola between their fingers, or playing guitar. The thing here is that you order and pay for each part of your meal with a different person. All these people rushing back and forth through the aisle are working, selling tortillas, salsas, grilled onions and chiles de agua (good flavor, sometimes spicy), chopped-up onions, cucumbers, tomatoes, and cilantro, and beverages.

El Pasillo de las Carnes Asadas

HOW TO ORDER

Order the carnes first. Your options are tasajo (beef), cecina enchilada (seasoned, or "chilied" pork), chorizo, lomo (pork loin), and tripa (intestines).

While they grill it up right there for you, head to the big communal tables at the west end and order whatever else you want for your meal. They'll pile up the meat and grilled chiles on a big basket-like plate and bring it to you. It may seem hectic, but the servers here will make sure you get everything you need. Someone will come by with a tray of veggies and salsas, someone else will take your beverage order, and a different person will bring you tortillas.

Someone from the butcher will bring the bill for the meat, and you'll pay everyone else separately for each type of food item at the end of the meal. ¡Buen provecho!

meals from Oaxaca and beyond. You'll find fresh seafood, pastas, and stir-fries, and fresh juices, chocolate, and tejate, all made with organic ingredients. There is even a stand that sells cemitas, large, often messy sandwiches typical of the neighboring state of Puebla, brimming with quesillo (Oaxacan cheese) and flavored with epazote, a zesty herb that grows in the region.

Street Food

During the day, you'll find older women with baskets of **empanadas de amarillo,** large quesadilla-like things filled with mole amarillo and chicken or pork, on the sidewalks outside the Mercado 20 de Noviembre. They're a delicious treat on the go, but be careful: The filling is usually steaming hot and takes a while to cool down. These empanadas are the famed recipe from the town of San Antonino Castillo Velasco, so if you're not going there, don't miss your chance to try one here.

Chefinita

corner of Las Casas and 20 de Noviembre; tel. 951/228-5957; 5pm-4am Mon.-Sat., 5pm-midnight Sun.; US$2

In the afternoon, taco and pozole stands like Chefinita set up shop along 20 de Noviembre on the blocks by the market. On the pozole, con todo means cabbage and guacamole thrown on top of the soup.

NORTH OF THE ZÓCALO

The north side is where you'll find the fancier restaurants in Oaxaca City, where chefs are more into experimenting with recipes than presenting them traditionally. Catering to tourists, these restaurants sometimes seem to spend more time, effort, and money on their decor and website than they do on the menu—but you'll also find some affordable places where the experiments have produced delicious new twists on Oaxacan flavors.

Mexican

★ Las Quince Letras

Abasolo 300; tel. 951/514-3769; www.lasquincelwtras.mx; 8am-10pm Mon.-Sat., 8am-7pm Sun.; US$8-12

The food of owner/head chef Celia Florian will have you head over heels. Relax in the shady, cactus-lined courtyard with a refreshing agua fresca and watch the chefs prepare the tortillas for tetelas (corn tortilla with beans, hierba santa, and cheese) and other tasty local delicacies. The menu's absolute musts include the chiles de agua a la vinagreta, stuffed spicy chiles prepared with a vinaigrette, and the chef's flavorful trilogía de moles, which includes mole negro, mole coloradito, and mole estofado de almendras. For dessert, try her ingenious tamal de chocolate (chocolate tamale).

La Olla

Reforma 402; tel. 951/516-6668; www.laolla.com.mx; noon-9:30pm Tues.-Sun.; US$7-20

Esteemed Oaxacan chef Pilar Cabrera runs the kitchen at a restaurant named after cooking pots. La Olla changes out its menu three to four times a year in order to exhibit the range of possibilities from all the ingredients available in Oaxaca. The rooftop terrace has an excellent view of Santo Domingo, perfect for cocktails at sunset.

★ Tierra del Sol

Reforma 411; tel. 951/516-8641; www.tierradelsol.mx; 7:30am-11pm daily; US$12-25

If you can't make it out to La Mixteca on this trip, get a taste of the region's delicious recipes in the cozy, ranch-style home setting at Tierra del Sol (Land of the Sun). Head chef Olga Cabrera Oropeza, originally from Huajuapan de León, brings the homestyle cooking she learned from her grandmothers to Oaxaca City and beyond, having presented dishes from La Mixteca at international culinary festivals in New York and elsewhere. The mole de tres generaciones is her homage to one of her grandmothers, from whom she gained much of the knowledge she uses in the kitchen.

Street Food

Empanadas del Carmen Alto

Jesus Carranza 102; no tel.; 5pm-11pm Thurs.-Tues.; US$3.50

Not too long after we moved to Oaxaca, my family was wandering around one evening, trying to find our way back to Santo Domingo (we were lost—and later realized, only a couple of blocks away!). Feeling peckish, we decided to give a bustling food cart a try—and I'm so glad we did. We found some of the most delicious memelas, quesadillas, and empanadas in the whole city. And apparently Netflix agrees: This spot was featured on the docuseries *Street Food: Latin American.* Be sure to try the empanadas de mole amarillo and quesadillas with flor de calabaza (squash blossom).

Asian

Mini Taj

Santos Degollado 512; tel. 951/109-6960; 11am-9pm Mon.-Sat., 1pm-8:30pm Sun.; US$8-10

Ramesh Radheshyam, owner of Mini Taj, has been firing up the tandoor and serving popular Indian dishes since 2010, including curries, naan, samosas, lassis, and more. His curries are made the way they're supposed to be: packed as full of spices and flavors as complex as mole.

Sakura Shokudou

Porfirio Díaz 507; tel. 951/145-6261; 1:30pm-7pm Mon.-Fri., 1:30pm-8pm Sat.; US$6-12

Nestled in the cluster of printmakers on Porfirio Díaz, Sakura Shokudou serves up ramen, udon, tempura, yakimeshi (a fried rice dish), and, of course, sushi—but only for a few hours a day, so it'll have to be lunch or an early dinner.

Oaxaca City for Vegetarians and Vegans

No meat? No problem! You will not be left out in the enjoyment of Oaxacan cuisine. Not only do some of the best restaurants in the city have vegetarian and vegan offerings on their menu, the city has several quality restaurants that are completely meat free:

CASA OAXACA

Constitución 104-A; tel. 951/516-8531; www.casaoaxacaelrestaurante.com; 1pm-11pm Mon.-Sat., 1pm-9pm Sun.; US$16-32

Casa Oaxaca, across the street from the Jardín Etnobotánico, may be better-known for its ribs and rabbit dishes, but Casa Oaxaca hasn't forgotten about meat-free eaters. In addition to some tasty salads and soups, Chef Alejandro Ruiz actually dedicated menu space for vegan plates, such as grilled tomatoes served hoja santo pesto and a macadamia nut "cheese" sauce.

CASA DEL ELFO

Reforma 703-Local 9; tel. 951/516-1480; www.linktr.ee/casadelelfo; 8:30am-11pm Mon.-Sat., 10am-6pm Sun.; US$6-12

Casa Del Elfo has tasty dishes like vegetarian burritos and hummus plates but also serves up some wonderful vibes. A diverse lineup of live music, salsa nights, and even an intercambio to brush up on your Spanish round out a great restaurant experience.

HIERBA DULCE

Porfirio Diaz 311; tel. 951/516-5374; www.hierba-dulce.com; 2pm-9:30pm Thurs.-Tues.; US$6-12

Hierba Dulce, set in the picturesque courtyard of an old colonial home, serves as a vegan oasis with a delicious variety of traditional Oaxacan delights, including several moles. The cocktails are tasty and pack a punch; if you're a lightweight like me, try the tepache (fermented pineapple drink) instead.

TAJ MAHAL

Fiallo 314; tel. 951/527-4242; 9am-10pm daily; US$8

Many vegan and vegetarian dishes are on the buffet at Taj Mahal, which is served noon-7pm. The menu also has vegan options, in case you don't make it for the buffet. The restaurant is two blocks east and one block south of the southeast corner of the Zócalo.

MERCADO ORGÁNICO LA COSECHA

Alcalá 806; no tel.; 9am-5pm Wed.-Sun.

Many stalls serve vegan food in the Mercado Orgánico La Cosecha, two blocks north of Santo Domingo.

Tapas

El Olivo Gastrobar

Constitución 207; tel. 951/501-0333; tasca.elolivo@gmail.com; 1pm-midnight Tues.-Sat., 1pm-11pm Sun.; US$8-10

The ample terrace at El Olivo Gastrobar has an open, friendly atmosphere for tapas next to the olive and pochote trees. The stylish horseshoe-shaped bar downstairs serves draft beer brewed in-house, as well as other local beers. Also on the menu are delicious Spanish-style tortillas, pastas, and gazpacho.

Gourmand

Porfirio Díaz 410-A; tel. 951/516-4435; deli.gourmand@gmail.com; 9am-midnight Mon.-Thurs., 9am-12:30am Fri.-Sat.; US$7-12

El Olivo's spin-off delicatessen and café two blocks west of Santo Domingo, Gourmand serves tapas, as well as sandwiches, burgers,

Comida Corrida

Of Mexico's eating customs, one of my favorites is the comida corrida. Translating to something like "meal on the go," comida corrida is a set menu of around five options of premade meals kept hot and ready to be served. It will include an agua de sabor (fruit drink), a soup or fruit salad, and guisado (literally "stew" or "gravy," but in this case, "main course") options like chiles rellenos, enchiladas, moles, and huevos al gusto ("eggs how you want 'em"). Comida corrida is usually served from breakfast to around 2pm or 3pm, sometimes later. It isn't really a dinner option, and it is rarely offered on Sundays.

comida corrida

WHERE TO TRY IT

The blocks south of the Zócalo are home to a number of delicious comida corrida options, where you can eat what is basically a fresh, home-cooked meal for US$3-5. Here are some of my favorite places:

- **La Rana Feliz** (Aldama 217; no tel.; 8am-7pm daily)
- **El Girasol de Castillo** (J. P. García 404; tel. 951/508-9321; 8am-11pm Mon.-Sat.)
- **Café Alex** (Díaz Ordaz 218; tel. 951/501-2020; 7am-9pm daily)

Spanish tortillas, gazpacho, sausages, charcuterie, and other Spanish delicacies.

Cafés

Most cafés tend to focus on the coffee and serve only bakery snacks like cookies, cakes, and muffins, but some have full menus with delicious breakfasts, salads, sandwiches, and more.

★ Café Brújula

Alcalá 104 and 407; tel. 951/424-0907; www.cafebrujula.com; 7:30am-10pm Mon.-Sat., 8:30am-9pm Sun.; US$4

Oaxaca's most reputable café chain, Café Brújula, has two locations on the Andador, one near Santo Domingo and the other near the Zócalo (with a mini bonus one inside the Stamp Museum). Since 2006, the chain has offered the highest-quality coffees from all regions of Oaxaca, in settings that add a hip, modern touch to the venerable surroundings. Brújula's master roasters extract full-bodied, never-bitter flavors from the beans.

Pan Con Madre

Quetzalcóatl 205-D; tel. 951/228-1154; 8am-8:30pm Mon.-Sat.; US$3-5

Who doesn't love bread? Here you can find everything from their sourdough loaves, croissants, and baguettes to sweeter favorites such as conchas (Mexican sweet bread), cinnamon rolls, and their oh so tasty empanada de guayaba (guava empanada). Grab a coffee or chocolate to enjoy with your treat in their adorable courtyard patio.

La Selva de Los Gatos

Abasolo 710; tel. 951/430-4231; Thurs.-Tues. 10am-6pm; US$5-10

There are kitties galore in this outdoor cat café that serves as a rescue and adoption center. The menu features vegan sandwiches, snacks, desserts, and beverages.

OUTSIDE OF CENTRO

Mexican

Los Pacos

Belisario Domínguez 108, Colonia Reforma; tel. 951/515-3573; 9am-8:30pm Mon.-Sat., 9am-6:30pm Sun.; US$12-18

It's a family affair spanning three generations at this restaurant known for its mouthwatering moles—and the self-proclaimed originator of the "degustación de moles" ("mole tasting"). The original restaurant in Colonia Reforma was on the family's compound, where patriarch Francisco Conseco decided to open a restaurant at the age of 50 with two other Franciscos—his uncle and cousin. Like *Bill* for *William*, *Paco* is a nickname for *Francisco*, hence "Los Pacos." His wife, Doña Maria del Socorro, used all their family's recipes, drawing on the best of the region's traditions. Daughter Laura Conseco and her son Hugo Santos now continue the family's legacy of rico (rich) mole, pleasant ambiance, and attentive service.

Bars and Nightlife

A unique staple of Oaxaca City nightlife is the mezcalería, a bar dedicated to promoting knowledge about Oaxaca's signature spirit. The recent economic boom in the mezcal industry has led to new mezcalerías sprouting up all over town like wild agave. The idea behind these usually small, intimate bars is to inform visitors about the culture, production, and types of mezcal, not necessarily to get drunk—that is to say, sip it, don't shoot it.

Most of the mezcalerías in Oaxaca City are north of the Zócalo, but there are a few south of the Zócalo worth checking out.

SOUTH OF THE ZÓCALO

Mezcalerías (Mezcal Bars)

Cuish

Díaz Ordaz 712; tel. 951/516-8791; www.mezcalescuish.mx; 2pm-9pm Mon., 2pm-10pm Tues.-Sat., noon-7pm Sun.

It's a little out of the way, but Cuish is worth the trek, especially if you can't find room at the smaller mezcalerías. It is five blocks south and three blocks west of the Zócalo, almost to the periférico (bypass highway). Cuish also has an expendio (store, and much smaller bar) of the same name on the Centro's north side, a block north of Santo Domingo (Alcalá 802; 1pm-10pm Wed.-Mon.). They boast many types of mezcal. Try the cuish, a mezcal made from the agave karwinskii plant. They make it so well, they decided to name the company after it.

NORTH OF THE ZÓCALO

Mezcalerías (Mezcal Bars)

Mezcalogia

García Vigil 509; tel. 951/514-0115; 5pm-1am daily

On García Vigil, a block west of Santo Domingo, Mezcalogia hosts regular catas de mezal (mezcal tastings) and boasts an imaginative menu of cocktails. Signature mixed drinks like the Mercado (espadín mezcal, lime, green Chartreuse, and mint), and the soft glow of candlelight on dark-stained wood, attract enough folks to keep the tables full.

La Mezcaloteca

Reforma 506; tel. 951/514-0082; www.mezcaloteca.com; 4pm-9pm daily

Take a national tasting tour at Mezcaloteca, where the curators have broadened their search for mezcal to include the entire country. The apothecary-style bar shelves have bottles from Miahuatlán, Matatlán, and Zoquitlán (all in Oaxaca) alongside agave distillates from Durango, Michoacán, Jalisco, and other Mexican states known (though not as well as Oaxaca) for mezcal.

El Cortijo

5 de Mayo 305; tel. 951/514-3939; www.mezcalelcortijo.com; 3pm-9:30pm daily

Juan Carlos Mendez opened El Cortijo to honor and spread awareness of the work of his grandparents, who hail from Matatlán, the world capital of mezcal. Juan likes to think of himself as a "guide to your mezcal adventure" and uses the compact but cozy space to foment friendship, as well as knowledge of mezcal. The late, world-renowned Oaxacan artist Francisco Toledo designed the stylized bats in the floor tiles, and tin sacred hearts adorn the wall behind the bar.

Bar-Cafés

Cafés by day, bars by night, these cozy little establishments in Oaxaca City tend to have a similar studio-style layout: bar and tables on the ground floor, and a loft-style second floor built above it with seating space on the floor.

La Nueva Babel

Porfirio Díaz 224; no tel.; cafelanuevababel@hotmail.com; 10am-2am daily

At La Nueva Babel, the bar is often full of musicians, poets, actors, and dancers, either drinking at the tables or performing on the small ground-floor stage.

Txalaparta

Matamoros 208; no tel.; 1pm-3am Mon.-Sat., 1pm-2:30am Sun.; occasional cover US$1-2

Around the corner, Txalaparta is a bit hard to categorize. The difference in the bar's atmosphere from day to night is, well, night and day. When the sun is out, you can sit around relaxing, puffing away at a hookah; after sunset, you can throw back beers and cocktails and dance through numerous rooms with vintage furniture and decor.

Nightclubs

La Tentación

Matamoros 101; tel. 951/313-3769; 9:30pm-3am Wed.-Sat.; cover charged

If the rhythm has still got you after the marimba band in the Zócalo has gone home, head up the Andador to Matamoros and take a left. Halfway down the block, La Tentación has live salsa, cumbia, and merengue Wednesday to Saturday nights.

In Situ

Desestresse

Alcalá 401; tel. 951/108-3193; 4pm-midnight daily; cover charged

A block south of Santo Domingo, next to the Iglesia Sangre de Cristo, Desestresse is known for its drink specials and its very loud techno and house music. Its sublime location gives partiers instant access to the late-night street food along the Andador.

EAST OF THE ZÓCALO

Mezcalerías (Mezcal Bars)

In Situ

Guerrero 413; tel. 951/514-1811; www.insitumezcaleria.com; 2pm-11pm Mon.-Sat.

The one not to miss is In Situ. Owners Ulises Torrentera and Sandra Ortíz Brena have worked as hard as museum curators since opening the bar in 2011. Now In Situ boasts the largest selection of mezcals of any bar of its type in the world.

Accommodations

All but a couple of the hotels listed here are family-run businesses with generations of hard work and great stories behind them. Many are masterpieces of architecture and design, and all are staffed by friendly locals and offer a memorable, authentic experience. Perhaps you're considering a peer-to-peer property rental in Oaxaca City. These have their allure and can be tempting, but this type of accommodations simply isn't fair for locals because it drives up rents for those living in an area. Landlords begin to realize that they can make more money renting nightly to tourists than monthly to residents. Furthermore, it can be difficult to tell if a property is owned by an actual resident of the area or a development corporation looking to skirt hotel taxes.

As a general rule, you can expect to find higher hotel rates on the north side of the Centro and more economical ones in the south, but there are a few exceptions. If your trip is during a big festival season, such as Día de Muertos, the Guelaguetza, Christmas, or Easter, book at least a few months in advance to get your top pick. Oaxaca City is brimming with visitors during these periods. Rates are generally 10-20 percent higher at these times, as well.

THE ZÓCALO

The area near the Zócalo has a number of great hotel options for those who want to stay in the heart of the action.

US$50-100

Casona Oaxaca

Trujano 206; tel. 951/516-4811; www.lacasonaoaxaca.com; US$78 s, US$104 d

Casona Oaxaca, a block west of the Zócalo, has over a century of hospitality experience. Established in 1896 under the name Hotel Francia, it has 25 large, high-ceilinged rooms with air-conditioning, TV, and Wi-Fi. On top of the four-star government rating attained after the remodeling and name change in 2013, the hotel's bragging rights include a stay by English poet and novelist D. H. Lawrence, who mentioned Hotel Francia in published letters to friends.

Over US$100

★ Marqués del Valle

Portal de Clavería; tel. 951/514-0688, 951/516-3474; www.hotelmarquesdelvalle.com.mx; US$143 d, US$205 suite

The balconies here serve as front-row seats to all the action going on in the Zócalo. Cloudy green onyx veined with red adorns the lobby, and the sunroof over the interior common area provides a bright, open environment. The Zócalo is rarely uneventful and can be noisy, but even street-facing rooms do an excellent job of keeping it quiet inside.

SOUTH OF THE ZÓCALO

Affordable accommodations abound in the lively blocks south of the Zócalo. It's the perfect area for shoestring budgeteers—you're not gonna get free shoeshines or a pillow menu, but neither do you have to sacrifice cleanliness or safety.

Under US$50

★ Posada El Chapulín

Aldama 317; tel. 951/516-1646; US$27 d

This economical hotel, while spartan in its accommodations, has a friendly, helpful staff. You can count on the water being hot, as advertised (not always the case in the bargain lodging here) and the ceiling fans are sufficient to keep you cool at night. El Chapulín's bang for your buck makes it a top budget choice, especially when you factor in its proximity to money-saving comedores, the food market, and the taco and pozole stands on a number of corners on 20 de Noviembre.

Villa Vazari

Aldama 409-A; tel. 951/514-6607; US$36 d

Also in this area are the basic but comfortable rooms at Villa Vazari, with its castle-like bare stone walls and ample light wells that usher the afternoon sunlight in and right up to your doorstep. A big plus is on-site parking rather than the use of a parking lot in another location, as is the case with many hotels in the Centro.

★ Hotel Chocolate Posada

Mina 212; tel. 951/516-3807 or 951/516-5760; www.chocolateymolelasoledad.com/posada; US$30 d twin beds, US$40 t, US$45 d en suite

No other hotel in the city embodies the magic of Oaxaca quite like Hotel Chocolate, on the south side of the Mercado 20 de Noviembre. Owned by the chocolate company Chocolate La Soledad, the small cacao-processing plant and store on the ground floor keep the whole place smelling like the Food of the Gods all day long. To be truthful, what you're paying for here is this aromatic novelty. Guests in the eight two- and three-bed rooms (which feature two or three twin beds, Wi-Fi, TV, and fans) use shared bathrooms, and the service is about what you'd expect for the rates. There are two rooms with en suite baths. Even if you're not a guest, stop in to enjoy a chocomil (chocolate milk) or traditional hot chocolate on the terrace and take in the view of the sacred hill of Monte Albán at sunset.

Hotel Villa Alta

Miguel Cabrera 303; tel. 951/516-2444; US$31-43 d

Four blocks directly south of the Zócalo, Hotel Villa Alta has no-frills but clean budget rooms with private bathrooms and an enviable location. The main markets are just around the corner, the Zócalo a five-minute walk away, and the north side just beyond that. This is a great option for those planning an early morning trip south the following day, as the Líneas Unidas suburban (van) station is less than two blocks away, on the corner of Bustamante and Xóchitl.

Over US$100

Hotel Trébol

Flores Magón 201; tel. 951/516-1256; www.hoteltrebol.mx; US$104 d

Just one block south of the Zócalo, award-winning Hotel Trébol is an oasis of luxury in the hustle and bustle just outside the Mercado Benito Juárez. Bare red brick and dark wrought-iron furnishings lend the rooms an air of rustic class. A continental breakfast is included, and the on-site travel agency can help with transportation or tour planning.

★ Hotel Boutique Casa Garay

Miguel Cabrera 110; tel. 951/516-4322; www.hotelcasagaray.com; US$130 d

Opened in 2017, the hotel is a tribute to the Garay family, owners of the colonial house-turned-hotel, with each of the 10 rooms named after a family member. The hallways are domed with miniature vaulted ceilings, and images of the Virgen de Guadalupe and the Sacred Heart of Jesus adorn the walls. Book nerds and antiques lovers should ask for a quick tour of the private library of the family patriarch, Miguel Jiménez Garay, whose shelves are brimming with leather-bound tomes.

NORTH OF THE ZÓCALO

Accommodations north of the Zócalo are generally more expensive than the blocks to the south, but a few budget gems still exist.

Under US$50

Iguana Hostel

Morelos 1008; tel. 951/435-6777; www.iguanahosteloaxaca.com; US$12-15 dorm, $35 s

This very social hostel in the heart of Centro is a great spot if you want to make friends on your Oaxacan adventure. The atmosphere is as warm, welcoming, and colorful as the city, with plenty of activities and hangouts organized by Iguana Hostel's friendly staff. Complimentary breakfast awaits you in the morning, and rooftop drinks on the terrace provide a perfect end (or beginning?) to your night.

★ La Casa de los Abuelos Studio Apartments

Reforma 410; tel. 951/516-1982, 951/514-9815; www.casadelosabuelos.net; US$45 s, US$70 studio

Perfect for longer stays, La Casa de los Abuelos has simple but comfy single rooms and furnished studio apartments with full kitchens (US$465/week), all pleasantly adorned with Oaxacan ceramics and paintings. I'm a sucker for houses painted yellow, and this one is a paragon of my predilection for sunnier colors: buttery-gold walls in harmony with sky-blue moldings and lime-green pillars. Built at the turn of the 18th century, the house was seized from its owner during the Reform Laws of the 1850s. Ita and Rosa, the current owners, run the property as an homage to their brother Luis, and to what their ancestors passed down to them. Just a block from Santo Domingo, it is right in the heart of the Centro's action.

★ Las Mariposas

Pino Suárez 517; tel. 951/515-5854; www.hotellasmariposas.com; US$50 s, US$75 studio

Eco-conscious visitors will find their utopia at Las Mariposas, just south of the broad, leafy plazas of Parque El Llano. Every detail here was designed to minimize the hotel's impact on the environment and maximize sustainability and the reuse of resources. The gutter system collects summer rains to water the multiple gardens and clean the restrooms. Small hourglasses on suction cups promote sustainable bathing practices, trash is separated and recycled, and food waste composted. A communal kitchen for guests allows them to prepare meals (studios include a kitchenette), and all rooms include

courtyard of La Casa de los Abuelos

a continental breakfast. The seven studios and 13 rooms are trimmed with dark-stained wood and bright Mexican ceramic tiles, and the ceiling and standing fans are more than sufficient for cooling down in the desert heat. The hotel arranges tours and transportation and offers services like lending sun hats, umbrellas, and shopping bags.

US$50-100

★ Hotel Casa del Sótano

Tinoco y Palacios 414; tel. 951/128-1186; www.guelaguetzaoaxaca.com; US$65 d, US$104 d king

The sylvan courtyards and cool covered patios of Hotel Casa del Sótano may surprise you, considering the hotel's name (*sótano* means "basement"), but this brightly painted 17th-century house is no dank, dark cellar. The stairs from the reception area lead down into a jungle of elephantine leaves and polychromatic petals, and the 23 rooms flanking it and the second courtyard beyond are airy and full of sun. The on-site restaurant serves coffee, chocolate, mezcal, and Oaxacan meals in the shade on the patios. Newly added temazcal spa services offer more opportunities for decompression. This is an ideal hotel for those in need of rest and relaxation after the hustle and bustle of exploring Oaxaca.

Over US$100

★ Hotel Boutique NaNa Vida

Murguía 405; tel. 951/501-1285; www.nanavida.com; US$140 d, US$176 junior suite, US$188 junior suite king

Named after a saying from the Zapotec people of El Istmo meaning "what a blessing," Hotel Boutique NaNa Vida truly lives up to the sentiment. Very few hotels in the Centro combine art, culture, service, and location like this. Within a 10-minute walk of both Santo Domingo and the Zócalo, it is right in the heart of the action, but the shade beneath the mango, grapefruit, and pomegranate trees offers a quiet respite. Bare green limestone columns and decor from Oaxaca's most famous folk-art villages add to NaNa Vida's Oaxacan aesthetic. Each of the 14 rooms has a QR code that can be scanned with a cell phone to provide information on the Oaxacan artists whose work decorates the room. Service goes above and beyond expectations. The hotel makes its own artisanal soaps, and guests get to choose from many aromas and ingredients, like chocolate and agave. Kids receive free bracelets from the Istmo, and women receive free huipiles with stays of two nights or more.

★ Hotel Azul

Abasolo 313; tel. 951/501-0016; www.hotelazuloaxaca.com; US$260 s, US$284 d, US$325-625 suite

Of the hotels in Oaxaca that marry modern design with traditional Oaxacan art, perhaps the best is the visually stunning Hotel Azul. Established in 2010, Hotel Azul boasts design by Oaxaca's most famous artist, the late Francisco Toledo, that blends seamlessly into the original colonial architecture. The Toledo Suite is fully decked out with his trademark style, epitomized by the backlit wall design above the king-size bed, a tessellation of his signature papalotes (kites). Along with fellow Oaxacan visual artist Luis Zárate, he designed the mosaics and water fountain that are the centerpiece of the main courtyard. Rubén Leyva and José Villalobos, also prominent local artists, provided the stylized tiles, colorful floor rugs, and other art for the spacious, airy twin and king twin rooms. The service is as impeccable as one would expect for the price, and each room comes with a gift of a straw sombrero and woven scarf.

★ Hotel Quinta Real

5 de Mayo 300; tel. 951/501-6100; www.caminoreal.com/quintareal; US$391 d, US$493-598 suites

The building now home to Hotel Quinta Real was built in 1576 as a monastery. The nuns were ejected as a result of the Reform Laws of the mid-19th century, and the premises served as a prison, movie theater, and governmental offices until its restoration and conversion into a hotel in 1976. Historical experts worked with the National Institute of Anthropology and History (INAH) to restore fading frescoes and to incorporate the old structure as much as possible into the design, such as the restaurant's Sala de los Cántaros (Pitcher Room), the western wall of which is covered in the clay oil jugs that were found discarded in a corner of the room. Oaxaca City's gorgeous iteration of the luxury hotel brand Quinta Real has 81 rooms and 10 suites richly decorated with dark wood furnishings and gracefully artistic lamps and other fittings. Bright blankets and pillows on the beds add a touch of color to the earth tones of the decor. The hotel's rates definitely reflect the comfort and services, but if you can afford it, stay here. If you can't, at least stop by and ask to look around the ground floor.

EAST OF THE ZÓCALO

Over US$100

Casa Antonieta

Hidalgo 911; tel. 951/688-8517; www.casaantonieta.com; US$288 standard, US$326 junior suite, US$370 suite

In a house that was part of one of the first construction projects in Oaxaca, the 16th-century Ex-Convento de San Pablo, Casa Antonieta has six luxury rooms and suites around a sunny courtyard lined with bare limestone columns and decorated with ferns, vines, and other endemic Oaxacan plants. Like many newer boutique hotels, Antonieta is pet-friendly and offers only a handful of rooms in order to provide superb attention to guests' needs.

OUTSIDE OF CENTRO

US$50-100

La Soley

Pdte. Gral. Martín Carrera 113, Miguel Alemán Valdez; tel. 951/615-4802; www.lasoley.com; US$60 studio, US$60 1 bdrm, US$80 2 bdrm

The comfort of these bespoke accommodations makes for a great longer visit. La Soley offers spacious studios and one- or two-bedroom apartments, so it feels like a home away from home. Their blend of curated tours and service options make for an unforgettable stay.

City Centro

Aldama 410, Barrio de Jalatlaco; tel. 951/502-2270; www.cityexpress.com; US$170 s, US$175 d

Farther northeast is the unapologetically Mexican pink City Centro. Although the hotel is part of the City Express chain, the design of the rooms and common areas speaks more to its location than its corporate ownership. It may be more subtle than at other hotels, but the Oaxacan touch is here. A gigantic pochote (ceiba) tree stands majestic and thorny as the centerpiece of the main courtyard, and the upper terrace boasts a swimming pool as well as a front-row-seat view of the 17th-century Templo de San Matías Jalatlaco. The price includes a traditional Oaxacan breakfast, and the hotel also loans bicycles to guests free of charge.

Information and Services

TOURIST INFORMATION

Coordinación Municipal de Culturas, Turismo y Economía

Matamoros 102; tel. 951/514-2882; 9am-5pm Mon.-Fri.

The Coordinación Municipal de Culturas, Turismo y Economía (Municipal Tourism Office) is a block west of the Andador. They operate **tourist information booths** (9am-6pm daily) in the Alameda de León and Calle Allende, in front of Santo Domingo.

State Secretary of Tourism

Juárez 703; tel. 951/502-1200; www.oaxaca.travel; 8am-8pm daily

The office of the State Secretary of Tourism (SECTUR) is across from Parque El Llano, northeast of Santo Domingo. They offer lots of information on their Tourist Routes, such as the Ruta de las Artesanías (Crafts Route), Ruta del Mezcal (Mezcal Route), and Ruta Dominica (Dominican Church Route), but this information is more easily accessed on their website.

TOURS AND GUIDES

Many hotels and Spanish schools offer day tours of the city, so check with your hotel (or school if you're taking classes) to see what they offer.

4 Seasons Tours and Travel Oaxaca

tel. 951/231-4840; oaxaca4seasons.toursandtravel@gmail.com

For the folks at 4 Seasons Tours and Travel, clients are not mere customers—they are guests, and owner Eduardo Negrete Solis loves treating his guests to authentic Oaxacan experiences, both in and outside the city. I can personally attest to this—every moment my family and I spent exploring with Eduardo, he uncovered a new side to Oaxaca that I hadn't seen before. Small group (1-3 people) tours for a full 8-hour day are US$145.

Chimalli Travel

Murguía 102; tel. 951/547-3656 or 951/501-2387; www.chimalli.travel; 10am-6pm Mon.-Sat.

Chimalli Travel operates a two-hour walking tour (US$25) through the vibrant streets of the Centro Histórico.

Free Tour Oaxaca

freetouroaxaca@gmail.com; www.freetouroaxaca.com

"Look for the purple umbrella!" If you're really on a budget, take a general walking tour of the Centro with Free Tour Oaxaca, which meets up outside the Catedral de Nuestra Señora de la Asunción (also called the Catedral de Oaxaca) at 10am daily. There is no charge for this tour, which runs about two hours, but you must reserve online first (tips are encouraged). They also operate a street food tour (US$10) of the city and a mezcal-tasting tour (US$20).

Bus Tours

If you're looking for a one-hour bus tour of the city, head to Calle Morelos, just to the west of the Andador. **TuriBus Oaxaca** (Morelos 700; tel. 951/253-1041), **Optimus Tours** (tel. 951/122-2896; www.optimuscar.net) and **El Andador** (Morelos 701; tel. 951/205-9986; contacto@elandador.com.mx; www.elandador.com.mx) run several times a day for about US$5.

CONSULATES AND IMMIGRATION

US Consulate

Alcalá 407; tel. 558/526-2561, toll-free US tel. 844/528-6611; conagencyoaxaca@state.gov; 10am-3pm Mon.-Thurs.

The US Consulate is in the Plaza Santo Domingo, across from the famous church of the same name. Contact them if you lose your passport. The office's hours (which would make a bank teller jealous) make it highly likely that it will be closed in the case you have an emergency. In such an event, call the **US Embassy in Mexico City.** During business hours (8:30am-5:30pm Mon.-Fri.), they can be reached at tel. 558/526-2561. For emergencies outside of business hours, call tel. 555/080-2000.

Other Consulates

Canada does not have a consulate in Oaxaca, so Canadians will have to call the **Canadian Embassy in Mexico City** (tel. 01-55/5724-7900; mex@international.gc.ca). Citizens of the United Kingdom are in the same boat. They will have to call the **British Embassy in Mexico City** (tel. 01-55/1670-3200; mexico.consulate@fco.gov.uk). For information on embassies of other countries, visit www.embassypages.com.

HEALTH AND EMERGENCY SERVICES

The likelihood of personal safety problems in the Centro is reasonably low. However, if you do find yourself in a dangerous or emergency situation, there are **Security Kiosks** (Módulos de Seguridad) outside Santo Domingo and the Alameda de León. There are officers at these two locations 24 hours a day, and 9am-6pm daily at the kiosk on Allende, also close to Santo Domingo. Officers of the

Municipal Police (tel. 951/514-4525) and **Tourist Police** (who don white shirts reading Policía Turística) have a strong presence in the Centro too. As in many countries around the world, the **emergency telephone number** in Mexico is 911.

Medical Services

The cheapest option for things like stomach bugs and colds is the consultorio médico (doctor's office) at a pharmacy in the **Farmacias del Ahorro** chain. Consultations are free but require speaking Spanish with the doctor, so you'll need someone to translate if you don't. There are branches all over the city. The Alcalá location is in the heart of downtown (Murgia 101; tel. 951/515-5000; 7am-10pm daily), and the doc is in 9am-2pm and 4pm-9pm Monday-Saturday.

For emergencies and serious conditions, there are highly qualified bilingual doctors at **Hospital Reforma** (Reforma 613; tel. 951/516-0989), on the block north of the Jardín Etnobotánico, and **Hospital Molina** (García Vigil 317; tel. 951/516-5468), a block west of the Andador at the corner of García Vigil and M. Bravo.

SEISMIC ALERT

As in many other parts of Mexico, Oaxaca City has an early alert system that sounds an alarm up to a minute before an earthquake. The **Alerta Sísmica** (Seismic Alert) is designed to be distinct from other urban noise, so if you haven't heard it (and don't speak Spanish), you won't recognize it. I highly recommend searching "alerta sísmica México" on YouTube and familiarizing yourself with the distinctly creepy tone before you come, so you'll be ready to act if the earth begins to rattle. It's also prudent to ask about your hotel's Punto de Reunión (Meeting Point), usually marked by a green sign with four white arrows pointing to a central spot.

MONEY

There are a number of **ATMs** clustered around the Zócalo. **Banamex** has 24-hour ATMs at its branches on the corner of Hidalgo and Armenta y López (bank hrs 9am-4pm Mon.-Sat.), a block east of the northeast corner of the Zócalo, and on the corner of Morelos and Porfirio Díaz, two blocks north of the Alameda de León (tel. 951/514-0832; bank hrs 9am-4pm Mon.-Fri.). A stand-alone 24-hour Banamex ATM is a block north of the Zócalo on Valdivieso, across from the back of the Catedral de Oaxaca.

Banco Santander (tel. 951/513-9874; 9am-4pm Mon.-Fri., 9am-2pm Sat.) has a 24-hour ATM on Independencia, just north of the Alameda de León, and **Scotiabank** (tel. 951/501-5720; 8:30am-4pm Mon.-Fri., 10am-3pm Sat.) has an ATM on Independencia, just east of the corner with the Andador Alcalá. South of the Zócalo, **Bancomer** (toll-free Mex. tel. 800/226-2663; 8:30am-4pm Mon.-Fri.) has 24-hour ATMs across from the east entrance to the Mercado 20 de Noviembre. Whatever ATM you choose, be sure to decline the conversion rate to save a little money.

On the rare occasion that I've had to exchange money, I prefer banks. The lines can be an aggravating lesson in patience, though, so another option is the casas de cambio (currency exchanges), which are just to the northeast of the Zócalo. **Euro Dolar** (no tel.; 8:30am-7pm Mon.-Sat., 9am-2pm Sun.) is on Valdivieso, across from the east wall of the Catedral de Oaxaca. On the south side of Hidalgo, on the block to the east of the Zócalo, are two places that both simply say **Money Exchange.** The one closest to the Zócalo is open 8:30am-7:30pm daily, and the other, a few storefronts to the east, is open 8am-8pm daily.

LAUNDRY

Pricier hotels will offer on-site laundry services. If yours doesn't (or if you don't want to pay US$2 per shirt), there are many lavanderías (laundries) around the Centro, many of which are also tintorerías (dry cleaners). They all charge around US$5 a load (charged per kilo) and usually have clothes clean and folded the next day.

On the north side of the Centro, your options are **Azteca Lavandería** (Hidalgo 404; tel. 951/514-7951; 9am-7pm Mon.-Sat.), **Antequera Tintorería y Lavandería** (Murguía 408; tel. 951/516-5694; 9am-7pm Mon.-Sat.), and **Lavandería Lavasolas** (Independencia 1307-A; tel. 951/196-0511; 9am-8pm Mon.-Sat.).

South of the Zócalo, look for **Lavandería Hole** (Fiallo 413; tel. 951/516-4622; 8am-7pm Mon.-Fri., 8am-3pm Sat.) and **Lavanet** (Aldama 301-A; tel. 951/514-4269; 8:30am-7:30pm Mon.-Sat.). They do not wash socks or underwear, but there are self-service machines so you can do your own loads.

LUGGAGE STORAGE

Most hotels will hold on to your luggage for a while after you check out at no extra cost if you stayed with them, and some will do so for nonguests for a fee. Also, suburban (van) stations like **Atlántida** (corner of Bustamante and Zaragoza; tel. 951/390-5319; 7am-10pm Mon.-Sat., 8am-7pm Sun.) and **Líneas Unidas** (corner of Bustamante and Xólotl; tel. 951/516-2472 or 951/187-5511; 24 hrs daily) offer guarda equipaje (luggage storage) service for minimal fees.

Transportation

GETTING THERE

With more airlines adding direct flights from US cities and highways being improved and expanded, it has never been easier to get to Oaxaca.

Air

Xoxocotlán International Airport

OAX; tel. 951/511-5088; contactos@asur.com.mx

The Xoxocotlán International Airport is about 7 km (4.3 mi) south of Oaxaca City.

United Airlines (local tel. 555/283-5500, toll-free Mex. tel. 800/900-5000), via the regional branch United Express, offers direct flights from Houston that take 2.5 hours; American Eagle, a similar subsidiary of **American Airlines** (local tel. 555/209-1400, toll-free Mex. tel. 800/904-6000), flies directly from Dallas/Fort Worth. Mexican airline **Volaris** (local tel. 551/102-8000, toll-free US tel. 800/865-2747) has added a direct route from Los Angeles that gets to Oaxaca in 4 hours.

Aeromexico (Mex. tel. 555/133-4000, US tel. 404/305-8200) and **Interjet** (toll-free Mex. tel. 800/011-2345, toll-free U.S tel. 866/285-9525) operate flights from many cities in the United States that connect in Mexico City. For flying from Oaxaca City to other destinations in Mexico, there are **Viva Aerobus** (toll-free Mex. tel. 818/215-0150, toll-free US tel. 888/935-9848), which flies to Monterrey; **TAR Aerolíneas** (tel. 552/629-5272; www.tarmexico.com), with routes to Guadalajara and Querétaro; and **Volaris** (local tel. 551/102-8000, toll-free US tel. 800/865-2747), which connects to many domestic destinations via Mexico City, Guadalajara, and Tijuana.

The regional airline **Aerotucán** (local tel. 951/502-0840, toll-free Mex. tel. 800/640-4148; www.aerotucan.com) operates flights to Puerto Escondido and Huatulco, on the Oaxacan coast, as well as flights to Tuxtla Gutiérrez, in neighboring Chiapas. The company's 10-14-passenger Cessna Grand Caravan planes are authorized to operate as air taxis, which means Aerotucán doesn't have to adhere to fixed flight schedules, allowing the company to be more flexible for clients. Flights are short, scenic, and safe.

Car

A number of highways, from wide, modern toll roads to winding, narrow strips of pavement barely two lanes wide and full of potholes, connect Oaxaca City to other destinations in the state, as well as to major cities in neighboring states. Average drive times to Oaxaca City are given in parentheses.

A quick note on highway driving in Mexico: As a general rule for anywhere in the country, I recommend limiting your drive times to the daylight hours, especially on smaller, isolated highways like 125 and 160. Highway bandits are not uncommon; overnight buses are usually safe, but private automobiles are another story.

From Mexico City

The fastest and safest way from Mexico City (6 hrs), 465 km (290 mi) from Oaxaca City, is via **Highway 150D,** a tollway, which leaves the capital via Calzada Ignacio Zaragoza and passes through Puebla City (4 hrs). About 75 km (47 mi) east of Puebla, take **Highway 135D** south until it meets up with **Highway 190** in the Valle de Etla, about 12 km (7.5 mi) northwest of Oaxaca City. This is a nice, scenic route, especially when it passes through the mountainous area on the border of Oaxaca and Puebla states, where weird, branchless forests of columnar cacti dominate the vistas. Be especially vigilant on mountain passes, as this stunning landscape also makes the road dangerous at times; rockslides aren't uncommon.

A more leisurely route from Mexico City takes **Highway 95D** south, via Calzada de Tlalpan, to Cuernavaca and Morelos, and follows **Highway 160** and later Highway 190 to Oaxaca City. There are toll roads at the beginning and end of this route (488 km/305 mi), which can run 8.5-11 hours, depending on traffic and conditions. It is best to do this route road-trip style, stopping for the night in Huajuapan de León, saving the last three hours of the drive for the next day.

From the North

From the north, **Highway 135** connects Oaxaca City to **Huautla de Jiménez** (241 km/149 mi; 5 hrs) via Highway 182, and **Highway 175** winds through the Sierra Norte from **Tuxtepec** (218 km/135 mi; 4.5 hrs) and the neighboring state of Veracruz. I recommend extreme caution on this and other mountain "highways," as they are narrow, serpentine, and not in the best condition. The unnerving tendency of some Oaxacan drivers to take blind curves in the opposing lane adds another hazard to these roads. Landslides are possible in the rainy season, so check the weather. It is best to avoid these routes if storms are in the forecast.

From the East

Farther east, the mountains are traversed by **Highway 179,** also coming from Veracruz state. Both **Tuxtla Gutiérrez** (541 km/335 mi; 8 hrs), the largest city in the neighboring state of Chiapas to the east, and the **Istmo de Tehuantepec** (Juchitán; 278 km/175 mi; 5 hrs) are connected to Oaxaca City via **Highway 190.**

From The South

The main route from the coast is **Highway 175,** which connects with coastal **Highway 200** at **Pochutla** (239 km/148 mi; 5.5 hrs). After about 3.5 hours of winding through tropical and evergreen cloud forests, the highway stretches through 100 km (62 mi) of rugged desert landscapes; green fields of corn, maguey, and nopal cactus; and hazy vistas of blue mountains beyond, before arriving in Oaxaca City. This is the fastest route from the beaches at Mazunte, Zipolite, and Puerto Ángel, all about six hours away. The **Oaxaca El Zapote-Copalita Highway** zigzags through 47 km (29 mi) of jungle from the Huatulco airport (245 km/152 mi; 5.5 hrs) before meeting up with Highway 175 just north of **Pluma Hidalgo** (210 km/130 mi; 4.5 hrs).

Autopista Barranca Larga-Ventanilla (104 km/65 mi; 3 hrs) is the new highway that has slashed the drive time from Puerto Escondido to Oaxaca in half. It's a straight shot from the coast to the city, the winding hills and curves a memory of the past.

From **Pinotepa Nacional** (336 km/210 mi; 8.5 hrs), scenic **Highway 125** squiggles north through La Mixteca until it meets up with the 135D toll road to Oaxaca. However, it's faster (7.5 hrs) to take Highway 200 east, connecting with Highway 131 via the **Río Grande-Juquila Highway** (turnoff in Río Grande O Piedra Parada).

Bus

Terminal ADO

5 de Mayo 900, Barrio de Jalatlaco; tel. 951/502-0560

Oaxaca's main first-class bus station is the conveniently located Terminal ADO, in the northeast corner of the Centro. It's a quick 10-minute taxi ride (US$4) or a half-hour walk to the Zócalo.

Operators

The main bus company here is **Autobuses de Oriente,** or ADO (toll-free Mex. tel. 818/354-3521; www.ado.com.mx), which operates the subsidiary companies **Ómnibus Cristobal Colón** (OCC) and **Autobuses Unidos** (AU), ADO's economy line, as well as the luxury brand **ADO Plantino.**

These three brands operate multiple daily buses to major cities outside the state, such as Mexico City (6 hrs); Puebla (5 hrs); Veracruz (7-8 hrs); Tuxtla Gutiérrez, Chiapas (10 hrs); and Acapulco, Guerrero (1 daily, 12 hrs). I recommend the smaller vans, called suburbans or camionetas, for overland travel within the state, as larger buses take longer on curving mountain roads (one exception being the new ADO route to Puerto Escondido). In addition, suburban stations tend to be more strategically located in the Centro, cutting down on time spent in city traffic. However, ADO and its subsidiaries run all over the state, with daily trips to and from Pochutla (9.5 hrs), Huatulco (8 hrs), Puerto Escondido (3 hrs), Tuxtepec (5.5 hrs), Juchitán (5 hrs), and other destinations.

To get your bus tickets without trekking out to the terminal, stop by one of the **ADO ticket booths** (puntos de venta) in the Centro. There is one at Valdivieso 106 (7:30am-9:30pm daily) and another a block west of the Alameda de León (20 de Noviembre 103-D; 8am-10pm daily). You can also download the ADO app and pay online.

Suburban

Central de Autobuses de Segunda Clase

Calle Juárez Mara, just north of the Central de Abastos; tel. 951/516-5326

The suburban (small, 12-15-passenger van) is the main type of interregional transportation in Oaxaca. They aren't the most comfortable trips, but they are very affordable. You can get anywhere in the state from the Central de Autobuses de Segunda Clase. The great thing about this kind of travel is that it is so common here that companies run multiple routes daily, so you can basically show up and get on a van, usually within the hour. However, if you want a coveted first-row seat by the window, it's best to buy your ticket at least a day in advance.

Operators

You don't have to go all the way to the Segunda Clase station for most destinations. Six blocks south of the Zócalo, the companies **Atlántida** (corner of Bustamante and Zaragoza; tel. 951/390-5319; 7am-10pm Mon.-Sat., 8am-7pm Sun.) and **Líneas Unidas** (corner of Bustamante and Xólotl; tel. 951/516-2472 or 951/187-5511; 24 hrs daily) both go to the coast. From the north side of the Centro, **Transjuar** (Calzada Héroes de Chapultepec 801, Colonia Reforma, Oaxaca City; tel. 951/132-7227) suburbans head north to Tuxtepec. On the west side of the Centro, companies like **Autotransportes Flechador del Sol** (to Nochixtlán; Periférico 408, Oaxaca City; tel. 951/220-9289), **Servicios Turísticos de Huajuapan** (Valerio Trujano 420, Oaxaca City; tel. 951/516-5759), and **Autotransportes de Tlaxiaco** (Trujano 505, Oaxaca City; tel. 951/516-4030) have routes to various locations in La Mixteca.

GETTING AROUND

Nothing in the Centro is really more than a half hour away on foot, which is why highly recommend **walking** as much as possible. Everywhere you go, you turn a corner and... wow! So meander as much as possible.

To and from the Airport

Depending on traffic, the Oaxaca airport is only 20-30 minutes from the Centro. Many hotels offer transportation, either included in the reservation or at an extra fee, usually around US$20. Consult your hotel to make arrangements before arriving.

You can get a **secure taxi** at the airport. **Colectivo** service, vans taking groups of 10-12 passengers, goes to the Centro for US$6.50 per person, and privado taxis of up to four people cost around US$22.50 per person. You can always rely on this service, as taxis wait until the last arrival of the night, even for delays.

When you depart, the cheapest way to get to the airport is via the buses run by **Transportación Terrestre** (Alameda de León 1-G; tel. 951/514-1071; 4:45am-6pm Mon.-Sat.). They run 12-passenger vans eight times a day from the Centro to the airport for US$5 per person (the same company runs the secure taxi and colectivo services from the airport). If you make reservations beforehand, they will pick you up at your hotel. The office can be a little difficult to see. It's in the building directly across from the Catedral de Oaxaca, tucked behind the small, narrow textile market. If you're in a group of three or four, it is cheaper to get a taxi from **Sitio Alameda** (tel. 951/516-2190 or 951/516-2685) on the north side of the Alameda; the charge is US$11 total for the trip to the airport.

Taxi

Taxis in Oaxaca City are safe and inexpensive. Drivers don't use meters, but prices are fairly consistent. You shouldn't be charged more than US$4 to get anywhere within Centro. It's a good idea to ask about the fare before getting in. If you don't like the price, you can always try negotiating or just find another taxi. Taxis can be hailed on the street. The main companies (referred to as sitios) are **Multitaxi ADO** (tel. 951/516-0503 or 951/516-1572), **Sitio Antequera** (tel. 951/503-8434 or 951/515-4355), and **Sitio Reforma** (tel. 951/515-5638 or 951/518-7484). These are all yellow cabs. You can also download the rideshare app **Didi.** It works like Uber, but, surprise, are only driven by yellow taxis. The maroon ones you'll see (mostly around the southern half of the Centro) are colectivo taxis that load up with as many passengers as possible on their way out to towns in the Valles Centrales and beyond.

Bus

Buses are a cheap way (US$0.50) to get around Oaxaca City, with two bus lines servicing the city. The older line looks, well, old, but the buses run regularly, have several routes, and display their stops on the windshield (a young man usually hangs by the front door shouting out the bus's destinations). Bus stops aren't always clearly marked, but generally pick up passengers wherever someone tries to flag them down. Before you pay, ask your driver if he's going to your destination. If it's not your bus (different routes share the same bus stop), don't worry—the next will come around in 15 minutes or so.

The newer buses are the **CityBus line** (tel. 951/567-1087; www.oaxaca.gob.mx/citybus/rutas-citybus). These modern buses are emblazoned with the "CityBus" logo on the side are comfortable, pet friendly, and accessible for people in wheelchairs. There are four different routes that run about every 30 minutes about 9am-10pm (extended hours on weekends). Routes cut through downtown east to west on main streets such as Avenida de la Independencia, and north to south on Avenida Benito Juárez and others, and go all the way into surrounding towns of the Valles Centrales.

Car

Driving in Oaxaca is not for the timid. Drivers are in a hurry, and they'll let you know it. It is actually safer to be a somewhat aggressive driver yourself (when in Rome, right?). In addition to dealing with the pell-mell pace of traffic, you must be alert for speed bumps. These keep people from speeding too much but can be excessive on some roads. Many speed bumps are painted with yellow stripes and have a sign reading either "Tope" or "Reductor," and many just pop up out of nowhere and toss everything and everyone in the car around like beans in a maraca.

Rental Agencies

There are three car rental companies in the Oaxaca airport. **Alamo** (tel. 951/503-3618; 7am-11pm daily), with prices starting around US$50 a day, has the cheapest rates of the three. **Hertz** (toll-free Mex. tel. 800/709-5000; 7am-11pm daily; US$90-680 per day) has the widest selection of vehicles. The rates at **Europcar** (tel. 951/143-8340; 6am-10:30pm daily) run US$115-185 per day. When it comes to customer satisfaction with these airport rentals however, your mileage (pun intended) may vary.

For the most affordable car rental options and much better service, go into town to rent a car from a local company. **Triada Rental Car** (Quintana Roo 111; tel. 951/291-3554 or 951/419-1807; 8am-8pm daily; US$50-230/day) is a younger company that promises low rates, transparency, and ease of service. **Only Rent-A-Car** (Matamoros 101-5; tel. 951/226-1517; 8am-8pm daily) is another local company; its rates are similar to those of the companies with airport offices.

Parking

Street parking in the Centro is free but scarce, and even scarcer the more central you get. However, if you don't mind walking, the more peripheral blocks usually have space. Many hotels offer on-site or valet parking included with reservations. Safer than the street, especially for overnight parking, are privately owned parking lots, usually marked with the word *Estacionamiento* (parking lot) or a large capital *E* inside a red circle. They sometimes charge discounted rates the longer your car stays in the lot. There is one (at least) on just about every block in the Centro. Ask if they close at night or if they are a 24-hour lot. You don't want to accidentally miss closing time and not be able to get your car out until morning.

Valles Centrales

Some places cultivate tradition like a living, growing thing. In these three valleys that extend east, south, and northwest from Oaxaca City, tradition is alive and well. Buried in the soil of these rolling hills that almost burn green when the summer rains come, the roots of crafts, cuisines, rituals, and commerce—some going back thousands of years—still nurture the work of modern hands.

The weavers of Teotitlán and other communities in the Valle de Tlacolula to the east have produced wool rugs embellished with Zapotec glyphs since the arrival of the Spanish (and their sheep) 500 years ago, and artists here today are still pushing the boundaries of what can be done with thread and loom. The bright, intricately painted wooden figures of fantastic animals called alebrijes have their roots in

Highlights

Look for ★ to find recommended sights, activities, dining, and lodging.

★ **Monte Albán:** Take a quick day trip from the current regional capital to the ancient one, as these 2,500-year-old ruins of the seat of pre-Hispanic Zapotec culture and politics still dominate a hilltop just outside the city (page 102).

★ **Árbol del Tule:** You'll be waxing philosophical about the brevity of human life under the boughs of this colossal 2,000-year-old cypress (page 108).

★ **Teotitlán del Valle:** Immerse yourself in the colors, textures, and stories of this quaint town whose people have dedicated themselves to making gorgeous rugs, tapestries, and other high-quality wool products for half a millennium (page 109).

★ **Tlacolula Sunday Market:** A shopper's paradise, the Sunday market of Tlacolula is one of Oaxaca's oldest (think centuries old) and largest traditional markets (page 113).

★ **Mitla:** Visit the religious capital of the Zapotec civilization, or the "Place of the Dead" as they called it, where the walls are adorned with unique, mortarless stone mosaics (page 117).

★ **Hierve El Agua:** These strange, towering "frozen waterfalls" might have you double-checking what planet you're on (page 121).

★ **San Martín Tilcajete:** It's alebrijes galore in this village that's the source of many of Oaxaca's colorful, wooden creatures, both real and imagined (page 127).

more recent history. The art began less than a century ago, and the towns of Arrazola and San Martín Tilcajete in the Valle de Ocotlán have only been famous for making them since the late 1970s. And it is simply hard to describe the feeling you'll get standing over a 2,000-year-old kiln at the ruins at Atzompa, overlooking the Valle de Etla, when your next stop is the town of Santa María Atzompa, where you can buy ceramic coffee mugs in the green-glazed style that has made the town famous.

To see where it all began, visit the big sites, like Monte Albán and Mitla, but try to make it to the lesser-visited ones, like Yagul and Atzompa, as well. They are a wealth of information, and much less crowded. These ruined towns are where people from the surrounding areas used to gather to socialize and trade, a custom that is still alive today in towns like Zaachila, Ocotlán, and Tlacolula.

The past is so close here, you almost feel like you're trespassing through time to a place you didn't know you were allowed to visit. And the connection doesn't lie only in the human-made. The giant Moctezuma cypress called El Árbol del Tule sprouted over 2,000 years ago, when much of these valleys were under the waters of a great lake. At Hierve El Agua, you can go swimming atop "frozen waterfalls" that have been formed by "boiling" mineral springs for millennia.

You may come to the Valles Centrales to buy pretty pottery or a bottle of authentic mezcal, but after experiencing this fascinating place for yourself, you might realize the most valuable things you take home with you are the stories. Come here to see. Come here to shop. Come here to eat. But most of all, come here to learn.

ORIENTATION

Think of Oaxaca City as the hub of a wheel, and the surrounding valleys as its spokes. **Monte Albán** is located just southwest of the city. To the east is the **Valle de Tlacolula,** famous for the tourist favorites of Mitla and Hierve del Agua. South of the city is the **Valle de Zimatlán-Ocotlán,** home to the Ruta de las Artesanías (Crafts Route) with its many small towns specializing in a particular craft. To the northwest of the city lies the smallest of the surrounding valleys, **Valle de Etla.**

PLANNING YOUR TIME

The traditional way to see the Valles Centrales is by staying in Oaxaca City and visiting destinations on day trips, for which you would need to devote at least three days of your trip in order to take in the highlights of this region. Tour agencies in Oaxaca City make this a very viable option, with tours that take in multiple sights a day, but it is also very possible by public transport.

It is becoming more popular for people to stay out in the valleys and explore them from towns like **Mitla, Teotitlán del Valle,** and **San Agustín Etla.** This is a great way to get to know a place better than a quick tour will allow.

You might plan your trips according to **market days** around the valleys. The markets in **Zaachila,** on Thursday, **Ocotlán,** on Friday, and **Tlacolula,** on Sunday, are the ones to see. It's best to make the market town your first stop on these days, as they have a better selection and are more lively in the morning.

GETTING AROUND

Tours and Guides

Very little English is spoken in the Valles Centrales, so those who don't have at least a basic level of Spanish will need guides to experience the place properly.

4 Seasons Tours and Travel Oaxaca

tel. 951/231-4840; oaxaca4seasons.toursandtravel@gmail.com; group tours from US$145 for 1-3 people

For private tours to the Valles Centrales,

Previous: Monte Albán; Zapotec ruin in Mitla; embroidery of San Antonino Castillo Velasco.

Valles Centrales

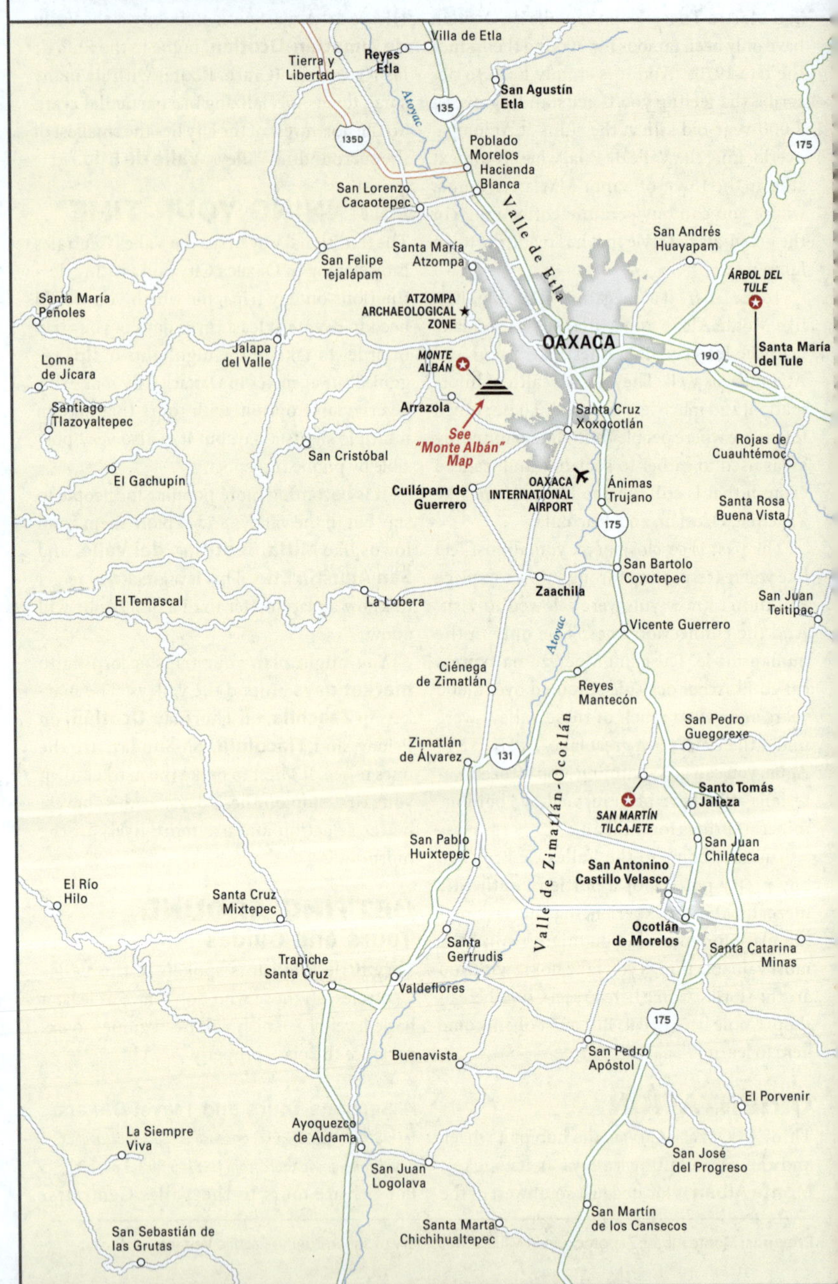

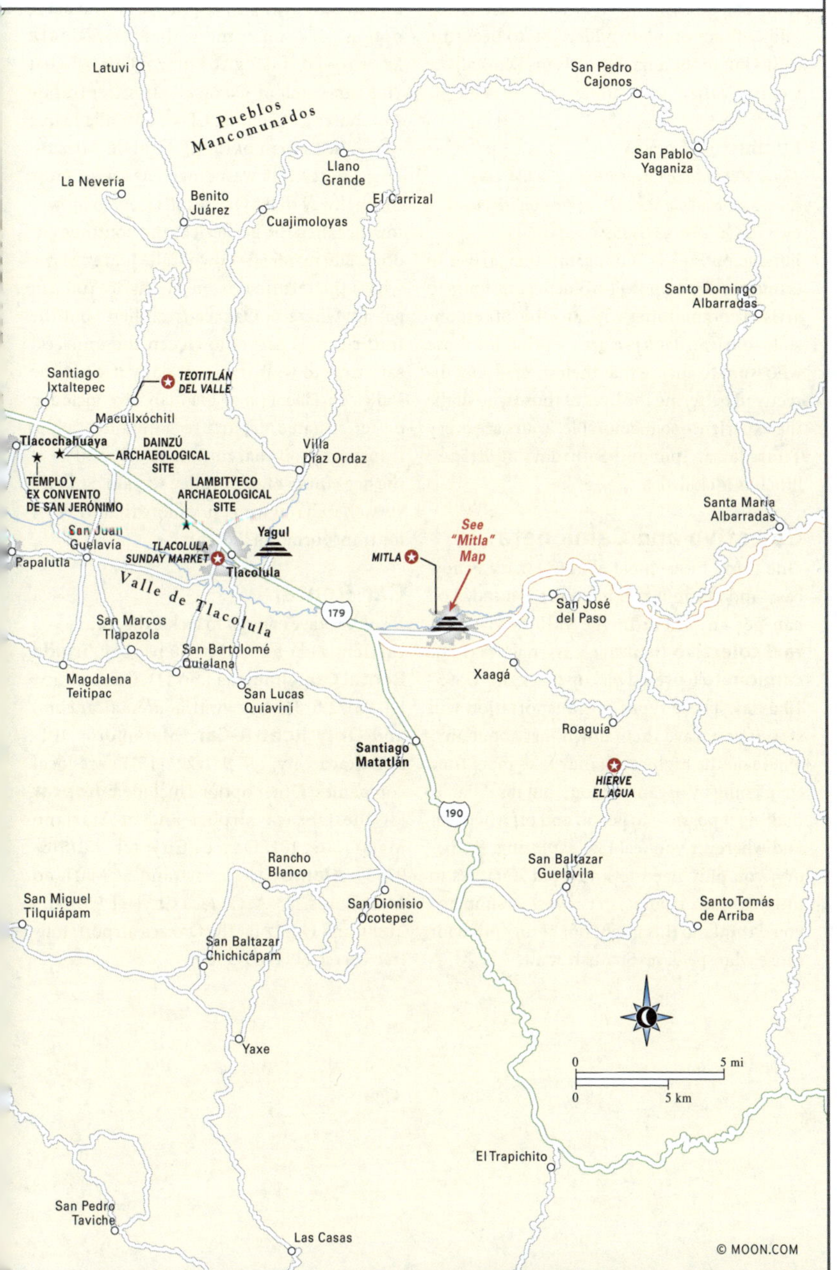
Latuvi
Pueblos Mancomunados
San Pedro Cajonos
San Pablo Yaganiza
La Nevería
Benito Juárez
Llano Grande
El Carrizal
Cuajimoloyas
Santo Domingo Albarradas
Santiago Ixtaltepec
TEOTITLÁN DEL VALLE
Macuilxóchitl
Tlacochahuaya
DAINZÚ ARCHAEOLOGICAL SITE
Villa Díaz Ordaz
TEMPLO Y EX CONVENTO DE SAN JERÓNIMO
LAMBITYECO ARCHAEOLOGICAL SITE
Santa María Albarradas
San Juan Guelavía
Yagul
See "Mitla" Map
Papalutla
TLACOLULA SUNDAY MARKET
Tlacolula
MITLA
Valle de Tlacolula
San José del Paso
179
San Marcos Tlapazola
San Bartolomé Quialana
Magdalena Teitipac
Xaagá
San Lucas Quiaviní
Roaguía
Santiago Matatlán
HIERVE EL AGUA
190
Rancho Blanco
San Baltazar Guelavila
San Miguel Tilquiápam
San Dionisio Ocotepec
Santo Tomás de Arriba
San Baltazar Chichicápam
Yaxe
0
5 mi
0
5 km
El Trapichito
San Pedro Taviche
Las Casas
© MOON.COM

Eduardo and his team at 4 Seasons Tours and Travel have you covered. His full-day tours can be customized to your preferences, and will not only introduce you to beautiful sights but to the amazing artisans who call the Central Valleys their home.

Fundación En Vía

Juárez 909, Oaxaca City; tel. 951/515-2424; www.envia.org; 9am-6pm Mon.-Fri.; half-day microfinance tours US$90, children US$55

Fundación En Vía, a nonprofit that strives to economically empower women, runs tours to artisan communities with an ethic of responsible tourism. This is a great option for those who want to ensure that their money goes directly to bettering the lives of those who make the experience so memorable. Tours are every Thursday at 1pm and Saturdays at 9:15am; lunch is included.

Colectivo and Camioneta

One thing I love most about Oaxaca is how easy and cheap it can be to get around. You can get anywhere in the valleys via **bus, taxi colectivo** (multiple passenger taxi), or **camioneta** (covered pickup truck) for US$5-10 a day. These types of transportation will stop if you wave them down just about anywhere on the highway. It may take more time than going by organized tour, but it's reliable, making it possible to get on and off whenever and wherever you feel like exploring. In theory, you only need to know place names to use this system, but it isn't always as simple as you'd think, so this might not be an option for those who speak no Spanish at all.

Suburban

Another mode of public transport called the **suburban** (van) is also a very affordable option. (It's sometimes called **camioneta** as well—confusing, I know.) This is what you can catch at Oaxaca City's Central de Autobuses de Segunda Clase, on Calle Juárez Maza, just north of the Central de Abastos. To get here, walk west down Las Casas, cross the highway that bypasses the Centro (downtown), called the periférico, and continue another 200 m (650 ft) down Calle Juárez Maza, where the terminal is on the right. You can get anywhere in Oaxaca from here, but the traffic in this part of town can add unnecessary time to your trip, especially if it's to the Valles de Tlacolula or Ocotlán. I've included better-situated departure points for public transportation that minimize city traffic at the beginning of each valley section. Still, it's very cheap. You won't pay more than US$3-4 for transportation like this.

Car Rental

If you're brave enough to tackle the traffic, you can rent a car for US$40-50 per day. **Triada Rental Car** (Quintana Roo 111, Oaxaca City; tel. 951/291-3554; www.triadarentalcar.com) and **Only Rent-A-Car** (Matamoros 101-5, Oaxaca City; tel. 951/226-1517) are local companies. Other options include **Europcar** (at the Oaxaca airport and at Mariano Matamoros 101, Oaxaca City; tel. 951/516-9305), **Alamo** (at airport and at Mariano Matamoros 203-A, Oaxaca City; tel. 951/501-2188), and **Hertz** (at the Oaxaca airport; toll-free US tel. 800/709-5000).

Itinerary Ideas

To visit the Valles Centrales is to experience a trifecta of gastronomical, archaeological, and cultural delights. Lucky for us all, visiting the towns of Oaxaca's central valleys is incredibly accessible.

But first, dedicate a day to visit Oaxaca's ancient sky-high capital, **Monte Albán.** Coming to Oaxaca without seeing Monte Albán would be akin to visiting Egypt but skipping the pyramids—you just don't do it! Although it's possible to visit some of the nearby artisan villages after exploring Monte Albán, your time is better spent soaking in the wonders of the site and relaxing afterward. Then, spend the rest of your time exploring the towns of the Valles Centrales, covered in the following itinerary.

It's easy to find tours that hit up the highlights, but if you're more of a DIYer, each day of the itinerary can be done via public transit, as outlined in this chapter. To maximize your time, however, you may want to rent a car or contact a tour guide who will take you where you want to go.

DAY 1: VALLE DE ZIMÁTLAN-OCOTLÁN DAY TRIP

This first day, ease into things with a day trip on the **Ruta de las Artesanías** (Artisan Route).

1 Begin the day with ready appetites at Zaachila's **Mercado Gastronómico.** (The best day to visit is Thursday, for Zaachila's speciality barbocoa en rollo.) Grab a cup of espuma, and a little nieve this early never hurt anyone.

2 Walk off breakfast at the neighboring **Zaachila Archaeological Zone.**

3 Next stop is the town of barro negro, San Bartolo Coyotepec. Head to **Alfarería Doña Rosa** to see a demonstration of how black clay pottery is made and to pick up a souvenir or two.

4 Drive 15 minutes down the road to San Martín Tilcajete, known for its alebrijes. Visit **Taller Una Inspiración de mi Vida** to learn about your personal tonas y nahuales (spirit guides) and see how alebrijes are made.

5 Time for a quick snack at **Empanadas Carmelita** in San Antonino Castillo Velasco.

6 Admire the flores immortales (immortal flowers) of **Biushita.**

7 Visit **Taller Manos Que Ven** to meet Master Potter José García Antonio (who crafts without sight) and his talented wife, Maestra Santa Reyna Teresita.

8 On your way out of town, stop by **La Casa del Bordado** to admire the delicate embroidery the town is known for.

9 Last stop of the day is Ocotlán de Morelos. At **Templo y Ex-Convento de Santo Domingo,** see how hometown artist Rodolfo Morales beautifully restored the church.

10 End your trip with mole estofado or chile rellenos at **La Cocina de Frida.**

DAY 2: VALLE DE TLACOLULA

Today in the Valley of Tlacolula, explore the archaeological treasures and natural beauty of the area.

1 I'm not an early bird myself, but you'll want to rise with the sun to get to **Hierve El Agua** before the crowds—which means arriving before 9am (at the latest) for peaceful views.

2 Enjoy a breakfast of enmoladas at **Don Cenobio** in Mitla.

3 Spend the next hour or so exploring the ruins at **Mitla.**

4 Head into Tlacolula and enjoy a hearty lunch of barbacoa at the **Mercado Municipal Martín González.**

5 Make your way to Teotitlán del Valle. Visit **Tapetes Nelson Perez Mendoza** to learn how natural dyes are used to create the gorgeous rugs the town is known for.

6 Final stop of the day is **Arbol del Tule.** Relax in the charming plaza and admire the figures in the gargantuan tree trunk.

DAY 3: VALLE DE ETLA

You've seen a lot the last couple of days! Time to relax and take a slower pace in the Etlas.

1 After a leisurely drive into San Agustín Etla, stop and have some chilaquiles or memelas for breakfast at **Comedor Campestre.**

2 Afterward, enjoy the beautiful grounds at **Centro de las Artes de San Agustín (CaSa).** Head inside to see the exhibitions or catch a class if you're lucky.

3 Stroll down to **Arte Papel Vista Hermosa** to see a demo of how they make their artisan paper from natural materials.

4 Have a delicious lunch at **Frida Libre.** Try the mushroom risotto or the fish tacos.

5 Drive 15 minutes to Villa de Etla to the **Mercado Municipal.** Wednesday is the big market day; if you miss it, no worries, there will still be plenty of the town's famous quesillo to choose from.

Monte Albán and Vicinity

When the Zapotecs first arrived here over 2,500 years ago, they built their sophisticated capital, in alignment with their advanced knowledge of the stars, atop the tallest hill they could find in the crux of three great valleys, and looked out over what would be their domain for the next two millennia.

The ruins of Monte Albán, impressive as they are, are merely what's been found of this great capital's downtown district. Packed into the dirt of these hills just to the southwest of Oaxaca City, much of the city lies under modern-day construction. However, more recently discovered sites like Atzompa are shining new light on the extent of this extraordinary pre-Hispanic metropolis.

TOP EXPERIENCE

★ MONTE ALBÁN

tel. 951/516-7707; 8am-5pm daily; US$5.60

The Zapotec name for the city they built at Monte Albán is Dani Baá, which means "Sacred Mountain," and from the views

Monte Albán

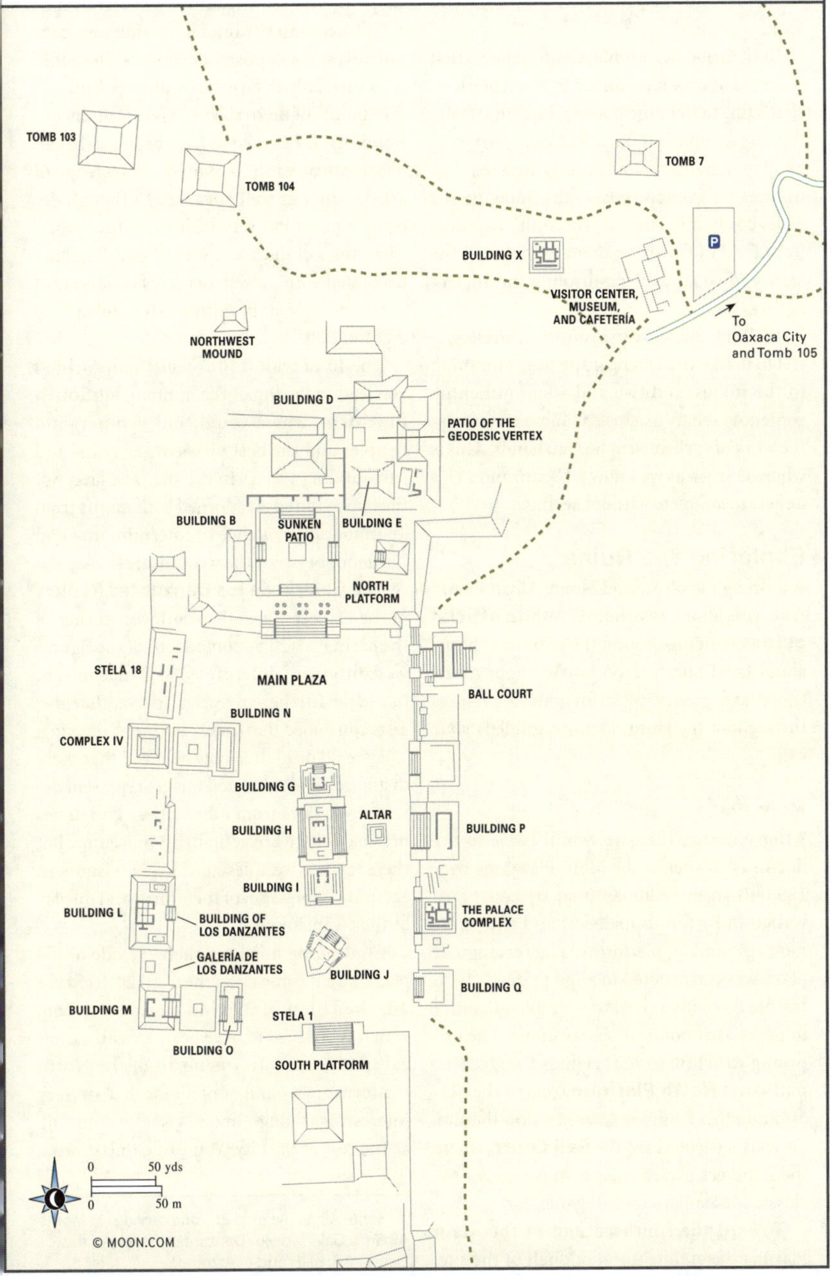

TOMB 103
TOMB 104
TOMB 7
P
BUILDING X
VISITOR CENTER, MUSEUM, AND CAFETERÍA
To Oaxaca City and Tomb 105
NORTHWEST MOUND
BUILDING D
PATIO OF THE GEODESIC VERTEX
BUILDING B
SUNKEN PATIO
BUILDING E
NORTH PLATFORM
STELA 18
MAIN PLAZA
BALL COURT
BUILDING N
COMPLEX IV
BUILDING G
BUILDING H
ALTAR
BUILDING P
BUILDING I
BUILDING L
BUILDING OF LOS DANZANTES
THE PALACE COMPLEX
GALERÍA DE LOS DANZANTES
BUILDING J
BUILDING Q
BUILDING M
STELA 1
BUILDING O
SOUTH PLATFORM
0
50 yds
0
50 m

alone it's easy to see why. Distance paints the hills blue as sunlight pours into the Valles Centrales, no matter which direction you look.

Built in 500 BC, Monte Albán is the earliest example of urban planning in the Americas, so it's fun to imagine it as the bustling, functional metropolis it once was. See tourists as busy merchants, flamboyantly dressed dignitaries, or excited sports fans. Imagine the walls covered in the red stucco the Zapotecs were fond of finishing them with. Smell the smoke of copal drifting through the ancient hallways.

Walking this close to history has an electric feel to it, like you can hear the time humming in the stones, and two and a half millennia somehow seems as close as memory among the work of such ancient human hands. This is where Oaxaca as we know it began, and a trip here is incomplete without seeing it.

Exploring the Ruins

A thorough stroll around Monte Albán should take you about two hours. While **official guides** hanging around the entrance charge about US$12 per person for two-hour tours, there are plenty of informative plaques throughout the ruins; hiring a guide is your call.

Main Plaza

After entering the gate, you'll come to the northeast corner of the Main Plaza, the over 185,000-sq-m (2,000,000-sq-ft) courtyard walled in by tombs, palaces, and two enormous pyramidal platforms. The rectangular plaza was constructed to align perfectly with the north-south axis of the compass in order to make astronomical observations. The imposing structure to your right is the gigantic, multilevel **North Platform,** one of the oldest and most complex structures on the site. To your left you'll see the **Ball Court,** where the Zapotecs played their own version of the classic Mesoamerican ball game.

Toward the southern end of the Main Plaza is the architectural oddball of the site, **Building J,** which stands out for its shape and orientation. It is five-sided and resembles the shape of an arrowhead. Its walls are vertical, rather than pyramidal. Its stairway faces northwest, as opposed to those of the other structures, which face the cardinal points, and the "point" of the arrowhead faces southwest. Building J is believed to have been used as an observatory, as the Zapotecs' knowledge of astronomy was well advanced, although definitive proof has yet to confirm this theory. The stones of the south wall of Building J are decorated with carved images of conquests of surrounding communities that date back to AD 100-200.

The 40-m-wide (130-ft-wide) stairs behind you lead to the top of the humongous **South Platform,** where you'll find two pyramid temples and the best views of the ruins and surrounding valleys in the site. The larger of the two pyramids is adorned with motifs from Teotihuacán, evidence of intermingling and influence between the two cultures.

The **Galería de los Danzantes** (Gallery of the Dancers) is at the southwest corner of the Main Plaza. The contortions of the figures were originally interpreted as dance moves; but after further investigation, archaeologists concluded that these men aren't dancing. They're all dead. It is now believed that these disfigured and mutilated images represent defeated warriors from other cities. The stones originally here are actually in museums, but these replicas were designed to give visitors an accurate impression of their form and display as they were found.

Continuing north on the west side of the plaza, you'll come upon the 6-m (20-ft) **Stela 18,** the tallest of its kind at Monte Albán, which is believed to have been an astronomical instrument. To the north of the North Platform are a number of tombs that are very interesting, though not as visually stunning as the rest of the city. You can climb down a

1: Monte Albán pyramid **2:** stone carvings at Monte Albán **3:** Galería de los Danzantes (Gallery of the Dancers) **4:** ball court at Atzompa

1
2
3
4

couple of them and peer into the small spaces where Zapotec kings and priests were laid to rest. Before heading back to the exit, make sure to stop by **Tomb 7,** one that was reused by Mixtecs after the decline of Monte Albán. It is here that archaeologists found the trove of gold, silver, alabaster, and jade that is now on display in the Museo de las Culturas, in the Santo Domingo Convent in Oaxaca City.

Monte Albán Visitor Center

tel. 951/516-7707; 8am-4pm daily

The visitor center at the entrance to the park houses a **cafetería** (8am-4pm daily; US$8-15) with a breezy terrace and food that is better than one expects from a tourist attraction such as this. There are also a jewelry store and a gift shop that is well-stocked with literature about the site, which are open the same hours as the site.

Monte Albán Museum

8am-5pm daily; admission included in entrance fee

The Monte Albán Museum, in the same building as the visitor center, is an interesting walk-through for anyone wanting to learn more about what was found here. Fascinating artifacts are on display, some dating as far back to AD 300. For sensitive travelers, be advised that in addition to the customary artifacts (household items, musical instruments, statues of Zapotec gods, etc.) you'd expect to see, there are also displays of child remains, including skulls and skeletons.

Getting There

The Monte Albán ruins are on a hill less than 9 km (5.6 mi) southwest of the Zócalo in Oaxaca City.

Bus

The cheapest way to get to Monte Albán from Oaxaca City is by one of the buses that leave from the corner of Minas and García, just two blocks west of the Mercado 20 de Noviembre. Buses run by **Hotel Riviera del Ángel** (Mina 518; tel. 951/516-6666; round-trip US$5) start at 8:30am and run every hour until 3:30pm. The trip takes about 45 minutes, and the last one leaves Monte Albán at 5pm. Hold on to your ticket—you'll need it for the return trip. Just across the street, **Viajes Turísticos Mitla** (Mina 501; tel. 951/516-6175; round-trip US$4) runs the same schedule.

Car

Drivers take Miguel Cabrera (which is called Flores Magón north of Aldama) south to the periférico and follow the Monte Albán signs across the Río Atoyac bridge. Take another right after the bridge and follow the road to the top of the hill. The road could probably use a few more signs, but it's not hard to stay on course. Just follow the tour buses. The drive takes about 30 minutes, depending on traffic.

ATZOMPA ARCHAEOLOGICAL ZONE

Cerro de la Campana; tel. 951/513-3346; 8am-5pm daily; free

To get a more complete idea of life in Monte Albán, visit the uncrowded ruins at Atzompa, which can be thought of as one of the first suburbs in the Americas. The suburb was founded during Monte Albán's peak, sometime around AD 700. At Monte Albán, you get a good impression of the political and ideological lifestyle of its inhabitants, while Atzompa contains much more information on their daily lives.

Give yourself about an hour to explore the site. The **East House** is one of two residences of upper-class families found on the site, and eight other housing units were found here as well. Attached to the East House is the service area where food was prepared and other domestic tasks were carried out. The **Altar House** is another structure where archaeologists found lots of evidence of daily activities. The ruins consist of square rooms around a central plaza, and a room at the back of the house was used as a pottery workshop.

The second **Ball Court** up the hill is the biggest of the six that are documented in the Monte Albán complex. There are two others in Atzompa, both on the properties of the aforementioned houses, which suggests they were for private use. The big one is believed to have been a public court, where the game was both ritual and political propaganda used to bolster power.

Here you can also observe the origins of ancient traditions still alive today. At the top of the site, archaeologists discovered a kiln dating back thousands of years. It is quite simply incredible to stand over it and consider how you can head right down the hill to the town of Santa María Atzompa and buy the products of a tradition that began here over 2,000 years ago. The aisles of the **Mercado de Artesanías de Santa María Atzompa,** also known as Mercado La Asunción, (Libertad 303; tel. 951/558-9232; 8am-7pm daily) brim with the **green-glazed pottery** the town is now famous for.

Getting There

The Atzompa ruins are about 4 km (2.5 mi) north-northwest of Monte Albán. The site has only been open to the public since 2012, so it hasn't had much time to garner a reputation and draw the crowds and access options Monte Albán does.

Taxi

If you take public transportation to Monte Albán, you can negotiate a deal with a taxi driver to take you to Atzompa and wait while you explore the site. The price will vary depending on the driver, but somewhere around US$16 is fair.

Car

The easiest way to get to Atzompa from Monte Albán is by driving. A little over 1 km (0.7 mi) from the Monte Albán Visitor Center, take a left at the fork in the road, which will be the one you did not come in on if you followed my directions to Monte Albán. The turn at the bottom of the hill can be tricky, as the road feeds directly into the traffic going right on Ignacio Bernal, but you'll need to turn left. The safest thing to do is let the highway take you to the right and then pull a U-turn in the broad, three-way intersection just a ways down the hill. The sign to turn right is about 1 km (0.6 mi) in the other direction, and from there it's a scenic 10-minute drive to the top. To get to the artisans market, head back down the hill and take a left, back in the direction you came. Take another left at the intersection about 2 km (1.2 mi) down the road and follow the Atzompa Highway 4 km (2.5 mi), where you'll see the artisans market on the right.

Public Transit

If you're feeling adventurous (and have at least some basic Spanish), you can take a colectivo to Atzompa from Oaxaca Centro. You'll need to head over to Central de Abastos across the periférico, where all the colectivos heading to nearby pueblos congregate (you can't miss the sea of maroon and white). Ask around for the colectivo to Atzompa, and you'll be directed to a maroon and white taxi with "Atzompa" emblazoned across the windshield. You'll share the ride with at least four other people, but at about US$1, you can endure. Once you're dropped off in Atzompa, it won't be difficult to find a taxi or mototaxi up to the ruins (US$1.50).

Tours and Guides

To visit the site from Oaxaca City, without seeing Monte Albán, your best bet is to organize transportation through an agency. It's not yet on the regular itineraries, but agencies are willing to work with you. **4 Seasons Tours and Travel Oaxaca** (tel. 951/231-4840; oaxaca4seasons.toursandtravel@gmail.com) offers an immersive tour that visits Atzompa's archaeological zone, green pottery workshops with demonstrations, and the artisan market.

Valle de Tlacolula

Extending east from Oaxaca City, the Valle de Tlacolula is home to some of the state's greatest hits, like the intricately adorned ruins at Mitla and the "frozen waterfalls" of Hierve El Agua. Santiago Matatlán, aka "The World Capital of Mezcal," is here, as well as one of the region's oldest weekly markets in Tlacolula de Matamoros. And the 500-year-old tradition of wool weaving is alive and well (and evolving) in Teotitlán del Valle and neighboring towns in the valley.

The best way to explore this valley via public transport from Oaxaca City is by grabbing a bus or taxi colectivo at a stop at the northeast corner of the Centro, on the corner of Calle de los Derechos Humanos and Highway 190. The stop is just to the east of the baseball stadium, between it and the McDonald's. Check the vehicles' windshields for destinations. You can expect to spend around US$5-10 a day traveling the valley in colectivos, depending on where you go and how many stops you make.

SANTA MARÍA DEL TULE

The harlequin gardens and tidy lawns of the zócalo at Santa María del Tule set a charming foreground to the town's main attraction, a monumental ahuehuete (Nahuatl for the Montezuma cypress) that boasts the largest trunk diameter of any tree in the world. The only thing bigger than the tree is the imagination of the niños guías (child guides). Don't expect them to answer your lame grown-up questions about the tree's circumference or the year the church was built. These kids' specialty is pointing out the shapes they see in the whorls and gnarls of the trunk and branches.

★ Árbol del Tule

no tel.; 8am-8pm daily; US$1.20

This area was a big lake when El Árbol del Tule sprouted on its shore over 2,000 years ago. Since then, it has grown to a diameter of 14 m (46 ft).

The 17th-century Templo de Santa María de la Asunción is a toothsome sight next to the ancient tree. It opens at 4pm, but don't worry if you miss it. The church you really want to see is right down the road.

Getting There

El Tule is about 11 km (7 mi) east of Oaxaca City. Taxi colectivo passengers should make sure their taxi stops in El Tule, about 20 minutes down the road. Taxis that go to towns beyond El Tule stay on the highway and skip the town completely. Drivers take Highway 190 east. The exit for El Tule is on the right about 5 km (3 mi) east of the Centro. The drive takes about 20-30 minutes, depending on traffic.

TEMPLO Y EX-CONVENTO DE SAN JERÓNIMO

8am-6pm daily; US$1.20

Legend has it that a Zapotec warrior named Cochicahuala ("He who fights at night") founded **Tlacochahuaya** after a great victory. When the Spanish arrived, they oversaw the construction of the remarkably ornate Templo y Ex-Convento de San Jerónimo. You'll be asked to give a 20 peso "cooperation," which supports the maintenance and restoration of the church and convent in back.

The mid-16th-century church houses a series of fine paintings depicting the revelation of the Virgen of Guadalupe to Juan Diego, the first Indigenous saint in the Americas, but the real feast for the eyes is overhead. The vaulted ceiling is covered in a pattern of floral designs and baby angel faces that inspires true wonder. Don't leave without climbing the narrow spiral staircase to the balcony to see the still-functioning organ that is nearly as old as the church.

Getting There

Many tours include Tlacochahuaya's Templo y Ex-Convento de San Jerónimo in their itineraries, or it can easily be added to an independent trip to other sites in the valley. About 8 km (5 mi) east of El Tule, you'll see a sign for the town at a crossroads with a pedestrian bridge. Mototaxis charge about US$1 for the ride into town from the crucero (crossroads). Drivers turn right. The town is about five minutes down the road.

★ TEOTITLÁN DEL VALLE

Although a few neighboring communities claim otherwise, Teotitlán del Valle is considered the birthplace of the nearly 500-year-old tradition of **wool weaving** that the Valle de Tlacolula is famous for. Zapotec people here have been weaving high-quality tapetes (rugs), tapices (tapestries), and other wool products since Juan López Zárate, the state's first bishop, introduced European sheep to the region in the mid-16th century. Traditionally, the tapetes are decorated with Zapotec glyphs and other abstract designs; newer generations, however, have begun to weave suns, hummingbirds, and other images into their rugs. Constantino Lazo, a local weaver who makes rugs for competitions, uses materials like thread, cotton, silk, and even feathers to work 3-D images into his pieces.

Some use synthetic dyes, but most weavers use natural ones in their rugs. Grinding the little scale insects called cochinilla (cochineal) that grow on nopal cactuses all over the valley produces the deep scarlets you'll see lining the walls of the tapete stores. Blue comes from the pulp of the leaves of the indigo plant, which grows in the Istmo de Tehuantepec. Pomegranate rinds and zacatlascal, a parasitic plant that grows like spilled spaghetti on treetops, produce yellow, and materials like pecan shells and a moss called musgo cuapascle yield brown. It truly is extraordinary to see how these and other natural materials are combined to create any color on the spectrum the artist desires, and many talleres (textile workshops with stores) give demonstrations for voluntary tips.

Sights

Templo de la Preciosa Sangre de Cristo

Teotitlán's Templo de la Preciosa Sangre de Cristo was constructed in 1518 on the site of a Zapotec temple once dedicated to the feathered serpent god Quetzalcoatl. If you take a closer look, you'll see that some of the stones in the facade are from that original temple, carved with images of him. The churchyard gets lively with food, fun, and dancing during its annual festival in July. The ruins of the original temple are down the stairs on the south side of the churchyard and to the left, behind the municipal government offices.

Museo Comunitario Balaa Xtee Guech Gulal

corner of Hidalgo and 20 de Noviembre; tel. 951/524-4463; 10am-6pm Tues.-Sun.; US$1

The Balaa Xtee Guech Gulal Community Museum may be small, but the "House (or Shadow) of the Old Town," as its name translates from the Zapotec, contains a wealth of information about Teotitlán and the surrounding valley. The first exhibit begins with a collection of Zapotec carved stonework depicting symbolic glyphs, jaguars, masked figures, and elaborately adorned gods.

The majority of the space, however, is dedicated to Teotitlán's long tradition of rug and tapestry weaving. The history and processes of the art are explained in detail. The last exhibit displays the history of arranged marriage traditions in Teotitlán, which included roaming groups of townsfolk armed with clubs, ready to clobber any man other than the groom caught chatting it up with the bride.

Centro Cultural Comunitario

Hidalgo s/n, next to artisan market south of churchyard; tel. 951/305-4580; 1pm-7pm Tues.-Fri., 11am-7pm Sat.-Sun. (11am-7pm Tues.-Sun. vacation seasons); US$1.50

Inaugurated in August 2018, Teotitlán's

1

2

3

Centro Cultural Comunitario houses a museum displaying rugs and explaining the town's weaving traditions. There is also an exhibit on the Danza de la Pluma (Dance of the Feather).

Festivals and Events

Annual Church Festival

July

If your visit is in July, head to Teotitlán on the first Wednesday of the month, when the town begins its annual church celebration dedicated to the Holy Blood of Christ. The highlight of the festival are its convites (parades), where boys with mini marmotas (spinning white globes on a stick) and girls clad in crisp huipils (embroidered blouses) hold decorated religious icons aloft as they parade through the village. You'll find local delights that aren't made during the rest of the year, like tamales de amarillo (made with chicken and yellow mole) and a savory chicken soup flavored with cumin called higadito. Don't let the name of this soup fool you—despite its similarity to the word for liver (hígado), there is no offal in the ingredients. It is made with chicken meat and eggs cooked casserole style and added to a rich broth.

During the church festival and **Lunes del Cerro** (cultural heritage celebrations held on the last two Mondays in July), you'll be able to catch the **Danza de la Pluma** (Dance of the Feather), arguably Oaxaca's most visually stunning dance. Teotitlán claims to be the origin of the dance, though folks from Cuilapam de Guerrero tend to disagree.

Shopping

Dulízùn Café

Hidalgo 26; tel. 951/524-4021; 8am-6pm daily

According to local weaver Manuel Lazo (Constantino's brother), 80 percent of Teotitlán's population works in weaving, and this is apparent almost as soon as you turn off the highway. Families all over town, especially along Benito Juárez and Hidalgo, sell their homemade tapetes, ponchos, and other fine wool products. The Bazán family converted part of their home into Dulízùn Café, where vivid and intricate rugs line the walls of the store and courtyard beyond. (*Dulízùn* is Zapotec for "Our House.") Ask Señora Teresa for a demonstration of how they make the natural dyes (and leave a tip in the jar). Manuel sells his work here. If he's around, he'll tell you about his personal style.

Tapetes Nelson Perez Mendoza

B. Juárez km 1-1/2; tel. 951/117-4728; 9am-6pm daily

Arte y Tradicion (art and tradition) are the watchwords of this workshop spanning four generations of extraordinary talent. Master Weaver Nelson Perez Mendoza's craftsmanship has earned him international awards, and when you visit his family's workshop you will see why—the details of the rugs, some double-sided, are just remarkable. A visit to the taller includes a walkthrough of how natural dyes are made, how the weaving process works, and the meaning behind the intricate Zapotec designs.

Food and Accommodations

★ Dulízùn Café

Hidalgo 26; tel. 951/524-4021; 8am-6pm daily; lunch US$4-6

If you're already shopping at Dulízùn Café, you might as well stay for lunch in the courtyard. Octogenarian Señora Juana still grinds cacao by hand to make the chocolate you should order. Grab a shady table and have a plate of mole and a cup of Juana's famous chocolate. For a unique treat, ask for a chocolate-atole, a sweet mixture of hot chocolate and the corn-based drink atole.

Café Vid

Benito Juárez 47; tel. 951/511-7626; 7:30am-10pm daily; US$5-8

If you're looking for a serious caffeine kick, stop by Café Vid for espresso-based drinks. The café buys its organically grown coffee

1: Templo de la Preciosa Sangre de Cristo
2: the vibrant natural colors of Teotitlán del Valle
3: Árbol del Tule

Tejate: The Drink of the Gods

Strolling through the markets, you're bound to see women behind large tubs of a strange-looking drink with white foam floating at the top. This is tejate, "la bebida de los dioses" (the drink of the gods), a pre-Hispanic drink that hails from **San Andrés Huayapam,** just north of Oaxaca City, and is still very popular in Oaxaca today. Don't let the odd look fool you. This stuff is delicious.

tejate

HOW IT'S MADE

It is made from fermented cacao beans, toasted corn flour, seeds of the mamey fruit, and the flowers of a tree called flor de cacao, which literally translates to "cacao flower" but is actually a different tree entirely. These ingredients are ground to a thick paste, then mixed with cold water, usually by hand. The mixture is set aside, and after a while, the flor de cacao rises to the top, forming the weird-looking foam that you'll end up craving again and again after you try it.

WHERE TO TRY IT

- San Andrés Huayapam, which is a quick 20-minute drive from downtown Oaxaca City, holds a tejate festival at the end of March.
- The **Feria del Tejate y el Tamal** (Tejate and Tamale Fair) is at the end of Guelaguetza season, usually in the beginning of August, in the Plaza de la Danza in Oaxaca City (page 66).
- The **Sunday Market** in Tlacolula (page 113) and the **Benito Juárez market** in downtown Oaxaca City (page 69) are great places to try this ancient drink, if you can't make it to the festivals.

beans directly from the Sierra Mazateca, in the north of the state, which ensures the growers get paid a fair price for their product. They also serve baguettes and sandwiches. If you stay the night in town, check in to see if they're hosting live music.

El Descanso

B. Juárez 51; tel. 951/524-4152; 9am-6pm daily; US$6-12

The verdant courtyard at El Descanso, where the Santiago family also has a rug gallery, is another great place for typical Oaxacan fare.

Casa de Huéspedes "Elim"

Pino Suarez 32; tel. 951/166-6289; US$38-42

Accommodations options in Teotitlán are limited. However, the town is gorgeous and the people warm, so if you have time, it's definitely worth staying a night at the Casa de Huéspedes "Elim." The spacious, rustic rooms offer beautiful mountain or garden views, set around a sunny courtyard. Continental breakfast is included.

Getting There

Teotitlán is 29 km (18 mi) east of Oaxaca City, and many tours include it in their itineraries. The total **drive** time is 45 minutes. **Colectivos** stop at the corner by the baseball stadium in Oaxaca City all day long and also take about 45 minutes. Drivers (and passengers aboard colectivos bound for other destinations) should keep an eye out for the sign to

Teotitlán del Valle about 18 km (11 mi) east of El Tule. You shouldn't have to wait too long for a **taxi** (US$0.50) into town from the crucero (crossroads).

TLACOLULA

When the Zapotecs arrived in this valley in the second century BC, they didn't live in what is now Tlacolula de Matamoros. They lived in Yagul, on a hilltop a couple of miles east of town. The Spanish moved the population to the site of present-day Tlacolula in the 16th century. Some scholars believe the name Tlacolula comes from a Nahuatl name meaning "Within the Place Full of Sticks," others "Crooked Thing." The Zapotec name for Tlacolula is Guichiibaa, which means "The Town Close to Heaven."

★ Sunday Market

The market that sprawls through the streets of Tlacolula is the oldest of its kind in Oaxaca, almost in all of Mesoamerica. People from the surrounding communities in the valley and the mountains to the north have been coming here since the Zapotecs settled the region, and some practices, such as bartering, have survived to this day. The tarps spread out from the Mercado Municipal, covering most of downtown to shade the stalls of everything from produce to artisan crafts to household items to coffee "that smells like the mountains," as one woman likes to advertise. This is a great place to try **tejate,** the sweet, foamy drink made from cacao, nuts, and cacao flowers. There is a whole aisle dedicated to cacao in the main market, and many vendors in the street sell tejate, as well as one made with coconuts.

Food

Mercado Municipal Martín González

Galeana 2; no tel.; 6am-6pm daily; US$4-6

Carnivores should visit Tlacolula whether they can make it to the Sunday market or not. You can find just about anything at this market, including pan de nuez (bread filled with pecan paste) and tejate (cacao and corn flour beverage), but the gastronomic specialty here is **barbacoa de chivo y borrego,** goat and lamb slow-roasted up to eight hours in an earthen oven and served in a consomé (stew) made from the blood and offal. Head to the barbacoa stalls on the north side of the Mercado Municipal Martín González to try it in tacos or in a stew. The smoky stalls are an organized chaos of vendors tending steaming pots of consomé, families squeezing in to

basket maker at the Tlacolula Sunday Market

The Slow-Roasted Flavors of Barbacoa

Foods like mole, quesillo, and chapulines (fried grasshoppers) are what usually come to mind when it comes to Oaxacan gastronomy, but with such a rich culinary tradition, it's no surprise that the Valles Centrales are full of mouthwatering barbacoa. Families in towns like Tlacolula, Zaachila, and Ocotlán have for generations perfected this technique of slow-roasting meat in ovens dug into the earth. It's not a meal unique to this part of Mexico, but it sure is delicious.

barbacoa stalls in the Tlacolula market

HOW IT'S MADE

The process usually begins the day before cooking, when the goat or sheep (the primary meats used in barbacoa here, though some places specialize in pork and beef) is slaughtered, skinned, and bled. The organs are set aside for use in the **consomé** (stew), and sometimes **sangrita,** a blood soup prepared with offal and seasoned with onions, chiles, cumin, and hierba buena (a type of mint).

For many families, cooking barbacoa is more than preparing a meal. It's spiritual. There are a few rituals to be performed before cooking. To avoid any malas vibras (bad vibes), points of maguey leaves in the form of a cross, or the meat of the chile de árbol, are placed in the oven before lighting the fire. El mal del ojo (The Evil Eye) is cast out by tossing the seeds and veins of the guajillo chile into the oven as well. And the cross is drawn over the pot of consomé ingredients before cooking, just in case a stranger stops by the house, possibly bringing bad vibes.

As early as 3am, it's time to prepare the oven, usually a brick-lined hole dug in the earth. A fire is lit in the bottom with wood from mesquite, laurel, and oak trees, and as the fire grows, more bricks are thrown into it to heat them up to cook the meat. After about two hours, the fire has died down to coals and the oven is ready. The bricks and coals are covered with a layer of avocado leaves, and then the meat is placed in the oven. The oven is covered with maguey leaves and dirt, which when dampened with water alerts the chefs to any leaks allowing heat out. The meat cooks in six to eight hours and is tender and flavorful by lunchtime.

HOW TO ORDER

When ordering barbacoa, you'll be asked questions like "Surtida o pura carne?" or "Roja o blanca?" If that bit about offal doesn't sit well with you, stick to **pura carne** (just meat) or **blanca** (white meat). The other options, **surtida** (assortment) and **roja** (red meat), include the chewier stuff.

You can order the meat in tacos or in a steaming bowl of savory consomé. Toss on some crunchy cabbage, cilantro, lime, and salsa, and ¡Buen provecho! (Enjoy your meal!).

eat, and guitar-toting musicians busking in the crowded aisles.

Getting There

Tlacolula is 32 km (20 mi) east of Oaxaca City on Highway 190. Many tours go on Sunday for the market. Drivers keep an eye out for the sign that says Tlacolula Centro about five minutes after the Teotitlán crossroads. Take Zaragoza straight into town. Total drive time is about 50 minutes. Colectivo passengers wait a bit farther and get out at the stoplight just before the highway climbs a hill. This option takes about an hour. The Plaza Municipal is six blocks south down Juárez, and there are mototaxis (US$1) if you're not feeling the walk.

DAINZÚ AND LAMBITYECO ARCHAEOLOGICAL SITES

The lesser-visited ruins at Dainzú and Lambityeco may not be as impressive as some of their neighbors, but that actually works to their advantage, because they draw fewer visitors. If you're pressed for time, or aren't overly interested in the finer archaeological details of the Valle de Tlacolula, then you might do better focusing your attention elsewhere. However, they're both just off the highway, so it's worth stopping by, especially if you're driving.

You won't find tour guides at these sites, but there are informational plaques in both Spanish and English.

Dainzú

Carretera a Tlacolula Hwy. 190 km. 17; tel. 951/568-0316; 8am-5pm daily; US$4.50

The Zapotecs named Dainzú "the Hill of the Organ Cactus" for the tall, prickly, pipe-like succulents that mark the landscape. Founded around 700 BC, a couple of centuries before the great capital Monte Albán, it was an important Zapotec settlement throughout the Classic Period (AD 250-900). The ruins, set in the west-facing slope of the hill, include religious and residential areas, tombs, bas-relief carvings, and a well-preserved ball court.

Lambityeco

Hwy. 190; no tel.; 8am-5pm daily; US$4.50

The ruins at Lambityeco may be small, but what they lack in size, they make up for in accessibility, as they're right on the highway. They date from 700 BC-AD 750. Part of a larger settlement called Yegüi (Zapotec for "Small Hill"), Lambityeco was a major producer of salt in the region, at one point filling 90 percent of the demand in Oaxaca. Salt was produced here as recently as 1940 by running river water through the soil and evaporating it to extract the minerals. The name Lambityeco has something to do with this process, though its etymology is uncertain. Some scholars assert that it is a Zapotec term for "hollow hill," while others claim it is a compound of the Zapotec word for hill and the Spanish word *alambique*, or alembic, a distillation apparatus from days of old. The highlight here is the pair of impressively carved masks of Cocijo, the Zapotec god of rain, thunder, and lightning. They are large carvings on a mound at the southeast corner of the site.

Getting There

Not very many tours stop at these sites (but Zapotrek does!), so you'll probably be on your own if you want to see them.

The sign for Dainzú, about 10 km (6 mi) east of El Tule, is white (in contrast to the blue signage for towns). The road from the highway is rough, but fine for cars at slow speeds. Colectivo passengers will have a nice 15-minute walk to the ruins along the dirt road through the valley scrub. Keep an eye out for the sign about 10 minutes after leaving El Tule.

To get to Lambityeco, go back to the highway and flag down a passing colectivo. The ruins are 7.5 km (4.5 mi) east of Dainzú, right on the southern side of the highway, just after the turnoff to Teotitlán.

YAGUL

Hwy. 190; no tel.; 9am-5pm daily; US$5.70

Founded sometime around 1500 BC, Yagul was an important cultural and governmental hub in the region, especially after the decline of Monte Albán. The name is believed to mean "Old Tree." The city was built on top of (and into) a steep cliff, resembling the civic planning of the great Zapotec capital to the west. Yagul remained an important and thriving urban area until the 16th century, when the Spaniards forced the Zapotecs out to form the current town of Tlacolula. Current residents of Tlacolula call the ruins Yugul, which means "Old Town."

You'll find structures similar to those at other sites like Monte Albán, such as a ball court, tombs, religious and residential buildings, and palatial patios, but what you won't see are the crowds. Yagul has the advantage of being a very interesting site that is slightly overshadowed by the grandeur of the region's most prominent ancient settlements. After the multitudes that flock to Monte Albán and Mitla, it can be a breath of fresh air to have a site that is (almost) as impressive (almost) all to yourself. The hill behind the main cluster of ruins is covered with trails and filled with more ruins. Up here you can peek into the entrance of **La Fortaleza** (The Fortress), an underground bunker where citizens hid out during times of conflict. The views from up here are phenomenal, as well.

And these ruins aren't even the oldest traces of human life here. On the road from the highway is a small site called **Caballito Blanco** (Little White Horse), where nomadic groups of hunter-gatherers left paintings in caves and rock hollows over 7,000 years ago. You can spy one on a cliff wall to the right of the entrance from the highway.

Getting There

Some tours that go to Mitla or Hierve El Agua also include Yagul on their itineraries. The turnoff to the site is about 2 km (1.2 mi) east of Tlacolula. Drivers and colectivo passengers shouldn't have a hard time seeing the large sign on the left side of the highway about five minutes outside the town. If you're going via public transport, be ready for a 20-minute, partly uphill walk from the highway, as there are no taxis or mototaxis working the 1.5-km (1-mi) road to the ruins.

SANTIAGO MATATLÁN

Wood smoke from the numerous pit ovens around town licks the yellow walls of the houses of Santiago Matatlán, "The World Capital of Mezcal," as you pass under the welcome sign decorated with a copper still. This is an essential stop for any lover of Oaxaca's favorite spirit. Like other artisan towns, the majority of the population of Matatlán works with the local specialty, and **palenques** (distilleries) and **expendios de mezcal** (mezcal stores) are around every corner.

Sights

Museo Comunitario Ta Guiil Reiñ

corner of Independencia and Niño Artillero; tel. 951/518-3003; 9am-noon and 1pm-6pm daily; donations accepted

Your first stop should be the Ta Guiil Reiñ Community Museum, where you'll get a better idea of the mezcal culture in Matatlán. The ground floor has displays on local celebrations

Yagul ruins

involving mezcal and the process of making the drink. Upstairs is a sizable collection of artifacts found at a local archaeological site called El Palmillo, which dates from 200-300 BC.

Mezcal Tours

El Rey Zapoteco

Carretera Internacional km 49; tel. 951/518-3020; www.elreyzapoteco.com.mx; 8am-8pm daily; free with purchase of mezcal

Founded by Don Serafín Hernández, El Rey Zapoteco is one of the most respected palenques in town. Mezcal is continually being made here, and the Hernández family offers tours of their palenque, demonstrations, and tastings. If you buy some mezcal, they'll show you around for free, but if not, it'll cost about US$3. They also have their world-famous mezcal for sale. They're by far not the only palenque in town, though, so take your time and visit a few to find one you like.

Getting There

Matatlán is located 47 km (29 mi) east of Oaxaca City. Total drive time is just over one hour. It is on many mezcal-themed tours run by agencies all over town. Drivers take Highway 190 east from the city and keep an eye out for the exit about 40 km (25 mi) from town. It is the same exit to go to Mitla, just hang right. Colectivos pick up passengers in the city at the corner stop by the baseball stadium. They take about 1.25 hours.

★ MITLA

Humans settled in Mitla sometime between AD 0 and 200. The Zapotecs call this place Lyobaam, which means "Place of the Dead." Both during and after the decline of Monte Albán, Mitla was the religious capital of the Zapotec civilization, and it flourished until the conquest in the 16th century. Today, it's one of Oaxaca's Pueblos Mágicos.

The modern town of **San Pablo Villa de Mitla** is built right on top of the ancient settlement. Some of the compounds can be seen in town, existing right next to residences and shops.

Exploring the Ruins

Mitla Archaeological Zone

Camino Nacional; tel. 951/502-1200; 8am-5pm daily; US$5.70

There are five architectural compounds, but the main cluster of ruins at the Mitla Archaeological Zone is where you'll find the unique, mortarless geometric mosaic stonework the site is famous for. You can view the walls and columns of the former administrative buildings now called the **North Group,** on top of which the **Templo de San Pablo Villa de Mitla** was constructed in the 17th century, without a ticket. They are just outside the ticket booth.

Buy a ticket and cross through the artisans market to enter the area called the **Columns Group,** a pair of open patios surrounded by structures elaborately adorned with Zapotec glyphs. At the top of the stairs in the patio to the north is the **Hall of Columns,** where six monolithic columns that once supported the roof still stand. A small passageway leads from this room to another small courtyard and a set of rooms, the walls of which are also covered in Mitla's distinct stonework. To get an idea of what it all looked like, try to imagine the floors and facades covered in red stucco. These were the palaces of high-ranking priests and other religious officials.

The patio just to the southwest of this one is home to what the Zapotecs named the place for: tombs. You can enter two of them, and you'll notice that here they decorated as lavishly for the dead as they did for the living. These tombs meant for high-ranking members of the priesthood also boast elaborate mosaics. Funerary tradition called for successive burials, in which the remains and offerings of previous burials were moved aside to make room for the newly departed.

Independent travelers can expect to spend about an hour in the Columns Group, and the other three compounds scattered around town can be seen in about a half hour by mototaxi.

Mitla

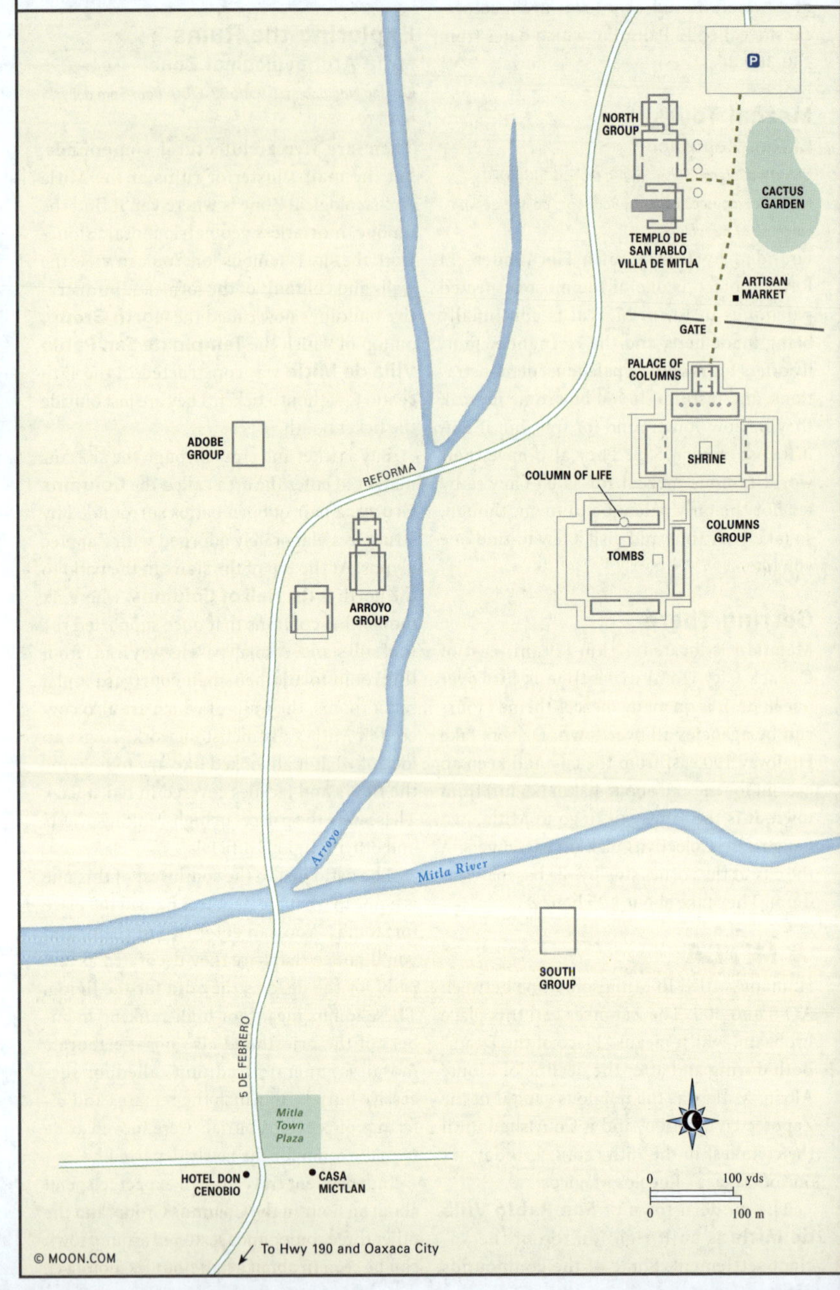

NORTH GROUP
CACTUS GARDEN
TEMPLO DE SAN PABLO VILLA DE MITLA
ARTISAN MARKET
GATE
PALACE OF COLUMNS
ADOBE GROUP
SHRINE
REFORMA
COLUMN OF LIFE
COLUMNS GROUP
TOMBS
ARROYO GROUP
Arroyo
Mitla River
SOUTH GROUP
5 DE FEBRERO
Mitla Town Plaza
HOTEL DON CENOBIO
CASA MICTLAN
0
100 yds
0
100 m
To Hwy 190 and Oaxaca City
© MOON.COM

They are not as impressive as the Columns Group, but it is interesting to see them alongside modernity. The **Arroyo Group,** on 5 de Febrero on the way to the main site, is little more than the rocky walls of what were once the residences of high-ranking priests. The sign for the **Adobe Group,** also called the Calvary, reads "El Calvario" and is at the bottom of the last rise in the road to the site. It is a short, squat stone building at the top of a set of stairs that offers a nice view of the town and Columns Group below. Not much more than a large pile of rocks among the surrounding houses, the **South Group** is just to the south of the Mitla River, a block east of 5 de Febrero. The Adobe Group and South Group structures were used for religious ceremonies.

Shopping

Artisan Market

8am-5pm daily

Mitla's main draw is the ruins, but it is also a hub for artisans from the surrounding communities in the valley to sell their work. You won't miss the artisan market, as you have to walk through it to get to the main ruins. The stalls are full of products from all over Oaxaca. Shops selling textiles, mezcal, and other Oaxacan products also line 5 de Febrero and Reforma, the main route to the archaeological zone.

Food and Accommodations

Mitla is another great town to consider spending a night in, conserving your energy to visit Hierve El Agua the following day, or to use as a base to explore the valley. There are **food stalls** just outside the artisan market, where you can get tacos, tlayudas (large tortillas topped with meat and cheese), and other typical street food for around US$3-4.

★ Doña Chica

Morelos 41; tel. 951/568-0683; 10am-8pm daily; US$6-12

Your best bet for dinner is Doña Chica, which serves up tasty moles, tacos dorados, memelas (tortillas topped with pork lard—say "sin asiento" if you don't get down with pork—salsas, cheese, and other ingredients), and more in a clean, casual setting among bamboo-lined walls and columns of bare green limestone. The service is impeccable, and the dining room stays nice and cool even in the heat of the day.

Casa Mictlan

Independencia 2; tel. 951/365-1444; www.artesaniasarely.com/casa-mictlan-habitaciones; US$40

Simple rooms are offered at this centrally located hotel, right across the street from the municipal plaza. The quiet and comfortable guesthouse with rooms equipped with TV and Wi-Fi is owned by a family of artisans. While you're staying with them, drop in their family's textile workshop a block from their store (5 de Febrero 2).

Hotel Don Cenobio

Juárez 3; tel. 951/568-0330; www.hoteldoncenobio.com; US$70 d, junior suite US$105 s or d, master suite US$116

For a bit of pizzazz, head to Hotel Don Cenobio, which the current Don Cenobio built around the 90-year-old house of his grandfather. Part of the original adobe walls remain among the newly remodeled structure. The lush courtyard is a comfortable escape from the midday heat, with a pool, a small playground for kids, and a **restaurant** (8am-6pm daily; US$5-10) that boasts a large menu of all kinds of Mexican food.

Getting There and Around

As it's one of Oaxaca's greatest hits, finding a tour that goes to Mitla is not a difficult task. It is usually included on itineraries that also stop at Hierve El Agua, Teotitlán, and other popular destinations.

Car

Mitla is 47 km (29 mi) east of Oaxaca City on Highway 190. The drive takes a little over an hour. Drivers will find the exit to Highway 179 10 km (6 mi) east of Tlacolula, but don't get on 179. The signage is pretty clear. You'll take a

left and cross over the highway onto the road that leads into town. If you don't want to deal with the traffic of the main drag to the ruins, keep an eye out for a sign that says "Zona Arqueológica" as you start to enter the town. Take a left and you'll follow a route that avoids the hustle and bustle. The main route is a little farther down the road, through the archway that says "Bienvenidos a Mitla" on the left.

Colectivo and Camionetas

If you're going directly to Mitla via colectivo, hail one at the corner by the baseball stadium in Oaxaca City. It'll get you there in about 1.25 hours. They'll drop you off at the archway. Camionetas that go to Matatlán and Hierve El Agua stop at the archway. Hierve El Agua is a 30-45-minute camioneta ride from Mitla.

Mototaxi

It's not really common practice, since few people visit the three groups of ruins in town, but if you want to check them out, you can ask a mototaxi driver to take you around (though they are walkable). Something like US$5 should be fair for a quick half-hour tour of them. There is not much to see at these sites, and don't expect the driver to be a tour guide, but it doesn't take long, and it is interesting to see them right next to people's houses and businesses. From the highway, stop by the **South Group** first, then the **Arroyo Group,** and finally the **Adobe Group.** Then just walk down the hill to see the main event.

★ HIERVE EL AGUA

no tel.; 7am-5pm daily; US$3

Despite what its name (which translates as "The Water Boils") implies, it's not really boiling, but the water in the mineral springs at Hierve El Agua sure looks like it is. For millennia, these springs have been gurgling up water laden with calcium carbonate and other mineral salts, which then flows over the edge of the cliffs, depositing the salts along the way. Slow as stalactites, these "petrified waterfalls" eventually grew to become the huge frozen water flows that spill down into the valley in uncanny formations.

1: Mitla's Columns Group **2:** Templo de San Pablo Villa de Mitla **3:** Hierve El Agua **4:** swimming hole at Hierve El Agua

The Springs

Make sure to bring your swimsuit—you can change into it in the restrooms (US$0.25) down by the pool. Coming down the hill from the food stands, you'll see the swimming pools of the **cascada chica** (little waterfall), where you can cool off in the heat of the afternoon. From here you can enjoy breathtaking views of the valley below, as well as the other "waterfall," known as the **cascada grande.** There are many springs bubbling to the surface here, trickling into the swimming pools and down the base of the formation.

Trails lead up and over another rise to the cascada grande, which does not have swimming pools but is an excellent perch for photos. From here, trails lead down to the valley floor, where you can explore around the bases of the falls. When climbing back up from the cascada grande, you can get to the parking lot more easily by continuing to climb instead of taking the trail that leads back down to the cascada chica. This way you can avoid having to go back down and up to the side with the food stalls. The trails are moderately steep and require a bit of effort in the heat of the day.

Food and Accommodations

The **food stands** (9am-6pm daily; US$4-8) up above the falls all have cocos frios (cold coconuts) and sodas to cool off in the heat, as well as quesadillas, tacos, tlayudas, and other street food favorites. Try a piña loca, an entire pineapple hollowed out, cut up, and served in the skin with orange juice, or, if you need the extra kick, a bit of mezcal.

Cabañas Ecoturísticas

tel. 951/561-4189; US$12 pp

Staying the night at Hierve El Agua is a rustic experience. The cabañas ecoturísticas just to the north of the food stands come with spectacular views and almost all the bare necessities, and camping is also an option. They have private bathrooms, but bring your own towels, soap, and toilet paper, just in case. If you'd rather pitch a tent than sleep in a cabin, it costs about US$3. Don't forget to bring your own food for when the food stands are closed.

Getting There

Car

Hierve El Agua is about 52 km (32 mi) southeast of Oaxaca City. Drivers take Highway 190 east from Oaxaca City. Take the Highway 179 exit about 39 km (24 mi) outside town. This route includes a toll (US$1.50), but it's worth it for the views. At km marker 62, take a right and follow the signs. The drive takes about 1.75 hours, and the last bit includes going up a mountain road without guardrails.

Camioneta

Public transport passengers can catch a camioneta from the main junction in Mitla; it takes 30-45 minutes and costs about US$2.50.

Tours and Guides

Like Monte Albán and Mitla, it's next to impossible not to find a tour to Hierve El Agua walking the streets of Oaxaca City. Most include it as the final stop on full-day tours with sites like El Tule, Teotitlán del Valle, and Mitla. However, to experience Hierve El Agua in a way that no other agency offers, call Eric Ramirez at **Zapotrek** (Aldama 304-A, Oaxaca City; tel. 951/257-7712; www.zapotrek.mx).

Valle de Zimatlán-Ocotlán

Home of the **Ruta de las Artesanías (Crafts Route),** the Valle de Zimatlán-Ocotlán extends south from Oaxaca City. It is rich with artisanal traditions both young and old, from alebrijes (the brightly painted figures of fantastic animals for which Oaxaca is renowned worldwide) to the various styles of alfarería (pottery) made here, which all have their roots in pre-Hispanic soil.

Getting There

Public transport travelers can reach any of these destinations (except San Sebastián de las Grutas) from Oaxaca City's **Automorsa bus station,** six blocks south of the Zócalo, at the corner of Bustamante and Xóchitl. Buses charge US$1-2 and leave every 8-10 minutes. You can get off these at any stop along the way, and then just wait for another one, or a taxi colectivo, by the side of the highway when you're ready to move on or return to the city. Make sure to confirm your destination with the driver before getting on, as there are two routes to take from here.

The Oaxaca-Zimatlán Highway and Highway 175 are the two major highways running through this valley. Drivers access the Oaxaca-Zimatlán Highway by heading south on Miguel Cabrera and crossing the periférico and Río Atoyac bridge. For Highway 175, cross the periférico at Calle Armenta y López.

ARRAZOLA

The concept of **alebrijes,** the brightly painted figures of fantastic animals for which Oaxaca is renowned worldwide, actually began in Mexico City, where Pedro Linares made them out of papier-mâché in the mid-20th century. But here in San Antonio Arrazola is where the art form took off. To pass the time while tending sheep, young Manuel Jiménez carved animals and other figures he saw in his dreams. Inspired by Linares's work, he began carving alebrijes out of wood, and the rest is history. You can easily pass a pleasant couple of hours strolling the hilly streets in town, searching for the style that calls to you.

Sights

El Tallador de Sueños

Álvaro Obregón 1; tel. 951/322-2505; www.eltalladordesueños.com; 8am-6pm daily; free

For the complete story of Manuel Jiménez (1919-2005) and his art, ask Manuel's son Isaías to show you around the small museum he made to his father's legacy at El Tallador de Sueños. They also have pieces for sale and host demonstrations on the process of making **alebrijes.**

Getting There

To get to Arrazola on public transport from Oaxaca City, take a Zaachila-bound Automorsa bus from the stop at Bustamante and Xóchitl (US$1). You'll have to get off in Santa Cruz Xoxocotlán, about 20 minutes out of the city, and get a taxi to Arrazola at the crossroads (big green sign). From here, it's a quick 15-minute cab ride (US$2) to Arrazola.

Drivers cross the periférico at Miguel Cabrera, then cross the Río Atoyac bridge but steer clear of the walled-off right lane. After the bridge, turn left onto the Oaxaca-Zimatlán Highway. In about 3 km (2 mi), turn right at the sign for Arrazola in Santa Cruz Xoxocotlán. Follow the signs for the next 7 km (4.3 mi) to Arrazola. The drive takes about 40 minutes.

CUILAPAM DE GUERRERO

Originally a town of Mixtec origin called Sahayuco, meaning "The Foot of the Hill," Cuilapam (sometimes Cuilapan) de Guerrero is now named after Afro-Mexican president Vicente Guerrero, who was assassinated here in 1831 during the political turmoil that followed Mexico's war of independence.

Sights

Ex-Convento de Santiago Apóstol

Vicente Guerrero; no tel.; 9am-6pm daily; US$2.50

The Ex-Convento de Santiago Apóstol is considered a masterpiece of Dominican architecture despite being left unfinished. The long, roof-less chapel you see as you first enter the courtyard was meant to be covered, but costs became too much for the Spanish crown, and construction was halted in 1568. You can wander around the courtyard free of charge, but it's worth paying to see inside. If it's not high season, there's a good chance you'll have the place mostly, if not all, to yourself. The quietness beneath the arches and vaulted ceilings is a great place to get away from it all and contemplate for a while, or not at all.

Festivals and Events

Lunes del Cerro

July

In the last week of July, Cuilapam holds its patron saint and Lunes del Cerro festivities, during which you can see performances of the **Danza de la Pluma** (Dance of the Feather). Cuilapam has a rivalry with Teotitlán del Valle over ownership of the dance's creation, and dancers here put their all into staking their claim.

Getting There

Cuilapam de Guerrero is about 10 km (6.2 mi) southwest of Oaxaca City. Zaachila-bound Automorsa buses stop in Cuilapam de Guerrero, just outside the Ex-Convento. They take about 30-40 minutes from Oaxaca City (US$1). Drivers cross the periférico and Río Atoyac bridge at Miguel Cabrera and turn left (south) onto the Oaxaca-Zimatlán Highway. The turn to Cuilapam de Guerrero is 3 km (1.9 mi) down the road, in Santa Cruz Xoxocotlán. The town is 7 km (4.3 mi) down the road from here. The drive takes about 30 minutes.

ZAACHILA

Zaachila was the last political capital of the Zapotec civilization after the decline of Monte Albán. It was named after the dynasty that began here sometime around the 14th century. Murals both here and in Mitla depict the divine lineage of the royal house of Zaachila.

Mercado de artesanías
de Barro Negro
fundado desde 1974
1
2 
3

Sights

Zaachila Archaeological Zone

Alarii 30; tel. 951/162-5065; 9am-6pm daily; US$3

What's left of this once great city can be seen at the Zaachila Archaeological Zone. You'll find the entrance just to the north of the bright-yellow church above the main square. Occupied in AD 1200-1521, it was one of the few inhabited Zapotec-Mixtec capitals when the Spanish arrived in Oaxaca. The Zapotecs and Mixtecs intermarried for political reasons. Much of the ruins have not been excavated, due to their locations beneath current residences, but you will be able to see a pair of tombs, one of which is decorated with human and animal representations of death. There are also a few aboveground platforms.

Festivals and Events

Lunes del Cerro

July

The hill where the ruins are located is the site where Zaachila holds its Lunes del Cerro festivities on the last two Mondays in July. At this lively festival, you can watch the stunning dance called the **Danza de los Zancudos** (Dance of the Stilted Ones), in which the participants dance on stilts over 2 m (6.5 ft) tall. If you get a chance to see this cultural gem, don't pass it up.

Food

Zaachila is an essential stop for those who come to Oaxaca to eat. The town specializes in its own twists on regional favorites. It's worth coming to Zaachila any day of the week, but Thursday is best, when the tarps of the weekly **día de plaza** cover the downtown streets for blocks.

★ Mercado Municipal Alarii

Plaza Municipal; no tel.; 6am-6pm daily

The goat and lamb barbacoa here rivals that of Tlacolula, but the **barbacoa en rollo,** beef wrapped in avocado tree leaves and slow-roasted for eight hours or more, is Zaachila's claim to fame. It is only made on Thursdays. In the Mercado Municipal Alarii, you'll find a number of stalls like **Cholita,** where the fourth generation of the Martínez family still serves this local delicacy. Along the walls of the market you'll find women selling tortillas and salsas. You can take all the goodies out to the park and picnic.

Outside the market building, tarps cover the streets for blocks, shading vendors selling fresh fruits and vegetables, tejate, aguas frescas, ice cream, folk art, and much, much more.

Mercado Gastronómico

Oaxaca-Zimatlán Hwy.; no tel.; 8am-7pm daily; US$2-4

If you happen to be in Zaachila on any day other than a Thursday and want to try **goat and lamb barbacoa,** you can find it in the Mercado Gastronómico, to the west of the cemetery. Chocolate lovers will want to try a cup of **espuma,** literally "foam," a frothy, sweet cacao and corn-based drink unique to Zaachila. You can find it any day of the week at the Mercado Gastronómico.

Save room for dessert at one of the **ice cream stands** (9am-7pm daily; US$1-2) in the Plaza Municipal. Zaachila simply puts a little more TLC into its nieves (ice cream similar to shaved ice) than other places around here do, and the result is delicious.

Getting There

Buses to Zaachila from the Automorsa stop in Oaxaca City take about 45 minutes to an hour (US$1). Drivers cross the periférico and Río Atoyac bridge at Miguel Cabrera and turn left (south) onto the Oaxaca-Zimatlán Highway. Zaachila is 11 km (7 mi) down the road. Stay on this highway, and in about 20 minutes, you'll see the Mercado Gastronómico on your left. The drive takes about 30 minutes.

SAN BARTOLO COYOTEPEC

Of the various styles of pottery in the Valles Centrales, the most striking, and arguably most popular, is the **barro negro (black**

1: Plaza Artesanal de Barro Negro **2:** alebrije hummingbird **3:** Ex-Convento de Santiago Apóstol

Días de Plaza: Weekly Markets

handicrafts at a market

Of all the ancient traditions still practiced in Oaxaca, the día de plaza (weekly market), also called a tianguis (more so elsewhere in Mexico) or simply mercado, is definitely one of the oldest. Towns all over the state host weekly markets that occupy the blocks surrounding the Plaza Municipal, selling everything from fresh meat and produce to household items to handicrafts and other artisanal products.

This practice dates back to before the founding of Monte Albán, when subjects of what the Spanish later called señoríos (chiefdoms) met in the chief's town to pay tribute and trade with each other as well. The día de plaza in Tlacolula is one of Oaxaca's oldest continuously running weekly markets, and here, as well as in Zaachila, traditions run so deep that many people still barter, rather than shop.

Between the Valles Centrales and Oaxaca City, you could fill each day of the week with a new street market. Although similar in many ways, each market day has something special that makes it stand out. Vendors set up shop early, and things are usually in full swing by 8am. Make the market your first stop on these days to get the best selection and freshest food. They begin packing things up in mid- to late afternoon.

SUNDAY: TLACOLULA

Renowned for its goat and lamb barbacoa, but also an excellent place to sample Oaxacan specialty drinks like tejate and mezcal.

MONDAY: TEOTITLÁN DEL VALLE

Artisans market where the wide diversity of styles of Teotitlán's expert weavers is on full display.

TUESDAY: SANTA ANA DEL VALLE

Also an artisans market specializing in the wool products of local weavers with styles distinct from those in Teotitlán.

WEDNESDAY: VILLA DE ETLA

Market known for the quality of its quesillo, a cheese that was accidentally invented by a forgetful teenager in neighboring Reyes Etla in the 1880s.

THURSDAY: ZAACHILA

Home of the one-of-a-kind barbacoa en rollo, made from beef and cooked with avocado tree leaves, and also known for its nieves (artisanal ice cream).

FRIDAY: OCOTLÁN

Great place to shop for the embroidered blouses made in neighboring San Antonino Castillo Velasco, and home of La Cocina de Frida, where Beatriz Vázquez dresses up like Mexico's most iconic painter to serve clients.

SATURDAY: OAXACA CITY (CENTRAL DE ABASTOS)

Largest of its type in Oaxaca, and known for having products from all over the state. One of my favorites, but pickpockets are known to quietly lift items from oblivious tourists, so move accordingly.

clay pottery) of San Bartolo Coyotepec. It was here, in the 1950s, that Doña Rosa Real de Nieto pioneered the glossy black pottery style that is now found in shops all over town. Artists here don't use a potter's wheel but stick to the traditional shaping method of a concave plate balanced and spun atop a convex one, spinning the piece with their hands.

Black clay pottery is primarily decorative, as the clay must be double-cooked in order to hold water, and a second cooking results in a dull-gray finish. Shops and markets all over town are full of vases, candleholders, figurines, skulls, and various other designs.

Sights

Museo Estatal de Arte Popular de Oaxaca

Oaxaca State Folk Art Museum; Independencia; tel. 951/551-0036; museoartepopular@gmail.com; 10am-6pm Tues.-Sun.; US$1

The Museo Estatal de Arte Popular de Oaxaca, on the south side of the Community Park, has devoted one of its four exhibition rooms to black clay pottery. This permanent exhibit shows off the extremely detailed work of San Bartolo Coyotepec's most talented artists. There's more than vases on display here, and what can be done with this clay is truly remarkable. The other three rooms host temporary exhibits of art from other regions of Oaxaca. Keep an eye out for the work of artists or artisans you've met elsewhere.

Shopping

Alfarería Doña Rosa

Juárez 24; tel. 951/551-0011; 9am-7pm daily

Your first stop should be at the place where the tradition began. At Alfarería Doña Rosa, the potter's grandchildren honor and continue her legacy. They offer demonstrations of Doña Rosa's innovative technique, and their large stock of gleaming vases and figurines are for sale in the ample courtyard-turned-showroom.

Plaza Artesanal de Barro Negro

Benito Juárez 37; no tel.; 10am-7pm daily

For a broad selection from alfareros (potters) from all over town, take an hour strolling the rustic yellow booths of the Plaza Artesanal de Barro Negro. This market boasts the widest range of styles in one place in town, and has a nice, laid-back atmosphere that invites you to take your time and find just the piece you're looking for.

Getting There

San Bartolo Coyotepec is 13 km (8 mi) south of Oaxaca City, a quick 25-minute drive. It is a big hit on the tourist circuit, and there really isn't an agency in the city that doesn't stop here. Drivers cross the periférico at Calle Armenta y López and take Highway 175 south. The main artisans market and signs for Doña Rosa are very conspicuous. The turn for the Plaza Artesanal is a few hundred meters (or yards) before this turn. Keep an eye out for the sign on the left side of the highway. The Automorsa buses that leave from the station on Bustamante and Xóchitl stop here on the way to Ocotlán; they take about 30 minutes (US$1).

★ SAN MARTÍN TILCAJETE

As the **alebrijes** craze spread in the 1980s, artists from the surrounding communities began to take up the craft. One such artist, Isidro Cruz, took what he'd learned in Arrazola to San Martín Tilcajete, and the art form took off. Now, like in Arrazola, the majority of the population works making and selling alebrijes, each with his or her own distinct style of carving and painting the figures.

Festivals and Events

Carnaval

Tuesday before Lent

Dancing with the devil is always risky business, but it'll be hard to resist the temptation at one of Oaxaca's one-of-a-kind carnival celebrations. In a blend of pre-Hispanic Zapotec tradition and Catholic folk practices, revelers take to the streets of San Martín Tilcajete for a riotous good time. Participants of all ages cover themselves with body paint—some with acrylic, but others the traditional way with oil. The oil is mixed with charcoal to make black (representing the underworld), corn flour to create yellow (representing this world), and brick dust for red (representing infinity). Hand-carved wooden masks with devil horns and ghastly visages complete the eerie ensemble. These aceitados (oiled ones) cause friendly havoc throughout the town, scaring neighbors and trying to sully anyone hapless enough to come into reach of their colorful hands. As with most Oaxaca festivities, the partying lasts day and night. Then it's off to church to repent of the devilry in the morning.

Shopping

Taller Una Inspiración de mi Vida

Calle del Tanque s/n; tel. 951/224-8778 or 951/183-3578; www.oaxacaunainspiraciondemivida.com; 8am-6pm daily

For over 40 years, this workshop has been creating chimerical alebrijes inspired by, well, life itself. As Maestro Victor Fabian Ortega explains, creating alebrijes isn't just about making a mash-up of animals and slapping paint on wood. Every day the artist must seek to create a different and fantastic being, but to do so they need to find an inspiration, a connection, in order to give life to these beings. Spirituality and tradition play a role, too. Before there were alebrijes, the Zapotec people had tonas y nahuales, animal spirit guides who protect individuals in this life and the life to come. In a zodiac-like system, your birth year and month dictate which animals are your guardians, and also influence your personality. (I was a bit put out that one of my spirit guides is an opossum—but that means I'm loving, so I guess that's great?) A blending of the two animals creates the fantastical creatures that fill this workshop in a rainbow of wonder. Free tours are given to explore the in-depth creation process from start to finish, and you will have a chance to find out about your own tonas and nahuales in this inspirational workshop.

Getting There

San Martín Tilcajete is located 26 km (16 mi) south of Oaxaca City. **Drivers** take Highway 175 south and turn right at the sign after about 35 minutes. The **Automorsa bus** takes 45 minutes. You can get a **mototaxi** (US$0.50) from the highway or walk into town; it's about 20 minutes on foot.

SANTO TOMÁS JALIEZA

This small town informally goes by the nickname "La Ciudad de los Cinturones" (The City of Belts). Weavers here have been producing colorful **cotton belts** and other **textile products** decorated with pre-Hispanic glyphs distinct to the area for generations.

Shopping

Artisans Market

Plaza Municipal; no tel.; 10am-6pm daily

Belts are the specialty here, but you'll also find table runners, shawls, bags, bracelets, even backpacks and laptop cases, all for a fraction of the price of what you'd find in the city. Weavers here yoke their telar de cintura (long, skinny backstrap looms) to a corner of the market, hands moving to the rhythm of their voices as they chat.

Getting There

Santo Tomás Jalieza is 27 km (17 mi) south of Oaxaca City and just two minutes down the highway from the turnoff to Tilcajete. Drivers take Highway 175 south, turn left at the sign, and follow the paved road to the artisans market in the Plaza Municipal. The Automorsa bus takes about 50 minutes (US$1). You can get a mototaxi (US$0.50) from the highway or enjoy the 10-minute walk into town.

SAN ANTONINO CASTILLO VELASCO

You might be asked why you visited this mouthful of a town, but you'll have fascinating ways to answer. San Antonino Castillo Velasco is known regionally for its unique style of **huipil** (embroidered blouse), with designs inspired by local birds and flowers.

The designs here are daintier than what you'll see on blouses made elsewhere in Oaxaca. The town is also known for a workshop where you'll find **barro rojo** (red clay pottery) sculptures.

With its checkerboard domes and pleasant pale-blue facade that in spots lets bare stone peek through, the 17th-century **Cuasiparroquia de San Antonino Obispo** (parish church dedicated to Anthony of Padua) in the town center is a fetching sight, so don't miss it on your way to go shopping and eating.

Shopping

Aguja de Plata

Macedonio Alcalá 32; tel. 951/539-6243; 8am-9pm daily

Three blocks east of the church, Marta Serna runs Aguja de Plata, a small textile shop where she passes down the knowledge she learned from her mother to the next generation. She embroiders intricate and colorful floral designs on clothing for women, children, and even men, as well.

La Casa del Bordado

Castillo Velasco 12; tel. 951/571-0623; 10am-6pm daily

There are a few textile shops on the road leading in from the highway. Stop by La Casa del Bordado (The House of Embroidery) on your way in or out of town for more beautiful embroidered dresses, blouses, and men's shirts. The selection here is large and varied.

Taller Manos Que Ven

Libertad 24; tel. 951/422-3371; tallermanosqueven@gmail.com; 8am-6pm daily

Master Potter José García Antonio contracted glaucoma in his 50s, and his vision began to fade. Within a few years, the artist, known regionally and internationally as **El Señor de las Sirenas** (The Mermaid Man) for his penchant for sculpting the mythical creatures, was completely blind. This, however, did not deter the man, who continues to work to this day, imbuing the life he recorded in his mind while he still had his vision and imprinting those images in **barro rojo** (red clay). His wife, Maestra Santa Reyna Teresita, is his eternal muse (all his female figures have a mole between the eyebrows, just as his beloved—I nearly swooned from the romance of it all) and sculpts alongside him. Their children are taking the craft in their own unique directions, as well. Maestro José and his family sell their work and give demonstrations at the Taller Manos Que Ven (Hands That See Workshop), also the family home.

Biushita

Independencia 57; 951/395-6535 or 951/196-8306; 10am-6pm Tues.-Sun.

San Antonino Castillo Velasco is an important cultivator of decorative flowers in Oaxaca, and the most awe-inspiring blooms here are the **flores inmortales** (immortal flowers), which keep their form and colors up to 45 years after they are cut. The Raymundo Sánchez family creates gorgeous statues, figurines, and religious items with these colorful natural wonders.

Food

★ Empanadas Carmelita

Albino Zertuche 21; tel. 951/505-3427; 9am-3:30pm Tues.-Sun.; US$3

There are lots of tasty bites in the **Mercado Progreso,** just east of the main square, but if you've come all the way here, you've got to eat an **empanada de amarillo,** the town's specialty. And there's no better place to try them than Empanadas Carmelita, where the chef-owner takes her vocation seriously. Distinct from other empanadas in Oaxaca, these are made with pork and include cilantro and other herbs that jazz up the delicious amarillo sauce.

Getting There

The turnoff to San Antonino is 32 km (20 mi) south of Oaxaca City on Highway 175, just before you reach Ocotlán. The drive takes about an hour. If you arrive via Automorsa bus, which takes about an hour (US$1), there are mototaxis (US$0.50) that will take you

Santo Tomas
JALIEZ

into town from the highway. If you say you're going to visit El Señor de las Sirenas, they will know exactly where to go.

OCOTLÁN DE MORELOS

Templo y Ex-Convento de Santo Domingo

Maximiliano Amador 1; no tel.; 9am-6pm daily

Church lovers must stop by the beautifully restored Templo y Ex-Convento de Santo Domingo. This 16th-century Dominican church was in drastic disrepair until the 1980s, when Ocotlán's most famous citizen, the painter Rodolfo Morales (1925-2001), restored it to the bright blue and white facade we see today. The interior is decorated with silver and gold from the neighboring town of Santa Catarina Minas. The shady church courtyard is a nice place to take food from the market and have a picnic.

Food

Friday is the day that tarps take over the central streets of Ocotlán de Morelos. Like the markets at Zaachila and Tlacolula, the **Friday market** features phenomenal barbacoa.

★ La Cocina de Frida

Mercado Morelos; tel. 951/222-2683; 9:30am-6pm daily; US$5-8

For a truly unique meal, head to La Cocina de Frida. This stall inside the main market on the west side of the Plaza Principal is run by Beatriz Vázquez, a woman who bears a striking resemblance to Frida Kahlo. She dresses up as the famous painter and serves up her specialties of chiles rellenos and mole estofado (stewed mole).

Getting There

Ocotlán is located 33 km (20 mi) south of Oaxaca City on Highway 175. The **drive** takes about an hour. Automorsa **buses** leave from the stop at Bustamante and Xóchitl every 10 minutes and take about an hour (US$1.25).

1: weaving on a telar de cintura **2:** cave at San Sebastián de las Grutas **3:** barro rojo creations from Taller Manos Que Ven **4:** Templo y Ex-Convento de Santo Domingo

SAN SEBASTIÁN DE LAS GRUTAS

San Sebastián de las Grutas technically isn't in the Valle de Zimatlán-Ocotlán. It is tucked away in the rolling green foothills of the Sierra Madre del Sur mountain range that divides the Valles Centrales from the coast. The main attraction here is the system of **caves** (grutas) in a hill just to the west of town. This 400-m (1,300-ft) cave has five rooms ranging 20-70 m (66-230 ft) in height. The shapes of the countless stalactites and stalagmites have inspired names like "The Lovers," "The Rhinoceros Fossil," and "The Bell" (because of the sound it makes when struck). There is also an underground river that runs below the caves. During the rainy season (June-Sept.), it is too dangerous to explore, but at other times of the year, the **Centro Ecoturístico San Sebastián de las Grutas** (tel. 951/118-2423 or 951/454-2656; office open 24 hrs) runs tours that rappel down into this part of the cave system. The center can also facilitate booking other activities that include hiking, visiting pre-Hispanic tombs, and Mezcal tastings.

Food and Accommodations

The ecotourism center has **cabañas ecoturísticas** with room for 5-8 people, which include hot water and Wi-Fi. The cost is US$12 per person for a group of 3 or more; for 1 or 2 people, it's US$30 for the cabin (pets are allowed for an extra US$5 per animal). The comedor on-site (9am-9pm daily; US$9-12) has the usual fare of chiles rellenos, quesadillas, huevos al gusto, and so on. Eating options in town can be quite limited, but there are a couple of comedores here, as well. You can grab a mototaxi on the highway, or enjoy the 15-minute walk into town. It's a pretty sleepy little community, so your best option is to make sure you get to the comedor at the cabañas before it closes.

Getting to the Caves

The cheapest way to get to the caves from Oaxaca City is on a suburban (12-passenger van) from the Central de Autobuses Segunda Clase, on the west side of the Centro, by the Central de Abastos. They cost US$3, leave hourly, and take a little over two hours to get to the cabañas. The driver will drop you off at the turnoff just west of town, and the cabañas are a five-minute walk from the highway.

The caves are about 53 km (33 mi) southwest of Oaxaca City. **Drivers** take Highway 175 south from the city. The junction with Highway 131 is 15 km (9 mi) down the highway. From here, follow Highway 131 for 55 km (34 mi), until you see the sign to turn right. The town is another 12 km (7.5 mi) from this junction, and the caves and cabañas are about 1 km (0.5 mi) west of town. Total drive time is a little over two hours.

Valle de Etla

Extending northwest from Oaxaca City, the Valle de Etla is the smallest of the Valles Centrales. Although it draws the least attention from tourism agencies, it is also home to treasured Oaxacan traditions. The fortunate accident that gave the world quesillo happened here toward the end of the 19th century. And Monte Albán is believed to have been founded by people formerly living in a settlement at San José El Mogote, which can be visited to this day.

Any destination in the Valle de Etla can be reached from Oaxaca City by getting a **taxi colectivo** on Calle Valerio Trujano, seven blocks west of the Zócalo, just on the other side of the periférico. It looks chaotic, and it is, but just ask a driver to help you find one for where you're going if you have any trouble. These taxis will get you anywhere in the valley and back for US$2-5 per day.

SAN AGUSTÍN ETLA

Two freshwater springs keep water flowing through the river at San Agustín Etla year-round, making the town a leafy green oasis in the winter, when much of the surrounding landscape has turned brown for the season. Only half an hour from downtown Oaxaca, it's a great place to get away from the heat of the city and cool off at one of the local **balnearios,** public swimming pools that can often look like mini-waterparks.

Sights

Centro de las Artes de San Agustín (CaSa)

Independencia next to Iglesia de SoSoledaVista Hermosa; tel. 951/521-3043; www.casa.oaxaca.gob.mx; 9am-6pm daily; free

San Agustín is the home of the Centro de las Artes de San Agustín (CaSa), founded by the world-renowned Oaxacan visual artist Francisco Toledo (1940-2019). In 2006, with the help of a grant from the Oaxacan government, Toledo bought and renovated the abandoned 19th-century textile mill on the north side of town, and turned it into a thriving arts and educational space. The center hosts temporary exhibits of art, photography, and video made in its many workshops, and the building itself is beautiful enough to warrant a visit.

CaSa offers a variety of cultural and artistic courses and workshops, from seminars on border issues to classes in painting, photography, theater, and other visual arts. Check their website for a list of available courses. There is no charge, but you must apply to enroll.

Arte Papel Vista Hermosa

tel. 951/521-2394; 10am-6pm Mon.-Sat.; free

From CaSa, the signs that say "Taller de Papel" (Paper Workshop) will lead you down the hill to the Vista Hermosa Paper Factory.

1: Centro de las Artes de San Agustín (CaSa) **2:** Arte Papel Vista Hermosa **3:** Frida Libre

1

2

3

In the workshop just below the store, you can get a demonstration of how they make paper out of recycled materials, much of which was used in Toledo's own projects. The store sells notebooks, jewelry, kites, and other pieces of art designed by Toledo.

Festivals and Events

La Muerteada

November

On November 1, when other towns in Oaxaca are solemnly observing Day of the Dead rites in the cemeteries, the citizens of San Agustín Etla do the complete opposite with a raucous, ghoulish parade called La Muerteada. Locals don homemade costumes and gather at the fittingly gothic **Iglesia de Soledad Vista Hermosa,** just next to the Centro de las Artes. Since its roots go back to the days of haciendas (large family-owned ranches), there is a classic list of characters representing members and ranch hands of the Ruiz Leyva family, who are said to have started the tradition. La Viuda (the widow) and El Muerto (her dead husband) are accompanied by El Viejo (the father of the deceased patriarch), the Butler, and others, who are corralled through the streets by the whip-wielding Chivero, or goatherd. This troupe from beyond the grave parades riotously through town until the sun comes up, when they return to the church full of mezcal and tamales, ready for another year of rest after dancing through the night.

Food and Accommodations

Comedor Campestre

Colón 1; tel. 951/251-2148; 8am-5pm daily; US$3-5

The most reliable option in town is Comedor Campestre. They serve the usual breakfast and lunch fare, but will also prepare vegetarian and vegan meals if you call ahead of time.

Frida Libre

Independencia 47; tel. 951/379-5981; 2pm-8pm Wed.-Mon.; US$5-13

Frida Libre opened its doors in March 2023 with fresh, international flavors. Staples include 100 percent angus hamburgers, ceviche and fish tacos with fish straight from the coast, and a vegetarian mushroom risotto. The menu really shines with its rotating specials, featuring soul food classics like shrimp 'n' grits or homey plates of gnocchi. Frida Libre is also an inclusive and friendly space for LGBTQ travelers.

Posada Villa Loohvana

Independencia 11; tel. 951/306-1367; villa_loohvana@hotmail.com; US$30-42

To save some dough without sacrificing aesthetics, try Posada Villa Loohvana, in the home of polyglot Michelle Tommi. The large white stucco house overlooks the green rolling hills of the Valle de Etla, and the sweet aroma of the azucena flowers (Madonna lily) permeates the terraced gardens at sunset. The house's four guestrooms are cozy yet spacious; all have private bathrooms.

El Rincón de San Agustín Etla

Calle Reforma; tel. 951/309-6591 or 951/521-2526; www.rincondesanagustin.jimdofree.com; private bungalows US$40 d, US$45 with kitchen, camping US$12

Amalia Cruz at El Rincón de San Agustín Etla has a wide range of private bungalow options that include ecological bathrooms with solar heating. The common area has a ping-pong table and a fireplace for guests to enjoy. And there's lots of space to pitch a tent. She also arranges hikes to a nearby lake and will fill the pond upon request if you need to cool off.

Getting There

Car

Drivers take Highway 190 west from Oaxaca City. After about 14 km (9 mi), turn right onto the unnamed road just after the Instituto Euro Americano. Take the next left and follow the road lined with towering jacaranda trees another 3 km (2 mi) to San Agustín Etla. The drive takes about 30 minutes. Public transport passengers can get here from the taxi colectivo stop on Valerio Trujano in about half an hour (US$1.50).

Tours and Guides

4 Seasons Tours and Travel Oaxaca (tel. 951/231-4840; oaxaca4seasons.toursandtravel@gmail.com) runs a full-day tour that stops at the Centro de las Artes and other places in the Valle de Etla.

VILLA DE ETLA

Villa de Etla is a charming town located about 30 minutes northwest of Oaxaca City, about 5.5 km (3.4 mi) from San Agustín Etla. Known for producing quesillo (a white, semihard cheese) and its vibrant Wednesday market, the town is a key part of Oaxaca's culinary and artisanal traditions.

Food

Mercado Municipal Porfirio Díaz

Independencia; no tel.; 7am-6pm daily

As legend has it, sometime in the 1880s, a cheesemaker from the neighboring village of Reyes Etla left his 14-year-old daughter in charge of the curds while he and his wife went into Villa de Etla for the day. Fortunately for us all, she forgot to tend to the cheese, and what her parents found when they got home looked strange, but tasted delicious. This classic teenage mishap was the birth of the sharp, stringy cheese Oaxaca is famous for, called **quesillo.**

The Mercado Municipal Porfirio Díaz has a number of booths selling this locally made cheese, and it is the hub of the town's weekly Wednesday market.

Getting There

Villa de Etla is right on Highway 190, 20 km (12 mi) northwest of Oaxaca City. The drive from Oaxaca City takes about 40 minutes. The taxis colectivos that leave from the stop on Valerio Trujano also take about 40 minutes and cost about US$2.50.

La Costa and Istmo de Tehuantepec

Oaxaca's two southernmost regions, La Costa and Istmo de Tehuantepec, share a coastline of over 480 km (300 mi), so you can bet that there's a beach for everyone. Playa Zicatela in Puerto Escondido offers the best surfing in the country. Only experienced surfers should tackle the world-class beach break here—but the calmer point break at Punta Zicatela, farther down the beach, is perfect for learning the ropes.

The beaches of Mazunte, San Agustinillo, and Zipolite are popular destinations for hippies, nudists, yoga retreaters, and sea turtles alike. Seven of the world's eight sea turtle species swim to Oaxaca's shores to lay eggs, and Mazunte, home of the Centro Mexicano de la Tortuga (Mexican Turtle Center), is a great place to learn about these incredible

Highlights

Look for ★ to find recommended sights, activities, dining, and lodging.

★ **Playa Zicatela:** Home of the world-famous "Mexican Pipeline," this surfer's paradise offers roaring waves by day and a vibrant party scene by night (page 144).

★ **Parque Nacional Lagunas de Chacahua:** Near the Afro-Mexican village that bears the same name, make sure you grab a tamale de tichinda as you explore the seven lagoons of this lovely corner of the coast (page 158).

★ **Mazunte:** The epitome of "chill vibes," this beachside Pueblo Mágico is a haven for those looking to slow down and unwind (page 170).

★ **San José del Pacífico:** A mystical respite above the clouds holds plenty of magic among its mist-shrouded alpine peaks ... in more ways than one (page 174).

★ **Playas La Entrega and Maguey:** See how many shades of blue you can spot as you lounge beside some of Oaxaca's calmest waters—or make a splash and go snorkeling (pages 185 and 186).

★ **Casa Museo Shunashi:** This gorgeous 17th-century home turned museum gives you an in-depth, yet personal, introduction to Istmeño culture and traditions (page 193).

La Costa and Istmo de Tehuantepec

and endangered animals, and even observe them in the wild.

Billed as the "Cancún of the Oaxacan coast" when it was planned by the federal government in the 1980s, Bahías de Huatulco has everything from virgin beaches to five-star, all-inclusive resorts to the ebullient and colorful La Crucecita, the pint-sized urban heartbeat of the place. Huatulco is the kind of place where you can live in the lap of luxury one night, and the next pitch a tent at the campground right next door. With nine bays, a national park, 2,000-year-old ruins, more surfing, and waterfalls all within reach, Huatulco, like the rest of the gorgeous Oaxacan coast, truly does have something for everyone.

ORIENTATION

In La Costa, also known as La Costa Chica (The Little Coast), the main three beach hubs of **Puerto Escondido, Puerto Ángel,** and **Bahías de Huatulco** dot the coastline, from west to east. North of Puerto Ángel—and worth a detour inland—the two mountain towns of **San José del Pacifico** and **Pluma Hidalgo** sit nestled in the towering cloud-forested peaks of the Sierra Madre del Sur,

Previous: Playa Zicatela; La Tehuana statue by artist Miguel Hernández Urbán in Tehuantepec; mirador in San José del Pacifico.

which run the entire coast of Oaxaca, terminating in the **Istmo de Tehuantepec** to the east, and to the west running through the state of Guerrero and on into southern Michoacán.

PLANNING YOUR TIME

How does one plan a stay in paradise? Ideally, give yourself at least two weeks. If you've only got one week, choose one of the three major tourist centers on the coast to explore (you can always take a day trip to visit one of the other two areas).

Puerto Escondido is Mexico's top surfing destination, where the monstrous beach break at **Zicatela** has world-class riding year-round. Day-trip options include tours in the wildlife-rich **Lagunas de Chacahua** and **Laguna de Manialtepec,** or cultural excursions to towns like **Santa Catarina Juquila.**

The beaches from **Puerto Ángel** west to **Mazunte** are Oaxaca's de facto "hippie beaches," and beach bumming is the primary activity here. For a little more excitement, take a boat ride through the croc-filled waters at **La Ventanilla.**

Bahías de Huatulco has a little something for everyone. If you can peel yourself away from the sand, splashing in the **Cascadas Mágicas** (Magical Waterfalls) or mountain biking through the dense jungle of **Parque Nacional Huatulco** is a fun excursion.

As for the mountains, you're going to want to stay at least a night or two in the foggy heights of **San José del Pacifico,** catching your breath at soaring vistas everywhere you turn. Coffee pilgrims absolutely must visit **Pluma Hidalgo,** the birthplace of Oaxaca's coffee love affair.

How you plan your time in **El Istmo** will depend on the calendar. The famous velas of **Juchitán** and **Tehuantepec** are mostly in April and May, but El Istmo has plenty of celebrations year-round, especially in the festive months of January, September, and December. In Tehuantepec, a visit to **Casa Museo Shunashi** is also in order and will immerse you in the rich culture and history of the region.

I recommend visiting **Salina Cruz** only if you've booked a surf camp trip; the surf camp guides know where all the good waves are, and packages include transportation to them.

High season corresponds with major national holidays. Book at least a month in advance of the Christmas and Semana Santa. The coast is also very busy in the months of July and August, when school is out for summer vacation.

Itinerary Ideas

Although it would be a dream to luxuriate on the beaches of Oaxaca for a month or more, sometimes time just doesn't allow. This three-day itinerary will give you an idea of what to expect for your next trip—because you know you'll be back. You may want to rent a car for ease of travel between beach towns.

DAY 1: PUERTO ESCONDIDO

1 Start the day with a fresh juice and fruit bowl at **El Sultán** in Rinconada.

2 Mosey on down to beautiful **Playa Carrizalillo** to relax, swim, or catch a surf lesson.

3 After rinsing off the salt and sand, make your way to La Punta. Grab a couple of fish or shrimp tacos at **Fish Shack** and explore the beach.

4 After hanging out on the beach and taking in bohemian vibes, be sure to catch sunset at **La Punta.**

5 End the night with a seafood pizza and drinks (and if you're lucky, a party) at **Cactus Bar and Restaurant** in Zicatela.

DAY 2: MAZUNTE

1 Upon arriving in Mazunte, wake up with a good coffee at **Café Duva.**

2 Head across the street and check out the sea turtles at **Centro Mexicano de la Tortuga.**

3 Enjoy a lunch of tacos dorados de camarón at **Doña Meche.**

4 Relax on **Playa Rinconcito.**

5 Make the trek up to the southernmost point of Oaxaca at **La Punta Cometa** and enjoy a dazzling sunset.

6 Have ceviche and unwind with a cocktail at **La Tertulia.**

DAY 3: BAHÍAS DE HUATULCO

1 Start your day with a cheerful breakfast at **Campestre Santa Clara.** For something different, order the tlacoyos.

2 Go to **Playa La Entrega** and enjoy snorkeling, swimming, or sunbathing.

3 Take a five-minute taxi to **Playa Maguey** for a palapa lunch and more beach fun.

4 Once the sun sets, take the **Tran Via El Huatulqueño** bus tour through the city.

5 Have dinner at **Terra-Cotta** and enjoy an evening in the zócalo.

Puerto Escondido and Vicinity

Puerto Escondido, Oaxaca's Hidden Port, is a secret no longer. Once a sleepy fishing village named after a kidnapped runaway (La Escondida), it has transformed into an international mecca for surfers and travelers drawn to its bohemian vibes. Catching morning waves, drinking in sherbet-shaded sunsets, evening adventuring to glowing lagoons, late-night partying under the stars… It's a charmed experience. No, magic like this definitely couldn't stay hidden forever.

The danger of popularity is when what makes the place special is bottled up, labeled, packaged, and sold off to the highest bidder. But this is Oaxaca we're talking about. The people's pride and tenacious stronghold on their culture just can't be commodified. And that's what will keep Puerto Escondido's intoxicating identity secure as it rides the wave of its growing appeal.

Orientation

Puerto Escondido stretches across 15 km (9 mi) of coastline, encompassing eight beaches, from Playa Bacocho to the west, curving south at the Bahía Principal, to Punta Zicatela, or La Punta, at its southeastern limit. The central coastal point is the **Bahía Principal,** which contains the Playas Principal and Marinero, with Playa Zicatela and La Punta to the south, and Playas Manzanillo, Puerto Angelito, Carrizalillo, and Bacocho to the west.

The tourist area of the Bahía Principal is the last cobblestone-covered stretch of Avenida Gasga, referred to as **El Adoquín** (The Paving Stone), which is closed to car traffic every night 5pm-6am. Coastal Highway 200 separates the beaches from the Centro and town proper, which fans out over the sylvan foothills to the north of the Bahía Principal; this north side of Highway 200 is where you'll find the town market and municipal bus station. The highway intersection with Avenida Gasga (called Avenida Oaxaca north of Hwy. 200) is the local crucero (crossroads).

Safety Concerns

Puerto Escondido is fairly safe, but still has a bit of an edge to it—a Disneyfied beach town this is not. That's part of its charm, but it is important to take a couple of precautions. Walking the beaches late at night isn't recommended due to crimes of opportunity and, unfortunately, unscrupulous police who pad their meager salaries by shaking down tourists. Just be aware of your surroundings, use common sense, and you should be fine. Personal thefts are more likely during the hustle and bustle of high season.

Your biggest safety concern in Puerto, however, isn't on land. The **undertows** on many of the beaches are extremely powerful and should be taken seriously. Anyone who is not an experienced surfer should steer clear of the water at Playa Zicatela completely. The water off La Punta is okay for experienced swimmers (maybe), but even here the undertow can

Puerto Escondido

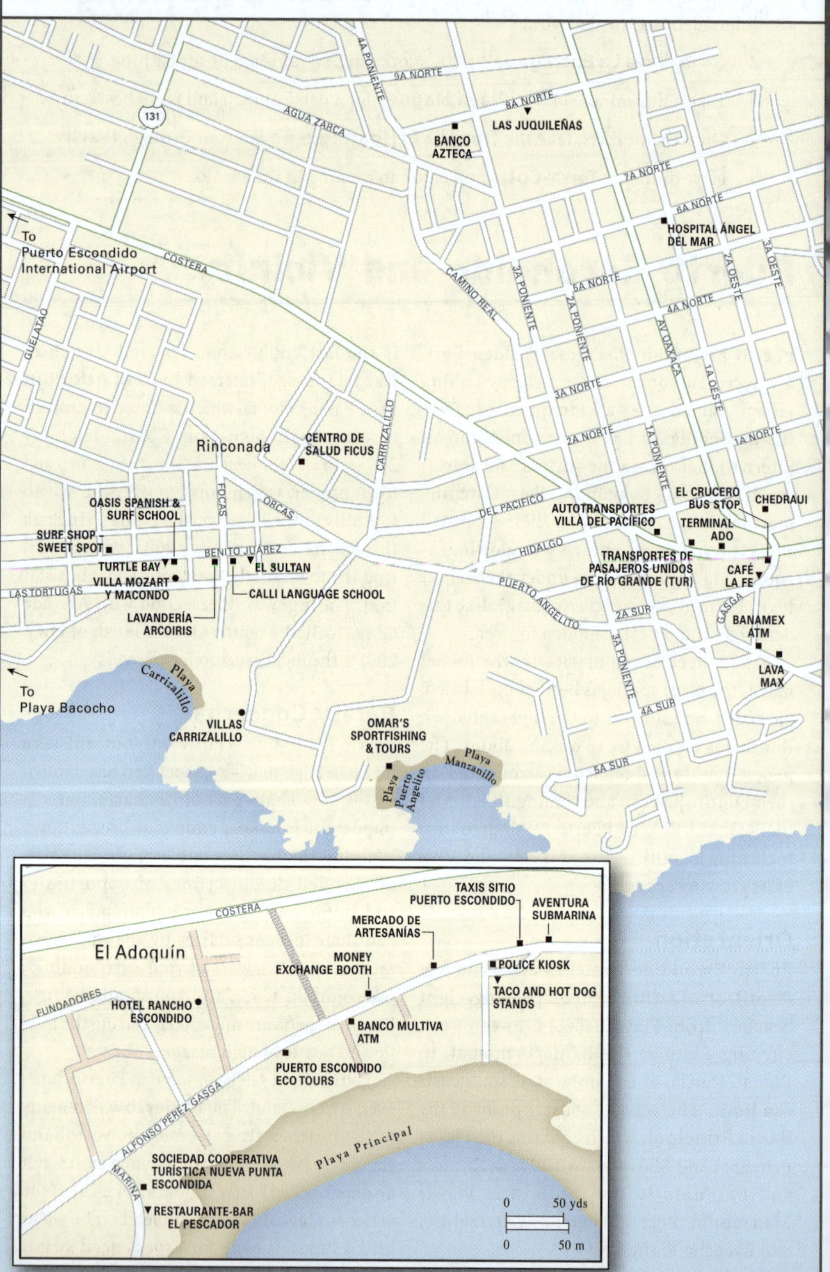

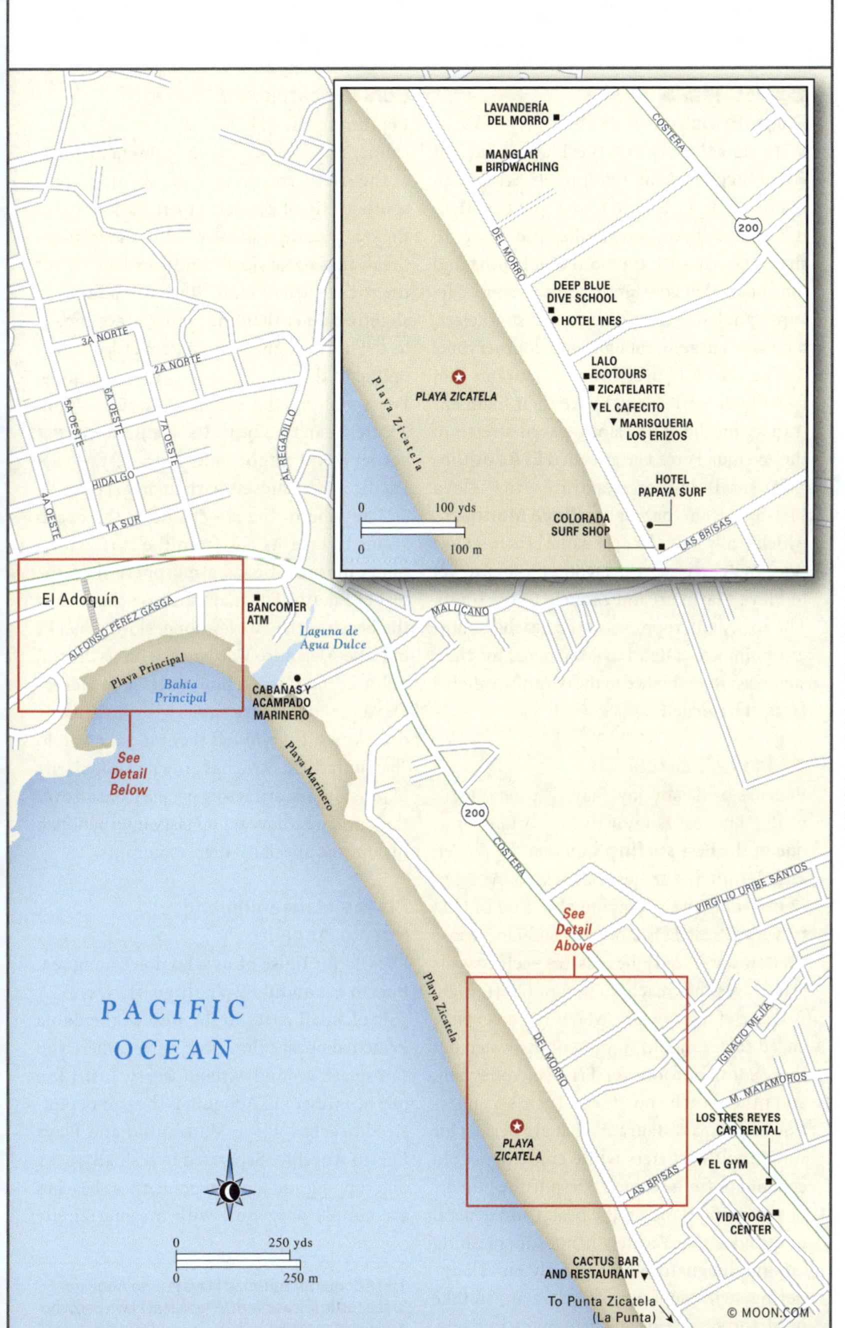
LAVANDERÍA DEL MORRO
MANGLAR BIRDWACHING
COSTERA
200
DEL MORRO
DEEP BLUE DIVE SCHOOL
HOTEL INES
LALO ECOTOURS
ZICATELARTE
EL CAFECITO
MARISQUERIA LOS ERIZOS
PLAYA ZICATELA
Playa Zicatela
HOTEL PAPAYA SURF
COLORADA SURF SHOP
LAS BRISAS
0 100 yds
0 100 m
3A NORTE
2A NORTE
5A OESTE
6A OESTE
7A OESTE
AL REGADILLO
HIDALGO
4A OESTE
1A SUR
El Adoquín
ALFONSO PÉREZ GASGA
BANCOMER ATM
Laguna de Agua Dulce
MALUCANO
Playa Principal
Bahía Principal
CABAÑAS Y ACAMPADO MARINERO
See Detail Below
Playa Marinero
200
COSTERA
VIRGILIO URIBE SANTOS
See Detail Above
PACIFIC OCEAN
Playa Zicatela
DEL MORRO
IGNACIO MEJIA
M. MATAMOROS
LOS TRES REYES CAR RENTAL
PLAYA ZICATELA
EL GYM
LAS BRISAS
VIDA YOGA CENTER
0 250 yds
0 250 m
CACTUS BAR AND RESTAURANT
To Punta Zicatela (La Punta)
© MOON.COM

be a formidable force. Playa Bacocho is also not recommended for novice swimmers.

BEACHES

Playa Principal

With its calm waters, the Playa Principal is the biggest of the swimmable beaches in Puerto, so it is easier to find a spot here than in Carrizalillo or Manzanilla. You'll have to share the bay with the flotilla of fishing and tour boats that constantly come to shore carrying anglers, scuba divers, and snorkelers, but there's usually enough room for everyone.

The cluster of beachfront restaurants that face the Bahía Principal have their main entrances on the cobblestone-paved stretch of the Avenida Pérez Gasga called **El Adoquín.**

A small lagoon separates the Playa Principal from the smaller **Playa Marinero,** which really looks like the same beach. At low tide, you can cross the lagoon on foot to get to Playa Marinero and Zicatela to the south. The rocky outcroppings at the beach's southern point are called Los Marineros for their supposed resemblance to the ocean-weathered faces of hardened sailors.

★ Playa Zicatela

Puerto's pride and joy, Playa Zicatela (Place of Big Thorns) is known the world over as one of the best **surfing** spots on the planet, and definitely the best in Mexico. At 3 km (2 mi) long and averaging about 60 m (197 ft) wide, Zicatela is a broad, flat giant whose shallow waters curl the massive Pacific swells into waves that reach up to 6 m (20 ft) high. Because of this, anyone who is not an experienced surfer should stay out of the water, but there's lots of room for Frisbee, volleyball, and other beach sports, and there's a collection of palapa restaurants that are perfect for watching the surfers while enjoying a cold coconut or fresh seafood. Despite the numerous warning signs on the beach and general knowledge that Zicatela is not for splashing around, lifeguards still regularly pull floundering swimmers out of the waves, so take heed and be safe here. Once nighttime hits, you can have a good time enjoying Zicatela's raucous **nightlife** scene.

Punta Zicatela (La Punta)

Beginning surfers should start out on the calmer waves off the beach at Punta Zicatela, at the southern end of Playa Zicatela. This southern tip of Zicatela tapers back out into the sea, creating a smaller "left-hander" point break that peels slowly and consistently off the rocky barb of land. Since the waters are slightly calmer than the raging beach breaks to the north, some swim here, but I still recommend the calmer beaches for swimming. For watching the sunset, however, Punta Zicatela can't be beat. Its dramatic coastal scenery and panoramic vista of the vast Pacific makes sunsets particularly special.

The vibe in the streets along the beach seems to take its cue from the surf, with a much more laid-back atmosphere than the rest of Puerto. The main drag on this end of the beach is the last few long, skinny blocks of Calle Alejandro Cárdenas, with its central point at the intersection with Calle Héroes Oaxaqueños, where taxis will most likely drop you off if you tell them to take you to "La Punta." This area has grown in popularity in recent years, attracting people from all over the world who have set up tasty international, fusion, and specialty-diet restaurants.

Playas Manzanillo and Puerto Angelito

Luckily for those of us who don't hang ten, Puerto Escondido isn't all gnarly waves. A pair of small coves to the west of the Bahía Principal boast calm, clear waters where you can splash around without worry. Just 1 km (0.6 mi) west of El Adoquín is the pair of pint-sized beaches, Playa Manzanillo and Playa Puerto Angelito. Separated by a small, rocky outcropping and lookout point, these beaches are simply gorgeous, with mesmerizingly

1: El Adoquín at sunset **2:** Playa Puerto Angelito **3:** sea turtle release with Vive Mar at Playa Bacocho **4:** Playa Manzanillo

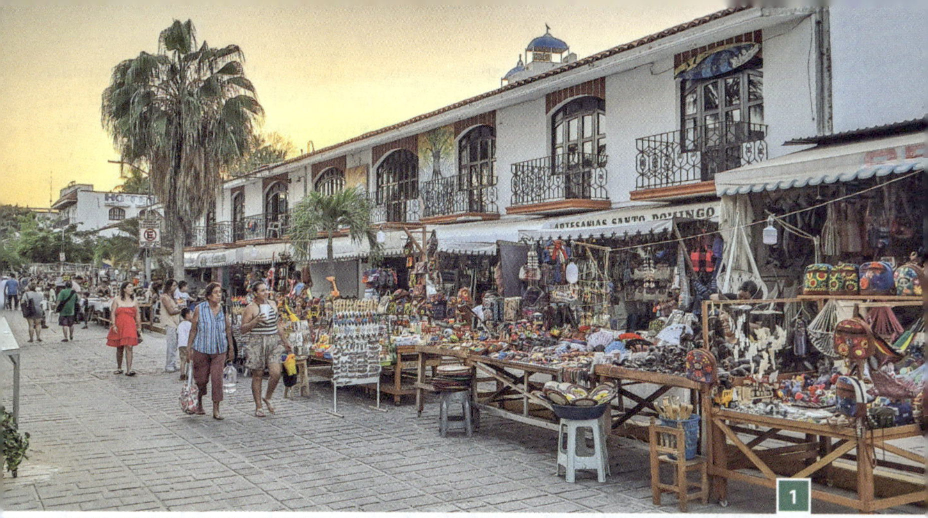

1

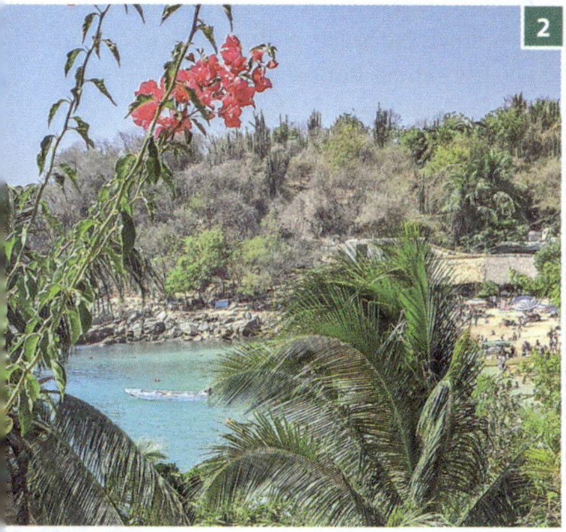

2

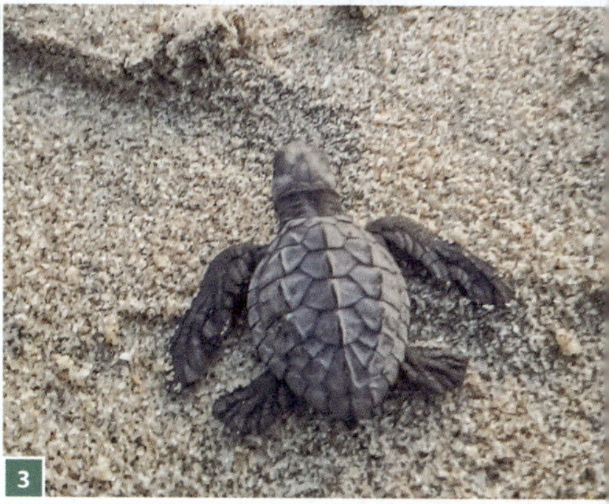

3

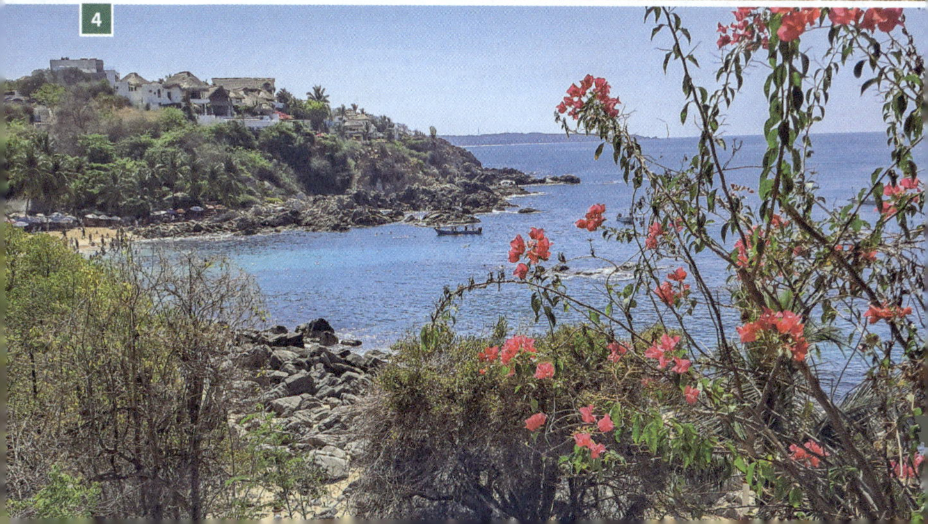

4

clear waters and a smattering of palapa restaurants on each. If the boats bug you, stay on Manzanillo, which is for swimmers only, but if you're looking for activities, head across the rocks to Puerto Angelito for fishing excursions, snorkeling, and banana boats. Both beaches are a quick 15-minute walk from El Adoquín. A stairway at the west end of Calle Cuarta Sur leads down to Manzanillo, and Camino A Puerto Angelito (Road to Puerto Angelito) leads exactly where its name says.

Playa Carrizalillo

Another 0.5 km (0.3 mi) west, a steep stone staircase leads down to Playa Carrizalillo, a compact stretch of sand tucked into the rocky coastline. The view from the top of the stairs is spectacular, especially as the afternoon sun goes down over the western point of the bay. At the west end of the beach, there is a little foot trail that leads to a tiny, hidden "lovers' beach."

The residential and tourist area above Carrizalillo is called **Rinconada,** where many new hotels, hostels, restaurants, and surf/Spanish schools have popped up in recent years. These are mostly concentrated in the outlet mall lining the southern side of Calle Benito Juárez, with a few new hostels in the blocks just to the north.

Playa Bacocho

About 1.5 km (1 mi) west of Carrizalillo, Puerto Escondido's westernmost beach is long, windy Playa Bacocho. Save for a couple of resorts, the majority of Bacocho's soft, fine sand is undeveloped, so it's a good idea to bring your own parasol or other shade. Bacocho is usually less crowded than Puerto's other beaches, especially during low season, so you shouldn't have any trouble finding a place to post up. For an unforgettable view, come at least an hour before sunset and watch the sun slowly disappear over the horizon. The temperament of the water, however, is somewhat similar to Zicatela's, with massive waves and an undertow that should not be underestimated. What makes this beach extra special is the nonprofit organization Vive Mar's **baby sea turtle release.** Every day around 5pm (tel. 954/544-1330; suggested donation US$8.50) anyone can come and participate.

TOP EXPERIENCE

SURFING

The best surfing in the entire country is at **Playa Zicatela,** where a long sandbar forms massive tubular beach breaks in the mornings and evenings. You need to be an experienced surfer to ride the towering waves, which can reach up to 6 m (20 ft) in height, so Zicatela is not the place to learn to ride. The waves farther down the beach, at **Punta Zicatela,** are usually calmer but sometimes get too hairy for learners. The gentle but ridable reef breaks at the entrance of the bay that shelters **Playa Carrizalillo** are the best waves on which to learn the ropes.

Surf Schools

Oasis Spanish and Surf School

Benito Juárez 6; tel. 954/582-1445; www.spanishandsurflessonsmexico.com; 8am-6:30pm Mon.-Fri., 8am-3pm Sat.

Oasis Spanish and Surf School has been providing professional surf coaching to students of all levels since 2006. Their team of expert instructors is led by Mexican Pipeline legend Roger Ramírez. Part of the first generation professional Mexican surfers, Roger has been riding Puerto's waves his entire life and has won numerous international competitions. He also shapes the custom boards used by Oasis students at his nearby workshop. Casual lessons start at US$45 and weeklong packages with accommodations start at US$735. One-on-one Spanish classes by certified, native-speaking teachers are also available. Surfboards rentals are available for US$25 a day (or US$17 for 5 hours).

1: Playa Carrizalillo **2:** world-class surfer and Puerto Escondido resident Roger Ramírez

1

2

Experiencia Puerto Escondido

La Punta, corner of Héroes Oaxaqueños and Nuevo Leon; tel. 954/205-0965; www.experienciamexico.mx; 8am-3pm Mon.-Fri.; from US$45

If you want to learn how to hang ten down on La Punta, you can schedule anything from daily classes to two-week intensive courses (US$390) at Experiencia Puerto Escondido, which also offers Spanish classes (US$230-315), accommodations, homestays, and volunteer opportunities at dog shelters or teaching English (donation request of US$70) through its campus on the corner of Colima and Morelos.

Surf Shops and Rentals

Colorada Surf Shop

corner of del Morro and Las Brisas; tel. 954/182-9167; 9am-10pm daily; US$14/day

On Avenida del Morro, the main drag of Zicatela, head to Colorada Puerto Escondido for boards, gear, repairs, and rentals.

Surf Shop - Sweet Spot

corner of Benito Juárez and Marlins; tel. 954/157-7970; 8am-4pm Wed.-Mon.

Part surf shop and rental outfitter, part surf school, part vegan restaurant, part coworking space—hey, you can even rent a scooter or snorkel equipment here. It's a one stop shop! Book a surf lesson, rent a board, and then come back and refuel with delicious vegan goodness.

SNORKELING AND SCUBA DIVING

As you might expect, the calmer beaches like Manzanillo, Puerto Angelito, and Carrizalillo are the best places to echarle un vistazo (have a look) at what's going on under the surface. Many of the palapa restaurants on these beaches rent snorkeling equipment and offer tours for around US$30-40, and many hostels and hotels lend goggles, snorkels, and flippers to guests free of charge, so it never hurts to ask at reception before heading to the beach.

Puerto's dive sites are almost exclusively igneous rock formations and shallow-water reefs, where you'll see a wide variety of tropical fish, such as trigger, parrot, angel, and butterfly fish, puffers, groupers, and various species of moray eels. Winter is the best time to dive in Puerto, November-February. During these months, although the water is cooler than the rest of the year (22-24°C/72-75°F), it's very likely you'll see humpback whales, giant manta rays, and, with a little luck, whale sharks. The water begins to warm up in May and still has good visibility until September.

Deep Blue Dive School

in Hotel Ines on Playa Zicatela; tel. 954/134-3466; www.deepbluedivemexico.com; 8:30am-1:30pm and 4pm-7:30pm Mon.-Sat., 9am-2pm Sun.; US$45-115

There are a couple of dive centers in Puerto who have maintained admirable reputations for safety and quality for years. Since 2003, Italian Master Scuba Diver Trainer Lorenzo Biny has run Deep Blue Dive School, offering everything from snorkel tours (US$45) to fun dives (US$70-115) to certification courses (US$255-485). Lorenzo and his crew of divemasters always adhere to PADI safety regulations, ensuring the best-quality experience beneath the waves.

Aventura Submarina

corner of 4a Poniente and 8a Norte; tel. 954/544-4862; bravoescondido@gmail.com; 9am-6pm daily; US$125

Aventura Submarina is also well regarded and offers fun dives for around US$125 and three-day open water certification courses for US$510.

FISHING

Fishing is Puerto's forte, and you can trust just about anyone with a boat to know where they're biting. The waters off Puerto's shores are full of black and blue marlin, albacore tuna, dorado (mahimahi), red snapper, sea bass, Mexican needlefish, and many other edible species.

Sociedad Cooperativa Turística Nueva Punta Escondida

tel. 954/102-4090 or 954/132-3422; www.tomzap.com/pe-coop.html; US$70/hour, 4-hr min.

Highly regarded for their knowledge and skill, Gume and the guys at Sociedad Cooperativa Turística Nueva Punta Escondida operate out of the restaurant El Pescador, at the west end of Playa Principal, where your fresh catch is grilled after you come back to shore. Gume has sailed all over the world, and has never seen a coastline with more sea turtles than Oaxaca's, which is why he likes to include a lot of information about turtle conservation on his fishing and dolphin-, whale-, and turtle-watching tours.

Omar's Sportfishing

Playa Puerto Angelito; tel. 954/559-4406; www.omarsportfishing.com; 7am-10pm daily; US$255-410

Another very well-respected agency in town is Omar's Sportfishing. Born and raised in Puerto Escondido, Captain Omar Ramírez has a lifetime of fishing experience and nearly three decades of experience operating fishing tours. The agency will send a taxi to your hotel to pick you up bright and early for the trip. Omar's fishing charters run US$395 for half-day (7am-noon) tours and US$565 for the full day (7am-3pm) for tours up to four people max.

ECOTOURISM

Manglar Birdwatching

in Hotel Las Olas, Avenida del Morro 15; tel. 954/180-3315, 954/108-2641, or 954/167-2546; 9am-10pm Mon.-Fri., 10am-6pm Sat.-Sun.; US$75 pp

The Oaxacan coast isn't only popular with humans. The Chacahua and Manialtepec lagoons, to the west of Puerto, are important stopovers on the migratory routes of herons, ibis, storks, roseate spoonbills, and many other species of avian nomads. Manglar Birdwatching focuses primarily on bird-watching tours and also offers surf lessons, coffee plantation tours, baby sea turtle releases, and other ecotourism activities. They also do day trips to beaches all over the coast. You can find their second office on El Adoquín in Hotel Rocamar.

Lalo Ecotours

in Rockaway shopping center on Zicatela; tel. 954/582-1611 or 954/588-9164; www.lalo-ecotours.com; 9am-8pm daily; US$25-75 pp

One of the most popular ecotours around Puerto is the quick trip to see and swim among the bioluminescent plankton of Laguna de Manialtepec, about a half hour away from Puerto. Lalo Ecotours runs evening tours out to Manialtepec (US$25 pp) for the bioluminescence, as well as in the mornings and afternoons for kayaking and bird-watching (US$60 pp). Horseback riding, baby sea turtle releases, and waterfall and boat tours are also on the menu (US$25-75).

YOGA AND MEDITATION

The majority of yoga classes in Puerto are in Zicatela and out in La Punta.

Vida Yoga Center

Vista Hermosa 4; tel. 954/114-7675; www.vidayogacenter.com; US$11.50

Vida Yoga Center, in Casa Mandala Apartments, holds hatha yoga classes every weekday morning. They also offer 200-hour and 100-hour teacher certifications endorsed by Yoga Alliance.

LANGUAGE SCHOOLS AND CLASSES

Calli Language School

Benito Juárez 13 and 14; tel. 954/103-9190; www.callilanguageschool.com; US$215-370

In Rinconada, Calli Language School offers 10-hour and 20-hour language program packages, along with tours and cultural experiences.

Spanish Immersion School

Puebla 161, La Punta; tel. 954/145-0927; www.spanishschoolinmexico.com; oaxacaimmersion@gmail.com; US$305-795

The Puerto Escondido branch of Oaxaca City-based Spanish Immersion School will have you chatting away en español in no time. Classes run US$180-280 per week.

SHOPPING

Gifts and Souvenirs

Mercado de Artesanías

El Adoquín; no tel.; 10am-10pm daily

The storefronts and sidewalks—and, at night, the middle of the street—of El Adoquín are stocked full of handicrafts from the coast and the state at large. Garishly bright inflatables, buckets, and swimsuits clutter the artesanías shops, many of which focus on textiles from weavers in Puerto Escondido and other coastal communities. The Mercado de Artesanías is at the east end of El Adoquín, just before the corner with Andador Azucenas.

Zicatelarte

in Rockaway shopping center; tel. 954/108-4041; 9am-10pm daily

In Zicatela, head to Zicatelarte for more unique silver and precious stone jewelry. In 2011, owner and silversmith Alan González took his custom gem and jewelry business from the streets to this little beachfront store, where he makes custom silver pieces and also has lots of rare stones and fossils for sale.

FOOD

Playa Principal and El Adoquín

For late-night snacks, hit up the **taco and hotdog stands** on Andador Azucenas. They set up around sundown and usually stay open until the drinking crowd goes home.

Restaurante-Bar El Pescador

north end of Playa Principal; tel. 954/582-1678; 7am-7pm daily; US$10-15

Run by the fishermen of the Sociedad Cooperativa Turística Nueva Punta Escondida, everything on the menu is fresh out of the sea. Savor a shrimp cocktail on their breezy terrace that looks out over Playas Principal and Marinero.

Café La Fe

Gasga 106; tel. 954/104-4595; 8:30am-2pm Mon.-Fri.

Head to Café La Fe for top-notch espresso. They buy their coffee from Mixe growers in the Sierra Norte, a region that produces beans with a sharp bite that flirts with acidity without slipping into bitterness. You'll see the café to your right from the top of Andador Unión.

Playa Zicatela

For lovely ocean views and tasty food for

arts and crafts for sale on El Adoquín

great prices, check out the fondas at Mercado Zicatela (7am-6pm).

Marisquería Los Erizos

Avenida del Morro; tel. 954/108-9934; 2pm-10pm Wed.-Mon.; US$5-7

Marisquería Los Erizos is a favorite with locals craving ceviche, Baja-style shrimp tacos, or the local specialty tiritas de pescado (tangy lime-cured strips of fish). Other seasonal treats include clams, oysters, and fresh salty seaweeds to top off their towering shrimp cocktails.

El Gym

Hwy. 200 at La Punta; tel. 954/141-0538; 4pm-11pm Thurs.-Tues.; US$5-12

A great place for burgers and barbecue is El Gym, originally opened by Miguel Ángel Ramírez and his lovely mother, Leticia Velasquez Mendoza. Though he has passed, his legacy of amiable service and mouthwatering dishes live on, with his mother and uncles at the helm. Fish-and-chips and the catch of the day are other favorites of the local and tourist crowd that fills the place.

El Cafecito

Avenida del Morro; tel. 954/119-3739; elcafecitozicatela@hotmail.com; 7am-10:30pm daily; US$7-10

A favorite of locals and visitors alike, El Cafecito is almost always busy—and is the only place to get a good espresso on the Zicatela strip. Food offerings include tacos, enchiladas, Mexican breakfasts, and international staples like cheeseburgers and club sandwiches. It's a great choice if you get bothered by cigarette smoke in other alfresco restaurants, as all the street-side tables are non-smoking. If you want to light up, you'll be sequestered in the tables in the pleasant garden patio in back. You can check out their second location in Rinconada (Benito Juárez 1; tel. 954/124-5162).

Punta Zicatela (La Punta)

For cheap, tasty eats, hit up one of the comedores that stay open late on Héroes Oaxaqueños.

Fish Shack la Punta

Alejandro Cárdenas; tel. 954/148-9932; www.shackslapunta.com; noon-11pm Tues.-Sun.; US$4.50-11.50

Blink and you may miss it, but you'd be missing out. Right across the street from Café Ole and tucked down a little alleyway, finding the Fish Shack is half the fun. The other half is sitting on barstools in the sand, chowing down on some of the tastiest shrimp and fish tacos you'll find in this part of Puerto. Try to save room for the camarones al coco (coconut shrimp).

Chicama

corner of Héroes Oaxaqueños and Alejandro Cárdenas Peralta; tel. 954/167-8874; noon-11pm Wed.-Mon.; US$15

Just a stone's throw from the beach, you'll find Chicama, named after one of the most stunning surfing destinations in Peru, and true to its name, serving up delectable Peruvian dishes. The soft sand floors and high thatched roof gives the perfect dreamy beach ambiance for enjoying a fine Peruvian ceviche with leche de tigre.

Rinconada

El Sultán

corner of Benito Juárez and Pargos; tel. 954/582-0512; 8am-10pm Mon.-Sat.; US$5-7

Kebabs, shawarmas, falafel, hummus, tabbouleh, and other Mediterranean delights are served up daily at El Sultán. They also serve fresh juices, amazing customizable fruit bowls, and flavorful coffees from both Mexico and abroad.

★ Turtle Bay

Benito Juárez 9; tel. 954/147-7469; www.turtlebay.com.mx; 1pm-10pm Tues.-Sun.; US$15-30

Heavily influenced by the gastronomy of California, talented chef Alejandro Hernández Aquino runs the open kitchen at Turtle Bay, where he applies the North

American coastal culinary style to his extensive knowledge of the ingredients and recipes of Oaxaca. Shrimp and octopus tostadas and aguachile (raw shrimp in super-spicy green salsa) share menu space with jalapeño burgers, rib-eye sandwiches, and mahimahi cooked in chardonnay. Speaking of chardonnay, their dark wood wine shelves along the walls boast the widest selection in Puerto, and Alejandro and his staff know just what to pair with whatever you order from the rich, inventive menu. The humble tables and chairs of the same polished wood create a date-night ambience while keeping things comfy.

Centro

★ Las Juquileñas

Octava Norte; tel. 954/582-1231; 7:30am-4:30pm daily

At Las Juquileñas, a small army of servers donning white scarves on their heads keep the colorful communal tables piled high with delicious local specialties while bright papel picado flags flutter overhead. Try an empanada de amarillo and an embarrada (literally, muddied tortilla, but it means with sauce) with cheese and mole, and wash it all down with the restaurant's signature agua de cacahuate, a delicious agua fresca made with peanuts.

BARS AND NIGHTLIFE

The warm-up starts in La Punta, with its chill, hippie-chic bars, but most of those close around midnight. That's when the party moves down to Zicatela, where the fiesta lasts into the wee hours of the morning.

The Boneyard

La Punta, Guanajuato 111; tel. 954/145-7910; 5pm-11pm Mon.-Sat.; US$11-16

I don't think I've seen anything like this place—a restaurant where you can grab a burger or a pizza, knock back a beer or cocktail at the bar, and the next moment hop on a skateboard and do your best moves in Puerto Escondido's first skate bowl. This place definitely wins points for being one of the most unique venues in La Punta.

Cactus Bar and Restaurant

Zicatela, Calle del Morro; tel. 954/131-4160; 10:30am-11pm Wed.-Mon.; $9-20

Located right on the beach, this is a fun spot to come any night of the week, with delicious food options (try the seafood pizza or generous fish tacos), live music, and smokin'-hot DJ sets, but Monday night is when the party goes on till the break of dawn (if you make it before midnight, the cover is free).

ACCOMMODATIONS

From rustic jungle cabins to luxury villas, Puerto Escondido has enough accommodations options to suit any budget or taste.

The prices listed below are for low season, since that is the vast majority of the year here. During high season, you can expect prices to be 25-50 percent higher, and some even double. Contact hotels directly if you're visiting around the Christmas or Easter holidays.

Playa Principal and El Adoquín

Hotel Rancho Escondido

Andador Revolución 21; tel. 954/582-1818; hotelranchoescondido@gmail.com; US$55 d, US$58 t

Just a short walk from Playa Principal, this charming hotel lives up to its tagline, "Encuentra la felicidad oculta!" (find the hidden happiness). The cheery yellows and blues of the hotel's facade and the cobblestone courtyard filled with leafy plants give the perfect rustic ambiance for a beachside stay. The affordable prices, convenient location, and lovely atmosphere make this a true gem in the area.

Playa Zicatela

Hotel Papaya Surf

Avenida del Morro; tel. 954/582-1168; www.papayasurf.com.mx; papayasurf@papayasurf.com; from US$55

At the southern end of the Zicatela strip and right in front of the waves, Hotel Papaya Surf is the perfect place to crash after a day of surfing and a night of partying. The rooms are set around a cozy courtyard with cacti, palms, and papaya trees and have all the bare necessities: queen beds, fans, air-conditioning (for an extra US$5), small patio areas (some strung with hammocks), some units with a kitchen, Wi-Fi and a cafeteria.

Hotel Ines

Avenida del Morro; tel. 954/582-0792 or 954/582-0416; www.hotelines.com; US$65 d, US$195 suite

Hotel Ines has options for everyone from groups of surfers to vacationing families. The 45 units built around the large pool and restaurant area, surrounded by tropical fronds and towering palm trees, run the spectrum from simple (but clean, spacious, and fetching) hotel rooms to cabañas to deluxe suites with broad, private ocean-view terraces hung with hammocks.

Punta Zicatela (La Punta)

Osa Mariposa

Privada de Cancún; tel. +1 720/419-8267; info@osamariposa.com; US$30-40

Close to the beach is the backpacker favorite Hotelito Osa Mariposa. Formally a hostel, Osa Mariposa went through major renovations and is now a delightful seven room guesthouse, four with queen beds, one with a king bed, and two with single beds. Shared areas include, bathrooms, kitchen, and the pool. The staff is super friendly and helpful.

★ One Love

two blocks from the beach on Calle Tamaulipas; tel. 954/129-8582; www.hostalpuertoescondido.com; US$50 bungalow, US$66.50 suite

One Love is an oasis of rest and tranquility within the hustle and bustle of the vibrant life of La Punta. Although named after '60s rock-n-roll greats such as Jimi Hendrix, Jim Morrison, Bob Dylan, and Bob Marley, it is not a party hostel. Its private bungalows, large terrace with ocean views, and plentiful hammocks offer a relaxed and comfortable vibe. Attached to the hostel is a mixology bar that serves up Mexican-style snacks, as well as Mexipipe beer, their proprietary brand of craft beer. It's renowned among travelers and locals alike for its value and quality.

Rinconada

★ Villa Mozart y Macondo

Las Tortugas 77; tel. 954/104-2295 or 954/113-0849; www.hotelmozartymacondo.com; US$72-110

Upon entering the sandy tropical garden that is home to the cabañas at Villa Mozart y Macondo, you'll be confronted with the possibility that this place may be just as prone to fantastical occurrences as the Colombian town from *One Hundred Years of Solitude* from which it takes half of its name. Large

Hotel Papaya Surf

wooden statues stand among the tropical ferns and flowers, ready to groan to life at any moment. With only four little fetching bungalows set in this tropical garden, Mozart y Macondo is intimate and secluded, despite its proximity to the commerce on Benito Juárez. This adults-only hotel is for the lovers; it's not an option for families (no kids or pets) or groups of surfers (max. two people per bungalow).

Villas Carrizalillo

Avenida Carrizalillo; tel. 954/582-1735; www.villascarrizalillo.com; US$230-290 villa

Perched atop the cliffs overlooking the gorgeous turquoise and green waters of Playa Carrizalillo below, there isn't a bad view from any of the 12 whitewashed deluxe villas at Villas Carrizalillo, all but two of which come equipped with fully stocked kitchenettes. Villas range in size from one bedroom for two people, to large three-bedroom, two-bath units for up to six people. Despite its beauty, comfort, amenities, and the phenomenal surf and turf on the menu at the on-site restaurant Espadín, the superlative feature at Villas Carrizalillo is the private beach access that descends through the forested hillside to the sandy bank below.

Apartments and Long-Term Rentals

Casamar Suites

Puebla 407; tel. 954/582-2593; www.casamarsuites.com; US$105-140

Originally begun as private vacation apartments for the owner's family, Casamar Suites has grown into a complex of 20 fully stocked and furnished apartments decorated with hand-painted ceramic tiles from Puebla and furniture and other interior design features by local carpenters and artisans. Although they're also rented out nightly, Casamar welcomes longer stays, offering weekly and monthly discounts. Recreational and relaxation facilities and amenities include the swimming pool, meticulously tended garden, ping-pong tables, movie nights, communal cookouts, massages, reflexology, and yoga classes.

Trailer Parks and Camping

Cabañas y Acampado Marinero

Calle Marinero; tel. 954/107-1716; US$6.50 pp

For camping spots hidden away in the middle of all the action, head to Cabañas y Acampado Marinero, where you can pitch a tent right in the sand between a pair of windblown palm trees for only US$6.50 per person. Cabaña guests and campers share bathrooms. From the beach, head toward the jungle on the east side of the lagoon, where you'll find them at the end of the cobblestone road to the highway. From Highway 200, get off on the east side of the Regadío bridge and take Calle Marinero down to the beach, where the campground will be on your right.

INFORMATION AND SERVICES

Medical Services

For emergencies, your best bet is the private **Hospital Ángel del Mar** (corner of Sexta Norte and Primera Oriente in the Centro; tel. 954/104-2270 or 954/582-1026; www.hospitalangeldelmar.com.mx). It is seven blocks north of the crucero (crossroads), and one block east of Avenida Oaxaca.

The government-run **Centro de Salud Ficus** (Health Center, Calle Puerto Vallarta; tel. 954/582-2360) accepts regular doctor visits 8am-6:30pm daily, and emergencies 24 hours.

Money

Banks, ATMs, and casas de cambio in Puerto Escondido are mostly located in El Adoquín and along Highway 200, with a pair of options in Zicatela. If you're staying out in La Punta, you'll have to come to town to withdraw or change money, so be aware of that before you get in a taxi.

Around El Adoquín, there is a **Banamex** (Gasga 314; 9am-4pm Mon.-Fri., ATM 24 hrs) on Gasga, where the road curves and climbs the hill on the west side of the main drag on the corner with Andador Unión. At the other end of El Adoquín, you'll find a **Bancomer ATM** in the Azul Plaza shopping center at the east end of the street. There is also a **Banco Multiva ATM** to the left of the ice cream shop next to Hotel Las Palmas. Change dollars at the **Money Exchange Booth** (10am-9pm Mon.-Sat.) a little farther east and across El Adoquín. In the Centro, you can change dollars at **Banco Azteca** (across from Benito Juárez market on Calle Octava Norte; toll-free Mex. tel. 800/040-7777; www.bancoazteca.com.mx; 9am-9pm daily), inside the Elektra appliance store. You can also use the ATMs in the supermarket **Chedraui** (Oaxaca 105).

Laundry

Most lavanderías in Puerto charge a little under US$1 per kg. If you're staying on El Adoquín, drop your dirty rags off at **Lava Max** (Gasga 405; tel. 954/582-3406; 8am-4pm Mon.-Sat.), or you can opt for the self-service option. It's a few storefronts down the hill from the Banamex.

In Zicatela, head to **Lavandería del Morro** (Andador Gaviotas; tel. 954/137-3443; 9am-10pm daily), just a ways down Andador Gaviotas, by Bungalows Zicatela. Down in La Punta, **Lavandería Michoacán** (Michoacán 371; no tel.; 8am-5pm Mon.-Sat.) has you covered.

In Rinconada, **Lavandería Arcoiris** (east end of Benito Juárez; tel. 954/126-5449; 8am-4pm Mon.-Thurs., 9am-4pm Fri., 9am-noon Sat.), right next to El Sultán, offers delivery service, as well as alterations and mending.

GETTING THERE

Air

A little over a mile from Playa Bacocho, the **Puerto Escondido International Airport** (PXM; tel. 954/582-2023 or 954/582-2024) is a quick 5-20-minute drive from anywhere you're going in town. The small terminal has a couple of snack bars and a bar and grill. There is also a Banco Multiva ATM and a small artesanías shop.

Los Tres Reyes (tel. 954/582-3335 or 954/134-9235; www.lostresreyescarrent.com) has a booth located within the airport, which has a wide selection of cars for around US$60-160 a day. If you drive a car to the airport and stay longer than 10 minutes, make sure to pay for parking at the booth inside before leaving.

Secure taxis from the airport charge US$15-21 per person for up to four people, and US$18-26 for six or seven, to anywhere in town. If you're not too weighed down with luggage, you can make the five-minute, 0.5-km (0.3-mi) walk to the highway and grab a taxi that shouldn't charge more than US$5-9 to anywhere in town.

Flights run by **Interjet** (toll-free US tel. 866/285-9525, toll-free Mex. tel. 800/011-2345; www.interjet.com) connect through Mexico City to 10 major U.S cities. The Mexican low-cost airline **Viva Aerobus** (toll-free US tel. 888/935-9848, toll-free Mex. tel. 818/215-0150; www.vivaaerobus.com) connects to Houston, Las Vegas, and Los Angeles via Mexico City, Guadalajara, and its hub in Monterrey.

Based in Mexico City, **Aeromar** (toll-free US tel. 844/237-6629, toll-free Mex. tel. 800/237-6627; www.aeromar.com) operates super-cheap flights between Puerto and the nation's capital, which connect to other major cities in the country, and even McAllen, Texas. Especially during low season, check for flights to Mexico City before buying bus tickets, since flights cost only slightly more than bus trips, which take 17-19 hours.

Air travel from Oaxaca City is superfluous at this point, with Puerto Escondido only a three-hour drive away. But if you want the novelty of a visually stunning flight over the Sierra Sur in a small Cessna, check out regional airline **Aerotucán** (tel. 951/502-0840, toll-free Mex. tel. 800/640-4148; www.aerotucan.com).

Bus

The **ADO bus station** (tel. 954/582-1073; www.ado.com.mx) is centrally located on the coastal highway, just to the west of the crucero (crossroads). From here, there are regular trips to Oaxaca City (3 hrs; US$17-29),

Huatulco (2.5 hrs; US$8-14), Tehuantepec (6 hrs; US$30), Mexico City (12 hrs; US$55-70), and numerous other destinations in the south of Mexico. The shops, restaurants, and hotels of El Adoquín are a 5-10-minute walk from the station, and taxis charge US$3-6 to other destinations in Puerto (some taxis will over-charge travelers coming from the station, so if you're traveling light and don't like the price you're given, just catch a taxi a block or two away on the street).

For shorter travel along the coast, your most economical option is to board an **urbano** (local/regional bus) at the crucero, or flag one down anywhere along the highway. This is your best option for getting out to the Lagunas de Manialtepec and Chacahua to the west, and Mazunte and Puerto Ángel to the east. They pass by every 20-30 minutes and charge a maximum of US$5, depending on your destination.

Suburban

From the crucero west along the highway, a couple of suburban companies run routes to destinations all over Oaxaca. About 140 m (460 ft) west of the ADO station, **Autotransportes Villa Del Pacífico** (Hwy. 200 between Hidalgo and Calle Primera Norte; tel. 954/132-5643) leaves for Oaxaca City (US$16) hourly on the half hour 3:30am-11pm daily. The trip takes about three hours.

To get out to the lagunas, Jamiltepec, or Pinotepa Nacional, grab a suburban from **Transportes de Pasajeros Unidos de Rio Grande,** or **TUR** (corner of Hwy. 200 and Calle Primera Poniente; tel. 954/582-2605), whose terminal is just to the west of the ADO station on the coastal highway. Vans leave every half hour or so all day and cost US$3.50-9, depending on your destination.

Car

West from Puerto Escondido, Highway 200 winds through verdant palm, papaya, and pineapple orchards out to Pinotepa Nacional (141 km/87 mi; 2.75 hrs), and on into the neighboring state of Guerrero to Acapulco (391 km/240 mi; 7 hrs) and Zihuatanejo (641 km/395 mi; 11 hrs).

To the east, Highway 200 will take you to the turnoff to Mazunte (57 km/35 mi; 1 hr), where you'll turn right at the Oxxo onto Highway 175 and drive another 11 minutes (7 km/4 mi) to get to Mazunte. Playas San Agustinillo, Zipolite, and Puerto Ángel are farther down this highway. The drive from Puerto to the Pochutla junction of Highway 175 (70 km/43 mi) takes a little over an hour, and Puerto Ángel (8 km/5 mi from crucero) is another 15 minutes from here. Total drive time to Huatulco (113 km/70 mi) is about two hours.

The most direct route from Puerto to Oaxaca City (104 km/65 mi; 3 hrs) is via the new Autopista Barranca Larga-Ventanilla. Just finished in February 2024, this highway has been decades in the making and cuts the original winding drive time in half. Though the highway is free as of this writing, it may turn into a toll road in the near future. The highway starts just 13 km (8 mi) east of Puerto Escondido and it's a straight shot from there. There are no gas stations or services along the highway, so fill up in Puerto before heading out.

GETTING AROUND

Many of Puerto's beaches are within walking distance of each other. Heading south from the Playa Principal, Zicatela is a 10-15-minute walk along the beach between the wave-battered stones of Playa Marinero and the Mirador Romance de Verano (Summer Romance Lookout Point) at the north end of Zicatela. It's possible to walk to La Punta, but Zicatela's length makes it a good 45-minute trip on foot from the mirador. Heading west from the Bahía Principal, Playas Manzanillo and Puerto Angelito can be reached in 15 minutes by walking through the residential neighborhoods. There is a stairway to Manzanillo at the west end of Calle Cuarta (4a) Sur. Puerto Angelito is just west of Manzanillo. Playa Carrizalillo is another 20-minute walk from Puerto Angelito, and Playa Bacocho is a 30-minute walk from Carrizalillo.

The folks at **Puerto Escondido Ecotours** (on Adoquín in front of Súper Precios; tel. 954/103-1177; www.puertoescondidoecotours.com.mx; 7am-midnight daily) rent scooters (US$27) and 250cc motorcycles (US$37). Prices are for 24-hour periods.

Numerous colectivo taxis, buses, and vans travel Highway 200 all day long, for trips out to the lagoons.

Taxi

The quickest way between beaches is via taxi. The green-and-white taxis operated by **Sitio Puerto Escondido** (tel. 954/582-0990, 954/582-0876, or 954/128-1620) charge US$3-10, depending on your origin, destination, and time of day (and honestly, how much they want to "tourist tax" you, which is unfortunately happening more often). If you're unsure of around how much you should be paying for a taxi, ask a hotel or restaurant worker, and they can at least give you a benchmark.

If you would like to make reservations with a taxi in advance, you can call/text **Servicio de Taxi PXM** (tel. 954/103-7717). They offer services around town for US$5.50 and a ride to or from the airport won't be more than US$16.50 max.

Car

Or you could rent a car from **Los Tres Reyes** (The Three Kings; in airport and on Hwy. 200 above Zicatela; tel. 954/582-3335 or 954/134-9235; www.lostresreyescarrent.com) for around US$60-180 per day.

West of Puerto Escondido

Lagoons full of crocodiles, bioluminescent plankton, and dozens of bird species lie to the west of Puerto Escondido, along with towns rich in traditions. I know it's hard to leave the beach once you've gotten in the zone, but this area of the coast has much to offer, from bird-watching tours to visiting Santa Catarina Juquila, a place of pilgrimage. Or you could just take your board and that beach lounging with you to Chacahua and rent a cabaña for an indeterminate amount of time.

LAGUNA DE MANIALTEPEC

Less than a half-hour drive from Puerto Escondido, Laguna de Manialtepec is a haven for an outrageous variety of migratory fowl, such as pelicans, roseate spoonbills, parrots, wattled jacanas, falcons, and herons in all kinds of colors. Most nights of the year, you can also see and swim among the glowing schools of phytoplankton that light up the water of the lagoon (new moon nights and the days surrounding are best).

Tours

Lalo Ecotours

in Rockaway shopping center on Zicatela; tel. 954/582-1611 or 954/588-9164; www.lalo-ecotours.com; 9am-8pm daily; US$25-75 pp

Based in Puerto Escondido, Lalo Ecotours offers an array of options, including morning and afternoon tours for kayaking and bird-watching and evening tours for the bioluminescence.

Manglar Birdwatching

in Hotel Las Olas, Avenida del Morro 15; tel. 954/180-3315, 954/108-2641, or 954/167-2546; 9am-10pm Mon.-Fri., 10am-6pm Sat.-Sun.; US$75 pp

With two offices in Puerto Escondido (the other in Hotel Rocamar, Gasga 601A), Manglar has bird-watching and bioluminescence tours.

La Puesta del Sol

east end of the lagoon; tel. 954/124-7001 or 954/124-700; ulises53212@gmail.com; 8am-6pm daily

If you get to Manialtepec all by yourself, stop by the restaurant La Puesta del Sol, where

Señora Elvira and her son Ulises run sunset boat tours that include bird-watching, a bonfire on the undeveloped beach Playa Puerto Suelo, and bioluminescence. Tours cost about US$140 for up to five people. They also rent kayaks for US$16-22 per hour.

Getting There

Getting out to Laguna de Manialtepec is really easy. In Puerto Escondido, board a suburban at **TUR** (corner of Hwy. 200 and Calle Primera Poniente; tel. 954/582-2605), just to the west of the ADO station. They leave every half hour or so and charge about US$3.50 for the 25-minute ride.

★ PARQUE NACIONAL LAGUNAS DE CHACAHUA

The Parque Nacional Lagunas de Chacahua comprises 140 sq km (55 sq mi) of lush tropical vegetation and mangrove forests and seven salty lagoons. Tens of thousands of migratory birds call this a temporary home, and some, just like some of us, become so enamored of the place that they never leave. You'll see many pelicans, herons, and other birds that also stop by Manialtepec. The Afro-Mexican town of **Chacahua,** on Isla Chacahua, has cabañas, palapa restaurants, and unmatched hospitality that will tempt you to pause your travels as well.

Sights

El Zapotalito and Laguna de Pastoria

The easiest access to the lagoons is at El Zapotalito, a small village on the eastern side of Laguna de Pastoria, the largest of the lagoons. From here, you can get to Isla Chacahua by lancha (boat), either colectivo style or on a tour that takes you around to some of the numerous mangrove islands in the lagoon.

Isla Chacahua

Long, skinny Isla Chacahua separates Laguna de Pastoria from the open ocean. Only the western tip of its 16 km (10 mi) of pristine coastline is developed, with several cabaña hotels and palapa restaurants offering economic beds and grub to beach loungers and surfers alike. Be sure to try a **tamale de tichinda** (mussel tamale); they look a little wild, but they're absolutely delicious. The waters of the little strait that leads from Laguna Chacahua to the sea are calm and crystal blue, perfect for taking a dip. Private boat owners will take you across the channel for about US$3.

Surfing

There is a long, slow, right-breaking wave just off the westernmost side of the beach on Isla Chacahua, where all the cabañas are located. You can haul your board down the jetty and hop right in. There's also a short but fun beach break on the mainland, just across the channel from the beach on Isla Chacahua.

Boat Tours

Adventure Lagunas de Chacahua

tel. 954/114-9030; 7am-10pm daily; US$25 pp

The best boat tours leave from Zapotalito. Adventure Lagunas de Chacahua will take you around the numerous islands of red and white mangrove forests before dropping you off on the east end of Isla Chacahua. Guides (Spanish only) are very knowledgeable of local bird species, and if you're lucky, you might see a crocodile.

Food and Accommodations

Just about any of the palapa places will let you **pitch a tent** if they've got the space for about US$5 per person. All have shared bathrooms. But it's not all hammocks here. There are cabins of varying levels of comfort, and new developments are being built all the time. Wherever you choose to stay, I encourage everyone to seek out accommodations owned by locals of the town. That keeps things fair, keep prices reasonable, and supports the folks who make being able to enjoy this little slice of paradise possible.

★ Delfines de Chacahua

west end of the beach; tel. 954/203-0404; US$26-37

Friendly and helpful Juana at Delfines de

Parque Nacional Lagunas de Chacahua

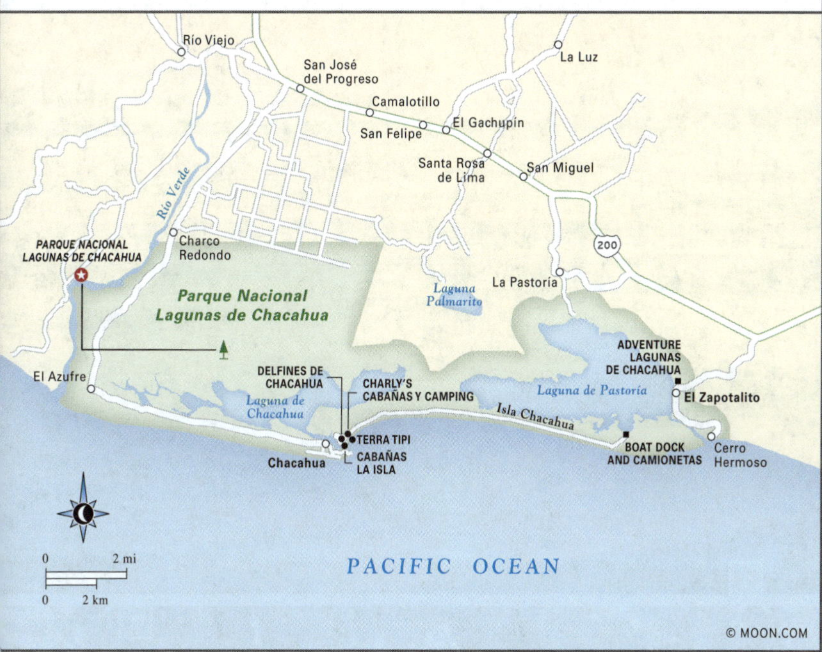

Chacahua has 19 simple cabañas with fans, mosquito nets, and private bathrooms, both on the beach and tucked back on the lagoon side of the island. Juana also rents hammocks for US$5 per night.

Cabañas La Isla

west end of the beach; tel. 954/130-5168; US$41-66

At the westernmost end of the beach, Cabañas La Isla has a few cabañas with private bathrooms and fans or air-conditioning, with views of both the beach and the crystalline channel on the other side. Offerings at the adjoining palapa restaurant include delicious shrimp cocktails and fish. The miscelania (convenience store) just up the road that runs parallel to the channel has fruit, snacks, beer, and a few other necessities, as well as a variable schedule.

Charly's Cabañas y Camping

east end of developed section of the beach; tel. 954/132-3860; charlychacahua@gmail.com; US$21 pp

Charly, of Charly's Cabañas y Camping, is an amiable host and has ample camping space available, with hammocks to rent. Cabins come outfitted with fans, Wi-Fi, and private bathrooms.

Terra Tipi

east end of the beach; tel. 954/151-3485; US$27-43

Gorgeous views, delicious food, and matchless hospitality await guests at Terra Tipi. It's only US$5.50 to spend the night in a hammock. Aside from costing next to nothing, spending the night swaying in the sea breeze is a unique and fun experience. You can also opt to spend the night in one of their comfortable rooms.

1
2

Getting There

TUR vans from Puerto Escondido (corner of Hwy. 200 and Calle Primera Poniente; tel. 954/582-2605) charge about US$4 for the trip out to the turnoff to Zapotalito, which runs just a little over an hour. From here, colectivo taxis wait to fill up before setting out on the five-minute ride to Zapotalito, and charge a little over US$1.50 per person.

You have a few options for the last leg of the journey. The long way is via the highly recommended tour by **Adventure Lagunas de Chacahua** (tel. 954/114-9032; 7am-10pm daily), which gets you to the beach in about three hours, after wending through the various islets and narrow mangrove canals of Lagunas Pastoria and Chacahua. This route will run you about US$25 per person.

For US$17 per person, you catch a direct 45 minute ride through the mangrove with Turismo Lagunas de Chacahua. This is a colectivo ride, so you'll have to wait until the boat fills up (if you're with a group, it may be a good idea to split the $85 cost to buy out the whole boat).

To get there the cheap, colectivo way, continue down the main road, up over the small rise about 300 m (1,000 ft), until you see a sign on your right that reads **"Lanchas Colectivas."** Boats from here charge about US$2.80 to take you to the east end of Isla Chacahua, where you'll board a camioneta that also charges about US$2.80 to take you the rest of the way overland. The whole journey takes about an hour.

SANTA CATARINA JUQUILA

Founded in 1272 by inhabitants of La Mixteca, Santa Catarina Juquila is a place of pilgrimage for many Oaxacans who come to venerate the Virgen de Juquila, affectionately called "La Juquilita" for her small stature.

Town folklore tells of a Spanish priest named Brother Jordán, who in the 1500s was serving in the neighboring village, Amialtepec. When it was time for Jordán to leave his post, he gave the local Indigenous farmer who had given him room and board during his stay a little figurine of the Virgen de la Purísima Concepción (Virgin of the Immaculate Conception). The farmer placed the Virgin in a little shrine, and she came to be revered by the local Chatino people.

While the Virgen performed many miracles among the people, the big miracle happened over a century later. A slash-and-burn fire in the fields got out of control and burned the huts of the town to the ground, including the one housing the relic. When the flames died down, the people returned and were shocked to see the little wooden statue still standing among the ashes. Not only that, her skin was turned as dark as theirs from the flames, earning her a second endearing nickname, La Morenita (the little brown one). Friars in the larger town of Santa Catarina Juquila moved La Juquilita to her current home in 1719.

To this day, devout Oaxacans from all over the state leave their homes on foot in November to make the pilgrimage to venerate the blessed virgin on December 8, the town's main festival in celebration of her honor. Santa Catarina Juquila is also one of Oaxaca's Pueblos Mágicos.

Sights

Santuario de Nuestra Señora de Juquila

Constructed in the mid-18th century, the Santuario de Nuestra Señora de Juquila is a brilliant white masterpiece of neoclassical architecture that is a stunning sight to see when lit up at night. The simple but intricate geometrical designs of the facade, once a burgundy red, are now outlined in gold.

The neoclassicism is apparent inside as well, with large, gold-lined columns along the blank white walls of the cross-shaped, dome-topped nave. A unique feature of this church is that there are no pews. You'll find La Juquilita above the altar at the back of

1: Parque Nacional Lagunas de Chacahua at sunrise
2: lanchas in El Zapotalito

The Mayordomías of Pinotepa Nacional

It's a ways out there, but the trip to Pinotepa Nacional is worth it if you can make it during a festival. If you went to the Guelaguetza in Oaxaca City, you most likely saw los sones y chilenas de Pinotepa Nacional, a dance and musical genre from the Costa Chica region of Oaxaca and Guerrero that has its roots in Chile in South America. Get ready to see that and more during Pinotepa's Fiestas, called mayordomías. The word denotes both the parties and the "stewardship" system used in many Oaxacan communities to organize and fund them. The person in charge of everything from changing out the flowers in the church altars all year to making sure the fireworks go off for the finale is called the mayordomo (steward). Each year, the mayordomo (or mayordoma) chooses the following year's master of ceremonies.

Mayordomías are thrown for various saints and virgins year-round, but Pinotepa's biggest one is the Semana Santa (Holy Week) holiday leading up to El Día de Pascua (Easter Sunday). This weeklong festival of solemn religious observances, lively dances, and community building honors Tatchu, the local Mixtec name for Jesus Christ, as well as Our Lady of Solitude. Another lively mayordomía to try and catch in Pinotepa is La Fiesta Patronal en honor a Santiago Apóstol, when the town venerates its patron saint James, son of Zebedee, or as he's called in the local Mixtec dialect, Tata Santiagu. It is held on June 25.

GETTING THERE

Pinotepa is 140 km (87 mi) west of Puerto Escondido on Coastal Highway 200, a 2.5-hour drive. **TUR** vans (corner of Hwy. 200 and Calle Primera Poniente; tel. 954/582-2605; transtur01@hotmail.com) from Puerto Escondido charge about US$8.50 for the three-hour trip. Vans leave every half hour.

the church, clothed in her unique triangle-shaped, gold-embroidered silk robe, and surrounded by flowers brought by the faithful.

El Pedimento

Pilgrims to Juquila also usually make a stop and leave an offering at El Pedimento, a hilltop chapel east of town (which happens to be near the original site of La Juquilita's first abode). Pilgrims bring offerings for the life-sized Virgen de Juquila outside the chapel, usually little figurines made out of clay, to accompany their pedimentos (petitions) to the virgin. You'll see the sign for it about 7 km (4 mi) east of town on the north side of the road. It's 30 minutes from the junction with Highway 131, and about 25 minutes from Juquila.

Festivals and Events

Día de Plaza

Friday

Friday is Santa Catarina Juquila's día de plaza, or market day, when farmers and vendors from the neighboring communities set up shop in the downtown streets.

Fiesta de la Virgen de Juquila

November-December

Pilgrims begin arriving in late November and early December, leaving offerings and lighting candles for the virgin, attending daily early morning masses, and leading religious processions through the streets. From then the celebration grows into a riot of fireworks, music, food, parades, and religious ceremonies until December 8, the day of the Fiesta de la Virgen de Juquila. Her sanctuary brims with flowers during the festivities, adding a harlequin touch to the austere interior. And since the day to honor the Virgen de Guadalupe, the patron saint of Mexico, is December 12, the fun usually continues until then.

Getting There

Public Transit

Getting to Juquila can be a bit hairy. By public transport from Puerto Escondido, your fastest route is to take an **urbano** from the crucero (crossroads) in Puerto or a suburban from the **TUR station** (corner of Hwy. 200 and Calle Primera Poniente; tel. 954/582-2605) west on Highway 200 to Rio Grande. From here, grab a taxi colectivo from the crucero for the trip north to Juquila. All in all, this can take three hours or more. If you take this route, you'll need to get a colectivo going east to Highway 131 when you leave Juquila in order to stop by El Pedimento. This trip should cost around US$6-8.

Alternatively, you could get in a suburban destined for Oaxaca at **Autotransportes Villa Del Pacífico** (Hwy. 200 between Hidalgo and Calle Primera Norte; tel. 954/132-5643) and tell the driver to drop you off at the turnoff to Juquila from Highway 131. Grab a colectivo from here, and you can stop by El Pedimento on the way into town. This route also costs around US$6-8.

Tours and Guides

To make things easier, call **Puerto Escondido Ecotours** (tel. 954/103-1177; www.puertoescondidoecotours.com.mx), who will take care of the transportation and take you to all the necessary sights. The tour costs around US$160 for up to four people and runs 8am-4pm.

Car

Drivers take Highway 200 west from Puerto Escondido. In 50 km (31 mi), turn onto the Rio Grande-Santa Catarina Juquila Highway at Rio Grande. Follow this road 48 km (30 mi) to Santa Catarina Juquila. The drive takes about 2.25 hours.

Puerto Ángel and Vicinity

The string of beaches from Puerto Ángel west to Mazunte are unofficially known as Oaxaca's "hippie beaches." The main activity on this part of the coast is good old-fashioned beach bumming, and sights like the crocodile hatchery in La Ventanilla and turtle center in Mazunte offer fun, educational ecotourism opportunities.

Despite its growing popularity with visitors both foreign and domestic, Puerto Ángel and its neighboring beaches have retained their essence of the isolation. If you're looking for an escape, this is where you want to come.

Orientation

From Pochutla to the north of Puerto Ángel, Highway 175 crosses the coastal highway and winds south through tight, jungled curves toward the sea. **Puerto Ángel** is 10 km (6 mi) south of the junction with Highway 200, and here Highway 175 turns west and runs along the coast, passing through the small beach towns of **Zipolite** (4 km/2.5 mi from Puerto Ángel), **San Agustinillo** (8 km/5 mi), and **Mazunte** (10 km/6 mi), which grow increasingly more "hippie" as you move west, before curving back north to meet up once again with Highway 200. **La Ventanilla** is 3 km (2 mi) west of Mazunte.

Getting Around

Travel between these beaches is cheap and easy. Anytime you want to head up or down the coast, just wait along the main road (Hwy. 175) for a **camioneta** to come along. The trucks charge US$1.50 or less, depending on where you're going.

PUERTO ÁNGEL

Beaches

Playa Estacahuite

Tucked away in a sheltered cove to the east of Puerto Ángel, the waters at Playa Estacahuite are turquoise, tranquil, and oh-so-inviting.

Puerto Ángel

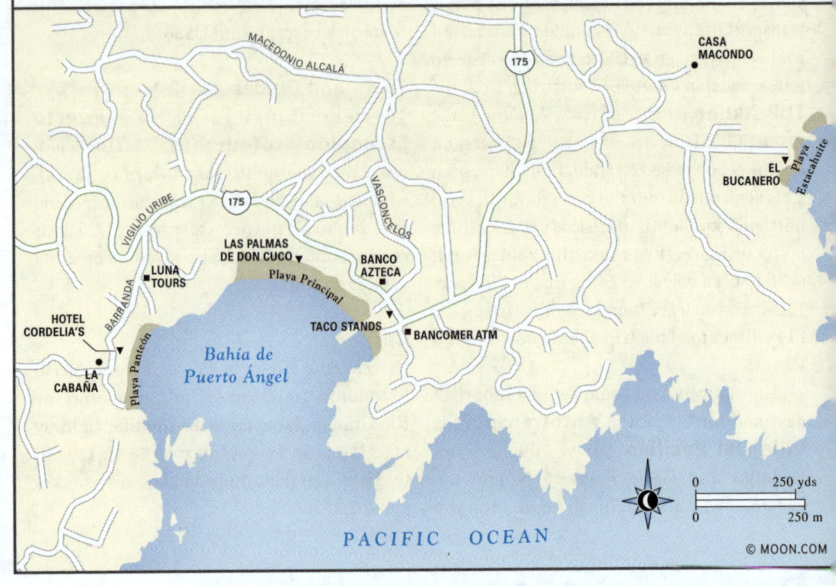

The beach of soft, fine sand is split in two by a rocky outcropping that extends into the gentle waves. Rock formations farther out in the small bay offer good snorkeling opportunities. The turnoff to Estacahuite is at the north edge of Puerto Ángel.

Playas Principal and Panteón

The dock on Playa Principal, in Puerto Ángel's main bay, gets lively toward sundown, as fishermen line up shoulder to shoulder to toss their lines out into the bay, local families relax in the sand after the workday is done, and youngsters practice their penalty shots between two sticks stuck in the sand.

Across the pint-sized bay, and connected to the main beach via a cobblestone path that skirts the rocky cliff between the two, Playa Panteón (Graveyard Beach) also has boats bobbing in the water and pulled up onto the sand, but fewer of them, making it the better choice for swimming. But don't let the currently charming little Playa Panteón fool you. It has a rather spooky past. Its name comes from the fact that human bones were found in the sand when the modern development was put in. The remains were moved to the graveyard farther inland.

Snorkeling and Fishing

For scuba diving on the Oaxacan coast, you'll have to look to Huatulco or Puerto Escondido, but there are a few good snorkeling spots to be found among the hippie beaches. The best snorkeling is on **Playa Estacahuite,** which has calm, clear waters and lots of rocks for marine critters to hide in. You can rent equipment from the palapas on the beach.

Luna Tours

corner of road to Playa Panteón and public beach parking; tel. 958/117-7538 or 958/106-6062; www.lunatours.wordpress.com; lunatoursmexico@yahoo.com

For snorkeling tours, call Aaron Vásquez at Luna. He's a Puerto Ángel native who has lived here since before tourism reached these

1: Puerto Ángel sign **2:** Playa Estacahuite

1

2

shores. A free diver who dives down as far as 25 m (82 ft) below the surface without a tank, Aaron knows every nook and cranny of the local reefs, and will take you on a 3-4-hour snorkel tour (US$12) where you'll see lobsters, octopuses, crabs, and a wide variety of reef fish. Aaron says that they also regularly see dolphins, whales, turtles, manta rays, and an array of marine bird species.

Luna Tours also runs artisanal fishing tours (US$27/hour pp, up to 8 people). Tours run 2-3 hours and can be scheduled in the early morning (6am) or afternoon (4:30pm). It varies season to season, but you're likely to snag tuna, marlin, bonito, sea bass, and mahimahi, among others. They provide equipment traditionally used on the coast, or you can bring your own gear.

Food

For something quick and cheap, hit up the **taco stands** that set up on the main road behind the Playa Principal around 4pm or 5pm in the afternoon. You'll find fried fish, as well as pork, beef, and chicken tacos, for around US$2-3.

Las Palmas de Don Cuco

Playa Principal; tel. 958/584-3140; 9am-6pm daily; US$9-13

On the Playa Principal, Las Palmas serves fresh fish, shrimp, and other seafood caught daily. The fish fillet stuffed with cheese is delicious. Portions are big here, and the location on the beach is perfect for watching the action of the fishermen on the dock in the evening.

Hotel Cordelia's

Playa Panteón; tel. 958/584-3021 or 958/106-0420; www.hotelcordelias.com.mx; 7:30am-10pm daily; US$10-12

Over on Playa Panteón, the restaurant at Hotel Cordelia's has been serving fresh, delicious coastal Oaxacan seafood since 1972. Steamed lobster, shrimp cocktails, and pescado a la talla (red snapper grilled with chile guajillo) are just a few of the plates Cordelia's has perfected in their decades of service.

El Bucanero

Playa Estacahuite; no tel.; 9am-9pm Mon.-Sat.; US$10-13

Your most reliable option on Playa Estacahuite is El Bucanero (The Buccaneer). As is the norm for this type of restaurant, the fish is fresh, the portions big, and the view breathtaking.

Accommodations

Casa Macondo

hill above the beach; tel. 958/587-5081; US$30-35 studio, US$50-75 apartment

Two of the three studios at Casa Macondo have fully stocked kitchenettes, as do the two apartments, and all have their own private terrace or semi-private patio space. All this is packed into a big, mango-colored house up the hill from the beach, with hammocks hanging wherever they'll fit and an ocean-view swimming pool out front. No air-conditioning here, this is a fans-and-mosquito-net kind of place, but the sea breeze keeps everything nice and cool at night.

★ La Cabaña

Playa Panteón; tel. 958/584-3105 or 958/584-3448; www.lacabanapuertoangel.com; US$57 d

On the other side of the bay, La Cabaña is a beautiful bright-orange house overlooking the beach. Lounge in the sun on the ocean-view terrace, or cool off in the swimming pool, spying the jungle-green hillside through the brick archways. All rooms have hot water (not always a guarantee down here), TV, Wi-Fi, and fans. Air-conditioning will cost you another US$10. The rooftop palapa restaurant serves breakfast and antojitos (snacks), but catch it early, as it's only open 8am-1pm.

Aside from its perfect location on Playa Panteón, La Cabaña accepts pets, offers onsite laundry service (about US$1/kg), and will even change out dollars for you. Extra services include outings to neighboring beaches, sportfishing tours, and whale-watching excursions.

Information and Services

In Puerto Ángel, you'll find a **Bancomer**

ATM in the municipal government building at the center of town, where the highway turns away from the Playa Principal to wind north toward Pochutla. You can change out dollars at **Banco Azteca** (Hwy. 175; toll-free Mex. tel. 800/040-7777; 8am-8pm daily), inside the Elektra appliance store on the main road behind the Playa Principal. For laundry services, the folks at **La Cabaña** (Playa Panteón; tel. 958/584-3105 or 958/584-3448; www.lacabanapuertoangel.com; 8am-6pm daily) will charge you a little under US$1 per kg.

The closest hospital to these beaches is the **Hospital General San Pedro Pochutla** (Calle del Hospital 4; tel. 958/584-0236; 24 hrs daily), up in Pochutla. This is your best option for serious emergencies. Calle del Hospital is 0.6 km (0.3 mi) north of the junction of Highways 175 and 200. After you turn right, you'll see the hospital on your left about 50 m (165 ft) down the street.

Getting There

Air

If flying directly to the coast, your best bet location-wise is the airport in **Huatulco,** about 28 km (17 mi) east, just under an hour away from Puerto Ángel. You could also fly into **Puerto Escondido,** 73 km (45 mi) west down Highway 200, but the trip to Puerto Ángel from here takes 1.5 hours or longer. But flights from Mexico City to Puerto Escondido tend to be cheaper than to Huatulco, so it might be worth the extra ground travel time. Check both airports to see which will be best for your trip.

Bus

Thanks to the new supercarretera (highway) connecting Oaxaca City and Puerto Escondido, catching an bus to the area is easy. Take the ADO bus from Oaxaca City to Pochutla (US$21; 4 hrs), and then catch a taxi, camioneta, or colectivo to Puerto Angel.

Suburban

Líneas Unidas (Hwy. 175; tel. 958/119-6666; US$15) makes several trips daily and has a terminal set up in Zipolite. You'll find them on the main road, where it curves toward the beach just to the east of the Adoquín area. The ride on the new highway only takes 3.5 hours. (Only take the original, winding route over mountains if you plan on stopping overnight at San José del Pacifico.) Catch a taxi from there.

Car

From Oaxaca City, take the Barranca Larga-Ventanilla Highway to Puerto Escondido. Upon reaching Puerto Escondido, take Highway 200 east to Pochutla, turning left onto Highway 175, traveling south to Puerto Angel. The total driving time between Oaxaca City and Puerto Ángel is four hours (251 km/156 mi).

Ten km (6 mi) north of Puerto Ángel, Highway 175 meets up with Highway 200. From this junction, it's a curvy 45-minute drive east to La Crucecita and Bahías de Huatulco (42 km/26 mi), and three hours out to Salina Cruz (180 km/112 mi).

PLAYA ZIPOLITE

The most developed beach (though nowhere near as done-up as Huatulco or Puerto Escondido) along this stretch of coastline is Playa Zipolite, known as the place where your birthday suit is acceptable beachwear, if that's what you're into. Although **nudism** is allowed all along the beach (most hotels and restaurants ask that you cover up when you come in from the sand), you'll still see plenty of people in swimsuits. In Zapotec, the name means "Beach of the Dead," as legend has it that early inhabitants used to offer their dead to the sea here.

At the eastern edge of Zipolite you'll find **Playa del Amor,** a secluded notch of golden sand stashed away among large igneous boulders. It's perfect for more private enjoyment of hanging out in only what God gave you.

Festivals and Events

Zipolite Nudist Festival

February

On the first weekend in February, Zipolite plays host to the Zipolite Nudist Festival, a

Zipolite

three-day, stitch-free celebration that includes traditional dances, music, yoga, theater, calendas (street parades), and more.

Food

Orale! Café

Calle las Casitas; tel. 958/117-7129; oralecafe@hotmail.com; 8am-3pm Thurs.-Mon.; US$8-11

On the road toward El Alquimista, you'll see Orale! Café peeking out from the tropical foliage. Aside from super-cheap breakfast options, you'll find baguette and bagel sandwiches made with fresh, healthy ingredients, as well as fresh juices, aguas de sabor (fruit drinks), and rich, organic, locally sourced coffee.

El Alquimista

Calle Shambala; tel. 958/587-8961; www.el-alquimista.com; 8am-11pm daily; US$10-19

Tucked away in a secluded cove at the west end of the beach, El Alquimista has a massive menu of pizzas, pastas, salads, seafood, and other Mexican and international specialties, such as bistec a la pimiento (thin beef steak in black pepper sauce) or grilled chicken breast served in a cream of mushroom sauce. It's a great option if you're craving something different from the palapa-style seafood available on just about every beach on the coast.

Bars and Nightlife

The street behind the beachfront establishments, referred to as **El Adoquín,** is lined with bars and restaurants that get pretty lively during high season in July and August, which is a bit of a change of character for the beach.

A Nice Place On The Beach

Avenida Roca Blanca; tel. 958/584-3195; aniceplaceonthebeach@outlook.com; 7:30am-1:30am daily

The bar at A Nice Place On The Beach is, well, a nice, casual place on the beach for drinks both before and after the sun goes down. Popular among sundried foreign beach bums and friendly locals alike, A Nice Place is one of the few spots in Zipolite that still gets lively during the lazy low season.

Entropía

Avenida Roca Blanca; tel. 557/988-6210; 5pm-midnight Tues.-Sun.

Over on the east end of Roca Blanca, restaurant and bar Entropía has a good selection of mezcals, wines, cocktails, and more. The regular DJ sets and live music, ranging from blues to cumbia to gypsy swing, usually get folks on their feet to dance.

Accommodations

★ Casa Mixteca

Avenida Roca Blanca; tel. 958/688-5514; casamixtecazipolite@gmail.com; from US$90-114

Casa Mixteca has a strong focus on aesthetics. The verdant tropical plants of the meticulously tended interior garden strike a pleasing contrast with the vibrant orange of the courtyard walls, which are adorned with handwoven artisanal baskets and textiles. The upper bungalows and penthouse are reached via a bridge that spans the courtyard below. Hammocks hang inside the bungalows as well as on their private terraces, and the interior design is both comfortable and visually pleasing. The overall effect is one of relaxation and the simple enjoyment of the tasteful interaction of colors and textures.

Hotel Noga

Calle Shambala; tel. 954/138-9368; www.hnoga.com; US$130-173

Stay in a tree house just steps away from the ocean at Hotel Noga. These beautiful wooden bungalows are nestled in the dense green foliage of the mangroves, connected via catwalks raised above the forest floor. All rooms come with a refrigerator, air-conditioning, a safe, and TV, as well as hammocks on the terrace for relaxing in the shade. The on-site restaurant/bar (8am-11pm), set in a leafy nook on the beach, serves everything from delicious breakfasts to fresh seafood dinners.

Information and Services

There's a **Banco Multiva ATM** on El Adoquín. Take your clothes to the lavandería in **Posada Navidad** (Christmas Inn; Avenida Roca Blanca; tel. 958/584-3358; 8am-5pm daily). For medical services, call or stop by the office of **Doctora Rojas** (Avenida Roca Blanca; tel. 221/266-4947; 9am-9pm daily), across from Posada México.

Getting There

From Oaxaca City, the van line **Líneas Unidas** (Xóchitl 101; 951/516-2472; US$15) travels directly to Zipolite (and vice versa) several times daily.

From Puerto Escondido, take an **ADO bus** to Pochutla (US$10; 1.5 hrs) and catch a taxi, camioneta, or colectivo to Zipolite.

From Puerto Angel, a quick 10-minute **taxi** ride will bring you to Zipolite.

SAN AGUSTINILLO

Between Zipolite and Mazunte, Playa San Agustinillo has the best of both worlds. Not as active or naked as Zipolite, but neither as mellow as Mazunte, this broad, open sea beach is perfect for those who like to surf or bodyboard but also sometimes just want to splash around in some gentle waves. The west end of the beach curves out into the sea, and the rocky outcropping at sand's end creates a miniature bay that forms small but surfable waves when the ocean gets a little rowdy. At other times, the blue-green waters chill out and become perfect for snorkeling or just lazily cooling off in the afternoon heat.

The hilly terrain here snuggles up right next to the beach, forcing the main road to curve as closely as possible to the shore. Because of this, all the accommodations here are either right on the beach or just across the street from it, meaning you'll never have a long walk to the waves in San Agustinillo.

Fishing

Pacífico Mágico Tours

in Restaurante Alejandra on the main road; tel. 998/810-9446; US$27 pp

Call up Pacífico Mágico Tours, which comes highly recommended by locals and tourists alike. Dolphin and sea turtle watching tours are US$27 per person (whales can also be spotted November-April). Sportfishing tours are US$81 per hour for a minimum of three hours and begin bright and early at 6:30am.

Yoga and Meditation

Hridaya Yoga

on the hill between Mazunte and San Agustinillo; tel. 958/100-8958; www.hridaya-yoga.com; 8:30am-10:45am Mon.-Sat.; US$3-8 drop-in classes

Up on the hill between Mazunte and San Agustinillo, Hridaya Yoga offers hatha yoga classes in English 8:30am-10:30am Mondays and Fridays (Spanish classes are Wednesdays at the same time). They also offer three-day yoga retreats that start at US$250 for the course only, and you can choose to add meal plans and accommodations.

Restorative Alignment

in Cabañas Las 3 Marías on the main road; no tel.; www.restorativealignment.com

Brigitte Longueville runs Restorative Alignment (formerly known as Solstice Yoga), where she offers five-day yoga retreats, giving instruction in both Spanish and English. Check her website for the class schedule, teacher trainings, and retreat information.

Accommodations

Paraíso del Pescador

Hwy. 175; tel. 958/589-9517; US$57 d

The rooms and large terrace at Paraíso del Pescador (The Fisherman's Paradise) look right out over the golden expanse of Playa San Agustinillo. This is a hotel-style paradise, unlike the more popular cabañas elsewhere along the beach, but it's an excellent value. Most rooms have that aforementioned phenomenal view, private bathrooms, and fans, or air-conditioning for another US$5.

Cabañas Un Sueño

Hwy. 175; tel. 958/113-8749; www.unsueno.mx; US$112-147

The 17 units right on the beach at Cabañas Un Sueño (A Dream) are covered in brilliant white stucco and adorned with naturally finished wooden doors and window shutters, with comfy hammocks hung between the palm trees out front and a half dozen more strung beneath a large palapa on the beach (meals at the on-site restaurant can be enjoyed here from 8am-10pm). Ceiling fans and the sea breeze keep the bungalows cool at night. Just 150 m (500 ft) away is their second property, H20 Container Cabins (US$125-180), which is exactly what it sounds like—but absolutely gorgeous.

Getting There

From Zipolite, catch a **taxi** (US$11; 10 min.) or a **colectivo** or **camioneta** on Hwy. 175 ($US1-2; 20 min.). From Mazunte, take a leisurely 10-minute stroll up and down the hill.

★ MAZUNTE

Oaxaca's coastal Pueblo Mágico is mellow Mazunte. There is no better place along the coast for doing absolutely nothing, and there's lots of space to do it in. The larger **Playa Mazunte** is just one of the beaches here, but most of the (in)action is on **Playa Rinconcito,** just over the rocks on the west side of the beach, around which the majority of the town's bars, restaurants, and cabañas are located. Over the hill to the west of the main town, **Playa Mermejita** is good for watching a sunset, but swimming isn't allowed due to the roughness of the water, so the beach is usually empty.

Sights

La Punta Cometa

La Punta Cometa is arguably the best place to watch a sunset in Oaxaca. Also called Cerro Sagrado (Sacred Hill), it's the southernmost point in Oaxaca.

To get there, take the road that climbs the hill to Playa Mermejita from Calle Rinconcito in the town. At the top, you can follow the signs that lead through the forested area out to the promontory's cactus-covered rocks, or continue down the hill to Mermejita, where you'll climb up the hill at the east end of the beach. At the bottom of the south-facing cliffs lies a tidepool with a small opening to the sea. It's called "the Jacuzzi" because of the rambunctious nature of the water made by waves splashing through the opening in the rocks. It's safe(ish) to wade or swim in—just steer

San Agustinillo and Mazunte

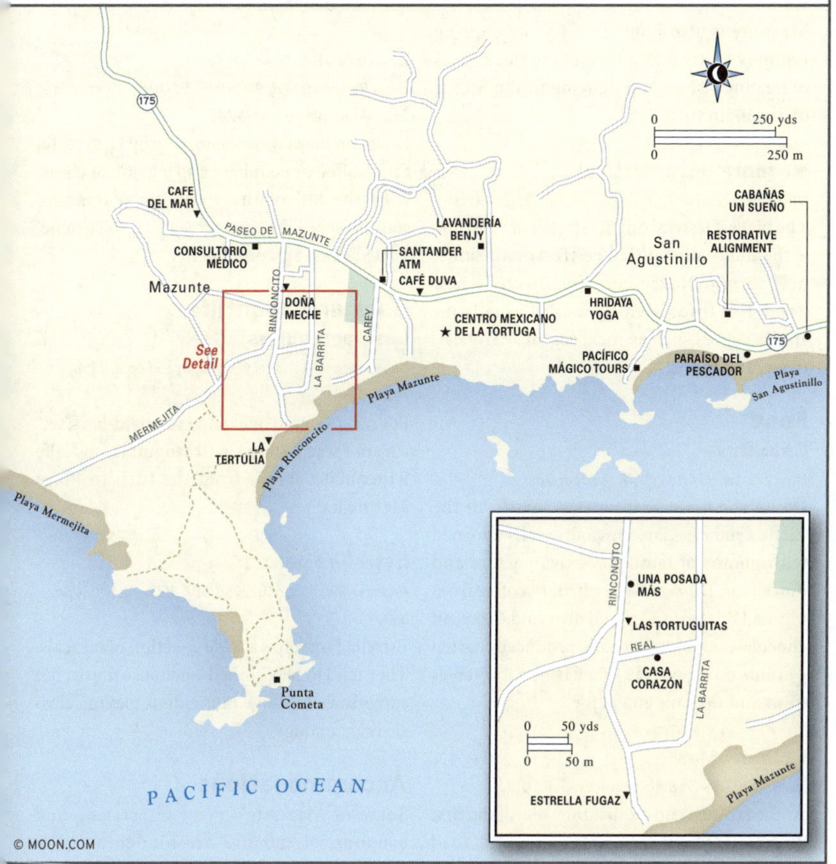

clear of the breach in the rocks; the water could pull you out to sea.

Centro Mexicano de la Tortuga

Hwy. 175; tel. 958/584-3376; www.tortugasmazunte.org; 10am-4:30pm Wed.-Sat., 10am-2pm Sun.; US$2.50, kids 12 and under free

You'd never know it now, but the facilities at the Centro Mexicano de la Tortuga were originally a sea turtle slaughterhouse and processing plant. Now it's an official institution of the Mexican federal government, dedicated to the conservation of marine, land, and freshwater turtles.

Fortunately, their efforts have had a positive effect the turtles' populations. The small on-site museum provides information about the various species that visit Mazunte, as well as the steps the center is taking to conserve them and their habitat. The aquarium houses a variety sea and freshwater turtles, many of which are rescues being prepared for release back into the wild. Kids especially love the baby sea turtle tanks.

Festivals and Events

Spring Equinox Festival

March

Mazunte is also home to a one-day Spring Equinox Festival that includes various types of healing rituals and dancing in the square on the main road.

Mazunte Jazz Festival

November

The biggest festival on this stretch of coastline is the International Jazz Festival of Mazunte, held in mid-November. Not strictly a jazz event, this three-evening festival usually includes genres such as rock, reggae, Afrobeat, trova, and more.

Food

Café Duva

Hwy. 175; tel. 954/133-8748; 7:30am-5pm

Down the main road, just across from the turtle center is Café Duva, its walls adorned with photos of famous Mexican actors and musicians. Duva serves rich, dark coffee from Pluma Hidalgo, and you'll also find Oaxacan chocolate, mole, and locally produced roasted peanuts on its shelves. They have a few tables to sit and sip your cup of joe.

Café del Mar

tel. 958/107-9942; 8am-4pm Tues.-Sun.; US$5

At the far west end of Mazunte, one of the first businesses you'll see coming in on the road from the highway is Café del Mar, with good coffee and a wide selection of vegan burgers and other plant-based options. Antique radios on the second-floor terrace pay decorative homage to the café's musical preference, jazz, which they play all day.

Doña Meche

Calle Rinconcito; tel. 958/109-8712; www.comedorlostraviesos.blogspot.com; 8am-11pm daily; US$5

You'll find cheap, tasty, traditional Mexican breakfasts at any of the restaurants along the main drag between Calles Rinconcito and Barrita. On Calle Rinconcito, Doña Meche has full breakfasts that include coffee or tea, fruit or juice, and a main dish of eggs cooked how you like them.

La Tertulia

Playa Rinconcito; tel. 958/113-8292; 10am-10pm Mon.-Sat., 10am-9pm Sun.; US$7-13

Down on Playa Rinconcito, stop by La Tertulia for a coffee or cold beer and a game of chess, with the lull of the waves for a relaxing soundtrack. They also serve up fresh ceviche, grilled tuna, and other delights.

Bars and Nightlife

Las Tortuguitas

Calle Rinconcito; no tel.; 9am-2pm and 6pm-10pm Thurs.-Tues.

For mezcal, grab one in the very laid-back setting of mezcal shop Las Tortuguitas, on Calle Rinconcito across from the turn to Playa Mermejita.

Estrella Fugaz

Andador Rinconcito; tel. 958/587-8133; 7am-11:30pm daily

Estrella Fugaz has a wide selection of mezcals. They tend to play chilled-out house music, but sometimes host live music duos playing classic reggae songs.

Accommodations

Some of Mazunte's most interesting and economical cabañas are hidden away in the mangrove forest just behind the rocky hill that separates Playas Mazunte and Rinconcito.

★ Casa Corazón

Calle Palma Real; tel. 983/168-5584; www.corazonmazunte.com; US$16-49

From Calle Palma Real, which runs east to west between Calles Barrita and Rinconcito, follow the raised wooden walkway through the mangrove trees to Casa Corazón, a small cluster of cabañas raised on stilts above the swampy ground below. The fairy lights hung in the trees along the way and the constant and surprisingly loud rustle of crabs in the grasses and mud below create a truly surreal experience. The bamboo and palm-frond cabañas have only mosquito netting for walls, allowing maximum ventilation, which will be necessary in the heat of the swamp. In the midst of this simple, natural setting, Casa Corazón still has modern amenities like Wi-Fi, a communal kitchen, and a dry toilet in the shared bathroom, so that the hotel and its guests have as little impact as possible on the environment. In fact, Casa Corazón's primary work is in conservation, particularly of those adorable crabs you hear rustling about. You can learn more about their conservation efforts on their website.

Una Posada Más

Calle Rinconcito; tel. 958/119-4504; www.unaposadamas.com; US$30-46

Una Posada Más literally means "One More Inn," but it has a more flippant connotation in Spanish, making a more accurate translation something like "Just Another Inn." But on passing through the bougainvillea-framed entrance, you'll see that this isn't just another hotel. The seven airy rooms of the inn overlook a small, jungly courtyard strung with hammocks in the shade of giant tropical fronds. It's like sneaking away from one paradise to another. All the rooms, which can accommodate 2-6 people, have private bathrooms, mosquito nets, and Wi-Fi access, and some are equipped with air-conditioning.

Information and Services

There's a **Santander ATM** on the main road next to the scooter rental/ice cream shop La Garrafita. The **consultorio medico** (doctor's office; Hwy. 175; tel. 669/262-3649; 8am-10pm daily) next to the natural cosmetics shop (stop in here, by the way, your skin will thank you) charges about US$5 for a doctor's visit. You can call the number listed anytime for emergencies.

For laundry services, head to **Lavandería Benjy** (Calle Tamarindos; tel. 958/107-0188; 7am-4pm Mon.-Sat.).

Getting There

From Oaxaca City, take an **ADO bus** to Pochutla (US$21; 4 hrs) and take a taxi, camioneta, or colectivo from there. You can also take a **Líneas Unidas van** directly to Zipolite and catch a taxi, camioneta, or colectivo on Hwy 175.

By **car,** take the Barranca Larga-Ventanilla Highway through Puerto Escondido and onto Hwy 175. The ride is 3.5 hours.

PLAYA LA VENTANILLA

About 2 km (1.2 mi) from Mazunte, Playa La Ventanilla is a long expanse of wave-battered sand, fully open to the gusts and swells of the powerful Pacific Ocean. But no big deal. You don't come here to swim. On an island in the mangrove swamps behind the beach is a crocodile hatchery that works to conserve the habitat and maintain populations of the scaly reptiles. You'll also see loads of sea turtles, migratory seabirds, deer, and iguanas on the little island, and the hatchery has other animals, like monkeys. There's a good chance you'll see crocs in the wild, too. The beach is called La Ventanilla (The Window) for the portal-shaped rock formation at the beach's east end, which can be clearly seen from the lookout point on La Punta Cometa.

Mangrove and Crocodile Tours

Sociedad Cooperativa Servicios Ecoturísticos de la Ventanilla

Playa La Ventanilla; tel. 958/220-5797 or 958/187-9412; www.laventanilla.com.mx; 9am-4pm daily; US$5-14

In La Ventanilla, the Sociedad Cooperativa Servicios Ecoturísticos de la Ventanilla (Cooperative Society of Ecotourism Services of La Ventanilla) offers boat tours of the mangrove swamps and visits to the crocodile hatchery and cocodrilario (crocodile farm) on the small island in the lagoon, as well as nighttime walks to observe nesting **sea turtles and baby turtle releases.** The boat tour (Spanish only) and visit to the island hatchery costs US$135 for a group of up to eight and takes about two hours. Nighttime turtle

Magic Mushrooms

For centuries, the inhabitants of the northern peaks of the Sierra Sur have used hongos (literally, "fungus," but in this context, "magic mushrooms") in spiritual ceremonies and to commune with nature.

Located at around 2,500 m (8,200 ft) above sea level, the town's cool, humid conditions are perfect for wild mushrooms, especially during the **rainy season (July-October).** Many visitors come to San José del Pacífico for guided or personal mushroom experiences, often in nature lodges or with local shamans.

RESPONSIBLE USE AND CONSIDERATIONS

- While magic mushrooms are part of the local culture, they **remain illegal under Mexican law,** though enforcement in San José del Pacífico is generally lax.
- It's essential to **respect local traditions and nature,** as well as approach the experience with **mindfulness and caution.**
- Some people may experience **intense emotions or hallucinations,** so being in a safe environment is crucial.

monitoring tours cost US$21. They also have rustic cabañas for US$65 a night.

The ecotourism cooperative offices are a quick 10-minute drive from Mazunte. Getting there is easy, even without a car. Just board a westbound camioneta anywhere along the main road and keep an eye out for the sign at the turnoff about 2.2 km (1.4 mi) west of Mazunte, about five minutes after leaving the town. The trip from Puerto Ángel takes a little over half an hour. The walk from the main road to the ecotourism cooperative offices takes about 15 minutes; the offices are on the left-hand side of the road.

Getting There

From Mazunte, Playa La Ventanilla is just a 10-minute drive. Head northwest on Hwy 175. About 2 km (1.2 km) down the road, look out for the sign for your left turn down the street to Ventanilla.

★ SAN JOSÉ DEL PACÍFICO

Perched atop the first row of the Sierra's towering peaks, the smoky cabañas of San José del Pacífico (elevation 2,500 m/8,200 ft) seem to be in another time and place entirely. During the rainy season (June-September), night and day here are mercurial concepts that don't stick to the rest of the world's circadian rhythms. Clouds regularly scud through the valley, blotting out the spectacular views and shrouding the early afternoon in a false twilight. If you're lucky, you'll see the famous mar de nubes, an effect that science calls a temperature inversion, when the valley below is filled with a "sea" of clouds.

This mountain town has its head in the clouds in more ways than one—it's been a popular destination for hippies since the 1970s due to the locals' use of psychedelic mushrooms. But even if you have no interest in magic mushrooms, the views, coffee, and cozy vibes in San José are also excellent reasons to come. And there are trails everywhere—through tunnels of fragrant pines and harlequin patches of wildflowers—perfect for strolling and taking in the beautiful scenery.

Hiking

San Mateo Río Hondo

Distance: *9 km (5.6 mi) one-way*
Duration: *2.5 hours*
Elevation gain: *286 m (938 ft)*
Effort: *easy to moderate*
Trailhead: *Biblioteca Publica*

Near San José del Pacífico, San Mateo Río Hondo is much more representative of a normal south Oaxacan mountain town. Although they're available, you won't find signs for magic mushrooms on every corner, like in

San José—just wood and brick houses up and down the slopes, and the bright-orange Plaza Municipal standing out against the background of green.

The most enjoyable way to get to San Mateo is on foot from San José. If you're not loaded down with luggage, take the road that climbs the hill just to the north of the main cluster of cafés and cabañas on the highway in San José. Take your first right at the local government building. From here, walk about 2 km (1.2 mi), or about half an hour, on the paved road until you see a sign to turn right onto a dirt road that says "San Mateo Río Hondo." From here, it's another 30-45-minute walk through tunnels of fragrant pine trees and dizzyingly high mountain vistas to the east side of San Mateo. The road is paved as it descends into town and terminates at its intersection with Calle Ixcotel. From here, the center of town is to the right, another 10 minutes downhill. To get to the cabañas, turn left and walk 100 m (330 ft), where you'll see the turnoff to Privada Ixcotel.

Food

Comedor La Morenita

Hwy. 175; tel. 951/290-6381; 7am-10:30pm daily; US$2-3

For breakfast, grab a steaming cup of café de olla and a plate of huevos al comal (eggs fried on a ceramic griddle called a comal) at Comedor La Morenita, just to the south of La Montaña, the store where the vans stop. A few other comedores line this part of the highway as well.

Cafetería Punto Sur

Cam. Al Cerro 1; tel. 951/197-6656; 9am-10pm Tues.-Sun.; US$3-8

You'll have to hike a bit to reach this café, but the panoramic views are well worth it. Fresh, delicious breakfasts can be enjoyed on the breezy terrace, and that crisp mountain air just makes everything taste that much better. It's also one of the best places to watch the spectacular sunsets here—grab a hot chocolate and enjoy.

La Casa del Arbol

Hwy. 175; tel. 951/174-6476; 7am-midnight daily; US$8-10

For meals anytime of day or night, stop by La Casa del Arbol, which serves up some tasty and innovative dishes, such as their signature "champiquiles" and fanciful drinks like "beso de hada" (fairy kiss). The homey aromas and tastes capture the flavor the this region perfectly. The atmosphere inside is perfectly cozy, or you can snag a table on the terrace to enjoy gorgeous forest views.

Accommodations

★ Cabañas La Cumbre

Camino al Cerro La Postema; tel. 951/126-3993; www.cabanaslacumbre.com; US$15 shared bathroom, US$49 en suite, US$68 family cabin

Cabañas La Cumbre offers pretty, wood-paneled cabañas, giving visitors the chance to stay on the hill with the best view in town. Many of the cabañas are in adorable geodesic dome shapes, with beautiful views of the forest and of the star-filled skies on clear nights. Prices are quite low, making it one of the best values up here in the clouds. They offer guided hikes and temazcal, information on hongos, and a 10 percent discount to the restaurant Cafetería Punto Sur.

Refugio Terraza de la Tierra

Hwy. 175; tel. 951/361-6590; www.terrazadelatierra.com.mx; terrazadelatierra11@gmail.com; US$39-51 d cabaña

About 4 km (2.5 mi) north of San José, a steep cobblestone road leads down to the aptly named Refugio Terraza de la Tierra, meaning "Earth's Terrace Refuge," and once you see the view, you'll know why. No cell service, Wi-Fi only in the restaurant, and the soothing sound of trickling water from the system of small canals around the cabañas make this the perfect refuge from the real world, which we all need every now and then. Yoga (US$8) and meditation classes (free) are offered daily. The on-site restaurant El Florecer is vegan and serves meals three times a day.

La Puesta del Sol

Hwy. 175; tel. 951/190-8256; www.sanjosedelpacifico.com; sanjose@sanjosedelpacifico.com; US$43-87

Just north of town, La Puesta del Sol has hotel-style rooms, as well as cabañas made of beautiful blonde pine and situated along the slope so as not to leave a bad seat in the house for a view of the sunset. All rooms have hot water in the showers and potable water in the taps (it's delicious), and cabañas include fireplaces, which are key for the chilly, high-altitude nights up here. Only about 1 km (0.5 mi) north of town, it's a pleasant 10-15-minute walk into town along the highway.

Getting There

San José del Pacífico is 136 km (84 mi) south of Oaxaca City on Highway 175. The **drive** takes a little less than three hours in a private car, and closer to three in one of the suburban vans run by **Líneas Unidas** (Bustamante 601, Oaxaca City; tel. 951/516-2472; US$10). The final hour of the drive is the ascent into the mountains and where you'll hit those infamous curves. If you're prone to getting carsick (honestly, even if you're not), make sure to have some anti-motion-sickness meds on hand.

If you're coming from Puerto Angel, Líneas Unidas will get you there in about 3-4 hours for around US$11. Unfortunately from the coast, the whole ride is as curvy as it is beautiful, so it may be best to pop a Dramamine (or chew on some ginger candy), take a nap, and wake up in San José del Pacifico.

PLUMA HIDALGO

Coffee grown in Pluma Hidalgo can be found in cafés all over the state, especially along the coast, but caffeine addicts should seriously consider making a pilgrimage to the mountaintop town on the misty southern slopes of the Sierra Madre del Sur. This, as they say, is where all the magic happens.

One of the local peaks is named Cerro de la Pluma (Hill of the Feather), either because it was in the habit of forming plume-shaped clouds at its peak when the town was founded, or because of the feathers that floated down from abandoned eagle nests when the raptors were more common there, depending on who you ask. The town's first name was derived from that. Its second name pays homage to Father Miguel Hidalgo, who famously kicked off the revolution in 1810 with a rousing speech remembered as the Grito de Dolores (Shout of Dolores) in the town of Dolores, Guanajuato, whose current second name also honors the insurgent priest.

Coffee from Pluma is referred to as café de altura, literally "coffee of heights," and it's exactly this altitude (Pluma averages around 1,300 m/4,300 ft above sea level) combined with the hot, humid tropical air that comes in from the coast that gives it its distinct full body and rich flavor. Some coffee is grown as high as 1,500 m (4,900 ft) above sea level. There are a few cafés in town where you can taste the local coffee, or you can tour a nearby finca (coffee plantation).

Sights

Cerro de la Pluma

Pluma Hidalgo zócalo; tel. 951/282-0405 or 951/115-1573; cafe_cerrodelapluma@hotmail.com; 9am-2pm and 4pm-10pm daily; US$27-37

To get a taste of what it's like to grow and process coffee in Pluma, contact Damián Ramírez or his sister Concepción of Cerro de la Pluma, whose café in town is right next to La Bóveda. The Ramírez family's finca (coffee plantation) is situated over 1,500 m (4,900 ft) above sea level, and everything from sowing to harvesting to drying and roasting is done using artisanal methods. Their customizable tours, or rutas (routes) as they call them, can include trips to waterfalls, finca tours, hikes, coffee tasting, samplings of local gastronomy, and more.

Tours range US$27-37 for the day, depending on the season and activities you want to do. The Ramírez family is more focused on spreading knowledge and awareness of coffee culture and production in Pluma than making a profit, so if you're interested in learning more, Damián will throw in a rustic night out on their plantation at no extra cost. They need at least a couple of days to prepare, so call or write them in advance.

Finca Don Gabriel

Colonia José Palogrande, Pluma Hidalgo; tel. 958/122-3000 or 958/116-1656; www.fincadongabriel.com; US$46 d, US$89 t

If roughing it isn't your preferred way of seeing a coffee farm, book a room at Finca Don Gabriel, about 1.5 km (1 mi) south of town. The bright-orange hotel-quality cabañas, with private bathrooms and hammocks strung on the porches, offer sprawling views of the southern slopes of the Sierra Sur as they descend to the sea. You can easily see the ocean from here. There is a small coffee museum, playground, spa, and swimming pool on the grounds. The on-site **restaurant** (8am-6pm daily) is good enough to draw locals from Pluma for weekend dinners of traditional Oaxacan fare. There's also a spa that offers massages, facials, temazcal, and other beauty and relaxation treatments.

For activities, they offer **tours** of the plantation grounds for US$5.50 per person, with discounts for groups. There's also lots of **hiking** in the surrounding hills, as well as a **tiorlesa (zip line),** which costs about US$8 a zip.

Food and Accommodations

La Bóveda

Pluma Hidalgo zócalo; tel. 958/103-8245; rosilaboveda@gmail.com; 8am-10pm daily

The espresso at La Bóveda is worth the trip to Pluma, as is the view of the verdant slopes of the Sierra Sur from the **lookout point** on the basketball court on the other side of the municipal government building on the west side of the zócalo.

Café Cerro de la Pluma

Pluma Hidalgo zócalo; tel. 951/282-0405 or 951/115-1573; cafe_cerrodelapluma@hotmail.com; 8am-8pm daily

Next door to La Bóveda, Café Cerro de la Pluma, the coffee shop of local finca Cerro de la Pluma, has a small selection of locally produced mezcals in addition to phenomenal cups of joe.

Café Origen Mágico

corner of Calle Allende and Calle Matamoros; tel. 958/525-8057; 8am-11pm Mon.-Sat., 9:30-11pm Sun.

You'll also find the Black Gold of Pluma at Café Origen Mágico, to the south of the Iglesia Ave María church. The café boasts a flowery terrace with a spectacular view of mountains below.

Posada Isabel

behind the Iglesia Ave María; tel. 958/525-8113; US$29

If you're charmed into staying a night in town, the seafoam-green Posada Isabel has clean private rooms with hot water, TV, internet, and gorgeous views of the valley to the south. The harlequin shades of sunset are best viewed from the second-floor room with big bay windows on three sides, so snag it if it's available.

Getting There

Suburban vans run by **Huatulco 2000** (Hidalgo 208, Oaxaca City; tel. 951/516-3154; US$11) leave Oaxaca City every two hours beginning at 7am. The trip takes about five hours. But you'll most likely be catching one of these on the main drag in San José de Pacífico. From here, the trip is a little over two hours and costs about US$6.

Drivers should keep an eye out for the junction at a sharp turn in the road on Highway 175 about 1.5 hours (61 km/38 mi) south of San José del Pacífico. From here, drive the last 9 km (5.6 mi) of the El Zapote-Copalita Highway to the vertiginously steep entrance to the town. Take a right at the top of the hill to get to the Centro.

To get to the Puerto Ángel-Mazunte beaches or Puerto Escondido, take a **colectivo** (US$1.50) back to Highway 175. From here, flag a passing suburban (US$2) to take you down to Pochutla and transfer from there.

To get to Bahías de Huatulco (not to be confused with Santa María Huatulco), hop on a suburban run by **Huatulco 2000** (US$7). They come through town every two hours, making a stop outside Café Origen Mágico. From Huatulco, catch a Huatulco 2000 van in La Crucecita (Chahué 46, in front of Plaza Madero)

Bahías de Huatulco and Vicinity

TOP EXPERIENCE

The Bahías de Huatulco, with its nine bays and 30-plus beaches, is brimming with arguably the state's (possibly the whole country's) most beautiful and pristine beaches. You'll find yourself enchanted by the shifting shades of turquoise and aquamarine of the calm waters, delighted by the rainbow-colored fish swimming just feet from the shore, or enjoying an untouched beach all by your happy lonesome.

As the "Cancún of Oaxaca," you'll find the best infrastructure and most luxurious resorts, with plenty of tours, day trips, and top-notch entertainment options if you inexplicably get bored in this earthly paradise. But don't worry—Huatulco still manages to retain a friendly, small-town feel.

Orientation

The town of **La Crucecita** is the central urban nucleus of Bahías de Huatulco. It is located about 1.5 km (1 mi) northwest of **Bahía Chahué,** which is accessed via the broad Boulevard Chahué, its median beautified with well-manicured lawns and pedestrian walkways. Huatulco's eight other bays are east and west of Chahué.

Just to the west of Bahía Chahué is **Bahía de Santa Cruz,** where many hotels and tourism agencies are located, as well as a long dock where cruise ships come to port throughout the week. The neighborhood of **Santa Cruz Huatulco** is home to a pleasant, shady central square, a small marina, and a tourist market stocked with water toys and other beach items.

West from Santa Cruz, the other bays are **Bahías Órgano, Maguey, Cacaluta, Chachacual,** and **San Agustín,** all within the borders of **Parque Nacional Huatulco.**

The bays to the east of Chahué are **Bahía Tangolunda** and **Bahía Conejos.** They are home to the fancier Huatulco resorts.

The area is served by its own airport, Aeropuerto Internacional Bahías de Huatulco.

LA CRUCECITA

La Crucecita has a much more "Mexican" feel to it than the hotel areas on the beaches, with delicious restaurants, colorful markets and crafts stores, and a profusion of charming low- to mid-range accommodations options, all set around a shady zócalo with its attendant church **Iglesia de la Crucecita** (which, interestingly, has the largest painting of the Virgen de Guadalupe in Mexico painted on its ceiling).

Forget about the luxury down on the beaches. La Crucecita is where all the life is. The Centro, little more than a couple of dozen blocks surrounding the zócalo, is a hive of activity, even during low season when other places on the coast are hearing crickets.

Although its excellent dining and accommodations options have recently made it more popular with tourists, La Crucecita is a town built and run by hardworking Mexican folks who aren't going to take the seeds out of the chiles to make the salsa more palatable to foreigners. With the calm, jewel-colored waters of Playa Santa Cruz a 20-minute walk across the andador turistico, a pedestrian walkway over the hill to the south of the Centro (also known as Quinta Avenida), and cheap taxi fares to almost anywhere in Huatulco's nine bays, La Crucecita is the

Bahías de Huatulco

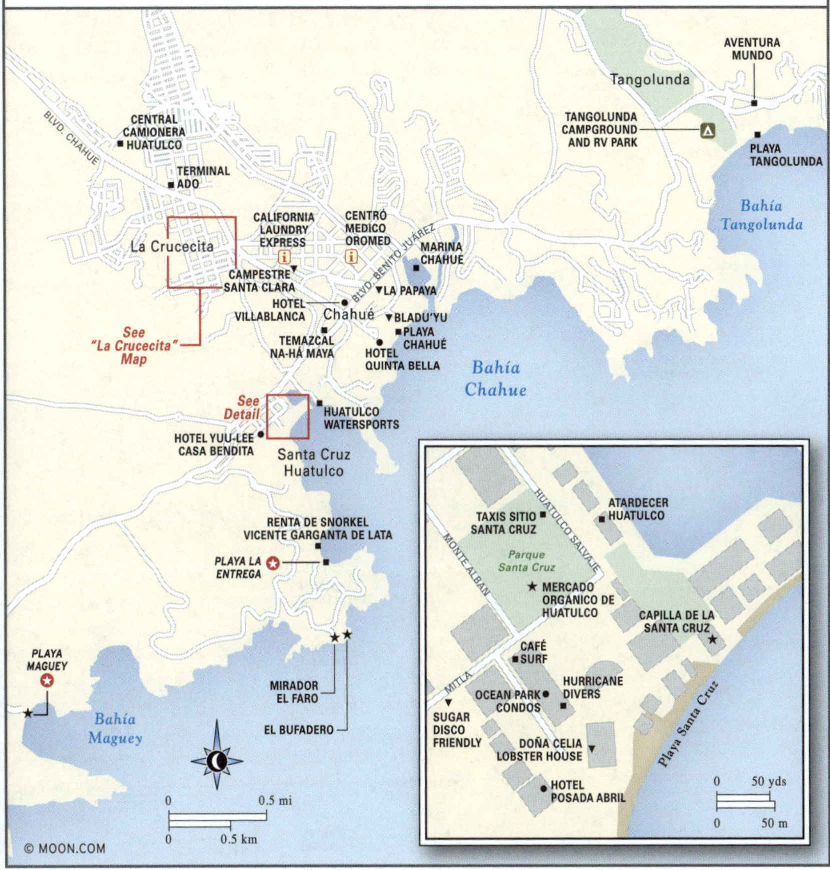

perfect base from which to explore this resplendent tropical paradise.

Biking

Descubre Huatulco

Chacah 210; tel. 958/119-7325 or 958/587-2195; www.descubrehuatulco.mx; 8am-8pm daily; US$50

If biking is your thing, you can't miss going on a bicycle tour with Miguel and the guys at Descubre Huatulco. Take a wild ride through the jungle at Huatulco National Park, or enjoy a nighttime ride to a pristine beach in the moonlight. The bilingual guides are very knowledgeable of these trails and the plants and wildlife found here.

Shopping

Mercado 3 de Mayo

Guamuchil 208; no tel.; 8am-8pm daily

The Mercado 3 de Mayo, just to the east of the main square, is a spacious and well-ventilated home for the plethora of stalls selling folk art, souvenirs, toys, beach gear, and much more. It's also a great place to grab a shrimp cocktail or smoothie during a shopping break.

El Buen Mezcal

Bugambilias 1202; tel. 958/123-2462; www.mezcalchahue.com; 8am-11pm daily

You'll also find good, locally produced mezcal at the aptly named El Buen Mezcal (formerly known as Casa Chahué). They offer tastings and have a wide selection of mezcals, from young to aged five years. They also have an Indigenous topical remedy for rheumatism, arthritis, and muscular pain they call Nep Viguú. This stuff isn't for drinking, as it contains scorpion venom at the bottom of the bottle. You can find their second location on Flamboyán 109, behind Plaza Madero.

La Casa del Alebrije

Chacah 203; tel. 958/100-1812; artblass925ley@gmail.com; 8:30am-10:15pm daily

For alebrijes (painted carved wooden figures), head to La Casa del Alebrije. César Blas and his family have been creating these fantastical creatures for over 30 years, each creation made with painstaking detail. A feature I find particularly endearing is that each piece is created from driftwood or fallen branches—no trees are cut for their creations, making their works not just beautiful but sustainable as well. They have a wide selection, ship worldwide, and take orders for custom pieces.

Food

Maré

Gardenia 1303; tel. 958/113-3106; 5:30pm-10:30pm Mon.-Fri., 5pm-10:30pm Sat.-Sun.; US$3-4

It's a bit strange to say that eating at an Italian restaurant in a small Mexican beach town feels like coming home, but eating at Maré is just such a warm experience. The owners, Alberto and Maria, are the sweetest couple you'd ever meet. Maria makes the delicious fresh-made pasta and cooks the seafood to perfection (have the mussels), while Alberto serves it all up with warmth and charm.

Campestre Santa Clara

Calle Mazateco; tel. 958/587-1047; 8am-6pm Thurs.-Tues.; US$5.50-11

When Doña Carolina opened up her restaurant over three decades ago, it was to serve the local workers who needed a good hearty meal. Her home-cooked, family-style meals gained popularity, and now Campestre Santa Clara is one of Huatulco's best restaurants for a traditional Oaxacan meal. The palapa-style restaurant gives a nice rustic setting, and there's a play area in the back for children to play while you savor your meal.

Terra-Cotta

Gardenia 902; tel. 958/587-1135; www.misiondelosarcos.website; 8am-11pm daily; US$10-17

The finest dining to be had in La Crucecita is at Terra-Cotta, the restaurant at Hotel Misión de los Arcos. The upscale ambience will make you think the prices should be higher, but you won't have to shell out a ton of clams for delicious gourmet soups, pastas, surf and turf, and imaginative twists on Mexican cuisine, such as the cuitlacoche crepes, made with corn fungus and smothered with a creamy poblano chile sauce.

La Crema

Flamboyán 210; tel. 958/587-0702; 4pm-1am Mon.-Sat., 6pm-1am Sun.; US$10-18

Named after the legendary trio that gave the world songs like "White Room" and "Sunshine of Your Love," La Crema is a hip, rock-and-roll-themed bar and pizzeria that is almost always busy. Try the La Crema Special, a pie topped with mushrooms, ham, pepperoni, green peppers, and sour cream. For dessert? More pizza! The banana pizzas are made with cinnamon and coconut cream.

Bars and Nightlife

After the sun sets, La Crucecita's zócalo gets quite lively, the bars, mezcalerias, restaurants and karaoke spots surrounding the square filled with people socializing late into the night.

Tran Via El Huatulqueño

Guamuchil H; tel. 958/584-7679; US$5.50

This is some nightlife that the kiddos can enjoy. Starting around 7pm, you can board one of these blazing neon buses that will take you on a mini tour through Huatulco. You'll go down through Santa Cruz, out to Tangolunda for photo ops at the Huatulco letters, and back into La Crucecita for some mezcal and chocolate sampling. It's not long, just about an hour, but sitting on top of a double-decker bus, ducking palm branches, and whooping it up is a fun way to end (or begin) the night.

La Papaya

Blvd. Benito Juárez, Bahía Chahué; tel. 958/115-7680; www.lapapayahuatulco.com; 10pm-5am Fri.-Sat.

Huatulco's premiere nightclub, checks all the boxes—hot music, cold drinks, jam-packed dance floor and ... mermaids swimming behind the bar. La Papaya is open every Friday and Saturday night.

Accommodations

A quick cab ride or pleasant half-hour walk from the beach in Santa Cruz, lively little Crucecita has a number of affordable accommodations options perfect for budget travelers, or for those looking for something more traditionally Mexican than the options close to the beach.

1
2
TRANVIA
HUATULQUEÑO
TRANVIA
PASEOS
RECREATIVOS
3
4

Hotel Posada Leo

Bugambilia 302; tel. 958/587-2601; posadaleo_hux@hotmail.com; US$40-54 d

Next to a small canal, you'll find a pair of hotels run by amiable Leonora Carmona. The smaller, more homey of the two, Hotel Posada Leo has six double rooms with air-conditioning, TV, Wi-Fi, and hot water.

Hotel Nonni

Bugambilia 203; tel. 958/587-0372; hotelnonni@gmail.com; US$49-65, US$60-87 d, US$75-108 t

Hotel Nonni has a few more options for larger groups. The rooms are bigger and slightly fancier, and the triple, with one king and two queen beds, sleeps up to six guests. The restaurant **La Chicatana** sits atop the hotel, offering breezy views and tasty eats.

★ Hotel Diamante

Colorín 404; tel. 958/587-2200 or 958/115-2266; www.travelbymexico.com/oaxa/diamante; US$62 d, US$95 t, US$120 suite

Three blocks south of the zócalo, the slender Hotel Diamante is a little odd, but in the best way. The narrowness of the building led to a refreshingly unique interior design: skinny, high-ceilinged rooms that fit up to four king-size beds. The rooms still manage to feel airy with this clever use of limited space. All rooms include air-conditioning, TV, and Wi-Fi, and most have a mini-fridge and coffeemaker. The rooftop pool is similarly unique, with its pyramid-shaped design and pleasant view of La Crucecita.

Information and Services

Medical Services

You can find consultorio services at various Farmacias Similares and Farmacias del Ahorro locations around town. For something more serious, you can go to **Centro Médico Oromed** (Sector L, Lote 13; tel. 958/121-4104; www.oromed.com.mx), which is open 24/7 and equipped to handle emergencies.

Laundry

For efficient self-service, head to **California Laundry Express** (Calle Salina Cruz; tel. 958/688-3012; 8am-10pm daily; US$7.50), where you can wash and dry your clothes in about an hour and a half. While you wait, get a bite to eat at Tacos D'Arbol on the corner.

Getting There

Air

The small size of the **Huatulco Airport** (Aeropuerto Internacional Bahías de Huatulco, HUX; tel. 958/581-9004) makes it easy to get in and out, and the white stucco terminals topped with thatched palapa-style roofs will get you in the coastal mood the minute you arrive.

Highway 200 connects the airport with the major destinations along the coast. The airport is located about 18 km (11 mi) west of La Crucecita, only a 15-minute drive. The popular surfing destination Barra de la Cruz, 40 km (25 mi) east, is a 45-minute drive down the coast. To Puerto Ángel, 38 km (24 mi) to the west, the drive takes about 50 minutes. Puerto Escondido, 100 km (62 mi) west, is about two hours down the highway.

Mexican airlines **Interjet** (toll-free US tel. 866/285-9525; www.interjet.com) and **Volaris** (tel. 551/102-8000, toll-free US tel. 855/865-2747; www.volaris.com) both run daily flights that connect Huatulco to various US destinations via Mexico City. Canadian airlines **Air Canada** (toll-free US/Can. tel. 888/247-2262; www.aircanada.com) and **West Jet** (toll-free US tel. 888/937-8538, toll-free Can. tel. 888/937-8538, toll-free Mex. tel. 855/269-2979; www.westjet.com) both have direct flights between Huatulco and Toronto, and connect Huatulco to many Canadian and US cities.

Aeromexico (tel. 555/133-4000; www.aeromexico.com) runs two daily flights between Huatulco and Mexico City, and, along with Interjet and Volaris, connect Huatulco to other major cities in Mexico. To fly within

1: street in La Crucecita **2:** Tran Via El Huatulqueño **3:** La Casa del Alebrije **4:** enfrijoladas at La Chicatana at Hotel Nonni

Oaxaca, book a flight with **Aerotucán** (tel. 951/502-0840, toll-free Mex. tel. 800/640-4148; www.aerotucan.com), whose fleet of small Cessna planes have air taxi privileges, making the company very flexible with scheduling.

For money matters, there is a **casa de cambio** in the arrivals hallway, as you leave baggage claim. If you need to change money upon arrival, make sure to do it before you exit the hallway to the parking lot, as you will not be allowed to reenter. To withdraw money, exit the arrivals palapa and turn right to head to the ticketing building, where you'll find **ATMs** for Banamex, Santander, and Bancomer.

A small, open-air **food court** between the departures and ticketing palapas serves burgers, sandwiches, and other food, as well as coffee and alcoholic drinks.

Taxis from the **official taxi stand** outside the arrivals terminal charge around US$32 to get to La Crucecita, but you'll be charged about half that if you walk the 450 m (1,500 ft) out to the highway and get a cab from **Sitio Fraccionamiento El Zapote** (tel. 958/589-3337 or 958/587-8126; info@taxihuatulco.com), which has an official stop in front of the gas station across the highway from the airport road. To save even more, flag down an eastbound **taxi colectivo** or **urbano** at this spot on the highway. These modes of transport only charge around US$2 to La Crucecita from here.

Bus

The **Terminal ADO** (Blvd. Chahué; tel. 958/108-6041; www.ado.com.mx) is on Boulevard Chahué, just north of downtown Crucecita. ADO routes connect Huatulco to Oaxaca City (5.5 hrs; US$25) and Puerto Escondido (2.5 hrs; US$11-17). Heading east, ADO buses go to Salina Cruz (2.5 hrs; US$17), Tehuantepec (3.5 hrs; US$18), Juchitán (4 hrs; US$20-24), and San Cristóbal de la Casas, Chiapas (11 hrs; US$51-55).

From Pochutla, the urbanos of **Transportes Rápidos de Pochutla** (across from Líneas Unidas on Lázaro Cárdenas, Pochutla; tel. 958/584-0159) only cost about US$3.50 for the speedy trip to La Crucecita, which takes just under an hour. Buses leave every 10 minutes 5am-8:30pm daily. The terminus in La Crucecita is the **Central Camionera** on Calle Carpinteros, northwest of the ADO station.

Car

Coastal Highway 200 connects Huatulco to the rest of the Oaxacan coast and beyond. To the west of Huatulco, the crucero (crossroads) with Highway 175 is about 42 km (26 mi) from La Crucecita through tight switchbacks in the tropical foothills; it's a 45-minute drive. From this junction, Puerto Ángel is 10 km (6.2 mi) south on Highway 175. Total drive time to Puerto Ángel is just over an hour. Puerto Escondido is another 72 km (45 mi) west down Highway 200 from the junction, two hours from La Crucecita.

If you're coming from San José del Pacífico (124 km/77 mi; 3 hrs), it's faster to take the El Zapote-Copalita Highway through Santa María Huatulco. The junction with Highway 175 is 62 km (38 mi) south of San José. From here, follow the highway 44 km (27 mi) to the junction with Highway 200. La Crucecita is 16 km (10 mi) east down Highway 200.

From Oaxaca City, take the Barranca Larga-Ventanilla Highway down to the coast and Highway 200 east to Huatulco.

You can rent a car in the airport terminal at **Alamo** (arrivals terminal; tel. 958/581-9134 or 951/160-3057; 8am-6pm; US$52-130 per day), but you'll save money by renting from local company **Los Tres Reyes** (next to gas station across the highway from airport road; tel. 958/109-8147 or 958/105-1376; www.losreyescarrent.com; 7am-8pm daily; US$42-105 per day). If you rent ahead of time, they can come into the airport to meet you with your rental.

SANTA CRUZ

Sights

Capilla de la Santa Cruz

The lazy waves of Playa Santa Cruz softly splash the foundation of the Capilla de la Santa Cruz (Chapel of the Holy Cross of Huatulco) all day long. This open-air chapel is dedicated to venerating Huatulco's piece of the mysterious, indestructible cross put on this beach by a mysterious, bearded man in a white robe some 2,000 years ago. The chapel is closed in the evenings, but you can always sneak a peek, since it has no walls.

Mirador El Faro

On your way to Playa La Entrega, stop at the Mirador El Faro (Lighthouse Lookout) to get a spectacular view of the coastline in both directions and the open sea to the south. If the waves are right, you should be able to see (and hear) **El Bufadero,** a rock formation that causes water to shoot up 10 m (33 ft) or more into the air. It's called El Bufadero, or The Snorter, because it makes a loud sound like someone raucously snorting. Ask your taxi driver to make a stop at the lookout. If you're in a car, keep an eye out for the lighthouse about 3 km (2 mi) after turning off Boulevard Benito Juárez west of Santa Cruz.

Hagia Sofia

Mitla 402-7; tel. 958/583-7943; www.hagiasofiahuatulco.com; 9am-2pm and 4pm-7pm Mon.-Sat.; US$85

The office of agro-ecological reserve Hagia Sofia is in central Santa Cruz, but all the adventure is out in the tropical foothills of the Sierra Madre del Sur, about 35 km (22 mi) northwest of Santa Cruz. On 130 hectares (320 acres) ranging 260-309 m (850-1,000 ft) above sea level, the reserve is the perfect venue to observe the wide spectrum of Oaxaca's polychromatic flora. You can choose between a flower tour or a zip line tour. Whatever your choice, you'll also see rainbows of butterfly and bird species as you hike out to a small waterfall for a swim. Their daylong tours include transportation, breakfast, and lunch, and cost around US$85 (children under 4 are free; kids 5-9 pay half).

Mercado Organico de Huatulco (M.O.H.)

Parque Santa Cruz; tel. 958/585-4145 or 958/107-1067; 8am-2pm Sat. (1st and 3rd Sat. May-Oct.)

Every Saturday is Santa Cruz's market day, but it's really more than a market. It's a weekly community gathering, a celebration of the bounty of the coastal region. Vendors come from neighboring coastal communities and mountain towns to sell the best of their organic produce, herbs, flowers, and more. Grab an exotic ice cream like yaca (jackfruit) or maracuya (passionfruit) as you stroll among the vendors selling crystals, copal, traditional medicines, handmade toys, and art, all while live music fills the air with a lively beat.

Beaches

Playa Santa Cruz

The pint-sized waves of Playa Santa Cruz rarely get more than ankle-high. A dock jutting over 300 m (984 ft) into the bay at the beach's east end separates the public beach from the small marina on the other side. Palapa restaurants line the beach, with the exception of the spot occupied by the chapel, providing shade, seafood, and cold beer and coconuts for tourists and local families alike. The beach is near the center of Santa Cruz Huatulco.

★ Playa La Entrega

Just south of Santa Cruz, Playa La Entrega is a miniature paradise of still turquoise waters, with a small dock on one end and palapas and snorkel equipment rental shacks along the short strip of sand. Reefs just 70 m (230 ft) from the beach offer lots of opportunities to see tropical fish and other coral-dwelling sea life. History buffs will be interested to know that this is the location of Mexico's Afro-Mexican president Vicente Guerrero's betrayal (La Entrega means "the delivery"—this is where he was delivered to his enemies). A statue at the entrance of La Entrega honors his memory. To get to La Entrega, follow Boulevard Benito Juárez west past Santa Cruz. You'll quickly see the sign to turn left to La Entrega.

★ Playa Maguey

Playa Maguey is within the boundaries of Parque Nacional Huatulco. Playa Maguey has a plethora of palapa restaurants to choose from, and snorkel shacks to rent fun beach gear from (my kids love renting the giant inflatables). Maguey's golden sand and gentle waves make it an ideal place to swim. To get to Playa Maguey, take Benito Juárez west, staying to the right, rather than turning left to get to La Entrega. It's easiest to just take a taxi.

Snorkeling and Scuba Diving

Renta de Snorkel Vicente Garganta de Lata

Playa La Entrega; tel. 958/106-5211; vicente_gargantadelata@hotmail.com; 8am-6pm daily; US$7

For snorkeling, head to Playa La Entrega. In a palapa at the end of the beach opposite the dock, you'll find Renta de Snorkel Vicente Garganta de Lata. They charge about US$7 for goggles, snorkel, and fins, and have lockers to stow your valuables while you snorkel around the reefs.

Huatulco Watersports

next to Pemex gas station at the end of Calle Tehuantepec; tel. 958/125-8666; www.huatulcowatersports.com; 8am-6pm daily; US$188

Huatulco Watersports' three-hour snorkeling tour visits four bays and includes hotel pickup and all the equipment.

Hurricane Divers

Playa Santa Cruz; tel. 958/587-1107; www.hurricanedivers.com; 8am-4pm Mon.-Fri., 8am-noon Sat.

In the shopping center by the beach in Santa Cruz, you'll find the offices of Hurricane Divers, a very well-respected dive center that offers everything from fun dives to all levels of PADI certifications. Check the website for prices and booking.

Surfing and Stand-Up Paddleboarding

The calm waters of Santa Cruz are perfect for paddleboarding, and there is good surfing on nearby beaches.

Café Surf

in shopping center next to Teatro del Mar; tel. 958/105-1806; www.huatulcosurftrip.com; 9am-5pm Mon.-Sat. (6am-5pm Oct.-May)

Café Surf rents equipment and offers lessons and tours, but they specialize in fully planned surfing trips that include two lessons a day, English-speaking instructors, all necessary transportation, and accommodations in the Ocean Park Condos in the same building as the office.

Fishing and Boat Tours

Atardecer Huatulco

Calle Mitla; tel. 958/688-1890

Just to the west of the central square in Santa Cruz, Atardecer Huatulco operates sportfishing and boat tours that include snorkeling and take you to many of Huatulco's beaches, as well as sights like El Bufadero. Contact them directly for pricing.

Spas and Temazcal

Temazcal Na-Há Maya

Vialidad 14; tel. 958/587-2179; www.nahamaya.com; 7am-10:30pm daily; massages US$30-65

Hidden away on a little corner street on the west side of the big intersection of Boulevards Juárez and Chahué, just east of Santa Cruz, Temazcal Na-Há Maya offers 30-90-minute massages for US$30-65, as well as temazcal (from US$33) and various packages that include aromatherapy, hydrotherapy, music therapy, and more.

Bars and Nightlife

Sugar Disco Friendly

Mitla 304, Bahía Santa Cruz; tel. 958/101-0332

Queer-friendly Sugar is a fun bar where you

1: Capilla de la Santa Cruz **2:** coconut with lime and chile **3:** Playa La Entrega **4:** palapa at Playa Maguey

1

2

can come drink, dance, and enjoy entertaining drag shows and theme nights. Drink specials are plentiful and the vibe is playful.

Food and Accommodations

Doña Celia Lobster House

Playa Santa Cruz; tel. 958/583-4876; www.restaurantdonacelia.com.mx; 8am-11pm daily; US$6-9

Down at the other end of the row of palapas, Doña Celia Lobster House is a great place to try its titular specialty, or a piña rellena (stuffed pineapple), loaded with shrimp, octopus, fish, veggies, and melted manchego cheese.

Hotel Posada Abril

Cerrada de Montealbán; tel. 958/587-2380 or 958/587-2260; www.hoteldabril.com; US$47 d

There isn't a hotel directly on Playa Santa Cruz, but the medium-sized Hotel Posada Abril is just 50 m (165 ft) from it. And there's a pool, in case the walk is too much. All 27 units have air-conditioning, TV, and Wi-Fi access.

Hotel Yuu-Lee Casa Bendita

Mitla 302; tel. 958/118-7347; US$49-87

A five-minute walk from the beach, Hotel Yuu-Lee Casa Bendita has a particular allure to it, especially for mezcal enthusiasts. This small, basic hotel is owned by El Buen Mezcal (whose store is in La Crucecita), and the hotel staff can put you in contact with the owners to arrange a visit to their palenque (distillery) about 30 minutes from Santa Cruz. All rooms have air-conditioning, TV, and Wi-Fi.

Ocean Park Condos

Mitla 402; tel. 958/587-0440 or US tel. 770/658-2113; www.oceanparkcondominiumshuatulco.com; rebeca@propiedadesideal.com; US$155-255 daily, US$1,400-3,500 monthly

Perfect for longer stays, Ocean Park Condos has all the comforts of home, and then some. All units are either studio apartments or full 1-2-bedroom condos, all have kitchenettes and balconies, and most have a washer and dryer. Manager Rebeca Anaya, a polyglot who speaks English, Spanish, and French, lives on the grounds and is available 24/7 to help with anything that may come up for her guests.

Getting Around

Taxis to anywhere in the Bahías de Huatulco (except Bahía San Agustín) won't charge more than US$4 from Santa Cruz. The stand for **Sitio Santa Cruz** (tel. 958/587-0888) is on the east side of Parque Santa Cruz.

EAST SIDE

The bays on Huatulco's east side cater more to luxury travelers. Here you'll find five-star all-inclusive resorts and a golf course, but you'll also find a campground and trailer park, as well as economical activities that will draw you here even if just for the day.

Beaches

Playa Chahué

Playa Chahué is a little less than 400 m (1,300 ft) of brilliant yellow sand with a slight gradation that sometimes causes red-flag swimming conditions. It is home to a few mid- to high-range resorts, beach clubs you can get a day pass for, spas, and a jetty at the east side of the beach separates it from the **Chahué Marina,** where you can dock a boat.

Playa Tangolunda

About 4.5 km (3 mi) east of Playa Chahué, Playa Tangolunda features golden sand that stretches along a curved bay. The water is a beautiful shade of turquoise, crystal clear, and calm, making it ideal for swimming and water activities. It's also a beach of extremes in terms of spending the night. You could do so in the lap of luxury in one of the five-star resorts, or rough it at the **camping** and trailer park area.

Playa La Bocana

Playa La Bocana is just the curled western end of a beach that stretches east to the mouth of the Copalita River and continues for nearly a mile beyond. It's also a "choose your adventure" kind of beach. There is some okay surfing off the rocks at Playa La Bocana; you can rent a board from **Bocana Surf School** (tel. 553/991-4414; US$16/hr), or take a class (US$81/hr). If you'd rather relax and pamper yourself, consider getting a mud treatment (around US$12), offered by the ladies at the entrance of the beach. After being plastered and rubbed down with healing mud from Copalita's riverbanks, rinse off in the waves, and maybe get a bite to eat at one of the restaurants by the entrance. My family's favorite activity is walking 10 minutes down to your left to where the Copalita River meets the sea. It's a beautiful sight and you're almost guaranteed to have the beach all to yourself. You can safely wade on the river side, and there are often half-erected little huts made from pieces of bamboo, driftwood, and palm fronds for some shade. Be sure to keep an eye on the tides though; the way back to the entrance may be a bit wetter. You'll see the turnoff about three minutes after the Secrets resort.

Adventure Sports

Aventura Mundo

Benito Juárez 25-1; tel. 958/581-0197; www.aventuramundo.net; 9am-7pm daily; US$35-125

Aventura Mundo (Adventure World), at the east end of the shopping center in Bahía Tangolunda, has you covered for all your ecotourism and adventure sports desires. The Aventura experience includes bike tours, hiking, ATV excursions, Jet Skis, kayaking, snorkeling, surf lessons, and more.

Horseback Riding

Rancho Caballo de Mar

Blvd. Benito Juárez; tel. 958/131-8137; 9am-5pm daily; US$45-95

Rancho Caballo de Mar runs horseback riding tours from its small ranch on the banks of the Copalita River. Tours trot along shady jungle roads, ford shallow rivers, and take you right out onto the sand of the beach. Owner María is very knowledgeable of local flora and fauna.

Food and Accommodations

Bladu'Yu

Bahía Chahué; tel. 958/109-2459; 8am-11pm daily; US$6-16

With its bright pink walls and eye-catching papel picada, Bladu'Yu provides a festive setting to enjoy the unique flavors of Istmeña cuisine. Typical Oaxacan meals are available, like mole and tlayudas, but you absolutely must try the Istmo dishes, like garnaches and my personal fave, their mouthwatering slow-cooked beef short ribs. The pride the dishes are made with is infused in each tasty bite, and at this price, really can't be beat. You can enjoy the cozy, colorful indoor seating, or catch an ocean breeze outside among palm trees and bougainvillea.

Hotel Villablanca

Benito Juárez 2; tel. 958/587-0606; www.hotelesvillablanca.com; US$73 d, US$90 suites

Gleaming white and centrally located, Hotel Villablanca is just a five-minute walk from Playa Chahué and offers a comfortable base to explore. The courtyard has a pool surrounded with palm trees—and you may catch a glimpse of the iguanas who call these trees their home. Service is always friendly and attentive; the on-site restaurant has delicious food, and there's live music on select nights.

Hotel Quinta Bella

Bahía Chahué; tel. 958/587-2466; www.quintabellahuatulco.com; from US$119 d

Hotel Quinta Bella is a modern, family-oriented resort right on Playa Chahué. Aside from the multiple pools for all guests, most rooms include a small splash pool on their private balcony. Day passes can be purchased for the day, and seven of Huatulco's best restaurants can be enjoyed by guests or others.

Tangolunda Campground and RV Park

Sandwiched between the extravagance of the Quinta Real and the last few holes of the golf course, you'll find the Tangolunda Campground and RV Park, where for around

US$3 per person you can pitch a tent or park an RV. The only services provided are bathrooms and showers; there are no water or electricity hookups for trailers. Camping is allowed on the beach, as well as in the area back behind the swamp. The 50 or so spots are first-come, first-served. If you don't see an attendant, just post up and someone will eventually come to you.

Getting Around

Taxis charge no more than US$4 for travel between these bays, and about US$1 more to get out to the horseback riding ranch. **Colectivo taxis** that zip up and down Benito Juárez will cost US$1 or less along this stretch of the road.

BARRA DE LA CRUZ

The sleepy surfer's paradise of Barra de la Cruz is only a half-hour drive from Tangolunda.

Surfing

The beach's west end curls like a claw out into the Pacific Ocean, and the clusters of igneous boulders on the point form the swells coming from the open ocean into one of the most reliable point breaks on the Oaxacan coast. Once it hits the point, this regular right-hander breaks slowly down the crest of the wave, allowing surfers to cut back and forth on it for a long time before splashing down.

The best time of year to surf in Barra de la Cruz is April-September, when swells are most consistent. The beach is open 7am-8pm daily, and access costs about US$1.50, which you'll be asked to pay at a roadside hut before descending to the beach.

Food and Accommodations

Down on the beach, a small **palapa restaurant** (no tel.; 9am-5pm daily; US$4-7) serves breakfast, seafood and more.

Pizzería El Dragón

San Pedro Huamelula; tel. 958/587-0702; 6pm-midnight daily; US$7.50-14

Up in the town scattered along the road in from the highway, Pizzería El Dragón is owned by former employees of La Crema bar and pizzeria in La Crucecita. La Crema has a long history of providing financial assistance to employees to start their own microenterprises, and El Dragón, along with the cabañas (US$16-41) on the property, is La Crema's flagship project. You'll find it 300 m (1,000 ft) down the dirt road.

Cabañas La Joya

main road, Barra de la Cruz; tel. 958/130-3980; US$8-40

The majority of accommodations in Barra de la Cruz are rustic wood cabins along the main road to the beach. Just down the road, Cabañas La Joya has rooms with a few more creature comforts, like private bathrooms and air-conditioning. But for those who can do without, the property has a camping area.

Surf Barra de la Cruz

Barra de la Cruz; tel. 958/128-6739; www.surfbarradelacruz.com; US$49

Surf Barra de la Cruz touts itself as a "one stop surf shop," and it truly does have everything you need for an amazing surf getaway. Native costeño Odi Barenca has been surfing these waters all his life, and he has created a comfortable place to rest just a five-minute walk from the shore. Each room has its own bathroom and kitchen (there's a restaurant if you don't feel like cooking), a/c, and Wi-Fi connection. Surf classes and camps are available for children and adults.

Getting There

A **private taxi** from Huatulco to Barra de la Cruz will cost about US$25. You can call dispatch at **Sitio La Crucecita** (tel. 958/587-1616 or 958/144-4092) to schedule a trip, or just hail a taxi on the street. All taxi companies here have the same fares. This is the best option, as they'll take you directly to the cabañas in town.

Alternatively, you could take **colectivos** to get out there. Your best bet is to catch one on Benito Juárez east of the intersection with Boulevard Chahué in Bahía Chahué; some of these go all the way out to Barra de la Cruz. It's possible you'll have to get off on Highway 200 before reaching Barra de la Cruz, in which case you just post up on the side of the road and wait for another to come by. If the colectivo doesn't go into Barra de la Cruz, you'll have to walk or hitch a ride the 2.5 km (1.5 mi) into town. All in all, you shouldn't pay more than US$2-3 for the whole trip.

By **car,** take Boulevard Benito Juárez east from anywhere in Bahías de Huatulco until it terminates at Highway 200. Take Highway 200 east for 14 km (8.7 mi), until you see the turn for Barra de la Cruz. From here, the beach is 4 km (2.5 mi) down the dirt road through town. Total drive time from Tangolunda is about 30-40 minutes.

LAS CASCADAS MÁGICAS AND FINCA LA GLORIA

The Copalita River snakes down from its source high up in the misty mountaintops of the Sierra Madre del Sur through hill after hill of the superabundant tropical vegetation before finally emptying into the Pacific at a very wide beach next to the ruins at Parque Copalita (unfortunately, not open to the public at the time of this writing, but hopefully that will change). Sixteen km (10 mi) inland, at **Las Cascadas Mágicas** (Magic Waterfalls), its contents tumble down a pile of boulders in a magical rush of white water that pools like liquid gemstones in a small clearing in the jungle. A swim in the cool water is exactly what you'll need in the sweltering tropical afternoon, and if you've been lugging a backpack around Oaxaca for a while, your shoulders could definitely use a brisk massage under the falls.

Just over 1 km (0.6 mi) from the Cascadas is **Finca La Gloria Coffee** (Llano Grande; tel. 958/587-0697), where robust arabica beans are grown in the sultry shade of the jungle canopy. Established early on in the coffee industry boom of the 19th century, La Gloria is one of the oldest coffee farms along the coast. Most of the tours from Huatulco to the Cascadas include a coffee tasting here, and you can also just show up and grab a cup of joe.

Getting There

Getting out to the waterfall is not easy, so I recommend taking a tour to do it. The daylong tour run by the bilingual guides at **Descubre Huatulco** (Chacah 210, La Crucecita; tel. 958/119-7325 or 958/587-2195; www.descubrehuatulco.com; 8am-8pm daily) costs about US$45 and includes transportation to and from the falls and a tour of the finca with a coffee production demonstration and tasting. The tour leaves at 10am and gets back to La Crucecita around 4pm.

If you have your own **car,** be aware that the dirt road is deeply rutted in parts and is not recommended (though not impossible) for sedans and other low cars. Take Highway 200 west from La Crucecita about 10 km (6 mi) until you see the sign for the turnoff on the right-hand side of the road. From here, follow the scant signage and trust your best judgment the slow rest of the way. The falls are another 30.5 km (19 mi) into the jungle. The drive takes about 1.5 hours.

Istmo de Tehuantepec

Here at the isthmus, the funnel of mainland Mexico thins out to just over 214 km (133 mi). Sparsely populated, misty mountains cover the north of Oaxaca's chunk of it, but most folks live in the windswept, semiarid lowlands between these low peaks and the Pacific coast. Natural springs dot the dusty landscape, crystalline oases in this sporadically soaked region, which experiences freak droughts even when the rest of the state is getting drenched.

Meanwhile, the citizens of El Istmo are as renowned for their indomitable spirit and energy for the fiesta as they are for those captivatingly colorful embroidery styles. These people know how to party. They even have their own word for it: *vela*. A typical vela in Tehuantepec or Juchitán is three nonstop days and nights of drinking, eating, and dancing to the regional musical style known as el son istmeño. Even the preparations—as early as six months before the fiesta—are turned into celebrations. Add the calendar of velas to that of the national and statewide festivities, and your chances of catching a raucous party are pretty good no matter what time of year you come.

Orientation

In Oaxaca's southeastern corner, bordering Chiapas to the east, Veracruz to the north, and the La Costa (the coast), is Istmo de Tehuantepec, one of Oaxaca's eight regions.

Two and a half hours northeast of Huatulco (165 km/103 mi) is one of Oaxaca's largest cities, Salina Cruz. A major, bustling port town, it lies right on the Pacific Ocean and is just west of the mouth of Rio Tehuantepec. Salina Cruz's surfing beaches and its resorts lie southwest of the city.

Just 25 minutes north of Salina Cruz (18 km/11 mi) is Tehuantepec. Tehuantepec is bisected by the Rio Tehuantepec, with its Centro laying on the eastern side.

Juchitán, the largest city of Istmo, is 30 minutes (27 km/17 mi) northeast of Tehuantepec. It lies on the Rio Juchitán.

TEHUANTEPEC

Citizens of Tehuantepec will tell you, rather haughtily, that their city is the cuna, or birthplace, of all that is considered Istmeño culture today. Whether or not these proprietary claims to tradition are historically accurate, Tehuantepec is currently the best place to experience and learn about the history, art, customs, and gastronomy of this unique region of Oaxaca.

Although it may not be as rebellious today as it has been in the past, Tehuantepec is still a raucous firecracker of a town—one that knows how to party. A sense of mystery pervades the crumbling colonial buildings of the Centro, with its defunct railroad tracks and rich history hidden behind bustling market stalls. What you'll find, however, are friendly locals, delicious meals, and a festive spirit that refuses to quit.

Sights

Monumento a la Mujer Tehuana

On a highway median to the west of the Centro, the Monumento a la Mujer Tehuana stands 7 m (23 ft) tall and overlooks the broad banks of the Río Tehuantepec, welcoming visitors to town as they cross the bridge. Installed in 2008 by Mexico City artist Miguel Hernández Urbán and endearingly referred to as **La Tehuana** (the woman from Tehuantepec), the stainless steel statue depicts a woman in the traditional Tehuantepec gala dress, the fanciest and most elaborate of the region's many styles of embroidered dresses. Urban, who died in 2017, built the statue to honor the courage of the women of Tehuantepec, who have always fought alongside the men to defend their homes and customs during various incursions, rebellions, and other conflicts here.

Tehuantepec

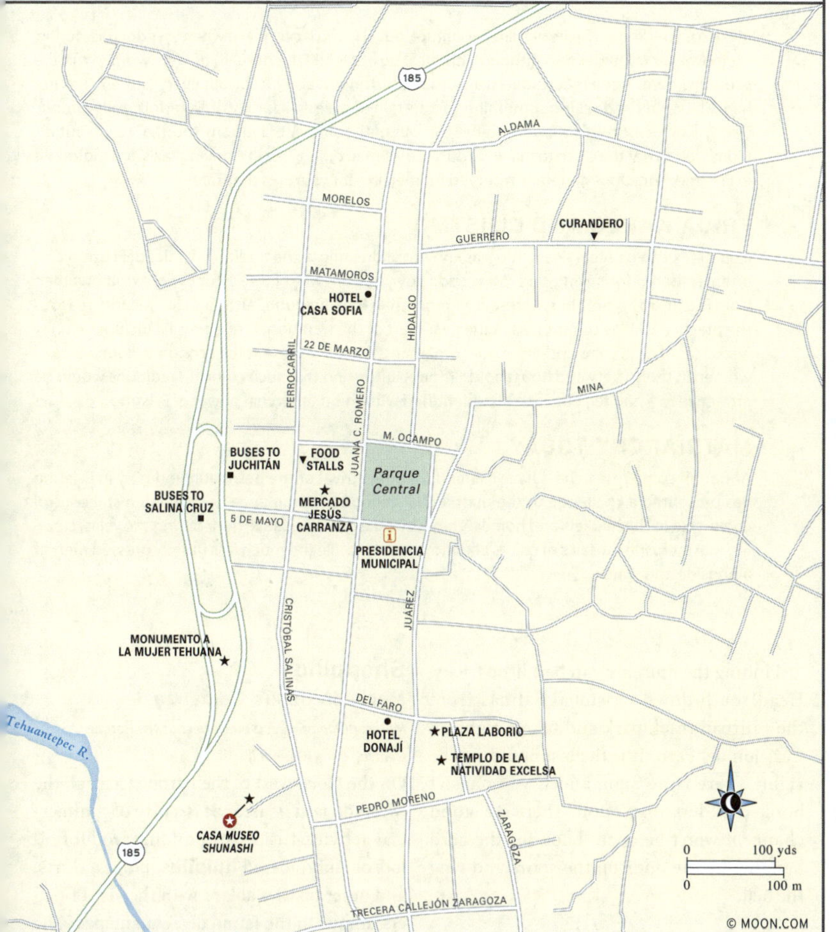

★ Casa Museo Shunashi

Callejón del Faro 1; tel. 971/161-1425 or 971/185-0222; noon-5pm daily; admission by donation, US$8-13 recommended

The gorgeous riverside home of ex-mayor José Manuel Villalobos and family is also the Casa Museo Shunashi, the perfect place to learn about the culture and food unique to the Istmo. The whitewashed 17th-century house is as sturdy as it is pretty, having withstood who knows how many quakes since it was built. It's also full of artifacts from the colonial period, including a pair of ancient wooden looms.

Showing up unannounced is not recommended. If you can book at least a week in advance, a whole show can be arranged with dancers in traditional dresses, a meal of regional foods, historical presentations, and more. For groups of 12 or more, the price should come out to around US$25 per person. No English is spoken.

Matriarchy in El Istmo

Mexico is well known for its patriarchal culture, but El Istmo is one place where gender roles follow their own set of guidelines. Although political power is still the domain of men, women run the economy here. Trade is considered a woman's birthright, and just about every istmeña has her hand in buying and selling something to a certain degree. In a family of fisherfolk, for example, Dad will be responsible for getting the fish out of the saltwater lagoons south of town, but it's Mom's job to get the catch to market. You'll see women doing jobs like driving taxis and mototaxis in El Istmo, vocations generally reserved for men in other parts of the state.

FRIDA KAHLO AND EL ISTMO

Iconic Mexican painter Frida Kahlo was known for dressing in the traditional trajes of El Istmo. She is remembered for having said "Mi vestido soy yo" (I am what I wear); for Frida, as with women from El Istmo, the clothing represented more than looking good. Although for security reasons the practice isn't as common as in the past, part of the traditional traje de gala includes clunky necklaces of gold coins and other gold ornaments, which represent the economic dominance of women in the society and households. It's not surprising that such colorful traditions would be attractive to a painter, but Frida also identified with this matriarchal power of El Istmo.

MATRIARCHY TODAY

Although some researchers have claimed that the arrival of the petroleum industry in El Istmo has presented a challenge to the matriarchal economic dominance here, women still control commerce in the markets and homes. They also take over the dance floor during the velas, creating mesmerizing mosaics of colors and movements, while the much less flashily dressed men sit alongside and watch.

Finding the museum can be a little tricky. Head south down Cristóbal Salinas from the railroad track park and take a right on Callejón del Faro. It is the last house on the right. There is no sign, and if you haven't booked a demonstration, there's a good chance it won't be open. Look for the cord hanging by the door up the stairs and ring the bell.

Plaza Laborio and Templo de la Natividad Excelsa

The pint-size Plaza Laborio and adjacent Templo de la Natividad Excelsa were damaged by the devastating 2017 quake, but repairs were made, and a new wooden playground for the kids was installed in the plaza. You'll find the church two blocks south of the main square, down Calle Juárez. You'll see the park on your left, and the church facade is on the next block to the east, on Calle Porfirio Díaz.

Shopping

Mercado Jesús Carranza

Melchor Ocampo 22, a block west of the Parque Central; 6am-10pm daily

On the block west of the Parque Central, the Mercado Jesús Carranza is a hive of commercial activity. Inside the building, you'll find lots of embroidered **huipiles,** purses, skirts, and other textiles ablaze with the vivid flowers unique to the Istmo de Tehuantepec. The only prepared food inside is from a couple of juice bars and refresquerías, little snack bars serving mostly tortas (Mexican sandwiches).

The alley on the west side of the market has more food stalls. Don't leave Tehuantepec without eating **garnachas** here. It's no surprise that the market building isn't big enough to hold all the commerce of Tehuantepec's

1: La Tehuana statue by artist Miguel Hernández Urbán **2:** dresses at Mercado Jesús Carranza **3:** Templo de la Natividad Excelsa **4:** Casa Museo Shunashi

1

2

Third Gender: The Muxes of El Istmo

Muxe (MOO-sheh) is a nonbinary gender fully accepted in the culture and society of El Istmo.

Muxes are men raised as females who follow the rigid gender norms that govern economic life in El Istmo. Much of the literature about muxes claims that they choose the identity themselves at an early age, but the choice is usually made by the parents, who assign the role to their firstborn son. Muxes are expected to care for their aging parents later in life. Many, but not all, consider the role to be a great honor. Others view it more as a burden than a privilege, a life they never asked for.

Still, the majority of muxes enjoy an esteemed social position in Istmeño society, and other big life choices are theirs to make, such as who to love and marry. Some muxes partner with men and play the female role in the household, while others marry women and raise children with them.

It is not as common, but some women also take on this gender role reversal. Called marimachas, they take on traditionally male attributes and mannerisms in both social and private life, and are accepted in Istmeño society.

enterprising citizenry. The callejón (alleyway) to the north is covered with tarps, under which vendors sell everything from housewares to huipiles to fresh ground coffee from the Sierra Mixe, the part of the Sierra Norte closest to El Istmo.

Food and Accommodations

Your first meal should be garnachas at one of the **food stalls** in the alley on the west side of the Mercado Jesús Carranza. The little tortillas are fried perfectly, giving them the flavor and texture distinct to this Istmeño specialty.

Curandero

Guerrero 19; tel. 971/137-4173; noon-8pm daily; US$6.50-10

Curandero functions as a breezy, stylish restaurant by day and a hip, fully stocked bar at night. The restaurant-bar is in the courtyard of a 200-year-old home and has murals by local artists. The food is a bit hipper than the traditional stuff in the market. Try the delicious, healthy fish tacos.

Hotel Casa Sofia

Romero 20; tel. 971/713-7747; US$32.50 d

Two blocks north of the main square, Hotel Casa Sofia enchants with its gold columns and white-walled hallways trimmed with the radiant floral patterns distinct to Tehuantepec. The 15 rooms themselves aren't as colorful, but they are comfortable, albeit a bit quirky—the walls facing the hallway aren't walls, but rather floor-to-ceiling windows and glass doors that make up the side of the room facing the hallway (there are curtains). The air-conditioning in the rooms is necessary, as they can get stuffy without it. The Internet works well, and credit cards are accepted.

Hotel Donají

Josefa Ortíz de Domínguez 10; tel. 971/715-0064; US$38 d

The rooms at Hotel Donají might be insufficiently lit, but the natural light filling the covered central courtyard makes up for it. Strands of green ivy hang from the mezzanine, over the restaurant (Café Yizu; 8am-11pm daily; US$5) that serves delicious Mexican staples. Book early if you're coming for a vela, as it fills up quickly due to its central location.

Information and Services

For tourist information, head to the **presidencia municipal** (Cinco de Mayo; no tel.; 9am-6pm Mon.-Fri.). There is no official information office, but the friendly staff will be available to help.

The **Hospital General de Tehuantepec** (Calle Universitario; tel. 971/715-0197; 24 hrs

Garnachas: An Istmeño Specialty

Just when you think Mexico has done everything there is to do with corn tortillas, you visit El Istmo and find more nuance in the country's vast gastronomic canon referred to as antojitos, or snack foods. Like tostadas, sopes, huaraches, and tacos, **garnachas** are a tortilla-based antojito topped with meat and a garnish, but the subtle differences create flavors and textures wholly distinct from those of the others.

The main difference is in the preparation of the tortilla itself. Garnachas use small, stout corn tortillas, usually thicker than taco tortillas, and instead of being heated in an oven or on a comal (traditional ceramic griddle), they are lightly fried in oil, which gives them a crunchy texture while still conserving the malleable nature of the tortilla. The meat commonly used is either a dry, shredded beef or something like picadillo (ground beef with diced potatoes). The garnish is a vinegary coleslaw made from cabbage that adds a delightful tang to the spice of the salsa.

daily) has doctors on call around the clock in case of emergencies. No English is spoken.

Getting There

Bus

For travel within El Istmo, board one of the rickety buses that stop at the **bus stop on the median** in Highway 185 just to the west of the Centro. Northbound buses get you to Juchitán in about a half hour and cost a little over US$1. The southbound ones go to Salina Cruz. They take a little bit longer and cost a few more pesos. Buses leave every 15-20 minutes.

For longer distances, head to the **Terminal ADO** on the highway north of the Centro. Take a taxi there for about US$2. Since Tehuantepec is a major stop on the route between Oaxaca City and the neighboring state of Chiapas, buses run frequently. Buses from Oaxaca City (US$15.50-22) leave from the main ADO station (Cinco de Mayo 900, Barrio de Jalatlaco, Oaxaca City; tel. 951/502-0560) on Highway 190 and take a little under five hours. To the east, in the state of Chiapas, the ADO routes run to San Cristóbal de las Casas (US$30-39; 7 hrs).

Car

Drivers from Oaxaca City head east on Highway 190. In about an hour, just before Mitla, stay on Highway 190 by taking the turnoff to Tehuantepec. You'll wind 251 km (156 mi) through the dry, scenic hill country for about 3.5 hours. If you're coming from the coast, take Highway 200 east to Salina Cruz. From here, head north on Highway 185 to Tehuantepec. The 18-km (11-mi) trip from Salina Cruz takes about a half hour. As with highways anywhere in Mexico, keep your long-distance driving confined to daylight hours.

Getting Around

Everything to see in Tehuantepec is in the cluster of downtown blocks around the main square. All the sights listed here are within easy walking distance of the square. To save a little time and effort, hop on one of the town's unique **motocarros.** Similar to the mototaxis found elsewhere in the state, these souped-up flatbed tricycles will putt-putt you anywhere around the Centro for US$2 or less.

JUCHITÁN AND VICINITY

Juchitán (hoo-chee-TAHN) means "Place of Flowers" in Nahuatl, which seems fitting given the big, bright blooms embroidered on the **huipiles** made here and elsewhere in the Istmo (though folks from Tehuantepec will tell you they thought of them first and Juchitán copied them). The two cities have historically had a rivalry fueled by claims to cultural and political power, one that at times has escalated to violence. Despite who started which tradition, Istmeño culture, music, art, and party ethic are just as vibrant here as they are in Tehuantepec, and bustling, business-oriented Juchitán is an excellent place to experience them.

Sights

Parque Benito Juárez

In Juchitán's main square, Parque Benito Juárez, you'll see a bust of Benito Juárez on the park's east side, and one of his wife, Margarita Maza, on the opposite (west) side of the plaza. On the north side, a statue of Juárez and a majestic eagle honor an 1866 battle hard fought against the French. For a snack unique to Juchitán, head to the plaza's east side when the market closes, around 6pm. Here women sell the pre-Hispanic drink bupu ("foam" in Zapotec), a super-sweet and frothy corn-based beverage flavored with chocolate.

Parque Charis

Gómez 10; 24 hours daily

Juchitán's oldest park and originally the town's zócalo, this charming little plaza is a great place to grab an ice cream or a snack in the evening, admire the beautiful murals, and, if you have kids, let them run around and play on the geometric climbing structure.

Festivals and Events

Fiestas de Mayo

April-May

The main vela season is in May, during the Fiestas de Mayo, with the first velas beginning at the end of April. There are also important velas in September and January.

Shopping

Mercado 5 de Septiembre

16 de Septiembre, just east of Parque Benito Juárez; no tel.; 8am-8pm daily

The Mercado 5 de Septiembre is a labyrinth of steamy food stalls; tunnels of vivid, kaleidoscopic textiles; vendors of housewares; and pungent, meat-strung aisles of the carniceros (butchers). From fresh produce and seafood to tacos to **garnachas,** the best of Juchitán's gastronomic offerings are here.

Food

Mariscos Toñita

5 de Septiembre 123; no tel.; 8am-6pm daily; US$5.50-11

Try a coctel de mariscos (seafood cocktail) at a little stall called Mariscos Toñita. Toñita prepares her delicious cocktails differently than they're made elsewhere in the state, with more lime juice and less ketchup. Now, don't get confused—despite the market's name being Mercado 5 de Septiembre, it is not on the street called 5 de Septiembre, and this seafood stall is not in the market. The stall is six blocks north of the Parque Benito Juárez on Calle 5 de Septiembre, which runs along the park's west side.

★ La Tequita

Ruiz 181; tel. 971/170-6376; 10:30am-5:30pm daily; US$7-11

Due to its proximity to the fishing villages on the lagoons, Juchitán is renowned for its fish dishes, the best of which are at La Tequita; the specialty is pescado al horno (oven-baked fish). The palapa-style restaurant gets pretty lively at lunchtime, when folks chow down on robalo (fried sea bass) and camarones a la diabla (devilishly spicy shrimp). The fruits of the sea are not considered a dinner meal in this part of the world, and seafood restaurants close even earlier here than on the coast. Be sure you get there for lunch at the latest.

Accommodations

Hotel Central

Gómez 30; tel. 971/712-2019; www.hotelcentral.com.mx; US$33 d, US$45 t

Just down the street from the Parque Benito Juárez, Hotel Central is your best budget option. All 18 rooms include air-conditioning, TVs, and Wi-Fi, and are spotlessly clean. Staff are friendly and helpful, and there are computers with Internet connections and printers in the lobby.

1: flor de mayo blooms **2:** fish tacos **3:** Parque Charis

1

2

3

Velas

People from El Istmo are renowned state-wide and around the nation for their ability to celebrate, which is saying something in a country like Mexico. Nightlong parties aren't unique to this part of the country, but nowhere else are they as common as in Juchitán and other Istmeño communities.

In El Istmo, these all-nighters are called velas, most likely a cheeky abbreviation of the word *velada* (evening party). These fiestas, however, are much more than social evenings. Velas are scheduled to last all through the night, for multiple nights in a row. When the dishes from one have been washed and put back in the cupboard, it's usually time to start another.

ORGANIZING THE VELAS

The velas are generally organized by occupational or social guilds called gremios. So one will be thrown by the fisherfolk, the next by firework manufacturers, then muxes, and so on. Velas often honor a patron saint of a particular barrio (district). Like parties elsewhere in Oaxaca, velas are overseen by mayordomos, a couple in charge of the festivities, and it is customary for guests to bring an offering to the couple. Men bring a case of beer, and women give botanas (snacks) and a monetary offering (US$5-10 recommended) to the female host.

MAIN EVENTS

As on a good journey, much of the fun is had en route to the party. Preparations, such as making the tamales and candles for the shindig, are festive, social events. Main events include the mesmerizing dances of women in their colorful trajes de gala; raucous parades with floats and processions of horsemen and bulls; and, of course, a mass for the patron saint. Even the cleanup on the final day has been turned into a party, the main dance of which is called lavada de ollas (cleaning of the pots). Some of the events are public, some are private, and some are a mix of both. Some events are in homes, and some are in the street.

TRADITIONAL MUSIC

Essential to the velas is the **son istmeño,** or traditional music played for the dances. The unofficial anthem of El Istmo is "La Zandunga," a song penned by musician Máximo Ramón Ortíz, the onetime governor of the unofficial (depending on whom you ask) sovereign state of El Istmo de Tehuantepec when it attempted to secede from the state of Oaxaca in the mid-19th century.

★ Hotel Santa Cruz

Carretera Transístmica, km 818; tel. 971/712-1326 or 971/712-0707; hotelsantacruzjuchitan.com; reservaciones@hotelsantacruzjuchitan.com; US$61 d

Hotel Santa Cruz is the most comfortable accommodation option in Juchitán. All rooms have air-conditioning units, TVs, private bathrooms, and coffee makers for that morning jolt. My kids were big fans of the swimming pool, and my husband and I were big fans of the on-site restaurant. The hotel offers guidance to help guests navigate velas and other of Juchitán's must-see points of interest.

Information and Services

For medical emergencies, head to **Clínica Hospital Sinaí** (16 de Septiembre 87; tel. 971/711-1342; 24 hrs daily), five blocks north of the main square. No English is spoken.

Getting There

Bus

The **Terminal ADO** (16 de Septiembre, tel. 971/711-1022) connects Juchitán to Oaxaca City (US$23-32), a 5.5-hour trip. Buses coming and going run all night long, so this is a good option for night bus travelers. Leave at midnight or later, and wake up in Juchitán. Buses from Oaxaca City leave from the main **ADO station** on Highway 190. ADO buses will also get you here from Tehuantepec (US$6; 30 minutes), Salina Cruz (US$7; 1.25

hrs), Huatulco (US$20; 4 hrs), and Puerto Escondido (US$32-41; 6.5 hrs). If you're continuing on to Chiapas, San Cristóbal de las Casas (US$30-43) is six hours away.

For traveling within the Istmo, it's cheaper and easier to take the local buses run by **Autotransportes Istmeños** (16 de Septiembre 5; tel. 971/711-4300), which leave from the corner of 16 de Septiembre and Callejón Angélica Pipi every five minutes or so. The trip to Tehuantepec takes half an hour and costs about US$2.50. The fare to Salina Cruz, a little over an hour away, costs about US$3. Buses run 4:30am-10pm daily.

Car

From Tehuantepec, head north from the statue La Tehuana and stay on Highway 185. Juchitán is a straight shot 28 km (17 mi) across the tropical plain, about half an hour away from Tehuantepec.

Getting Around

If your feet get too tired to carry you around town any longer, you'll have no problem hailing a **mototaxi** on the street. It shouldn't cost you more than US$2.50 to get anywhere you need to go in town.

SALINA CRUZ

Oaxaca's third-largest city, Salina Cruz is home to a large oil refinery, and despite the pollution, the beaches around Salina Cruz boast some of the best surfing on Mexico's Pacific coast. The locally owned surf camps provide the best accommodation options in the area, and their guides can show you where all the good waves are.

When you're not riding the waves, you can admire the otherworldly effect of the strong winds on the dunes—they blow the soft sand up and over the crests in ghost-like strands—and on the patches of rocks that look like they'd fit right in on Mars. But if you're not a surfer and want to do some beach lounging, swimming, and exploring, any of the other destinations along the coast will suit you better.

Beaches

Playa La Ventosa

The winds of Playa La Ventosa (Windy Beach) promise adventure for kite surfers looking to catch some air. The gusty conditions are caused by the Venturi effect, the same amplifying effect that occurs between two buildings on a windy day. The mountains on either side of El Istmo funnel the strong Atlantic winds from the north, increasing their speed on their way out over the Pacific. Most of the year, wind speeds here average 20 to 35 knots (23-40 mph), but they calm down a little bit between August and October.

Surfing

The rugged coastline between Salina Cruz and Huatulco, 100 km (62 mi) to the west, is home to over two dozen surf spots, among which surfers of all skill sets will find the perfect wave to ride. From powerful point and beach breaks to jetty and other natural wedge waves, this stretch of coast is basically a buffet for surfers. A number of well-established surf camps offer all-inclusive tours that maximize your time in the water. Most of the spots are on undeveloped shoreline only accessible via 4x4 vehicles, and the surf camps provide the best accommodations in and around Salina Cruz; if you're coming here, this is the way to do it. The surf season runs April-October.

Las Palmeras Surf Camp

Playa Brasil; US tel. 831/588-1306; www.surflaspalmeras.com; josh@mulcoytravel.com; US$175-200

You'll find the most accumulated experience at Las Palmeras Surf Camp, where David Ramírez has been surfing these waves his whole life and leading tours here since 1992. David's deep knowledge of the local spots is enhanced by the experience of the camp's resident pro, Josh Mulcoy, who has spent over two decades traveling the globe in search of waves.

Las Palmeras offers 5- to 10-night packages starting at US$1,150, depending on the size of your group. For stays shorter than five days, the nightly rate is US$220-240. These prices include food, accommodations in the camp's four-star beach hotel, guides, and transportation to the surf spots. Airfare and transportation to and from the airport are not included. David and his crew can arrange airport pickup from Huatulco in a car (US$190, up to three people) or an SUV (US$290, up to five people). Also not included, but enticing, are the optional cooking and dance classes led by camp manager and native of Tehuantepec Karla Gutiérrez.

Salina Cruz Surf Camp

Calle Monte Bello; tel. 971/107-0918, US tel. 714/916-9663; www.salinacruzsurfcamp.com; surfingmexico@me.com; from US$175 pp

Another well-respected and experienced camp is Salina Cruz Surf Camp, where local surfer César Ramírez and his crew of guides have been taking both amateur and pro riders to the area's best spots since the camp opened in 2000. Like those offered by Las Palmeras, Salina Cruz Surf Camp tours include food, accommodations, and travel to and from surf spots. The nightly rate is slightly cheaper, but here they have a five-night minimum. Nightly rates start at US$175 per person in a group of five, increasing up to US$210 for two-surfer groups. The camp's hotel, Casa El Mirador, is on the hill between Salina Cruz and the beaches to the west, offering stunning views of the bays and port below.

Food

Peso-pinching travelers might want to stick to the food stalls at the **Mercado Ignacio Zaragoza.** One or two inside sell tortas, fresh juices, and licuados (smoothies), but the stalls in the streets on the market's west and south sides serve up delicious garnachas, quesadillas, and other antojitos, as well as hearty shrimp cocktails and other fresh mariscos.

★ La Pasadita

Camacho 603; tel. 971/714-2848; 7am-10pm daily; US$8.50-12

Since you're this close to the ocean, you'll most likely have a hankering for fried fish or some spicy shrimp. Satisfy the craving at La Pasadita. The large, breezy dining area has a casual, family-style feel, with the usual paintings of waterfalls and lilies hung on the avocado-colored walls. They have mountainous seafood parrilladas, hearty and flavorful seafood stews, and tangy ceviches and shrimp cocktails. Portions are large, so make sure to bring your appetite.

Accommodations

If you've come to Salina Cruz, you're really only here for one thing: surfing. You've most likely booked a trip with one of the camps, so take this hotel option as more a contingency plan than a recommendation. Salina Cruz is great for surf trips, but can be dicey for anything else.

Hotel Boutique San Francisco

Camacho 705; tel. 971/714-0796 or 971/720-3052; US$38 d, US$46 king bed

Near the ADO station and catering to traveling business folk, Hotel San Francisco has rooms comfortably decorated with dark-wood furnishings, as well as services like fast, dependable Wi-Fi, TVs, air-conditioning, safes, hair dryers, and more. It's an especially convenient option for those taking an ADO bus, as the station is two blocks away.

Medical Services

The best emergency medical services in town are at the **Hospital General con Especialidades** (Camino a San Antonio Monterrey; tel. 971/281-3232; 24 hrs daily). It is 8 km (5 mi) north of town, up Highway 185. Take a right at the Nissan dealership, and you'll see the hospital about 400 m (0.2 mi) down the road on your left. Taxis in town should know how to get here, but if not, tell the driver about the Nissan dealership. No English is spoken.

Getting There

Bus

For travel within El Istmo, the cheapest option is a bus run by **Autotransportes Istmeños**

(Avenida Tampico; tel. 971/711-1751). Their base is north of the Centro, on Avenida Tampico, just before the road meets up with the highway. There is an Oxxo convenience store next to it. A cab from the center of town will cost you about US$2.50. These buses charge a little over US$1 to Tehuantepec (30 minutes), and a little over US$2 to Juchitán (1 hour). Buses leave every 15-20 minutes.

If you're headed elsewhere in Oaxaca or Mexico, take a bus from the **Terminal ADO** (Primero de Mayo 32; tel. 971/714-1441). Buses to Oaxaca City (US$20-23; 5.5 hrs) leave daily and nightly. Buses leave even more frequently for destinations along the coast. Huatulco (US$17) is a little under 3 hours away, and Puerto Escondido (US$27) is about 5.5 hours away. If you're going to Puerto Ángel or one of the neighboring beaches, you'll have to take a bus to Pochutla (US$21), which takes about 4 hours, and get to the beach from there.

ADO buses will also get you to Chiapas. The trip to San Cristóbal de las Casas (US$40) takes 7-8 hours. These routes also make stops in Tehuantepec (US$3; 30 minutes) and Juchitán (US$5; 1 hour), but the extra comfort makes the trip more expensive than the bouncier, hotter Autotransportes Istmeños buses.

Car

Both highways that lead to Salina Cruz are in very good condition. If you're driving from Oaxaca City, take Highway 190 to Tehuantepec, turn south on Highway 185, and continue for another half hour or so to town. The 266-km (165-mi) drive takes about five hours total. From anywhere along the coast, take Highway 200 (which locals refer to as la costera) east to reach Salina Cruz.

Salina Cruz is 254 km (160 mi) from Puerto Escondido, a four-hour drive. Between Puerto Escondido and Pochutla, Highway 200 is mostly straight, cutting through coastal plains full of papaya and pineapple fields. Between Pochutla and Huatulco, the rough foothills of the Sierra Madre del Sur run all the way to the sea, making the road very curvy. These foothills continue east of Huatulco for a while. The hills then begin to give way to more extensive coastal plains, creating bays bounded by rocky points that crinkle the highway again, in between long, straight stretches of road.

Getting Around

It's best to take a **taxi** for any distances longer than four or five blocks, especially at night. Take taxis to any of the bus stations from the Centro.

La Mixteca

There is something to the blood-red color of the sunsets here that makes you wonder if the Mixtec tale of a warrior piercing the sun with an arrow is more than a myth. La Mixteca (meeks-TEH-kah) is usually presented to the world with a focus on its majestic human achievements, namely the architecture of the Dominican churches and convents. But travel these lands zippered with rough, rocky hills and valleys, and nature's hand might impress you even more.

The towering crags of the Apoala Valley will cause your imagination to run wild with the local legends about the gigantic two-headed eagles that are said to have once haunted these peaks. The colors in the sunset appear in some places to have tie-dyed the earth with their brilliance.

Highlights

Look for ★ to find recommended sights, activities, dining, and lodging.

★ **Apoala:** The spiritual birthplace of the Mixteca, this gorgeous valley is home to soaring cliffs, beguiling rivers, stunning waterfalls, sacred caves, and miles of some of Oaxaca's most scenic hiking trails (page 212).

★ **Templo y Ex-Convento de Santo Domingo Yanhuitlán:** Seated atop a hill, with vaulted ceilings soaring to 25 m (82 ft), this stunning work of architecture will turn your inner and outer gaze heavenward (page 216).

★ **Balneario Atonaltzin:** Sapphire waters from a sulfurous spring invite the weary traveler to soak in beautiful, healing pools (page 218).

★ **Templo y Ex-Convento de San Pedro y San Pablo:** This 16th-century masterpiece of Dominican architecture is the largest capilla abierta (open chapel) in Latin America (page 220).

La Mixteca

PUEBLA
Cosoltepec
Petlalcingo
Tepejillo
Chila
Santiago Ayuquililla
Santa María Camotlán
San Simón Zahuatlán
La Mixteca Baja
Huajuapan de León
Santiago Huajolotitlán
See "Huajuapan de León" Map
San Marcos Arteaga
Santo Domingo Tonalá
CAÑÓN EL BOQUERÓN
Tezoatlán de Segura y Luna
Tamazulapan
BALNEARIO ATONALTZIN
Villa Tejúpam de la Unión
Coixtlahuaca
APOALA
TEMPLO Y EX-CONVENTO DE SANTO DOMINGO YANHUITLÁN
San Agustín Atenango
Villa de Chilapa de Díaz
El Fortín Alto
Yucunama
Yanhuitlán
Santiago Amatlán
Ixpantepec Nieves
Teposcolula
See "Teposcolula" Map
Santiago Yolomécatl
See "Nochixtlán" Map
Nochixtlán
TEMPLO Y EX-CONVENTO DE SAN PEDRO Y SAN PABLO
San Miguel Tlacotepec
Mixteco
San Martín Huamelúlpam
La Mixteca Alta
San Miguel Tecomatlán
San Miguel Achiutla
Santiago Juxtlahuaca
San Juan Diuxi
Magdalena Jaltepec
Tlaxiaco
San Bartolomé Yucuañe
See "Tlaxiaco" Map
San Agustín Tlacotepec
San Mateo Peñasco
San Miguel el Grande
Chalcatongo do Hidalgo
Yutanduchi de Guerrero
Putla Villa de Guerrero
Sierra Madre del Sur
Nochixtlán
Copala
Zapotitlán del Río
Infiernillo
Santa Cruz Itundujia
Santiago Yosondúa
Parque Natural Yosondúa
Santa María Zacatepec
Barrio del Toreo
Santa María Tecomavaca
Llano Grande
Independencia
190
125
15
135D
0
10 mi
10 km
© MOON.COM

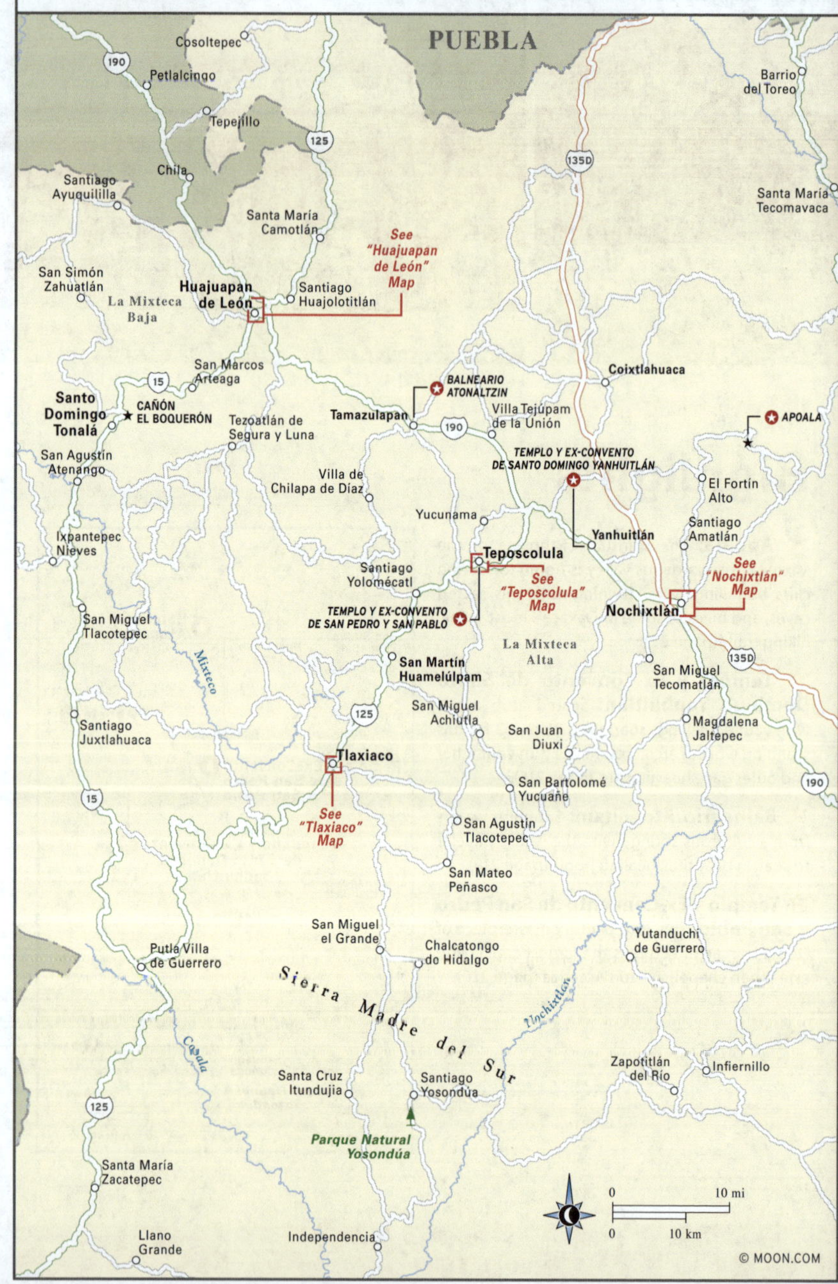

In the hills around Yanhuitlán, Coixtlahuaca, and neighboring towns, the hues in the earth range from deep wine reds to vision-searing yellows to eerie powdery greens.

That said, the work of human hands is nothing to disparage here. The monumental facades and capillas abiertas (open-air chapels) of the 16th-century cathedrals of La Mixteca's Dominican Route inspire awe, as well as curiosity about the history behind them.

Touring La Mixteca requires a bit more effort and patience than visiting more popular tourist destinations in Oaxaca. Very little English is spoken, and the advertised services don't always exist. But the payoff for your senses is worth it. If you're looking to explore a place that's off the beaten path, La Mixteca, a few hours from Oaxaca City, is a world away from your wildest expectations.

ORIENTATION

La Mixteca is divided into two parts—**La Mixteca Alta** (High Mixteca) and **La Mixteca Baja** (Low Mixteca). La Mixteca Alta includes the gateway town of **Nochixtlán,** the towns north of Nochixtlán that make up the **Dominican Route,** and **Tlaxiaco** nestled in the mountains of the southwest. The warm lowlands of La Mixteca Baja include **Huajuapan de Leon** in the northwest of the region.

PLANNING YOUR TIME

To see all the sights in La Mixteca, you'll need around two weeks, especially if you're coming here to see awe-inspiring natural wonders and out-of-the-way archaeological zones. Start in **Apoala.** The sights in Apoala can be seen in a few hours, making it a possible day trip from Oaxaca City, but a long one that will involve getting up quite early and coming back late. I recommend spending the night in the cabañas (mountain cabins).

If you've come to see the churches, your best base is Nochixtlán, where all the must-see architectural wonders are within about an hour's drive. All the churches in the **Dominican Route** section can be seen in two comfortable days of exploring. If you don't have time for them all, make sure to visit Yanhuitlán's **Templo y Ex-Convento de Santo Domingo Yanhuitlán** and the gargantuan open-air chapel of Teposcolula's **Templo y Ex-Convento de San Pedro y San Pablo.**

If you have less than two weeks, I suggest you pick either Tlaxiaco or Huajuapan de León, depending on what you'd like to do after your time in and around Nochixtlán. The hustle and bustle and delicious food of the **Saturday market in Tlaxiaco** are excellent reasons to head that way. The rushing cascades at the **Parque Natural Yosondúa** are worth the trek. Like Apoala, Yosondúa is not easy to get to, so plan on staying the night. Give yourself about three days to see the sights in and around Tlaxiaco.

On the way out to Huajuapan de León, you can stop off for a few hours in **Tamazulapan** to see the Parroquia de Santa María de la Natividad and take a dip in **Balneario Atonaltzin,** the local sulfur-spring-fed swimming hole. Give yourself a day in **Huajuapan de León,** making sure to walk to the ruins at **Cerro de las Minas.** The next day you could head down the highway to take the short hike through the **Cañón El Boquerón.** Return to Huajuapan in the evening, or spend a night in the small but lively little town of **Santo Domingo Tonalá,** where you should spend a tranquil hour or two in La Sabinera, the local park full of Montezuma cypress trees.

Previous: Balneario Atonaltzin; Templo y Ex-Convento de San Pedro y San Pablo; Santo Domingo Yanhuitlán.

Itinerary Ideas

A DAY ON THE DOMINICAN ROUTE

Spend a day exploring the best of La Mixteca's breathtaking architecture with this one-day itinerary. It's ideal by car but is still doable by public transit.

1 Start the morning in La Mixteca's gateway town, Nochixtlán. Admire the **Templo de La Asunción** and **Parque Miguel Hidalgo** before grabbing breakfast at **Restaurant Alameda.**

2 Head to Yanhuitlán to visit the **Templo y Ex-Convento de Santo Domingo Yanhuitlán.** Check out the regional museum in the convent.

3 Next stop is the Pueblo Mágico of Teposcolula. Take in the awe-inspiring **Templo y Ex-Convento de San Pedro y San Pablo.**

4 End the day in Tamazulapan. Assuage that appetite you've worked up at the **Mercado Lázaro Cárdenas** with delicious barbacoa and spicy pozole.

5 Take a walk to **Parroquia de Santa María de la Natividad** church and wonder at its buttery yellow walls.

6 End your evening with a relaxing dip in the pool at **Balneario Atonaltzin.**

Bonus: If you're so inclined and have a bit more time, spend the night in one of Balneario Atonaltzin's cozy cabins. You can head back to Oaxaca in the morning, or for further adventuring, go on to Huajuapan de Leon to explore the sights there.

Nochixtlán and Vicinity

Although technically part of La Mixteca Alta (High Mixteca), this gateway to the region is more like a multicolored middle ground between the heights of Tlaxiaco and the "Hot Country" of Huajuapan and the surrounding Mixteca Baja (Low Mixteca). Besides the small but busy city of Nochixtlán, the area includes stunning natural and human-made wonders, such as the waterfalls and caves of Apoala.

NOCHIXTLÁN

Nochixtlán (no-cheeks-TLAHN) is named for the scale insects used to make red dyes known as nochiztli in Nahuatl, nduko in Mixtec, and grana or cochinilla (cochineal) in Spanish. According to local legend, Viejo Nochixtlán (Old Nochixtlán) was a Mixtec military outpost founded around AD 900, but this settlement was virtually wiped out in 1521 and 1522 by outbreaks of cholera, measles, and smallpox.

Officially named Asunción Nochixtlán, the current town was founded in 1527 by conquistador Francisco de Orozco and 50 surviving Mixtec cochineal farmers, and the reputation it gained as "The Town of Merchants" remains to this day. For such a compact city, Nochis (as locals affectionately call it) usually bustles with mercantile activity, from the lively Sunday día de plaza, to the hardworking market vendors of the mercado municipal, to enterprising locals selling various wares off the hoods of their cars around **Parque Miguel Hidalgo,** the town's tree-laden main square.

Nochixtlán

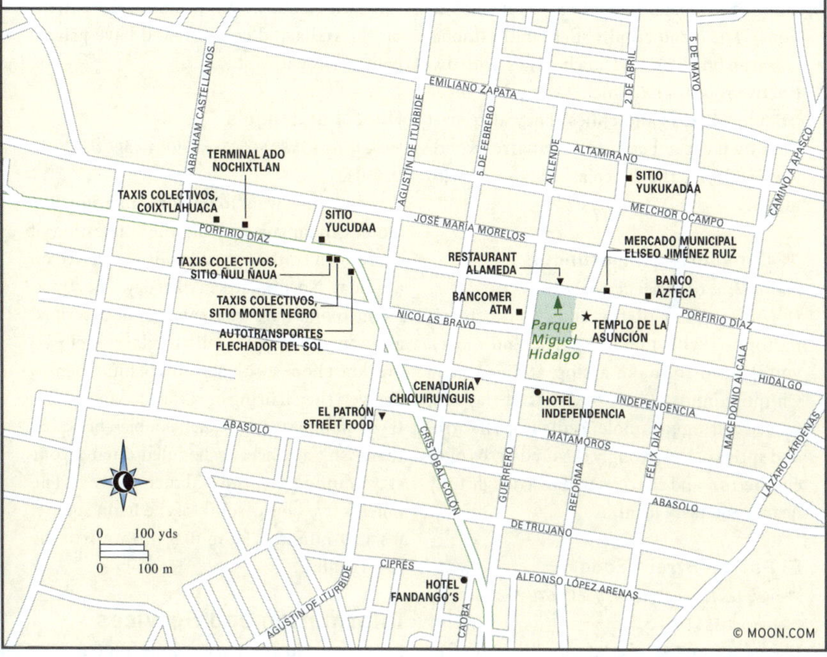

Templo de La Asunción

Dedicated to the Virgin Mary of the Assumption, the Templo de la Asunción is a great introduction to the religious architecture you're going to see in La Mixteca. Smaller and less ornate than the region's Dominican masterpieces, the church serves as an appetizer for the grandiose structures at Yanhuitlán and Teposcolula. The first mention of the church in the local registry dates back to 1581, and the facade and nave still date to that century, but the towers are not the originals. A pair of earthquakes in the first half of the 20th century toppled one and then the other, but both were restored in the 1990s. The green wooden cross in front of the facade was atop the right tower before it came down in the quake. Inside, you'll find a comparatively small but lavish altar and gilded retablo (altarpiece, or retable), as well as colorfully decorated vaulted ceilings. The church and its interior are fetching, but if you are short on time and seeking truly impressive Dominican architecture, you should look elsewhere.

Food

If you're in Nochis on a Sunday, the town's weekly market day, meander through the busy streets north of the zócalo (main square), where you'll find barbacoa (slow-cooked meat), tacos, quesadillas, empanadas, and more. Any other day of the week, you'll find the same kind of fare in the **Mercado Municipal Eliseo Jiménez Ruiz,** just across Calle Porfirio Díaz from the Templo de la Asunción. The stalls inside usually close around 6pm.

★ Restaurant Alameda

Porfirio Díaz 42; tel. 951/160-4402; 8am-7pm Mon.-Sat.; US$5

On the north side of the main square, you'll

find Restaurant Alameda, festooned with brightly colored ribbons, woven handicrafts, and papel picado (stenciled paper decorations). The menu usually sticks to traditional Oaxacan breakfast and lunch dishes, with distinctive touches like thick, tasty salsas made from local seeds and chiles. They also roast their own cacao beans on an anafre (wood-fired grill) for the chocolate they serve with meals.

★ Cenaduría Chiquirunguis

Libertad 3; no tel.; 10am-11pm daily; US$5

If you're a fan of tlayudas (large tortilla topped with meat, veggies, and more), you'll need to make a stop at Cenaduría Chiquirunguis. Their open-faced tlayuda, served with guacamole, radishes, cilantro, and sprigs of the strongly flavored herbs pipiche, berroz, and epazote, makes a delightfully hearty and tasty meal.

El Patrón Street Food

Plazuela Las Flores #2; tel. 951/561-0671; Wed.-Sun. 7pm-1am; US$5.50

If you're in need of a late-night meal after a day of exploration, there's no better option than El Patrón Street Food. Cheerily lit with hanging lights and papel picado, the taqueria opened in 2020 as a labor of love by owner Abimae Santiago Lopez to support his ailing mother, who, at the time, was told by doctors she had only a few days to live. Well, Señora Leonor is alive and well, helping in the kitchen, and giving everything an unmatched flavor and that little extra something that can only be love. Their specialty is Mediterranean-style tacos, loaded with shrimp, arrachera and bistec (two different cuts of beef), peppers, al pastor (pork), and, for a Oaxacan touch, quesillo. I recommend washing it all down with their deliciously refreshing té limon (lemongrass).

Accommodations

Hotel Independencia

Independencia 6; tel. 951/522-0463; US$20 d

Near the zócalo is Hotel Independencia, where the street-facing rooms offer a nice view of the Templo de la Asunción. All rooms are decorated with a quirky yellow-and-white pattern on the walls and ceilings, and have private bathrooms with hot water.

Hotel Fandango's

Roble 11; tel. 951/522-0545 or 951/164-4619; US$30 d, US$50 suite

Drivers might want to opt for something like Hotel Fandango's to avoid the congestion of downtown traffic, especially if you arrive on a Sunday, Nochixtlán's market day. The street-facing rooms have what can only be described as indoor balconies—little glass-enclosed breakfast nooks with curtains behind them—and yes, they'll bring breakfast to your room. If you want peace and quiet, double-check that there isn't a concert scheduled during your stay (*fandango* means "dance party"). The hotel is five blocks south of the main square; it's a 10-minute, 750-m (0.5-mi) walk to the town center.

Information and Services

Services in Nochixtlán are quite limited. This is not a tourist town, but if you do have questions about something in town, you can try to find someone to help in the **presidencia municipal** (local government offices) on the south side of the main square. The **post office** (Progreso 1; no tel.; 8am-4pm Mon.-Fri., 10am-2pm Sat.) is in the western corner of the same building.

Change money at the **Banco Azteca** (Porfirio Díaz 28; tel. 953/522-0374; www.bancoazteca.com.mx; 9am-9pm daily) in the Elektra department store. It has ATMs, as does **Bancomer** (Guerrero 4; tel. 800/226-2663; www.bancomer.com; 8:30am-4pm Mon.-Fri.) on the block west of the main square.

Hospital Básico Comunitario (Av. Carmen Zárate; tel. 951/522-0647; 24 hrs daily) has emergency services, but there is no

1: El Patrón Street Food **2:** waterfall in Apoala **3:** Nochixtlán's Parque Miguel Hidalgo

1

2

3

English-speaking staff. The hospital is a little over 1 km (0.6 mi) from the main square, about a 15-minute walk. Take Progreso south from the square until it meets Cristóbal Colón, continue south another 0.5 km (0.3 mi), and then turn left onto Lázaro Cárdenas. You'll see the hospital from Colón. Taxi drivers know how to get you there.

Getting There

All your transportation options are on Calle Porfirio Díaz, three blocks west of the zócalo. The trip from Oaxaca City takes a little over an hour. First-class **Ómnibus Cristobal Colón** (OCC) buses (toll-free Mex. tel. 818/354-3521; www.ado.com.mx; US$8) from the main bus station in Oaxaca City arrive at the **Terminal ADO** (Porfirio Díaz 78) in Nochixtlán.

To spend about a third of the first-class price, take a suburban (shared van) operated by **Autotransportes Flechador del Sol** (Periférico 408, Oaxaca City; tel. 951/292-9839; US$2.50). Vans leave for Nochis hourly. Get to their Oaxaca City terminal by walking west on Valerio Trujano until you get to the Periférico; then cross the street and take a right. It's on the third block north of Trujano. Their **terminal in Nochixtlán** (Porfirio Díaz; tel. 951/103-0360) is just east of the ADO station.

By **car** take Highway 190 west from Oaxaca City. In about half an hour (12 km/7.4 mi), you'll see the exit to Highway 135D, a toll road. From here it's another 65 km (40 mi) to the turnoff by the Pemex station, just after the overpass. Pull a U-turn through the dirt road by the gas station and take a left on Cristobal Colón. The center of Nochixtlán is about 1.6 km (1 mi) down this road. The drive takes a little over an hour.

To get here from Huajuapan, take a Oaxaca-bound suburban from **Servicios Turísticos de Huajuapan** (Nuyoó 36, Huajuapan; tel. 953/530-5204; US$3.50). The trip takes about 1.75 hours. Vans leave Huajuapan hourly, sometimes more frequently if there are more passengers.

★ APOALA

The legendary place of origin of the Mixtec people, Apoala is home to fantastic natural wonders including vertiginous canyons, circuitous caves, towering waterfalls, and what locals call bosques fantasmas (ghost forests), thickets of oak trees strung with wraithlike mosses that have a fun spookiness. According to Mixtec lore, this is the legendary cradle of the great civilization of the Ñuu Savi. It was here that the Mixtec gods summoned the waters of the River of Lineages, which watered the pair of trees that gave birth to the first Mixtecs.

Perched on a valley shelf about 1.5 hours north of Nochixtlán, **Santiago Apoala** is the small town used as a base for exploring the valley's canyons and waterfalls. It's a fun place to get away from the city and explore, especially if you want to do so on your own. Tourism has been developed insofar as it ostensibly exists, but beyond that, not so much. Don't trust signs like Wi-Fi Zone, for example. Still, if you need to disconnect and explore stunning natural areas, a day or two in Apoala is just the thing.

Before you begin your explorations, you'll need to stop at the **ecotourism office** (page 214) to check in and pay the access fee of US$5.50. You'll be assigned a guide to accompany you.

Sights

La Cueva de la Serpiente Oscuro

La Cueva de la Serpiente Oscuro (Cave of the Dark Serpent), or Yavi Ko O Maa in Mixtec, lives up to its name. After entering through a slim crack in the canyon wall, you take narrow twists and turns down the serpent's gullet. A natural spring and wishing well lie deeper in the canyon. This experience is not for claustrophobes or people who have issues with creepy critters (like spiders and bats), but if these things don't bother you, crawl on in.

After 10-15 minutes of crawling, the cave opens up into two larger galleries, and ultimately an underground lagoon. Bring a coin to make a wish. Guides can provide flashlights, but if you have a headlamp, bring it in order to free up both hands. Also be aware that guides are not necessarily trained in first aid or other emergency procedures, so take each step carefully. They do, however, know the cave intimately, as they've been exploring it since childhood.

Las Peñas Gemelas

Farther up the Río Apoala from the cave—past a narrow cut through 150-m (490-ft) vertical canyon walls studded with cliff-hanging magueys, bromeliads, and moss-strewn trees—the valley opens up. The brown earth turns to wine red where the trails snake through a green paradise of low shrubs, well-tended bean fields, and rainbow-colored wildflowers. By now you'll have noticed the 400-m (1,300-ft) peaks called Las Peñas Gemelas (Twin Crags) in the background. Here the river flows through an even thinner cut through sheer rock walls that shoot straight up from the canyon floor, and on either side of the narrow gorge, the pointed tops of the crags tower over the surrounding landscape.

To get to Las Peñas Gemelas, from the cabañas on the west side of town, just continue west (upstream) through the canyon for about half an hour. The easy walk is mostly flat, along the banks of the river. There's lots of good exploring to be done out this way. Trails run up the sides of the valley to the bases of the cliffs, and you can always find your way with the aid of the river.

La Peña Roja

The even taller cliff behind you is La Peña Roja (Red Crag). It measures a whopping 600 m (1,968 ft) tall and is the subject of a local tall tale. It is said that sometime before the Spanish conquest, a large two-headed eagle lived on this peak and made itself a menace to a local shepherd's flock. The shepherd brought his concerns to the townsfolk, and together they killed the double-beaked beast. The legend lives on in the imaginations of residents of Apoala, and a statue outside the agencia municipal commemorates the story. Although polycephaly has been observed in some animals, and the two-headed eagle is a common symbol in heraldry, no such bird has ever been scientifically recorded. Most Apoalans consider it no more than a fun story, but you never know.

Las Cascadas Cola de Serpiente and Cola de Caballo

Just to the east of town, the valley shelf ends, giving way once again to steep, narrow canyon slopes. The Río Apoala winds through tight turns that twist like a snake, ergo the first falls, measuring 25 m (82 ft), are called **La Cola de Serpiente** (The Snake's Tail). The second waterfall is called **La Cola de Caballo** because it looks like a horse's tail. It plummets 80 m (262 ft) into a misty pool of emerald-green water. Both here and in **pools** farther downstream are great places to take a dip in the afternoon heat, if you don't mind cold water. You can swim in the pool that the waters of the Cola de Caballo plunge into, but the pools another minute or so down the trail are deeper and much more tranquil. The largest is 3 m (10 ft) deep.

To get to the cascadas (waterfalls), head east (downstream) to the other side of town. Walk two blocks east from the ecotourism office (corner of Independencia and Pino Suárez) until you see a paved stone exit to the right that leads down to another dirt road. Loop around the cornfields and cross the little bridge to find the falls. You'll see La Cola de Serpiente winding alongside you to the left of the trail, and La Cola de Caballo is just another few minutes' walk down the trail. The walk from town to the falls takes about 20 minutes. Bring water and maybe a snack for the hike back up the stairs alongside the rushing water.

Ancient Rock Carvings and Paintings

The cliff with a cave at its base to the north of town is La Peña del Diablo (Devil's Crag), where you'll find interesting pre-Hispanic rock carvings. The carving called El Danzante

(The Dancer) has been busy busting a move for an unknown number of centuries. Other carvings represent the sun, moon, and a cornstalk. It is said that this was a ceremonial venue for rituals that thanked the gods for good harvests.

Food and Accommodations

There are limited food options in Apoala. At the ecotourism office is a **comedor** with the usual fare (7am-7pm daily; around US$5). A couple of little **misceláneas** (corner stores) have eggs, veggies, and tortillas, as well as water and snack foods. They'll be able to help you out in a pinch if you're camping, but I recommend shopping in the mercado in Nochixtlán before heading here.

Restaurante El Centauro

Calle Independencia; tel. 561/118-6004; 8am-7pm daily; US$7

Your main option is Restaurante El Centauro, just a few steps down Independencia from the ecotourism office. Along with amiable service, you'll find delicious comedor fare here, such as a simple but flavorful and spicy chile relleno. There's a comida corrida (set menu) option available and plenty of choices for vegetarians.

Cabañas

With a view of the towering gray and orange canyon walls, and the sound of the Río Apoala chugging through its lane of sabino (cypress) trees, the cabañas (US$30 d) on the west side of town are a pleasant escape from the buzzing streets of Nochixtlán. They are basic but clean. Someone from the ecotourism office will come by around 6pm to light the boiler, which runs until morning. I recommend giving it about half an hour and then checking how well it works (you might get a burst of steam and then cold water). If you absolutely need hot water, try to get to the office to ask them to check it before they close at 7pm. If not, shower during the day, when it is warm out.

Tourism is so sparse here that you don't need to reserve a cabaña beforehand. Just show up at the ecotourism office in town (corner of Independencia and Pino Suárez) to book one when you arrive.

Camping

In front of the cabañas is a small field where you can pitch a tent for about US$5 per night. You'll need to bring all your own equipment, but if you forgot a plate or a pan, just ask in the comedor at the ecotourism office; they might be able to lend you what you need. Bathrooms for campers are next to the cabañas.

Information and Services

Ecotourism Office

corner of Independencia and Pino Suárez; tel. 561/504-2660; 7am-7pm daily

The ecotourism office is staffed by gregarious locals. You'll need to stop here to check in and pay the access fee of US$5.50 before you begin your explorations. Guides are included in this price and assigned according to what you wish to see and explore. You'll need about three hours to see the sights.

Getting There

The easiest way to get here by public transport is a viaje especial (special trip) in a **taxi** (US$25 one-way) from **Sitio Yukukadáa,** in a yellow house on Calle 2 de Abril two blocks north of the mercado in Nochixtlán. It's a 1.5-hour ride on a newly paved road. Make arrangements with your driver to come back to pick you up later. It's best to stay a night or two, but if you're only day-tripping, make sure your driver knows you want him to return the same day before leaving Nochixtlán.

Santiago Apoala is about 44 km (27 mi) north of Nochixtlán. **Drivers** take Calle 5 de Mayo north from the mercado in Nochixtlán, a straight shot on a nicely paved road (as opposed to the rugged dirt nightmare that Google Maps might try to take you on).

The Dominican Route

TOP EXPERIENCE

After the arrival of Hernán Cortés in 1519, it didn't take long for the Spanish to turn up in La Mixteca. The Aztecs didn't have the treasure trove of gold the Spanish were looking for, so Moctezuma sent them in this direction to get rid of them. Although the first missionaries to arrive in the New World were Franciscans, the Spanish crown later chose Dominican friars to proselytize the Indigenous peoples of this region, due to the order's reputation for austerity and strict religious vows.

This process, of course, was not peaceful. The Mixtec people saw the Spanish mission for what it was—a militant takeover masked by the pretty flourishes of baroque church facades—and they resisted the destruction of their temples and construction of Christian ones for decades.

Five hundred years later, the impressive architectural results of this conversion campaign dot the countryside of La Mixteca, making up what the Oaxacan secretary of tourism has designated the Ruta Dominica (Dominican Route). The most outstanding examples are in Yanhuitlán, Coixtlahuaca, Tamazulapan, and Teposcolula. The 16th-century structures have considerable artistic and historical value, but they should be appreciated for what they really were, which, as one resident of Coixtlahuaca described them, were fortresses disguised as churches. This is not to take away from their beauty. Still, the full historical context is helpful when appreciating works of this kind.

These towns are quite close together and can be seen in a busy day, but if you want a slower pace, use Nochixtlán as your base. I've also included accommodations options in the pleasant town of Teposcolula, which has a bit more to see beyond its church.

Tours from Oaxaca City

The highlights of the Dominican Route can be seen in a day trip from Oaxaca City, but be prepared for a full day with the tour guides.

4 Seasons Tours and Travel Oaxaca

tel. 951/231-4840; oaxaca4seasons.toursandtravel@gmail.com; 8 hours

Eduardo of 4 Seasons Tours and Travel Oaxaca offers private tours for small groups on the Dominican Route (and beyond). The main sights of Yanhuitlán, Coixtlahuaca, and Teposcolula are of course included, and other sites can be chosen to your liking. Tours are US$145 for groups of 1-3 people, US$205 for groups of 4-6, and US$265 for groups of 7-10.

La Soley

tel. 951/615-4802; ateran@lasoley.com; 6-8 hrs; from US$60 pp

La Soley also runs shared and private tours. The shared tour is around US$75 per person for an 8-hour tour to the main sights. The private tour, for up to 4 people, is US$190-215 (depending on the distance and the time you want to travel).

YANHUITLÁN

While it might be tempting to deem it a miracle that the Dominican friars were able to build such marvelous architectural wonders in this isolated area of New Spain, it's important—and historically accurate—to keep in mind that such feats were achieved by unwilling human hands, not a divine one. The Spanish town council in Yanhuitlán (New Land) donated land for a Dominican convent in 1529, but the friars weren't able to call it a permanent home until decades later due to multiple successful acts of resistance by the local Mixtec people, on whose temple ruins the Christian edifice was being constructed. The church and monastery here is a stunning masterpiece of colonial religious architecture that should still be appreciated, with the context of its autocratic history in mind.

★ Templo y Ex-Convento de Santo Domingo Yanhuitlán

Set atop a low, flat hill in the center of town, the Templo y Ex-Convento de Santo Domingo Yanhuitlán commands attention from anywhere in the surrounding valley. Saints carved in pink limestone stand among the columns and flourishes of its towering facade. Big, stocky buttresses support its west-facing corners, and the stone hallways and flowered courtyards of the old convent are on the nave's east side.

The church's religious and political importance in the region was eclipsed only by the Santo Domingo church and convent in Oaxaca City. Formal construction began in 1550, when locals finally gave in to the political and physical force of the Catholic Church. The last stone was laid in 1575.

Despite a few modifications in the 18th century, many of the original sculptures and paintings remain intact, such as the altarpiece by Sevillian painter Andrés de la Concha. This gilded 11-m (36-ft) altar is adorned with de la Concha's depictions of the life of Saint Dominic. The original designer and construction date of the elaborate pipe organ in the balcony are unknown. Most likely built around 1700, the instrument shows signs of repairs over the centuries, such as a keyboard installed in 1886. It was fully restored to working condition in 1998 in a collaborative effort by Mexican and French organ builders.

Part of the convent has been turned into a **regional museum** (9am-3pm Sat.-Mon.; US$3), which houses lots of religious artwork and presents temporary exhibits. It also has an exact copy of the Yanhuitlán codex, a document dating from 1550 that depicts the history of Yanhuitlán and the Spanish intervention in Mixtec glyphs and transcriptions of Mixtec phrases in Spanish characters. The original is in the Academy of Fine Arts in Puebla.

Getting There

Yanhuitlán is a quick, straight shot from Nochixtlán, 16 km (10 mi) northwest on Highway 190. Drivers will be glad for the paved road in good condition, passengers in the back of **camionetas** (covered pickup trucks used as vans) will appreciate the smooth 20-minute ride, and all will enjoy the sprawling views of the valley. The camioneta terminal in Nochixtlán is a block north of the zócalo on Calle Allende, just before the corner with Morelos. They charge about US$1.75 to get to Yanhuitlán.

From Oaxaca City, grab a Huajuapan-bound suburban at **Servicios Turísticos de Huajuapan** (Valerio Trujano 420, Oaxaca City; tel. 951/516-5759; US$4) and get off after about 1.5 hours in Santo Domingo Yanhuitlán, about 20 minutes after Nochixtlán. The large pink church is striking against the green of the broad valley floor, so it's hard to miss.

COIXTLAHUACA

Coixtlahuaca (In the Field of Snakes) was founded around AD 37 by the Chocho people of La Mixteca Alta. It was an important commercial hub for the region in the centuries before the Spanish arrived, with a market that attracted both Mixtec and Chocho people from miles around. Coixtlahuaca is situated in gorgeous, multicolored hill country. The earth here holds all the hues you can think of, and a few others you never would have.

Templo y Ex-Convento de San Juan Bautista

Because of Coixtlahuaca's strategic cultural and commercial position in the region, the Spanish decided to build the spectacular Templo y Ex-Convento de San Juan Bautista, which was completed in 1576. It sits atop a low, flat hill in a valley, commanding spectacular views of the surrounding landscape, especially in the late afternoon when the west-facing

1: open-air chapel at Templo y Ex-Convento de San Juan Bautista **2:** Templo y Ex-Convento de Santo Domingo Yanhuitlán **3:** Balneario Atonaltzin **4:** Parroquia de Santa María de la Natividad

1
2
3
4

church facade turns to gold in the light of the setting sun.

As with other Indigenous peoples and most churches around here and in many parts of Mexico, the Chochos rightfully opposed the replacement of their temple with a Christian one and resisted for decades before finally giving in. Being obliged to build a temple to a god they did not serve, they took a few liberties with the design. They left signs of their displeasure in the bas-relief carvings of the facade and the archway of the open-air chapel, where you'll see symbols such as moons with faces and the plumed serpent Quetzalcoatl. The stage-like open-air chapel to the side of the main nave was where the Chochos were forced to hold their masses, as they were not allowed inside to worship with the European believers.

The on-site **museum** (10am-5pm Mon.-Sat., 11am-3pm Sun.) is free to enter, but you'll have to pay about US$2.50 if you want to shoot video (taking photos here or at the church costs US$1). The highlight inside is the lienzo de Coixtlahuaca, a 16th-century canvas map delineating the boundaries of the Coixtlahuaca chiefdom and the official recognition of Spanish authority over it. The main town is represented by a glyph of a snake, and the boundaries are in a patched, jaguar-print perimeter.

Getting There

Coixtlahuaca is about 40 km (25 mi) north of Nochixtlán. From here, Highway 135D (toll, about US$2) cuts straight through a firework-hued display of terra firma. Take Porfirio Díaz west out of Nochixtlán, then take the unmarked turnoff to the right, at the top of a low hill about 1.6 km (1 mi) past the ADO station. The toll booth is about half an hour down the highway. Turn right after exiting, and follow the road another 3.5 km (2.2 mi) into town. The total drive time is about 40 minutes.

Colectivo taxis leave from a car wash just to the west of the ADO station on Porfirio Díaz in Nochixtlán. They cost about US$3. If you hear the word "transbordar" (transfer), you'll have to get out at the toll booth and cross it on foot to change taxis, so that the drivers can avoid expensive tolls.

TAMAZULAPAN

In Nahuatl, *Tamazulapan* means "In the Water of the Toads," but don't worry. The crystal-clear water in the local swimming hole is toad-free. Boasting another fine example of Dominican architecture right on the highway, Tamazulapan is a nice place to stop for an afternoon on the way to Huajuapan de León.

Sights

Parroquia de Santa María de la Natividad

You should have no problem spotting the 16th-century Parroquia de Santa María de la Natividad, which stands out among the other churches on this route for its paint job. The cochineal-red baroque embellishments of the facade contrast delightfully with the soft, buttery yellow of the bricks.

Inside, you'll find a towering altarpiece of gold and a number of paintings in which a phalanx of saints surrounds the Virgin Mary. This church is home to two 16th-century organs, a large stationary one and a smaller processional organ that was designed to be carried during ambulatory celebrations. It is the smallest organ in Oaxaca, and one of only five of its kind in Mexico.

★ Balneario Atonaltzin

Hwy. to Tepelmeme, km 2; tel. 953/109-1908; 10am-6pm daily; entry US$6 adults, US$3 children

When the Mixtec sun gets to baking, folks from Tamazulapan head to Balneario Atonaltzin, just north of town. The three swimming pools, one of which is Olympic size, are fed by sulfur springs that cycle water through them constantly, maintaining an average water temperature of 26°C (79°F). A craggy slope of boulders lines one side of the large pool, and atop it sits a terrace where you can look out over the gemstone-hued waters while you enjoy a meal. Green gardens and palapas (thatched huts) provide shade around the pools. There is also a children's area with a splash pad and water slides.

You'll pay extra to rent tables, chairs, and other services (around US$5.50). You also pay if you bring your own snacks. Might as well not worry about packing a picnic, and enjoy the burgers, fries, nachos, and other snack-bar fare at the pool.

To get here, grab a **mototaxi** (US$1.50) at the northeast corner of the zócalo or walk the 2 km (1.2 mi) from town. Walk north on Calle Independencia, follow the curve and cross the river, and you're there. If you take a right onto the dirt road just after the bridge, you'll get to another spring called **El Ojo de Agua Chico** (Little Spring), where you can take a dip. It's about 0.8 km (0.5 mi) from the main road.

Food and Accommodations

The **Mercado Lázaro Cárdenas,** just north of the main square, is full of fondas (food stalls) serving Mixtec delights such as barbacoa and pozole.

Cuzama Restaurante

Benito Juárez 19; tel. 953/533-0070; 8am-5pm Mon.-Fri.; US$7

Cuzama Restaurante, just two blocks north of the main square, with tokens of its Mixtec heritage adorning the walls, is a cozy comedor that offers traditional breakfast fare, a comida del dia menu for just US$4, and satisfying Oaxacan favorites.

Oaxacanita Chocolate

Plazuela Josefa Ortiz de Domínguez 5; tel. 951/417-1778; www.oaxacanitachocolate.com; 10am-8pm Mon.-Fri.

Walk two blocks north of the church to Oaxacanita Chocolate for delicious chocolate made with cacao grown in La Mixteca. Although the majority of raw cacao used to make it is sourced from Tabasco and Veracruz, the Oaxacan chocolate recipe is unique to the state. Oaxacanita is special in bringing the whole production process to their corner of Oaxaca, creating jobs and supporting local artists with the proceeds. The room next to their chocolate bar showcases the talents of local artists and artisans. Their cacao farm is a few hours away in the verdant hills around Tlaxiaco.

Balneario Atonaltzin

Hwy. to Tepelmeme, km 2; tel. 953/540-0185; US$43 2 people, US$86 4 people, US$130 6 people, US$220 10 people

There are a few basic hotels in town, but the cabañas at Balneario Atonaltzin are more relaxing and picturesque. Made of white limestone or rustic, cobbled stone with wood finishes, the cabañas have hot water, TVs, internet, coffee makers, and valley views. Plus, they're next to the spring-fed swimming pools (access is included in the price).

Getting There

From Oaxaca City, grab a Huajuapan-bound suburban at **Servicios Turísticos de Huajuapan** (Valerio Trujano 420, Oaxaca City; tel. 951/516-5759; US$5) and get off at Tamazulapan's lovely Parque Central. Vans leave hourly, and the trip takes about 2.5 hours. From Nochixtlán, get a colectivo from **Sitio Yucudaa** (Calle Porfirio Díaz, Nochixtlán; tel. 951/105-9000 or 951/177-5943; US$3), just after the bridge on Calle Porfirio Díaz.

By **car** take Highway 190 northwest of Nochixtlán. Tamazulapan is 52 km (32 mi) down this highway. The hour-long drive crosses low green valleys and twists through the variegated hills of La Mixteca Alta.

YUCUNAMA

If you've been paying attention to the toponyms in this part of Oaxaca, you might notice that Yucunama doesn't sound like the others, which are in Nahuatl, the language of the Aztecs. This is because Yucunama (Hill of Amole)—the name refers to a tuberous plant used to make soap—was never conquered by the Aztecs. The Spanish included Yucunama in the Teposcolula district when they arrived around 1520, but the Spanish viceroyalty endowed the settlement with political and territorial control in 1585, designating it an autonomous Indigenous republic. The town is small and quaint, with cobblestone streets in the center, and the 16th-century **Templo de San Pedro** boasts a fetching facade plastered and painted white and red.

Archaeologists have found artifacts here that date back 2,000 years. These can be viewed in the small **archaeological museum** (9am-6pm daily; free, donations appreciated) called Bee Ñuu (House of the People). Of note here is a copy of the **Codex Nuttall,** one of the principal pictographic documents relating the history and legends of the Mixtec people. Folded like an accordion, it details in full color the story of famed king Ocho Venado (Eight Deer). You'll also see a 14th-century receipt for tribute payments printed on amate, paper made from the bark of the wild fig tree. If the museum isn't open, head to the presidencia municipal across the plaza and ask someone to open it for you.

Getting There

To get to Yucunama, head to the junction of Highways 190 and 125, 29 km (18 mi) northeast of Nochixtlán. Take the dirt road with a sign for Yucunama that leads west from the intersection. It's a 20-minute **drive** through 9 km (5.6 mi) of low scrub- and pine-covered hills into town. At the junction, public transport passengers will find **colectivo taxis** (about US$4.50) for the ride into town. Get to the highway junction via a colectivo from Nochixtlán, which you'll find in front of a car wash just west of the ADO station on Porfirio Díaz; the ride takes about half an hour.

If you're headed to Teposcolula next, take the road that leads south out of town. Teposcolula is about 8 km (5 mi) south. A colectivo will charge US$4.50 for the trip.

SAN PEDRO Y SAN PABLO TEPOSCOLULA

When the Spanish arrived in this part of La Mixteca in the 1520s, they found the Ñuu Savi living on a nearby hill called Yucundaa (Hill of the Ancient People). By 1550, Yucundaa was completely abandoned, and the Ñuu Savi were displaced by the Spanish to form the town now known as Teposcolula (which means "Next to the Twist of Copper," but as hard as I tried, I could not find the exact reason for such a name). For the next couple of centuries, it was the most important trade hub in the region, with business connections that reached as far as Guatemala and even countries in South America.

As in other communities in the region, the people of Teposcolula resisted the Europeans' invasion of their lands and traditions. Their most notable artistic defiance, the Danza de las Mascaritas (Dance of the Masked Ones), is still practiced today. The dance has its origins in the European courtier dances the Spanish brought to the town. The colonized Native people made fun of the courtier dance through caricatured, hammy movements. They donned outrageous masks and costumes so that the insult would fly under the radar of the people they were mocking.

Other interesting traditions here include the games pelota Mixteca, a Mixtec ball game similar to that of other pre-Hispanic cultures but played with a heavy rubber glove, and the juego de batalla, a hockey-like game played with a ball that is on fire.

Sights

La Casa de la Cacica

For such a small town, Teposcolula is packed with sights to see, such as La Casa de la Cacica (House of the Chief's Wife), which was constructed around 1560 and stands out for its fusion of Postclassic Mixtec and Spanish Renaissance architectural styles. Considered the last construction of the Mixtec señorío, the building now houses a children's library with copies of the Codex of Yanhuitlán, which contains interesting, colorful Mixtec glyphs.

★ Templo y Ex-Convento de San Pedro y San Pablo

Teposcolula's main event, and the reason for its denomination as a Pueblo Mágico (Magic Town), is the 16th-century Templo y Ex-Convento de San Pedro y San Pablo. You can't

Teposcolula

GÓMEZ FARÍAS
J. MINA
FRANCISCO I. MADERO
RESTAURANTE EUNICE
ÁLVARO OBREGÓN
HOTEL CASA FRANCO/ RESTAURANTE DOÑA JOSEFINA
VICENTE GUERRERO
PORFIRIO DÍAZ
TRUJANO
BENITO JUÁREZ
VENUSTIANO CARRANZA
ITURBIDE
LA CASA DE LA CACICA
TEMPLO Y EX-CONVENTO DE SAN PEDRO Y SAN PABLO
Parque Central
SARABIA
ALLENDE
SERVICIOS TURÍSTICOS PLATINUM
HOTEL JUVI
125
To Restaurante Señora de Yucundaa
HIDALGO
0 50 yds
0 50 m
To Tlaxiaco
© MOON.COM

miss it, just to the west of the main square. Most notable here is the monumental **open-air chapel,** where colonized worshippers were forced to hold the ceremonies they were compelled to observe. Depending on whom you ask, it's either the largest in Latin America or the largest in the world, but either way, an impressive sight to behold.

Inside the church, a gigantic gilded altar is adorned with botanical flourishes, flanked by smaller altars that include imagery of saints and the Eye of Providence. The ex-convent contains paintings of the life of Saint Dominic by Spanish painters Simón Pereyns and Andrés de la Concha; the latter also painted pieces in the temple in Yanhuitlán. Outside the eastern wall of the complex is the **Portal de Dolores,** a small arcade once used for religious ceremonies that is now a small artisans market.

Festivals and Events

Feria Anual

Teposcolula's nearly three-week-long Feria Anual (Annual Fair) lasts from the end of February through the middle of March.

PUEBLO MÁGICO
1
2
3
4

During the Feria Anual, you can experience the games pelota Mixteca, a Mixtec ball game similar to that of other pre-Hispanic cultures but played with a heavy rubber glove, and the juego de batalla, a hockey-like game played with a ball that is on fire. The festivities also include riotous calendas (street parades), live music, regional foods, and more.

Food and Accommodations

Restaurante Eunice

Álvaro Obregón 28; tel. 953/518-2017; 8am-6pm Sun.-Fri.; US$6

Eunice and family serve up traditional breakfast and lunch meals made with fresh, flavorful ingredients and an extra helping of homemade TLC. It's fun to appreciate, among the various calendars and pictures of churches on the walls, the framed, embroidered textile that dates back to 1868.

Restaurante Señora de Yucundaa

Hwy. 125; tel. 951/188-2257; 7:30am-10pm daily; US$5-7

About 3.5 km (2.2 mi) east of town, Restaurante Señora de Yucundaa is a colorful setting for enjoying the local take on a chile relleno or creole hen soup. Doña Cholita's chiles rellenos are served in a soupy, piquant red sauce with olives, potatoes, and other veggies.

Restaurante Doña Josefina

Iturbide 20; tel. 953/552-7017; 8:30am-3:30pm daily; US$7-10

Enjoy the chef's local take on mole negro in a room filled with 19th-century artifacts, pianos, documents, and family photos. They have extensive menus for breakfast and lunch, as well as a full bar. You'll find the restaurant in Hotel Casa Franco.

Hotel Juvi

Hwy. 125; tel. 953/518-2064; US$20 d

The best view in town is at Hotel Juvi, located across from the grassy field of the church complex. The windows of the street-facing rooms overlook the grandeur of the open-air chapel and baroque facade of the main nave. All rooms include hot water, TVs, and Wi-Fi, but if you need internet, check to see if it's working first.

★ Hotel Casa Franco

Iturbide 20; tel. 953/552-7017; www.hotelcasafranco.com; US$50 d, US$59 king bed, US$85 junior suite

This restored Independence-era villa was home to Lieutenant Colonel Justo Franco, whose descendants opened Hotel Casa Franco in 2017. The 11 sleek, modern rooms are set around a lovely courtyard with sponge-textured orange walls that contrast delightfully with columns of green limestone, similar to the stone predominantly used in Oaxaca City. Deluxe rooms and the hotel's one suite are equipped with coffee makers and bubbling whirlpool tubs.

Getting There

The cheapest way to get to Teposcolula from Nochixtlán is by **colectivo,** which you'll find outside a car wash on Calle Porfirio Díaz, just west of the main bus station. They'll take you to the junction of Highways 190 and 125, where suburban vans wait to take you the rest of the way. All in all, the trip takes about an hour and will cost you about US$4.

To get here from Huajuapan de León, board a Tlaxiaco-bound suburban at **Servicios Turísticos Platinum** (Nuyoó 36-A, Huajuapan de León; tel. 953/503-4836; 1.5 hrs; US$4), a couple of blocks north of the churchyard. Vans leave every half hour. If you're coming from Tlaxiaco, take the Huajuapan-bound **Platinum** suburban (Hidalgo 3, Tlaxiaco; tel. 953/552-0124; 1 hr; US$3) from their station on Calle Hidalgo, one block west of the Plaza de la Constitución. They also leave every half hour. Their station in Teposcolula is across from the southeast corner of the main square.

Drivers shouldn't have a hard time noticing the junction of Highways 190 and 125.

1: Teposcolula **2:** Portal de Dolores **3:** open-air chapel at Templo y Ex-Convento de San Pedro y San Pablo **4:** Casa de la Cacica

Teposcolula is just 13 km (8 mi) from the junction, a 15-minute drive on Highway 125 through wildflower-strewn fields. From Nochixtlán, take Highway 190 northeast 29 km (18 mi) to the junction. From Huajuapan, turn onto Highway 190 four blocks north of the main square, and follow it for 63 km (39 mi) to the junction.

If you're driving from Tlaxiaco, take Highway 190 north out of town. The 44-km (27-mi) drive through verdant, pine-covered peaks takes about an hour.

La Mixteca Alta

Although Nochixtlán and the towns of the Dominican Route are in the region called La Mixteca Alta (High Mixteca), it isn't until you head south from Teposcolula that the road begins to climb to mountainous altitudes. Lofty pine trees strung with spectral mosses rise over bright patches of wildflowers on the way to Tlaxiaco, the town of the perpetual street market. Tlaxiaco makes an excellent base from which to explore the surrounding attractions, such as the ruins at San Martín Huamelulpam and the rushing cascades and stunning vistas of Yosondúa.

TLAXIACO

In Nahuatl, *Tlaxiaco* means "The Place Where It Rains over the Ball Court." Its name in Mixtec is Ndiji (Good View). Like Nochixtlán, the current Heroic City of Tlaxiaco did not exist before the conquest but was formed by moving the inhabitants of two nearby settlements after devastating outbreaks of fatal diseases. It earned its valiant name in a battle won here against the French during their Second Intervention in the 1860s. (Incidentally, the town acquired the nickname "El Paris Chiquito," Little Paris, due to the influence of the French.)

Tlaxiaco today is known for its majestic four-faced **Reloj** (clock tower) located in the **Plaza de la Constitución,** which serves as a handsome symbol of the city. And of course if you've traveled all to the way to this corner of Oaxaca, you probably know of Tlaxiaco's Saturday market. What you may not know is that Tlaxiaco is the birthplace to two of Oaxaca's most beloved stars—singer-songwriter Lila Downs and Academy Award nominee Yalitza Aparicio.

Saturday Market

Vendors begin arriving from the surrounding slopes and beyond on Friday night, claiming their spots and setting up beforehand to be ready for the early-morning rush. Tlaxiaco's Saturday market is a behemoth, commencing around the Plaza de la Constitución, the tarps spreading to fill the neighboring streets to the south for blocks, including the garden in front of the 18th-century Templo de Santa María de la Asunción.

It's easy to spend hours winding through the narrow, congested aisles and alleyways, shopping, socializing, and eating. Although a few stalls sell gifts and souvenirs, this market is not aimed at tourists. Like other markets of this kind in Oaxaca, though, it is an excellent place to eat. Everywhere you turn are tacos, tamales, coconuts prepared with lime and chile served in the half shell, local raw honey, and much, much more. The selection of fresh produce, meats, and dried chiles is impressively diverse. Other finds include broad selections of spices, herbs, barks, roots, seeds, and elixirs used in traditional medicines, as well as bags, shoes, artisanal soaps, and cool retro watches. Some unique locally produced artisanal products include canastas (reed baskets), tenates (smaller woven baskets with tops), and petates (woven reed mats), as well as belts, hats, and other accessories.

Food and Accommodations

★ Antojitos Los Abuelos

corner of Fray Lucero and 5 de Mayo; tel. 953/107-2952; 6pm-11:30pm Sun.-Fri.; US$3

Any day of the week, the tianguis is full of delicious, affordable food. Any night except Saturday, stop by the food stall Antojitos Los Abuelos at the tarp intersection at the southwest corner of the Plaza de la Constitución. Enjoy fantastic pozole, tostadas, and tlayudas served with a side of chapulines (grasshoppers), pods of the guaje tree, and spicy slices of chile de agua. There are six stools to elbow into, or you can eat standing in the din of the market traffic.

★ Restaurante El Patio

Hotel del Portal, Plaza de la Constitución 2-A; tel. 953/552-1723; 7:30am-9pm daily; US$7

You should have a meal at Restaurante El Patio, where the thoughtful menu showcases the best of what the region has to offer. The plates are a feast for the eyes as well as the stomach. The casually elegant dining area in the hotel's covered courtyard holds a dozen tables and a small jungle of leafy plants beneath a canopy of undulating papel picado decorations.

Hotel México

Hidalgo 13; tel. 953/552-0086; US$25 shared bathroom, US$30 en suite

Just around the corner from the market is Hotel México, which is cash-only and also on a hot water schedule. The rooms are set around a courtyard with gardens of bougainvillea and other flowers and dark green fronds. Even the central parking area is colorful and pleasing, with columns and arches painted the colors of the sunset.

Hotel del Portal

Plaza de la Constitución 2-A; tel. 953/552-0154; US$27-32 d (cash only)

Hotel del Portal beckons with blue, orange, yellow, and white walls and earthy red in the tiles. Oddly, the rooms themselves, while clean and comfortable, are a little anticlimactic after the gorgeous lobby and restaurant. If you're here in the winter months, pay the couple of dollars extra for a room with carpet, which stays warmer.

Information and Services

You won't find a tourist information booth or office in Tlaxiaco, but you can stop by the **presidencia municipal,** opposite the Templo de Nuestra Señora de la Asunción on Calle Fray Lucero, if you have a pressing question. The **post office** (Alejandro Méndez Aquino; no tel.; 8am-4:30pm Mon.-Fri., 8am-noon Sat.) is in the northeast corner of this same building.

Change money at the **Banco Azteca** (Colón 13; tel. 555/447-8810; www.bancoazteca.com.mx; 9am-9pm daily) in the big, yellow Elektra department store two blocks east of Hotel del Portal. It has ATMs, and there are 24-hour ATMs at the **Bancomer** (Claudio Cruz 8; tel. 800/226-2663; 8:30am-4pm Mon.-Fri.) one block west of Hotel del Portal.

For 24-hour emergency medical services, head to the **Unidad Médica Hidalgo** (Hidalgo 5; tel. 953/552-0221; 24 hrs daily). Staff is Spanish-speaking only.

Getting There

To get directly to Tlaxiaco from Oaxaca City, board a suburban at the base for **Autotransportes de Tlaxiaco** (Trujano 505, Oaxaca City; tel. 951/516-4030; US$4). They leave every 15 minutes or so all day, taking about 3 hours to arrive at the Tlaxiaco station (Colón 19; tel. 953/552-0088).

From Nochixtlán, you can flag down a passing suburban that has a Tlaxiaco sign in the windshield. Just wait by the road on Calle Porfirio Díaz. You can also take any colectivo that will get you to the junction of Highways 190 and 125, and from here grab a suburban headed for Tlaxiaco. You'll be charged around US$2.50 for the 1.75-hour trip.

To get here from Huajuapan, take a suburban run by **Servicios Turísticos Platinum** (Nuyoó 36-A, Huajuapan; tel. 953/503-4836; 2.5 hrs; US$6). The vans go directly to Tlaxiaco (Hidalgo 3; tel. 953/552-1024), stopping in Tamazulapan and Teposcolula on the way. Vans leave every half hour.

Drivers from Oaxaca City take Highway 190 west out of the city and use the left lanes to exit onto Highway 135D (toll) 11 km (7 mi) outside the city. Stay on this highway another 69 km (43 mi) and exit onto Highway 190 just outside Nochixtlán. Drivers from Nochixtlán head west on Porfirio Díaz to get on Highway 190. From this junction, continue 29 km (18 mi) until you reach the junction of Highways 190 and 125. Turn south onto Highway 125 and follow it for 57 km (35 mi) to reach Tlaxiaco. Total drive time from Oaxaca City is 2.75 hours, and 1.75 hours from Nochixtlán.

If you're driving from Huajuapan de León, turn onto Highway 190 four blocks north of the main square, and follow it for 63 km (39 mi) until you get to the junction of Highways 190 and 125. Turn south onto Highway 125 and follow it for 57 km (35 mi) to reach Tlaxiaco. Total drive time is 2.5 hours.

SAN MARTÍN HUAMELULPAM

The town of San Martín Huamelulpam was founded around 400 BC and became a political and economic center that may have been the largest Mesoamerican city at the time. Huamelulpam, its Nahuatl name, means "Hillock of Amaranth," which is derived from a pair of amaranth trees (huautli in Nahuatl) that grew into the shape of an *H* and lived that way for centuries. Its Mixtec name, Yucunindaba, means "Hill That Flew."

Just half an hour from Tlaxiaco, it is perfect for a short day trip to the ruins of the old town and the small but interesting community museum.

Yucunindaba Archaeological Zone

The town of Yucunindaba was a Mixtec señorío to which surrounding communities made tribute. The ruins date back to its founding in 400 BC. Its trade network extended north as far as Tehuacán in Puebla, and south all the way to the Pacific coast of Oaxaca. The many Zapotec urns found here show that the Mixtecs also traded with Zapotec settlements to the east. The people here also carved monoliths in a style found nowhere else in La Mixteca. You can view these and other artifacts at the **Museo Comunitario Hitalulu** (tel. 953/106-9842; 10am-5pm daily; free), next to the municipal government building at the center of town.

The ruins are just east of town. The largest of the structures is the **Church Group,** now little more than a few terraces and a couple of damaged platforms. Many of the stones from this structure were used to build the present-day church on the hill.

Getting There

San Martín Huamelulpam is half an hour (21 km/13 mi) north of Tlaxiaco on Highway 125. Drive or grab a suburban bound for Oaxaca and tell them you want to get off at the Huamelulpam turnoff. Vans run by **Autotransportes de Tlaxiaco** (Colón 19; tel. 953/552-0088) leave every 15 minutes and will charge about US$2. From here you can walk the 1 km (0.6 mi) into town or flag down a passing taxi.

PARQUE NATURAL YOSONDÚA

It isn't easy to get to, but the vertiginous waterfalls, breathtaking views, and endless exploring opportunities at the Parque Natural Yosondúa are definitely worth the trip. With lots of ecotourism activities such as hiking, mountain biking, and zip-lining, the park offers more than enough to fill a couple of days with action, excitement, and discovery. There is a 30 peso (about US$1.70) entrance fee for the park unless you stay in the cabañas.

Although there's little chance of accommodations or services being booked up, call ahead to check because it is such a trek to get to Yosondúa. Call Edilberto Martínez Sánchez (tel. 953/157-5123 or 951/212-2417 via WhatsApp), the park's head of communications, for information or to book tours, cabañas, or other services. (If you don't speak Spanish, it's best to use Google Translate and send a message on WhatsApp.)

Sights

La Cascada Esmeralda

You'll hear the waters of La Cascada Esmeralda (Emerald Falls) rushing over the edge of the canyon as you begin to descend from the canyon rim toward the park entrance. From here, the waters of the river (also called Esmeralda) spill 100 m (328 ft) to the canyon floor in a spectacular show of tiered splashdowns, for which there are numerous excellent viewing points.

Suspension Bridge

The **park office/snack bar** (6am-5pm Mon.-Fri.) is perched on a ridge just to the left of the falls, and from here a 131-m (430-ft) suspension bridge spans the width of the canyon, offering mesmerizing views no matter where you look. On one side, La Cascada Esmeralda surges down the canyon walls and through the forest hundreds of feet below, and on the other side, the canyon opens up to a panoramic view of the imposing ridges of the Sierra Sur. The distinctive peak in the distance that resembles El Cerro de la Silla (Saddle Hill) in Monterrey is called Yuku Yuu, which means "Hill of Stone" in the local Mixtec dialect.

Hiking and Swimming

The park has many marked and easy-to-follow trails, most of which descend into the canyon from the cabañas area, but there are also less frequently hiked trails that involve a bit more bushwhacking to satisfy your urge for adventure. No matter where you are along the slopes, you can orient yourself by the sound of rushing water. In calmer parts, the Río Esmeralda stalls in brilliant green pools that justify its luxurious name and offer paradisiacal settings for cooling off in the afternoon heat. But use your best judgment and stick to the calmer pools. The falls all through the canyon are quite strong and aren't really for splashing around in.

Zip-Lining

Also spanning the vertiginous heights of the canyon is a 300-m (984-ft) zip line, in case the suspension bridge doesn't elicit enough adrenaline in you. You'll pay about US$5.45 a zip.

Tours

Edilberto Martínez Sánchez and the folks at the park offer four different hiking tours called rutas (routes), some of which venture beyond the boundaries of the park into the surrounding rancherías (rural neighborhoods). Other sights on these tours include caves, pinturas rupestres (cave paintings), lagoons and other waterfalls, and a ton of miradores with phenomenal vistas. Contact Edilberto (tel. 953/157-5123, or 951/212-2417 via WhatsApp; if you don't speak Spanish, use Google Translate and send a message on WhatsApp) for more information and to book tours.

Food and Accommodations

The one downside to staying in the park is that, aside from soda pop and Cheetos, there's nothing to eat here. Luckily, the nearby town of **Santiago Yosondúa,** about 10 minutes away in a taxi, has a few hotels and restaurants.

Restaurante El Manantial

Nicolás Régules 8, Santiago Yosondúa; tel. 953/100-2463; 7am-10pm daily; US$3

Your most reliable option is Restaurante El Manantial, with a comedor-style rotating daily menu of delicious home-cooked Oaxacan meals. From the Parque Central, head two blocks south to Nicolás Régules and take this east a block and a half. A handful of other comedores dot this street, but El Manantial is the most consistent.

Cabañas

Although there are a few hotels in town that would be closer to more restaurants, the best place to stay is at the park's cabañas (US$50). The two cabins that sleep four people each are rustic, for sure, but they have solar-powered electricity and private bathrooms with hot water; all are surrounded by the lush, semiarid vegetation of the canyon. Unlike cabañas in other parts of the state, they don't have fireplaces, which are less necessary here than at higher altitudes. It isn't likely that the cabañas will be booked up, but call beforehand since it's a trek to get here. To head into town to eat, ask the park office to call you a taxi.

Getting There

This is the hard part. In Tlaxiaco, head to the **Terminal de Autobuses Yosondúa** but don't get on a bus (they go to Mexico City). You'll find the terminal on Calle Hipódromo, one block east of Calle Independencia. You can walk here from the Plaza de la Constitución by heading two blocks east on 5 de Mayo to Independencia, where you'll take a right. Walk four blocks south until you get to Calle Hipódromo. Take a left, walk one block, and cross the little bridge. You'll see the terminal on your left. Note: It's easier to just take a taxi.

At the ticket window, say you want to take a **taxi colectivo** to Santiago Yosondúa. The trip costs about US$6, takes about 1.75 hours, and is not comfortable; but as stated earlier, it is worth it. From Santiago Yosondúa, taxis to the park cost about US$3.50 and get you there in about 10 minutes.

Drivers don't have it much easier. I'm going to describe the long way from Tlaxiaco to Santiago Yosondúa, because the route the taxi drivers take is confusing. Take Calle Independencia south until you see the sign for Chalcatongo (you might have to ask for directions). Chalcatongo is 57 km (35 mi) from Tlaxiaco, and you should reach it in a little under two hours. Continue south from here 22 km (13.7 mi) until you get to Santiago Yosondúa, about 40 minutes down the road. From town, drive west on any road until you get to the unnamed dirt road that borders the west side of town. Take this road south; about 4 km (2.5 mi) outside town, you'll see the sign for Parque Yosondúa. Turn right to descend into the canyon. The park office is about 130 m (425 ft) down the road, on your left.

La Mixteca Baja

The Mixtec name for La Mixteca Baja (Low Mixteca) is Ñuiñe (nyoo-EE-nyeh), "Hot Country." As the name suggests, the climate of this lower region of La Mixteca is warmer than up in the pine forests of Tlaxiaco and Teposcolula. Out here are more stunning landscapes such as the 400-m (1,300-ft) vertical walls of Cañón El Boquerón, as well as the ruins of Cerro de las Minas in Huajuapan de León and places to try more local culinary delicacies.

HUAJUAPAN DE LEÓN AND VICINITY

Although folks had already been living here for a couple thousand years, Huajuapan de León as we know it was founded in 1561. A group of brave locals who defended the town during the fight for Mexico's independence from Spain earned it the title "The Heroic City of Huajuapan de León" when it was officially designated a city in 1884. In Nahuatl, Huajuapan means "Place of Huaje Trees Next to the River," using an alternate spelling of the guaje tree for which the state is named. Its Mixtec name, Ñudee, means "Land of the Brave." Huajuapan is the perfect base for exploring La Mixteca Baja.

Sights

Parque Independencia

At the center of Huajuapan is Parque Independencia, a virtual forest of a zócalo that is shaded by towering ficus and jacaranda trees. A statue of town hero Antonio de León stands guard at its north side, watching over the Catedral de San Juan Bautista, a 17th-century neoclassical church built of rosy red limestone.

Museo Regional de Huajuapan (MUREH)

Nuyoó 15; tel. 953/536-1069; 10am-2pm and 4pm-8pm Tues.-Sun.; free

Just a five-minute walk north of Parque Independencia is the Museo Regional de Huajuapan, a small museum dedicated to the preservation and celebration of Mixtec heritage and culture. Here you'll find a collection of Mixtec artifacts and modern exhibits filled with pieces created by local artists. The museum also hosts concerts, plays, workshops, and a number of other events that you may be lucky enough to catch. You'll need to stop here anyway to see Lic. Austerlitz Sanchez Mendez, the cultural heritage manager, before heading to Cerro de las Minas, so spend half an hour or so exploring the museum's offerings.

Huajuapan de León

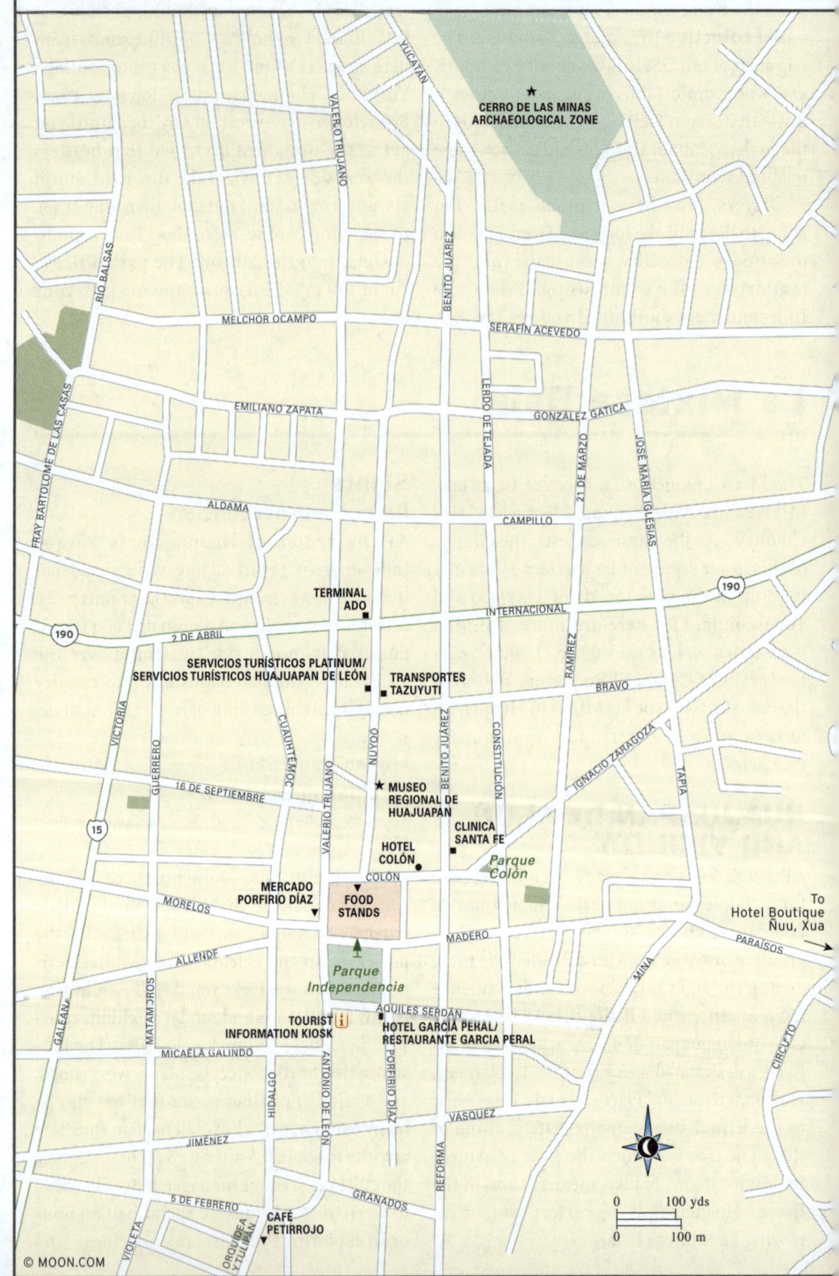

Cerro de las Minas Archaeological Zone

The place now called Cerro de las Minas (Hill of Mines) was founded sometime around 400 BC by early Mixtec people known as the Ñuu Yate, Mixtec for "The Ancient People." Its strategic location atop a hill surrounded by broad tracts of arable land made it the major economic, political, and sociocultural center for the surrounding communities, and within a couple of centuries it reached a population of 1,000-2,000 inhabitants. In contrast to other pre-Hispanic sites in Oaxaca, which center around one large central plaza, Ñuiñe urban planning at Cerro de las Minas and other ancient settlements in La Mixteca included numerous smaller plazas with temples, tombs, and housing for the elite around them.

The most notable finds uncovered by archaeological excavations in the 1980s are the bas-relief Ñuiñe glyphs carved into limestone slabs. Generally consisting of a central glyph, most likely a person's name, surrounded by calendrical characters, this early Mixtec writing system is one of five documented Mesoamerican scripts. The best examples of these glyphs are on the walls inside Tomb 5.

It doesn't take more than about half an hour to explore the ruins, but trails crisscrossing the hill allow for a bit of exploration among guaje trees and patches of bright wildflowers. The ruins' location offers gorgeous 360-degree views of the surrounding landscape of La Mixteca Baja, which shines a vibrant green in the rainy season.

To check in and get a tour of the site, stop by the Regional Museum of Huajuapan (MUREH; Nuyoó 15; tel. 953/536-1069; 10am-2pm and 4pm-8pm Tues.-Sun.) and see Lic. Austerlitz Sánchez Méndez. He'll get you set up with a guided tour, which is mandatory for seeing the site.

Food

After sundown, **food stands** set up shop on the north side Cathedral de San Juan (across from Parque Independencia), selling tacos, quesadillas, tostadas, elotes (roasted corn), and other local treats for those nighttime snack attacks. Try a triangulito, a local specialty that is (surprise) a tortilla in the shape of (surprise) a triangle and filled with (surprise) beans. They'll top it off with salsa, cream, and cheese, and meat if you want it. These vendors pack it up around 11pm.

Café Petirrojo

Orquídea y Tulipán 2; tel. 953/142-5718; 8am-10:30pm daily; US$5-10

The best place in town for a good espresso is Café Petirrojo (Robin Red Breast). It's a bit of a walk from the zócalo, but if you need good coffee, it's worth the trip. They use deliciously dark beans from the famous coffee-growing town of Coatepec in Veracruz (an adorable Pueblo Mágico where the aroma of coffee fills the streets). The café also serves full breakfasts, sandwiches, and snack foods and has a children's menu. You'll find their second location on Guerrero 8 (tel. 953/124-8745).

★ Restaurante García Peral

Heroico Colegio Militar 1; tel. 953/532-1532; www.hotelgarciaperal.com; 8am-10:30pm Mon.-Sat., 8am-10pm Sun.; US$11-16

The best place in town to try local and seasonal delicacies like mole de caderas is definitely Restaurante García Peral, the sleek, lily-decorated eatery in the hotel of the same name. For a unique and flavorful breakfast, try the chile relleno stuffed with a cheese omelet, made with meaty chile poblano. In the evening, you might be lucky and catch a live musical performance.

Mercado Porfirio Díaz

tel. 953/102-0202; 8:30am-7:30pm daily; US$5-7

For cheaper eats, head to the Mercado Porfirio Díaz, across the churchyard from the cathedral. The fondas on the north side of the market serve fresh and tasty antojitos (snacks), pozole, barbacoa, and more. Inside, booths of fresh-baked breads, chocolates, mezcal, and more are piled mountainously high around the vendors hollering to grab the attention of people passing by.

Accommodations

Hotel Colón

Colón 10; tel. 953/532-0817; US$25-32 d, US$32 t

Just a block north of Parque Independencia, Hotel Colón is the best value in town. The 50 basic but clean rooms are set around its ample parking space. Again, it's bare-bones, but this place has TVs, hot water, fans, and it'll do for a night.

Hotel Boutique Ñuu, Xua

Eucaliptos 4; tel. 953/532-5070; US$68 d, US$110 suite

Drivers who don't want to deal with the congested traffic of the centro should consider staying at Hotel Boutique Ñuu, Xua, whose name means "New Town" in Mixtec. Just two blocks west of Highway 190 on the east side of town, it offers easy access when arriving and leaving. The 1.5-km (1-mi) walk to the Centro takes around 20 minutes. Ñuu, Xua artistically combines modern luxury with ancient tradition, with white stucco juxtaposed with red stone walls that resemble the town's hilltop ruins. Inside, the rooms are furnished in a sleek, contemporary style that tastefully accents the bare bricks in the walls. Amenities include parking, air-conditioning, TVs, and Wi-Fi. The on-site **restaurant** (9am-5pm) is another good place for mole de caderas when it's in season, and the tables in the courtyard next to the grand staircase are perfect for a romantic alfresco dinner.

Hotel García Peral

Heroico Colegio Militar 1; tel. 953/532-0777; US$78 d, US$111 suite

Hotel García Peral has been in business since 1945, but that doesn't mean they rest on their laurels. They are constantly adapting to new services and technology, most recently by using solar power to generate electricity. Aside from its excellent location at the southeast corner of the zócalo, the hotel boasts a gym, swimming pool, and lush garden areas for relaxation. Locals hail the on-site restaurant as the best food in town.

Information and Services

For information on the ruins and other local attractions, stop by the **tourism kiosk** (in the Casa de Cultura, Calle Heroico Militar #1, across from the southwest corner of the zócalo; tel. 953/532-2740; 8am-4pm Mon.-Fri., 9am-2pm Sat.) on the south side of the main square.

For medical services and emergencies, **Clínica Santa Fe** (Benito Juárez 2; tel. 953/532-0902; 24 hrs daily) has round-the-clock emergency care. Doctors only speak Spanish.

The **post office** (5 de Febrero 16; no tel.; 8am-4pm Mon.-Fri., 8:30am-11:30am Sat.) is a few blocks south of the main square. From its southwest corner, walk south on Antonio de León until it curves to the right and becomes 5 de Febrero. The post office is a block and a half down the street on the left.

Getting There

To get to Huajuapan from Oaxaca City by bus, you have limited choices. Autobuses SUR runs two daily routes from **Terminal Periférico** (Periférico 1006, Oaxaca City; no tel.; US$10) in the southwest corner of the Centro, about three blocks south of the Centro de Abastos, but they leave at 5am and 11pm for the three-hour trip. The **ADO Terminal in Huajuapan** is on the corner of Calle Nuyoó and Highway 190, three blocks north of the churchyard.

Your best option from Oaxaca City is to take a suburban run by **Servicios Turísticos de Huajuapan** (Valerio Trujano 420, Oaxaca City; tel. 951/516-5759; US$6). Vans run every 1.25 hours, beginning around 4am. They will take you to their **terminal in Huajuapan** (Nuyoó 36; tel. 953/530-5204), a couple of blocks north of the main square. From Nochixtlán, you'll have to take a taxi to the gas station west of town on Highway 190 and hop on one of these suburbanes. The trip from here takes about 1.5 hours and costs around US$5.

Drivers from Oaxaca City take Highway 190 west out of the city and take the left lanes to exit onto Highway 135D (toll)

11 km (6.8 mi) outside of the city. Stay on this highway another 69 km (43 mi), then exit onto Highway 190 just outside Nochixtlán. Drivers from Nochixtlán head west on Porfirio Díaz to get on Highway 190. Huajuapan is 91 km (57 mi) down Highway 190 from this junction. Total drive time from Oaxaca City is 2.5 hours, and 1.5 hours from Nochixtlán.

SANTO DOMINGO TONALÁ

The small farming town of Santo Domingo Tonalá is the perfect escape from the busy streets of Huajuapan de León. Mototaxis cruise the town's broad, palm-lined avenues, ferrying residents around the tranquil, traffic-free couple dozen blocks that make up town. Even the short hike through the canyon north of town is a rather laid-back activity.

Tonalá is Nahuatl for "The Place Where It Gets Hot," but don't worry. If you need to cool off, you can find some shade in the jungly churchyard in front of the 16th-century neo-classical **Iglesia de Santo Domingo,** or among the massive ahuehuete (Montezuma cypress) trees in **La Sabinera,** a small park two blocks east of the zócalo. The largest of these trees is at the far west end of the park, with a diameter of 4.5 m (14.8 ft) and a girth of 15 m (49 ft).

Cañón El Boquerón

You'll pass the entrance to the Cañón El Boquerón (Bigmouth Canyon) when you cross the bridge over the Río Salado on your way into town. Decreed a protected area in 2008, this awe-inspiring gorge is home to hundreds of species of flora and fauna, although you're not likely to see many animals besides lizards, weird caterpillars, and a spectrum of colorful butterflies on the trail. Much of the walking path is cantilevered over the river below, hugging the sheer canyon walls that tower more than 400 m (1,300 ft) above the canyon floor. Other stretches of the trail run under lines of jacaranda trees, which are stunning in spring when their leafless branches are ablaze with pinkish-purple blossoms that fall to the ground like magical snow.

It takes only about an hour to walk the flat, easy 2-km (1.2-mi) trail, but since there's little else to do, you might make a leisurely afternoon of it with a picnic or just chilling out on the riverbank. To get here from Tonalá, grab a colectivo bound for Huajuapan on the highway (about US$1). The bridge is about 4 km (2.5 mi) north of town; you'll find the entrance to the trail on the north side of the bridge.

Food and Accommodations

During the day, head to the **open-air food market** (9am-6pm Mon.-Sat.) next to the main plaza for delicious antojitos like quesadillas and tacos, as well as richly flavored moles and other guisados (sauce-based dishes) like chileajo, a pork dish made with guajillo and chicoxtle peppers.

La Casita

Niños Heroes; tel. 953/127-6884; 9am-10pm Tues.-Sun.; US$8-12

This breezy palapa-style restaurant serves a plethora of tasty seafood dishes with rather fetching presentations. Sure, there's chicken and beef on the menu, too, but the lovely view and bamboo-thatched walls will have you in the mood for an aguachile de mango (think a spicier ceviche) or camarones zarandeados (shrimp made with a cooking technique that hails from Nayarit). You can wash it all down with margaritas made with fresh fruit (or with candy for my relentless sweet tooths).

Hotel California

Melchor Ocampo; tel. 953/531-0026; US$24 d

Alí Martínez and family run Hotel California, with five basic but clean rooms stocked with TVs, fans, and double beds. They also run **Cabañas Garra de Jaguar** (Jaguar Claw Cabañas; US$27), a quaint collection of cabins in a field south of town.

Ocho Venado

Eight Deer; tel. 953/531-0026; 8am-9pm daily; US$4-6

They have comfy beds, fans, and hot water, but no kitchens at the cabins, so you'll have to eat in town—or call up Alí and he'll bring you food (I recommend the burritos) from the hotel restaurant, Ocho Venado, named after the powerful Mixtec warrior-king.

Getting There

Santo Domingo Tonalá is a scenic, one-hour drive from Huajuapan through forested hills with columnar cacti poking their spiny heads above the treetops. Take Highway 15 south from Huajuapan for 47 km (29 mi) until you reach Tonalá.

A suburban run by **Transportes Tazuyuti** (Nuyoó 29, Huajuapan; tel. 953/155-3180) will cost you a bit over US$2. They leave Huajuapan every half hour and take a little over an hour. If you're planning to visit just the canyon, not Tonalá, tell the driver to let you off before the Puente Morelos (Morelos Bridge), or Cañón El Boquerón. The Tazuyuti terminal in Tonalá is right off the highway on the south side of town, five blocks from the zócalo.

Sierra Norte, El Papaloapan, and La Cañada

From vertiginous, pine-forested peaks shrouded in almost constant cloud cover to hot, humid lowlands full of sugarcane and rubber tree fields, Oaxaca's northern regions call out to adventure-seekers. The altitude of the mountains combined with humid air from the Gulf of Mexico is the perfect combination for an ecosystem so varied that it earned Mexico a place on Conservation International's list of the world's 17 megadiverse countries.

Up in the Sierra Norte, an oak tree will be home to half a dozen other plants, many of which you've likely never seen before. Entire forests are full of ghostly mosses or the bright flowers of bromeliads, so many that there's a good chance you'll witness bromeliads falling from branches they grew too big for. Hirsute ferns grow into 6-m-tall (20-ft-tall) trees

Highlights

Look for ★ to find recommended sights, activities, dining, and lodging.

★ **Pueblos Mancomunados:** Experience community-led ecotourism at its finest, in a connected group of Zapotec villages offering hiking, zip-lining, biking, and cultural educational opportunities in the gorgeous Sierra Norte mountains (page 240).

★ **Mirador de Cristal:** Not for the faint of heart, this lookout point is one of the highest in Latin America, and with its see-through floor, one of the most heart-stopping (page 256).

★ **Parque Ecoturixtlán:** A cozy cabin in the forest is the idyllic setting to explore this serene park full of caves, waterfalls, and peaceful woodland (page 258).

★ **Huautla de Jiménez:** On the slopes of the Sierra Mazateca, come pay homage to famed traditional healer curandera Maria Sabina at her birthplace (page 270).

★ **Las Regaderas:** Just outside Huautla, these twin waterfalls cascading down from the Sierra Mazateca make a striking sight against the green woodlands they're nestled in (page 277)

★ **Cañón del Sabino:** Witness the emerald flight of flocks of green macaws against the verdant backdrop of this awe-inspiring canyon in La Cañada (page 276).

and cover entire mountainsides in what look like dark-green waterfalls. And you've probably never seen so many different orchids blooming in one place as you do in the Sierra Mazateca, at the western end of the range. It's not an exaggeration to say that something astonishing lies around nearly every bend in the highway.

The only reason so few tourists make it to El Papaloapan is because the region's coastline is in the neighboring state of Veracruz. But these tropical lowlands on the north side of the mountains are full of lush, untouched natural beauty, and the seafood is as good as that of Oaxaca's Pacific coast.

The arid canyon country of La Cañada, to the west of the mountains, has been off the radar of foreign visitors for some time, but that should really change. Home to the Oaxacan half of the Tehuacán-Cuicatlán Biosphere Reserve, this region is home to sprawling cactus forests, stupefyingly deep canyons, and huge flocks of green macaws, not to mention some of the rarer recipes in the Oaxacan cookbook.

Lots of the places here are out of the way and therefore require a bit more effort than other parts of the state. However, as anyone who has driven these highways will tell you, the journey, as well as the destination, is worth it. If you're after adventure and adrenaline, head north from Oaxaca City.

ORIENTATION

The term **Sierra Norte** refers generally to the mountains in the north, which have regional names, as well. The mountains at the western end of the range are the **Sierra Mazateca,** named for the main Indigenous group who has called them home for centuries. Directly north and east of Oaxaca City is the **Sierra Juárez,** home to admirably organized ecotourism spots like the Pueblos Mancomunados and Ixtlán de Juárez. The mountains to the east are called the **Sierra Mixe,** also for the Indigenous group calling them home. On the north side of the mountains is **El Papaloapan,** a vast swath of tropical lowlands named for the Río Papaloapan, the region's largest river. **La Cañada** is the canyon country to the west of the Sierra Mazateca.

PLANNING YOUR TIME

Give yourself about two weeks to see all the highlights here. The conventional route starts off in the **Pueblos Mancomunados,** whose high-altitude flagship town, **Cuajimoloyas,** has lots of hikes, bike routes, and other outdoor and cultural activities to keep you busy for days. Or you could hike to one of the other Pueblos Mancomunados via the over 100 km (62 mi) of nature trails that connect them all. (If you only have a few days to get a taste of the region, the Pueblos Mancomunados are where you should focus your time.) After three days or so in these villages, head north to **Ixtlán de Juárez** to spend a couple of days exploring the bromeliad forests and caves in **Parque Ecoturixtlán.** The charming Pueblo Mágico (magic town) of **Capulálpam de Méndez** is also worth a day's exploration (or two if you become as enamored as I did).

After checking out Oaxaca's second-largest city, Tuxtepec, head north to **San Pedro Ixcatlán,** on a peninsula that juts out into Lake Miguel Alemán, and take a boat tour to **La Isla del Viejo Soyaltepec.** You'll see lots of migrating large birds on the way, and exploring the island and chatting with locals is a fun way to pass some afternoon hours.

Spend the night in Ixcatlán, or head up the mountains to **Huautla de Jiménez.** Plan for one or two days here, seeing nearby sights like the hilltop worship area Cerro de la Adoración and the waterfalls called **Las Regaderas.**

Finally, head down to La Cañada, "Canyon Country," to trek through the 600-m-deep (2,000-ft-deep) **Cañón del Sabino,** home to numerous flocks of green macaws. Don't forget to try the delicious local specialties, such as pilte (marinated meat cooked in a

Previous: highway in the Sierra Norte; sunset over the Sierra Mazateca; flowers in the Sierra Norte.

Sierra Norte, El Papaloapan, and La Cañada

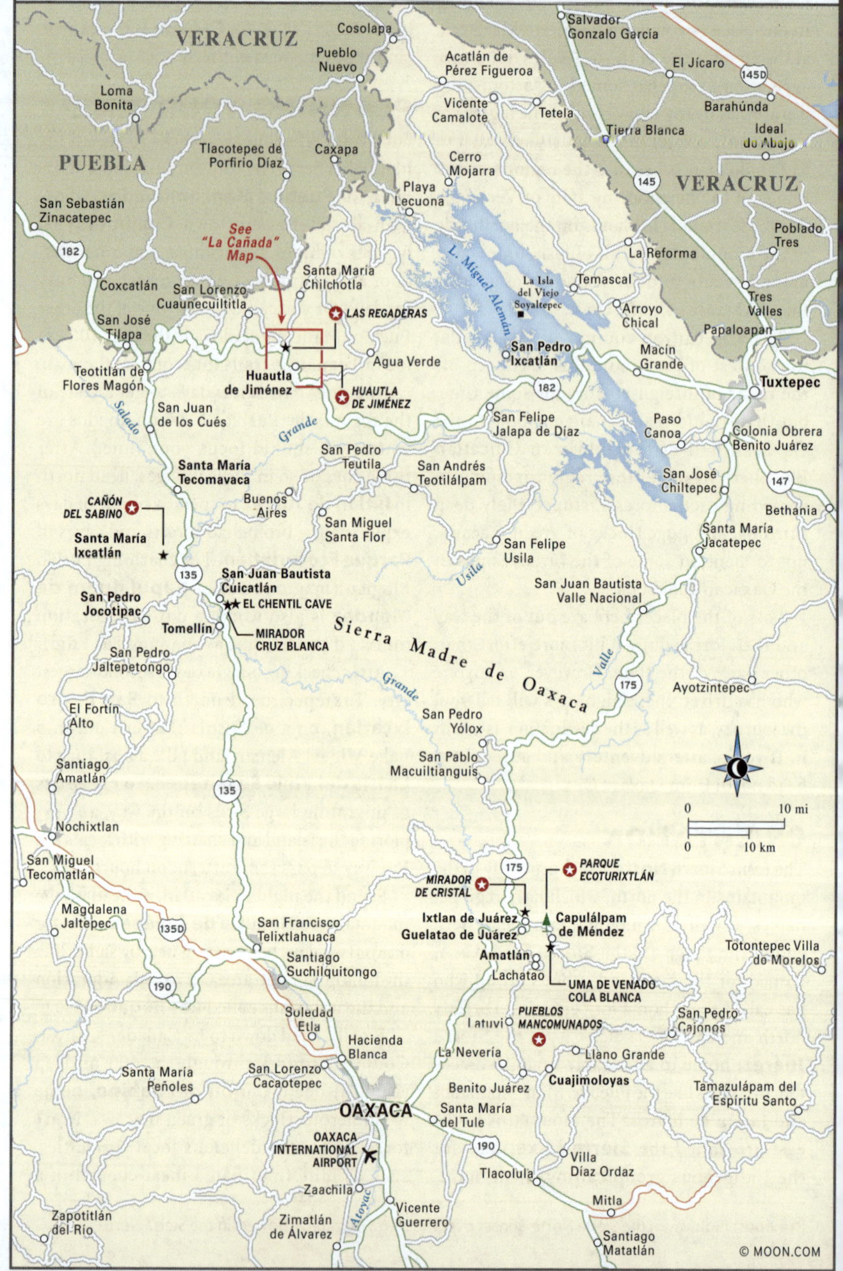

banana-leaf wrapper on hot coals) and mole chichilo, which gets its rich, smoky flavor from ground tortillas made of charred corn.

That should be enough, though you'll probably see many things that will make you want to stay longer.

Itinerary Ideas

A trip to the pueblos of the Sierra Juárez is less about doing and more about being. The gorgeous views, enchanting towns, and delicious mountain air are an invitation to unplug and unwind. Traveling between the three towns in this itinerary can easily be done by rental car or by using colectivos and taxis.

DAY 1: GUELATAO, IXTLÁN, AND ECOTURIXTLÁN

1 History buffs will appreciate beginning the day by paying homage to beloved Zapotec president Benito Juárez in his quiet hometown of Guelatao. In the main square, visit the **Sala Homenaje a Juárez,** peek inside the **Museo Casa Replica Benito Juárez,** and take a leisurely stroll around the **Laguna Encantada.**

2 Head 10 minutes north to Ixtlán de Juárez. Stop by the **Templo de Santo Tomás Apóstol** on your way to brunch a couple of blocks away at **Restaurante de la Calzada.**

3 Catch a mototaxi up to **Mirador de Cristal** to take in heart-stopping views.

4 Enjoy the grounds of **Truchería Cuachirindoo** and fill up on a delicious trout dinner.

5 Time to head to **Parque Ecoturixtlán!** Check in to your cabin and enjoy a peaceful night.

DAY 2: ECOTURIXTLÁN AND CAPULÁLPAM

1 Start with a hearty breakfast at **Restaurante Los Duendes.**

2 Explore all **Parque Ecoturixtlán** has to offer. Caves, orchid gardens, forest hikes, ziplines, obstacle courses, and of course, plain old relaxing.

3 Enjoy lunch at **Restaurante Los Duendes.**

4 Make your way to Capulálpam. Check in to **Hotel Los Sabinos.**

5 Catch the sunset with dinner and dessert at **El Verbo de Méndez Café.**

DAY 3: CAPULÁLPAM DE MÉNDEZ

1 Eat a scrumptious breakfast of mole coloradito at the **Mercado Municipal.**

2 Stop by the traditional medicine hospital and **Taller y Galería de Juguete y Arte** to pick up unique souvenirs.

3 Have a riverside lunch at **Restaurante Los Molinos.** The trout is fresh and the tostadas are huge. If you're up to it, you can rappel or climb the cliffs behind the restaurant.

4 Go back into town before sunset to visit the **White Deer Wildlife Reserve** and feed the deer as you learn about their conservation efforts.

5 Enjoy a rooftop dinner back at **Hotel Los Sabinos.**

★ Pueblos Mancomunados

TOP EXPERIENCE

Oaxaca's best example of community organizing for responsible ecotourism is the Pueblos Mancomunados (United Villages) in the cloud-covered peaks of the Sierra Norte. The town of Benito Juárez was the first to begin offering ecotourism services here in 1994, and the neighboring towns of Cuajimoloyas, Llano Grande, La Nevería, Latuvi, Amatlán, Lachatao, and Yavesía joined the organization four years later. (At the time of this writing, Yavesía was not offering ecotourism services.) This community organizing has benefited both the land and the people living on it by bringing new economic opportunities that promote sustainable treatment of the natural resources they depend on in order to be profitable.

Now over 100 km (62 mi) of two-track dirt roads and hiking trails snake up and down the piney slopes and steep valleys of cornfields and wildflower patches to connect all eight member communities. Local trails in each community offer even more hiking and mountain biking opportunities to visitors. Home to over 2,000 plant species, 400 bird species, 350 different types of butterflies, and six classes of wild mountain cats, this region is recognized by the World Wildlife Fund for its high biodiversity.

Planning Your Time

Peaks here reach as high as 3,330 m (10,925 ft) above sea level, with minimum daytime temperatures averaging 8-10°C (46-50°F) and nightly lows as cold as 1°C (34°F), so don't forget to bring warm clothes. When the sun is out, however, you can expect temperatures as high as 28°C (82°F). The rainy season roughly runs June-November, with the heaviest rains falling between July and September. The best time to visit is October-December, when the views are green and full of life. When the skies are clear, such heights receive intense sunlight, so pack sunscreen and a hat, as well as lighter clothing for daytime.

Access Fee

Once you get up here, you'll want to stay a night or two, but if you've only got a day to explore, you'll have to pay an access fee of US$5.50 to enter the Pueblos Mancomunados. You can arrange this beforehand or simply show up at the ecotourism office in the town you arrive in and pay the fee.

In each town you visit, check in with the local ecotourism office. If you're in town for the day, you'll need to pay the access fee; if you're staying overnight, the fee is included in the price of the accommodations, for which you'll need to stop by the ecotourism office to check in anyway.

Local Guides

Expediciones Sierra Norte

M. Bravo 210-F, Oaxaca City; tel. 951/226-8395 or 951/310-3904; www.sierranorte.org.mx; sierranorteoaxaca@gmail.com

All tourism activities in the Pueblos Mancomunados are operated by Expediciones Sierra Norte. You can organize trips with them beforehand or stop in at their offices in the towns. The guías comunitarios (community guides) are locals from the villages who know the mountain trails, including local flora and fauna, better than anyone. English-speaking guides are available. For shorter routes (8-13 km/5-8 mi), they charge around US$20 for groups of up to seven hikers. Longer routes (15-25 km/9-16 mi) cost around US$60 per group.

HIKING

A hike through the Sierra Norte takes in sprawling vistas of sawtooth mountain ranges painted blue by distance; friendly farmers tending fields of corn, beans, and other crops; an array of orchids, wildflowers, ferns, bromeliads, and mosses; and whole choruses of crooning songbirds. In addition to the roads and trails that connect the Pueblos Mancomunados, each town has smaller hikes to miradores (lookout points), waterfalls, canyons, caves, and other impressive natural features. Most trails are marked, albeit sporadically and insufficiently; the recommended option for hikes here is to hire a guide. It is easy to take a wrong turn, and you don't want to get lost.

Besides the local hikes around each town, there are eight **Rutas de Naturaleza** (Nature Routes). These routes go from town to town, linking the pueblos with hikes of about 7-20 km (4.3-12.4 mi) one-way.

Ruta Loma de Cucharilla

Distance: *15.7 km (9.8 mi) one-way*
Duration: *4 hours*
Difficulty: *difficult*
Trailhead: *Cuajimoloyas, signed gate on the ridge west of town*

Linking Cuajimoloyas to Latuvi, the Ruta Loma de Cucharilla is named for the plant called cucharilla (little spoon), which grows in abundance along the route. Its spoon-shaped leaves are used to make decorations for religious celebrations in the region. This hike descends through pine and oak forests and past colorful meadows, babbling brooks, and the campgrounds north of Cuajimoloyas. Most of the hike is flat, but there are descents at the beginning and end, the latter of which is quite steep; good physical condition is required.

Ruta Yaa-Tini

Distance: *19.8 km (12.3 mi) one-way*
Duration: *5 hours*
Difficulty: *difficult*
Trailhead: *Llano Grande*

The Ruta Yaa-Tini links Llano Grande to Lachatao and Amatlán in the north. With an elevation drop of nearly 1,100 m (3,600 ft), this is the best hike for observing the Sierra Norte's spectacular range of the biodiversity. There is quite a bit of up and down, so depending on your walking speed, this hike can take as long as five hours. Good physical condition is recommended.

Ruta Shoo Raa

Distance: *14.7 km (9.1 mi) one-way*
Duration: *4 hours*
Difficulty: *difficult*
Trailhead: *north side of Llano Grande*

Heading north from Llano Grande, the Ruta Shoo Raa will take you to Yavesía. The first 8 km (5 mi) or so descends gently about 300 m (984 ft). The second half of the hike is much steeper, descending all the way to 1,900 m (6,234 ft) at Yavesía. This four-hour hike is another great opportunity to observe the changes in vegetation at various altitudes.

Ruta Camino Real

Distance: *11.9 km (7.4 mi) one-way*
Duration: *4 hours*
Difficulty: *easy*
Trailhead: *Latuvi, bottom of the hill from the ecotourism office, to the right*

The Ruta Camino Real is believed to have been part of a much longer pre-Hispanic thoroughfare that connected the Zapotec settlements in the Sierra Norte and the Valles Centrales to villages in the Gulf Coast region of Mexico. In some parts, the original stones of the road are still intact. The Camino Real runs from Latuvi north to Lachatao and Amatlán, much of it along the banks of the Río Cara de León (Lion's Face River). With little elevation change, it's a relatively easy hike that takes about four hours.

Ruta Cipriano Cabrera

Distance: *10.9 km (6.8 mi) one-way*
Duration: *2.5-3 hours*
Difficulty: *moderate*
Trailhead: *north side of La Nevería*

The Ruta Cipriano Cabrera runs north from the pine forests of La Nevería to the warmer oak woods of Latuvi. After a slight ascent at the beginning, the quaint rural footpath descends almost 500 m (1,640 ft) in just a few kilometers, offering stunning views of the surrounding landscape.

1
2
3
4
PUEBLOS MANCOMUNADOS

Ruta Needa-Queta-Miru

Distance: *8.2 km (5.1 mi) one-way*
Duration: *2 hours*
Difficulty: *easy*
Trailhead: *Benito Juárez*

Running from Benito Juárez to La Nevería, the Ruta Needa-Queta-Miru is used by many local farmers to get to and from their fields. It's mostly downhill, but around the 6-km (3.7-mi) mark it begins to climb back up to La Nevería, so conserve your energy for the end. The easy walk, mostly through fields of beans and corn, takes about two hours.

Ruta Latzi-Hroo-Lii

Distance: *8.2 km (5.1 mi) one-way*
Duration: *2 hours*
Difficulty: *easy*
Trailhead: *Cuajimoloyas*

The flattest route is the Ruta Latzi-Hroo-Lii, which runs along a high ridge between Cuajimoloyas and Llano Grande. Since it doesn't change elevation much, the entire trail runs through forests of towering, moss-covered pine trees.

Ruta Needa-Yaa-Lagashxi

Distance: *6.6 km (4.1 mi) one-way*
Duration: *2 hours*
Difficulty: *moderate*
Trailhead: *west side of Cuajimoloyas*

The shortest Ruta de Naturaleza, the Ruta Needa-Yaa-Lagashxi, leads west from Cuajimoloyas to Benito Juárez. This trail heads down the steep slopes west of Cuajimoloyas through farmland and pastures, bottoming out in a valley with a crystal-clear river. The trail ascends about halfway back up to reach Benito Juárez. As on the Ruta Needa-Queta-Miru, you'll probably meet local farmers heading to or from their fields or working in them.

1: wildflowers on the hillsides of Benito Juárez **2:** a hike through the pine forests **3:** blooming maguey plant **4:** trail marker in the Pueblos Mancomunados

MOUNTAIN BIKING

There are miles and miles of double-track and single-track trails up in these mountains, and Expediciones Sierra Norte (M. Bravo 210-F, Oaxaca City; tel. 951/226-8395 or 951/310-3904; www.sierranorte.org.mx; sierranorteoaxaca@gmail.com) has all the gear you'll need, as well as highly trained and knowledgeable guides to show you the way. Biking tours are charged per person, and can include up to twelve riders in a group. Easier routes cost US$100, and more technical rides run about US$150. These prices include the bike rental, transportation, food, access to the area, and insurance. Call ahead to ensure the staff and equipment will be ready.

Circuito Taurino Mecinas Ceballos

The Circuito Taurino Mecinas Ceballos has three sections that connect Benito Juárez, La Nevería, and Latuvi. Experienced riders who don't like pit stops can complete the circuit in a little over three hours. If you prefer a more casual pace and stops for sightseeing and meals, you can expect the trip to take up to twice as long.

Benito Juárez to La Nevería

The first is the shortest and least technical, running 7.7 km (4.8 mi) along the high ridge between Benito Juárez and La Nevería. After about 5 km (3 mi) of short climbs and descents, the rest of the trail slopes down to the terminus, which is only slightly lower in elevation than Benito Juárez. The ride takes half an hour to an hour, depending on your experience and condition.

La Nevería to Latuvi

From La Nevería, the second section climbs about 50 m (164 ft) in about 0.5 km (0.3 mi), then descends steeply for 5 km (3 mi) before beginning a slight ascent the rest of the way to Latuvi. This is one of the more technical routes, as more than half of the 10.9-km (6.8-mi) trail is single-track, requiring a bit more experience than the first part. This leg takes 45 minutes or more.

Latuvi to Benito Juárez

The third section runs between Benito Juárez and Latuvi, descending from lofty pine forests that gradually fill with moss-covered oak trees in the lower elevations. The 12-km (7.4-mi) route drops about 600 m (1,968 ft) on a two-track road. Be aware that, although they're infrequent, cars are allowed on roads like this. You can expect this leg to take 45 minutes to an hour.

Ruta Ka-Yezzi-Daa-Vii

The fourth and longest bike route here is the Ruta Ka-Yezzi-Daa-Vii, which runs 28 km (17 mi) north from Cuajimoloyas to the towns of Lachatao and Amatlán on the north side of the Pueblos Mancomunados. This is not for inexperienced riders. Starting from an elevation of 3,100 m (10,170 ft), the trail descends, often steeply, a total of 900 m (2,950 ft), and loose rocks and gravel cover some stretches. Also, vehicles are allowed on these roads. The one-way ride takes about three hours and is a great way to see various geographies and vegetation zones.

Biking Tours

Zapotrek Tours

Aldama 304-A, Barrio de Jalatlaco, Oaxaca City; tel. 951/257-7712; www.zapotrek.mx; 9am-8pm Mon.-Fri., 2pm-6pm Sat.-Sun.; from US$110 pp

For biking tours from Oaxaca City, contact Eric Ramírez at Zapotrek Tours. You can choose an itinerary of 1-7 days. Each package includes transportation, lodging, meals, snacks, access fees, and an English-speaking guide.

FOOD

The hatcheries serve mouthwatering trout, and you can find snack foods in the little corner shops called misceláneas, but most of your meals in the Pueblos Mancomunados will be in little home-style restaurants called **comedores.** They are generally open 8am-ish to 8pm-ish (emphasis on the *-ish*), and usually charge around US$5 for a set meal.

Although many comedores will have a whole list of dishes they potentially serve, the actual menu changes daily. It's customary to enter and ask what's available. The usual fare includes chiles rellenos, moles, quesadillas, beans, rice, and various guisados (meat stewing in a rich, flavorful sauce). Also, many folks prefer to save money and conserve energy by leaving the lights off if no one is dining inside. If you come upon a darkened comedor, just knock or enter and ask if they're serving food.

ACCOMMODATIONS

Cabañas

Cozy mountain cabins called cabañas (US$40 for 1-2 people, US$50 for 3 people, $60 for 4 people) are the primary accommodations in the Pueblos Mancomunados. These brick structures are all run by Expediciones Sierra Norte. Book ahead or inquire in the local ecotourism office when you arrive. They all include a private bathroom with hot water, comfy queen- or king-size beds, and fireplaces with a load of firewood for the chilly nights. All of these communities have cabañas, but Cuajimoloyas, Latuvi, and Amatlán offer stunning views of the surrounding landscape. If you want to be more nestled in the woods, try Llano Grande or La Nevería.

Casa del Turista

Benito Juárez; tel. 951/172-1581; US$13.50 pp

Unique to Benito Juárez is the Casa del Turista (Tourist House), a large, four-room cabin for up to 22 people with a glass roof over the living room that has a fantastic view of the stars as you fall asleep. The sky is so clear you can see the creamy splash of the Milky Way spill across the night sky. Aside from the bedrooms with dorm-style sleeping arrangements, the cabin has a loft-like second floor, multiple balconies, a beautiful green garden in front, and spectacular views of the valley below.

Hotels

Hotel Yaa-Cuetzi

Cuajimoloyas; tel. 951/524-5024; US$19 pp

Across the street from the ecotourism office in Cuajimoloyas, Hotel Yaa-Cuetzi has simple rooms with twin or queen beds and lots of windows to take in the gorgeous views of the town below and the fog-shrouded peaks beyond. All have shared bathrooms. It's the only hotel in the Pueblos Mancomunados and keeps you in close range of all the delicious food in the comedores. Book through Expediciones Sierra Norte, or inquire in the ecotourism office in Cuajimoloyas.

Camping

All the Pueblos Mancomunados have campgrounds (US$5.50 pp), and many have more than one, giving you the option to stay closer to town or a bit farther away. If you're not traveling with a tent, you can rent one for US$8. The only amenity at all these campgrounds is a dry toilet, but some have access to fresh potable water.

Nighttime temperatures, especially in the higher-altitude communities, get pretty low, occasionally freezing. Make sure you bring the proper clothing and equipment to suit such temperatures. For warmer nighttime temperatures, camp in the towns at lower elevations (Latuvi, Lachatao, and Amatlán).

Larger groups and families should consider the Llano de Tarajeas campgrounds, some 4.5 km (2.8 mi) north of Cuajimoloyas. On the Ruta Ka-Yezzi-Daa-Vii, which leads to Lachatao, the broad clearing has room for dozens of tents, and there is an on-site trout hatchery and comedor, as well as playground equipment for the kids.

CUAJIMOLOYAS

A plaque in town tells the story of Spanish conquistadores who, when they arrived here centuries ago, joked that it was so cold that "el mole cuaja en la olla" (the mole sets in the pot). The phrase was amalgamated to form the town's name. Only rarely does it get below freezing up here, but at 3,200 m (10,500 ft) above sea level, it is one of the highest towns in the Pueblos Mancomunados—so it can get chilly! Squat concrete houses fill the small valley and are stacked up its steep slopes, with ribbons of gray woodsmoke rising from fires set for cooking or just to keep warm. At this altitude, you can expect temperatures in the high 20s Celsius (80s Fahrenheit) when the sun is out, and lows that flirt with the freezing point at night. Pack accordingly.

Hiking

Mirador Yaa-Cuetzi

Distance: *1 km (0.6 mi) one-way*
Duration: *20 minutes*
Difficulty: *easy*
Trailhead: *ecotourism office, heading west*

It's recommended that you just take it easy the first day you get up here, to get adjusted to the high altitude. Try something easy like a short sunset hike up to the Mirador Yaa-Cuetzi, on a pointed crag on the west side of town. The walk from the ecotourism office takes about 20 minutes. Since you're up here, take the fun way down on the 1-km-long (0.6-mi-long) **zip line** (US$13.50), or tirolesa, that soars 100 m (328 ft) above the smoky town below; make arrangements in the ecotourism office.

Mirador Xi-Nudaa

Distance: *14 km (8.7 mi) round-trip*
Duration: *7 hours*
Difficulty: *difficult*
Trailhead: *landing side of the zip line on the east side of town*

Located 7 km (4.3 mi) northeast of town, at an altitude of 3,000 m (9,842 ft), the Mirador Xi-Nudaa offers spectacular 360-degree views of dramatic alpine landscapes, pine and oak forests, winding valleys, and the neighboring villages of Benito Juárez and Latuvi. The cross on the peak commemorates the appearance and tactical support of Saint Michael the Archangel at a battle here during the Mexican Revolution. The route begins at the landing side of the zip line, on the east side of town, and takes about seven hours round-trip.

Cañón del Coyote

Distance: *5 km (3.1 mi) round-trip*
Duration: *3 hours*
Difficulty: *moderate to difficult*
Trailhead: *Cuajimoloyas*

During the hike to Cañón del Coyote, you'll take in stops at a natural spring issuing forth from a rocky outcropping, the Cuevas del Coyote (Coyote Caves), and a number of miradores throughout the canyon, whose walls rise 30 m (98 ft) overhead.

Llano del Fraile

Distance: *3 km (1.9 mi) round-trip*
Duration: *1 hour*
Difficulty: *easy*
Trailhead: *Cuajimoloyas*

The Llano del Fraile (Plain of the Friar) is a quick hike that will take you out to a cave of the same name, as well as to rushing waterfalls and babbling brooks during the rainy season.

Mountain Biking

Aside from being the trailhead for the Ruta Ka-Yezzi-Daa-Vii, Cuajimoloyas has shorter bike routes, such as Tarajeas and Benito Juárez.

Tarajeas

The Tarajeas route descends 4.4 km (2.7 mi) to the Llano de Tarajeas campgrounds. The outbound journey through maguey-fenced cornfields and forests of towering pines only takes about half an hour since it is almost all downhill, but you'll have to go back the way you came. Allow up to two hours or more for the round-trip ride.

Benito Juárez

The Benito Juárez route descends 9 km (5.6 mi) from Cuajimoloyas and squiggles through a valley of fertile fields, terminating in the neighboring town to the west after an hour's ride or so.

Zip-Lining

The 1-km-long (0.6-mi-long) zip line over Cuajimoloyas is Oaxaca's longest. It stretches from the Mirador Yaa-Cuetzi on the south side of town and soars 100 m (328 ft) to the north, offering a speedy, bird's-eye view of the smoky little village. Head to the ecotourism office to make arrangements and get equipment (US$13.50).

Cultural Activities

The inhabitants of Cuajimoloyas invite guests to learn about their crafts and traditions. There are **classes** (US$11-25) on making pan serrano (artisanal "mountain" bread), medicinal and edible mushrooms, traditional medicine, and basket weaving with fibers made from pine needles.

For **traditional medicine,** ask in the ecotourism office for directions or a guide to the house of Señora Esther, a local curandera (medicine woman) trusted by the community to provide traditional healing. She is bilingual and leads a medicinal plant tour with a tea tasting at the end (US$11 pp, two-person minimum). Call the ecotourism office ahead of time to plan other workshops and activities.

Festivals and Events

Feria Regional de Hongos Silvestres

July

In the penultimate weekend of July, Cuajimoloyas hosts the Feria Regional de Hongos Silvestres (Regional Wild Mushroom Fair), a two-day festival of workshops, classes, and hikes focused on identifying, preparing, and consuming edible wild mushrooms. Cuajimoloyas bills itself as "the capital of wild mushrooms," as the surrounding mountainsides are the perfect habitat for a wide range of uncultivated fungi. This is not a magic mushroom festival. Some species that grow here have medicinal properties, but the majority are for plain old cooking and enjoying.

Food

Most of the comedores are located around the agencia municipal (local government offices), less than 0.8 km (0.5 mi) east of the ecotourism office.

Trout Hatcheries

On the way to the Llano de Tarajeas campgrounds north of town, a few criaderos de truchas (trout hatcheries) serve fresh trout in a variety of recipes, such as al mojo de ajo (in garlic), enchipotlado (in chipotle sauce), and a la diabla (in super spicy chile sauce). The one in the Llano de Tarajeas campgrounds is about 4.5 km (2.8 mi) north of town.

Information and Services

Centro Ecoturístico Yaa-Cuetzi

tel. 951/524-5024; cuaji_yaacuetzi@hotmail.com; 9am-8pm daily

The ecotourism office is on the highway just as you enter town. The unnamed highway becomes Calle Oaxaca when it enters Cuajimoloyas. Stop here before you do anything to get information, reserve cabañas or campsites, or to pay the US$5.50 access fee (only if you're not paying for accommodations).

Getting There

Cuajimoloyas is 56 km (35 mi) from Oaxaca City. Drivers head east from the city on Highway 190. At Tlacolula, take a left at the main intersection onto the road that leads to the town of Díaz Ordáz (you'll see a big green sign for it over the intersection). From there it's another 45 minutes through tightly coiled switchbacks that quickly get you up to the soaring heights of the Sierra Norte. The road is in mostly good condition; just drive with caution and hug the turns. Total drive time is about 1.5 hours.

You could take a suburban (shared van) from Oaxaca City's **Central de Autobuses de Segunda Clase** (Calle Juárez Mara, just north of the Central de Abastos; tel. 951/516-5326) to get up here in one shot, but the location of the second-class bus station makes it necessary to cross the whole city after getting out of the crazy traffic that buzzes around the Central de Abastos. This option is only viable for those already staying on the south side of the Zócalo. They charge about US$3 for the trip, but the traffic congestion around the terminal prolongs the trip to two hours or more. Vans leave hourly.

To opt out of this hectic city traffic, walk or take a taxi to the **bus and colectivo taxi stop** on the northeast side of the Centro, in between the baseball stadium and the McDonald's. Grab a colectivo (shared taxi van) bound for Tlacolula or beyond, and in Tlacolula, wait for a taxi, suburban, or camioneta (covered pickup truck) on the north side of the main intersection to take you the rest of the way. You shouldn't have to wait too long for a ride at these stops, so the journey shouldn't be much longer than 1.5 hours. In total, you'll spend US$5-6 to get up the mountain.

Expediciones Sierra Norte (tel. tel. 951/226-8395 or 951/310-3904; www.sierranorte.org.mx; sierranorteoaxaca@gmail.com) offers transportation from Oaxaca City to the Pueblos Mancomunados, but it is a bit pricier than the public transport options, costing around US$30 for up to four people.

LLANO GRANDE

With an elevation just below that of Cuajimoloyas, Llano Grande (3,050 m/10,000 ft above sea level) is also one of the higher villages in the Pueblos Mancomunados. It is the smallest village in the cooperative, and because of its conscientious citizenry, it is one of the cleanest communities in Mexico. Most of the small town is tucked away in the tranquility of the surrounding woods.

Hiking

Cascada Pinovete

Distance: *8 km (5 mi) round-trip*
Duration: *2 hours*
Difficulty: *easy*
Trailhead: *north side of Llano Grande*

Up in the high pine-oak forests north of Llano Grande, the Cascada Pinovete tumbles 30 m (98 ft) down moss-covered stone to the riverbed below. The easy hike out to the falls and back can be done in just over two hours, depending on how fast you make your way through the forest. With the sweet smell of pennyroyals and the songs of kingfishers and goldfinches permeating the clear mountain air, you might want to take your time.

Caminata El Amanecer

Distance: *6.3 km (3.9 mi) round-trip*
Duration: *3 hours*
Difficulty: *easy*
Trailhead: *Llano Grande*

The Caminata El Amanecer (Daybreak Hike) begins around 4:30am. This hike takes about three hours round-trip and is a spectacular way to see the sunrise at nearly 3,350 m (10,990 ft). The outbound leg climbs through dense pine forests until you reach the peak at sunrise, and the return home is an easy descent.

La Sepultura

Distance: *12 km (7.5 mi) round-trip*
Duration: *3 hours*
Difficulty: *easy*
Trailhead: *Llano Grande*

Another route full of miradores with panoramic views and a wide range of flora and fauna is La Sepultura, a stroll through one of the highest regions of the Sierra Norte. The trail circles through the high-altitude pine forests north of town (no oaks this high up). It's a flat, easy hike that takes about three hours.

Mountain Biking

Ruta Latzi-Hroo-Lii

Instead of walking, you could take a bike along the forested Ruta Latzi-Hroo-Lii (8 km/5 mi) west to Cuajimoloyas. With very little elevation change, it's an easy ride that takes just under an hour. You can rent the bike in Llano Grande and arrange to leave it at the ecotourism office in Cuajimoloyas, or just ride back to Llano Grande.

Cultural Activities

Local cooks offer **cooking classes** (US$19 pp, two-person minimum) that feature regional specialties, as well as **workshops** on making tortillas and artisanal breads (US$27 per group of up to four people). Other cultural activities include bird-watching excursions, environmental education workshops, and classes about local legends and stories. Call ahead to give them time to prepare.

Food

Comedor Martínez

Calle Benito Juárez 2 (behind the primary school); tel. 951/393-9945; 7am-9pm Mon.-Sat.; US$4-6

There are a few comedores in town to choose from, and the closest to the office is Comedor Martínez. The Martínez family serves up traditional eats with the freshest ingredients the Sierra Juárez has to offer. Be sure to try their freshly baked bread.

Information and Services

Ecotourism Office

Calle Constitución; tel. 951/524-5089 or 951/598-5086; adecordillera@hotmail.com; 9am-8pm daily

The ecotourism office is on Calle Constitución, the first left upon entering town from the west, so make it your first stop.

Getting There

Llano Grande is 10 km (6 mi) down the highway east from Cuajimoloyas. If you wait for a **colectivo** (both taxis and trucks run this route) by the highway next to the Cuajimoloyas ecotourism office, it'll get you to Llano Grande in about 20 minutes (US$1). If you're not in a rush, why not walk it? The **Ruta Latzi-Hroo-Lii** is an easy 8-km (5-mi) walk that takes about 2.5 hours.

BENITO JUÁREZ

At 3,000 m (9,800 ft) above sea level, Benito Juárez rounds out the trio of high-altitude towns in the Pueblos Mancomunados. At this altitude, deciduous trees like oak, fir, and strawberry trees begin to elbow in among the pines that dominate the higher peaks. The pine trees here grow up 30 m (98 ft) tall during their lifespan of 250-300 years.

Sights

Mirador and Suspension Bridge

From a peak northeast of the center of town, the view from the mirador stretches over the town's houses, basketball court, school, and governmental building, as well as miles and miles of green beyond. The one-way walk up the dirt road from town takes about 40 minutes. You'll find it by heading north from the ecotourism office and taking a right at the three forks in the road that you come across. There is also a **cafeteria** (8am-4pm daily; US$5) at the mirador, for lunch with a view.

From the mirador, a 150-m-long (492-ft-long) long suspension bridge (puente colgante) stretches through the tops of the pine trees with their roots in the dirt of the gorge 30 m (98 ft) below.

Hiking

Benito Juárez is the trailhead for the **Ruta Needa-Queta-Miru** (page 243), which heads west to La Nevería, and the **Ruta Needa-Yaa-Lagashxi** (page 243), which climbs up to Cuajimoloyas to the east.

Piedra Larga

Distance: *3 km (1.9 mi) round-trip*
Duration: *2 hours*
Difficulty: *easy*
Trailhead: *Benito Juárez, east side of town*

Staying local, you could hike out to the Piedra Larga (Long Rock), a vertiginous crag offering panoramic vistas east of town. At just under 3 km (1.9 mi) from town, the easy trek to the rock and back takes about two hours.

Mountain Biking

From Benito Juárez, you could bike to either La Nevería (7.7 km/4.8 mi) or Latuvi (12 km/7.4 mi) via the **Circuito Taurino Mecinas Ceballos** (page 243). The section from Benito Juárez to La Nevería is the less technical and takes half an hour to an hour. The ride to Latuvi can be done in about an hour. Finish the whole circuit, and you'll be back in Benito Juárez in 3-5 hours, depending on your pace.

Zip-Lining

Up by the mirador and suspension bridge, a set of three zip lines stretches a total of 300 m (984 ft) back and forth across the gorge. The tallest of the three is over 80 m (262 ft) high. Inquire in the ecotourism office for operators and equipment. Zip-lining the set of three costs about US$10.

suspension bridge at Benito Juárez

Cultural Activities

Cultural activities (US$11-25) in Benito Juárez include medicinal mushroom production and preparation, cooking classes, and classes in making pan serrano. Unique to Benito Juárez is a trip to the farm of **Señor Eli** (US$19, two-person minimum), a local farmer who invites visitors to spend a day with him and his family, learning the ins and outs of daily agrarian life in the Pueblos Mancomunados and preparing a traditional meal. Guides from Expediciones Sierra Norte can translate. Always call ahead to plan cultural activities.

Food

There are a number of **comedores** in the small town center and throughout the town to enjoy a simple but hearty meal that are open around 8am-8pm. The comedor located inside the ecotourism office is a solid and convenient option.

Information and Services

Ecotourism Office

tel. 951/172-1581; 9am-8pm daily

The ecotourism office is in the center of town, just north of the basketball court and municipal government building. It is at the intersection of the road from Cuajimoloyas and the one that climbs up the mountains from Teotitlán del Valle. Make this your first stop upon arrival.

Getting There

Drivers who aren't in a hurry can take the scenic route from Teotitlán del Valle, which is 29 km (18 mi) east of Oaxaca City via Highway 190. About half an hour after leaving the city, take the turnoff to Teotitlán del Valle and pass through town. This road, Avenida Benito Juárez, is unpaved north of Teotitlán, where it begins to wind up the southern slopes of the Sierra Norte. Benito Juárez is 20 km (12.4 mi) from Teotitlán, about an hour's drive up the mountain. From Cuajimoloyas, it's about 15 minutes away. Head south on Highway 17 for 2.5 km (1.5 mi) and take the signed turn to the right. Benito Juárez is another 3.5 km (2.2 mi) down the dirt road.

By public transport, the best way to get here from Oaxaca City is to arrive at Cuajimoloyas; from there you can organize transport at the ecotourism office. The trip costs about US$15, so it is more economical for groups of three or four. The best way to get around up here is on foot, so I recommend bringing only what you can carry in a backpack and taking the **Ruta Needa-Yaa-Lagashxi** from Cuajimoloyas to Benito Juárez on foot. The walk takes about two hours.

LA NEVERÍA

Set in the cradle of a small valley surrounded by oak- and pine-forested peaks, La Nevería (elevation 2,700 m/8,900 ft) gets its name (Ice House) from the intense cold that used to come with winters at the turn of the 20th century. The weather fostered the production of ice that was delivered on donkeys to the capital. Although the effects of climate change have caused average temperatures here and elsewhere in the Sierra Norte to rise, winter temperatures still flirt closely with freezing, so pack accordingly.

Hiking

Recorrido de Plantas Medicinales

Distance: *2 km (1.2 mi) round-trip*
Duration: *3 hours*
Difficulty: *easy*
Trailhead: *La Nevería*

Ask in the ecotourism office about the Recorrido de Plantas Medicinales (Medicinal Plant Route), a guided tour (US$19) through the forests north of town, which abound in orchids, bromeliads, and an array of plants used in traditional medicine in the Sierra Norte. Your guide will tell you the names of the plants, as well as how they are used to treat medical conditions.

Río Las Guacamayas

Distance: *3 km (1.9 mi) round-trip*
Duration: *3 hours*
Difficulty: *moderate*
Trailhead: *La Nevería, on the north side of town*

This hike leads to a waterfall on the Río Las Guacamayas (Macaw River) north of town, which is about 5 m (16 ft) tall. The return to town passes through fields of beans, peas, mustard greens, and other crops; cultivated fields of big, bright calla lilies, gladiolas, geraniums, and daisies; and apple and hawthorn tree orchards. If you take the tour with the English-speaking guides from Expediciones Sierra Norte, the excursion includes a delicious meal in the community restaurant before the trek.

Cultural Activities

You'll find tortilla making and organic cooking classes, but what stands out in La Nevería are the agricultural tours and workshops. You can **tour the greenhouses** (US$5.50) where locals cultivate berros (watercress), an herb that is often served with tlayudas (large tortillas topped with meat and cheese) in other parts of the state. This tour also visits fields of maize and beans, as well as a reforestation area.

To gain a deeper knowledge of the farming and sustainability practices here, you can arrange to **volunteer with local farmers** in the fields and greenhouses. Locals will need to plan for this, so call ahead (it's easiest to call the Expediciones Sierra Norte office in Oaxaca City; tel. 951/226-8395 or 951/310-3904) and make sure everyone is ready upon your arrival.

Food

Restaurante Comunitario

tel. 951/172-4651; 8am-8pm daily; US$5.50

The restaurante comunitario (community restaurant) serves delicious regional recipes, the most notable of which are the tortitas de berro (US$3), a kind of fritter made with locally grown, organic watercress, served with beans, tortillas, and a fresh salad and salsa. The restaurant usually closes around 8pm, but it's always a good idea to let them know when you plan on eating dinner, to be sure they don't close earlier due to lack of diners.

Information and Services

Ecotourism Office

Hidalgo 1; tel. 951/172-4651; ecoturismolaneveria@gmail.com; 9am-8pm daily

Follow the sign as you enter town to get to the ecotourism office, the first place you should go. It's in the local government building next to the basketball court.

Getting There

La Nevería is 8 km (5 mi) west of Benito Juárez. **Drivers** head south from the ecotourism office in Benito Juárez, past the basketball court, and follow the signage down the unnamed dirt road to La Nevería. The drive takes a little over 20 minutes.

Get to La Nevería from Benito Juárez on foot via the **Ruta Needa-Queta-Miru.** The walk takes about two hours. You can also arrange transport in the ecotourism office in Benito Juárez (US$18 for up to four people).

LATUVI

At 2,400 m (7,900 ft) above sea level, Latuvi ("rolled leaf" in Zapotec) is the gateway community to the even lower towns of Lachatao and Amatlán to the north. Spread along the top of a ridge descending from the higher elevations, the town is generally warmer and sunnier than the often cloud-veiled towns to the south. This is the southern trailhead for the famed **Camino Real,** a trail believed to be part of a longer pre-Hispanic commercial route that connected the Valles Centrales with communities near the Gulf of Mexico.

Sights

El Molcajete

In the valley on the east side of town, the waters of the Río Cara de León (Lion's Face River) have perforated the rocks over millions of years to form the waterfalls called El Molcajete, named for the classic Mexican mortar and pestle. An English-speaking local guide (US$15 for up to seven people) can take you there, telling local history and legends, as well as explaining the various flora and fauna along the way. The tour can take 3-5 hours, depending on your preference, and it makes a stop at a truchería for a trout lunch. The toughest part of this moderately difficult 10-km (6.2-mi) hike is the uphill return to Latuvi, so conserve your energy for the end.

Hiking

You'll find the trailhead to the **Ruta Camino Real** (page 241) to the right at the bottom of the hill from the ecotourism office. From here, the towns of Lachatao and Amatlán are about four hours away.

Ruta El Manzanal

Distance: *6 km (3.7 mi)*
Duration: *3 hours*
Difficulty: *moderate*
Trailhead: *bottom of the hill from the ecotourism office, to the left*

The trailhead for Ruta El Manzanal (Apple Orchard Route) is to the left at the bottom of the aforementioned hill. Aside from the trail's namesake, you'll also pass through orchards of apricot trees and fields of corn, beans, and other crops until you reach the Río Guacamayas. Here, you can stop in at the truchería El Manzanal and enjoy a meal of fresh trout and locally grown veggies. A guided tour (US$19 for up to seven people) can be arranged in the ecotourism office.

Ruta Piedra del Corredor

Distance: *16 km (10 mi) round-trip*
Duration: *6 hours*
Difficulty: *difficult*
Trailhead: *Latuvi*

The Ruta Piedra del Corredor (Runner's Stone Route) is a great hike for observing the various bromeliads, cacti, orchids, and other flowering plants that thrive in this region. It also passes through a forest called Las Canteras (The Quarries), where ghostly white mosses cover the oak trees.

Mountain Biking

You can also take a bike on the **Ruta El Manzanal** or just pedal around the surrounding hills. Bike rentals at the ecotourism office cost about US$18 a day. Call ahead to arrange and ensure that the equipment is ready when you arrive.

Cultural Activities

Local fruit farmers invite visitors to join them for a day in the fields. They offer **workshops** (US$20 for up to four people) on sustainable farming, fruit picking, and making jam. If you're going to be in town in the latter half of July, inquire about the exact dates of the **Feria de la Manzana** (Apple Fair), which hosts agricultural workshops, guided apple orchard tours, mountain biking excursions, live music, and lots and lots of delicious food.

Those interested in traditional alcoholic beverages should plan a visit with **Señora Julia,** a local producer of tepache, made from fermented pineapple rinds, and pulque, a fermented beverage made from maguey. She offers demonstrations (US$11 for up to four people) on the production processes and tastings of these low-alcohol drinks.

Latuvi is also a great place to do a **temazcal** (US$43), a traditional pre-Hispanic sweat bath with massage included. As with all cultural activities here, arrange everything with Expediciones Sierra Norte before your arrival.

Food

Restaurant Linda Vista

across from the cabins; tel. 951/408-9209; 7am-9pm; US$5

Across the street from the cabins, Restaurant Linda Vista (Beautiful View) lives up to its name. Señora Marta creates a warm and welcoming atmosphere for travelers to refresh and refuel from adventuring on the trails. This cozy restaurant serves up amazing views of the valley, along with its flavorful and healthy meals.

Trout Hatcheries

Take just about any road down the eastern slope of the ridge from town and you'll find one of a number of truchérias that all serve delicious trout-based meals. They don't really have set hours. As long as the folks are up, they'll cook you a fish. Don't be unreasonably late, though.

Information and Services

Ecotourism Office

tel. 951/506-7903; lat_eco@hotmail.com; 9am-8pm daily

You'll find the ecotourism office down the hill from the elementary school, on the second rise of paved road in town as you enter from the south. Stop in to pay and get info.

Getting There

Latuvi is 11 km (6.8 mi) north of Benito Juárez. **Drivers** head north from the ecotourism office and take Avenida Benito Juárez, the unmarked road that descends to the left at the first fork you see. Stick to this main road and you'll get here in about half an hour. Transportation arranged in the ecotourism office costs US$15 for up to four people.

Walk to Latuvi from Benito Juárez via the **Circuito Taurino Mecinas Ceballos** (12 km/7.4 mi), a relatively easy, mostly downhill walk that takes a little over two hours. With an elevation change of almost 600 m (1,968 ft), it is a great way to observe the changes in vegetation at different altitudes in this part of the Sierra Norte. You could also rent a bike in Benito Juárez (US$15/day) to make the trip. Just make sure to arrange this ahead of time.

From La Nevería, walk the 10.9-km (6.8-mi) **Ruta Cipriano Cabrera,** which will get you to Latuvi in 2.5 hours or so, or take a bike down the second section of the **Circuito Taurino Mecinas Ceballos.**

LACHATAO

Lachatao definitely lives up to its name, which means "enchanted valley" or "enchanted plain" in Zapotec. At 2,200 m (7,200 ft) above sea level, it is one of the lowest towns in the Pueblos Mancomunados. This quaint valley town stands out for its attractive, colonial-style cobblestone streets and colorfully painted adobe houses.

Sights

Templo de Santa Catarina de Alejandría

La Asunción

At the center of town, the baroque Templo de Santa Catarina de Alejandría was built at the behest of Dominican friars in the 17th century. The gold-plated altarpieces and retablos depicting the martyrdom of Saint Catherine of Alexandria are in very good condition. The town celebrates its patron saint on November 25 with religious processions, music, and plenty of food.

Museo Comunitario

next to the church; tel. 951/517-6058; 9am-5pm; free

To the left of the church facade, the museo comunitario (community museum) is the town's way of connecting with its history and sharing it with others. The museum divides the history of Lachatao into four stages, beginning with an exhibit of carved stone and other pre-Hispanic artifacts from the region. The next exhibit focuses on the colonial period, with a small collection of 16th-century religious paintings and baroque sculptures. A photo of Benito Juárez is the principal piece in the section concerning the Reform Era of the mid-19th century; turn-of-the-20th-century radios, wall telephones, sewing machines, and a cannon make up the final period represented in the museum, the Mexican Revolution. All signage is in Spanish.

Ex-Hacienda Cinco Señores

tel. 951/517 6058; 9am 6pm daily; US$25 for up to 4 people

The Ex-Hacienda Cinco Señores is another place in Lachatao to steep yourself in Mexican history. Built in 1750, it was once home to Faustino Díaz, father of infamous dictator and native Oaxacan Porfirio Díaz. Later, in the mid-19th century, hacienda owner Miguel Castro gave refuge to Margarita Maza de Juárez, wife of Benito Juárez, during his two-year exile to Cuba and New Orleans. And it finally ended up in the hands of Díaz's brother Felix in the last decades of that century. You'll have to book a tour (US$25 for up to four people) through the ecotourism office to visit. Book early to request an English-speaking guide. The tour will take you back to the village's colonial period, when it was a small but bustling mining community.

Food

Your best food option in town is at the **community restaurant** in the western end of the museum building. A local specialty here is mole chichilo, a rich, dark mole of a soupier consistency than its six Oaxacan siblings. It gets its dark color from the mixture of smoked peppers such as pasilla, guajillo, and the rarer chile chilhuacle, as well as from its most interesting ingredient, charred and ground-up corn tortillas. It is usually served with pork and often with small balls of cornmeal called chochoyotes. Comedores don't always have everything on the menu, so if you're set on trying this dish, call ahead and have the folks at the ecotourism office make plans for the meal before your arrival.

Information and Services

Ecotourism Office

tel. 951/517-6058; ecoturlachatao@hotmail.com; 9am-8pm daily

The ecotourism office is in a charming brick and adobe house to the south of the church in the center of town. As always, stop by here first.

Getting There

Get to Lachatao on foot from Latuvi in about four hours via the **Ruta Camino Real** (page 241). Get here from either Cuajimoloyas or Llano Grande via the **Ruta Yaa-Tini** (page 241); you'll find the turnoff to the Ruta Yaa-Tini about halfway (4 km/2.5 mi) between Cuajimoloyas and Llano Grande on the Ruta Latzi-Hroo-Lii. Plan ahead, however, as this route connecting the highest and lowest elevations in the Pueblos Mancomunados can take as long as five hours. Transport arranged by the ecotourism offices can cost up to US$35 for up to four people, so it is really an option for groups.

Experienced cyclists can take the **Ruta Ka-Yezzi-Daa-Vii** (page 244) from either Cuajimoloyas or Llano Grande. Call ahead to arrange rentals (US$15/day) and/or a guide (US$36 for up to four people) with the ecotourism office in Oaxaca City or in your starting point to ensure everything is ready when you arrive.

From Oaxaca City, **drivers** take Highway 190 4 km (2.5 mi) east from the Centro and take a left onto Highway 175 at the Benito Juárez Monument. Head north 53 km (33 mi) until you see the turnoff to Amatlán and Lachatao, just before a bridge over the Río Yavesía. Lachatao is another 11 km (6.8 mi) down the unnamed dirt road, through distractingly beautiful vistas of green valleys, steep and rocky canyons, and picturesque hilltop chapels. Total drive time is just under two hours. You'll pass through Amatlán, and there's a good chance you'll get lost or be unsure of where to go in town, as there is little signage about which road to take to get to Lachatao. You can always ask a friendly local if you're headed in the right direction or not. Lachatao is 1.5 km (0.9 mi) south of Amatlán.

If you're driving from Latuvi, take Avenida Benito Juárez north until it hits Highway 175. Turn north onto the highway and make the turn at the river about 15 km (9.3 mi) up the road. This route takes about an hour.

AMATLÁN

The Nahuatl name Amatlán means "place of the amate tree," a type of ficus with alien-like roots that grow like tentacles sunk in earth or wrapped threateningly over huge boulders. The bark of this tree was used in pre-Hispanic times to make paper. The town's name in Zapotec, Yagaa-Tzi, means "yellow tree" in English, an allusion to the encino amarillo. This species of oak endemic to Mexico has yellowish hairs on the undersides of the leaves and is also abundant in and around town.

At 2,000 m (6,600 ft) above sea level, Amatlán has the lowest elevation of the Pueblos Mancomunados, and it's no surprise that the names for the town are inspired by trees. Warmer temperatures at this altitude, combined with the humid air from the Gulf of Mexico, foster a broad variety of floral diversity, and orchids, bromeliads, mosses, and wild magueys thrive in this northernmost part of the Pueblos Mancomunados.

Sights

Museo Comunitario

tel. 951/189-0453; 9am-5pm; free

Just down the street from the church is the museo comunitario (community museum), where you can learn the pre-Hispanic and colonial history of Amatlán, as well as the history of the formation of the Pueblos Mancomunados, which were officially delineated in 1961. Although the original is now in the National Anthropology Museum in Mexico City, you can see a copy of the 17th-century Códice San Lucas Yataú, a pictographic account of the pre-Hispanic history of the town, painted in oil on a piece of cloth.

Hiking

Ruta La Vida del Minero

Distance: *14 km (8.7 mi) round-trip*
Duration: *5 hours*
Difficulty: *moderate to difficult*
Trailhead: *Amatlán*

As in Lachatao, gold and silver mining were once big business in Amatlán, and the Ruta La Vida del Minero (Life of the Miner Route) will take you back through that history. After passing through a verdant path of bromeliad-laden yellow oaks and patches of wild-growing medicinal plants, you'll stop at the Mirador Loma Amarilla (Yellow Hill Lookout Point), where you take in the view of the town and observe a natural spring that flows into the Río Papaloapan. Finally, you'll stop by an old mine that you can enter if you're on the **guided tour** (US$27 for up to seven people). The 200-m (656-ft) tunnel still shows the open veins where miners extracted the precious metals over a century ago. This moderately difficult, 14-km (8.7-mi) hike takes about five hours.

An interesting trek offered here is a **guided nighttime hike** (US$20 for up to seven people) around town, in which you'll observe and identify the various bat species that call Amatlán home.

Mountain Biking

You can also rent a bicycle (US$15/day) to explore the surrounding countryside and old architecture. On the south side of town, you can visit old haciendas like El Socorro (Help), which was built in 1827. Keep heading south until you find the trails that follow the banks of the Río El Arco. They're a good way to see the rich biodiversity of the region.

Cultural Activities

Cultural workshops (US$10-23 for up to four people) available in Amatlán include cooking classes, embroidery demonstrations and classes with local women artisans, mushroom cultivation, organic farming, and artisanal bread-baking courses. Local **curanderas** offer massages, limpias, and temazcal sweat baths (US$27).

Food

Like nearby Lachatao, Amatlán is a great place to try mole chichilo, much rarer than the traditional moles negro (black), amarillo (yellow), and coloradito (red), which are also regional delights. Give them a try in the **comedor** next to the ecotourism office. As with other gastronomic and cultural services in the Pueblos Mancomunados, it's not guaranteed that the restaurant will be serving something like mole chichilo every day. If you are set on tasting it, call ahead and plan a meal or cooking class before you trek up the mountains.

Information and Services

Ecotourism Office

tel. 951/344-1228; ecoturismoamatlan@hotmail.com; 9am-8pm daily

The ecotourism office where you'll check in is perched on a ridge on the north side of town, about 350 m (1,148 ft) up the road from the church and government building.

Getting There

Amatlán is the northern terminus of the **Ruta Camino Real** (page 241), which will get you here on foot from Latuvi in about four hours, as well as the **Ruta Yaa-Tini** (page 241), which will get you here from Llano Grande or Cuajimoloyas in around five hours. The ecotourism cooperative will organize transport from the other villages for you, but it can cost as much as US$33 for up to four people, so it is more economical if you have a small group, if you don't want to travel on foot.

Drivers from Oaxaca City can take the same route via Highway 175 to get to both Amatlán and Lachatao. Take Highway 190 4 km (2.5 mi) east from the Centro and take a left onto Highway 175 at the Benito Juárez Monument. Head north 53 km (33 mi) until you see the turnoff to Amatlán and Lachatao, just before a bridge over the Río Yavesía. Amatlán is another 9.5 km (5.9 mi) down the unnamed dirt road, just before Lachatao. Total drive time is just under two hours.

If you're driving from Latuvi, take Avenida Benito Juárez north until it hits Highway 175. Turn north onto the highway and make the turn at the river about 15 km (9.3 mi) up the road. This route takes about an hour.

Sierra Juárez

The middle section of the Sierra Norte, which includes the Pueblos Mancomunados, is referred to regionally as the Sierra Juárez because it is home to the birthplace of legendary 19th-century president Benito Juárez. This route, up Highway 175 from Oaxaca City, is one of the most scenic routes in the whole state, with views that will have you rubbernecking around every curve. As you wind through tight tunnels of pine and oak trees, visibility is often limited to a mere couple of meters when dense clouds cloak the entire mountainside. The experience is made more surreal when the highway rises above the mantle of vapor, and the breathtaking phenomenon of thermal inversion pushes the wet air of the Gulf of Mexico down to lower elevations, filling the valley below with the spectacular mar de nubes (sea of clouds).

The forests around this part of the Sierra Norte are so biologically rich and diverse that they have earned Mexico a spot among the 17 megadiverse countries in the world, as identified by the U.S.-based nonprofit Conservation International.

IXTLÁN DE JUÁREZ

In Nahuatl, the name Ixtlán means "place of the maguey fibers," and the town's Zapotec name, Laa Yetzi, means "thick leaf" or "maguey leaf." It later became Ixtlán de Juárez to honor Oaxaca's worthiest citizen, Benito Juárez, who was born in the small town of Guelatao, just 4 km (2.5 mi) down the road.

Sights

Templo de Santo Tomás Apóstol

corner of Calle Revolución and Calle Campos

Just across the street from the main square, you'll see a clock tower made of cantera verde, or green (very green) limestone, in the courtyard outside the Templo de Santo Tomás Apóstol. This churrigueresque (a type of baroque architectural style) cathedral is lavishly adorned inside and out with finely detailed statues and flourishes in the facade, and large, elaborate, gold-plated altarpieces shining inside the dome-topped nave. Since it's across the street from the ecotourism office, you can quickly stop by to admire the architecture before leaving town to explore.

★ Mirador de Cristal

Cerro de Cuachirindoo; tel. 951/405-4118; 10am-7pm daily; US$5.50

This heart-stopping sight may give those who fear heights a run for their money, but trust me, it's worth a visit. With a walkway that's entirely see-through, it's the highest outdoor mirador (lookout point) in all of Latin America. The Mirador is perched on top of the Cerro de Cuachirindoo (Cuachirindoo Hill), named in honor of a Zapotec warrior whose statue you'll pass on the way to the lookout. At 30 m (98 ft) long and 200 m (656 ft) high, it offers breathtaking views of the Sierra Juárez and Ixtlán de Juárez (way, way down) below.

The fee is $5.50 to walk the horseshoe loop (no shoes—don't want to scuff up the glass floor). The lookout sways a bit with the wind sometimes, but it's perfectly safe, and only adds to the thrill.

But if this thrill sounds more like "terror" and you, like me, arrive only to find yourself breaking into a cold sweat, don't worry, you have a couple of options. You can hang around the statue of Cuachirindoo and admire the equally lovely views there, or eat at the little restaurant (US$3-6) above the Mirador, where you can enjoy the same views, seated and with a snack.

Hiking

Cerro de Cuachirindoo

Distance: *8 km (5 mi) round-trip*
Duration: *3 hours*
Difficulty: *moderate*
Trailhead: *bottom of Cerro de Cuachirindoo, north side of Ixtlán*

For a short hike just outside town, ask in the ecotourism office about the trip to the Cerro de Cuachirindoo (US$15 for up to four people). This hike takes you up the hill north of town, stopping at a monument to the Zapotec warriors Juppa and Cuachirindoo, who fought valiantly against the Aztecs when they invaded Oaxaca just before the Spanish did. The tour then proceeds to a mirador that offers an impressive view of the town below. This tour can also be done in a vehicle (1.5 hrs; US$24 for up to four people).

Bosque Mesófilo

Distance: *9 km (5.6 mi) round-trip*
Duration: *3 hours*
Difficulty: *moderate*
Trailhead: *just north of Ixtlán de Juárez*

A trip to the bosque mesófilo (cloud forest) north of town is another unforgettable experience in nature. Often shrouded in dense clouds, the oak trees are dripping with wraith-like mosses that add to the forest's eerie, fantastical atmosphere. The tour (US$25 for up to four people) is capped off by a visit to the **Mirador Shiaa Rua Via,** a lookout point 3,125 m (10,253 ft) above sea level. From here, on a clear day you'll be able to see the Pico de Orizaba, Mexico's highest peak, over 200 km (124 mi) to the northwest in the state of Puebla. But don't worry: If there are clouds, there's a good chance you'll be above them, in awe of the Sierra Norte's mar de nubes.

Food and Accommodations

★ Restaurante de la Calzada

corner of Calzada La Eternidad and Francisco Villa; tel. 951/182-4550; 8am-5pm daily; US$5

Restaurante de la Calzada's slogan says it all: El Sazón de Mamá (Mom's Flavor). Whether it's eggs for breakfast, a chile relleno for lunch, or a tlayuda for dinner, everything here has that special, homey touch. The setting, in a quaintly decorated room and part of the patio of the family home, is a pleasant place to enjoy such a meal. You'll find it on the Calzada La Eternidad, a block south from the church.

★ Truchería Cuachirindoo

tel. 951/186-4763; 10am-6pm daily; US$9

The taxi ride (US$3.50) out to Truchería Cuachirindoo, a trout hatchery 3.5 km (2.2 mi) north of town, is worth the trip. Their alfresco dining area perched on a hillside, a perfect position for being wowed by the sunset, is one of the most pleasant settings in the Sierra Norte. The trout cooked in aluminum foil with mushrooms and quesillo is absolutely delicious. If the stunning views and scrumptious dining wasn't enough, there's a **recreation area** that includes a playground, pool, and zip line. You can even spend the night in their **cabañas** (US$19 for 2 people, US$37 for 4).

Hostal Laa Yetzi

Av. 16 de Septiembre #5; tel. 951/553-6392 or 951/346-0631; US$27 d

Honestly, it's more likely that you'll be staying the night in Parque Ecoturixtlán's cabins or the more charming Capulálpam de Méndez. But a stay at the Hostal Laa Yetzi will save you a little money and give you easy access to the food and services in town (there's even a restaurant conveniently located next door that has pizza and hamburgers). The rooms are simple, but the hot water works and there's space for parking.

Getting There

From Oaxaca City, drivers take Highway 190 4 km (2.5 mi) east from the Centro and take a left onto Highway 175 at the Benito Juárez Monument. From here it's 59 km (37 mi) up this scenic and snaking road to Ixtlán. Total travel time from Oaxaca City is about 1.5 hours.

You can also get to Ixtlán from Oaxaca City via colectivo (US$3.75) from the Benito Juárez Monument. Look for the taxis from Sitio Laa-Yetzi. With frequent stops along the way, this mode of transportation takes around two hours. The Cuenca bus line (US$6) that operates from the ADO bus station (5 de Mayo 1016, Ruta de Independencia, Oaxaca City) makes a stop in Ixtlán before continuing on to Tuxtepec; the ride is an hour and a half.

★ PARQUE ECOTURIXTLÁN

tel. 951/553-6075 or 951/592-4162; 9am-5pm daily; US$1.50 day access

Just 5 km (3 mi) east of Ixtlán de Juárez, Parque Ecoturixtlán is the perfect alpine getaway, whether for just the afternoon or for a day or two with an overnight stay camping or in one of their cabañas. Don't miss both ends of the **Gruta El Arco,** a cave that cuts over 150 m (492 ft) from one side of a mountain to the other and is home to a number of bat species as well as large flights of swallows.

Head up the hill from the park office, past the family-size cabañas, to get to the **orquideario** (orchid garden), where park employees work to conserve these fantastical flowers. The best time of year to see them bloom in this part of the Sierra Norte is in April and May.

The park has numerous **hiking trails** and a **bike route** that wend through this impressively biodiverse region. It is easy to fill a day or two exploring the countryside. Aside from orchids, you'll find a variety of bromeliads, tree ferns, parlor palms, mosses, lichens, fungi, and many other examples of the region's 6,000 plant species. **Guides** can accompany you for any part of your visit for US$3.25.

Hiking

Bosque de Bromelias

Distance: *6 km (3.7 mi) round-trip*
Duration: *2 hours*
Difficulty: *easy*
Trailhead: *office at Ecoturixtlán*

Visitors to Parque Ecoturixtlán shouldn't leave without taking a tour to the bosque de bromelias (bromeliad forest), where these exotic, tree-climbing cousins of the pineapple are so abundant that you might witness one or two fall off of branches they outgrew. The 6-km (3.7-mi) walk takes about two hours and costs around US$10 for one person. Add another US$2.50 or so for each person in your group.

Zip-Lining

The zip line at Ecoturixtlán shoots 200 m (656 ft) from a tower atop a hill above the western entrance to the caves, going through the treetops and over the obstacle course 29 m (95 ft) below. A quick zip will cost you only US$3.50.

Rappelling

Park staff also have all the equipment necessary to rappel down a 28-m (92-ft) cliff within the park. Staff are well trained, and the

1: Templo de Santo Tomás Apóstol **2:** Mirador de Cristal **3:** recreation area in Parque Ecoturixtlán **4:** Restaurante Los Duendes in Parque Ecoturixtlán

1

2

equipment is all in good condition. A bajada (trip down) costs about US$3.50.

Obstacle Course

Test your balance and nerve on the park's obstacle course (juegos de destreza), built 3 m (10 ft) up in the trees. Hop, hang, and swing your way from tree to tree, trying not to fall. But don't worry: The park has harnesses and helmets to make sure that one missed step isn't your last. A trip through the course costs US$3.50.

Food and Accommodations

Restaurante Los Duendes

Ecoturixtlán, Carretera Capulálpam; tel. 951/553-6075; 9am-5pm daily; US$4

If you're staying out in the cabañas in the ecotourism park, you can have breakfast or lunch at Restaurante Los Duendes (duendes are elf- or gnome-like beings who inhabit, among other places, forests such as these). But for dinner, you'll have to head into town. If you don't have your own wheels, you can arrange transport with park staff in the office.

Cabañas

Parque Ecoturixtlán; tel. 951/553-6075 or 951/592-4162; US$37 d

Parque Ecoturixtlán is home to the most luxurious cabañas in the Sierra Norte. The group of duplex-style cabañas down by the park office and restaurant are for one to two people, and each boasts a comfortable king-size bed, fireplace, bathroom with hot water, and shared patio space. White stones line the pathways between the structures, and ground lights fetchingly brighten the way after the sun goes down. Contact Ecoturixtlán to make reservations.

Camping

Parque Ecoturixtlán; tel. 961/553-6075 or 951/592-4162; US$3 pp

Parque Ecoturixtlán has three campgrounds. You can pitch a tent in the small field next to the obstacle course and small suspension bridge, though the other two sites are more inviting. You'll find the second nestled among the towering pines below the official conservation zone about 0.5 km (0.3 mi) down the main road. Continue down this road to get to the prime camping real estate next to the river at the bottom of the gorge. All three have access to dry toilets. From here you'll have quick access to a number of trails leading into the surrounding forest, as well as the eastern opening of the Gruta El Arco, through which water flows to meet with the main river next to the campgrounds. Contact Ecoturixtlán to make reservations.

Information and Services

Ecoturixtlán

16 de Septiembre s/n; tel. 951/553-6075 or 951/592-4162; 9am-5pm daily

The office of the local ecotourism organization Ecoturixtlán is one block south of the main square, just to the east of the church in Ixtlán. They administer the nearby nature park and operate tours to cloud forests, miradores, and other sights around Ixtlán de Juárez.

Getting There

From Oaxaca City, **drivers** head to Ixtlán, taking Highway 190 4 km (2.5 mi) east from the Centro and take a left onto Highway 175 at the Benito Juárez Monument. From here it's 59 km (37 mi) to Ixtlán. Once you reach Ixtlán, it's only a 10-minute drive to the park. At the Monumento Ixtlán, (across the street from the Pemex) turn right onto Calle Benito Juárez. Take Benito Juárez through the center of town and take a right on Calle Fidencio Hernández Campos. When the road forks, keep left, going onto the Carretera a Capulálpam. When the road forks again in 90 m (300 ft), take another left. Follow signs to the park.

You can also reach Ecoturixtlán via **taxi** or **mototaxi** from Ixtlán de Juárez for US$3.75.

CAPULÁLPAM DE MÉNDEZ

Probably the prettiest town in the Sierra Norte, Capulálpam de Méndez gleams on its perch on a sunny mountaintop 10 km (6 mi) east of Ixtlán de Juárez. The cobblestone streets and 16th-century **Templo de San Mateo** are built of luminous cantera amarilla (yellow limestone) that looks like bricks of hardened sunlight. The houses, hotels, and restaurants boast vividly painted adobe walls, wavy red clay roof tiles, and enough spectacular views of the valley below to earn it a designation as a Pueblo Mágico (Magic Town) by Mexico's secretary of tourism. Capulálpam is more than just a pretty face, though. From hiking to climbing to cultural walking tours, there's lots more to do here than take in the view.

Sights

UMA de Venado Cola Blanca (White Tailed Deer Reserve)

For a truly unique experience, book a tour (US$9.50) with the ecotourism office to Unidad de Manejo Ambiental (UMA) de Venado Cola Blanca (White-Tailed Deer Environmental Management Unit), which is much more fun than it sounds, especially if you have kiddos with you. UMA runs a wildlife reserve within the town dedicated to the conservation of the white-tailed deer. You'll visit their outdoor "museum" of nature art and photography and hear a bit about their work. Then comes the fun stuff—going out to see and feed the deer. Being able to observe such graceful creatures up close and feed them was easily the highlight of our time in the Sierra Juárez for my kids, and it was pretty high up there for me, too.

Tours

Descubriendo Capulálpam

If the quaint, colorful architecture of Capulálpam enchants you, ask in the ecotourism office about a tour called Descubriendo Capulálpam (Discovering Capulálpam; US$10), a 2.5-hour stroll through town, during which you'll stop by the **Templo de San Mateo,** with its mix of baroque and neoclassical design, and enjoy a meal in the local market. Tours don't run regularly but are offered on demand, so make sure to call ahead to make arrangements, especially if you need an English-speaking guide. You can inquire about temazcal, massages, and other pre-Hispanic treatments during the stop at the **traditional medicine hospital,** and search for souvenirs in the **Taller y Galería de Juguete y Arte** (Toy and Art Workshop and Gallery). The tour's final stop is at the **Mirador El Calvario,** where you can take in a panoramic view of this gorgeous little town. If you have time and enjoyed the tour, check out their other offerings, which include bird-watching hikes, cave exploration, and more.

Recreation and Activities

For a bit more adrenaline, **rent a bike** (US$11/hr) from the ecotourism office and take a ride through the surrounding pine and oak forests. They have a three-hour **biking tour** (US$17) that ends up at a swimming hole, so don't forget to bring your swimsuit. Other ecotourism options include **ziplining** (US$4.50), **rappelling** (US$6), **rock climbing** (US$8/hr), and **hiking** the many trails.

Food and Accommodations

Mercado Municipal

Calle Miguel Méndez; no tel.; 8am-6pm daily; US$5

In town, grab breakfast, lunch, or dinner a block and a half south of the main square at the local market with a number of comedores to choose from. Each has more or less the same regional favorites, and main dishes seem to change daily. If they're making mole coloradito when you stop by, order it.

1
2
3
4

El Verbo de Méndez Café

Emiliano Zapata 3; tel. 951/539-2045 or 951/173-6877; elverbodemendezcafe.com; 4pm-10pm Mon.-Fri., 8am-10pm Sat.-Sun.; US$8

Pretty views aren't hard to come by in Capulálpam, but my favorite place to enjoy them is El Verbo de Méndez Café, just four blocks north from the main square on Miguel Méndez. The amiable owners serve Oaxacan favorites, coffee grown in the Sierra Norte, sandwiches, and crepes (try the one with caramelized quinces) in a cozy, welcoming setting with panoramic views of Capulálpam and the mountains beyond. After your meal, there's a delightful trail that loops through their orchards, along a stream, and back to their spacious terrace.

Restaurante Los Molinos

tel. 951/539-2168; 10am-6pm daily; US$11

Restaurante Los Molinos, tucked in a small gorge carved out by the river of the same name, is a great place to work up an appetite rappelling or climbing on the cliff behind the restaurant, and then satisfy it with a delicious grilled trout or a gigantic tostada. There's also a playground on the banks of the river for the kids.

You'll find Los Molinos about 1 km (0.6 mi) down the road past the **cabañas** (US$22 pp) perched on a hilltop glade 1 km (0.6 mi) north of town. Follow the ample signage on Miguel Méndez to get here. You can pick a cabin in the sunny clearing or one tucked into the shade of the pines beyond. It doesn't get as cold at night here as in the higher elevations, but all cabins include hot water and a fireplace. Book through the ecotourism office in town.

Hotel Los Sabinos

Hidalgo 4; tel. 951/539-2154; lossabinos2014@hotmail.com; US$27 d, US$38 king bed

In town, stay on the charming main square at the peach-colored Hotel Los Sabinos. It has nine comfortable rooms, as well as a terrace café and restaurant for dinner or evening drinks that has a view of the square in the yellow streetlights. Rooms with king beds have street-facing balconies.

1: feeding deer at the UMA de Venado Cola Blanca
2: Templo de San Mateo in Capulálpam de Méndez
3: Mirador El Calvario 4: Capulálpam's cobblestone streets

Information and Services

Ecotourism Office

tel. 951/539-2168 or 558/441-3285; contacto@turismocapulalpam.com; 10am-4pm daily

Stop by the ecotourism office to learn about all the tours available. It's at the corner of Calle Hidalgo and Calle Carranza, next to the colectivo station and just a couple blocks west of the church.

Getting There

Drivers take the picturesque route from Oaxaca City up Highway 175 to Ixtlán de Juárez (about 1.5 hrs), where you'll head east on Avenida Campos or 16 de Septiembre. Capulálpam is 10 km (6 mi) east of Ixtlán, a curvy and enjoyable 20-minute drive through the pines.

You can also get to Capulálpam from Oaxaca City via **colectivo.** Grab one of these shared taxis (US$3.50) at the Benito Juárez Monument, at the junction of Highways 190 and 175. The ones that go to Capulálpam are green and white. The trip takes a little over two hours. These colectivos take Calle Benito Juárez through Ixtlán until it terminates at Avenida Campos, and then turn right toward Capulálpam. If they've got an empty seat, they'll take you there for about US$1. A private taxi ride will cost you US$8-10.

GUELATAO DE JUÁREZ

There are a number of towns with "de Juárez" in their name to commemorate Benito Juárez, but Guelatao de Juárez is the only one that can call itself the birthplace of the renowned Mexican statesman. The town's first name has two meanings in Zapotec: "the place where hope abounds" and "embrace power."

Sights

Sala Homenaje a Juárez

main square on Avenida Juárez; no tel.; 10am-5pm Tues.-Sun.; free

Just a 10-minute drive from Ixtlán, and half an hour from Capulálpam, this is perfect for a quick day trip to brush up on Mexican history. The exhibition at the Sala Homenaje a Juárez (Room in Homage to Juárez) tells the story of the politician's life through a series of informational plaques (in Spanish) written in first person. On display are government documents dating back to the Reform Era in the mid-19th century, as well as a collection of woodcut prints that tell a visual story of the life of this man who changed the country forever.

Statue of Juárez

After the museum, make sure to check out the statue of Juárez in the seated position, as he is usually depicted in statues in Mexico. He sits in the lowest level of the tiered main square, to the north of the museum. The text above the fountain to the right of the statue is part of Juárez's most famous quotation. It reads: "Respect for the rights of others is peace."

Laguna Encantada

From the statue of Juárez, head up the stairs on the east side of the plaza and stop by the Laguna Encantada, where Benito's humble beginnings as a shepherd are memorialized in a statue of the child with the sheep he brought here to drink from the enchanted waters of the pond.

Getting There

Guelatao de Juárez is 4 km (2.5 mi) south of Ixtlán de Juárez on Highway 175. **Drivers** have an easy 10-minute trip from the center of Ixtlán. If you're coming from Oaxaca City, you'll see the sign just before Ixtlán.

Take a private **taxi** (US$7) from the center of Ixtlán, or wait for a southbound colectivo (US$1) on Highway 175 next to the gas station and entrance archway to Ixtlán. Keep an eye out for the Guelatao sign about five minutes down the road. The museum is just two blocks from the highway.

Laguna Encantada

El Papaloapan

Cascades of gigantic ferns blanket the steep hillsides on the northern slopes of the Sierra Norte, as altitudes drop and you get closer to the hot, humid climate of the Gulf of Mexico. You won't be needing any of the warm clothing you brought for camping up in the mountains in El Papaloapan (or "La Cuenca," the basin, as the locals call it), a fertile tropical lowland with cane fields, rubber tree farms, and fruit tree orchards.

Agriculture, commerce, and industry, as opposed to tourism, move the economy of this most industrialized region of the state, but there are still a few gems for those determined to see a different side of Oaxaca.

TUXTEPEC

Although its name means "Hill of Rabbits," you won't find too many hills in Tuxtepec. Oaxaca's second-largest city, with an elevation of only 20 m (66 ft) above sea level, is centered around a pronounced bend in the Río Papaloapan, which has become quite polluted as a result of the industry that is the base of the region's economy. For someone on vacation, you probably won't spend too much time in the city itself. But if you're exploring this far north in Oaxaca and spending the night, you might as well check out a few of its gems.

Sights

Museo Regional de Tuxtepec "Casa Verde"

corner of Calle Guerrero and Calle Libertad; museotuxtepec@gmail.com; 10am-6pm Tues.-Sat.; free

You can't miss the bright emerald facade of the aptly named Casa Verde. Right across the street from Parque Juárez, Tuxtepec's main square, it tells the cultural story of La Cuenca (the basin). The airy halls are home to a myriad of pre-Hispanic artifacts, art exhibitions, an open-air garden, and my favorite, a gallery of colorful and intricately embroidered huipils, unique to the region. Cultural presentations are given on topics as varied as the Afro-Mexican diaspora presence in northern Oaxaca and celebrations highlighting the area's Indigenous villages and their traditions.

an intricately woven huipil

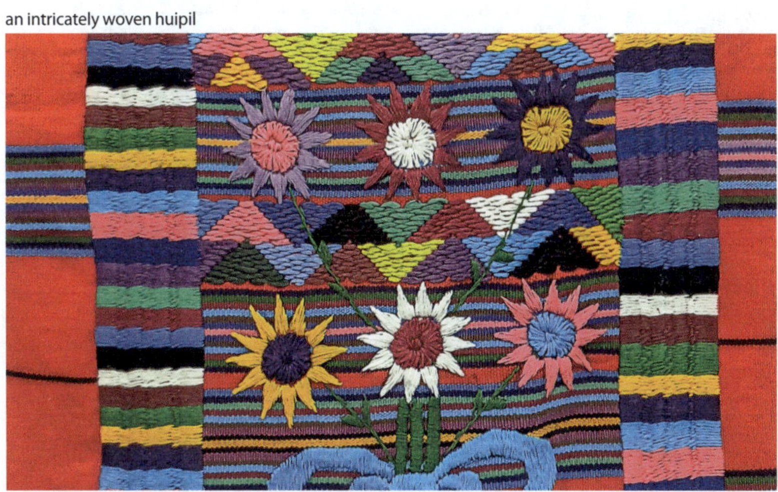

Ruinas del Castillo

corner of Calle Las Ruinas and Calle Tabasco; 24 hrs daily

The Papaloapan region is a lush land rich in resources, which made it a strategic site for the Aztec empire hundreds of years ago. In fact, Moctezuma I built a site at what was called Moctezuma's Castle. After the Spanish conquest, the "castle" was abandoned and subsequently looted. All that remains now are the mysterious ruins that lay forgotten by most of the outside world, but which the inhabitants of this neighborhood (called, no surprise, El Castillo) lovingly and proudly maintain. As I was walking around the perimeter of the rubble, an elder from across the street came over to share the story of the ruins with me. With a conspiratorial glint in his eye, he told me of rumors that not all the treasures were stolen, but lay buried in tunnels and caverns underground that haven't been discovered yet. Is it true? Who knows? But being in such a historically significant space was special in itself. Catch a cab from Centro and have the driver wait for you; the visit shouldn't take more than 15 minutes, but if you're into history, it's worth seeing.

Festivals and Events

Fiestas de Mayo

May

May is a good month for festivals here. The Fiestas de Mayo (May Parties) begin with a carnival-style parade through town. During these and other national and local festivals, you're likely to see Tuxtepec's **Flor de Piña (Pineapple Flower) dance,** which is always a hit at the Guelaguetza, a festival that celebrates regional cultures.

Fiestas de San Juan

June

Like many communities in El Papaloapan, Tuxtepec's patron saint is Saint John the Baptist, who is celebrated on June 24. But in true Oaxacan fashion, the celebrations go on all month, with parades, processions, fandangos (a tradition also shared with neighboring Veracruz), and other festivities.

Food and Accommodations

Restaurante El Legado

Sebastián Ortiz 849; tel. 287/162-0544; 7am-11pm daily; US$8-12

Enjoy a well-made Oaxacan mole or fresh seafood dish at Restaurante El Legado. The empanadas especiales (fried dumplings of plantains and ground beef) are a big hit. The service is impeccable, and some waiters speak English.

Saboreando Oaxaca

Miguel Hidalgo 350, Colonia San Bartolo; tel. 287/101-3000; noon-6:30pm Mon.-Fri., 10am-6:30pm Sat.-Sun.; US$11

Work up an appetite at the zip line and aerial obstacle course on-site, then proceed to fill up on a buffet of tacos, moles, mondongo, tlayudas, empanadas, memelas, carne asadas, fried plantains, and much more at the festive Saboreando Oaxaca. There's even an endless supply of pizza and fries if you have picky adventurers in tow. Did I mention the all-you-can-eat desserts?

Hotel María de Lourdes

corner of 5 de Mayo and Santos Degollado; tel. 287/875-0410; US$25 d

The 43 clean, comfy rooms of Hotele María de Lourdes are set around a charming inner courtyard and have air-conditioning, TVs, and Wi-Fi.

★ Hotel El Rancho

Camacho 435; tel. 287/875-9500; www.hotelelranchotuxtepec.com; US$40 d, US$52 country room, US$55 suite

You'll feel a world away from Oaxaca's second-largest urban area at Hotel El Rancho, which puts a rustic touch on modern comfort. Inside the entrance, you'll see an old horse-drawn carriage covered in potted succulents, cacti, and tropical flowers. Distinctive among its 52

1: Río Papaloapan **2:** Flor de Piña dance

1

2

Caldo de Piedra (Stone Soup)

El Papaloapan is home to one of the most interesting pre-Hispanic dishes from Oaxaca, the caldo de piedra, or stone soup, a recipe of the Chinantec peoples of Veracruz and northern Oaxaca.

HOW IT'S MADE

This seafood stew, made with shrimp, fish, tomatoes, cilantro, onions, dried chiles, and a potent herb called epazote, is prepared by tossing the raw ingredients in a bowl, and the cooking is done by fire-heated river rocks that are dropped into the broth, bringing the water to boil. The fish, shrimp, and fresh vegetables are ready to eat in about three minutes.

CULTURAL HISTORY

Caldo de piedra is traditionally made only by men, who serve the soup to the women. The meal is a way of giving Mom a break and showing gratitude for the work she does for the family. Interestingly, however, a bowl is not part of the traditional preparation method. In the town of **San Felipe Usila,** the ingredients and broth are put in a bowl-shaped hollow in a rock, or a hole dug in the sand and lined with banana leaves.

Because of this, anthropologists believe this recipe predates the use of ceramics in Mexico, which by some estimates dates as far back as 2300 BC. This makes caldo de piedra a contender for one of the oldest traditions in Oaxaca, and possibly in the Americas.

STONE SOUP TODAY

Usila is recognized as the cuna, or birthplace, of this intriguing soup, but the small village is very out of the way, and as a result, it has no restaurants that serve the soup.

However, the **Comedor Prehispánico Caldo de Piedra** (tel. 951/114-1234; www.caldodepiedra.com.mx; 9am-6pm Tues.-Sun.; US$13.50), founded in Usila by the Gachupín Velasco family in 1996, moved to the **Valles Centrales** in 1999. You'll find this location in Tlalixtac de Cabrera on Highway 190, 7 km (4.3 mi) west of Oaxaca City's Centro. It's just before Tule, but don't take the Tule exit. The restaurant is about 1 km (0.6 mi) past the Tule exit.

César Gachupín Velasco was chosen by the town council of Usila as the "ambassador" of Chinantecan stone soup to the outside world, and he and his children are doing just that. Señor César and his family have dedicated their lives to conserving and promoting this fun and caring gastronomic tradition that dates back thousands of years.

units are its "country rooms," with dark cedar finishing on the walls and support beams overhead; cut stone walls add a bucolic counterpoint to the luxurious suites.

Getting There

From Oaxaca City, get to Tuxtepec on a **Cuenca** or **AU bus** (6 hrs; US$17) from the city's main bus station. Both lines make several trips daily. The trip is quicker in a suburban run by **Transjuar** (Calzada Héroes de Chapultepec 801, Colonia Reforma, Oaxaca City; tel. 951/132-7227; 5.5 hrs; US$12). Their base in Tuxtepec is at Melchor Ocampo 74 (tel. 287/875-1513).

However, it's highly unlikely that you'll make the trip directly from Oaxaca City, so if you're coming from the mountains, wait by the highway and flag down a passing Transjuar van or any other colectivo that passes by. Transjuar vans make a stop outside the gas station in Ixtlán de Juárez (4.5 hrs; US$7).

Drivers take Highway 175 north from Ixtlán de Juárez, climbing and descending the vertiginous slopes of the Sierra Norte for a couple hours until the road finally bottoms out in the humid, tropical valley that snakes its way to Tuxtepec. The 155-km (96-mi) drive takes about 4.25 hours.

SAN PEDRO IXCATLÁN AND LA ISLA DEL VIEJO SOYALTEPEC

Created by a pair of dams in the 1970s, **Lake Miguel Alemán** covers 4,300 sq km (1,660 sq mi) of lush valley and is home to a wide variety of tropical birds and freshwater fish, including catfish, bass, and tilapia. The small fishing village of San Pedro Ixcatlán is on a peninsula jutting into the lake from the southern shore. It's a good option for an afternoon meal en route to the Sierra Mazateca to the west, or a calm overnight respite for those who'd rather take their time.

Once an isolated hilltop town, La Isla del Viejo Soyaltepec became even more isolated when the waters of the reservoir cut it off from the surrounding landscape. Walk down the western slope of the peninsula from the church to find the **embarcadero** (boat dock), where you can hire a boat (US$35 for 3 hrs) to take you out to the island. During the half-hour trip, you'll see large flocks of ducks, cranes, herons, and other migrating birds that turn into a riot of wings and quacks when the noisy motorboat roars by. Almost always shrouded in clouds, the peak rising out of the lake north of Ixcatlán is called Cerro Rabón.

For a few decades after Soyaltepec's transformation into an island, the town mostly spoke Mazatec. However, the industry and tourism that have come as a result of the reservoir have brought Spanish to the island, and most folks are bilingual. You'll be hard-pressed to hear any English, though. As of this writing, its unique isolation is earning it talks of possibly giving it a Pueblo Mágico designation.

Sights

Iglesia de San Miguel Arcángel

16 de Septiembre; Sat.-Sun.

Overlooking the lake to the west of the island stands the weathered Iglesia de San Miguel Arcángel. You'll only be able to see inside on Saturdays and Sundays, when locals gather for mass. Surrounded by the usual pious cohort, Saint Michael slays his dragon inside a modest, concrete altar painted a pastel orange. Head through the grass-covered main streets of town and take a left to get to a rocky outcropping that serves as a mirador; it's at the far end of the soccer field. From here, you'll have a fantastic view of the lake below and an even larger, uninhabited island to the north. Keep your ears on alert for women artisans calling from their windows to sell huipiles distinct to the region.

Food and Accommodations

Restaurante El Paraiso

Calle Otilio Montaño; 287/889-0427; 10am-6pm Mon.-Sat.; US$7

Ixcatlán is a fishing village, so having some seafood here is a must. At Restaurante El Paraiso you can enjoy a fresh grilled mojarra (tilapia) or ceviche (seafood salad of fish cured in lime juice). A few folks with grills set up along the main drag, Benito Juárez, selling tacos and tlayudas, and some homes had signs on front doors advertising homemade tlayudas.

Hotel Villa del Lago

Benito Juárez; tel. 287/152-4847; US$20 fan, US$22 a/c

The quaint Hotel Villa del Lago in Ixcatlán is on Benito Juárez about 0.5 km (0.3 mi) north of the church. Rooms are basic but clean, and boast pleasant views of the lake and islands. There is also a swimming pool to cool off in the sweltering sun of El Papaloapan.

Getting There

From Tuxtepec, board a **camioneta** behind the Pemex station at the Glorieta de la Piña, the junction of Highways 175 and 182. The base is a few storefronts down Highway 182 from the gas station. The sign reading San Pedro Ixcatlán is pretty conspicuous, making it easy to find, and the pickup trucks are white with a blue stripe. The 1.5-hour drive costs about US$2.50.

San Pedro Ixcatlán is about 60 km (37 mi) from Tuxtepec. **Drivers** take Highway 182 west from Tuxtepec and take the turnoff to San Pedro Ixcatlán in about 1.5 hours. The town is perched on a peninsula about 15 minutes from the highway. Or you might stop off for a meal at one of the comedores on either side of the **Puente Pescadito,** the bridge that spans the channel connecting the two reservoirs that constitute Lake Miguel Alemán. The bridge is on Highway 182, about 40 minutes from Tuxtepec.

La Cañada

With the rugged Sierra Mazateca on its eastern side, and a long arm of the Valle de Tehuacán-Cuicatlán to the west, La Cañada (Canyon Country) is a land of extremes. The valley may not boast the level of megadiversity of the mountains, where a single oak tree can be home to six or seven other colorful and rare plant species, but there is still an extraordinary abundance of life here. It boasts gullies teeming with succulents and massive colonies of green macaws, and is home to one of the highest concentrations of columnar cacti in the world. This lesser-visited region of Oaxaca truly deserves more attention from travelers, and not just those looking to get trippy in Huautla (hey, no judgment). Down in the valley there are lots of spectacular natural sites and ecotourism opportunities. It's a bit off the beaten tourist path in Oaxaca, but a visit to La Cañada doesn't disappoint. The variety in the natural setting, people, and food all follow the Oaxacan traditions of being completely unique and consistently awe-inspiring.

★ HUAUTLA DE JIMÉNEZ

Sprawled across a steep slope of the Sierra Mazateca, Huautla de Jiménez has been a destination for psychedelic thrill seekers since the 1960s, when hippies came in droves to visit local curandera María Sabina. The Mazatecs had long used hallucinogenic mushrooms in their healing and spiritual ceremonies, but folk healer María Sabina was the first to openly share with the outside world the skills and knowledge passed down to her from her maternal grandparents.

Huautla was founded sometime between AD 1200 and 1375 by Mazatec people. The origin of the name Huautla ("Among the Eagles" in Nahuatl) comes from an ancient Mazatec legend of a pair of gigantic eagles that lived in the nearby caves and used to trouble the townsfolk.

Tourism is still driven primarily by María Sabina's magic mushrooms, still called niños santos (holy children) by the Mazatecs who carry on her tradition today. But the mushrooms aren't the only things that are magical in this Pueblo Mágico. My first day in Huautla, I experienced its magic firsthand when I was whisked away by my camioneta driver who insisted I go with his family to what he said was dinner. "Dinner" turned into a trek to a hilltop barrio, where the lively music of an orchestra and heart-stopping bangs of firecrackers could be heard streets away. It was a mayordomia, a religious fiesta, this one in honor of El Cristo Negro. We were taken to a copal filled room and brushed down with herbs, incense and prayers before being sat down to enjoy a hearty meal of tamales wrapped in hoja santa leaves, spicy beef stew, and shots of mezcal. Sitting, a stranger welcomed into the heart of this community, surrounded by the lilting and whispering tones of Mazateca, as tendrils of copal still swirled in the air, I felt the thrum of magic. The surreal day ended with watching the sun paint the viridian mountains vermillion, as a sea of clouds slowly rolled in.

Hopefully, as more outsiders come looking for the magic not only in the ñinos santos but in the rich culture, hospitality, and natural beauty of Huautla, demand will lead to not only more options for visitors to enjoy, but

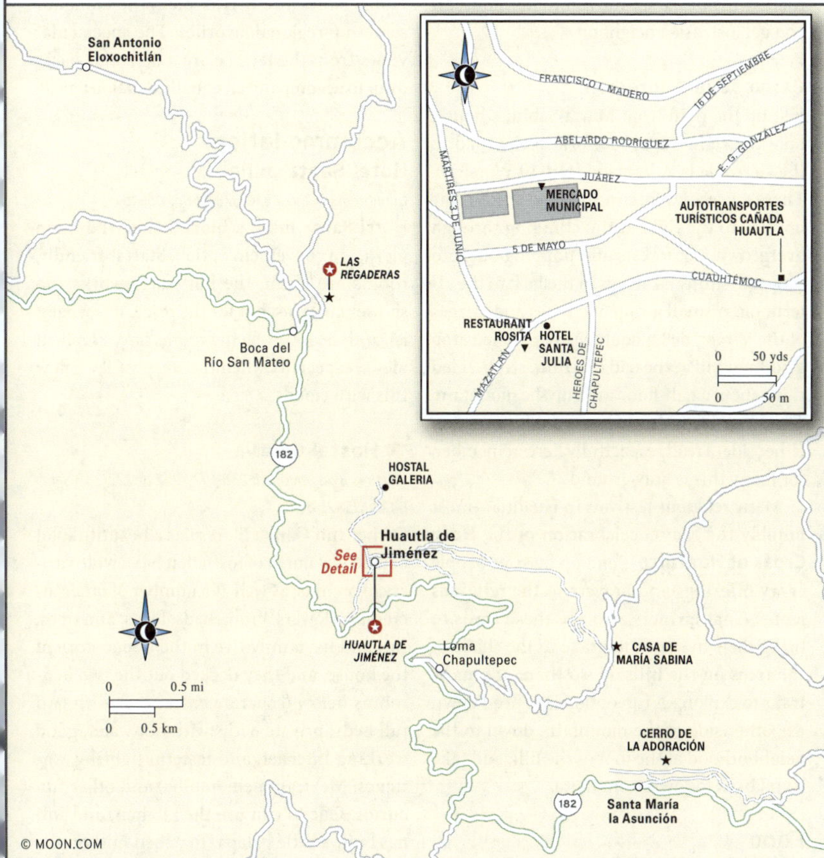

also more jobs and more money in the local economy overall.

Sights

Casa de María Sabina

Carretera María Sabina; tel. 236/102-8567 or 236/108-6151; museum US$2, cabañas US$3.50 pp, camping US$3

The descendants of María Sabina carry on her healing traditions at the Casa de María Sabina, where she used to hold mushroom ceremonies with visitors. They have a small museum dedicated to her life, which is mostly photos and paintings, and they also have some very rustic tin-sided cabañas and space for camping. Call or just stop in and ask about accommodations, ceremonies, and other traditional medicine treatments.

The best way to get up here is to take a **taxi** (US$2.50). All drivers will know exactly where you want to go. On foot, the 4-km (2.5-mi) walk takes a little over an hour and gets steeper as you near the house. Driving in Huautla can be a stressful experience, so I recommend a taxi or a hike even if you drove here. If you're intent on **driving,** however, take Benito Juárez east from the town center until it turns into Carretera María Sabina. The road switchbacks up the hill to her house. If you get lost, ask a neighbor.

Cerro de la Adoración

Just up the road from María Sabina's house, take the right leg of the fork in the road to the Cerro de la Adoración (Hill of Worship). There's a second fork in the road a little way up; stay to the right again, climbing through overgrown oak forests and popping out into tranquil, sunny clearings in the heat of the afternoon. A small group of crosses and images of the Virgen de Guadalupe are perched atop a pointed hill at the end of a thin, steep-sided ridge about a half-hour walk up the mountain. The views from the ridge extend for miles on either side. Tread respectfully here; remember, for many this is holy ground.

Many religious festivals in Huautla—most notably the May 3 celebration of the **Holy Cross of Huatulco**—end up here, as people carry offerings and prayers to the religious icons. Goat farmers also use these trails to bring their livestock to graze in the shade of the trees on the hillside, so there are many trails to explore. A fun option is to head down the other side of the mountain, down to the neighborhood at the foot of the hill, and take a taxi back to town from there.

Food

Huautla's main plaza has several vendors who sell prepared food like tamales de mole. My favorite is **Antojitos Vero** (tel. 236/117-3701 or 236/102-9929) where you'll find tacos, tostadas, memelas, empanadas, and agua frescas. You'll find more fondas (food stalls), produce, and butchers in the **mercado municipal,** in the building on the east side of the local government offices.

★ Restaurant Rosita

Mazatlan 2; tel. 236/378-0386; 8am-6pm Mon.-Sat.; US$5

Restaurant owner Rosa (Rosita) Estrada is the sister of Álvaro Estrada, author of the international bestseller *Vida de Maria Sabina* (Life of Maria Sabina). Just a minute west of Hotel Santa Julia, this pleasant comedor serves up regional favorites. The spectacular views from the terrace are a delicious backdrop to accompany an equally delicious meal.

Accommodations

Hotel Santa Julia

Cuauhtémoc 12; tel. 236/378-0586; US$16 d

Hotel Santa Julia, a block below the main plaza, is a convenient option. Staff is friendly, rooms are clean, the hot water works (no shower curtains, but for the price, it is what it is), and the south-facing rooms have excellent views, especially when the steep valley below fills with clouds.

★ Hostal Galería

Mártires 3 de Junio; tel. 236/102-7252 or 222/349-8423; US$25 d

Owner Inti García Flores has a beautiful plot of land just north of town that has a wide variety of orchids, as well as a number of other incredible flowers, bromeliads, ferns, and trees. Inti and his family live in the upper story of the house, and they decked out the two bedrooms below (separate entrances) with two full beds, private baths with hot water, good working Internet, and tasteful lighting, antiques, Mexican memorabilia, and other fun curios. Guests can use the kitchen, and Inti has built a little palapa (thatched hut) on the hillside at the back of his property, where he invites visitors to read, do yoga, or just relax, take in the view, and listen to the wind in the sycamore trees.

Getting There

Get to Huautla from Oaxaca City on a suburban run by **Autotransportes Turísticos Cañada-Huautla** (Trujano 600, Oaxaca City; tel. 951/284-5960; US$14). The very curvy trip takes about five hours. They make five trips daily (six on Sunday), beginning at 8:30am. Their base in Huautla (Cuauhtémoc 21; tel. 236/106-8555) is down the street from Hotel Santa Julia.

Camionetas and **colectivos** leave Tuxtepec regularly from the Glorieta de la Piña, the junction of Highways 175 and 182. There's no direct trip to Huautla, though; you'll have to transfer to another camioneta at Jalapa de Díaz, about an hour and a half away. From Jalapa to Huautla is another hour and a half. It costs about US$8 total.

Drivers will have an amazing time driving through the Sierra Mazateca, but use caution. Landslides are not uncommon during the rainy season, so wait until the rain stops to drive. It's also a good idea not to drive after the sun goes down, as bands of carjackers are known to stop private vehicles late at night. Don't be in a rush when driving through the clouds, which can limit visibility to no more than a few feet in front of the car. Just go very slow and hug the yellow line.

Huautla is a 239-km (148-mi) drive from Oaxaca City. Take Highway 190 west and take Highway 135 (not 135D, the toll road that goes to Puebla) at Telixtlahuaca. From here it's 140 km (87 mi) on serpentine Highway 135 through canyon country to Teotitlán de Flores Magón, where you'll turn east onto Highway 182. Total drive time is about five hours. If you're coming from Tuxtepec, you've only got 123 km (76 mi) to drive. Take Highway 182 west from Tuxtepec and stay on it for about three hours, or maybe longer if you get snagged by a cloud and have to slow to a crawl for a while.

★ LAS REGADERAS

At the western base of the peak on which Huautla is located, a pair of waterfalls called Las Regaderas (The Showers) flow out of the rock in the neighboring hill and fall 30 m (98 ft) to the river below. There is a suspension bridge that I was personally suspicious of; instead of crossing it, I opted to climb down to the base of the river to admire the falls from below.

Local Guides

Tropical Sabina

tel. 236/104-7095; tropicalsabina22@gmail.com; US$40

Pedro of Tropical Sabina, a proud Mazateco born and raised in Huautla de Jiménez, loves sharing the richness of his culture with visitors. I highly recommend his tours of his lovely hometown that include a visit to Las Regaderas, Casa Museo Maria Sabina, a guided walk to Cerro de la Adoración, and any cultural events going on. And you may even learn a little Mazatec, too.

Inti García

tel. 236/102-7252 or 222/349-8423; US$20

Make an activity of Las Regaderas by hiking down to the falls. Inti García at Hostal Galería will take you on a walk down through the lush oak forests to the falls that takes about two hours round-trip (US$20).

Getting There

A **taxi** from Huautla will cost you about US$5. The falls can be thoroughly appreciated in 15 or so minutes, so just ask your driver to wait while you snap pictures.

Drivers take a right onto Highway 182 after leaving from Huautla's main gateway. Zigzag down the road about 7 km (4.3 mi) until you see the sign for Santa María Chilchotla, just before the bridge. You'll see the falls on your left in about 0.8 km (0.5 mi).

CUICATLÁN

The original inhabitants of Cuicatlán are believed to have migrated from the Toltec settlement of Tula, north of Mexico City, after its fall in AD 1150, but much of their history was destroyed during the conquest. The Cuicatecs named it Yabaham (Earthen House). The Nahuatl name Cuicatlán means "Land of Poems."

Sights

El Chentil Cave

Just a 30-minute walk from Cuicatlán, a cave called El Chentil is a natural gallery of pinturas rupestres, or ancient cave paintings. The paintings haven't been officially dated, but locals say they were chipped into the rocks as far back as 12,000 years ago. The easy hike to the cave is a great opportunity to observe local

1
2
3

flora and fauna, and a local guide (US$7) can tell you what the paintings are believed to say about the origins of the Cuicatec people, if you speak Spanish (no English-speaking guides). Get here by taking Calle Mina east from the Hotel Real Sochiapam and making a U-turn onto Calle Juárez, which leads into the mountains east of town. The cave is a 5-10-minute drive from town.

Mirador Cruz Blanca

From the town's main square, head up the hill to the east (behind the church) to get to the Mirador Cruz Blanca (White Cross Lookout Point), which offers a nice view of the center of town and the 17th-century Iglesia de San Juan Bautista. The walk up the hill takes about five minutes.

Food and Accommodations

Find delicious comida corrida (set menu) meals at any of the **comedores** around the main square, as well as in the market to the northeast of the square.

Taquería El Borracho Loco

Calle Hidalgo; tel. 951/425-3711; 3pm-midnight daily; US$5

Tasty tacos can be found in town at Taquería El Borracho Loco (The Crazy Drunk Taco Restaurant). Rather than drunk, you're more likely to waddle away from this place a glotón loco (crazy glutton). You'll find it about two blocks north of Hotel Real Sochiapam.

★ Comedor La Abuelita

Calzada de la Juventud; tel. 236/374-0203; 7am-7pm daily; US$5-7

To get a taste of the best of Cuicatecan gastronomy, head to Comedor La Abuelita in the old railroad station across the highway from the main gateway into town. Traditional moles, empanadas de amarillo, chile rellenos, memelitas (corn tortillas with a sauce), and more are served up with care. Try anything they've made that day with the rare chile chilhuacle (a moderately spicy pepper) in it.

Hotel Real Sochiapam

Hidalgo 50; tel. 236/374-0001; reservaciones@hotelrealsochiapam.com.mx; US$30 d

Your best hotel option in town is Hotel Real Sochiapam, a few blocks south of the main square. The comfortable, airy rooms all have hot water and are cooled with fans. South-facing second-floor rooms have nice views of the valley. There is an on-site restaurant, and all rooms have a little rotating door for discreetly passing snacks and drinks ordered from reception. The hotel has ample parking space and a pleasant gazebo with tables and chairs for reading, writing, or just relaxing.

Information and Services

Presidencia Municipal

Juárez 5; tel. 236/106-1457; sanjuanbautistacuicatlan177@gmail.com

Call or stop by the presidencia municipal (local government offices) to get more information and to hire guides to local sights and day trips to nearby villages. It is actually a good idea to call beforehand for any ecotourism activities in this part of Oaxaca. Tourism here is so slow that most offices don't keep regular hours, and people will need time to prepare activities and accommodations.

Getting There

Cuicatlán is 121 km (75 mi) northwest of Oaxaca City. Get here on a suburban run by **Transportes Turísticos Teoax** (Periférico 408, Oaxaca City; tel. 951/268-1192; US$5.50). Vans leave Oaxaca City hourly from early in the morning to 8pm (10pm on Sunday). The trip takes about 2.5 hours. Their base in Cuicatlán (tel. 236/374-0026) is on Calle Hidalgo, three blocks south of the main square. Bigger buses leave Oaxaca City from the **Terminal Periférico** (Periférico 1006, Oaxaca City; no tel.; US$5) twice a day, arriving at the station in Cuicatlán, also on

---

1: clock tower in Huautla de Jiménez 2: waterfalls at Las Regaderas 3: Tehuacán-Cuicatlán Biosphere Reserve

Calle Hidalgo, a block north of Hotel Real Sochiapam. The bus trip takes about 3 hours.

Drivers head west on Highway 190 from Oaxaca City. Stay on Highway 190 until you get to Telixtlahuaca, about 35 km (22 mi) from Oaxaca City, which takes about an hour. From here, turn right onto Highway 135 (do not confuse it with the toll road 135D) and follow this twisty stretch of desert road for another 1.5 hours to Cuicatlán. Cuicatlán is 85 km (53 mi) from Telixtlahuaca.

TEHUACÁN-CUICATLÁN BIOSPHERE RESERVE

Cuicatlán is a good base for exploring the Tehuacán-Cuicatlán Biosphere Reserve, a 4,900-sq-km (1,900-sq-mi) protected natural area with breathtaking topography and rich biodiversity in both plant and animal life. Shielded from rain by the Sierra Mazateca to the northeast and a ridge of mountains referred to as the Sierras Centrales de Oaxaca to the southwest, this arm of the Valle de Tehuacán-Cuicatlán is a hot, dry desert where 6-m (20-ft) columnar and organ cacti thrive on the rugged hills lining the valley. This region is home to one of the world's greatest concentrations of columnar cacti. Despite the area's aridity, the waters of the Río Cuicatlán allow for agriculture to thrive along its banks. Oranges, lemons, limes, papayas, beans, and especially chiles, which like the hot, dry weather, are all cultivated here, and the food is correspondingly delicious. On a walk through this area, you might see badgers, possums, snakes, iguanas, doves, and other desert-dwelling creatures.

To enjoy the wonders of this corner of Oaxaca, hire a **guide** at the presidencia municipal in Cuicatlán, or check down the road in Santa María Tecomavaca.

SANTA MARÍA TECOMAVACA

The small town of Santa María Tecomavaca is the gateway to the astounding landscapes of not only the larger Biosphere but the Cañón de Sabinos (Cypress Canyon) within, with its towering, sheer rock walls and large flocks of green macaws. During the colonial period, the Spanish mispronounced the Nahuatl name Tecomahuaca, which means "where the possessors of the calabash tree live," adding the *V* with which it is pronounced today.

Local culinary specialties include moles rojo y verde (red and green moles), tesmole (a mole-like sauce made from guajillo and chiltepec chiles, pumpkin seeds, and achiote, a dark-red fruit), and pipián, another sauce with a base of roasted ground pumpkin seeds.

Sights

★ Cañón del Sabino

Tecomavaca's main attraction is the awe-inspiring Cañón del Sabino (Cypress Canyon), where some of the cliff walls shoot up 600 m (1,968 ft) from the canyon floor. The sides of these vertiginous crags are home to the nests of what locals call esmeraldas voladoras (flying emeralds), or guacamayas verdes (green macaws).

The best times to see them are in the early morning and late afternoon, as the colorful birds escape the midday heat in the cool nests they've made in the cliffs. You'll see entire flocks (at their largest between March and August) fly by with the spectacular view of the canyon in the background.

Since the canyon (about half an hour from Tecomavaca) is in the Tehuacán-Cuicatlán Biosphere Reserve, you'll have to hire a **guide** in town. To do this requires speaking Spanish, as committee members do not speak English. Call the Oficina de Bienes Comunales (tel. 951/294-3360). The tour (US$25 for two people) goes from 2pm-8pm and includes transport to the canyon from town and back.

Coming out here also requires patience. Tourism is not the primary activity of this and other areas in the valley, and cell phone service is spotty. Begin making arrangements well before you plan to come, as it may take a few calls just to get someone to pick up.

Ruta de los Compadres

September-December are the best months for seeing macaws along the Ruta de los Compadres (Route of the Buddies), a three-hour car trip through the deciduous forests of the lowlands. Various types of copal trees abound, one of which was the first species used to make alebrijes (painted carved wooden figurines) when they became popular in the 1970s. Another, called lináloe, was once used to make an aromatic essential oil for aromatherapies and perfumes. The tour costs US$20 for up to four people. Inquire in the Oficina de Bienes Comunales.

Hiking

Ruta de las Echeverías

Distance: *2 km (1.2 mi) one-way*
Duration: *2 hours*
Difficulty: *easy*
Trailhead: *east side of Santa María Tecomavaca*

This short hike is called the Ruta de las Echeverías for the profusion of the namesake succulents that grow in the area to the east of town. Their soft green rosettes and pink flower stalks are all over the place here. Just 2 km (1.2 mi) outside town, this hike can be done in a couple of hours at a relaxed pace. A guided tour (Spanish only) costs about US$7. Inquire in the Oficina de Bienes Comunales about the tour, or to alert them to your presence and get info on where to find the trailhead east of town.

Information and Services

Oficina de Bienes Comunales

Tecomavaca main square; tel. 951/294-3360

Ecotourism activities are administered by a committee in the local government's Oficina de Bienes Comunales (Office of Common Property). The office is next to the basketball court in the main square, but call ahead to make sure those on the ecotourism committee have time to prepare for your arrival.

Presidencia Municipal

Tecomavaca main square; tel. 236/372-2048; 10am-4pm Mon.-Sat.

If you have trouble getting in touch with this office, call the presidencia municipal. No English is spoken in these local government offices.

Getting There

AU buses leave Oaxaca City from the **Terminal Periférico** (Periférico 1006, Oaxaca City; no tel.; US$8) multiple times a day. These buses make three stops daily in Cuicatlán, at 7:45am, 11am, and 10:50pm. The half-hour trip costs about US$3.50. The station in Cuicatlán is on Hidalgo, a block north of Hotel Real Sochiapam. From Huautla, board a Oaxaca-bound suburban run by **Autotransportes Turísticos Cañada-Huautla** (Cuauhtémoc 21; tel. 236/106-8555; US$8) and tell them you want to get off in Cuicatlán. They'll probably just drop you off on the highway, but it's only a 5-minute walk to the hotel, and 10 minutes to the main plaza.

Drivers take the same route to Cuicatlán. If you're coming from Oaxaca City, continue up Highway 135 another half an hour to get to Tecomavaca, a total drive time of about two hours. From Huautla, the drive takes a little over two hours.

Background

The Landscape

Oaxaca's rich, vibrant culture has as much to do with the rugged landscape as it does with the people living on it. The rim of mountains surrounding the Valles Centrales has made access to certain areas difficult for centuries, creating pockets of isolation where human life developed into traditions, recipes, and languages wholly unique from anywhere else in the world. It wasn't until the latter half of the 20th century that highways and other modern development began to connect Oaxaca's more out-of-the-way places with each other and the rest of Mexico.

The bright, broad color spectrum of Oaxaca's traditions comes as

no surprise when considering the fireworks-colored earth of La Mixteca, the brilliant blooms of the orchids in the Sierra Mazateca, the pinks and greens in the limestone bricks of the old churches, and the indigo plant, cochineal insects, pomegranate rinds, pecan shells, mosses, and other sources of natural dyes. Oaxacans are deeply rooted in the land they call home, and everything from ecotourism to parties to clothes to the food on the table to the toponym itself is a reflection of that link with this diverse and fertile part of Mexico.

GEOGRAPHY

At 93,757 square km (36,200 sq mi), Oaxaca is the fifth-largest state in Mexico. The rugged ranges that hem in the Valles Centrales are the southernmost curves of the two great chains in Mexico, the Sierra Madre Oriental and the Sierra Madre Occidental, which stretch over 1,600 km (1,000 mi) to the north, all the way to the border with the United States.

In Oaxaca, these mountains are referred to as the Sierra Madre de Oaxaca in the north (or, more casually, the Sierra Norte or Sierra Juárez), and the Sierra Madre del Sur in the south. Together they constitute 36 percent of the state's landmass and boast 20 summits higher than 3,000 m (9,843 ft).

Inside this nest of craggy peaks, Oaxaca City and the surrounding Valles Centrales have an average elevation of 1,500 m (4,921 ft). To the west, La Mixteca ranges 1,200-2,300 m (3,937-7,546 ft) above sea level, dividing it nominally into the High Mixteca (La Mixteca Alta) and the Low Mixteca (La Mixteca Baja).

To the north of La Mixteca, the canyon country called La Cañada abuts the foothills of the western part of the Sierra Norte, known regionally as the Sierra Mazateca for the people who have called it home for generations. Peaks here don't get as high as in the Sierra Juárez and Sierra Mixe (also named for the local Indigenous people) to the east, but these mountains are just as rough and rich in biodiversity.

The lofty heights of the Sierra Norte give way to the broad, tropical lowlands of Oaxaca's northernmost region named after Oaxaca's largest river, El Papaloapan. Average altitudes here are only 10-20 m (33-66 ft) above sea level. Oaxaca's easternmost region, El Istmo de Tehuantepec, is also mostly tropical lowlands and short, squat hills.

Most of Oaxaca's Pacific Coast is rough and rocky, as the Sierra Madre del Sur lines the vast majority of it, in some places tumbling all the way into the sea. The Sierra Madre del Sur is home to the Cerro Nube (Cloud Peak), Oaxaca's highest, and the tallest non-volcanic summit in Mexico, with an altitude of 3,750 m (12,303 ft) above sea level.

CLIMATE

Although over half of Oaxaca's landmass has a hot, tropical humid or subhumid climate, the mountains and seasonal rains keep average temperatures within moderate ranges. This rough terrain creates a number of different climate zones. Nearly half of Oaxaca is a hot, subhumid climate zone, which is found on the coast and in El Istmo to the east. Seasonal rains averaging 79-99 cm (31-39 in) annually turn the hills green May-October, but by January the lack of moisture turns them brown until April. Average temperatures here range 22-35°C (72-95°F) year-round. Just about any day of the year, you can expect temperatures on the coast to climb into the mid-30s (90s F) by mid-afternoon.

The tropical region of El Papaloapan, in the north of the state, receives an average of 206 cm (81 in) of rain during the same months. Average temperatures range from 21.5°C (71°F) in January to 33°C (90°F) in May. Temperatures can get into the mid-30s (90s F) here in the hot months, but highs usually range 27-32°C (80s F). The humidity might make it feel warmer, though.

Previous: an iguana in a mangrove on the coast.

In Oaxaca City and the Valles Centrales, you'll find a hot, semiarid climate where average temperatures range from 17.5°C (64°F) in January to 29.5°C (85°F) in May. Highs in the hot months are around 30°C (the upper 80s F). The rainy season here is also April or May-October, but these desert areas only receive about 68.5 cm (27 in) of rain per year.

If you plan on staying up in the higher altitudes of the mountains, you'll need to plan for colder, often wetter weather. In Cuajimoloyas and other towns at and above 3,000 m (9,843 ft), the lows average 8-12°C (46-54°F) throughout the year, and in the winter months it can even freeze at night. Still, when the sun is out, it gets hot up here. Average highs run 20-25°C (68-77°F) in April and May, and it can get as hot as 28°C (82°F) at the hottest time of day.

ENVIRONMENTAL ISSUES

The main environmental problem Oaxaca faces today is drought. Due to a mix of several factors, including outdated infrastructure struggling to keep up with the demands of increased tourism, inadequate rainy seasons, misappropriation of government funds, and deforestation, locals are paying the price. During the dry season, Oaxacans often go without water for days, if not weeks.

Pollution is another malady, due to industry, agriculture, and government corruption. Salina Cruz is home to one of Mexico's biggest oil refineries, which has negatively affected the local environment and wildlife, with numerous oil spills taking a toll on the sea turtle population.

Although lots of Oaxaca may seem empty, the reality in many areas is that human activity has had a negative effect on the environment. Destructive wildfires, some caused by drought, others by slash-and-burn practices gone awry, ravage the countryside. Fires started to burn trash have also contributed to deforestation, but that practice's main effect is on the air quality.

Plants and Animals

Oaxaca is partly to thank for Mexico ranking among the 17 countries designated by Conservation International as megadiverse. With 707 species, Mexico tops the world list of reptilian biodiversity. The country also boasts 438 mammalian species (second on the list), 290 amphibian species (fourth), and 26,000 different species of flowers, the fourth-highest on the floral diversity list.

VEGETATION ZONES

Semiarid Scrub

Visitors to Oaxaca City and the Valles Centrales will be familiar with this type of vegetation zone. The Valle de Tehuacán-Cuicatlán, in La Cañada, also has this type of ecosystem. Found at altitudes between 1,400 and 1,700 m (4,595-5,575 ft) above sea level, the mountains that hem in these deserts keep out the majority of the wet air from the Gulf of Mexico to the north and the Pacific Ocean to the south. These parts of Oaxaca average only about 33 cm (13 in) of rain annually.

Trees here tend to be short scrubs, such as the guaje (*Leucaena leucocephala*), from which Oaxaca derives its name. The little seeds are edible, and you might be served a pod of them with a tlayuda or plate of tacos. Taller trees here include jacarandas (*Jacaranda mimosifolia*), which fill with lilac-colored blooms at the beginning of spring, and Montezuma cypress (*Taxodium mucronatum*), which prefer the wet earth of riverbanks and creek beds. Although the monumental Árbol del Tule is no longer close to a body of water, it started out next to a great lake that filled parts of the Valles Centrales when it sprouted over 2,000 years ago. In Oaxaca, people call this cypress sabino or ahuehuete.

The plantlife that dominates this ecosystem by far is shrubs, grasses, and succulents. Morning glory plants are common in this ecosystem. Of the 10 species that grow here, one of the most common is the cazahuate (*Ipomoea paucifora*), which spreads its fetching white blooms in November and December.

Cactuses that thrive here include the emblematic nopal (*Opuntia ficus-indica*), various parts of which are staples in the Mexican diet. The broad, flat leaves are eaten grilled on tacos, fried with eggs, beef, or other ingredients, or fresh in chunky salsas that the cactus turns slimy and a little sweet. The super-sweet prickly pears, called *tuna* in Spanish, range from green to yellow to red to a deep wine purple, and are eaten fresh or used to make aguas de sabor (fruit drinks). Like great, green candelabra towering as high as 7 m (23 ft) over the critters on the desert floor, the garambullo blanco (*Myrtillocactus schenckii*) is also common in this vegetation zone, especially in the Valle de Tehuacán-Cuicatlán. This valley is also home to one of the highest concentrations of ceroid, or columnar cactus (of the *Pachycereus* genus), in the world.

Other non-cactus succulents common here include various types of yucca, such as Joshua trees (*Yucca brevifolia*) and *Yucca mixtecana*, but the Valles Centrales are known for having the perfect conditions for a variety of **agave** species, called maguey here in Oaxaca. Many of these species are used to make mezcal.

Pine-Oak Forest

The majority of forested land in Oaxaca is covered in lush pine-oak forests, which you'll find in both the Sierra Norte and Sierra Sur at altitudes starting around 2,000 m (6,562 ft). Oaks prefer lower, drier elevations, and they gradually mix with pines as the altitude rises. By the time you get to 3,000 m (9,843 ft) above sea level, it's too cold for the oaks, and pines and sacred firs (*Abies religiosa*), here called oyamel, cover the slopes. Much of these forests are considered cloud forests, as giant clouds often sweep in and shroud the peaks in a dense fog.

The mountains of Oaxaca are home to more than 10 species of pine, the more common of which are Mexican white pine, Chiapas white pine, and Montezuma pine. The most common oak tree is the yellow oak, but you'll also see the netleaf oak. The latter is sometimes called encino chicharron (pork rind oak), as some locals see a similarity between its leaves and the crunchy pigskin snacks Mexicans love so much.

In many parts of Oaxaca's pine-oak forests, especially in the Sierra Norte, oaks are often covered in a number of other plants, such as mosses, ferns, agaves, bromeliads, orchids, and other various wildflowers. Spend enough time in these forests and you'll hear them falling from branches they grow too big for. Ixtlán de Juárez is a good place to go to see these kinds of plants. The oaks of the bosque mesófilo (mesophyll, or cloud forest) west of the city are usually shrouded in mist, and their branches are covered with spectral mosses. North of the Parque Ecoturixtlán, the bosque de bromelias (bromeliad forest) is likewise full of bromeliads and other epiphytes. The Sierra Mazateca, in the northwest of the state, has the perfect conditions for various species of orchids to bloom at the same time.

Tropical Deciduous Forest

These color-changing tropical forests of primarily short trees and scrubs cover the foothills along the coast, as well as parts of El Istmo. They'll be burning a brilliant green if you visit during the rainy season, but come January, that vivacious luster will have faded to brown until the rains come back. But the bougainvilleas, flor de mayo, passion flowers, and other vibrant blossoms keep the place colorful year-round.

The more common scrub trees in these forests are rosa amarilla, Pacific Coast mahogany, and Mexican plumeria, or as it is more commonly called here, flor de mayo (May flower). The taller trees with trunks covered in large thorns and what looks more like green skin than bark are called pochotes in Oaxaca, in English known as the silk cotton or Kapok

The Maguey Plant: Emblem of Oaxaca

The importance of the maguey plant to Oaxacan people can be summed up in the common adage "Para todo mal, un mezcal, para todo bien, también" (For all the bad, mezcal, and for all the good, as well). This succulent, generally called agave elsewhere in Mexico, is vital to the Oaxacan cultural identity and livelihood.

MAGUEY'S MANY USES

Aside from alcoholic drinks (mezcal isn't the only one), maguey plants have been used here for thousands of years to create various necessities. The fibers of the plant, called ixtle, come with their own needle, and can be used to make cords, ropes, bags, hammocks, paper, and more. Some people place a pair of maguey leaf points in the form of a cross in the earthen oven before they cook barbacoa as a way to ward off malign spirits. In the mountains, farmers use a species that grows up to 2.5 m (8.2 ft) as fences to delineate the boundaries of their fields.

PULQUE

Less popular than mezcal, the alcoholic beverage pulque is also made from certain types of maguey. This is made by fermenting the sap of the maguey heart, which is called aguamiel (honey water), collected by boring a hole in the piña (heart) and collecting it in a gourd. The aguamiel can also be drunk. It is very sweet and does not contain alcohol.

SPECIES USED FOR MEZCAL

Despite these various uses, say the word "maguey" to a Oaxacan, and you can bet that the first thing that comes to mind is mezcal. Types of mezcals depend on the species of maguey used to make them. The most common type is made from the **espadín** maguey (*Agave angustifolia*), with swordlike, hazy-blue leaves.

One called **cuishe, madre cuish,** or **tobaziche** is made from an endemic species to Oaxaca called *Agave karwinskii*. This one grows in long, skinny stalks, yielding more tubular piñas than its cousins that stay closer to the ground. **Tobalá** (*Agave potatorum*), a wild species common around Sola de Vega, is another in-demand type for mezcal. Popularity in the 1980s and 1990s took a heavy toll on the populations of this wild species, and farmers began to look for ways to cultivate it. The cultivated plant is now common in mezcal-producing towns.

Other types of maguey commonly used for mezcal include **coyote** (*Agave americana*), **arroqueño** (*Agave americana oaxacensis*), **jabalí** (*Agave convallis*), and **tepeztate** or **tepextate** (*Agave marmorata*).

NEW SPECIES

To this day, botanists continue to discover new species of maguey in Oaxaca. Scientists in the Institute of Biology at the National Autonomous University of Mexico found four new species in 2017, bringing the total for the 35 years preceding 2018 to 44 previously undiscovered species.

trees. The Aztecs named Pochutla, just north of Puerto Ángel, "place of the pochotes."

Savanna and Mangrove Forests

Along much of the coast, the rocky, forested foothills of the Sierra Madre del Sur tumble straight into the sea, but in some places between the hills, you can find broad, flat grasslands speckled with palm trees. These savannas are mostly found around the Lagunas de Chacahua and in between Huatulco and Salina Cruz, where the mountains become much sparser. This is one of Oaxaca's ecosystems on which agriculture has taken its toll, as much has been converted to fields or grazing pastures.

Common palms here include many types of

fan palms, with broad fan-shaped leaves, and of course an array of coconut palm species. These types of trees are some of the most useful in the state. The fruit is eaten, the trunks and leaves are used to build all the palapas on the beaches, and mats, baskets, hats, and a laundry list of other useful items are produced with materials from palms.

Around the Lagunas de Chacahua and La Ventanilla you'll find mangrove swamps. The two most common mangrove trees here are the red mangrove and white mangrove.

Tropical Evergreen Forest

Highway 175, which squiggles its way through the Sierra Norte from Oaxaca City to Tuxtepec, gets a bit tricky about half an hour before you reach Valle Nacional. Once it dips below 1,500 m (4,921 ft) above sea level, the forest is wet enough, either by rain or being enveloped in thick fog, for plants to sport healthy green leaves year-round. Not only are the curves tight, there's a good chance rain has made the road slick and limited visibility, and entire slopes like green waterfalls of gigantic ferns are so impressive as to be a potentially dangerous distraction.

These tree ferns thrive in the tropical evergreen forests that blanket the northern slopes of the Sierra Norte, growing up to 6 m (20 ft) or taller. Their leaf stalks grow up to 1.2 m long (4 ft) and 0.9 m wide (3 ft), and the new fronds slowly uncurl from the top like thick, hairy tails.

The rubber tree, called palo de hule (rubber stick) in these parts, is among the taller trees here, growing up to 50 m (164 ft) tall. Coffee trees thrive in this environment too. And growing on all the trees are thick vines and the holey-leafed climber plant ceriman, or as it's called around here, piñanona. It has a marvelous scientific name: *Monstera deliciosa*.

Also growing on lots of trees in this forest is a species of the very alien-like strangler fig, which sprouts from a notch in another tree and slowly grows around it, eventually killing it and taking the place it once held in the earth. Another type of fig tree common here, called amate, has thick, twisted, tendon-like roots dug into the ground.

Flowers in these forests are equally as otherworldly. The famed bird of paradise grows here. There are also lots of species of heliconia in these forests, whose flowers resemble those of the bird of paradise but grow in strings of alternating blooms that get so heavy they fall over and hang from the plant like the tail of a creature born of imagination.

Tropical Rainforest

The lowlands to the north of the Sierra Norte are covered in dense tropical rainforest. A number of fig species thrive here, as well as mahogany trees. Also important to this type of ecosystem are sapodillas, which bear the fruit zapote, and their cousin in the genus, *Manilkara chicle,* which bears a natural chewing gum called chicle.

A number of other fruit-bearing trees also thrive here, such as mango, banana, papaya, and coconut palms, and lots of land is used in the cultivation of these fruits. Other cultivated plants here include rubber trees, sugarcane, and pineapples.

The tropical rainforest is so important to Oaxacans (and the rest of us) because this is the favorite rooting grounds of the cacao tree. Smaller than the figs and mahoganies, the cacao trees are found beneath the canopy with their branches full of yellow pods about 25 cm (10 in) long, which are full of the beans from which chocolate is produced. So we can all be thankful for the tropical rainforests of Oaxaca and elsewhere in southern Mexico. Can you imagine life without chocolate?

BIRDS

Birds are the most common type of wildlife you'll see in Oaxaca, and there are a lot to see. With 741 known species in the state, Oaxaca is home to two-thirds of the country's bird species. Some to look out for in the Valles Centrales are the vermillion flycatcher, gray-breasted woodpecker, and ocellated thrasher. Birds like the bridled sparrow,

Oaxaca sparrow, and white-throated towhee forage for food among the cacti and shrubs of the desert.

The pine-oak forests of the mountains are home to mockingbirds, red warblers, mountain trogons, and various types of hummingbirds. Populations of the dwarf jay, found only in the state of Oaxaca, are low enough to almost put them on the endangered species list.

Hundreds of bird species call the tropical deciduous forests of the Sierra Sur foothills and Pacific coast home. Some that stand out are the golden-cheeked woodpecker, orange-breasted bunting, russet-crowned motmot, and white-throated magpie-jay. Bird-watching is a popular tourist activity on the coast.

A wide array of colorful and unusual birds inhabit the tropical evergreen forests and tropical rainforests of the Sierra Norte and El Papaloapan. In the evergreen forest, you'll see and hear the white-winged tanager, gartered trogon, Lesson's marmot, band-backed wren, red-legged honeycreeper, emerald-chinned hummingbird, and many, many more. Among the hundreds of species known to live in the Oaxacan rainforest, some rather spectacular ones include the olive-throated parakeet, keel-billed toucan, red-throated ant tanager, and Amazon kingfisher.

Parrots, Parakeets, and Macaws

You'll mostly find parrots and macaws along the Pacific coast. They enjoy the subhumid foothills of the Sierra Sur. They also like parts of the Sierra Norte, and a large population of green military macaws inhabits the Cañón del Sabino, in the Valle de Tehuacán-Cuicatlán in the northwest of the state. Parakeets are also very common in Oaxaca. The olive-throated parakeet is found in the northern slopes of the Sierra Norte and the tropical lowlands beyond. Green and Pacific parakeets are abundant in the coastal regions. The orange-fronted parakeet, white-fronted parrot, and yellow-headed parrot are also common in this region.

Seabirds

Oaxaca's Pacific coast is an ornithologist's utopia. The Lagunas de Manialtepec and Chacahua are the best places to go bird-watching in this region. They are home, either temporarily or permanently, to dozens of species, including fantastic-looking birds like the roseate spoonbill, blue heron, and the yellow-crowned night heron. Other birds that either live here or stop by on their migrations are American white pelicans, brown pelicans, royal terns, wood storks, tricolored herons, bare-throated tiger herons, red-billed tropicbirds, brown boobies, and many, many more.

REPTILES AND AMPHIBIANS

While Mexico tops the worldwide list of diversity of reptile and amphibian species, Oaxaca tops the nationwide list. Mexican scientists have identified at least 245 reptilian species and 133 amphibian species in the state.

The dry Valles Centrales region isn't the best place for amphibians, but it is perfect for the over 60 species of reptiles that call it home. Take a hike through the Valle de Tlacolula, and you're most likely to see lizards like Sack's giant whiptail lizard and the eastern spiny lizard. You might see a snake, but your chances are much less likely. The Oaxacan coral snake is endemic to this region. Amphibians do live here, though. The Mexican tree frog, southern highland tree frog, and giant toad are a few of the species that like the foothills and wetter areas.

On a hike through the pine-oak forests of the mountains, you might see an emerald spiny lizard or a southern crevice spiny lizard. You probably won't, but if you do see the Oaxacan subspecies of the pygmy rattlesnake, steer clear. Like all rattlesnakes, they're poisonous, but unlike other rattlesnakes, they aren't as inclined to give you a warning before they bite. Near streams, you might see a shiny peeping frog or a Cochran's false brook salamander.

In the forests on the Pacific Coast, check the trees for green iguanas and the rocks for spiny-tailed iguanas. These forests are also home to the brown basilisk lizard, which uses its webbed feet to run across the surface of water. The lagoons at Chacahua and La Ventanilla are home to caimans and swamp and river crocodiles. In the rainy season, Mexican giant tree frogs hop down from the branches to breed in ponds and still pools. You might also see a marbled toad.

The brown basilisk also walks on water in the higher-elevation tropical evergreen forest, and the red coffee snake, Mexican jumping pit viper, and greater scaly anole call this type of forest home as well. Down in the rainforest, dozens of lizard species thrive, as well as the Central American crocodile and the Central American boa. The classic lime-green red-eyed tree frog lives down here, too. The Mexican burrowing caecilian, an amphibian that looks like an overgrown earthworm, burrows under the plant debris of the jungle floor.

SEALIFE

Fish

The waters of the Pacific Coast of Oaxaca are equally rich in fish species. At the dinner table, you'll see huachinango (red snapper), róbalo (sea bass), pez vela (sailfish), lisa (mullet), atún amarilla (yellowfin tuna), dorado (dolphin fish), and marlin (pronounced mar-LEEN in Spanish). Other fish that swim these waters include angelfish, bonito, barracuda, stingrays, swordfish, triggerfish, spadefish, yellowtail, parrotfish, mackerel, pufferfish, and many more.

More than a few species of tiburón (shark) like to call these waters home, but don't worry. They are not known to attack humans. These include the angel shark, scalloped hammerhead shark, whitetip shark, and blacktip shark.

Sea Turtles

Four of the world's seven sea turtle species come to the Oaxacan coast to lay their eggs. The most abundant is the olive ridley (golfina), whose favorite nesting beach in the world by far is La Escobilla in Puerto Escondido. Thousands of them crawl up the beach June-September to lay eggs, a spectacular event the locals call the arribazón (great arrival). This is how La Escobilla earned the nickname Playa Tortuguera (Turtle Beach).

Green sea turtles (tortuga verde or blanca) and hawksbills (tortuga carey) also come here to nest, as well as the gigantic leatherbacks (tortuga laud, also called garapacho and machincuepo in some areas), which can reach a length of 2.5 m (8.2 ft). Other popular nesting sites along the coast include Mazunte, La Ventanilla, and Playa Morro Ayuta, near San Pedro Huamelula. The name Mazunte is actually derived from a Nahuatl word meaning "Please lay eggs!"

INSECTS AND ARACHNIDS

There are lots of creepy crawlers in Oaxaca. Insects run the gamut from houseflies to mosquitoes to tropical and exotic species like rhinoceros beetles and footlong stick-bugs. Chiapas has the highest rate of butterfly biodiversity in Mexico, but Oaxaca, especially in the Sierra Madre del Sur, has the highest number of endemic species, such as the mariposa esperanza Oaxaqueña (Oaxacan hope butterfly). The cute little yellow ones that are regular companions on hikes through the pine-oak forests are called cloudless sulfur butterflies (mariposa azufre). Some rather spectacular-looking ones to keep an eye out for are the kites, such as the Mexican kite swallowtail, or as it's called here, cometa cebra (zebra kite), with white and sky-blue wings with black stripes and pointy, tail-like wingtips.

One of the most common spiders you'll see in Oaxaca are wolf spiders. (Since wolf spiders and tarantulas are both hairy, people call them both tarántulas.) If you don't want to know exactly how numerous these guys are, don't wear a headlamp at night in the forests along the coast. Also common here are spiders of the Selenops genus. These flat, crab-looking spiders were the first in which scientists observed the ability to glide and somewhat steer themselves when falling in order to land on branches (cue my internal screaming). They like the dry desert and foothills of the Valles Centrales. Other common desert spiders here include black widows (check your shoes) and the aforementioned tarantulas, which can grow to be bigger than your hand. If you don't want to see firsthand just how big spiders can get in Oaxaca, do not enter the Cueva de la Serpiente Oscuro (Cave of the Dark Serpent) in Apoala. Some of the stranger species here include the spined micrathena (araña espinosa), which has a bulbous, oversized abdomen with ten spines, and the golden orb-weavers (araña seda dorada), whose silk has a yellow pigment that shines gold in the right light. They like arid regions as well.

MAMMALS

The richest areas of mammal biodiversity are the Sierra Norte, followed by El Istmo and the Sierra Sur. Human activity such as agriculture, logging, and development have encroached on the natural habitats of mammals, and they have learned to avoid us. Aside from squirrels, rabbits, bats, and the possible deer, there is little chance you'll be able to observe very many mammals in the wild in Oaxaca.

Pumas, Jaguars, and El Tigrillo

You may not see the pumas, jaguars, ocelots, lynxes, and other wild cats when hiking through the mountains, but you can bet they see you. These cats are masters at stealth, and will almost always avoid you altogether.

The tigrillo, a smaller wildcat native to forests from here to Brazil, has spotted fur similar to that of a jaguar. The jaguarundi is another small wildcat endemic to Mexico and Central and South America, with monotone gray, red, or black fur. The tigrillo is considered a vulnerable species, but populations of jaguarundis in the Amazon Basin are large enough that the species does not worry conservationists.

Monkeys

What would a jungle be without monkeys? The tropical rainforest of El Papaloapan is home to the black-handed spider monkey, one of the largest monkey species in the Americas. Spider monkeys have prehensile tails and hooked fingers that they use to swing from branch to branch with ease. As more and more of El Papaloapan gets claimed for human use, the less room there is for the spider monkeys. The species is considered endangered.

Black howler monkeys are sometimes spotted in the rainforests of El Papaloapan, but they tend to mostly hang out in those in the states of Veracruz and Tabasco, closer to the Gulf Coast. Unlike their neighbors the spider monkeys, howler populations are large enough for them not to appear on the endangered species list.

Armadillos, Tamandúas, Coatis, and Cacomixtles

Armadillos are common in many parts of Oaxaca. Of the 20 armadillo species in the Americas, the nine-banded armadillo, found in Oaxaca and elsewhere in Mexico, is the only species whose populations are on the rise. It is one of only two species that lives outside of South America. Armadillo is a part of the traditional diet in El Istmo. One of its cousins, the anteaters called tamandúas, also live in Oaxaca, preferring the southeast-facing part of the coast east of Mazunte.

Raccoons have a couple of cousins that call Oaxaca home. The ring-tailed cacomixtle prefers the tropical humid and subhumid forests in the north and on the coast. Its name comes from the Nahuatl, meaning "half lion." The other cousin, the white-nosed coati, has a larger habitat in Oaxaca, as coatis venture deeper into the pine-oak forests of the mountains than cacomixtles.

Bats

There are at least 82 species of bats in Oaxaca, and they have found homes all over the state. One species in Oaxaca is endangered, and 16 others are either under special protection or considered threatened.

Vampire bats like the semiarid foothills around the Valles Centrales and La Mixteca, as well as the muggier regions of the coast and El Papaloapan. Cases are rare, but vampire bats here and elsewhere in the world are known to bite people and spread rabies. Other rarer bats in Oaxaca include the Aztec fruit-eating bat, Parnell's mustached bat, and Salvin's big-eyed bat. Oaxaca is at the southern tip of the habitat of the funny-looking Townsend's big-eared bat, which, well, has big ears.

History

PRE-HISPANIC OAXACA

The earliest known evidence of crop domesticating in the Americas were found in the **Guilá Naquitz** cave outside **Mitla** in the 1960s. Paleobotanists date the cucurbita (type of squash native to Mesoamerica) seeds found here as far back as 8000 BC. Beans and teocintle (predecessor to maize) didn't become domesticated until 4,000 years after squash, so the presence of those seeds in these caves has led archaeologists to conjecture that the caves hosted a succession of seasonal residents over the millennia. The evidence suggests that Oaxaca might be the epicenter of agriculture in the Americas.

Marcus Winter, US archaeologist and author of *Oaxaca: The Archaeological Record* (1989), has broken down the history of Oaxaca into four stages. The seeds from Guilá Naquitz date back to the Agricultural Phase (9500-1500 BC). As agriculture ensured more dependable food supplies, the hunter-gatherers began to prefer to stay put, forming villages and building the foundations for the great societies to come.

The Village Era

The Village Stage of Oaxacan history was from 1500 BC to AD 500. These peoples had quite a bit more time on their hands, now that they did not have to hunt or migrate as much in search of food. Small villages formed, and people began forming the customs and traditions that would go on to define their cultural identities in the phases to come.

The most important site from this era is **San José Mogote,** just north of Monte Albán, in the Valle de Etla. This is the first known Zapotec settlement, and it was here that they began to create some of the cultural characteristics of their descendants. The layout of the constructions leads archaeologists to believe that the residents of San José Mogote were already performing impressive astronomical calculations, and the hieroglyphic inscriptions found here make the Zapotecs one of the primary candidates for the earliest writing system in the Americas.

Monte Albán

Winter's third phase, the **Urban Stage** (AD 500-750), begins with the founding of the greatest of pre-Hispanic Zapotec cities, Monte Albán. By this time, the Aztecs had founded Teotihuacán, in the Valley of Mexico, and the Maya were taking care of business in Tikal, in Guatemala. Evidence of influence from both cultures has been found in Monte Albán.

Citizens of Monte Albán continued to study astronomy and develop their writing system, and by AD 200, the city was an economic and political powerhouse in the region, being known as the capital of the Zapotec empire and reaching a peak population estimated by some to be as high as 100,000 people around AD 600.

The Zapotec religious center **Mitla,** in the Valle de Tlacolula, came along a few centuries after the founding of Monte Albán. Mitla was home to Zapotec high priests, and was the final resting place for many important political and religious figures. All of its names have to do with passing on. In Nahuatl and Mixtec, its names mean "place of the dead," and the Zapotec word for it means "place of rest."

Archaeologists believe that sometime around AD 500 Monte Albán's importance in the region began to decline, and by the year 900, the city was completely abandoned. The reason or reasons remain a mystery to this day. Mitla and the nearby city of **Yagul** became the important Zapotec centers. This period represents the beginning of the fourth and final stage of Winter's pre-Hispanic Oaxacan history, the **City-State Stage** (AD 750-1521).

Oaxaca's second most powerful group at this time, the Mixtecs, had founded their important centers, such as **Monte Negro** and **Yucuita,** around the same time as Monte Albán, and invaded Zapotec territory in 1325, occupying Mitla and bringing life back to Monte Albán. In the early 1490s, the Aztecs invaded Oaxaca, setting up a military outpost on the **Cerro del Fortín,** the hill just to the northwest of the Centro of Oaxaca City, and giving the place the name we know it by today, named after the abundance of guaje trees they found there. The Aztecs' colonial aspirations were short-lived, as the arrival of the Spanish three decades later thwarted the designs they had on Oaxaca.

THE CONQUEST

Spanish conquistador **Hernán Cortés** (1485-1547) made his first landing in Mexico in Cozumel, an island off the Caribbean Coast, in 1519. Pop history will have you believe that the Aztecs were a gullible people, easily duped into believing that Cortés was the reincarnation of their plumed serpent god **Quetzalcoatl,** making them fearful and more inclined to welcome the outsiders. This notion was actually propagated by the Spanish themselves in the 1540s as a way to justify what they had done in the New World. The word *Quetzalcoatl* was also the Toltec term for high priests and other elites. **Moctezuma II,** the Aztec emperor at the time of the arrival of the Spanish, did not think that Cortés and his men were gods but rather the descendants of **Ce Ácatl Topiltzin Quetzalcóatl,** a Toltec king who had been exiled by the Aztecs in 987, and that they had come back to reclaim power in the region. Well aware of these fears before his arrival in Tenochtitlán, Cortés used them to his advantage, claiming that **King Charles of Spain** (1500-1558) was indeed divine, and that the conquistadores had been sent to bring the true word of god back to the Aztecs.

By 1521, European diseases introduced by the Spanish had helped them conquer Tenochitítlán and other important Aztec cities and towns, and Cortés began to go after the rest of the Aztec empire. Outbreaks of smallpox in 1520, 1531, and 1545 would go on to kill over five million Mexicans before it finally ran its course.

Into Oaxaca

Their first excursions into Oaxaca were into La Mixteca, led by **Francisco de Orozco y Tovar,** first taking towns like Yucundaa, which was subsequently relocated to form the town of **Teposcolula.** Conquistador **Pedro de Alvarado** also played a hand in the colonization of Oaxaca, as he passed through the region on his way to conquer Guatemala. The town of **Huaxyacac,** now Oaxaca City, fell to the Spanish in 1521, marking the beginning of a new era for Oaxaca. The diocese of **Antequera** was established in Oaxaca City in 1535.

COLONIAL OAXACA

The Spanish saw some of the fiercest resistance to their presence in Mexico in the peoples of Oaxaca, the majority of whom fought against colonization for decades. Some churches in La Mixteca took decades to complete, as many Mixtec tribes organized uprisings in response to the forced labor imposed on them and the construction of the Christian temples on the foundations of their own. Many towns today are not in the same location as the pre-Hispanic towns of the same names, as many were moved after smallpox and other diseases took root in them. This also served political purposes, and was done even when not made necessary by disease. The system called congregación (congregation) displaced Indigenous communities, forcing them to live under the administrative stipulations imposed by the colonizers.

The Caste System and Population Decline

Disease and overwork killed millions of people in Mexico during the colonial period. It is estimated that in 1500, the Indigenous population of Mexico was anywhere from 15 to 25 million people, around 2 million of those in Oaxaca. By the mid-17th century, those numbers had dropped to 1.3 million and 150,000, respectively. Because of this, the Spanish began to enslave Africans to make up for the lost labor and save their economy. Critical to the colonial economy was the red dye cochineal, of which Oaxaca was Mexico's, and for a while the world's, largest producer.

Colonial Mexican society was broken down into three distinct social groups: the peninsulares or blancos, white people born in Spain who moved to Mexico; the indios, Indigenous Mexicans; and the negros, slaves brought from Africa. The subsequent Spanish generations born in Mexico were called criollos, and were a notch down from the peninsulares in the social hierarchy. There was much discord between these two groups, as the criollos, who considered themselves to be fully Spanish, were often denied the perks they felt their skin color earned them. From the intermixing of these groups, the Spanish created a caste system that was more than racial classification; it was also a form of economic control. Tributes were based on a people's caste, with the larger sums unsurprisingly falling to the lower levels.

MEXICAN INDEPENDENCE

At the beginning of the 19th century, Spain was experiencing political instability and started to see its power wane. A power vacuum was created in New Spain, with the peninsulares pitted against the criollos.

Conspiratorial Book Clubs

Luckily for the criollos, they had a majority in the Mexico City Council, and a criollo-controlled junta of municipalities was also established. Criollos all over New Spain began attending "literary clubs" that were merely a front for conspiratorial meetings, where the main word whispered was "revolución." Their intentions were not to make an independent Mexico for the people, but rather for themselves.

Spanish captain **Ignacio Allende** (1769-1811) sympathized with the criollos and their movement for independence. Allende knew the movement needed the support of high-ranking religious and political officials in New Spain, so he appealed to a priest from Dolores, Guanajuato, named **Miguel Hidalgo** (1753-1811). The plan was for Hidalgo to lead the movement, while Allende would take care of the coup, which they planned for December 1 in Jalisco. But word got out, and on September 13, Spanish authorities arrested many involved.

The Grito de Dolores and Rise of the Insurgency

Father Hidalgo was at home in Dolores when word of the arrests got to him. Early in the morning on the September 16, he gave a rousing call-to-arms that has gone down in Mexican history as the Grito de Dolores (Shout of Dolores), which lit the fire in the people that grew into the **Mexican War for Independence** (1810-1821).

Ten Years of War

The next 10 years in Mexico were volatile and bloody. In Oaxaca, the royalists had control of the capital, suppressing an 1811 insurrection in the city led by **Felipe Tinioco** and **José Palacios,** but the insurgents had traction elsewhere in the state. A mule driver turned insurgent soldier named **Valerio Trujano** (1676-1812) led rebel forces in La Mixteca, holding out in Huajuapan de León. Oaxaca City finally fell to the rebels in 1812, led by **José María Morelos** (1765-1815).

After taking Oaxaca, Morelos marched to Huajuapan, where he and his men helped Trujano fight off the royalist troops besieging the city.

Despite his early victories, Morelos was captured and executed in 1815, and his place at the head of the insurgency was taken by **Vicente Guerrero** (1782-1831). He was so successful in leading the insurgents that the royal government offered him amnesty to capitulate, but he refused. Royalist general **Agustín de Iturbide** (1783-1824) was sent to take on Guerrero's rebel forces, but seeing that the tide was turning, he turned himself, and the two wrote up the **Plan de Iguala** on February 24, 1821. This revolutionary proclamation announced the official independence of Mexico from Spain and guaranteed "Religion, Independence, and Union" in the country. On August 24 of that year, the Plan de Iguala was ratified by the signing of the Treaty of Córdoba in Veracruz.

Emperor Iturbide and the Constitution of 1824

The insurgents had achieved their goal of ousting the royalists from power, but once they had it, they found themselves faced with a new problem. The peasants and farmers who had won the fight with sheer determination and ingenuity had no experience running governments. In the political instability that followed the war, Iturbide was elected emperor of Mexico. His sovereignty was short-lived, however, and two years later, he abdicated power after former allies turned against him.

Mexico's first constitution was signed in 1824, officially forming the Estados Unidos Mexicanos (United Mexican States). Oaxaca had been a government department since the end of the war, but that year, the department wrote up its own constitution and was granted statehood. This year also saw the founding of the Institute of Sciences and Arts of Oaxaca, which would go on to educate two of the most important figures in Mexican history.

Santa Anna and War with the United States

The rest of the decade was plagued by political instability, a number of failed coups, and more plots. Renowned military leader **Antonio López de Santa Anna** (1794-1876), who had crossed over to the side of the insurgents when Iturbide did so, was declared president by the congress. His reputation in Mexico was pretty good at the time, but that good standing went down the drain when Santa Anna lost Texas to the United States. Santa Anna never recognized Texas independence, and disputes over the territory led to the Mexican-American War (1846-1848). As part of the **Treaty of Guadalupe Hidalgo,** which brought an end to the conflict, Mexico lost the states now called Colorado, New Mexico, Arizona, Utah, Nevada, and California.

Santa Anna hopped in and out of the president's office 11 times between 1833 and 1855. By the time he was done, Mexico had lost over half its territory to the United States, whether by insurrection, treaties, or transactions.

REFORM, CIVIL WAR, AND FRENCH INVASION

While Santa Anna dealt disastrously with the United States, **Benito Juárez** (1806-1872) was doing good things in the Oaxacan governor's office. During his tenure from 1848 to 1852, he greatly improved the state's infrastructure and revived the economy by attracting foreign investment. After a Santa Anna-imposed two-year exile spent working in a cigar factory in New Orleans, Juárez returned to Mexico. He and other liberals wrote the Plan of Ayutla, which forced Santa Anna to step down and called for a new constitution to be written.

Juárez went to work as the provisional government's Minister of Justice, but what he did there would put into question his status as a man of the people. He drafted the Juárez Law, which restricted the jurisdiction of the church and military and declared all citizens equal before the law, but part of the limitations on the church included large divestments of church-owned land. The idea was to redistribute lands among the people, but as it worked out, the only ones with means to buy the land were elites with money, defeating the purpose of the law. Juárez's legacy went on to be that of a spotless, sometimes almost godlike figure in the formation of the country as it is known today. While more recent scrutiny of his time in power has called into question these myths, his overall track record suggests that his intentions were always good, even when the results weren't what was planned.

The Reform Law sowed even more discord between liberals and conservatives, and the latter organized an uprising in 1858 that lasted for three years. When the liberals finally won out in 1861, Juárez assumed the presidency.

Juárez and Maximillian

Unfortunately, Juárez's term was short-lived. In 1862, Napoleon invaded Mexico. The most famous battle of this period was the Battle of Puebla on May 5, 1862, led by Oaxacan **Porfirio Díaz** (1830-1915), the battle that is the origin of the 5 de Mayo celebration in the United States, whether revelers know it or not. The holiday was first celebrated on May 5, 1863, by residents of Puebla who had moved to California.

Despite Díaz's best efforts on the battlefield, the French took a number of state capitals, including Oaxaca, and ultimately Mexico City by 1864. Austrian archduke **Maximillian** and his wife, Carlota, were instated as emperor and empress of the Second Mexican Empire. The United States continued to recognize Juárez as the president, and he fled to the mountains to set up a government-in-exile. Pressure from the United States caused the French to begin pulling out of Mexico in 1866, and by the next year, the Mexican army had taken back Mexico City. Juárez ordered Maximillian's execution by firing squad on June 19, 1867.

Juárez was reelected with little opposition that year, but fellow Oaxaqueño Porfirio Díaz started talking trash, claiming Juárez had violated the constitution. Juárez continued his attempts at reform, but Díaz would not relent. A tough, stressful life had taken its toll on Juárez, and he died of a heart attack in the National Palace in Mexico City on July 18, 1872.

THE PORFIRIATO

After Juárez's death, the office of president was assumed by the Supreme Court chief justice, Sebastián Lerdo de Tejada. Díaz opposed Lerdo de Tejada's appointment as well, and when the liberal announced he was running for reelection in 1876, Díaz picked up the refrain he'd shouted during Juárez's term: ¡No reelección! (No reelection!). He issued the Plan of Tuxtepec Díaz in 1876, sparking a nationwide revolt against the Lerdo administration.

When he finally made it to the presidency in 1877, Díaz began to change his perspective on reelection, and he ended up serving seven presidential terms over 31 years. Díaz's main goal was to bring peace to the country, no matter the cost. He created a provincial police force call the rurales, who were ordered to be as ruthless with bandits as Díaz's soldiers were with the French. Even low-level crimes were often punished with a bullet in the back.

Díaz attracted foreign investments in the railroad and other industries, and the economy prospered. The British-built Ferrocarril Mexicano del Sur (Southern Mexican Railroad), which connected Oaxaca City with the nation's capital, was inaugurated in 1892. The economic stability and peace came to be known as the Pax Porfiriana.

Such progress came at loggerheads with the communal landownership common in Oaxaca, and many communities only pretended to accept privatization. This conflict was very prevalent in the coffee boom on the coast. Many communally owned Indigenous lands were appropriated during this time in order to establish coffee plantations. In the north, around the town of Valle Nacional, tobacco cultivation became popular, and both Indigenous people from the region and elsewhere were brought in to work the fields.

Porfirio Díaz: National Villain, Local Hero

The Battle of Puebla was Díaz's main military claim to fame, but the citizens of Miahuatlán de Porfirio Díaz remember him for chasing the French out of their town on October 3, 1866.

Many Mexicans villainize Díaz for what he did during the Porfiriato, but to this day, Miahuatecos celebrate his victory every October 3 with a cabalgata (cavalcade of horses), foam and confetti fights, and lots and lots of tacos and mezcal. One interesting aspect of this party is the practice of setting bamboo cages around the zócalo. Throughout the night, distracted partiers get nabbed and locked up in these jaulas. The jailers charge a coin or two for freedom.

Exploitation, malnutrition, and abuse was rampant.

THE MEXICAN REVOLUTION

In 1909, Díaz saw a formidable electoral opponent in acting National Anti-reelectionist Party president **Francisco I. Madero** (1873-1913), who began to stir up trouble for Díaz. In December of that year, after releasing a manifesto directed toward Oaxacans, Madero came to Oaxaca City, where he planned a mutiny. The mob gathered on the Cerro del Fortín, prompting the city leadership to send in police. The protestors moved their function to a private residence and began sowing the seeds of revolution.

Although Díaz tried to suppress this and similar movements in La Mixteca, La Cañada, El Istmo, and La Costa, the stage was set, and his nephew, **Felix Díaz** (1868-1945), was ultimately ousted as governor of Oaxaca. Discontent was rife among the poor populations of Mexico, and two firebrand rebels would soon bring back the chaos Díaz had worked so violently to control.

Villa and Zapata

While Oaxacans were revolting in the south, farmhands, cattle rustlers, miners, and other poor workers joined the cause of **Francisco "Pancho" Villa** (1878-1923), who was leading them around Chihuahua, attacking rurales and wealthy landowners.

Also at the same time, in the state of Morelos, just south of Mexico City, **Emiliano Zapata** (1879-1919) was rounding up loyal Indigenous followers under the slogan ¡Tierra y Libertad! (Land and Liberty!). He and his Indigenous army violently retook ancestral lands from the wealthy hacendados who had bought it up during the Reform, eventually taking the capital, Cuernavaca.

Madero, who had been in exile in the United States, saw the turning tide and crossed back over the Rio Grande to join in. Díaz's troops began deserting the federal army in droves, and Díaz resigned on May 25, 1911. He went into exile in Paris, France, where he died four years later. When Madero's deputy, General Victoriano Huerta, escorted Díaz to the ship that would take him to Europe, he said to the ousted dictator, "Madero has unleashed a tiger. We'll see if he can control it."

The Mexican Civil War

By 1912, the beast that Madero had created turned against him. Zapata and his followers wanted to see a faster redistribution of lands, but Madero was taking his time. His army in Mexico City turned against him, and Huerta ordered both his resignation on February 18, 1913, and his execution four days later.

War raged on in Mexico. In Oaxaca, liberals and conservatives duked it out. By now, Villa and Zapata, along with revolutionary generals **Álvaro Obregón** (1880-1928) and **Venustiano Carranza** (1859-1920), were a group known as the "Big Four," but Oaxaca's revolutionary leaders weren't on board. They denounced the Big Four and proclaimed

Oaxaca a sovereign republic, denying outside revolutionaries entry into the state.

In 1917, Carranza had majority power in the country, and he called a convention in Querétaro to write up a new constitution. It reformed labor laws, limited the presidential term to one four-year term (which would later be changed to a six-year term in 1927), and prioritized public over private landownership. It has been amended since, but this is the constitution that governs Mexico to this day.

Obregón Brings Stability

In 1920, Álvaro Obregón found himself president of a country battered and bruised by 10 years of bloody civil war. He and the rest of the country badly wanted peace. He instituted land and labor reforms, and built over 1,000 rural schools and 2,000 public libraries around the country.

Oaxacan governor Manuel García Vigil followed suit, writing up the constitution the state still uses today. It included tax reforms that were not popular among wealthy landowners in the state.

Obregón was succeeded by Plutarco Elias Calles in 1924, a liberal turned conservative. He stepped down, and Obregón hopped back in, but the term was short-lived, as Obregón was assassinated two weeks after the election. The next three presidents were mere puppets of Calles, who called the shots off-stage.

THE REIGN OF THE PRI

In 1929, Calles formed the political party that would rule over Mexican politics for the rest of the century. The Partido Revolucionario Institucional (Institutional Revolutionary Party, PRI) was originally formed of workers, the rural poor, and the middle class, but the party moved closer to the right, becoming known as a corrupt party for the rich by the end of the century.

Lázaro Cárdenas, a True People's President

Previously governor of Michoacán, Lázaro Cárdenas (1895-1970) did much to create a government that served the people. During his term, he reverted 20 million hectares (49 million acres) of land to public ownership, improved education, and enacted more labor reform. He even cut his own salary in half, and turned the opulent Chapultepec Castle, previously the residency of the president, into a museum that can be enjoyed to this day. However, he is most remembered as the president who nationalized Mexico's petroleum industry. Cárdenas created the national oil company, Petróleos Mexicanos (Pemex) in 1938.

Manuel Ávila Camacho

Successor to Cárdenas was Manuel Ávila Camacho (1897-1955), who did much to improve relations with the United States. He was the second Mexican president to meet a US president on Mexican soil, when Franklin D. Roosevelt visited him in Monterrey in April 1943. During World War II, his economy sent raw materials north of the border, and the United States sent manufactured consumer goods south.

Political Unrest in Oaxaca

New taxes designed to be used to modernize agriculture in the state began to cause political trouble in the 1940s and 1950s. A coalition of farmers, merchants, students, and others organized uprisings across the state in protest. One student protest resulted in the deaths of two students at the hands of police, and Oaxaca City erupted in protests by various groups. President **Miguel Alemán** (1900-1983) sent the federal army into the state to control the situation, but this was just the beginning.

Political Activism in the 1960s and 1970s

Women voted in Mexico for the first time in 1958, helping elect **Adolfo López Mateos** (1908-1969). A leftist, he redistributed farmland to the tune of 16 million hectares (40 million acres), constructed thousands of new schools and stocked them with millions of new textbooks, and set a minimum of at least 60 percent of gross domestic product for car manufacturing. He also nationalized the country's power companies and founded the National Museum of Anthropology upon leaving the presidency in 1964.

Despite also being from the PRI, his successor, **Gustavo Díaz Ordaz** (1911-1979), had much different political ideals than Mateos. His authoritarian style of leadership didn't fly with liberals, especially students. The disagreements came to a head in 1968, when student activists from the National Autonomous University of Mexico gathered in the Plaza de las Tres Culturas (Plaza of the Three Cultures), in the Tlatelolco neighborhood of Mexico City 10 days before the Summer Olympics were to be held there. Government forces massacred up to 400 people that day in order to suppress the protests. Although the government told media outlets that the students began firing first, documents released in 2000 make it all but certain that there were federal snipers in the buildings around the square.

Students in Oaxaca were also fired up, and they teamed up with unions to form a coalition based on their Indigenous Zapotec heritage. They organized boycotts, strikes, protests, and marches, and some more-radical factions applied terroristic tactics with explosives. Their efforts ended up forcing the government to improve working conditions in rural areas. The success was especially seen in Juchitán, which in 1980 voted leftists into the local government offices, making it one of very few towns in the country to not be governed by the PRI. The turbulent climate in the state also caused Mexico City to respond by sending more funds and resources Oaxaca's way, which improved the highways and health and education services and connected many small rural towns to the electrical grid for the first time.

The Maquiladora Industry

During this time, the United States and Mexico continued to exchange goods and develop their trade relations further. The most significant development was the creation of the maquiladora industry. These duty-free factories built in Mexican towns along the border allow US companies to take advantage of cheap labor without having to provide the kinds of salaries, working conditions, and infrastructure they would north of the border. This industry, which produces many of the separate parts of "American-made" automobiles, which are then assembled in the United States, is notoriously corrupt and exploitative. Maquiladora workers all along the border work in unsafe conditions, are underpaid, and are often forced into debt slavery disguised as home ownership.

Oil Boom and the Inevitable Bust

In 1972, colossal oil reserves were found in the Gulf of Mexico, bringing about rapid economic growth in the 1970s. Oaxaca saw the results of this boom in construction of the trans-isthmus pipeline and one of the country's biggest refineries in Salina Cruz. The business grew the small coastal town into the state's current fourth-largest city.

But, of course, all the infrastructure to suck that oil out of the ground had to come from somewhere. Mexico had turned to the United States for that loan, but in the 1980s, when the interest payments were due, the global market was glutted with oil and the barrel price plummeted. Mexico's oil industry couldn't pay its debt, and the peso collapsed, sending inflation sky-high. Try as he might, President Miguel de la Madrid was unable to curb inflation, and in 1988 one US dollar was worth 2,500 Mexican pesos. As they always do, the macroeconomic games of the rich hit the poor hardest, worsening the already extreme poverty in Oaxaca.

NAFTA

The PRI candidate to win the presidency in 1988 was Carlos Salinas de Gortari, who broadened the trade landscape with the United States and Canada by signing the North American Free Trade Agreement, or NAFTA, on January 1, 1994. All of a sudden, US products flooded the Mexican market, and

Mexican farms kept US supermarkets stocked with fresh fruits and veggies year-round. The most notable effect of NAFTA was the reduction in prices for these agricultural products. The price of corn, for example, plummeted, putting thousands of poor Mexican farmers out of work. As a result, many began to seek the means to support their families north of the border.

The Zapatistas

The signing of NAFTA didn't go over well in the state of Chiapas. On the day of its signing, a guerilla army of Indigenous citizens who called themselves the Ejército Zapatista de Liberación Nacional (Zapatista Army of National Liberation, EZLN), or the Zapatistas for short, stormed and occupied a number of towns in the state, and took one of its former governors hostage.

The movement inspired communities in Oaxaca to organize to ensure their rights, as well. Many formed communal work programs designed to foster local economies by keeping money in the community. The Zapatistas' activity has waned since, but they continue to declare war on the Mexican state to this day, and the repercussions of their struggle can be seen in the Indigenous community-organizing seen in Oaxaca and elsewhere in Mexico.

Another Peso Crisis

Luis Donaldo Colosio (1950-1994) was the PRI's first candidate for the 1994 elections, but he was assassinated. Instead of destroying the party, the assassination elicited grief across the country and from his would-be opponents. **Ernesto Zedillo** (b. 1951) took his place on the PRI stump and won, ensuring the PRI's grip on Mexican politics for the rest of the century.

Zedillo didn't have long to celebrate, though, for the peso collapsed again by the time he took office, devaluing by half by January 1995. US president Bill Clinton put together a massive loan package that gave the Mexican economy a lifeline, but did not stop inflation from soaring and causing Mexico's poor to once again have to worry about putting food on the table.

This caused more guerilla activity in Oaxaca, Chiapas, and Guerrero. One guerilla army, the **Ejército Popular Revolucionario** (Popular Revolutionary Army, EPR), coordinated attacks in Guerrero, Puebla, Guanajuato, Tabasco, Mexico City, and Oaxaca. On August 28, 1996, EPR soldiers attacked Tlaxiaco first, and others attacked Huatulco two hours later. As a result of these attacks, the Mexican naval officers watching for turtle poachers at Playa Escobilla, in Puerto Escondido, were called away to address the threat in Huatulco. The word quickly spread, and poachers flocked to the beach, killing thousands of olive ridley turtles.

Zedillo saved his reputation by commissioning over a billion US dollars on public works and infrastructure projects. The economy began to recover, and inflation began to fall by 1998. Mexico repaid the debt it owed the United States, and the peso returned to stable values.

The political climate began to change as well. For the first time in Mexican history, primary elections were held in 1998, putting the choice of candidate in the hands of the people, rather than the political parties themselves. Non-PRI candidates began winning more elections, and the party saw its grip on the nation's government slacking.

21ST-CENTURY OAXACA

The PRI's luck did indeed change when the country elected **Vicente Fox** (b. 1942) as president. A member of the **Partido Acción Nacional** (National Action Party, PAN), Fox was the first non-PRI president in 71 years. Fox was a right-wing populist and neoliberal businessman who had already had a profound effect on Mexico before becoming president. During the 1970s he had been the president and CEO of Coca-Cola in Mexico, and the soda's sales skyrocketed under his leadership. Now Mexico is the largest consumer of Coca-Cola in the world.

The Disappeared: Mexico's Desaparecidos

The Iguala 43 (sometimes Ayotzinapa 43) were a group of students from the Rural Teachers' College in Ayotzinapa, Guerrero, whose disappearance and presumed murders shocked the country in 2014. The politically active students of these left-leaning schools, called escuelas normales, were known to commandeer passenger buses for transportation to and from their rallies and protests. It was more or less tolerated by the bus companies, who could usually count on the students to bring them back.

On September 26, the group from Ayotzinapa went to the town of Iguala to nab the buses they were planning to use to drive to Mexico City in October for protests, as well as disrupt a party thrown to celebrate the public works of María de los Ángeles Pineda, wife of the mayor of Iguala. Pineda had been widely accused of being connected to organized crime in Guerrero, one of Mexico's most active states for gang activity. Investigations revealed that in order to save her fiesta from embarrassment, she ordered the municipal police to stop them at any cost.

The details that follow are uncertain, but what is known is that those 43 young men haven't been seen again, and it is generally accepted that they have been murdered. The movement that has grown out of this tragedy to denounce those involved, from the governor of Iguala and his wife to then-president Peña Nieto, uses the slogans "Nos faltan 43" (We're missing 43) and "¡Vivos los llevaron, vivos los queremos!" (They took them alive, and we want them back alive).

This kind of state violence is unfortunately not uncommon in Mexico. In Oaxaca City, there is a good chance you'll see people from one or more of the state's Indigenous peoples either in Zócalo or around the Santo Domingo complex protesting the disappearances of friends and loved ones. If you speak some Spanish, take a little time to ask them about their experiences, and maybe buy something they're selling. It is shocking that the international community has not taken notice. There is power in knowing, and more outside attention on this problem could possibly open the doors to change.

Despite his wealth and status, Fox struck a chord with poor and Indigenous communities. He had campaigned heavily in poor barrios and rural villages, and one of his first acts in office was to visit Indigenous leaders in Chiapas, where he significantly scaled down the federal military presence. He also presented Congress with a bill of rights for Indigenous people. The Zapatistas visited Mexico City and spoke to Congress with their faces hidden behind their black masks, and the two sides worked out a plan for Indigenous rights, despite the complaints by some Zapatista leaders that it wasn't enough.

Fox also went after government corruption, signing the country's first freedom of information act and founding a transparency committee to investigate cases of administrative unscrupulousness.

The 2006 Oaxacan Teachers Revolts

In May 2006, Oaxacan members of the **Sindicato Nacional de Trabajadores de la Educación** (National Education Workers Union, SNTE) organized their 25th annual strike for better conditions and funding for rural schools. Unofficial tallies counted as many as 80,000 teachers occupying the Centro in Oaxaca City. During the strike, protestors also took up the cause of demanding the resignation of PRI governor Ulises Ruiz Ortiz, who many accused of rigging the 2004 election. In response, Ortiz sent in 3,000 federal police to disperse the protestors on the morning of June 14, and violence ensued, but luckily there were no deaths.

Protestors responded by forming the **Asamblea Popular de los Pueblos de Oaxaca** (Popular Assembly of the Peoples of Oaxaca, APPO), which went on to boycott the Guelaguetza celebrations in July, ultimately forcing the government to cancel the festival by blocking access to the Auditorio Guelaguetza with burned buses and trash. The first deaths in the conflict came in August, when people later identified as plain-clothes police officers and members of organizations supporting the PRI began to raid APPO-controlled radio stations. Ortiz fled to Mexico City for a few months. He would later be arrested for embezzlement in 2014.

Teachers still strike each year in May and June, and protests have grown violent in recent years, with highway blockades, burned buses, and clashes between police and protestors. It is not necessarily dangerous for tourists, but the last two weeks in May and the first two in June really aren't the best time to plan trips here.

Calderón and the Drug War

The 2006 presidential election was so close as to require a recount. The country was split right down the middle between the more conservative PAN candidate Felipe Calderón (b. 1962), and the leftist former mayor of Mexico City **Andrés Manuel López Obrador** (b. 1953), or as he's known colloquially, **AMLO.** The recount came up Calderón, and for weeks Obrador pulled strings in Congress to obstruct Calderón at every turn, going so far as to make him unable to deliver the state of the union address his first year. But Obrador's tactics backfired on him, and public opinion was adamantly against him.

Unlike his predecessor, who had a rather laissez-faire attitude toward drug trafficking in the country, Calderón decided to amp up military action against narcotraffickers, but with disastrous consequences. His first year saw the escalation of drug-related violence and put Mexico in the international spotlight for the number of murders, femicides, disappearances, mass graves, and other atrocities that happened as a result. The scourge of drug violence still plagues much of Mexico.

The PRI Makes a Comeback

The 2012 presidential elections saw the return of the PRI with the election of **Enrique Peña Nieto** (b. 1966), or as he was called, EPN (eh-peh-EH-ne). Again, his biggest opponent was López Obrador, who staged over a month of protests in the city after Nieto was named the winner. Widespread allegations of fraud plagued his campaign.

It was apparent from the beginning of his presidency that EPN, with his wax-figure smile and telenovela-star wife, was going to be a pretty face and little more. His approval rating went from 50 percent when he took office to a meager 12 percent by the last year of his term. The angry refrain ¡Fuera Peña! (Out Peña!) was shouted at protests throughout his presidency.

AMLO Makes a Comeback

The third time was the charm for López Obrador, who ran again in 2018. After the unpopular presidency of Peña Nieto, he didn't have to worry too much about the PRI, or anyone else, for that matter. He won the vote by a landslide, taking in over 53 percent of the popular vote.

Like liberal presidents before him, López Obrador took a pay cut of 60 percent. He also declined to live in the presidential residence called Los Pinos (The Pines) in Chapultepec Park in Mexico City, opting to continue living in his personal home and opening up Los Pinos as a public cultural center. One of his first acts in office was to create a truth commission to investigate the disappearance and presumed murders of the Iguala 43, a group of teachers' college students who were attacked by state police in Guerrero during Peña Nieto's administration.

He remained a widely popular president throughout his presidency, despite mixed feelings on his handling of the Covid pandemic and "hugs, not bullets" stance toward cartels. His legacy will be that of solidifying the power and popularity of the political party created by his own hand, the left-wing populist MORENA party (Movimiento de Regeneración Nacional).

Mexico's First Woman President

While its neighbor to the north had the opportunity once again to elect its first woman president, Mexico already beat it to the punch. Former mayor of Mexico City, and endorsed by AMLO, Claudia Sheinbaum (b. 1962) of the Morena party was elected president in June 2024 and took office in October 2024.

Government and Economy

ORGANIZATION

Before the conquest, the regions of Oaxaca were divided into señoríos, chiefdoms in which a ruling cacique (chief) held sovereignty over a group of tributary towns. The organization of the señoríos at the time of the arrival of the Spanish dictate the borders of Oaxaca's districts and municipalities even into the present. Modern Oaxaca now boasts more municipalities (municipios) than any other Mexican state, with a grand total of 570.

These municipalities are grouped into larger administrative branches called districts (distritos). In 1950, the federal government applied the traditional regional divisions in Oaxaca to its official political map in order to both improve administrative functions and preserve the cultural identity of the people here. You might hear talk of the seven regions of Oaxaca, the traditional number, but today they are considered to add up to eight, after the Sierra Region was divided into the Sierra Norte and Sierra Sur. The other six regions in the state are the Valles Centrales, La Costa, La Mixteca, La Cañada, El Papaloapan, and El Istmo de Tehuantepec.

At the state level, the governor holds the office of the executive branch. A unicameral legislative branch makes statewide laws, and the judiciary branch consists of seven judges who preside over the supreme court.

POLITICAL PARTIES

Mexico's four dominant political parties are the Movimiento de Regeneración Nacional (Morena), the Institutional Revolutionary Party (PRI), the National Action Party (PAN), and the Party of the Democratic Revolution (PRD). Since the Revolution, the PRI has been the party to occupy the governor's seat in Oaxaca, until recently.

In Oaxaca, the PRI lost gubernatorial power in 2010, when Gabino Cué Monteagudo (b. 1966), of the more recently formed Citizen's Movement, a self-described social-democratic party, was elected to power, but the change didn't last. In 2016, PRI candidate Alejandro Murat Hinojosa (b. 1975) was elected governor, bringing the state once again under PRI control.

But the winds of change are finally blowing through Oaxaca's political scene. The Oaxacan governor as of this writing is Salomón Jara Cruz (b. 1959), of the Morena party. More than half of Mexico's governors are Morena, and a sizable percentage of senate is as well.

THE OAXACAN ECONOMY

According to Mexico's National Council for the Evaluation of Social Development, Oaxaca has the third-highest poverty rate in the nation. The gap between Oaxacans and economic opportunities at home has driven many to migrate north to the United States in search of ways to support their families.

Agriculture is the main economic option for most of Oaxaca's poor rural communities. Much of it is subsistence, and the majority is for consumption within the state, such as corn, chiles, and beans. Tropical fruits such as pineapples, mangoes, and coconuts are also grown, as well as sugarcane. Mining and oil production are other significant industries here.

Much of Oaxaca's economy has its roots in its pre-Hispanic culture. The weekly markets known as tianguis or día de plaza (market day) come from traditions based in the tributary systems of the señoríos of the Indigenous groups here. The Sunday market in Tlacolula is one of the oldest continuously running markets in Mexico, and ergo, the Americas. Commerce among Oaxacans is vital to the economy all over the state.

Tourism

The largest chunk of Oaxaca's economic activity is categorized in the tertiary sector, or service industry. Tourism is a vital part of the state's economy, intrinsically linked with all the primary economic activities here. Because so many foods and artisanal products in Oaxaca are sourced from within the state, you can be sure that just about any purchase you make puts money into the local economy.

People and Culture

Cave paintings at places like Yagul and Apoala reveal signs of human habitation here as far back as 6,000 years ago. Half a millennium ago, these pre-Hispanic cultures combined their rich Indigenous traditions with the new customs and goods introduced by the Spanish to create a land teeming with art, craftworkers' products, festivals, dances, and recipes wholly unique from anywhere else in the world.

DEMOGRAPHY AND DIVERSITY

Nearly 70 percent of Oaxaca's population has its roots in one of the state's 17 distinct Indigenous groups, making it the state with the highest percentage of Indigenous peoples in Mexico.

The geographic isolation caused by Oaxaca's mountainous terrain also led to cultural and linguistic isolation, creating practices unique to a certain region, or even to one small town, some of which survive to this day. One of the most striking examples of this is the caldo de piedra (stone soup) of San Felipe Usila, in El Papaloapan. Since it is traditionally served in a bowl-shaped hollow in a boulder or in the sand next to the river, anthropologists believe this recipe to predate the making of ceramics in Mexico, which is estimated to have begun as far back as 2300 BC.

Every region in the state has created its own cultural identity, each with its own dances, music, traditional vestments, recipes, ingredients, and more that represent it. If you study up on the embroidery styles of the various regions, for example, you'll be able to identify the region, sometimes the specific town, that a person wearing them calls home. This rich cultural diversity really is what makes getting to know Oaxaca so much fun. Around just about every corner, you'll find something new.

INDIGENOUS CULTURES

This section covers 17 Indigenous cultures, including the Tacuates, who speak a dialect of Mixtec but are a different ethnic group.

The annual festivals known as the **Guelaguetza,** or sometimes **Los Lunes del Cerro** (Mondays on the Hill), revel in the vibrancy and diversity of Oaxaca's Indigenous traditions with folk dance extravaganzas and colorful processions. The official Guelaguetza is held in Oaxaca City on the last two Mondays of July, but communities all over the state have their own Guelaguetza at other times of the year. One of the most popular is in Zaachila and is also held in July.

Zapotecs

The Zapotecs didn't name themselves as such.

The Spanish word *zapoteco* comes from the exonym the Aztecs gave them during their colonization campaign just before Cortés and company arrived in Mexico. The Aztecs called them tzapotēcah, which means "inhabitants of the land of the zapote," for the region's abundance of the zapote fruit, a type of persimmon.

Most Zapotecs call themselves "The People of the Clouds" in their various dialects. Those of the Valles Centrales call themselves Ben Zaa; those of El Istmo, Binni Zaa; and those of the Sierra Norte, Bene Xhon. The Zapotecs of the Sierra Sur call themselves Mén Diiste, which means "People of the Old Language."

With over 400,000 speakers in Oaxaca, Zapotecs make up the largest Indigenous group in the state. Although many people will identify as Zapotec, they will identify more strongly with the region from which they hail.

Their heartland is the Valles Centrales, where you'll find the remains of their greatest pre-Hispanic urban centers, such as Monte Albán, Mitla, and Yagul. Along with the Mixtecs, they put up the strongest resistance to the Aztec invasion of the late 15th century, ultimately reaching a peace treaty after a lengthy battle at Guiengola, near present-day Tehuantepec, in El Istmo.

Zapotecs had a polytheistic religion, which, like many Mesoamerican religions, had gods that represented natural forces. The most important god was Cocijo, whose name means "lightning bolt." Similar to the Aztec god Tlaloc, Cocijo's domain was the lightning, thunder, and, most importantly, rain, and was also credited with having created the world. In ceramics and other artwork found at pre-Hispanic Zapotec sites, he is represented as a short, squat deity with a porcine nose and forked snake's tongue curled over his chin. His headdress features traditional Zapotec glyphs. You can see statues of him in the museum at Monte Albán and large stone masks of his face at Lambityeco, in the Valle de Tlacolula.

The Zapotecs were one of the first Mesoamerican peoples to have a writing system, but aside from a few details about calendric symbols, linguists are still unable to decipher the true nature and meaning of their pictographic characters. Instead of left to right, Zapotec glyphs are read from top to bottom.

It could easily be said that the Zapotec huipiles (embroidered blouses) of El Istmo are the most popular in Oaxaca. Technically part of a full traje de gala (party dress), they feature big, brightly colored flowers on a background of black velvet. Other traditional dresses of El Istmo include the geometrically intricate traje de costura (sewing suit) and the much less elaborate traje de luto (mourning dress). Zapotec embroidery from other parts of the state tends to also feature flowers, though with different designs, as well as other inspirations from nature, such as birds, foxes, and other animals, including people. Some feature monochrome embroidery on a white cotton fabric, while others, such as the much smaller and more delicate stitching of San Antonino Castillo Velasco, in the Valles Centrales, are as multicolored as the flower fields outside the town.

Zapotec communities tend to have a communal political organization, and many in the Sierra Norte have abolished the practice of private landownership altogether, instead preferring to work the land together and benefit the community as a whole. Zapotecs have played a pivotal political role in Mexico. Benito Juárez (1806-1872), born in Guelatao, in the Sierra Norte, served as governor of Oaxaca and president of Mexico multiple times during his turbulent career.

Women in Zapotec society are traditionally in charge of a household's economy and finances, especially in El Istmo. While the male head of household may be in charge of working the fields, animal husbandry, or fishing, his wife manages the process of getting the goods to market. Nontraditional gender roles have been taken a step further in El Istmo, where the muxes (MOO-shehs), a third gender of men raised to take on the roles of women, are widely accepted in society there.

Mixtecs

With around 267,000 speakers, the Mixtecs are the second-largest Indigenous group in Oaxaca, accounting for just over 22 percent of the Indigenous population. Like the Zapotecs, Mixtecs did not choose that name for themselves. The Aztecs called them the mixtecah, which means (possibly to the chagrin of the Zapotecs) "People of the Clouds," and they weren't far off. The Mixtecs called themselves the Ñuu Savi, or one of its dialectical variations, which means "People of the Rain."

Because of the similarity in their languages and names for themselves, it is widely believed that Zapotecs and Mixtecs were once the same people, and that their languages began to diversify sometime around 4400 BC in the Valle de Tehuacán, which now straddles the border of Puebla and Oaxaca. Their heartland is called La Mixteca, which is in the western part of Oaxaca, and includes the neighboring parts of Guerrero and Puebla. It is divided into highlands (La Mixteca Alta), lowlands (La Mixteca Baja), and the coast (La Mixteca de la Costa).

According to Mixtec legend, their people were conceived from trees along a river summoned up from the depths of the earth by the gods, and they conquered their land, La Mixteca, with the help of El Flechador del Sol (The One Who Wounded the Sun with an Arrow), a mythical warrior who made the western sun bleed red when he aimed his dart skyward. When you see the red hillsides of La Mixteca at sunset, the myth kind of starts to make sense.

Mixtec codices tell of a great ruler named Eight-Deer Jaguar Claw, who is now remembered as the great unifier of the previously disparate Mixtec señoríos. Born in AD 1063 in Tilantongo, Eight-Deer left town at the age of 18 with the specific purpose to create his own dynasty. He moved south, toward the coast, where he took advantage of political instability and the region's agricultural resources, valuable to those in the highlands, and founded the señorío of Tututepec. In 1098, he returned to his hometown of Tilantongo to become the cacique there. Using a series of military campaigns and politically motivated marriages, he ruled over and unified the señoríos of Tututepec, in La Mixteca de la Costa; Tilantongo, in La Mixteca Alta; and Teozacualco, in La Mixteca Baja.

Mixtecs are known for their economy. Many pre-Hispanic towns in La Mixteca were large regional trading hubs that connected commerce with civilizations all over the Americas, even as far south as Peru. La Mixteca was once the largest global producer of the cactus-dwelling scale insects called cochinilla (cochineal), which was used for red dyes before the invention of synthetic ones in the 19th century. They were also renowned for their skills as goldsmiths, and many of the intricately filigreed pieces found in Monte Albán and Zaachila are believed to have been of Mixtec design.

Traditional Mixtec clothing varies widely, depending on region, and often features images of birds, scorpions, deer, winged horses, or people, but geometrical designs are just as prominent. Common, but not ubiquitous, among the various Mixtec embroidery styles are elaborately designed collars. One style from Pinotepa Nacional, for example, features embroidery only along the collar.

More recently, Mixtecs have been known for their ability to stick together even after migrating thousands of miles. Mixtecs are estimated to be the largest Indigenous immigrant population in the United States, and have been organizing migration while maintaining social and familial bonds since the 1980s, despite the challenges presented by diaspora. Because of this, academic researchers have applied labels such as "transnational" and "transborder" to the Mixtec community.

Mazatecs

The western slopes of the Sierra Norte (part of the La Cañada region), parts of El Papaloapan, and the bordering areas of Puebla and Veracruz are home to the Mazatecs. Like *Zapotec* and *Mixtec*, *Mazatec* is an exonym that comes from the Nahuatl, the language of the Aztecs, meaning "People of the Deer." Their endonym for themselves is Ha Shuta Enima, which means "Humble People of Traditions Who Work in the Mountains." Their homeland is one of the most biodiverse areas in Oaxaca, and the world. Farmers here cultivate some of the rarest chiles in Mexico, some of which face the threat of extinction.

Mazatecs make up the third-largest Indigenous group in Oaxaca, with around 180,000 speakers of the language, or about 15 percent of the Indigenous population. Mazatec identity lies primarily in knowledge of their oral language, which currently has 10 distinct regional dialects, some of which are mutually unintelligible. Despite this lack of semantic understanding between dialects, speaking one of them still identifies one as pertaining to the group and its customs. The Mazatec language is considered to be a branch of the Popolcan linguistic tree, along with the Ixcatec, Chocholtec, and Popolcan tongues.

Mazatec embroidery is quite fond of the colors blue and pink, such as those of Huautla de Jiménez, which often feature floral and avian designs, like peacocks, and blue and pink ribbons woven through. Also quite popular are the two-tone blouses from towns like San Bartolomé Ayautla and San Felipe Jalapa de Díaz. These feature large embroidered designs of birds and flowers that cover the majority of the shirt and are generally of one hue that stands out against the color of the fabric.

Because of their isolation on the steep slopes and ravines of the northern Oaxacan mountains, many Mazatec communities have preserved ancient traditions and languages. With up to 40 percent of the Mazatec-speaking population speaking little or no Spanish, they are considered among the least Hispanicized Indigenous peoples in Oaxaca. This lack of interaction with the Mazatec community reached a critical point in the mid-19th century, when the Río Papaloapan was dammed to create Lake Miguel Alemán, which forced over 22,000 Mazatec people to migrate elsewhere, as their homes were now underwater.

One tradition that has lasted and garnered much global attention is the use of hallucinogenic mushrooms in traditional medicinal and spiritual practices. The curandera (traditional medicine woman) María Sabina garnered worldwide notoriety for herself and her hometown of Huautla de Jiménez when she openly welcomed outsiders to participate in her traditional ceremonies. Like the filling of Lake Miguel Alemán at the foot of the mountains, this event changed Mazatec life in Huautla de Jiménez forever, and hallucinogenic experiences are now the main tourist attraction here.

Chinantecs

Inhabitants of the northern foothills of the Sierra Norte and the hot, humid tropical lowlands of El Papaloapan, the Chinantecs call themselves Tsa Ju Jmí, which means "People of the Ancient Word." They call their traditional homeland La Chinantla, which includes the towns of Valle Nacional, San Felipe Usila, San Pedro Sochiapam, and other small communities tucked away in the sultry ravines of the foothills. With just over 107,000 speakers of one of the tonal languages called Chinantec (linguists have a hard time fully classifying them as dialects), Chinantecs are the fifth-largest Indigenous group in Oaxaca.

Like their Mazatec neighbors, Chinantec weavers are fond of using ribbons to decorate their huipiles. Whereas other regions tend to find inspiration for their designs in nature, Chinantec huipiles are a reflection of their religion, much of which has to do with cosmogony and elemental opposites—night and day, animal and human, good and bad, body and soul. Common design motifs include a sun and moon, two-headed eagles, plumed serpents, and traditional Chinantec grecas, geometric patterns used to represent various elements, such as the four cardinal directions or concepts like protection or punishment. Although the majority of Chinantecs are now Catholic, much of their old religion has been syncretized into that of those who conquered them centuries ago.

Around AD 999, a Chinantec king named Quiana founded a señorío (chiefdom) in La Chinantla, but internal conflicts caused a rift in the sovereignty he established, and La Chinantla was subsequently divided into two señoríos, La Chinantla Grande, comprised of the tropical lowlands to the east, and La Chinantla Pichinche, in the rough, hilly west. Around 1300, part of the population of La Chinantla Pichinche seceded and formed its own señorío based in Usila. In the mid-15th century, the Aztecs established an outpost at Tuxtepec, and from there led campaigns to conquer the Chinantecs and other native inhabitants of northern Oaxaca.

When the Spanish arrived, they began to enforce their policy of congregación, which involved displacing Indigenous populations and forcing them to live in communities organized by the conquistadors. After decades of paying tribute to the Aztecs, the Chinantecs had had enough of colonization, and many put the past behind them and united once again to rise up against the Spanish. The first of these uprisings was in the town of Tepetotutla in 1530. Despite their resistance to the colonizers, the Spanish eventually won out, forcing Chinantecs to work on tobacco, sugarcane, and fruit plantations and cattle ranches for the next three centuries.

Like the Mazatecs to the west, the Chinantecs once again faced displacement in the 20th century, when the Cerro de Oro Dam was built in the 1970s and 1980s. This reservoir, now connected to the Miguel Alemán reservoir, displaced over 26,000 people. That being said, both reservoirs paved the way to the industrialization of El Papaloapan, bringing jobs, schools, and agriculture and connecting once remote communities to the outside world. Today the Chinantec heartland is Oaxaca's biggest industrial center, producing pineapples, bananas, mangoes, and other tropical fruits, as well as sugar, paper, and other important products.

Mixes and Zoques

Although they are distinct, the languages of the Mixes and Zoques are considered to be part of the same linguistic family. With about 115,000 speakers, Mixes make up 9.5 percent of Oaxaca's Indigenous population. Zoque speakers make up a much smaller percentage, with only about 11,000 native speakers. Some linguists have theorized that the Mixe-Zoque peoples came from the Olmecs of the Gulf Coast, but others claim that evidence traces their origins as far south as Peru.

According to Mixe legend, they migrated to their lands under the leadership of a great king named Condoy, who settled them in the lands around the sacred, cloud-covered Cerro Cempoaltépetl (sem-poh-ahl-TEH-peh-tl), which in Nahuatl means "20 Winds Mountain." It is believed that the Mixes once occupied an area much larger than their current homeland in the eastern Sierra Norte (known as the Sierra Mixe) and northern part of El Istmo, but much of their territory was lost due to the imperial forces of the neighboring Zapotecs, Mixtecs, Zoques, and Popolocas, as well as the Aztecs and Spanish. The political turbulence of Mexican independence also had a hand in shrinking the boundaries of Mixe domain.

Little archaeological evidence exists in the Sierra Mixe, but it is known that the pre-Hispanic and colonial-era Mixes were fierce defenders of the land their legendary king bequeathed them. Neither the Zaachila of the Zapotecs, Ahuitzotl of the Aztecs, or Cortés of the Spanish conquistadors were able to subdue the Mixe completely. After two failed attempts to put them under his thumb, Hernán Cortés mentioned the tenacity of the Mixes and Zapotecs in a letter to the King of Spain, writing that his men failed "because of the roughness of the terrain, and because the warriors are very fierce and well-armed."

Cortés eventually turned to religion to further Spanish dominance, finally reaching a peace agreement in 1555, when Dominican friars began proselytizing and building in the region. Despite the success of the conquest's spiritual element here and elsewhere in Oaxaca, the Mixe pride themselves on never having been conquered by outside forces. Like many other Indigenous peoples in Mexico, their brand of Catholicism is heavily syncretized with elements of their native spiritual beliefs. Deities such as Poj 'Enee (Thunder Wind), the Mixe rain god, and Naaxwiiñ (Earth Surface), a fertility goddess, are in their pantheon alongside Jesus Christ, the Virgin Mary, and the host of saints.

The Zoques did not have the same luck against invaders. In pre-Hispanic times, the Zoques occupied much of Chiapas, part of Tabasco, and the northern part of El Istmo, in Oaxaca. Until the end of the 15th century, they maintained peaceful social and economic ties with the Aztecs, but in 1494, Aztec emperor Ahuitzotl wanted more and invaded the Selva Zoque (Zoque Jungle). They were unable to defend themselves as fiercely as the Mixes, and were quickly subjected to pay tributes to the Mexica empire. Cortés also found success in colonizing the Zoques. His dispatch to the region, led by conquistador Luis Marín, divided the Zoque land up into encomiendas and promptly put the people to work for the Spanish crown.

In the early 20th century, Mixe towns were still run like chiefdoms, with caciques (chiefs) in the towns of Cacalotepec, Ayutla, and Zacatepec, but were not united politically. Each belonged to different neighboring administrative districts. In the 1920s, the cacique of Zacatepec, Manuel Rodríguez, began to get a taste for non-Mixe comforts and luxuries, like fancy dress, riches, even emigration, but his son Luis, however, was not on board. In 1926, Luis ran his father out of town and usurped his position as cacique of Zacatepec. This was only the beginning of Luis Rodríguez's devious, power-hungry political career.

Twelve years later, when the Oaxacan legislature was persuaded by President Lázaro Cárdenas to give the Mixe their own administrative district in Oaxaca in honor of their bravery on the battlefield against the French in 1865, the three Mixe seats of power began to fight over which would be named the capital. Luis Rodríguez used violence to grab power over the Mixe communities, and even hired his godson to shoot his main rival, Daniel Martínez, cacique of Ayutla. Most likely in an attempt to cover his tracks, Rodríguez then banished his godson to Mexico City, but the scorned hitman instead returned to the villages, organizing an uprising that proved to be the bloodiest battle of the conflict. Even at war, Luis Rodríguez liked to have a good time, and during a patronal festival reportedly ate too much barbacoa, for which he was transported to Oaxaca City, where he died of an embolism.

However, aside from bloodshed, his legacy also included the formation of the Association of Progressive Town Councils of the Sierra Mixe, which collected data on the communities that could be taken to the state and federal governments to request funding for schools, clinics, and other services.

Today, Mixes are known as the producers of the rare chile pasilla mixe, sometimes called chile pasilla oaxaqueño. Pasilla is the dried form of a chile called chilaca, but the cloudy alpine conditions of the Sierra Mixe make it impossible for the chiles to air dry completely. To finish the drying process, Mixe growers smoke the chiles in adobe huts. The pasilla mixe is one of the Oaxacan chiles you will have an extremely hard time finding outside the state. Mixe embroidery sometimes features floral or anthropomorphic designs, but tends to stick to finely stitched geometric patterns. Zoque huipiles tend to be less elaborate, usually white cotton blouses with hand-stitched embroidery along the collar. Zoque weavers also work with wool and silk.

Chatinos

Chatinos make up a little over 4 percent of Oaxaca's population, with about 50,700 speakers. The low, tropical foothills around Santa Catarina Juquila and neighboring communities in this small slice of the coast are where the Chatinos call home. Like many native Oaxacans, the majority of Chatinos work in agriculture, primarily on coffee plantations.

If you have trouble pronouncing their name for themselves, Qne-a Tnya-e, or one of its dialectical variations, don't worry. In all of its forms, it means something like "People of the Language That Takes Some Work."

Chatinos have a number of linguistic and cultural commonalities with the Zapotecs. Their language is considered to be in the same branch as that of the Zapotecs. Linguistic evidence linking the Chatinos to the Zapotecs is very scant but points to language divergence from the Zapotecs anywhere between 4000 BC and AD 200. They began to break cultural and political ties with their linguistic descendants toward the end of that period.

Much of what is known about the Chatinos is found in the codices of the Mixtec people. It is written that they made an alliance with the kingdom of Mixtec unifier Eight-Deer Jaguar Claw during his reign in the 11th century. The Chatino were still tributaries to the Mixtec kingdom when Spanish conquistador Pedro de Alvarado arrived in Tututepec in 1522. The foreign diseases brought by the European explorers had devastating consequences for the Chatinos, who are estimated to have numbered as many as 250,000 before the conquest. By 1544, a pair of voracious epidemics had shrunk that number to as low as 35,000 people.

The Spanish put the Chatinos to work in fields, basically appropriating the tribute system already in place, but redirecting its benefits from the Mixtec to the Spanish crown. Many farmers began producing cochineal, which was then New Spain's second most valuable export, outshined only by silver. The Spanish exploited Chatino labor and goods through a system of credit and inflated prices euphemistically called repartimientos de comercio (commercial distribution).

Like the Mixtecs and Zapotecs, who also relied on cochineal, the Chatinos had to find other sources of income when synthetic dyes took over the market in the 19th century. After the Miahuatecos (Zapotecs from Miahuatlán) brought the coffee plant to the Sierra Sur, many Chatinos also began to plant the crop in the shady, tropical hillsides they called home. This brought more money to the people, but also led to more privatization of the land, and this, along with the repartition of landholdings of the Reform Era, caused many Chatinos to lose the rights to the land they had lived on for generations. This economic subjugation continued into the 20th century, and by the 1980s, subsistence and coffee farmers began to leave their previous crops behind to focus on one much more profitable, marijuana. Despite the hundreds of hectares devoted to marijuana cultivation here and elsewhere in Oaxaca, the state has seen relatively less violence related to narcotrafficking than neighboring Guerrero and states in the north.

Chatino huipiles are white cotton blouses with crocheted designs of flowers and/or birds along the collar, shoulders, and upper chest, with a sternum-shaped strip of crochet down the middle. Chatino artisans also work with ceramics, and weave the fibers of the maguey plant, called ixtle, into ropes, strings, nets, and hammocks.

Chatino religion is based on an equilibrium between human society, the natural world, and the divine, which they see as intrinsically linked. Many of their traditional gods, mostly based in nature and natural forces, have been syncretized with Catholic saints and deities. The most famous celebration in the region is the patronal festival for the Virgin of Juquila, held in Santa Catarina Juquila on December 8.

Triques

The Triques, or Triqui in Spanish, occupy a small 500-sq-km (193-sq-mi) patch of mountains in La Mixteca, in the districts of Tlaxiaco, Putla, and Juxtlahuaca. With just over 18,000 speakers, Triques make up 1.5 percent of Oaxaca's population. Their territory spans the slopes delineating the High and Low Mixteca, ranging 800-2,500 m (2,600-8,200 ft) above sea level. The biggest Trique settlements are San Martín Itunyuoso, Santo Domingo del Estado, and San Juan Copala. A few theories speculate different origins of the Spanish name Triqui, but their own name for themselves, in its various dialects, means "Native Person."

According to their oral tradition, the descendants of the Trique hailed from Monte Albán and were forced to roam the Mixteca after being banished for disobeying a royal decree. They kept moving south, but were forced to stop around Putla and vicinity due to mosquitoes, rains, and other unforgiving natural barriers to settlement. The Mixtecs of Tlachquiauhco, modern-day Tlaxiaco, subjugated them and forced them to pay tribute, and when the Aztecs arrived, both Mixtecs and Triques were made tributaries to the outside regime.

With the Triques and Mixtecs, the Spanish had more luck with the word than the sword, but the Catholic religion didn't take root immediately. Communities such as Copala fiercely resisted the imposition of new beliefs. Their lot didn't improve much with independence, either. Triques remained under the yolk of the ruling class's various modes of labor exploitation, and rebelled in 1843. After five years of fighting, their leaders were captured and the uprising quelled. Triques lost more land to privatization after the introduction of coffee to this part of Oaxaca.

The Triques' struggle for land and civil rights continues to this day. In 1956, a struggle between Triques and government forces left a number of soldiers dead, and the federal government responded by bombing and firing machine gun rounds on the Indigenous residents of Copala. Since then, Triques have organized to demand an end to oppression.

Triques are known for their distinct red, full-body huipiles with horizontal stripes embellished with geometric designs and ribbons woven vertically the full length of the dress. Some will have multicolored ribbons hanging from the collar. Girls learn the art of weaving from a young age. Trique artisans also make ceramics, hats, baskets, mats, and other products for personal and commercial use.

Amuzgos and Tacuates

The Amuzgos and Tacuates occupy small patches of land in La Mixteca de la Costa, or what is also referred to as La Costa Chica (Small Coast), which spans the Oaxacan border with Guerrero. Only about 8,000 of the total 58,000 Amuzgo speakers live in Oaxaca. Their name comes from the Nahuatl word *amoxco*, which the prevailing theory states as meaning "place of books," most likely because the main pre-Hispanic Amuzgo settlement was once a large regional administrative center.

The true origin of the Amuzgos is unknown, but their linguistic link with Mixtecs leads researchers to infer that they were once the same people. The town of Xochistlahuaca, in Guerrero, was the Amuzgo capital in AD 1100, when the Mixtecs conquered and subjected them to tributaries. Later, when the Aztecs made their way to La Mixteca, the Amuzgos rebelled against their new colonizers, but uprisings in 1497, 1504, and 1507 were suppressed by the Aztecs.

The colonization by the Spanish had devastating consequences on the Amuzgos. Disease, state violence, and overwork nearly eradicated their populations completely, their numbers dwindling to a mere 200 people by 1582. As Indigenous populations declined in Mexico, the Spanish enslaved Africans, and brought them primarily to the port of Veracruz. Many slaves who escaped settled in areas along La Costa Chica, pushing the Amuzgo even farther inland than the Mixtecs and Spanish had.

The construction of highways in the 20th century opened up Amuzgo communities to the outside world, which opened up economic opportunities to the previously isolated inhabitants. Many opened transportation businesses, while others took their chance at immigration, many choosing to try their luck in the United States.

Numbering only about 3,300 people, the Tacuates inhabit a tiny patch of La Mixteca de la Costa east of Amuzgo land, in the towns of Santa María Zacatepec and Santiago Ixtayutla. Fond of snakes themselves, the Aztecs must have taken a liking to the Tacuates, calling them the same name they called themselves: Snake Men. The Tacuates are believed to have originated from Ixtayutla, but according to their legend, a giant eagle forced the original population to split, which formed the town of Zacatepec. The mythical eagle is not unique Tacuate lore. Legends of giant, sometimes two-headed eagles also appear in the oral traditions and artisanry of the Mazatecs, Mixtecs, and Chinantecs.

Although their language is considered a Mixtec dialect from Zacatepec, the Tacuates do not consider themselves Mixtec. Their language, which they call Tu'un Va'a, is at most only about 60 percent mutually intelligible with Mixtec dialects in neighboring towns.

Amuzgos and Tacuates share a style of huipil that is a blouse or full-length dress, usually white, but sometimes blue, black, or other colors, with two vertical stripes and rows of intricate, colorful floral embroidery. Tacuate women also wear huipiles that feature brightly colored animals embroidered on the chest and back.

Huaves

A little under 17,000 Huaves inhabit the large sandspits between the lagoons of El Istmo and the Gulf of Tehuantepec, principally in the communities of San Mateo del Mar, San Dionisio del Mar, Santa María del Mar, and San Francisco del Mar. Although they shared El Istmo with the Mixes and Zoques, before the arrival of the Zapotecs, the Huave language is considered an isolate, totally unrelated to other languages. Linguists have attempted to demonstrate connections to the Mixe-Zoque and Mayan families, but none of these theories have panned out.

Around AD 1300, the Aztecs came through El Istmo to open up a trade route to the Soconusco region in Chiapas, and the Zapotecs came on their heels to take advantage of the instability they left in their wake. This pushed the Huave as close to the coast as possible. The name Huave is actually a rather derogatory Zapotec exonym meaning "People Who Rot in the Humidity." During the colonial era, disease almost wiped them out completely, until toward the end of the 16th century, the Huave only numbered around 100 people.

Due to their precarious location between the sea and the lagoons, Huaves have learned to live with the water and other elements, earning them the nickname Mareños (Sea People). Year-round, they deal with fierce winds, either from the north or the south. Rains are scarce, but when they do come, they can cause deadly flooding. When they don't come for too long, the lagoons dry up. People's lives are intricately linked with the sea, and they are known as excellent fishermen. The pre-Hispanic Zapotecs basically viewed them as a cash cow, knowing that the Huave needed the corn, beans, and other fruits of the land, and would therefore keep their markets brimming with fresh seafood. The Spanish likewise took their pound of flesh in fish and shrimp.

Considering there is little else to do on the sandspit, the Huave continue fishing to this day. Census data shows that their numbers are growing, and toward the end of the 20th century, they even founded new communities, such as Cuauhtémoc and Benito Juárez, in between San Mateo del Mar and Salina Cruz.

Cuicatecs

Numbering just under 11,000, the Cuicatecs live on about 8,400 square km (3,200 sq mi) in the Cañada region, in the state's semiarid northwest. Their name in Nahuatl means "People of Song." The Cuicatec language is in the same family as Mixtec, and, like La Mixteca, their heartland is divided into the lowlands of the canyon country and the highlands to the west.

Little is known about the origins of the Cuicatecs, due to the Spanish having destroyed their codices, maps, and other texts, but archaeological findings in the region suggest that they are the descendants of the Toltec refugees fleeing the fall of Tula in 1064. When the Spanish arrived in this part of Oaxaca around 1526, the Cuicatecs had been weakened by Mixtec and Aztec incursions on their land, and were in no condition to put up a fight. The majority of Cuicatecs fled to the mountains west of present-day San Juan Bautista Cuicatlán, and now most live in mountain towns like Concepción Pápalo and San Juan Tepeuxila.

Dominican friars had a hard time with the Cuicatecs, and much of the naturalism of their native religion remains to this day. Their principal deity Sá Iko, now associated Jesus Christ, inhabits their sacred mountain, Cerro Cheve. Practices such as sacrificing livestock for favorable weather conditions are also still quite common. Cuicatecs are so fond of doing things their own way, that only one of the nine communities in which they live is governed by the official party system, whereas the others do so according to their ancestral customs.

Cuicatec land is very fertile, and many devote themselves to farming—cultivating beans, corn, chiles, squash, mangoes, oranges, apricots, and nuts. Coffee is grown in the highlands. This is the only region in Oaxaca, and the world, where the rare chile pepper chile chilhuacle is grown.

Chontals

According to the Documentation of Endangered Languages Archive (DOBES), the speakers of one of the two extant variations of Oaxacan Chontal number less than 5,000, and fluent first-language speakers are much fewer, and aging. They inhabit a chunk of the coast and foothills of the Sierra Sur measuring only 870 square km (336 sq mi), between Huatulco and Salina Cruz. This land is divided by name and by dialect into highlands and lowlands. The citizens of Santiago Astata and San Pedro Huamelula, closer to the coast, are called costeños. Chontals that live in towns like Magdalena Tequisistlán, Santa María Ecatepec, and San Carlos Yautepec, up in the hills, are called serranos (of the mountains).

Linguists have traced the genealogy of the Chontal language to that of the Hokan peoples of Arizona, California, and Baja California, as well as to the Jicaquean languages of Honduras. The Chontals of Oaxaca, however, are not related to the Chontals of Tabasco, who speak a language in the Mayan family. The word *chontal* is an Aztec exonym for a foreign people. The costeño dialect of Oaxacan Chontal, sometimes called Huamelulteco, is more endangered than its serrano version. The DOBES archive estimates there are only around 1,100 speakers of costeño Chontal, and all 100 or so of those who are fluent first-language speakers are over 70 years old. The Chontal of the highlands is sometimes called Tequistlateco, but linguists view this as erroneous. The true Tequistlateco, once spoken in Tequisistlán and considered a third dialect of Chontal, is now extinct.

Chontals are primarily subsistence farmers, depending on the rains that fall June-September to water their fields of corn, beans, squash, soursop, avocado, mamey, nache, and guava. Coffee is also grown on the shady hillsides in the Chontal highlands, which reach altitudes around 700 m (2,300 ft) above sea level.

Nahuas

Nahuatl is the most widely spoken pre-Hispanic language in Mexico, but in Oaxaca, there are only a couple small enclaves of people who speak the language of the Aztecs. Perhaps the colonial endeavors of the Aztecs at the end of the 15th century had insufficient time to root the language in Oaxaca before the arrival of the Spanish, or maybe the language found too much resistance among the headstrong native Oaxacans, but Nahuatl is now one of the lesser-spoken Indigenous tongues in the state.

The largest population of Nahuatl speakers is in the northwest corner of the state, on the border with Veracruz. Around 13,000 native Nahuatl speakers live primarily in the towns of Santiago Texcalcingo, Santa María Teopoxco, Capultitlán, Vigastepec, and San Bernandino. This community is bordered to the north, east, and south by Mazatec-speaking towns, like Huautla de Jiménez.

Nahuatl is also spoken by a small group of people in and around Tuxtepec, in the northeast corner of El Papaloapan. However, the language is at risk of dying out in the area, and in 2018, a group of teachers and concerned citizens of Tuxtepec began offering courses in Nahuatl to keep it alive in this part of Oaxaca.

Chocholtecs, Ixcatecs, and Popolocas

The Chocholtecs, Ixcatecs, and Popolocas live in the northwest of Oaxaca, in La Mixteca and the Valle de Tehuacán-Cuicatlán. According to the 2015 census, the most at-risk of these three languages is Ixcatec, spoken primarily, if not solely, by just under 150 people in Santa María Ixcatlán, about two hours through the rough canyon country west of Cuicatlán. *Ixcatlán* is a Nahuatl term meaning "place of cotton." When attempting to put Ixcatec on the family tree, linguists initially tried to relate it to Zapotec and Mixtec, but the final conclusion shows that it is more closely related to the tongues of the Chocholtecs and Popolocas.

Numbers of Chocholtec speakers are also quite meager. Also called Chochos, Chochones, or sometimes Chuchnones in Spanish, only about 730 native speakers of the language live in San Juan Bautista Coixtlahuaca and other nearby villages in La Mixteca Alta. Their traditional land has historically been quite isolated and not easy to live on. The first highway came through Chocholtec territory in 1945, and the main Chocholtec towns weren't connected to the electrical grid until 1967. Because of the poor quality of the soil and general lack of resources in their region, many Chocholtecs have turned to migration in order to survive. Oaxaca City and Huajuapan de León are popular destinations within Oaxaca for finding work, but many choose to make the perilous journey to the United States in search of a better life.

The largest of these three groups is the Popolocas, who inhabit the Valle de Tehuacán-Cuicatlán that straddles the border with Puebla, but only a fraction of them live in Oaxaca. Like the Chontals, the Popolocas get their name from a pejorative word (*popoluca*) the Aztecs used for foreigners who didn't speak a version of Nahuatl, the connotation of which implies stammering or stupidity. Linguists believe that the Chochos and Popolocas were once the same people, but that their languages and cultures began to diverge sometime around the 11th century. Only a small slice of Popoluca territory is in Oaxaca, primarily in the municipality of Santiago Chazumba.

AFRO-MEXICANS OF LA COSTA CHICA

The Afro-Mexicans of La Costa Chica constitute a significant ethnic group in the state, one which is often overlooked culturally and politically.

When disease began to whittle down Indigenous populations in Mexico, which the Spanish relied on for cheap or free labor, they began to bring people from Western Sudan in Africa, as well as from islands in the Caribbean, most of whom disembarked in Veracruz, to work as slave labor. Before President Vicente Guerrero (1782-1831), an Afro-Mexican himself, abolished slavery in 1829, escaped slaves from places like Veracruz fled to isolated spots along La Costa Chica of Oaxaca and Guerrero, and many others joined them once they were freed. In Oaxaca, they primarily inhabit the coastal area west of Puerto Escondido, including Lagunas de Chacahua, Rio Grande, Corralero, Pinotepa Nacional, going into Guerrero. Census data shows they also live in communities in La Cañada, El Papaloapan, El Istmo, and elsewhere along the coast.

Afro-Mexicans have historically had difficulty being accepted as truly Mexican by their countrymen, for they are neither considered Indigenous (though many have Indigenous ancestry) nor mestizo, which specifically means only a mix of Spanish and Indigenous. Deeply entrenched attitudes of colorism and anti-Black racism also contribute to their systematic sidelining. Hopeful strides were made in 2020, when Afro-Mexicans were finally added to the constitution and recognized at the government level.

The Afro-Mexicans of Oaxaca speak Spanish and celebrate the same holidays as elsewhere in Mexico, but they have retained elements of their African roots, which they combine with their Mexican traditions. The Danza de los Diablos (Dance of the Devils), which they perform during Day of the Dead celebrations, has a clear African influence. A visit to the pueblos of the Costa Chica will introduce you to a welcoming people with rich culinary, musical, and dancing traditions, while uniquely rooted in African ancestry, are wholly Mexican.

RELIGION

According to Mexico's National Institute for Statistics and Geography (INEGI), 81 percent of Oaxacans profess to be Catholic. However, the religion brought by the Spanish didn't fully supplant the old beliefs, so much of the Catholicism practiced in Oaxaca, especially in rural areas, is heavily syncretized and acculturated with elements from pre-Hispanic faiths. Jesus took over for supreme beings that inhabited sacred mountains, Mary took over the role as the mother goddess, and saints took the places of gods representing the sun, moon, rain, and other natural elements. Religions with oral traditions or dances depicting a god decapitating a snake, for example, could replace their god with Saint Michael the Archangel, who is often depicted as slaying a dragon.

Syncretism is notable in celebrations like Day of the Dead, practiced by many pre-Hispanic cultures, most notably the Aztecs. The Zapotecs of El Istmo call their ceremony for honoring the dead Xanduu 'Yaa. The pre-Hispanic ceremonies were made to coincide with the Catholic All Saints' Day, resulting in the modern Day of the Dead holiday.

INEGI reports that there are a total of 17 religions practiced in Oaxaca, but the second-largest religious affiliation in Oaxaca actually isn't a religion at all. Just under 170,000 people in Oaxaca claim to not be a member of any specified faith. A number of Protestant faiths, such as Pentecostal, Jehovah's Witnesses, and Seventh-Day Adventists, are next on the list. Also counted were Judaism, Islam, Indigenous religions, and spiritualism.

VISUAL ARTS

Oaxaca has produced some of Mexico's most famous visual artists. Historically, the most notable is **Rufino Tamayo** (1899-1991), born in Oaxaca City. His parents died when he was young, and he moved to Mexico City to live under the guardianship of his aunt, who worked as a fruit vendor in the markets there. This may have been where Tamayo obtained his artistic fondness for watermelons, a subject he painted often and for which he is remembered. In Mexico City, he worked and studied cubism and surrealism with another Oaxacan important to the arts, **José Vasconcelos** (1882-1959), a philosopher, writer, and politician known as the caudillo cultural (cultural leader) of the Mexican Revolution.

Although Tamayo was contemporary with and is remembered alongside Mexico's great painters of the Revolution, such as Diego Rivera (1886-1957), José Clemente Orozco (1883-1949), and David Alfaro Siqueiros (1896-1974), Tamayo did not have the same view of the Revolution as they did. Whereas Rivera, Orozco, and Siqueiros believed the Revolution was necessary for the future of their country, Tamayo was convinced it would only harm it. His painting *Niños jugando con fuego* (Children Playing with Fire, 1947) represents a pair of children being burned by the fire they started, an obvious metaphor for his opinion of the Revolution.

Tamayo's controversial attitudes toward the Revolution and the branch of Mexican art meant to support it led him to move to New York in 1926, but not before creating a buzz with a solo exhibition in Mexico City. When he returned in 1929, his work was met with much applause, and the media took notice. Tamayo began working with woodcuts,

Francisco Toledo: Pioneer and Patron of Oaxacan Art

Born in Juchitán, world-renowned artist Francisco Toledo (1940-2019) was a feverishly active player in the cultural, political, and artistic scenes in Oaxaca. In 1982, he founded the publisher Ediciones Toledo, which published books about Mexican history and culture with a focus on Oaxaca.

His most famous project was **IAGO,** the Instituto de Artes Gráficas de Oaxaca (Graphic Arts Institute of Oaxaca). Located in a gorgeous 18th-century house across from the Santo Domingo church in Oaxaca City, which the Toledo family donated to the National Institute of Fine Arts, IAGO has one of Latin America's most extensive graphic arts libraries and hosts temporary exhibits of both new and established Mexican artists. An on-site gift shop sells Toledo's famous work.

As a cultural activist, he campaigned to block the opening of a McDonald's in Oaxaca City's Centro to protect the city's gastronomical heritage.

In 2006, he founded the **Centro de Artes de San Agustín (CaSa),** a cultural and artistic center in San Agustín Etla that offers workshops in painting, writing, dance, filmmaking, and many other artistic pursuits free of charge to those accepted. Toledo was still very active in the arts scene in Oaxaca up until his death in 2019.

etchings, and lithographs, and even developed a new printmaking technique called mixografía, which resulted in prints with a three-dimensional texture. Tamayo's printmaking legacy lives on today in the numerous graphic arts galleries that have popped up in Oaxaca in recent years.

Also part of the legacy Tamayo left to his native Oaxaca is his rich collection of pre-Hispanic art, which is now on display in the **Museo de Arte Prehispánico de México Rufino Tamayo,** in Oaxaca City. With pieces chosen for their artistic rather than their archaeological value, the collection truly demonstrates the creative ability of the Indigenous peoples of Mexico. Some pieces still have the original paint from centuries ago.

Born in Ocotlán de Morelos, **Rodolfo Morales** (1925-2001) was another Oaxacan painter of Zapotec origins who reached worldwide recognition. He is remembered for his surrealist, oneiric canvases and collages that often depict the Zapotec women of his birthplace. It wasn't until he was 50 years old that he gained mainstream recognition, when his work at a solo exhibition in Cuernavaca caught Tamayo's keen artistic eye. Morales was introduced to the larger art world via the connections Tamayo had with galleries and critics all over the world.

The fame brought Morales some money, which he used to spruce up his hometown of Ocotlán, about an hour south of Oaxaca City. There, he founded the Rodolfo Morales Cultural Foundation, which dedicated itself to restoring the old buildings in town. The pretty, sky-blue Templo y Ex-Convento de Santo Domingo, now home to the town's municipal government offices, was the foundation's most important project. At the end of his life, Morales and fellow Oaxacan painter Francisco Toledo were considered Mexico's greatest living artists.

Like Tamayo and Morales, **Francisco Toledo** (1940-2019) was a world-famous graphic artist of Zapotec origins. As a young painter and sculptor, Toledo studied in the School of Fine Arts of Oaxaca, as well as the National Institute of Fine Arts (INBA) in Mexico City, where he studied under famous Colombian painter Guillermo Silva Santamaría (1921-2007).

Toledo's favorite subject was the natural world, especially the elements that normally give us the willies. Spiders, scorpions, crocodiles, and other creepy crawlers feature prominently in his tessellations, prints, and jewelry. One of his signature techniques was using lasers to cut materials like leather, gold plating, or X-ray film into visual representations of stylized bugs and beasts. One of his most famous works that demonstrated Toledo's ability to turn the repugnant into something aesthetically refined is his *Los cuadernos de la mierda* (The Shit Notebooks), which features 1,745 images of people, animals, and skeletons defecating. Drawn during Toledo's second stay in Paris, 1985-1987, the images are meant to explore the pre-Hispanic views toward this quotidian act that all of us have in common, no matter our wealth or social status. In Mexico, artists can pay certain taxes using their work, and Toledo did so with these images, possibly commenting on what he thought of taxation in his country.

The second decade of the 2000s saw a resurgence in the practice of **printmaking,** popularized by Oaxacan artists like Tamayo and Toledo. Now over a dozen printmaking workshops and galleries dot the map of the Centro in Oaxaca City, the majority of them located on Calle Porfirio Díaz, west of Santo Domingo. Artists in these galleries use xylography (woodcut), lithography, etching, engraving, and other techniques to create beautiful images representing political ideas or Oaxaca's wealth of cultural symbols. If you're really head-over-heels for this type of art, pick up a **Pasaporte Gráfico** (Graphic Passport) at one of the galleries and take it around to all included. If you get a stamp from each one, you get a discount at any of them.

MUSIC

Oaxaca's tireless creativity is heard in its music, as well. The conquest brought new instruments for people to tinker with, and people in regions all over the state have come up with their own genres of music, some of which take influences from music as far away as South America. The marimba, for example, re-created in the Americas by enslaved people brought from Africa, is very popular in Oaxaca, especially in Oaxaca City.

Oaxacan Brass Bands

The music you're most likely to hear in Oaxaca is the traditional Oaxacan brass band called **Tambora Oaxaqueña,** literally "Oaxacan Bass Drum." These groups of 15-20 musicians provide the lively accompaniment for the parades called **comparsas** and **calendas,** which are thrown to celebrate everything from major holidays to college graduations, so your chances of seeing and dancing in one in Oaxaca City are pretty good just about any time of year.

The songs these bands play have much in common with Balkan music—at one moment slow, introspective, and somewhat gloomy, and in the next exploding with energy and celebratory rhythms and melodies.

In La Costa Chica, an area of the coastline straddling the border with Guerrero, the popular music is called **La Chilena,** which combines music brought by Chilean sailors in the 19th century with traditional Mexican music. It is popular in Pinotepa Nacional and other towns on the coast, and is usually what accompanies their dancers in the Guelaguetza and other festivities.

Another popular Oaxacan music genre is the **son istmeño,** literally "sound of the Isthmus." *Son* is a Spanish word used for various regional types of folk music, the most well-known of which is the Son Cubano, from Cuba. The son istmeño is traditionally played with a trio of guitars: a normal six-string, a smaller six-string called a requinto, and a 10-string guitar called a bajoquinto. This genre from El Istmo de Tehuantepec contributed one of the most popular standards in Latin American music, called "La Llorona" (The Weeping Woman). Its poignant melody and hypnotizing pace have captivated musicians and listeners all over Latin America since its popularization by Oaxacan poet Andrés Henestrosa (1906-2008) in the 1940s.

The song has been part of the son istmeño

since the mid-19th century, and refers to the tradition of la llorona, a woman always searching for her lost children. This legend is said to come from the Aztec goddess of birth and motherhood, Cihuacóatl (see-wah-CO-at-l), who abandoned her son Mixcoatl at a crossroads and returned often in search of him, only to find a sacrificial knife. The legend became a metaphor for the conquest, and the traditional lyrics include the lines "Cover me with your shawl, Llorona, because I'm dying of the cold."

The song has been sung in El Istmo since the 1850s, but Henestrosa and others later added a number of verses that turned it into a tragic love story meant to represent the tumultuous Mexican Revolution. Mexican singer Susana Harp (b. 1968) has recorded it five times without repeating a verse. The most popular version was sung by Chavela Vargas (1919-2012), who was born in Costa Rica but found fame and fortune singing in Mexico. The song has become a sort of rite of passage or badge of honor for Spanish-language singers, and it has been interpreted by Mexican stars like Eugenia León (b. 1956), Natalia Lafourcade (b. 1984), and Oaxacan singer of Mixtec origin Lila Downs (b. 1968).

Lila Downs was born in Tlaxiaco to a Mixtec mother and an American father. Taking influences from both cultures, Downs's music runs a wide range of styles, genres, and languages. She is fluent Mixtec and often sings songs in the language, as well as Zapotec. She tours all over the world but also sings at many events in Oaxaca, like the Guelaguetza, the Mazunte Jazz Festival, and the Zipolite Nudist Festival. Lila has also lent her money, talent, and celebrity to the Fondo Guadalupe Musalem, which promotes and supports education for young women in Oaxaca's rural and Indigenous communities.

Oaxaca is also home to **Álvaro Carrillo** (1921-1969), who also contributed a song now considered a standard in Latin music—his "Sabor a mí" (Taste of Me). Popularized by the Latin romantic trio Los Panchos in 1959, the song has gone on to be sung by a number of famous Mexican singers, including Lila Downs, Luis Miguel (b. 1970), Javier Solís (1931-1966), José José (b. 1948), and even the US Latin rock band Los Lobos.

The Oaxaca City native **Macedonio Alcalá** (1831-1869) may not have gained the worldwide recognition of the previously mentioned artists, but he might be the most important to Oaxacans themselves. He was the composer of the waltz "Dios nunca muere" (God Never Dies, 1868), the de facto anthem of Oaxaca. The popular pedestrian walkway and downtown theater in Oaxaca City are named in his honor.

DANCE

Dance has been deeply rooted in Oaxacan culture for millennia. The Indigenous peoples of this land used dance to tell religious tales and allegories. When the Spanish arrived, many stories were kept alive via the dances, which were ostensibly changed to represent Christian elements. Some, like the **Danza de las Mascaritas** (Dance of the Masked Ones) of Teposcolula, in La Mixteca, were actually created to surreptitiously mock the dances brought by the conquistadors.

Dances are the main attraction at the **Guelaguetza.** The first dance is usually an homage to **Centéotl** (sen-TEH-oh-tl), the goddess of corn, which is then followed by dances from the invited delegations from all over the state. Dances represent the language, culture, food, and enterprise of a certain region. Tuxtepec, in the El Papaloapan region where lots of pineapples are grown, is known for its consistently crowd-pleasing **Flor de Piña** (Pineapple Flower). The star dance of Zaachila, in the Valles Centrales, is called the **Danza de los Zancudos** (Dance of the Stilted Ones), in which the dancers perform atop tall stilts, some over 2 m (6.5 ft) tall.

One of Oaxaca's most famous dances is the **Danza de la Pluma** (Dance of the Feather). Citizens of both Cuilapam de Guerrero and Zaachila claim the dance as originally from their respective towns, but now it is also performed by dancers from various towns in the

Valles Centrales, such as Teotitlán del Valle and Zimatlán de Álvarez. Like the Danza de las Mascaritas, this one is a product of the conquest, owing as much to its Indigenous influences as to its Spanish ones. The dance was invented by Dominican friars and Mixtec Christian converts to represent the triumph of Catholicism over the pagan religions of the Aztecs and other Indigenous peoples of Mexico.

Folk Art and Craftwork

TEXTILES AND CLOTHING

Hand-woven wool rugs, called **tapetes,** are one of the most popular artisanal products in Oaxaca, especially in the Valles Centrales, where the main centers of production are Teotitlán del Valle and Santa Ana del Valle. Weavers here use wool from La Mixteca, which is regarded as the softest in the state.

Using various dyeing techniques and ingredients, they produce all the colors of the rainbow, transferring the kaleidoscope of colors found in the land to their woven works. At first sight, the prices that weavers ask for their rugs can seem expensive, but when taking into account the time and skill that goes into creating a rug, as well as the quality of the product you're getting, the prices start to look like a steal. Weaving one rug can take an artist up to three months or more, depending on the size and style of a piece.

Embroidered blouses and dresses called **huipiles** (wee-PEEL-ehs) not only express a person's culture and origins in Oaxaca, they are now big business, being one of the most popular products for tourists and locals alike in the state. The most popular huipiles come from Tehuantepec and Juchitán, in El Istmo de Tehuantepec. These black velvet garments emblazoned with the fiery colors of bright tropical flowers are so popular that they could be considered the de facto emblem of Oaxaca.

Just about every Indigenous group in Oaxaca has its own style of huipil, giving garment shoppers a wide range of styles to choose from. The flowers embroidered on the huipiles made in San Antonino Castillo Velasco, south of Oaxaca City, for example, are much smaller than those from El Istmo, with finer details and images of people and birds, as well.

POTTERY

Pottery (alfarería) is probably the oldest and most dynamic craft practiced in Oaxaca. In Atzompa, for example, you can observe the remains of a 1,300-year-old kiln once used by the suburbanites of Monte Albán, then head down the hill to Santa María Atzompa, where the modern descendants of this tradition work day in and day out to keep it alive. The style currently popular in Santa María Atzompa is glazed an eye-catching forest green that highlights small imperfections, making each piece totally unique.

In the 1950s, a potter from San Bartolo Coyotepec named Doña Rosa came up with a technique of polishing the clay before firing it in the kiln, which produces a shimmery black finish to the decorative pieces. Her distinct style of **barro negro (black clay pottery)** lives on into the present day.

José García, the blind potter of San Antonino Castillo Velasco, creates unglazed **barro rojo (red clay pottery)** pieces, opting to keep the tone earthy and subdued.

Whether it's a decorative piece for a gift, or a new set of mugs for the kitchen cabinets, Oaxacan potters are sure to have something that will catch your eye.

ALEBRIJES

Although the origins of alebrijes, the psychedelically painted wooden statues of fantastic animals you'll find at just about any artisans market in the state, aren't completely Oaxacan, the figurines have come to be symbols for the creative impulse of the place. The concept came from a Mexico City-based artist named Pedro Linares (1906-1992), who claimed to have seen the fanciful creatures in a dream when he became ill at 30 years old. In his dream, the creatures shouted over and over again the word "¡alebrijes!"

Linares used wire frames and papier-mâché to bring his visions to life, but when the idea made it to Oaxaca and grabbed the attention of a shepherd named Manuel Jiménez, who had been whittling figurines out of wood since childhood, the alebrije as we know it today was born. Manuel initially didn't paint his figurines, but began to do so at the request of an English tourist who told the artist he wanted some color on them. The process took root in Manuel's hometown of Arrazola, and later in nearby San Martín Tilcajete, and artists have been developing new carving and painting styles ever since.

For many artists, alebrijes came to represent the Indigenous concept of tonas y nahuales, animals that represent and protect a person based on their date of birth. The tona is the animal based on the Zapotec calendar, and the nahual is based on one's specific day and year of birth. Some talleres (workshops) will find what animals are yours based on your birthday, and you can then seek out one that combines the two, or get one commissioned.

CANASTAS, TENATES, AND PETATES

Oaxacan artisans use reeds, palm fronds, plastic bands, maguey fibers, and other materials to make beautiful **canastas** (baskets), **tenates** (different style of baskets), **petates** (woven mats), and a number of other useful products, as well as decorative items. The most useful of these to visitors to the state are things like shopping bags, but you could also get a cool laundry basket or floor mat for the kitchen or patio.

You'll find that many of these products are named based on their usage. For example, a panera is a bread basket (*pan* is bread in Spanish), a frutero is a basket for holding fruits, and a florero is one for flowers. You'll also find canastas (small baskets) and canastos (bigger ones, usually with a lid). Artisans in towns like Etla, Ocotlán, and Tlacolula are famous for their products made with carrizo verde (green reed). Out in La Mixteca, craftworkers use palm fronds to create beautiful tapetes and petates (mats), bolsas (bags), sombreros (hats), sopladores (hand fans for stoking the cooking fire), and more.

Historically, the town of Santo Domingo Xagacía (sha-gah-SEE-ah), in the Sierra Norte, is the biggest producer of goods made with ixtle, the fiber of the maguey plant, but there are ixtle weavers in a number of other Oaxacan communities. You'll have a good chance of finding these products at the Sunday Market in Tlacolula, but places like Ixtlán de Juárez (which takes its name from the fiber), Teposcolula, Nochixtlán, and Miahuatlán also make things with ixtle. The fiber is known for its durability and pliability.

JEWELRY

Fine jewelry is another artisanal product that has its roots in pre-Hispanic Oaxacan culture. When archaeologist Alfonso Caso (1896-1970) and his team excavated Tomb 7 at Monte Albán, they found a treasure trove of gold jewelry fit for a movie scene. Among the riches were intricately filigreed earrings, rings, necklaces, chest plates, and little bells, as well as decorative or symbolic representations of birds, fish, and deities, like gods of happiness and light. One popular jewelry store has dedicated itself to purveying replicas of these pieces. Oro de Monte Albán has four stores in downtown Oaxaca, as well as one in the visitor center at the Monte Albán archaeological site.

Down on the coast, you'll find lots of jewelry made with **ámbar** (amber), as well as a cornucopia of hand-woven hippie trinkets, like bracelets, anklets, necklaces, earrings, and charms. Areas like El Adoquín in Puerto Escondido and La Crucecita in Bahías de Huatulco are great places to go shopping for **silver jewelry.**

LEATHER GOODS AND KNIVES

The craft of **talabartería** (leatherworking) is popular in Oaxaca City. Markets here are stocked to the brim with leather jackets, purses, coin purses, backpacks, hats, belts, wallets, shoes, and many other fine goods made from animal hide. Artisans in places like Ocotlán de Morelos and Miahuatlán de Porfirio Díaz are known for the fabrication of **sombreros de panza de burro,** wide-brimmed sunhats made from the bellies of donkeys.

Oaxaca City and Ocotlán are also home to makers of fine blades, such as **machetes, swords, knives, daggers,** and **silverware.** Many are more for showing that using, adorned with acid-etched images of Oaxacan landscapes and local proverbs.

Essentials

Transportation

GETTING THERE

Air

If you're coming straight to Oaxaca, your best travel option will be to fly directly here. US and Canadian airlines in recent years have begun to add more direct flights to Oaxaca City, Puerto Escondido, and Huatulco. This has made the trip easier and quicker for citizens of these countries, as well as those from others who connect via those countries. Visit September-early October and April-May to get the best deals on flights.

From the United States and Canada

Many airlines have either connecting or direct flights between Oaxaca City and major US and Canadian cities, such as Dallas, Houston, Austin, San Antonio, Albuquerque, Phoenix, Los Angeles, San Francisco, Chicago, Atlanta, New York, Miami, Toronto, and Vancouver. If you're coming from Southern California or close by, check for flights from Tijuana. It might be cheaper to fly domestically, and since 2015, flyers have been able to cross from San Diego directly to the Tijuana airport via the Cross Border Xpress international bridge.

For nonstop flights to Oaxaca City, you'll have to fly out of **Houston,** with **United Airlines** (toll-free US and Canada tel. 800/260-1952, toll-free UK tel. 0800/028-5003; www.united.com); **Dallas,** with **American Airlines** (toll-free US and Canada tel. 800/433-7300, UK tel. 0207/660-2300; www.aa.com); or **Los Angeles** or **Tijuana,** with **Volaris** (toll-free US tel. 855/865-2747, Mex. tel. 551/102-8000; www.volaris.com).

The only other Oaxacan city with direct flights from the United States and Canada is **Huatulco.** Canadian airline **Westjet** (toll-free US and Canada tel. 888/937-8538, toll-free UK tel. 0800/279-7072; www.westjet.com) has direct flights from **Toronto, Vancouver,** and **Calgary.**

Other major airlines with flights that connect via one of these cities, or **Mexico City,** include **Aeromexico** (toll-free US and Canada tel. 800/237-6639, toll-free UK tel. 0800/977-5533, Mex. tel. 555/133-4000; www.aeromexico.com), **Interjet** (toll-free US tel. 866/285-9525, toll-free Canada tel. 844/874-4053, international tel. +52 998/881-6836; www.interjet.com), and **Delta Airlines** (toll-free US and Canada tel. 800/221-1212, UK tel. 0207/660-0767). Flying into Mexico City and then booking a separate flight onward to Oaxaca (or even an ADO bus) can often be cheaper than booking a direct flight to Oaxaca City or the coast.

From Europe, Latin America, Australasia, and Asia

To get to Oaxaca from elsewhere in the world, your quickest option is to fly **Aeromexico** and connect via Mexico City. In Europe, Aeromexico flies directly to London, Paris, Madrid, Amsterdam, Frankfurt, Munich, and Rome. In Latin America, Aeromexico has direct flights to Mexico City from major cities in Cuba, the Dominican Republic, Belize, Guatemala, El Salvador, Honduras (San Pedro Sula), Nicaragua, Costa Rica, Panama, Colombia, Ecuador, Peru, Chile, Argentina, and Brazil (Sao Paulo). The only city in Asia with which Aeromexico offers nonstop flights to the capital is Tokyo.

Visitors from Australia and New Zealand have a long flight itinerary ahead of them. Aeromexico does not fly to Australasia, so you will have to fly one of the US airlines (**United, Delta,** or **American Airlines**) and connect either through one of the cities with direct flights to Oaxaca, or have one more stop in Mexico City.

Bus

Bus travel is the primary mode of long-distance transport in Mexico. Unlike the United States, where bus passengers are at the mercy and whim of a couple of companies, Mexico boasts over 50 major long-distance bus companies. With such a large, varied, and competitive market, you can generally expect to walk into a bus station almost anywhere in the country and board a bus in an hour or two.

The bus company that reigns supreme in Oaxaca is Autobuses del Oriente (Buses of the East), or **ADO**, pronounced by spelling the letters in Spanish: ah-DAY-oh (Mex. tel. 555/784-4652; www.ado.com.mx) and

Previous: view of Oaxaca from Monte Albán.

its subsidiaries Autobuses Unidos (United Buses), or **AU, Estrella de Oro** (Gold Star), Omnibuses Cristóbal Colón, or **OCC,** which, unlike its namesake, Christopher Columbus, actually knows where it's going. ADO buses come in three levels of comfort: the basic ADO, the slightly more upscale ADO GL (my usual go-to), and the crème de la crème ADO Platino. You can view schedules and buy tickets for all of these companies on ADO's website and app. If you're coming from Mexico City, Puebla, Chiapas, Veracruz, or even as far east as Quintana Roo, ADO and its daughter companies will be your main bus options. (Pro tip: bring a jacket or blanket—the AC on the bus is frosty.)

Car or RV

To see Oaxaca at your own pace, you might consider driving to Oaxaca. This option requires quite a bit more money than taking public transport in Mexico, as you will have to factor in expenses such as gas, insurance, permits, parking, and tolls.

Mexican Car Insurance

All vehicles in Mexico, foreign and domestic, are required to have an insurance policy issued by a Mexican company. One of the most experienced is **Sanborn's Mexico Auto Insurance** (2009 S. 10th St., McAllen, TX 78503; toll-free US tel. 800/222-0158; www.sanborns.com). Their tourist insurance includes civil liability, physical damage and theft, roadside and legal assistance, medical coverage, and more. They also insure motorcycles and other street-legal recreational vehicles. You can also get quotes and buy insurance at **Mexpro.com** (toll-free US tel. 855/639-7761).

Quotes vary, depending on your type of car and the amount of coverage you want. Get a quote for your vehicle on these companies' websites.

Gas

US, Canadian, and Australian drivers in Mexico will find higher gas prices in Mexico than they are used to back home. Gas is sold by the liter here, so keep your phone handy for conversions.

Drivers accustomed to gas prices in the United Kingdom and New Zealand can most likely expect to pay considerably less than they would for a liter back home. For up-to-date listings on gas prices in Mexico, check the website **GasolinaMX.com,** which reports daily average prices both state- and nationwide. You can even choose specific communities and find the updated prices at the gasolineras (gas stations) there. This will be your best resource in getting an idea of how much of your budget you will need to devote to fuel expenses. To get an idea of how they will compare to gas prices back home, check the website **GlobalPetrolPrices.com.** Buying gas in Mexico will be much more expensive than taking public transport here, so take this into account when planning your budget.

Tolls

Tolls are going to be another not insignificant expense if you drive to Oaxaca. For safety, time, and general comfort reasons, toll roads (indicated with a capital D after the highway number) are worth taking, but tolls at Mexican expressways on average tend to be higher per kilometer than many countries.

The main inconvenience of toll roads here is that they bottleneck traffic and cause long waits. Have games, music, audiobooks, or some other way to pass the time, just in case you get stuck in standstill traffic. **Pro tip:** Although it can be difficult to find change for larger bills even (especially) in chain convenience stores in Mexico, toll booth operators almost always have exact change in order to keep traffic moving. Take advantage of this and get those cumbersome 500-peso notes changed out at the toll booths, and you won't have to worry as much about this unfortunately frequent problem in Mexico.

Parking Tickets

One procedure in Oaxaca and other parts of Mexico to be aware of is that **officers will remove your front license plate** when they give you a parking ticket, to ensure that you pay the fine before moving your car. After paying your fine (multa, also the word for the paper ticket), make sure to ask where you retrieve your license plate (placa). Keep all paperwork, por si las moscas (just in case).

Roadside Assistance

Since the 1960s, **Los Ángeles Verdes (The Green Angels)** have provided free information and roadside assistance to tourists driving on Mexican highways. If you need assistance on a main highway, dial 078 to be connected with a representative and ask for help. Both Spanish- and English-speaking representatives are available.

If you don't have a cell phone with Mexican service, you can flag down a passing vehicle and ask them to call you some help, but I recommend having phone service if you are going to be driving to Oaxaca. If your phone will not accept SIM cards from other carriers, it might be best to just buy a cell phone to use in case of emergency. You can get an old button phone as cheap as US$25-30 at a cell phone distributor.

Highway Routes from the US Border

If you're driving from **Texas,** take the **central route,** for which the best place to cross is in Laredo, Texas, at the southern end of I-35. From here, take Highway 85 (part of which you have the option to take a toll road) to **Monterrey,** where you should see the **Barrio Antiguo** neighborhood and go for a stroll in the **Parque Fundidora.** There are also tons of great opportunities for outdoor activities within an hour or so of the city, from rock climbing or hiking at **El Potrero Chico** to skiing at the **Bosques de Monterreal** mountain resort.

From Monterrey, take Highway 40 toward Saltillo, and get on 57D (toll), which will turn into the free federal highway of the same number, and take it to **San Luís Potosí.** Spend the evening strolling its gorgeous colonial downtown streets.

From San Luís, you could reach **Mexico City** in about six hours via Highway 57 and its tolled stretches. If you've got another day available in your itinerary, though, you could head east on Highway 70 until you get to Highway 85, where you'll turn south to stop over in **Xilitla,** renowned for its location in the stunning natural area called **La Huasteca Potosina.** Alternatively, you could take Highway 57 toward **Guanajuato,** making a quick stop in **Dolores Hidalgo** to shout "¡Viva México!" on the same church steps where Don Miguel Hidalgo famously sparked the Mexican Revolution with his inspiring speech, now called El Grito de Dolores. Spend the night in colorful Guanajuato, maybe taking part in a callejonada, in which musicians from the local university sing songs and crack jokes as they guide you through the city's cobblestone streets.

From Mexico City, take Highway 150 and its tolled stretches to **Puebla.** About an hour outside of Puebla, take the exit for tolled Highway 135D, which will take you through **La Mixteca** to meet up with the free (libre) 135, about a half hour from **Oaxaca City.**

GETTING AROUND

Air

There are airports in **Oaxaca City, Puerto Escondido, Huatulco,** and **Ixtepec** (actually closer to Juchitán), but since this is the least common way for people to move around inside Oaxaca, any flight itinerary with large airlines will have you connecting via Mexico City or elsewhere.

However, Oaxaca-owned **Aerotucán** (Emilio Carranza 303, Colonia Reforma, Oaxaca City; tel. 951/502-0840, toll-free Mex. tel. 800/640-4148; www.aerotucan.com; 8am-8pm Mon.-Fri., 8am-6pm Sat.) offers flights between these cities. For a one-way flight from Oaxaca City to Puerto Escondido, you can expect to pay around US$185, to Huatulco, US$172, and to Ixtepec, US$150. All Aerotucán flights go between Oaxaca City, meaning you can't fly between airports on the coast, or to Ixtepec from there. It is

Highway Routes from US Border to Oaxaca

The projected total travel days in this chart have been estimated by considering driving by day and staying one night in the suggested stops. Of course, you'll miss a lot on the way if you just drive and sleep, so make sure to factor in time for fun along the way. If you're driving to Oaxaca, you're obviously not pressed for time, so enjoy the trip. Also, be advised that the only route I can comfortably recommend is the central route, due to the high safety risks of driving through certain states. Please do your due diligence.

Route	Via	Km (Mi)	Hours at the Wheel	Travel Days
Eastern	Matamoros or Reynosa-Tampico, Veracruz-Oaxaca City	1,421 km (883 mi)	20 hrs	3 days
Central	Nuevo Laredo-Monterrey, San Luís Potosí-Xilitla or Guanajuato, Mexico City-Oaxaca City	1,740-2,021 km (1,081-1,256 mi)	22-26 hrs	4-5 days
Alternate Central	Ciudad Juárez Chihuahua, Durango-Zacatecas, Guanajuato-Mexico City, Oaxaca City	2,393 km (1,487 mi)	30 hrs	5-6 days
Pacific	Nogales-Guaymas, Los Mochis-Mazatlán, Puerto Vallarta-Manzanillo, Zihuatanejo-Acapulco, Puerto Escondido	2,981 km (1,852 mi)	44 hrs	8 days
Pacific-Mexico City	Nogales-Mazatlán, Tepic-Guadalajara, Guanajuato-Mexico City, Oaxaca City	2,723 km (1,692 mi)	33 hrs	7 days
Baja California-Pacific	Tijuana-San Felipe, La Paz-Mazatlán, Puerto Vallarta-Manzanillo, Zihuatanejo-Acapulco, Puerto Escondido	3,987 km (2,477 mi)	62 hrs	8-9 days

definitely a unique way to see the magnitude and magnificence of the Sierra Madre del Sur.

Aside from their main office in Oaxaca City, you'll also find Aerotucán offices in the airports, as well as one in La Crucecita, **Huatulco** (Carrizal 603-H; tel. 958/581-9085; 11:30am-3pm Mon.-Sat.). The office is inside Plaza Madero, two blocks east of the main square.

Car

Road System

To travel between regions in Oaxaca, you'll take a paved **carretera federal (federal highway),** which will be designated with a police badge-shaped symbol with the word *Mexico* at the top and the number of the highway below. Speed limits on these roads range 60-90 km per hour (40-55 mph), and are lower in curvy stretches. It is not uncommon for drivers here to go well over the speed limit.

Conditions on these roads range from severely potholed to nice and smooth to nonexistent in cases of landslides in the mountains. Since they are so important to trade, they are usually repaired quickly. If you're planning on driving through mountains during the rainy season, pay attention to the weather forecast. Do not drive in the mountains during a rainstorm.

Toll roads in Oaxaca, and elsewhere in Mexico, are designated with a **capital D** after the number of the highway route they cover. At highway intersections where you must choose to get on the toll road or not, you will see the words *cuota* (toll) and *libre* (freeway), as well as the capital D, to distinguish the roads. Pay attention to the speed limits as you approach the caseta de cobro (toll booth). The maximum speed limit on toll roads is 110 km per hour (about 70 mph).

Road conditions in towns and cities also range from nice paved roads to fields of potholes to heavily rutted dirt roads, as well as many speed bumps. Many roads in the mountains are nice, two-track dirt roads with space to pass a car in the opposite direction. Be aware that you'll potentially be sharing these roads with bikers, hikers, and locals and their livestock, who use them to get to their fields or commute between villages.

Speed Bumps

Oaxaca's main method for speed regulation is the speed bump. They are everywhere, even on highways when passing through populated areas. In many cases, you'll see a sign that reads **Tope** or **Reductor,** and in some places they'll be painted yellow.

Rather frequently, they'll have neither and will jump right out of the road if you're not looking out for them. To avoid damage to your car or your rental, always be on the lookout for topes.

Car Rental

Although you can get anywhere in Oaxaca in public transport, you might consider renting a car to save time or have more freedom to explore. It can really come in handy in places with lesser-developed tourism sectors, such as La Mixteca and La Cañada, to get to those really out-of-the-way places.

You can expect to spend around US$60-90 per day to rent a car, but some local companies have rates as low as US$38 a day. Depending on what you want or need, prices can get as high as US$185 per day. Unless you are certain you will be going to very rugged terrain, you shouldn't need a 4x4, but get something with a good amount of clearance, just to avoid having to worry at every speed bump.

Your valid driver's license issued in your home country is valid for driving a rental car in Mexico. Your rental will include the necessary insurance to legally drive in Mexico, but you might want to consider getting the extra collision and theft coverage.

Suburban

The main mode of interurban transport in Oaxaca is the 12-15-passenger van called a suburban. These are your cheapest, fastest, and most widely available option. You'll see them and their stations (bases) everywhere. Prices generally range from about US$5 for a two-hour trip to US$12-15 for a six-hour trip. Suburban trips longer than six hours are rare in Oaxaca, unless there are unexpected hold-ups, such as a roadblock, accident, or construction.

Suburban passengers should be aware that one way these companies offer you such savings on time and money is by the drivers usually being in quite a hurry. They drive fast and pass a lot, even on mountain roads and in other situations with limited visibility. I've never been in an accident in one of these, but a quick search of Oaxacan news reports reveals that they do happen. Use your seatbelt, if there is one.

Safe Driving in Mexico

Rule number one: Do not drive on highways at night here in Oaxaca, or elsewhere in Mexico. It is not uncommon for highway bandits to wait for private automobiles to come along a secluded stretch of darkened highway and pull a rope across to stop drivers and rob them. Night buses, however, are generally safe. I've taken countless night buses in Mexico and have never had a problem like this.

Be very cautious in mountainous areas, and don't drive during rainstorms. We once took a cab through the mountains after a big rainstorm, only to come to an abrupt stop by a tree that had fallen in the middle of the road. My husband got out and joined the other drivers and passengers on either side of the tree in hacking away with machetes and dragging branches and pieces of the trunk off the road. Fallen trees and landslides aren't uncommon. If you're driving through the mountains and there is a big storm, just wait it out. You never know when a disaster like this will occur, so better safe than sorry.

On two-lane highways with shoulders, it is common for slower vehicles to ride the shoulder to allow faster ones to pass. This sometimes leads to some tight squeezes, when both lanes are jockeying for room. Be aware of this and practice caution. If you're not sure about a pass, don't do it, even if the driver behind you alerts you to his or her frustration.

Road blockages are also common in Oaxaca. They are mostly due to agrarian disputes between neighboring farm communities over land rights, and aren't directed toward tourists. If you're caught in one, just be patient, or try to find another route to get to your destination. Never get involved with these types of disputes. Also, pay attention to the news to see if there is a blockage on the road you plan to take. A good source is the app **Oaxaca iDubi** (https://oaxaca-idubi.en.softonic.com/android), which has up-to-date information on roadblocks and other traffic events in Oaxaca.

Taxi Colectivo and Camioneta

For shorter trips between towns within a region, you'll either have one or both of these options. Taxis colectivos are small, five-passenger sedans that follow a more-or-less fixed route. On just about any highway in the state, you can depend on these to be running their routes from early in the morning, until just after the sun goes down. Do not be on the highway trying to flag down a taxi colectivo (or for any reason) at night. They are five-passenger cars, so don't expect comfort, but with fares rarely over US$3-4, you can't really complain.

Camionetas are the same collective travel concept, but with covered pickup trucks with benches in the bed to accommodate more people and cargo. They often have ample seating in the cab, if you're not into riding in the back. Fares for camionetas are usually similar to taxis colectivos.

Visas and Officialdom

PASSPORTS AND TOURIST VISAS

Visitors from the United States, Canada, the United Kingdom, Australia, New Zealand, and dozens of other countries do not require a visa to enter Mexico for tourism purposes. This means that as long as your passport is valid for at least six months after the time you plan to depart, all you have to do is show up at a port of entry and present your passport to an immigration official.

Citizens of these countries are allowed to stay in Mexico up to 180 days for unremunerated activities. On your flight, or in the immigration office at the border, you will be given a bilingual Forma Migratoria Múltiple (FMM), on which you will state your purpose for visiting (check Tourism) and request the amount of time you plan to stay. If you're making a long trip, simply write 180 days, but if your trip is shorter (say, only a week long), I recommend requesting an extra week or so, just in case. You never know when you'll lose your passport, or miss a flight (or want to spend an extra few days on the beach), and have to stay longer. You'll also need to write the address of your hotel or person you're visiting, so have your accommodations information ready when filling out the form. You don't need to show proof of hotel reservations, but you will need the address, so if you haven't booked a room, have the guidebook handy and write the address of the place you plan to stay. (Mexico is slowly phasing out physical FMM forms, so instead of a FMM form, you may just get a stamp in your passport.)

If you fly to Oaxaca, or anywhere in Mexico, the fee for this card is included in your plane ticket. If you are crossing at the border, the form costs around US$20. Those traveling with children should note that Mexican law requires children under 18 to also have their own tourist card, so make sure everyone in the family has a valid passport.

REPLACING A LOST TOURIST CARD

You will be given a part of the form that the immigration official will tear off for you. Do not lose this small piece of paper. (Keep it in your passport or wallet.)

If this card is lost, stolen, or damaged beyond legibility, you will need to get it replaced before you leave. This is a tedious bureaucratic process, so avoid it at all costs. It is a good idea to make a copy of all your travel documentation (passport, tourist card, plane ticket, etc.) once you arrive, in order to make the process as easy as possible. You will need to go to the immigration offices at one of the airports in Oaxaca City, Puerto Escondido, or Huatulco with your passport and any other information that shows when you arrived in Mexico, such as your plane ticket.

The fee for replacing a lost tourist card is around US$40. If you are not close to an airport when you lose your card, and do not have too much time before you leave, it might be best to just sacrifice your last day to replacing your card. Again, this process could take a long time, so if you do it the day of your flight, make sure to get to the airport at least five hours before departure to ensure you don't miss your flight.

CUSTOMS

The customs process when entering Mexico from the United States, United Kingdom, European Union, Australia, and New Zealand is easy and streamlined. As long as you do not have the usual prohibited items (firearms, drugs, etc.), you should have no problem when entering the country. Things like food items could cause your bags to be searched and make the process take longer. For an extensive list of what you can and can't bring into Mexico, visit the **Foreign Relations Secretariat** website (https://consulmex.sre.gob.mx/reinounido); the list can be found with the information on entry requirements for foreign nationals.

After collecting your luggage from the baggage claim, you'll most likely pass through a gate where you're required to press a button to see if your bags will be inspected more closely. Get a green light, and you're good to go. Get a red one, and you'll have to wait a bit longer for them to search your luggage. Note that travelers flying in from a Central or South American country might be searched more thoroughly.

The general duty-free limits on goods brought from Mexico by country are as follows: United States, US$800; Canada, C$200; United Kingdom, £390; Australia, A$900; New Zealand, NZ$700.

The duty-free limits on alcohol by country are as follows: United States (age limit 21), 1 liter of alcohol; Canada (age limit 19), 1.5 liters of wine, 1.14 liters of hard liquor, or up to 8.5 liters of beer; United Kingdom (age limit 18), 1 liter of hard liquor, 2 liters of wine or beer; Australia (age limit 18), 2.5 liters of any alcohol; New Zealand (age limit 17), 4.5 liters of wine or beer, up to three bottles of liquor (max. 1.125 liters per bottle).

The duty-free limits on tobacco products by country are as follows: United States (age limit 18), 200 cigarettes or 100 cigars; Canada (age limit 21), 200 cigarettes, 100 cigars; United Kingdom (age limit 17), 200 cigarettes, 100 cigarillos, 50 cigars, 250 grams of tobacco; Australia (age limit 18), one open pack of cigarettes and one unopened pack of up to 25; New Zealand (age limit 17), 50 cigarettes or 50 grams of tobacco.

Bringing alcohol or tobacco may affect your overall duty-free amount. Check your government's customs website for specifics.

When exiting the country, stop by the immigration window. It's just a quick stop right before going through security. Sometimes you'll be processed out at the airline ticketing counter, but if not, they'll take care of you at the immigration window.

CONSULATES AND EMBASSIES

If you lose your passport or have an emergency, you will need to contact your government's consulate or embassy. The **US Consulate in Oaxaca City** (Alcalá 407; toll-free Mex. tel. 800/681-9374, 10am-3pm Mon.-Thurs.) is across the Andador from Santo Domingo.

Citizens of Canada, the United Kingdom, Australia, and New Zealand will have to contact their embassies in Mexico City. Their contact information is as follows: **Canada** (Schiller 529, Colonia Bosque de Chapultepec, Mexico City; tel. 555/724-7900; mxico@international.gc.ca; 9am-noon and 2:30pm-4pm Mon.-Fri.); **United Kingdom** (Río Lerma 71; tel. 555/242-8500; ukinmexico.info@fco.gov.uk; 8am-4pm Mon.-Thurs., 8am-1:30pm Fri.); **Australia** (Rubén Darío 55, Colonia Polanco; tel. 551/101-2200; embaustmex@yahoo.com.mx; 8:30am-5:15pm Mon.-Fri.); and **New Zealand** (Jaime Balmes 8, Colonia Polanco; tel. 555/283-9460; 9:30am-5pm Mon.-Fri.).

CAR PERMIT

If you plan on driving to Oaxaca, you will need to obtain a Mexico Temporary Vehicle Importation Permit (TIP), as well as a Mexican car insurance policy. The only institution that provides this permit is the national bank of the army called **Banjercito.** Banjercito has offices at border crossings, and can process your application when you arrive. You can also try to apply for the TIP online (www.banjercito.com.mx/registroVehiculos). The site is in both English and Spanish, but it sometimes doesn't work. Apply online at least 7-10 days in advance to allow time for the permit to arrive in the mail.

To obtain a TIP, you will need a valid passport, your driver's license, tourist visa, the original vehicle title as well as copies, vehicle registration, and proof of a Mexican car insurance policy. The fee for the permit is US$51 (US$45 online), and you will need to make a deposit of US$200-400, depending on how old your car is. Boats or RVs require a separate TIP. You'll find lots of detailed information about obtaining a TIP and buying insurance at **Mexpro.com.**

Your permit will be issued for as long as your tourist visa. This will be your most important document to hold on to in Mexico. Your vehicle can get confiscated without it, a process that could prove more difficult and/or costly than even replacing a passport.

Recreation

ECOTOURISM

Oaxaca is home to some of the best organized ecotourism organizations in Mexico. The megadiverse region of the Sierra Norte is the place to go to explore what both nature and the local cultures have to offer. These lofty peaks are home to more ecotourism centers than I have room for in this guidebook. The stars of the bunch are places like Ixtlán de Juárez, where the local organization Ecoturixtlán has activities both in and out of its ecotourism park just a few minutes out of town. Closer to the valley, the Pueblos Mancomunados are the most well organized in the state, probably in the country. I encourage visitors to take advantage of the guides and community workshops, to get to know the people and customs as much as the natural world.

A handful of more recently established tour agencies in Oaxaca City have begun to offer fun and culturally enriching tours of the Valles Centrales, as well. Instead of taking you through the main gate of an attraction so you can snap the required selfies to prove you've been there, these companies will have you hiking or biking through the valley to get there. They stop at rickety old highway comedores (restaurants), where the food is meant for Oaxacan palates, not simplified or made "safer" for picky tourists, or fused into hip new recipes.

Down on the coast, you'll find lots of bird-watching, sea turtle conservation, lagoon tours, and more. Destinations like Huatulco, Laguna Manialtepec, and the Lagunas de Chacahua are home to large and diverse avian populations that should be of interest to everyone from casual birders to professional ornithologists. Many agencies in Puerto Escondido offer tours to Laguna Manialtepec to see the bioluminescent phytoplankton that light up the water at night. Mazunte is the place to go to learn more about sea turtles and the local efforts to conserve their habitat. And La Ventanilla, just to the west of Mazunte, offers lagoon tours through crocodile-filled waters.

MOUNTAIN BIKING

Mountain biking in Oaxaca is very popular, and only growing more so each day. Agencies in Oaxaca City offer biking tours throughout the Valles Centrales, often combining them with cultural activities, such as stops at palenques (mezcal plantations) to learn about the process and taste the wares. Many of the ecotourism centers in the Sierra Norte, such as the Pueblos Mancomunados, offer mountain bike rentals and guides. Trails here range from wide, two-track mountain roads to rocky, expert-level single-track trails. There's something for everybody.

Down on the coast, don't miss the chance to take a bike through the Parque Nacional Huatulco, just to the west of the Bahías de Huatulco, the main tourist area. You can work up a sweat pedaling through the jungle, then cool off on one of the undeveloped beaches in the park.

With lots of trail maps, route testimonials, photos, and more, the Oaxaca-specific mountain biking website **OaxacaMTB.org** is the most extensive online resource for those who bring their own bike. If you don't bring your own equipment, don't worry, every rental and tour agency in this guide provides a casco (helmet) for riders.

During high season, you most likely won't be able to just walk into a tour agency and plan a mountain biking tour the next day. Make

The Sierra Norte's Communal Lands

Private property is forbidden by municipal law in many of the communities in the Sierra Norte. The trails you walk belong to everyone in the town; therefore, it is necessary to **check in with the local ecotourism office** (yes, in every new community you visit) and **pay a small entrance fee.** This fee is included in the price of cabañas and other accommodations (for which you'll have to pass by the office to check in anyway), but if you're just going to be in town for the day, stop in and pay the fee.

reservations well ahead of time with Oaxaca City operators. Even in lesser-visited areas, like the Sierra Norte, call ahead at least a few days to a week ahead of time to reserve, so that operators have time to get all the gear in safe, working order.

HORSEBACK RIDING

Through the company **Horseback Mexico** (Murguía 403, Oaxaca City; tel. 951/183-8768; www.horsebackmexico.com), you can do half-day, overnight, and weeklong rides in various locations throughout Oaxaca.

Lots of communities in the Sierra Norte also offer horseback riding. Take a ride from one town to another in the Pueblos Mancomunados. Call the communities' ecotourism offices well in advance to plan rides.

You can also trot through thick jungle and on the shores of rivers, lagoons, and beaches in Huatulco, Puerto Escondido, and Laguna de Manialtepec, on the coast.

SURFING, KAYAKING, AND BOAT TOURS

Your number one choice for surfing in Oaxaca is Puerto Escondido, where the beach break at Playa Zicatela is so powerful, consistent, and downright fun that Puerto is regularly in the top 10 of best surfing spots worldwide. Zicatela's waves are best left to the highly experienced and professionals, but the budding part of the beach called La Punta Zicatela has much milder waves for those learning the ropes. East down the coast, at Barra de la Cruz, you'll find a very consistent point break that curls slowly for hundreds of yards.

Farther east, in El Istmo de Tehuantepec, the town of Salina Cruz is home to a handful of very knowledgeable and experienced surf camps that take care of everything from accommodations to food to transportation to the almost two dozen varied and consistent waves between here and Huatulco. Salina Cruz is not as developed for tourism as Puerto Escondido, and there's not much else to do here besides surf, so it is better to plan a trip with the surf camps rather than just show up with your board.

One reason the sport is so popular here is because many places have long surf seasons in which wave conditions are perfect. A good online resource for finding when waves will be best is **Surf-Forecast.com.**

A couple of spots on the coast, such as Huatulco and Laguna de Manialtepec, offer sea and lagoon kayaking. This is an excellent way to see the mangrove forests of the lagoon and observe the flocks of seabirds that nest and feed there. And just about anybody with a boat on the beach will take you out to see dolphins or explore the secluded, undeveloped coves all up and down the coast.

SNORKELING AND SCUBA DIVING

Huatulco is the ideal spot on the coast to go snorkeling. The aquamarine waters of Playa La Entrega are calm and clear enough to see lots of tropical fish and other reef-dwelling creatures. Just be careful not to touch the corals. When the tide is low, there is only a few feet of water over them, and the effects of so many snorkelers and swimmers is apparent. Playa Puerto Angelito, in Puerto Escondido, is also calm and clear enough to observe sea life, but in general, the Pacific coast here is rough and murky.

Oaxaca isn't as ideal a destination for scuba diving, but there are a couple of options along the coast. Because of the often dangerous conditions of the water, I can't emphasize enough the importance of sticking to the dive centers listed in this guidebook (there aren't many others, anyway). Only centers that showed they follow PADI safety certifications have been included, and that they know where the good diving is. You'll find the best conditions in Huatulco.

As with diving anywhere, be insistent that all safety precautions are taken, and if something besides the ocean seems fishy, don't get in the water.

FISHING

When it comes to fishing, you really don't need a guidebook to find it on the coast. Go to a beach, and it'll find you. Fishermen have been pulling the catch of the day out of the Pacific up and down the coast for who knows how many generations. Just about any one of them who offers to take you out on his boat will know exactly what he's doing, but Puerto Escondido, Puerto Ángel, and Huatulco are the most popular destination for deep-sea fishing.

All fishing guides listed in this guidebook expressed a personal responsibility to adhere to responsible fishing practices. One in Puerto Escondido made it a priority to be vigilant on the water for illegal turtle fishing and educating his clients on the biology and conservation of this beautiful endangered species.

CLIMBING

There are a few great spots for climbing in Oaxaca, but the sport isn't practiced much here, and very few tourism agencies have the necessary equipment. If you come without your own, head to Ixtlán de Juárez, in the Sierra Norte, where there is climbing and rappelling in Parque Ecoturixtlán. The ecotourism center in Capulálpam de Méndez also has equipment and experienced guides for the cliffs outside town. These are not tall cliffs, and in these locations, climbing is more of a tourist activity than a serious sport.

The best spot for serious climbing is Apoala, in La Mixteca, where the cliffs tower as high as 600 m (1,970 ft) over the canyon floor. You will have to bring your own gear and experience with you, as the folks in town aren't climbers themselves, and they do not offer guides or equipment.

YOGA AND MEDITATION

Major tourist destinations in Oaxaca, such as Oaxaca City and Puerto Escondido, have lots of yoga studios and hotels that offer hatha, vinyasa, kundalini, and other styles of yoga, as well as meditation classes. But for full-on yoga retreats, there's no better place than Mazunte. If you really need to disconnect from the stress, worry, and technology of the daily grind, this is where to do it.

Food

For many travelers, the gastronomy of Oaxaca is so delicious, unique, and creative that it is reason enough to visit. Even within Mexico, Oaxacan cuisine is widely regarded as the best in the nation, causing Oaxaqueños and other Mexicans alike to emit yummy sounds when they talk about it. Oaxaca is truly an endless buffet for those in search of bold flavors, interesting recipes and cooking methods, and, of course, el picante (spicy food).

ANTOJITOS

Most of what the rest of the world thinks of as "Mexican food" is really just the tip of the iceberg. Tacos, quesadillas, and enchiladas belong to the subcategory of Mexican cuisine referred to as antojitos, or basically snack foods (don't get me wrong, they will fill you up) or fast foods, which is why you'll find so much of this on the street.

Many of the antojitos in Oaxaca aren't exclusively Oaxacan. There are lots of **tacos,**

tostadas, and **quesadillas** to be eaten here. As is Oaxaca's wont, however, they usually come with a regional twist that adds flavors distinct from other parts of Mexico. A simple quesadilla here will have a few leaves of the potent herb **epazote,** which, aside from the interesting flavor it lends to a dish, also helps reduce gasses during digestion (it is also often mixed in with beans). **Tortas,** or Mexican bread-roll sandwiches, are, in this author's obviously biased opinion, better in Oaxaca than in other parts of the country, as well.

Oaxaca also has a couple unique takes on the antojito. The most notable and most available statewide is the **tlayuda.** This overgrown monstrosity of a quesadilla (or tostada, depending on the cook's style) is the epitome of tortilla-based cuisine. The tortilla, also referred to simply as a tlayuda, is generally around 40 cm (16 in) in diameter, and usually a bit tougher than a regular crunchy tostada. Ingredients vary between cooks and regions, but they are most commonly filled or topped with meat, cheese, beans, lettuce or cabbage, tomatoes, avocados, and other veggies. A key ingredient, what sets the tlayuda apart from its sibling antojitos, is something called **asiento.** Asiento is what is left over after frying chicharrones (pork rinds), so vegans beware. (Don't worry. I don't eat pork, but tlayudas are just as tasty "sin asiento"—without asiento.)

Also unique to Oaxaca, but not as widespread, are the **garnachas** of El Istmo. Unlike their larger Oaxacan cousins, the tortillas for garnachas are small and stout. What sets them apart from other antojitos is that the tortilla is deep fried before the other ingredients are placed on top. When done right, the tortilla has a crunchy outer layer, but is still somewhat soft and pliable inside, and the light frying gives it a delicious flavor that complements the shredded beef or picadillo (ground beef with potatoes) and queso istmeño (a queso fresco, or "fresh cheese," from El Istmo). They are usually served with a tangy coleslaw that adds a fresh crunch to the greasy little things.

REGIONAL FOODS

Oaxaca's rugged landscape has kept communities more or less secluded for hundreds, even thousands of years. Because of this, people have had to work with what was close by, which in the gastronomical department means there are lots of regional dishes that one can only find in certain locations, despite the installation of highways in the 20th century that made travel between remote locations easier. This often makes eating here a full-on adventure, and not just one for the taste buds.

For example, you'll very rarely find the **chile de agua** outside Oaxaca City and the Valles Centrales, which means the chile relleno you order in the Mercado 20 de Noviembre, in downtown Oaxaca, will taste very different from one you order in the neighboring state of Puebla, which will most likely be a chile poblano. Don't leave Oaxaca City without trying one.

Places like the coast, El Istmo, and El Papaloapan in the north are renowned both state- and nationwide for their **seafood.** In these regions of Oaxaca, you can bet on the fact that the fish you ordered for lunch was caught that morning. Another great region for fish meals is the Sierra Norte, where countless trucherías (trout hatcheries) serve fresh trout in a number of tasty and interesting ways.

And then there's **mole.** Although the myth is that there are seven different mole recipes in Oaxaca, the truth is that there are so many nuanced regional recipes for the dish that the real number can't be counted. Chef Pilar Cabrera of the Oaxaca City restaurant La Olla once said that each tiny town in Oaxaca boasts at least one distinct mole recipe. One unique regional variation is the soupy, spicy **mole de caderas** (goat mole, literally, "mole of hips"), a recipe and tradition shared with the Tehuacán region of the neighboring state of Puebla. You'll only find this recipe, which uses the hip and spine bones of the goat and is made with the incredibly flavorful leaves of the avocado

Oaxacan Chile Peppers

Mexico's National System of Phytogenic Food Resources and Agriculture (SINAREFI) has counted 64 distinct chile pepper species that grow within the country's borders, making Mexico the nation with the most biodiversity of chiles worldwide. Oaxaca tops the list of states with 25 distinct pepper species that thrive in its deserts, valleys, mountainsides, and hot, humid tropical regions. Some can't be found outside Oaxaca, others are in danger of extinction. Some burn, others transform the soil into more dulcet tones. All are delicious. Here are a few you'll probably see a lot of, and a couple you might not.

CHILE DE AGUA

The chile de agua (water chile) is unique to the Valles Centrales. It's usually greenish yellow, and gets bright orange as it matures. These are what is used in all the chiles rellenos, and often in salsa de molcajete, a salsa made by grinding the ingredients in mortar and pestles made of igneous stone. Chile de agua isn't as easy to come by outside the Valles Centrales, so don't leave without trying one. They usually have a very mild spice.

CHILE PASILLA MIXE

Also called chile pasilla oaxaqueño, this species of one of Mexico's most complexly flavored chiles grows in the Mixe region of the Sierra Norte. When fresh, the pasilla is called chile chilaca. Growers smoke the peppers in wood-fired adobe ovens, and the cloudy days in the mountains don't fully dry them, so they are left in the oven longer than usual to finish the job. This puts the distinctive Oaxacan twist on a pepper whose flavor scuds from sweet to earthy to a distant spice behind it all, just like the clouds on the mountains where it grows. Like the chile de agua, you're only likely to find this pepper here in Oaxaca, primarily in the Valles Centrales and mountains to the north, so if you see it on a menu, say yes.

CHILE COSTEÑO

As you might guess from the name, you'll find lots of salsas on the coast made with the bright-red chile costeño, which usually has a mild spice to it. But terms in Oaxaca, and Mexico in general, can often be fluid and regional, sometimes used to refer to something different elsewhere. So if you see a yellow chile costeño, as they're called around the Jamiltepec region to the west, be warned that it can get pretty hot.

CHILE DE ONZA

This little firecracker, also grown in the Sierra Norte, is short and skinny, and usually packs a punch. Usually yellow, but sometimes flirting with reddish tones, this flame-colored pepper can get up to three times hotter than a jalapeño, so be careful.

CHILE TABICHE

This short, triangular pepper, mostly found in Miahualtlán and Ejutla, most often comes in a deep wine red. Fresh tabiches are used in salsas and mole verde. The dried peppers are used to make

tree, in La Mixteca, primarily in and around Huajuapan de León, and only mid-October-mid-November. The restaurant Tierra del Sol in Oaxaca City, which specializes in the cuisine of La Mixteca, also serves this dish at this time of year. You might also see it called huaxmole.

BEVERAGES

Oaxaca's most famous beverage (and my personal favorite) is hot chocolate, known here simply as **chocolate.** Rare will be the time that the comedor you're eating in will not have chocolate as a beverage option. When served hot, it is made with either dark-red salsa macha, a very spicy oil-based salsa with a pulp of dried peppers, herbs, and nuts that settles at the bottom.

CHILE ESCUCHITO

Also called chile paradito (standing chile) because the little dark-green conical pods grow sticking straight up off the plant. With a fire similar to chile serrano or chile de árbol, escuchitos are typically used in table salsas in Oaxaca City. In the tropical regions to the north, they are sometimes burned to create a smoke that repels mosquitoes, or in infusions that repel spiders, scorpions, and snakes.

CHILE CHILHUACLE

In Nahuatl, *chilhuacle* means "old chile." This moderately spicy pepper only grows around Cuicatlán, in the region known as La Cañada Chica, the low, arid canyon country to the west of the Sierra Mazateca. It is very rare and, as a consequence, quite expensive, as far as chiles go. Because of this, many of the dishes that traditionally include the chilhuacle will have chile guajillo as a substitute. If you are in La Cañada and find a plate that has this chile in it, do not miss your chance. If you're scouting the markets for them, the fresh ones are green, but they turn red as they mature. When dried, they turn a deeper wine red, and don't become wrinkly like pasillas or guajillos.

CHILE ACHILITO

This very rare chile pepper also only grows in La Cañada, tending to like the same conditions that favor the chilhuacle. It is generally used in dried form for salsas, or sometimes tossed whole into a batch of barbacoa de borrego (slow-roasted lamb barbecue). If you think you've had a hard time tracking down chilhuacles, you'll struggle even more to find achilitos. They are extremely hard to find, even in the communities where it is still cultivated, and not used often in restaurants.

CHILE GUAJILLO

Unlike the previous two, this pepper is by no means endemic to Oaxaca. You'll find it in states as far away as Jalisco and Colima, to the west. But you'll also find it a lot in Oaxaca, especially since it is used as a substitute in moles that traditionally call for the chilhuacle. This dark-red pepper, the dried form of a pepper called mirasol when fresh, is dark brownish red with a leathery texture. Although it tends to have a mild afterburn, it is usually sweeter than it is spicy, making it a great choice for those not accustomed to high amounts of capsaicin, the stuff that gives chiles their fire.

CHILE HABANERO

Like the guajillo, you'll find habaneros all over Mexico, and also in abundance in Oaxaca. Unlike the guajillo, however, the habanero is very spicy. Lots of salsas in Oaxaca, especially if they are orange, will have habaneros in them, so if you can't stand the heat, ask what's in the salsa before dousing your taco with it. It is also used as a condiment, usually sliced and mixed with sliced onions in vinegar. It comes in green and red, so be wary.

water (chocolate de agua) or milk (chocolate de leche), and you can also order it as a **malteada** or **chocomil,** what is generally referred to in the United States as chocolate milk. One of the things that makes Oaxaca so magical to me is that you don't have to wait until the holidays to have a hot chocolate. Here, you'll find the sweet, delicious drink year-round.

But simple hot chocolate or chocolate milk aren't the only drinks made with cacao here. Endemic to Oaxaca City and the Valles Centrales is the wholly Oaxacan drink **tejate.** Made with cacao, nuts, the seed of the

Pre-Hispanic Oaxacan Food

The Spanish influence on Oaxaca cuisine is clearly seen—or rather, tasted. They did bring the rice for the beans, after all, and without them, there'd be no beef for the mind-altering barbacoa en rollo of Zaachila, and no quesillo for the tacos, tlayudas, and quesadillas. However, if it weren't for the tendency of the Zapotecs, Mixtecs, Mixes, Triques, and the numerous other Indigenous peoples of Oaxaca to not let their culture and livelihood go down without a fight, the gastronomy here would be much less varied, creative, fun, and, most importantly, delicious.

The Spanish diet was part and parcel of the conquest, but the conquistadors' attempts to impose their European grub onto the native people of Mexico wasn't as successful as the political, linguistic, and religious components. The magnitude of the biodiversity here gave the creative cooks of pre-Hispanic Oaxaca much to work with, and a lot of what they prepared thousands of years ago is being made the same way today.

INSECTS

The practice of entomophagy (eating insects) dates back to, one would assume, the first time someone walked around this land and got hungry, the earliest signs of which are around 7,000 years ago. To this day, you can find women in the Mercado Benito Juárez and other markets all over Oaxaca with mounds of **chapulines** (fried grasshoppers) and **gusanos de maguey** (maguey worms) for sale. If your tlayuda is served the ideal way, it'll come with a side of chapulines, as well as a few piquant and uniquely flavored herbs like berroz, pipicha, and pápalo, and the seeds of the guaje tree, from which Oaxaca takes its name.

mamey fruit, and a flower called flor or rosita de cacao (which, funnily enough, is not actually the flower of the cacao plant), this foam-topped beverage may look strange at first glance, but don't let that deter you. It is absolutely delicious, and you won't find it anywhere in the world outside Central Oaxaca. One of the ingredients is the climate. Cool, dry conditions are needed for the ground petals of the flor de cacao to turn foamy and rise to the top, so you won't get this chance down on the sultry coast.

Other interesting drinks made with cacao include the **espuma** (literally, "foam") of Zaachila, and the **chocolate-atole** of Teotitlán del Valle and other communities in the Valle de Tlacolula. These are mixed with the corn-based drink called atole, a thick, sweet hot beverage sold on just about every street corner in the country.

The state's **coffee**-producing pride and joy is Pluma Hidalgo, in the Sierra Sur, and most of the coffee you try in the state will be from here. Pluma coffee is strong, with bold flavors and a heavy acidity, which, when roasted right (which it usually is), has the perfect acidic bite that doesn't overtake the other flavors in the brew. Other regions, however, such as the Sierra Norte and Sierra Mixe, as well as parts of La Mixteca, also have excellent coffee-growing conditions that tend to produce much milder coffees that don't come out as dark as the black gold of Pluma. No matter what kind of coffee you prefer, Oaxaca has a roast for you.

In regions like La Mixteca, the Sierra Norte, and El Istmo, you might have trouble finding espresso-based coffee drinks, as this is a relatively new way to prepare coffee here. Traditionally, and statewide, coffee is prepared in a large ceramic pot, a recipe called café de olla (pot coffee). This is usually a much weaker brew, but the Mexican form of brown sugar called piloncillo is commonly added to give it sweetness and make up for the lighter taste of the brew. It isn't always presweetened,

BEVERAGES

Women from San Andrés Huayapam, just north of Oaxaca City, have been passing down the recipe for the foamy, nutty drink **tejate** to their daughters since long before the town had either the Spanish or Nahuatl names it is known by today.

Chocolate was one of the items in the Mesoamerican diet that the Spanish actually had no desire to wipe out or replace. The English and Spanish word *chocolate* comes from the Nahuatl *xocolatl,* meaning "bitter water," and many chocolate companies today sell the addictively tasty stuff with chiles, honey, and other local ingredients used to flavor it centuries ago.

The sweet, viscous breakfast beverage **champurrado,** the corn-based drink atole flavored with chocolate, is likewise from before the conquest.

LOCAL FAUNA

People along the Coast and in El Istmo have likewise consumed local fauna, such as **iguanas, armadillos,** and **sea turtles** and their eggs, for millennia. The Afro-Mexicans of the Costa Chica serve these up, along with the fish, shrimp and mussels in fiery hot moles and spicy stews served up with boiled mashed plantains, reminiscent of West African culinary traditions.

CALDO DE PIEDRA

Probably the most interesting of pre-Hispanic dishes in Oaxaca is the caldo de piedra, a seafood stew cooked by dropping a fire-heated river stone into the broth and raw ingredients. Since the isolated town of San Felipe Usila, in El Papaloapan, was never conquered by the Spanish, the recipe has survived as it was thousands of years ago.

though, so I usually ask if it's already sweet (¿Ya está dulce?).

Anywhere you go in Oaxaca, especially in the mercados, you're sure to find a juguería (juice bar). In these stalls, you can find **fresh juice** made from the wide variety of tropical fruits that grow in this fertile region.

Oaxaca's most famous alcoholic beverage is **mezcal,** a distillate of the maguey (also called agave) plant. Mezcal is not exclusively Oaxacan. Other states, such as Michoacán and Jalisco (known for its tequila, a type of mezcal), produce quality mezcal, as well. The general consensus around the country, and world, however, is that palenqueros (mezcal producers) in Oaxaca do it best. Although you'll be able to find a bottle of the potent stuff anywhere in the state, the real mezcal-crazy region is the Valles Centrales, where conditions are best for the types of maguey used to make it. Other parts of Oaxaca, El Istmo for example, have high rates of alcohol consumption but tend to stick to beer, so if you are interested in tasting and learning more about mezcal, Oaxaca City and the surrounding communities are the places to do so. Mezcal culture in Oaxaca has more to do with flavors, culture, and production methods than with getting drunk. You don't shoot mezcal, you sip it.

PICNIC SUPPLIES AND GROCERIES

If you have dietary restrictions, are on a budget, or are just planning a picnic or asada (cookout), every single town in Oaxaca will have a mercado where fresh fruits, meats, cheeses, and other foodstuffs are sold daily. Since the best cooks in town tend to be in the markets as well, I've noted the markets in just about every town listed in this guide. (You can also find supermarkets such as Chedraui, Soriana, and Bodega Aurrera, but these are better for toiletries and odds and ends. The freshest, best-priced produce and meats are in the mercados.)

You'll find both organic produce and produce grown with pesticides, so take care in rinsing your fruits and veggies off thoroughly. Supermarkets and convenience stores here sell products you can mix with water to clean produce, but simple substances like lime juice or vinegar can be used, as well.

MEALS AND MEALTIMES

A staple of Mexican cuisine is what is called **comida corrida** (set meals, literally something like "food on the run"). This breakfast or lunch option will usually include a few courses, such as soup or pasta and a main dish, and an agua fresca. Also called agua de sabor, or in conversation, most often simply agua, these are juice-like drinks made with fresh fruit and immoderate amounts of sugar. If you want plain old water, you'll have to ask for agua natural. Most places that serve comida corrida close in the late afternoon, after the lunch rush.

Since the workday starts early for many Mexican folks, breakfast (el desayuno) is usually eaten quite early. For many people in Oaxaca, breakfast is just a cup of hot chocolate and a pan de yema (egg yolk bread served with chocolate). Egg plates, like huevos rancheros or chilaquiles, are on the whole called desayunos, but some folks will call them almuerzo, the word your Spanish textbook told you means "lunch." Some will call lunch either el almuerzo or simply la comida, the word for food. (Language is a very malleable thing in Oaxaca, used to suit hyperlocal needs for representation, and just when you think you're using the wrong term for something because people in one town call it one thing, you go to the next and everyone says the word you thought it was from the beginning.) Like many Latin American countries, lunch and dinner are generally later than those in the United States, Canada, and the United Kingdom. Dinner (la cena) is eaten much later as well.

Pay attention to the operating hours of restaurants, as in some places there are de facto rules as to when a certain cuisine is eaten. Many seafood places on the coast, for example, open at 8am and close by 8pm (or sooner). Tacos are more commonly available in the late afternoon until the wee hours of the night, though you shouldn't have problems finding them for lunch.

Accommodations

Take this as a disclaimer: The rates listed in this guide are an approximation of what you can expect to pay, more or less, when you come. Things like fluctuating exchange rates or changes of ownership or operational style may cause the prices to be different when you arrive. Do not argue for a rate quoted in the guidebook.

MAKING RESERVATIONS

Most of the year, you should be able to walk right into a hotel just about anywhere in Oaxaca and get a room. Even the busiest places in the state, like Oaxaca City, Puerto Escondido, and Huatulco, are pretty empty during low seasons, but if you have a specific hotel in mind, reserve anyway.

There are lots of great websites to get deals on hotels, but when booking online, keep the businesses in mind as much as your own vacation. I personally recommend booking directly with hotels. This will ensure they have your reservation. It may even be cheaper than the price listed online, plus it's a great way to practice your Spanish. Many hotels in Oaxaca City, Puerto Escondido, and Huatulco have English-speaking staff for booking rooms and other services.

You really shouldn't need reservations for regular hotels in regions like La Mixteca, the Sierra Norte, and El Istmo (except in May for El Istmo), but always reserve ahead of time for ecotourism options that include stays in

High Season in Oaxaca

Here's a quick rundown of the high tourist seasons in Oaxaca. If you're coming during these periods, book well in advance (i.e., months). Hotels in Oaxaca City book up months in advance for festivals such as Day of the Dead.

- **Late October and early November:** Day of the Dead
- **Late December and early January:** Christmas and New Year's
- **March/April:** Semana Santa, or Holy Week; very popular domestic tourism dates
- **May:** month with the most velas, traditional raging parties in El Istmo
- **July:** Guelaguetza, festivals in Oaxaca City and many other towns that celebrate local culture
- **July and August:** summertime!

If you want to **avoid the crowds,** May, September, and early October are the best months to come.

cabañas. This is more to ensure that the activities you want to do are ready when you arrive, but you never know. And you don't want to be stuck out of doors in these secluded communities.

And this may be an unpopular opinion, but if at all possible, avoid peer-to-peer rentals. Although convenient and giving the guise of supporting locals, peer-to-peer rentals have been pricing many local folks out of their own communities. Gentrification is a real and unfortunate reality in Oaxaca, as in many popular travel destinations in the world. Let's be pro-local travelers, and enjoy our vacations in ways that bring the least amount of harm.

HOTELS

Hotels in Oaxaca range from the basic to the unique and artsy upscale establishments owned by mezcal producers to five-star luxury beach resorts. You've got options here to suit whatever budget and traveling style you like.

When I describe a hotel as "basic," this usually means a bed, private bathroom, a fan, and sometimes TV and Wi-Fi, but don't bet on the internet functioning perfectly in out-of-the-way places like La Mixteca and the north. The best thing about hotels like this is the affordability of privacy. You can often get a private room and bath for less than US$25.

HOSTELS

The hostels listed are clean, welcoming, and social without being all-out nightly bacchanals. Most include at least a light breakfast, and many on the coast have full schedules of fun activities, like barbecues, social nights, language exchanges, and more.

CABAÑAS

The primary accommodations in the mountains are cabañas (cabins). In the higher altitudes, you can expect them to have a fireplace and your reservation to include a load of firewood. Many have potable water in the taps, so ask the manager when you check in. You can get a good idea of how nice a cabaña will be from the price.

Down on the coast, cabaña really means bungalow. Again, there is a wide range of cleanliness and amenities, from rustic shacks in the swampy areas to luxury hilltop villas with spectacular ocean views, balconies, internet, and more.

HOMESTAYS

For those looking to practice or perfect their Spanish, or to just meet amazing and friendly people and experience their unique culture, there is no better option than the homestay. Forcing yourself to use Spanish all day will increase your vocabulary (key to mastering a language) and get you accustomed to thinking and responding in Spanish. They usually include three home-cooked meals a day, as well. Can't beat that.

Some Spanish schools in Oaxaca City and Puerto Escondido offer homestays as part of their learning packages.

SHORT-TERM RENTALS

You'll find the most short-term rentals directed toward tourists in Oaxaca City and the popular destinations on the coast. Depending on the size, condition, amenities, and services offered, this could be the most affordable option for those spending at least a month in one location. You can expect to spend anywhere from US$400-1,500 a month, or more, depending on how luxurious you want your place to be.

You'll also find a lot of rooms for rent in non-touristy towns all over the state. If you're a DIY traveler like myself, and want to truly experience the daily life of a tiny Oaxacan city or town, keep an eye out for signs reading "Se rentan cuartos" (Rooms for rent). Deal directly with the property owner for rentals like this. Since these will be primarily targeting Oaxacan tenants, you can expect low rates. Just be aware that most of these come unfurnished and you get what you pay for.

GUEST RANCHES

The guest ranch option is one of the most limited here in Oaxaca. There is one just outside Oaxaca City that focuses on horseback riding. Down in the Sierra Sur, around Pluma Hidalgo, you'll find fincas de café (coffee plantations) that cater to tourists, offering tours of their coffee fields and other fun activities.

CAMPING

The fog-shrouded peaks of the Sierra Norte are the best places for camping in Oaxaca. Every ecotourism center listed in this guidebook has a camping option, some of which are more idyllic than others.

Lots of beach hostels in Puerto Escondido, Mazunte, and Zipolite offer space to pitch a tent, as well. And in Huatulco's Bahía Tangolunda, you can camp out in a small, jungly space between two gigantic five-star resorts, surrounded by huge populations of crabs, iguanas, and tropical seabirds.

I've heard of people just finding a secluded place on a beach somewhere on the coast and setting up a campsite there, but often with unwelcome results. Still, camping is much safer here than in the rest of Mexico, where it is often confined to fenced-in areas. Stick to the businesses listed in this guide, which offer the freedom of staying outdoors without feeling like a backyard campout.

HAMMOCKS

For the true budgeting beach lover, there is no more economic option than the hammock hung between a couple almond trees in the jungle—a practice that unfortunately is dying out. However, if people start to request it more, it will become more available again.

Obviously, this option is for those who travel very light and don't bring too many valuables. If you do have something of value you want to keep safe, you can always ask the hostel or hotel owner to lock it up in the office for you. The usual rate for a hammock is around 100 pesos (US$5.50), making this the cheapest way to beach bum it on the coast

Conduct and Customs

Oaxacans are very friendly people, and they respond well to friendly visitors. They like to laugh boisterously and have a good time. Be friendly with them in all your interactions, and you'll have a great trip full of memories of all the wonderful people you met here.

COMMUNICATION STYLES

This friendliness is apparent in your communication styles. It is customary in Mexico to wish someone "Buenos días" (Good morning), "Buenas tardes" (Good afternoon/evening), or "Buenas noches" (Good evening/Goodnight) before beginning a conversation, so always begin with one of these greetings, especially if you're going to make a request.

One of the main differences is that whereas English speakers tend to speak, and therefore think, in linear sequences (with a narrative-like beginning, middle, and end, even in everyday conversations), Spanish has a more cyclical pattern to it. Spanish speakers will often come back to a topic in a conversation that a linear-thinking English speaker assumes is finished. This is just a linguistic generality, and doesn't speak for how every Spanish-speaking person thinks and communicates, but the tendency is common enough that awareness of it can make it easier to keep up when learning the language.

BODY LANGUAGE

There really aren't any major differences in the meaning of body language in Mexico and countries like the United States, Canada, and the United Kingdom. The main one that I have noticed is the common gesture here for showing gratitude, which is to display the back of the hand with the fingers in rigid extension. It doesn't correlate directly with an offensive gesture from my culture, but it was slightly alarming at first, and did take a little practice for me to get accustomed to using it in social interactions. If it does take you aback, just remember that the person is saying "Thank you," and not threatening to slap you in the mouth.

One gesture that I find delightful is the use of the pointer finger in saying yes or no. When saying or meaning yes, make the tip of your finger "nod" a few times. To signify no, shake your finger back and forth, sometimes moving your whole hand.

TERMS OF ADDRESS

The same general politeness you would use at home in the United States or the United Kingdom is expected here in Oaxaca. For example, where you would say "Sir" or "Ma'am" back home, you'll say "Señor" or "Señora" here in Mexico. To address a younger woman you do not know, say, a waitress or girl in a vendor stall in the market, the diminutive "Señorita" is acceptable.

If you need to speak to a police officer, you can get their attention by saying "Oficial" (officer). You might hear people in casual conversation refer to the police as "poli," but do not say this directly to a police officer. It would be considered offensive.

When meeting a new person, it is customary and polite to say you're glad to meet them, so after introductions, give a genuine "Mucho gusto" to your new acquaintance to keep things cordial.

TABLE MANNERS

When it comes to mealtime in Mexico, politeness extends to strangers, and it is customary to wish that others at a restaurant enjoy their meal. When you both enter and leave a restaurant or food stall, wish the nearby diners a friendly "Buen provecho" (Enjoy your meal), and when others say this to you, it is polite to respond with "Gracias, igualmente" (Thank you, same to you).

Since a server's entire livelihood is not

wholly dependent on tips in Mexico, service can often be slower than foreign visitors would like. Just be patient if something takes longer than you'd like it to. One thing that ends up making wait times at tables longer than foreign visitors would prefer is the fact that servers in Mexico do not bring the check when they assume you are ready to go. This is considered rude here, like they are trying to kick you out. So when you're ready to head out, get your server's attention and say "La cuenta, por favor" (Check, please), or give them the writing-hand gesture that is more or less the international sign for this request.

On Mexican Time

One of the main cultural differences between Mexico and other countries, even Latin American ones, has to do with time. For example, the word *ahorita* (the somehow diminutive of "now") can mean anytime in the next two minutes to tomorrow morning. It is often joked that it can really mean "never." Arriving late for a party or dinner isn't always considered rude. So in general, it is best to know that you are on Mexican time and have patience.

PHOTO ETIQUETTE

Like most of us, Oaxacans doing everyday things like working or chilling in the park aren't too keen on having their picture taken without their knowledge or consent. No one wants to be considered a novelty when they're just doing what is normal to them. So in situations like this—say you want to take a picture of the woman selling chapulines (fried grasshoppers) in the market—it is polite to simply ask "¿Puedo sacar su foto?" (May I take your picture?) before snapping the shot. As for children, you always get their parent or guardian's permission first. This doesn't really apply, however, in public events where people are dressed up and out in public to show off their flashy, colorful costumes and other traditions. Revelers at calendas (parades) and other festivities are there for the show, and generally have no problems with their photos being taken.

Health and Safety

DON'T DRINK THE WATER

This may seem obvious to most travelers, but just about every pharmacy doctor in touristy areas will roll their eyes and tell you a story of a foreigner who thought his or her stomach was strong enough to take it. As a rule of thumb, stick to bottled water. If you're staying in one place for an extended period of time, the most economical option is to use a garrafón (20-liter hard plastic jug). After paying for a deposit (your rental may already have empty ones to use), you can take the empty jug to a convenience store and get a full one for cheap (about US$1). Or keep an ear out for the guy on his tricycle cruising the streets and shouting "¡Aguaaaaa!"

In some places in the Sierra Norte and Sierra Sur, potable water comes from clean mountain springs, and you can drink it straight out of the tap or hose. I've noted this where applicable, but always ask, just to be safe.

VACCINATIONS

There are no vaccine requirements for entering Mexico. However, all visitors to Oaxaca should make sure their routine vaccinations are up-to-date. Hepatitis A is a problem in Mexico, and travelers to any part of the country should have at least the first round of shots before entering. Hepatitis B is also recommended. If you're planning on going to more remote parts of the state, especially in tropical areas like the coast, El Istmo, and El Papaloapan, you should consider getting vaccinated for typhoid, dengue, and rabies. Also be aware that mosquitoes here can carry other diseases that do not yet have vaccines, such as zika and chikungunya, so don't forget bug repellent.

COMMON HEALTH PROBLEMS AND DISEASES

The most common stomach problem for visitors to Mexico is traveler's diarrhea, or what is jokingly called "Montezuma's Revenge" (even though the name of the Aztec emperor was actually Moctezuma). This is usually not caused by food prepared in unsanitary conditions, but simply because the stomach is coming into contact with a microbial environment it isn't used to. It usually isn't serious, though it can ruin a day or two of your trip. I recommend trying to wait it out for a day, and if it persists, go to a doctor.

If the problem persists longer, say you get sick every couple weeks for a couple months, it's possible you have a parasite, for which antibiotics obviously won't work. There are good one-dose, over-the-counter medications available in every pharmacy for this. Just ask for a desparasitante (antiparasitic). If you enjoy street food as much as I do, this information might come in handy.

HEALTH MAINTENANCE

To make sure that your gut bacteria are as strong and healthy as possible when you arrive, begin taking probiotics a month or two before your trip.

When you're down here, drink fresh coconut water as much as possible. It is naturally antiparasitic, and is also packed full of electrolytes to keep you hydrated. The small bottles of drinkable yogurt available in just about every miscelania (convenience store) are good for regulating your stomach bugs, as well (and quite tasty—my son always tries to sneak an extra two or three a day). The most popular and widely available brand is called Yakult. Drinking one a day can help prevent digestive problems. I also travel with activated charcoal tablets just in case I feel like I've eaten something funky.

Medications and Prescriptions

You should be able to find the same basic over-the-counter medications in pharmacies in Oaxaca that you can back home. Unless you prefer a specific brand, you shouldn't have to worry about bringing your own basic medicines with you. Mexican pharmacies will fill prescriptions from foreign doctors; just make sure that you have as much valid documentation as possible and that it is up-to-date. (There is a longstanding myth that Mexican pharmacies will just sell you whatever prescription medication you ask for without a doctor's note. This may have been true across the board long ago, but pharmacies are big business now in Mexico, and you may need paperwork in order to release the medication.) To save money, ask for the genérico (generic) version of the medication you are buying.

Birth control, both preventative and emergency, is available without a prescription in Mexico. In the pharmacy, ask for pastillas anticonceptivas (contraceptive pills). Condoms (condones) can be bought in any pharmacy and most convenience stores. The emergency contraceptive Plan-B is also called Plan-B here, but you'll have to pronounce the *B* in Spanish (beh). For these and other medications you think you will need while here, research online before you come to find out the equivalent Mexican brand, or at least know what the active ingredient's name is in Spanish.

BEACH SAFETY

The number one safety concern on the coast is the powerful Pacific Ocean. Take warnings about conditions seriously. Even skilled swimmers can get caught in an **undertow,** and undertows can exist even when the ocean seems relatively calm. Surfers, make sure your skill level and confidence are adequate for the waves you attempt to ride. And do not go swimming on Playa Zicatela, in Puerto Escondido—despite the world-renowned size and power of the Mexican Pipeline, lifeguards here still regularly have to pull out swimmers who thought they could hack it. If you just can't wait to take a dip, head to the calmer waters of Playas Marinero and Principal, right next to Zicatela.

As with any hot, tropical region, take the usual precautions to stay healthy. Bring sunscreen and stay hydrated, especially if you drink alcohol.

CREEPY CRAWLERS

Your biggest bug worry down here is going to be **mosquitoes,** which in Oaxaca are known to carry diseases like dengue, chikungunya, and zika (use bug repellent). Other insects here might be frightening in size or appearance but do not pose serious health risks. **Sand flies** on the beaches are a nuisance and often small enough to get through mosquito nets, so use bug spray if you don't want to itch for a few days.

Spiders, although very prevalent (and my personal nightmare fuel), are not a serious threat in Oaxaca, and shouldn't cause concern. The deserts of the Valles Centrales are a natural habitat for black widows and brown recluses, but you don't need to take any more precautions than checking your shoes before putting them on, or a towel hung outside to dry before using it. And this is really only a concern in rural areas or when camping. The rest of Oaxaca's spiders may look scary, but they generally won't bother you (unless you bother them), and if they do, their bite is similar to that of a mosquito. Take similar precautions with shoes and towels for **scorpions,** which are found in the warm regions of the deserts and the coast.

As for **snakes,** be aware that a species of coral snake endemic to Oaxaca lives in the tropical deciduous forests of the Pacific side of the Sierra Madre del Sur and the lowlands of the Istmo de Tehuantepec. A species of rattlesnake also lives in Oaxaca, primarily in the deserts of the Valles Centrales and the Valle de Tehuacán-Cuicatlán. Just be aware.

Very cheap accommodations, mostly in rural areas, might have **bedbugs.** Although they aren't known to spread diseases, their bites are itchy and irritating, so it is better to be aware. Check the mattress and bedframe for small, dark stains.

Finally, you may come across the dreaded **cockroach.** When you see them, it doesn't necessarily mean accommodations are filthy; they often come up through uncovered drains. Before going to sleep at night, if covers aren't provided, I lay something over the sink and shower drains and stuff a towel in front of the door if there's a crack.

MEDICAL SERVICES

The most widely available healthcare option is the consultorio medico (doctor's office) in many of the farmacias (pharmacies). These are adequate for stomach bugs, colds, the flu, minor injuries like small cuts or non-serious burns, and other maladies you'd go to a general practitioner for at home. A consult usually costs no more than US$3, and in some chains they're free, since they expect you to purchase the meds in the pharmacy next door. Private doctors, whose signs will also read consultorio medico, can also take care of these health issues.

For anything more serious you will need to go to a hospital. All the hospitals listed in this guidebook have 24-hour emergency rooms. Most hospitals in downtown Oaxaca, and those that see lots of tourists on the coast, have English-speaking doctors and staff. If you go to a pharmacy doctor, the visit will most likely be conducted in Spanish, so if you're not confident in your ability to communicate in the language, it's best to take a Spanish speaker with you.

INSURANCE

Since medical care is so affordable in Mexico, it isn't really necessary to take out a traveler's insurance plan, especially for short trips. If you have a medical condition that that

Oaxaca 911

Mexico uses the emergency telephone number 911 at the national level to connect people to police, fire, and other emergency services. In a situation where you need to think fast, try 911, but if it doesn't work, or the response time is too long, contact the local police department directly. In many small towns, this will be the agencia municipal, or local government offices in the center of town.

requires special attention and could affect you during your trip, however, it might be good to take out a policy. Many resources online state that if you feel you can afford medical expenses on your trip, it is best not to waste the money on insurance.

If your trip is longer than a few months, or if it involves physically risky activities like surfing, mountain biking, or rock climbing, you might consider taking out a policy. A top-tier global provider is **World Nomads** (www.worldnomads.com). On their website, you can choose your home country and select a plan that is right for your needs.

For the ultimate peace of mind, you can take out a policy with air ambulance provider **Medjet** (toll-free US tel. 800/527-7478; www.medjetassist.com). It's not cheap, but their network of hospitals and air ambulances can get you to the hospital of your choosing back home in case of serious medical conditions.

EARTHQUAKES

Oaxaca is a very seismically active part of the world, and it pays to know what to do in case of an earthquake. The most important thing to do in a seismic event is to remain calm. It might be harder than it sounds, but if you hear the alarm, take a deep breath, and think. Gas lines and appliances are very dangerous in these situations, so put out any flames around you, like stoves, candles, etc. Move away from windows that could break and other loose objects that could fall on you. If you can get to your hotel's Punto de Reunión (Meeting Point), make your way there in a calm, ordered fashion. During the actual shaking, however, moving through rooms of a house or being anywhere near an exterior wall is not recommended. The best thing to do is drop to your hands and knees so that the shaking won't knock you over. If there is a sturdy desk or table, scurry under it and hold on to a leg, prepared to move with the object, if necessary. If there is no such cover, make your way to an interior wall, away from windows and other objects that could fall on you, cover your neck and head with your arms, and wait out the quake.

There are certain myths about surviving a quake that aren't actually safe. The most enduring myth is that doorways are the safest parts of a house, but this is not the case. Neither is the "triangle of life" (crouching next to a piece of furniture in hopes that it will stop a collapsing wall) an effective or safe method. Although it is definitely the most terrifying possibility in an earthquake, total building collapse is extremely rare, and you are much more likely to be harmed by falling objects inside the house than the house itself.

DRUGS

Drugs such as cocaine, crystal meth, and heroin are illegal in Oaxaca. Marijuana use is against the law, as well. The consumption of **hallucinogenic mushrooms** is tolerated by the authorities in the towns of San José del Pacífico (in the Sierra Sur) and Huautla de Jiménez (in the Sierra Mazateca), due to their long-standing use in traditional medicine practices. A stipulation is that the mushrooms be collected, sold, and consumed within the communities. Flouting the stipulation could potentially jeopardize the de facto deals these communities have with the higher authorities, which would not be fair to the people who use the mushrooms religiously or medically, and who have gone through many troubles to preserve this aspect of their culture.

CRIME AND PERSONAL SAFETY

Crime against foreign tourists in Oaxaca is rare, but has been on the rise ever since the pandemic. But as long as you take the same general precautions you would elsewhere, you should not have a problem. Of course, flashy jewelry, iPhones, or other expensive-looking effects may make you a target, as they would anywhere, so leave this stuff at home. Things like nice cameras will not necessarily make you a target—just make sure to keep them on your person, and do not leave them sitting unattended in a public place. There is little chance that you will be violently assaulted for your belongings, but it's not unheard of. Just be aware of your surroundings, don't wander around late at night and keep an eye on your stuff.

As a rule of thumb, stay off the highways at night, unless you're in a bus or suburban. Do not drive your own car or a rental on the highways at night, as carjacking is a possibility and should not be underestimated.

Those familiar with other popular tourist destinations in Mexico, such as Cancún and Puerto Vallarta, will know about or maybe have experienced police trying to cheat or otherwise extract bribes from them. This is nowhere near as much a problem in Oaxaca as it is in other major tourist areas, but it has been known to happen in Puerto Escondido. Police in Oaxaca are generally friendly to tourists and will be polite and cordial with you, as long as you treat them with the same respect.

In general, treating people respectfully is one of the best ways to stay safe. You give respect to get respect. So stick to the Golden Rule, and you'll have a safe and fun trip to Oaxaca.

Practical Details

WHAT TO PACK

Pack warm clothing if you expect to spend some time in the mountains. Places like Cuajimoloyas and San José del Pacífico regularly get down to 5-10°C (40s F), so don't assume Mexico is all heat and pack nothing but shorts and T-shirts. You'll also want a jacket or sweater if you'll be traveling by bus or suburban.

Pharmacies here should have everything you can find in pharmacies at home, and can fill valid prescriptions. Bring extras if you take a harder-to-find medication, or prescriptions to refill while you're here

Sunscreen and contact solution are items that are likely to be more expensive in Mexico than back home. Make sure to buy these before coming here. Bug repellent is easy to find in pharmacies and supermarkets, with both chemical-based and those made with natural ingredients (like lemongrass) available.

MONEY

Currency

Mexico's national currency is the peso. Its symbol ($) is the same as US dollars, so don't freak out when you see that your hotel room costs $600 (about US$32). In bills, the peso comes in denominations of $20, $50, $100, $500, and the rarer $1,000. In coins, the peso comes in denominations of $20, $10, $5, $2, and $1. The smallest coins are worth $0.50, or 50 centavos (cents). Whenever possible, get change for your $500 peso bills, as they are nearly impossible to use in taxis, mercados, and smaller restaurants.

Exchange Rates

The prices listed in this guidebook are in the equivalent of US dollars at the time of research, during which the rate fluctuated between 17 and 19 pesos on the dollar. But given the capricious nature of the global economy, the rate could be totally different by the time of publication. Check the website www.xe.com for accurate and up-to-date exchange rates when planning your budget.

Changing Money and ATMs

A common question is whether it is better to change money at a casa de cambio (money exchange center) or withdraw from ATMs. It all depends on your personal banking situation. Check with your bank before coming to see what will be best for you. Some banks partner with Mexican banks so that you don't get charged international ATM fees, others reimburse fees, and some have more favorable exchange rates than others. A casa de cambio will charge a fee for the exchange, so depending on your bank's fee system, it might be better to stick to ATMs. That's what I do. And make sure to decline the conversion rate when the ATM gives you the option.

Because of bank fees, it makes more sense to take out larger sums of money. Just be careful doing so. Go immediately from the cash machine to your hotel and store what you don't need for the day in a safe place. For those who go the cash exchange route, be aware of the risk of traveling with so much cash on you, and prepare accordingly. Many hotels have personal safes in the rooms for storing money and other valuables.

Credit Cards and Tipping

Many hotels and restaurants in cities accept major credit cards, but cash is king in Oaxaca. Check your credit card provider's policy on foreign transactions. If it's high, use cash more than your card for purchases, so as not to rack up fees.

Tipping is not as common in Mexico as in the United States, Canada, and the United Kingdom, but as a foreigner, you're expected to tip. A tip of 10 to 15 percent is appropriate. Tipping when paying with a credit card is different from the process in the United States and Canada. Rather than swipe your card and return with a slip to sign that has a line for including the tip, the waiter brings a payment terminal to the table, and you will need to tell him or her how much you want to add as a tip. The easiest is to simply say, "Con el diez por ciento, por favor" (With 10 percent added, please). If they did an amazing job, switch out the diez for quince (15) or veinte (20) to show how much you appreciated the service.

COMMUNICATIONS

Phones and Cell Phones

Making Calls in Mexico

All phone numbers in Mexico have ten digits, the first two or three of which will be the area code, depending on the region. In Oaxaca, the area codes have three digits, as opposed to Mexico City, which has a two-digit area code and eight-digit phone numbers. Some of the numbers listed in this guide are cell phone numbers from Mexico City, but they have been presented in the three-digit area code format for consistency. All numbers listed that begin with 55 are technically Mexico City numbers.

With a Mexican cell phone number, all you have to do is dial the area code and number. Calling from landlines is a little trickier. To call another landline, dial 01 before the ten-digit phone number listed. The codes to call a mobile phone are 044 and 045, depending on the area codes of both numbers. If one doesn't work, try the other.

International Calls

The country code for Mexico is 52. If you're calling from a cell phone, you'll need to dial the plus sign (+) before the country code for the call to go through. This takes the place of the exit code, which you will need if calling from a landline. So the international call format is: + (or exit code), country code, area code, phone number.

If you're calling from the United States or Canada, your exit code is 011. The exit code for the United Kingdom is 00. Callers from Australia will use the exit code 0011, and those from New Zealand, 00. The exit code for all Central American countries is also 00, as is Mexico's. To call home from Oaxaca, use the same call format from the previous paragraph.

Cell Phones

Most populous places in Oaxaca have cell phone service, but don't count on it in the mountains or secluded stretches of highway. Check your roaming rates before you come. If you do need to have internet outside of Wi-Fi hot spots, and your roaming charges are high, you can get a SIM card (chip) at a **Telcel** outlet. You will need an official ID (preferably your passport) and a phone that allows you to use other cellular services.

I recommend downloading the phone and messaging app called **WhatsApp,** which is basically Latin America's exclusive communications tool. Many businesses here only use this app for calls and texts.

If your phone won't take another carrier's SIM card, you could just buy a cheap cell phone with a prepaid Mexican service plan. Although the racks at cell phone distributors are primarily filled with smartphones these days, they will still have a few old-timey button models for as low as US$30-40.

Internet Access

Just about every accommodations option in this guidebook is equipped with Wi-Fi internet; the exceptions have been noted. Internet is spotty in out-of-the-way places, such as in the mountains or lesser-touristed regions such as La Mixteca and El Istmo. If an internet connection is essential to your stay, make sure to check that it works before checking in to your hotel.

Since in-home internet service is relatively expensive in Mexico, many people here go to an internet café (ciber) to get online. They are not hard to find; there should be one close to a town's main square. They usually charge around US$1 per half hour.

Many towns, especially mountain towns, have opted for a central Wi-Fi connection that is usually based out of the main government building of the town. Local businesses will sell fichas, little slips of paper with sign-in information that give you a specified amount of Wi-Fi time. They are generally about US$1 per half hour. Some public places like parks and zócalos will have free Wi-Fi. Look for the network called "infinitum movil" and access the internet via your Facebook or email account.

Shipping and Postal Service

The Mexican postal service, **Correos de México,** is notorious for being a labyrinth of lost packages and envelopes. For anything more important than a postcard, I do not recommend using this service, especially if time is of the essence.

For important packages, I recommend using one of the international couriers, such as FedEx or DHL, the latter of which usually has slightly lower rates. Make sure to get a tracking number for your package. There's still a good chance it won't arrive on the exact day they tell you at the counter, but it will get there.

TOURIST INFORMATION

Places with the highest amounts of tourist traffic, such as Oaxaca City, Puerto Escondido, and Huatulco, have numerous tourist information booths in popular areas of town. In Spanish, they'll read Modulo de Información Turística, but they will most likely have information in English, as well. During high seasons in Oaxaca City, the Zócalo and Andador Macedonio Alcalá are crawling with English-speaking representatives from both the state and municipal tourism agencies.

Just about everywhere else in the state, head to local government offices to find tourist information. They are always located by the main square, either called a plaza (or jardín) central, and the offices will either be called the H. Ayuntamiento, or the presidencia (or agencia) municipal. Small towns without the resources to support a full-fledged tourism office, many of which are communities that have prohibited the private ownership of property, will coordinate tourism activities out of the oficina de bienes comunales (office of communal properties). These and other government offices usually close 2pm-4pm (-ish) for the siesta, so try to get there in the morning or late afternoon. These are usually quite sleepy communities, so don't be surprised if no one is in seven outside the siesta hours. You might have to ask in another office and spend a bit of time tracking down the right person.

Traveler Advice

OPPORTUNITIES FOR STUDY AND EMPLOYMENT

Studying Spanish in Oaxaca is high on my list of recommended activities here. Visiting Oaxaca is an incredible experience no matter how you do it, but being able to communicate with these kind, intelligent, funny, and infinitely surprising people takes the experience to another level.

Spanish schools in Oaxaca City offer everything from individual classes to weekly and monthly courses to packages that include accommodations, one-on-one instruction, travel planning, and loads of fun cultural activities like dance and cooking classes. Research schools thoroughly. Here you'll find something for all learning types. Some schools have a more traditional classroom style, some only offer one-on-one tutoring, while many focus on immersive, hands-on instruction. Your afternoon class could be something like a trip to the market, where you're in charge of communicating with vendors to buy the ingredients you'll need for the cooking class later. Puerto Escondido is another great place to consider learning Spanish. Schools here also offer immersive learning packages, which, of course, include classes on your board in the waves.

Alternatively, if you've already got a good base of Spanish, and just need to put it into practice, consider a homestay.

The most widely available (legal) employment for foreigners is teaching English. If Oaxaca hooks you as it has done me, teaching English is an excellent option. Immerse yourself in a community, force yourself to speak Spanish daily, and get to know this vibrant and varied culture more deeply than a vacation will allow. Look for universities belonging to the statewide system of higher learning institutions called **SUNEO** (Sistema de Universidades Estatales de Oaxaca; www.suneo.mx). There are SUNEO campuses in Huajuapan de León, Tuxtepec, Huatulco, Puerto Escondido, and many other parts of the state. Most have English departments. You could try looking for a position on **Idealist.org**, but if you don't see any posts there, you can contact the universities directly.

If the classroom isn't your kind of place, you could always try the classic working at a beachside hostel for room and board. This usually depends on luck, whether or not a place needs help, your level of Spanish, etc.

ACCESS FOR TRAVELERS WITH DISABILITIES

Although accessibility in Oaxaca, and Mexico in general, is not as universal as in countries like the United States, Canada, and the United Kingdom, travelers with disabilities shouldn't let that deter them from coming to experience what this place has to offer. Airlines and a good deal of hotels in Oaxaca City and on the coast are very accommodating to travelers' needs. Very few buildings, however, aside from large beach resorts, have elevators. The colonial architecture of Oaxaca City can present a challenge to those in wheelchairs, but the majority of street corners in the Centro have curb cuts, so mobility is possible.

It is against the law in Mexico for airlines to discriminate against people with disabilities, so you can expect the same accessibility options as in the United States, Canada, the United Kingdom, and elsewhere.

A good online resource for US travelers with disabilities is **Mobility International USA** (132 E. Broadway, Ste. 343, Eugene, OR 97401; tel. 541/343-1284; www.miusa.org). They can provide destination-specific tips, and also organize cultural, educational, and professional development exchange programs.

In the UK, travelers with disabilities can contact the friendly and experienced staff at **DisabledHolidays.com** (163-167 King St., Dukinfield, SK16 4LF; tel. 0161/260-2218). They can arrange flights, hotels, travel, and more, and guarantee accessibility in all the services they arrange.

For more information on accessibility in Oaxaca, contact the folks at **Piña Palmera** (Playa Zipolite; tel. 951/584-3147; www.pinapalmera.org; 9am-2pm Mon.-Fri.). For over three decades, they have worked to increase social awareness and inclusion and offer skills training to people with physical and mental disabilities in the rural communities of the coast and Sierra Sur. They accept donations and offer volunteer opportunities to those who want to support their very important work.

TRAVELING WITH CHILDREN

Oaxaca is a safe and enjoyable place for those traveling with children. Oaxaqueños love children, and have shown nothing but kindness to my kiddos (I'll never forget the woman we were sitting next to on the bus who shared a slice of cake with my son who was wailing about something or another). There are lots of fun cultural activities for them in Oaxaca City and the Valles Centrales, such as workshops on painting alebrijes (painted carved wooden figures) or making traditional Oaxacan chocolate. You could take them to the Árbol del Tule and have them name the shapes they see in the gigantic tree's trunk. The pyramids at Monte Albán and other sites are some of my daughter and son's favorite places to explore. But if your kids are anything like mine, they'll be content with just eating cup after cup of nieve, running around the zócalo, and playing with kids at the park.

I also recommend the ecotourism centers in the Sierra Norte for travelers with kids in tow. You might feel like a kid yourself exploring the cloudy peaks and endless trails in places like Ixtlán de Juárez and the Pueblos Mancomunados. Feeding the deer in the Pueblo Mágico Capulálpam is an experience my children will never forget. Most ecotourism centers have a zip line, and many have obstacle courses that look like a lot of fun for both children and parents.

It goes without saying that the beach is a kid's ultimate playspace. The beaches of Playas Entrega and Maguey in Huatulco and Carrizalillo, Manzanillo, and Angelito in Puerto Escondido are favored among families for their calm, shallow waters. Oaxaca's beaches offer snorkeling, giant inflatables in the shape of unicorns and flamingos, and even surf lessons tailored just for kids. As beautiful as the beach is, it's not without its dangers, especially for kiddos. I know it goes without saying, but stay near your kids and always keep them in sight. Opt for swimsuits bright colors that stand out in the aquamarines and turquoises of the ocean, like pink and orange. The sun can be brutal, so make sure kids are wearing rash guards and (preferably reef-friendly) sunscreen. Keep your kids hydrated with fresh coconut water.

It may be a hard sell to a kid who just started summer vacation, but learning Spanish is a great option for children. The earlier a child is exposed to a second language, the easier it will be to learn it. My daughter's Spanish is so good from her early exposure, she is my family's de facto translator! So many schools offer fun, hands-on, immersive instruction, so it won't be like going back to school while on vacation.

Every town in Oaxaca should have a good doctor, in case the children get sick. Basic stuff like stomach problems and colds can be taken care of at pharmacies with an attached doctor's office (consultorio médico). If you can't seem to find one, you can ask a local store owner or the nice older folks relaxing outside their homes, "¿Dónde hay un doctor/médico?"

If your kiddos are a little less excited than you to try mole, luckily there are options for, ahem, selective eaters. Chicken soup (caldo de pollo) is as Mexican as the taco, and you should be able to find it anywhere. A standard cheese-and-tortilla-only quesadilla is always a good option for satisfying a picky youngster. Simple memelas of "solo frijol y queso" (only beans and cheese) are my kids' go-to. Tasajo is a thin, soft, and tasty cut of beef that I've ordered many a time to accompany fresh tortillas. Hamburgers, hot dogs, and pizzas are also popular enough in Mexico to make them easy to find. If they are daring, try the salsa first, before putting it on their food. Sauces can get pretty spicy down here. When all else fails, the array of tropical fruits never fail to please.

WOMEN TRAVELING ALONE

Oaxaca is a safe enough place for women traveling alone. That said, harassment toward women both Mexican and foreign is common, mostly taking the form of whistles and piropos (catcalls) directed at women in the street. This is not to say that every single Mexican man is going to treat female travelers this way, but the chances of it happening are high, especially for women traveling solo (and more so in areas not as accustomed to foreign tourists).

The chances of physical violence against female travelers is very low. Violent attacks against foreign tourists in general, although not nonexistent, are rare. Practice the same caution you would at home. Be aware of your surroundings, and make that awareness apparent in your comportment.

SENIOR TRAVELERS

Being the popular snowbird's paradise that it is, Oaxaca City is no stranger to senior travelers, and it is very welcoming to tourists of the tercer edad (senior citizens; literally, "the third age"). Destinations on the coast like Puerto Escondido and Huatulco are also popular with senior travelers.

Tour agencies in Oaxaca are extremely accommodating and will customize tours to fit any ability level. Check with them to see how they can create a trip that best suits your interests and needs.

LGBTQ TRAVELERS

Oaxaca is open and welcoming to LGBTQ travelers. Same-sex marriage has been legal in Oaxaca since 2019 and you can find queer-friendly hotels, restaurants, and bars throughout the state. You may encounter curious stares in smaller communities, but by and large, you shouldn't have any problems.

Although tourism in general is less developed in El Istmo, the culture of muxes, the third gender widely accepted in that region, is of interest to LGBTQ travelers, and some newer hotels are beginning to target their services toward this traveler group. Zipolite on Oaxaca's coast is also well known for its vibrant LGBTQ scene.

There are lots of great Oaxaca-specific online resources for LGBTQ travelers. The "Gay Oaxaca Guide" at **QueerInTheWorld.com** has extensive information on hotel and nightlife options in Oaxaca City. Another excellent resource for Oaxaca and Mexico at large is **GayMexicoMap.com.**

BIPOC TRAVELERS

As a Black woman, I've found Oaxaca overall to be a delightful place to live and travel in. One reason my family was attracted to Oaxaca was its heavy Afro-Mexican presence on the coast in areas like Chacahua (which you absolutely must visit!). But being in Oaxaca is often an exercise in stamina for the introvert in me. My hair, often styled in an afro or braidout, is the object of admiration and much attention. If you wear your hair in a 'fro, in locs, or any other style not too often seen in Oaxaca, expect to hear appreciative exclamations of "Que bonito!" and more often than not, hands reaching out to touch.

Even though Oaxaca is culturally diverse, if you are Black or of Asian descent, you're going to stand out and get lots of attention. Don't be surprised if people want pictures of or with you (feel free to smile and say "No gracias" if you feel uncomfortable). Mexican culture is a bit more blunt in identifying people than folks from the US, Canada, or the UK are used to. If someone is on the bigger side, they're called Gordo. Light-skinned people are guero or guera. If you're Black, you may be referred to as moreno/morena, and if you're Asian, be prepared to hear chino (I know, I know)—Black folks with visibly curly hair are called chino, too. It can be a bit off-putting, but nothing offensive is meant by it.

Though my experience has been largely positive, xenophobia can, unfortunately, be found in all corners of the globe. Migration from Central America and island nations like Haiti has caused an uptick in anti-Blackness. If you're coming from the Global North, your privileged passport will largely protect you from any microaggressions, but on the chance you encounter anything less than stellar service, don't be afraid to speak up. I've always found situations like these to be rectified immediately.

Resources

Glossary

abarrotes: groceries, grocery store
Adoquín: paved pedestrian street, in places like Puerto Escondido and Zipolite
agua de sabor: highly sweetened fruit juice-based drink, also called agua fresca; often served with set meals called comida corrida
aguamiel: the sweet sap of the mature maguey plant
¡Aguas!: Watch out!
alegrías: literally "happinesses," these are sweet snacks made from amaranth, peanuts, cranberries, and other fruits and nuts; commonly sold by street vendors
alebrije: brightly painted carved wooden figures of fantastical creatures, made primarily in Arrazola and Tilcajete
alfarería: pottery
amarillo: literally "yellow," but in Oaxaca is a type of sauce used as filling in empanadas; the best are in San Antonino Castillo Velasco
andador: pedestrian walkway
antojitos: Mexican snack foods (e.g., tacos, tortas, quesadillas)
arte popular: folk art
artesanías: handicrafts
artesano, artesana: folk artist
asiento: the sediment of pork lard collected after frying the meat; used in tlayudas and memelas, it is the flavor that sets them apart from tacos, quesadillas, huaraches, and other antojitos
atole: thick, sweet, corn-based drink served often with breakfast and sweet breads
autopista: expressway
ayuntamiento: town council
balneario: swimming hole usually formed from a mineral spring or other natural water source, developed into a fun aquatic center
barbacoa: pork, lamb, goat, or sometimes beef (in Zaachila) barbecue; slow-roasted in an earthen oven for up to eight hours
barrio: neighborhood, unofficially; officially neighborhoods are called colonias
barro: mud or clay; in the context of folk art, the type of clay used in ceramics, e.g., barro negro (black clay) and barro rojo (red clay)
berros: watercress; often served with tacos and tlayudas
bienes raices: real estate
bola: small crowd of people
boleto: ticket, for bus, plane, admission, etc., but not a traffic ticket (multa)
bota: boot
bote: can refer to a small boat, and also a trash bin (bote de basura)
caballero: gentleman
cabaña: cabin
cabecera: town that is the seat of a municipality
cabrón: literally "cuckold," but used both derisively and affectionately among friends
cacique: chief of a señorío (pre-Hispanic chiefdom), and still used today for head elders in communities
café de olla: coffee made in a big clay pot; a staple of comida corrida meals, and usually seasoned with piloncillo
calavera, calaca: words for the skulls used to decorate altars and homes during Day of the Dead
calenda: riotous parade with costumes, danc-

ing, and live music; celebrates everything from university graduations to cultural festivities

caminata: hike

camionera: bus station

camioneta: covered pickup truck used to transport people and cargo colectivo style

campesino: farmworker

canasta: type of woven basket with a handle

canasto: bigger basket, like a hamper

cantera: literally, quarry, but used in Oaxaca to refer to the stone itself; many colonial buildings in Oaxaca City are made of cantera verde, green limestone

casa de huéspedes: guesthouse

cascada: waterfall

cecina: a tasty cut of pork; cecina enchilada is the cut marinated in red chiles and other seasonings

cempasúchil: Mexican marigold; the primary decorative flower for Day of the Dead

centro de salud: medical clinic

champurrado: corn-based drink similar to atole but flavored with chocolate

chapulines: grasshoppers; cooked with chiles, lime, garlic, and other ingredients, they are a common snack in Oaxaca

charro: horseman, or cowboy; also used to refer to the outfits worn by mariachi musicians

chicatana: a species of flying ant used seasonally in Oaxacan cooking

chilena: musical style popular on the coast near the border with Guerrero, takes heavy influence from a musical genre called cueca, brought to the Oaxacan coast by Chilean sailors in the 19th century

chingón: cool, really good

Churrigueresque: highly ornate baroque Spanish architectural style popular in the late 17th and early 18th centuries, used to decorate many of the Dominican churches in Oaxaca

Cocijo: Zapotec god of lightning, thunder, and rain; also referred to as El Rayo, or Lightning Bolt

colectivo: literally "collective"; used to describe various modes of public transport, such as taxis, camionetas, and subúrbanes; as opposed to viaje privado or especial (private or special trip)

colegio: preparatory school

colonia: official administrative neighborhood denomination

comal: flat ceramic griddle used to cook tortillas, eggs, and other foods

comedor: small, family-run restaurant serving set meals called comida corrida

comida casera: home-cooked food

comida corrida: set meal in a comedor, usually includes a few courses, such as soup or pasta and a main dish, and an agua de sabor

compadre: buddy, mate, pal

comparsa: group of musicians, dancers, and revelers in the parades called calendas

comunal: communal; much of village life in Oaxaca is communal, from event planning to administration to landownership

correo: mail, post office; also, informally, email

crucero: highway intersection

Cuaresma: the Catholic observance of Lent

cuota: toll

curandero, curandera: traditional medicine man or woman

dama: lady

desviación: another term used for a highway junction in some regions, most notably the junction of Highways 190 and 125 in La Mixteca

día de plaza: weekly market, also called a tianguis or simply mercado

Domingo de Ramos: Palm Sunday

ejido: communal farming system

empanada: baked hand pies filled with savory or sweet fillings; empanadas de amarillo are a unique Oaxacan food

enramada: word used in El Istmo for wood and palm-thatch huts, called palapas elsewhere

epazote: a piquant herb used often in Oaxacan cuisine, primarily in beans for its gas-reduction properties

espuma: literally "foam," but in Zaachila, a foamy chocolate-based beverage

expendio: store

farmacia: pharmacy

fiesta patronal: festival to honor a patron saint

finca: farm, ranch, plantation, especially for coffee in Oaxaca

flor de terciopelo: common name for the velvety, fuchsia cockscomb flowers used widely in Day of the Dead decorations

fonda: food stall in a market

fraccionamiento: housing subdivision

gasolinera: gas station, petrol station

grabado: print made from woodcut, linotype, acid etching, or other various carving methods

gringo: slightly offensive term to refer to citizens of the United States of America

grito: shout, or impassioned exclamation, as in the Grito de Dolores by Father Miguel Hidalgo, which sparked the War of Independence

guero: light-skinned person, but not offensive, as some often take it to be; Mexicans will call other light-skinned Mexicans guero

guías: the stems and leaves of various squash and chayote plants; this is a homonym for the word for "guides," but don't worry, your sopa de guías is not made of tour guides

hacienda: large ranch

hamaca: hammock

hojalata: tinplating; material used in a popular folk art in Oaxaca

hongos: literally "fungi," but used to refer to the mushrooms themselves; most often, but not always, hallucinogenic mushrooms

huarache: sandal; also, an antojito similar to a taco but bigger, named as such due to the tortilla's resemblance to the floppy footwear

huipil: traditional embroidered blouses or dresses, of which Oaxaca boasts many distinct styles

huitlacoche: tasty edible fungus that grows on corn; served on quesadillas and other antojitos

indígena: Indigenous person

jejenes: small sandflies that live in coastal wetlands; they bite and are often small enough to squeeze through mosquito nets

jícara; jicarita: calabash squash, and the bowls made from their dried shells; the smaller ones (jicaritas) are often used to sip mezcal

juguería: juice bar that usually sells tortas and other antojitos, as well

laguna: lagoon

lancha: small motorboat

licenciado: bachelor's degree; also used as a generic term for a professional person

machismo; macho: hyperbolic and toxic masculinity; a man who has this perception of himself and his manhood

maguey: succulent from which mezcal is made; generally called agave elsewhere in Mexico

mal de puerco: the sleepy feeling you get after a big meal; food coma or "the itis"

mañanitas: "Las mañanitas" is the song sung on a person's birthday in Mexico

mano: hand; also the pestle used to grind corn and other grains on a metate

marmotas de calenda: in the street parades called calendas, the marmotas (literally "marmots") are the large white globes sporting the name of the comparsa (group celebrating)

marquesitas: rolled crepe desserts originally from the Yucatán filled with cream cheese, jams, or cajeta (caramel spread); a common nighttime street snack in Oaxaca City

mayordomía; mayordomo: social system in which a person or group of people are chosen to fund and organize a local festival; the person chosen to organize the party

me enchilé: literally "I chilied myself"; said when you've had too much spicy (picante) salsa

memela: flat tortilla-based antojito topped with pork lard, salsas, cheese, and sometimes meat

mercado: market

mestizo: a person of mixed Spanish and Indigenous descent

metate: slightly concave grindstone made of igneous stone

mezcal: distillate of the baked hearts of the maguey plant

milagro: miracle; also a small religious icon offered at a saint's altar to accompany a prayer request

milpa: cornfield or the crop itself

mirador: lookout point

molcajete: bowl-shaped mortar and pestle made of igneous stone; the popular style in Oaxaca is carved to look like a pig

mole: from the Nahuatl word *mulli,* meaning "sauce" or "stew"; represents any one of an almost infinite number of complex sauces served with chicken, pork, or other meats or vegetables; the most well-known is mole negro (black mole), which includes such interesting ingredients as chocolate and ground-up, burnt-to-a-crisp corn tortillas

monos de calenda: in the street parades called calendas, the monos are the large puppets of men and women operated by dancing partygoers inside

mordida: little bite; slang word for a bribe; also shouted at birthday parties to egg on the guest of honor to take a bite directly from the cake, although it is widely known that someone is going to shove their face in it

moreno: a dark-skinned person of any nationality

mototaxi: a small, covered, three-wheeled vehicle with seating for two or three, used for transportation over short distances, such as within a town or to and from a highway to a nearby town

muxe: a person belonging to a third gender of men raised as women, who take on the social, economic, and labor roles of women in the Zapotec communities of El Istmo

Nahuatl: the language of the Aztecs

nanche: small orange fruit popular in Oaxaca with an interesting flavor

ofrenda: an altar in a home, business, or public space that honors the memory of loved ones who have passed on during the Day of the Dead; common decorations are marigolds, candles, skulls, and the favorite snacks of the deceased

olla: ceramic pot

padrino, padrina: godfather, godmother

palapa: wall-less wooden shack covered with a palm-thatch roof; popular on the coast as beach restaurants or simple structures for shade

palenque: distillery

palequeta: a candied peanut bar usually sold by vendors who sell alegrías and other snacks on the street

pan: bread

panadería: bakery

panteón: cemetery

pápalo, pipicha: common regional names in Oaxaca for a type of pigweed, or amaranth, of which the stems and leaves are served with tacos and tlayudas, especially in La Mixteca

Pascua: Easter holiday celebrated the week proceeding Easter Sunday; schools get this week off too, so always make reservations during the two-week Semana Santa/Pascua holiday

periférico: highway that bypasses a dense urban area; called a business loop in the United States

petate: woven palm-frond mat used for various household tasks

piciete: strain of tobacco (*Nicotiana rustica*) endemic to Mexico that is cultivated in the Sierra Mazateca; sometimes called Aztec tobacco

piloncillo: super-concentrated brown sugar made from boiled sugarcane, used to sweeten café de olla and various candies; goes by names like panela, papelón, pepa dulce, and many more in other Spanish-speaking countries

piñata: papier-mâché figure, usually human, animal, or pop culture character, filled with candy and whacked with sticks by blindfolded birthday partygoers to get to the sweets

plan: political manifesto, generally written and submitted by leaders of political parties or factions vying for power

Porfiriato: the 34-year dictatorship of Porfirio Díaz, which began in 1876 and ended with the Mexican Revolution in 1910

posada: the nine-day celebration leading up to Christmas, December 16-Christmas Eve; parades, parties, religious processions, and lots and lots of eating commemorate Mary and Joseph's trip to Bethlehem, where Jesus would be born

pozahuanco: an Indigenous female garment used like a skirt or dress, primarily in La Mixteca; generally striped with deep cochineal red, indigo blue, and purple

pozole: a hearty stew made with hominy and usually pork, but sometimes beef or chicken, served with shredded lettuce, radishes, oregano, and chili powder

presidencia municipal: the main government or town elder council offices of a town, almost always located beside the main square; also called the palacio municipal, or the H. Ayuntamiento (Town Council; the H stands for "Honorable")

pueblo: town, village

puente: bridge; also used to refer to a three-day weekend

pulque: alcoholic beverage made by fermenting the sap (aguamiel) of a mature maguey plant

quesillo: Oaxacan string cheese with a pleasing tang; perfect for melting right on the griddle

retablo: altarpiece, retable

retorno: highway turnaround

sal de gusano: worm salt; made with the worms that grow in the hearts (piñas) of maguey plants, and served alongside orange slices with glasses of mezcal

Semana Santa: Holy Week, celebrated the week preceding Easter

son istmeño: literally "sound of the Isthmus," this distinct musical genre is the accompaniment for the three-day parties of El Istmo, called velas

suburban: the main mode of interurban transport in Oaxaca, a 12-15-passenger van

taller: workshop for printmaking, ceramics, alebrijes, or other arts

tambora: lively bass brand that provides the tunes for the calendas (parades); named for the large bass drum called a tambor

tapete: rug; the weavers of Teotitlán del Valle, Santa Ana del Valle, and other communities are known for their colorful tapetes de lana (wool)

tasajo: a thin cut of beef for tacos, tlayudas, and other meals

tejate: foam-topped pre-Hispanic drink that originated in San Andrés Huayapam, just north of Oaxaca City; made with a number of interesting ingredients, it has a delightful nutty/chocolatey flavor, but is also sometimes flavored with coconuts

telar: loom

temazcal: traditional indigenous sweat lodge; a primary medicinal treatment for a number of ailments in Indigenous communities

tenate: woven palm-frond baskets, sometimes brightly colored, used for storing tortillas, fruits, or grains

tepache: an alcoholic beverage made from the fermented juice of pineapple skins and piloncillo

tianguis: street market; in Oaxaca, where some have run weekly for thousands of years, the market day is usually called día de mercado or día de plaza

tienda de campaña: camping tent; also called a casa de campaña

tlacoyo: an antojito made of a thick, usually blue corn tortilla, filled with beans or cheese and topped with nopal (cactus), queso fresco, and salsa

tlayuda: the paragon of tortilla-based gastronomy, this large quesadilla or tostada-shaped antojito is topped with asiento (type of pork lard), meat, veggies, cheese, and other ingredients; the term is also used to refer to the giant tortillas themselves

traje típico: traditional Indigenous dress or suit

vela: a three-day party thrown in El Istmo to celebrate a trade (e.g., fishermen, masons, farmers) or social group, such as the muxes

zócalo: common name for the Plaza de la Constitución, the main square in Mexico City, which has also come to refer to the main squares of cities elsewhere in Mexico; smaller towns have a plaza, parque, or jardín (garden) principal

Spanish Phrasebook

Spanish commonly uses 30 letters—the familiar English 26, plus four straightforward additions: ch, ll, ñ, and rr, which are explained in the "Consonants" section.

PRONUNCIATION

Once you learn them, Spanish pronunciation rules—in contrast to English—don't change. Spanish vowels generally sound softer than in English. (*Note:* The capitalized syllables below receive stronger accents.)

Vowels

a like ah, as in "hah": *agua* AH-gooah (water), *pan* PAHN (bread), and *casa* CAH-sah (house)

e like eh, as in "egg": *mesa* MEH-sah (table), *tela* TEH-lah (cloth), and *de* DEH (of, from)

i like ee, as in "need": *diez* dee-EHS (ten), *comida* ko-MEE-dah (meal), and *fin* FEEN (end)

o like oh, as in "go": *peso* PEH-soh (weight), *ocho* OH-choh (eight), and *poco* POH-koh (a bit)

u like oo, as in "cool": *uno* OO-noh (one), *hule* OO-leh (rubber), and *usted* oos-TEHD (you); when it follows a "q" the **u** is silent; when it follows a different letter and is followed by another vowel, or has an umlaut, it's pronounced like "w"

Consonants

b, d, f, k, l, m, n, p, q, s, t, v, w, x, y, ch pronounced almost as in English; **h** occurs, but is silent—not pronounced at all

c like k as in "keep": *cuarto* KWAR-toh (room), Tepic teh-PEEK (capital of Nayarit state); when it precedes "e" or "i," pronounce **c** like s, as in "sit": *cerveza* sayr-VEH-sah (beer), *encima* ehn-SEE-mah (atop)

g like g as in "gift" when it precedes "a," "o," "u," or a consonant: *gato* GAH-toh (cat), *hago* AH-goh (I do, make); otherwise, pronounce **g** like h as in "hat": *giro* HEE-roh (money order), *gente* HEHN-tay (people)

j like h, as in "has": *Jueves* HWEH-vehs (Thursday), *mejor* meh-HOR (better)

ll like y, as in "yes": *toalla* toh-AH-yah (towel), *ellos* EH-yohs (they, them)

ñ like ny, as in "canyon": *año* AH-nyo (year), *señor* seh-NYOR (Mr., sir)

r is lightly trilled, with tongue at the roof of your mouth like a very light English d, as in "ready": *pero* PEH-doh (but), *tres* TDAYS (three), *cuatro* KOOAH-tdoh (four)

rr like a Spanish r, but with much more emphasis and trill. Let your tongue flap. Practice with *burro* (donkey), *carretera* (highway), and Carrillo (proper name), then really let go with *ferrocarril* (railroad)

z like s, as in "see," never the buzzing sound of an English z: *zócalo* SOH-cah-loh (main square), *zapato* sah-PAH-toh (shoe)

Note: The single small but common exception to all of the above is the pronunciation of Spanish **y** when it's being used as the Spanish word for "and," as in "Ron y Kathy." In such case, pronounce it like the English ee, as in "keep": Ron "ee" Kathy (Ron and Kathy).

Accent

The rule for accent, the relative stress given to syllables within a given word, is straightforward. If a word ends in a vowel, an n, or an s, accent the next-to-last syllable; if not, accent the last syllable.

Pronounce *sombrero* som-BREH-roh (hat), *orden* OHR-dehn (order), and *carretera* kah-reh-TAY-rah (highway) with stress on the next-to-last syllable.

Emphasize the syllable before the -ia or -ias in words that end in these letters with no accent on the i, such as *gracias* GRAH-seeahas (thank you) and *farmacia* far-MAH-seeah (pharmacy). When the i is accented with a *tilde* (ac-

The Magic of Spanish Grammar

You may have heard your Spanish teacher ramble on in grammar lessons about reflexive verbs and their pronouns and blah, blah, blah. This can be a difficult aspect of the language to master, especially when you're thinking in grammatical terms. It's better to just think of the magic within the Spanish language, instead.

Reflexive verbs put the action in the object, rather than the person or subject. For example, the verb *gustar* translates to "to like," but it is not a literal one. In Spanish, you do not like pizza, pizza pleases you: Me gusta la pizza ("The pizza pleases me"). You don't like other people, other people "fall well" on you: Me cae bien ("I like him," but literally, "He falls well on me"). When *gustar* is used with people, it means a romantic or more-than-friendly interest: Me gustas ("I like you," in the "like-like" sense). Reflexive verbs can also be a neat linguistic way to avoid blame. For example, in Spanish, you don't drop objects, they fall from your hands: Se me cayó el celular ("I dropped my phone," but literally, "The phone fell from me").

Once you start to think about the outside world acting on you in Spanish much more than you act on it, things start to click and your learning will speed up significantly. With all this grammatical magic in the language, it's no wonder the literary movement called Magical Realism, popularized by writers such as Colombian Gabriel García Márquez (1927-2014) and Chilean Isabel Allende (b. 1942), originated in Spanish-language literature.

cent sign), put the emphasis on the i: *zapatería* sah-pah-the-REE-ah (shoe store), and *alegría* ah-leh-GREE-ah (happiness).

Otherwise, accent the last syllable: *venir* veh-NEER (to come), *ferrocarril* feh-roh-cah-REEL (railroad), *edad* eh-DAHD (age), and feliz feh-LEES (happy).

Exceptions to the accent rule are always marked with an accent sign: (á, é, í, ó, or ú), such as *teléfono* teh-LEH-foh-noh (telephone), *jabón* hah-BON (soap), and *rápido* RAH-pee-doh (rapid).

BASIC AND COURTEOUS EXPRESSIONS

Most Spanish-speaking people consider formalities important. Whenever approaching anyone for information or some other reason, do not forget the appropriate salutation—"Good morning, Good evening," etc. Standing alone, the greeting "Hola" (hello) can sound brusque.

Hello. *Hola.*
Good morning. *Buenos días.*
Good afternoon. *Buenas tardes.*
Good evening. *Buenas noches.*
How are you? *¿Cómo está usted?*
Very well, thank you. *Muy bien, gracias.*
Okay; good. *Bien.*
Not okay; bad. *Mal* or *feo.*
So-so. *Más o menos.*
And you? *¿Y usted?*
Thank you. *Gracias.*
Thank you very much. *Muchas gracias.*
You're very kind. *Muy amable.*
You're welcome. *De nada.*
Goodbye. *Adios.*
See you later. *Hasta luego.*
please *por favor*
yes *sí*
no *no*
I don't know. *No sé.*
Just a moment, please. *Momentito, por favor.*
Excuse me, please (when you're trying to get attention). *Disculpe* or *Con permiso.*
Excuse me (when you've made a boo-boo). *Lo siento* or *Perdón*
Pleased to meet you. *Mucho gusto.*
How do you say ... in Spanish? *¿Cómo se dice ... en español?*
What is your name? *¿Cómo se llama usted?*

Do you speak English? *¿Habla usted inglés?*

Is English spoken here? (Does anyone here speak English?) *¿Se habla inglés?*

I don't speak Spanish well. *No hablo bien el español.*

I don't understand. *No entiendo.*

My name is ... *Me llamo ...*

Would you like ... *¿Quisiera usted ...*

Let's go to ... *Vamos a ...*

TERMS OF ADDRESS

When in doubt, use the formal *usted* (you) as a form of address.

I *yo*

you (formal) *usted*

you (familiar) *tú*

he/him *él*

she/her *ella*

we/us *nosotros*

you (plural) *ustedes*

they/them *ellos* (all males or mixed gender); *ellas* (all females)

Mr., sir *señor*

Mrs., madam *señora*

miss, young lady *señorita*

wife *esposa*

husband *esposo*

friend *amigo* (male); *amiga* (female)

sweetheart *novio* (male); *novia* (female)

son; daughter *hijo; hija*

brother; sister *hermano; hermana*

father; mother *padre; madre*

grandfather; grandmother *abuelo; abuela*

SPEAK LIKE A CHAPULIÑERO

If you want to sound a little less like a gringo (foreigner) and more like a chapulinero (a Oaxacan), try sprinkling a few of these colloquial Spanish words and phrases into your conversation:

- **carnal:** a term of endearment for a friend, like "my brother" or "my dog"
- **fresa:** someone or something that is pretentious or rich and spoiled
- **güey/wey:** a ubiquitous slang term to refer to any person, similar to "dude" or "bro"
- **¡hijole!:** an exclamation of surprise that can mean wow, whoa, dang, oh my goodness (careful, while not exactly a curse word, it's not always said in polite company)
- **¿mande?:** What did you say?
- **¡no manches!:** No way!
- **nena/nene:** daughter/son
- **órale:** versatile Mexican Spanish word that can mean a number of things, from "right on" to "whoa" to "okay"
- **por fa/por fis:** a cute variation of por favor
- **pues:** a filler word similar to "just," "well," "I mean..." or "umm." When in doubt, just throw it in there.
- **¿qué onda (güey)?:** a common greeting used with friends, like *Que tal?*, especially young people. Usually paired with "güey." Means "What's up dude?" or "Whats good, bro?"
- **que padre/que chido:** Cool!
- **sale/sale vale:** a term of agreement. "Okay," "alright," "got it"

TRANSPORTATION

Where is ... ? *¿Dónde está ... ?*

How far is it to ... ? *¿A cuánto está ... ?*

from ... to ... *de ... a ...*

How many blocks? *¿Cuántas cuadras?*

Where (Which) is the way to ... ? *¿Dónde está el camino a ... ?* or *¿Cómo llega uno a ... ?* (How does one arrive at ...?)

the bus station *la terminal de autobuses*

the bus stop *la parada de autobuses*

Where is this bus going? *¿Adónde va este autobús?*

the taxi stand *la parada de taxis*

the train station *la estación de ferrocarril*

the boat *el barco*

the launch *lancha; tiburonera*

the dock *el muelle*

the airport *el aeropuerto*

I'd like a ticket to ... *Quisiera un boleto a ...*

first (second) class *primera (segunda) clase*

round-trip *ida y vuelta*

Getting the Server's Attention

The noun for waiter or waitress is *mesero* or *mesera*, but you won't actually use it when speaking to them, and the forms of address for waitstaff in Mexico might take you some getting used to. If your server is male, you will say "Jóven" to get his attention. This literally means "youngster," but it is the word to use no matter the waiter's age.

If your server is female, you will call her "Señorita," again, despite her age. It might seem a little awkward calling a person older than you a young man or young lady, but it won't be for them. It is the proper way to address them in Mexico. Oh, and don't forget to wish a hearty "¡Buen provecho!" (Enjoy your meal!) to the diners around you when you enter and/or leave a restaurant.

reservation *reservación*
baggage *equipaje*
Stop here, please. *Pare aquí, por favor.* Or, more commonly in Oaxaca, *Baja aquí, por favor.*
the entrance *la entrada*
the exit *la salida*
the ticket office *taquilla*
(very) near; far *(muy) cerca; lejos*
to; toward *a* or *hacia*
by; through *por*
from *de*
the right *la derecha*
the left *la izquierda*
straight ahead *derecho; directo*
in front *en frente*
beside *al lado*
behind *atrás*
the corner *la esquina*
the stoplight *la semáforo*
a turn *una vuelta*
right here *aquí* or *acá*
somewhere around here *por acá*
right there *allí* or *allá*
somewhere around there *por allá*
road *el camino*
street; boulevard *calle; bulevar*
block *la cuadra*
highway *carretera*
kilometer *kilómetro*
bridge; toll *puente; cuota*
address *dirección*
north; south *norte; sur*
east; west *oriente (este); poniente (oeste)*

ACCOMMODATIONS

hotel *hotel*
room *cuarto* or *habitación*
Is there a room? *¿Hay cuarto?*
May I (may we) see it? *¿Puedo (podemos) verlo?*
What is the rate? *¿Cuál es el precio?*
Is that your best rate? *¿Es su mejor precio?*
Is there something cheaper? *¿Hay algo más económico?*
a single room *un cuarto sencillo*
a double room *un cuarto doble*
double bed *cama matrimonial*
twin bed *cama individual*
with private bath *con baño privado*
hot water *agua caliente*
shower *ducha*
towels *toallas*
soap *jabón*
toilet paper *papel higiénico*
blanket *cobija; manta*
sheets *sábanas*
air-conditioned *aire acondicionado*
fan *abanico; ventilador*
key *llave*
manager *gerente*

FOOD

I'm hungry *Tengo hambre.*
I'm thirsty. *Tengo sed.*
menu *carta; menú*
order *orden*
glass *vaso*
fork *tenedor*

knife *cuchillo*
spoon *cuchara*
napkin *servilleta*
soft drink *refresco*
coffee *café*
tea *té*
drinking water *agua pura; agua potable*
bottled carbonated water *agua mineral*
bottled uncarbonated water *agua natural*
beer *cerveza*
wine *vino*
milk *leche*
juice *jugo*
cream *crema*
sugar *azúcar*
cheese *queso*
snack *antojito; botana*
breakfast *desayuno*
lunch *almuerzo* or *comida*
daily lunch special *comida corrida* (or *el menú del día* depending on region)
dinner *comida* (often eaten in late afternoon); *cena* (a late-night snack)
the check *la cuenta*
eggs *huevos*
bread *pan*
salad *ensalada*
fruit *fruta*
mango *mango*
watermelon *sandía*
papaya *papaya*
banana *plátano*
apple *manzana*
orange *naranja*
lime *limón*
fish *pescado*
shellfish *mariscos*
shrimp *camarones*
meat (without) *(sin) carne*
chicken *pollo*
pork *carne de puerco* or *carne de cerdo*
beef; steak *res; bistec*
bacon; ham *tocino; jamón*
fried *frito*
roasted *asada*
barbecue; barbecued *barbacoa; al carbon*

Don't Be a Puedotener!

In English, especially US English, we commonly request goods or services by opening with "Can I have...?" As a Spanish language learner, your initial instinct might be to translate this literally: *¿Puedo tener un taco de camarón?* While your meaning will be understood, it is not said like this in Spanish.

A good go-to for requesting things is *Me da* (Give me), but not in a commanding or pushy way. Say it with a slight intonation of a question and it is a nice, sensible way to get what you want. *Me da un taco de camarón, ¿por favor?* translates literally to "Give me a shrimp taco, please," but has the connotation of a phrase like "Can I have..." or "I'll take..."

SHOPPING

money *dinero*
money-exchange bureau *casa de cambio*
I would like to exchange traveler's checks. *Quisiera cambiar cheques de viajero.*
What is the exchange rate? *¿Cuál es el tipo de cambio?*
How much is the commission? *¿Cuánto cuesta la comisión?*
Do you accept credit cards? *¿Aceptan tarjetas de crédito?*
money order *remesa* or *giro*
How much does it cost? *¿Cuánto cuesta?*
What is your final price? *¿Cuál es su último precio?*
expensive *caro*
cheap *barato; económico*
more *más*
less *menos*
a little *un poco*
too much *demasiado*

HEALTH

Help me please. *Ayúdeme por favor.*
I am ill. *Estoy enfermo.*
Call a doctor. *Llame un doctor.*
Take me to ... *Lléveme a ...*

hospital *hospital*
drugstore *farmacia*
pain *dolor*
fever *fiebre*
headache *dolor de cabeza*
stomach ache *dolor de estómago*
burn *quemadura*
cramp *calambre*
nausea *náusea*
vomiting *vomitar*
medicine *medicina* or *medicamento*
antibiotic *antibiótico*
pill; tablet *pastilla*
aspirin *aspirina*
ointment; cream *pomada; crema*
bandage *venda*
cotton *algodón*
tampons *tampones*
sanitary napkins use brand name, e.g., Kotex
birth control pills *pastillas anticonceptivas*
contraceptive foam *espuma anticonceptiva*
condoms *preservativos; condones*
toothbrush *cepilla de dientesl*
dental floss *hilo dental*
toothpaste *crema* or *pasta dental*
dentist *dentista*
toothache *dolor de muelas*

POST OFFICE AND COMMUNICATIONS

long-distance phone call *llamada de larga distancia*
I would like to call ... *Quisiera llamar a ...*
collect *por cobrar*
station to station *a quien contesta*
person to person *persona a persona*
credit card *tarjeta de crédito*
post office *correo*
general delivery *lista de correo*
letter *carta*
stamp *estampilla, timbre*
postcard *tarjeta*
aerogram *aerograma*
air mail *correo aereo*
registered *registrado*
money order *remesa* or *giro*
package; box *paquete; caja*
string; tape *cuerda; cinta*

AT THE BORDER

border *frontera*
customs *aduana*
immigration *migración*
tourist card *tarjeta de turista*
inspection *inspección; revisión*
passport *pasaporte*
profession *profesión*
marital status *estado civil*
single *soltero*
married; divorced *casado; divorciado*
widowed *viudado*
insurance *seguros*
title *título*
driver's license *licencia de manejar*

AT THE GAS STATION

gas station *gasolinera*
gasoline *gasolina*
unleaded *sin plomo*
full, please *lleno, por favor*
tire *llanta*
tire repair shop *vulcanizadora*
air *aire*
water *agua*
oil (change) *aceite (cambio de)*
grease *grasa*
My ... doesn't work. *Mi ... no sirve.*
battery *batería*
radiator *radiador*
alternator *alternador*
generator *generador* or *dínamo*
tow truck *grúa*
repair shop *taller mecánico*
tune-up *afinación*
auto parts store *refaccionería*

VERBS

Verbs are the key to getting along in Spanish. The "you" forms included here are conjugated for the pronoun *usted*. (The regular conjugation for the informal *tú* has an s on the end, e.g., tú compras/you buy). Verbs employ mostly predictable forms and come in three classes, which end in *ar*, *er*, and *ir*, respectively:

to buy *comprar*
I buy, you (he, she, it) buys *compro, compra*
we buy, you (they) buy *compramos, compran*

to eat *comer*
I eat, you (he, she, it) eats *como, come*
we eat, you (they) eat *comemos, comen*

to climb *subir*
I climb, you (he, she, it) climbs *subo, sube*
we climb, you (they) climb *subimos, suben*

Here are more (with irregularities indicated):

to do or make *hacer* (regular except for *hago*, I do or make)
to go *ir* (very irregular: *voy, vas, va, vamos, van*)
to go (walk) *andar*
to love *amar*
to work *trabajar*
to want *desear, querer*
to need *necesitar*
to read *leer*
to write *escribir*
to repair *reparar*
to stop *parar*
to get off (the bus) *bajar*
to arrive *llegar*
to stay (remain) *quedarse*
to stay (lodge) *hospedarse*
to leave *salir* (regular except for *salgo*, I leave)
to look at *mirar*
to look for *buscar* (the "for" is in the verb already, so you don't have to say *por*. Don't say *Estoy buscando por*, just *Estoy buscando...*)
to give *dar* (regular except for *doy*, I give)
to carry *llevar*
to have *tener* (irregular but important: *tengo, tienes, tiene, tenemos, tienen*)
to come *venir* (similarly irregular: *vengo, vienes, viene, venimos, vienen*)

Spanish has two forms of "to be":

to be *estar* (regular except for *estoy*, I am)
to be *ser* (very irregular: *soy, es, somos, son*)

Use *estar* when speaking of location or a temporary state of being: "I am at home." *"Estoy en casa."* "I'm sick." *"Estoy enfermo."* Use *ser* for a permanent state of being: "I am a doctor." *"Soy doctora."*

NUMBERS

zero *cero*
one *uno*
two *dos*
three *tres*
four *cuatro*
five *cinco*
six *seis*
seven *siete*
eight *ocho*
nine *nueve*
10 *diez*
11 *once*
12 *doce*
13 *trece*
14 *catorce*
15 *quince*
16 *dieciseis*
17 *diecisiete*
18 *dieciocho*
19 *diecinueve*
20 *veinte*
21 *veinte y uno* or *veintiuno*
30 *treinta*
40 *cuarenta*
50 *cincuenta*
60 *sesenta*
70 *setenta*
80 *ochenta*
90 *noventa*
100 *ciento*
101 *ciento y uno* or *cientiuno*
200 *doscientos*
500 *quinientos*
1,000 *mil*
10,000 *diez mil*

100,000 *cien mil*
1,000,000 *millón*
billion *mil millones*
one half *medio* or *mitad*
one third *un tercio*
one fourth *un cuarto*

TIME

What time is it? *¿Qué hora es?*
It's one o'clock. *Es la una.*
It's three in the afternoon. *Son las tres de la tarde.*
It's 4am. *Son las cuatro de la mañana.*
six-thirty *seis y media*
a quarter till eleven *un cuarto para las once*
a quarter past five *las cinco y cuarto*
a minute *un minuto*
an hour *una hora*

DAYS AND MONTHS

Monday *lunes*
Tuesday *martes*
Wednesday *miércoles*
Thursday *jueves*
Friday *viernes*
Saturday *sábado*
Sunday *domingo*
today *hoy*
tomorrow *mañana*
yesterday *ayer*
January *enero*
February *febrero*
March *marzo*
April *abril*
May *mayo*
June *junio*
July *julio*
August *agosto*
September *septiembre*
October *octubre*
November *noviembre*
December *diciembre*
a week *una semana*
a month *un mes*
after *después*
before *antes*

Suggested Reading

HISTORY

Blanton, Richard, Gary Feinman, Stephen Kowalewski, and Linda Nicholas. *Ancient Oaxaca: The Monte Albán State*. Cambridge University Press, 1999. Although agriculture in the Americas most likely began in the Oaxaca Valley, and the Zapotecs created one of the first writing systems in Mesoamerica, many overall histories of the pre-Hispanic American cultures overlook these important details. The authors of *Ancient Oaxaca* aim to correct this oversight.

Pearce, Kenneth. *A Traveler's History of Mexico*, 2nd edition. Interlink Publishing, 2004. Pierce's condensed account of the convoluted history of Mexico is both precise and detailed where it counts. As the title conveys, the book is the perfect size for lugging around in a backpack while on the road.

Weeks, Charles A. *The Juárez Myth in Mexico*. University of Alabama Press, 1987. Benito Juárez was influential to the development of modern Mexico even after his death in 1872. In his examination of Juárez's life and legacy, Weeks studiously sheds light on how the national memory of Juárez has been altered to serve various political agendas in the century and a half since his presidency.

FICTION

Ford, Richard. *The Ultimate Good Luck*. Vintage Books, 1981. Pulitzer prize-winning American author Richard Ford's second novel is set in Oaxaca during the cocaine smuggling climate of the 1970s. In Oaxaca to bail his girlfriend's brother out of jail, Harry Quinn gets caught up in a menacing and erotic tale of violence and deception.

Sada, Daniel, and Katherine Silver, translator. *Almost Never.* Graywolf Press, 2012. Originally published in Spanish under the title *Casi Nunca* (2008), Katherine Silver's excellent translation brings the work of this highly respected Mexican author to an English-reading audience. Chilean novelist in Mexico Roberto Bolaño called Sada's work "the most daring" of the writers of his generation, and this novel of a torrid love triangle set on a ranch outside Oaxaca City is no exception to that description.

Wright, Lili. *Dancing with the Tiger.* G. P. Putnam's Sons, 2016. After a grave robber high on methamphetamines discovers what is possibly the death mask of Aztec emperor Moctezuma, Wright's heroine Anna Ramsey flies to Oaxaca to vindicate her father, a disgraced art collector, and discover the truth behind the mask. While chasing the looter, Anna gets mixed up in the criminal underbelly of Mexico's art scene, discovering that we all wear masks, whether they be literal or figurative.

POETRY

Moore, Roger. *Sun and Moon: Poems from Oaxaca, Mexico.* Mount Saint Vincent University Press, 2000. These verses by Canadian poet Roger Moore explore the lives and histories of the Indigenous peoples of Oaxaca, weaving ancient stories into the modern society in which Oaxacans find themselves today. Pre-Hispanic ceremonies are juxtaposed next to interactions between Oaxacans and the tourists that come to experience these cultures that have been overlooked politically, economically, and historically.

ARCHAEOLOGY

Ramos, Juan Arturo López, and Owen Ferguson, translator. *Oaxaca: Cradle and Destiny of American Civilization.* Fernández Pichardo Cultural Foundation, 2017. This recent translation of the Oaxacan historian and author's 2010 Spanish-language book of the same name draws on the best and latest archaeological evidence to reveal the roots of many modern conventions of civic life to Oaxacan origins. Agriculture, writing systems, and urban planning in the Americas have all been traced back to the rugged mountains and valleys of Oaxaca.

Winter, Marcus. *Oaxaca: The Archaeological Record.* Minutiae Mexicana, 1992. Winter's concise account of the peoples of Monte Albán, Mitla, Yagul, and other pre-Hispanic sites in Oaxaca is a good traveling companion for anyone looking to broaden their knowledge of the place's history. Begin your research here, and use the book from the previous entry to place these civilizations in the greater context of Mesoamerican history.

COOKBOOKS AND GASTRONOMY

Martínez, Zarela. *The Food and Life of Oaxaca: Traditional Recipes from Mexico's Heart.* Macmillan Publishing, 1997. An authority on Mexican food, Zarela Martínez got both her cooking and cookbook writing from her mother. More than just recipes, the book ties every dish to the people and history behind it.

Ruiz, Alejandro. *The Food of Oaxaca: Recipes and Stories from Mexico's Culinary Capital: A Cookbook.* Knopf Doubleday Publishing, 2021. Oaxacan native, esteemed chef, and award-winning restaurateur of Casa Oaxaca fame Alejandro Ruiz has created much more than just a cookbook. *The Food of Oaxaca* is a love song to Oaxaca's culinary traditions, with delicious recipes to try, essays to peruse, and glossy photos that you can nearly taste.

PEOPLE AND CULTURE

Iturbide, *Graciela. Juchitán de las mujeres: 1979-1989.* Editorial RM, 2010. This collection of images of the women of Juchitán by prolific Mexican photographer Graciela Iturbide includes bilingual essays about the pictures that have gone on to iconic representations of the city. A statue six blocks north of the main square in Juchitán honors her most striking photo of the series, *Nuestra Señora de las Iguanas* (Our Lady of the Iguanas), of a juchiteca with over a half dozen iguanas perched on her head.

Lawrence, D. H. *Mornings in Mexico.* Martin Secker, 1927. Although Lawrence's collection of travel essays from Mexico, four of which treat Oaxaca, occasionally dips into the colonially arrogant, even rude, his descriptions of the markets and street life of Oaxaca City are as rich and lively as the scenes they describe. He wrote some of the passages while staying in the hotel now called Casona Oaxaca.

ARTS, CRAFTS, AND ARCHITECTURE

Chibnik, Michael. *Crafting Tradition: The Making and Marketing of Oaxacan Wood Carvings.* University of Texas Press, 2003. Get the full scoop on the nascent tradition of alebrijes in Oaxaca with this, the most exhaustive examination of the very recent history and marketing techniques of this folk art. Chibnik's well-researched text is accompanied by gorgeous photos of these kaleidoscopic wooden creatures.

Mindling, Eric Sebastian. *Oaxaca Stories in Cloth.* Thrums Books, 2016. A quick look through the table of contents of Mindling's comprehensive study of the regional embroidery styles in Oaxaca reveals just how extensive his research was. The book introduces the English-speaking world to embroidery styles from all over the state, including many of the hardest-to-reach places.

Wasserspring, Lois. *Oaxacan Ceramics: Traditional Folk Art by Oaxacan Women.* Raincoast Books, 2000. Rather than an exhaustive investigation of the Oaxacan ceramics world at large, Wasserspring decided to focus on six female potters in Santa María Atzompa and Ocotlán de Morelos, connecting their art to their religions, legends, daily lives, and rich imaginations.

GOVERNMENT, POLITICS, AND ECONOMY

Denham, Diana, editor. *Teaching Rebellion: Stories from the Grassroots Mobilization in Oaxaca.* PM Press, 2008. Diana Denham is the coordinator of the CASA Collective, a Oaxaca-based international solidarity organization. This anthology collects firsthand accounts of stories from the 2006 political movements that erupted into violence and led to the formation of the Popular Assembly of the Peoples of Oaxaca (APPO).

Murphy, Arthur D., and Alex Stepick. *Social Inequality in Oaxaca: A History of Resistance and Change.* Temple University Press, 1991. Murphy and Stepick's socioeconomic study of Oaxaca in the 1970s and 1980s takes a neighborhood-based approach to follow the lives of residents of Oaxaca City and learn from the challenges they face to get by.

ENVIRONMENT

Grosselet, Manuel, and Georgita Ruiz. *Field Guide to the Birds of Mexico: Volume 2, Birds of Monte Albán and Yagul.* National Institute of Anthropology and History, 2010. The fact that the 173 different bird species included in this extensively detailed bilingual field guide are found on two hills in the Valles Centrales tells you just how rich the avian biodiversity here is. This is an essential guide for ornithologists amateur to professional.

Sacks, Oliver. *Oaxaca Journal*. National Geographic Society, 2002. Take a drive up to Tuxtepec and you'll understand neurologist and author Oliver Sacks's fascination with ferns. Visit anywhere in Oaxaca and you'll understand how the travelogue of his trip with a band of fellow fern fanatics ended up including his musings on the origins of mezcal, chocolate, and ceremonial use of hallucinogenic mushrooms, as well as vibrant descriptions of markets and other scenes of Oaxacan life.

Internet Resources

GENERAL INFORMATION

Oaxaca Mio

www.oaxaca-mio.com

Originally in Spanish, this tourism website uses Google's translation program to convert its pages into English. With lots of general information on festivals, activities, hotels, food, and more, it is a great place to browse and find something to fill a day or two on your itinerary.

Viva Oaxaca

www.vivaoaxaca.org

This independent site founded in 2011 by Mark Anthony Santiago Aquino is run by a team of collaborators dedicated to celebrating, highlighting, and preserving Oaxacan culture. The gorgeous site, originally in Spanish, also can be translated into English through Google Translate. There is a lot of broad information on visiting Oaxaca, as well as up-to-date information and coverage on cultural events throughout the state. A wealth of high-quality photos and videos accompany the entries, making this another great resource for trip planning. During Guelaguetza season, this site is a must.

Oaxaca Cultural Navigator

www.oaxacaculture.com

This extremely comprehensive site, featured by the *New York Times*, is a labor of love born from the work of American Norma Schafer and Teotitlan del Valle native Eric Chavez Santiago. It is a treasure trove of information, with articles dating back to 2007, and has articles on anything you could ever think of, from Oaxacan wedding customs, to the fine line between cultural appropriation and appreciation, to the origin of Tuxtepec's show-stopping dance Flor de Piña. They also offer in-depth cultural tours and services.

ARTS AND CULTURE

Friends of Oaxacan Folk Art

www.fofa.us

Friends of Oaxacan Folk Art (FOFA) is a nonprofit organization dedicated to the preservation and promotion of Oaxaca's rich and varied folk art traditions. Their website is the most extensive online English-language resource on Oaxacan folk art, with sections on ceramics, textiles, jewelry, and 10 other disciplines, as well as the various regional styles within them and profiles of the artists.

Un Huipil al Día

www.unhuipil.wordpress.com

This Spanish-language blog showcases the various regional embroidery styles of the blouses called huipiles. Each entry includes a high-resolution close-up photo of the embroidery, the town in which it was made, and a brief description of the piece. Even if your Spanish isn't on the level to fully understand the descriptions, the site is an excellent resource for learning to recognize these regional artistic styles.

NEWS AND EVENTS

Qué Pasa Oaxaca

www.quepasaoaxaca.com

The digital component of the free bilingual print magazine is the place to find art exhibitions, movie screenings, concerts, festivals, and other events in Oaxaca City. In addition to events listings, the site has articles from the magazine and sections on hotels and Spanish schools. Keep an eye out at businesses in Oaxaca City for a copy of the print edition.

Oaxaca Events

www.oaxacaevents.com

Hikes, walking tours, card games, poetry readings, mahjong, and much, much more make up the list of events on the calendar on this handy website. If you're doing an extended stay in Oaxaca City or the Valles Centrales, check Oaxaca Events often to get into the groove of social life here.

OAXACAN COAST

Puerto Escondido Real Estate and Vacation Rentals

www.puertorealestate.com

Plan your move to or extended stay in paradise with the help of Puerto Escondido Real Estate and Vacation Rentals. Their English-language site has extensive listings of houses, apartments, bungalows, and vacation rentals all over town. You'll also find tons of maps and information on activities, restaurants, transportation, and more.

Tomzap: The Pacific Coast of Mexico

www.tomzap.com/oaxaca.html

This English-language site is dedicated to the Pacific coast of Mexico, specifically the coasts in the states of Jalisco, Colima, and Oaxaca. The listings include information on many communities on the coast, as well as popular destinations in the Valles Centrales and other towns in Oaxaca. There is also lots of information about the wildlife of the region, as well as stories of the recent history of the Oaxacan coast.

The Eye

www.theeyehuatulco.com

This is the online component to the Huatulco-based print magazine that focuses on beach life, urban living, food, lifestyle, history, culture, and more on the coast. The magazine is free, and the website has links to the digital editions of the full magazine.

PARKS AND RECREATION

Ecoturismo Oaxaca

www.ecoturismoenoaxaca.com

Oaxaca is experiencing an ecotourism boom, and communities all over the state are organizing to showcase the best of what their geographies have to offer. This Spanish-language site has information on ecotourism centers big and small, broken up regionally into the coast, La Mixteca, the Valles Centrales, and the Sierras Norte and Sur.

Expediciones Sierra Norte

www.sierranorte.org.mx

This bilingual site is the promotional website for the organization Expediciones Sierra Norte, which coordinates ecotourism in the Pueblos Mancomunados, in the Sierra Norte. You can use it to book trips, but also just to get information about the pueblos, local traditions, and activities they have to offer.

Oaxaca MTB

www.oaxacamtb.org

Cycling is one of the fastest-growing activities in Oaxaca in recent years. Oaxaca MTB is a wealth of information on trails, rides, organizing, and more. The dozens of trails in its detailed and well-mapped directory are mostly in the hills around San Felipe del Agua, just a few miles north of Oaxaca City. Entries include information on the terrain, altitude, difficulty, and more of each ride.

Surfing in Oaxaca
www.srfer.com/surfing-in-oaxaca/

The Oaxaca section of srfer.com is a comprehensive collection of everything surfing along the coast. You'll find wave-specific information on surf spots up and down the coast, as well as seasonal weather details, wind and wave statistics, and profiles of hotels and surf camps.

Surf Forecast
www.surf-forecast.com

Surf Forecast is another global online surf network that has diligently updated information on surf conditions. Unlike Srfer, it doesn't include camp, hotel, or other information related to the sport, but the pull-down navigation menus let you browse specific conditions for 25 breaks along the Oaxacan coast.

Index

A

B

C

D

E

F

G

H

I

JK

L

M

NO

P

R

S

T

UV

WXYZ

List of Maps

Photo Credits

All interior photos © Ashley C. Roberts except: page 1 © Bernardo Ramonfaur | Dreamstime.com; page 5 © (top) Kmiragaya | Dreamstime.com; (left middle) William Perry | Dreamstime.com; (right middle) Antwon Mcmullen | Dreamstime.com; (bottom left) Arkadij Schell | Dreamstime.com; (bottom right) Andy Kramer | Dreamstime.com; page 6 © Aurora Esperanza Ángeles Flores | Dreamstime.com; page 8 © Jesus Eloy Ramos Lara | Dreamstime.com; page 10 © (top) Aleksandar Todorovic | Dreamstime.com; (bottom) megapress images / Alamy Stock Photo; page 11 © In Situ Mezcaleria; page 12 © Roberto Rios; page 14 © Jesus Eloy Ramos Lara | Dreamstime.com; page 15 © (top) Birdiegal717 | Dreamstime.com; (bottom) Kobby Dagan | Dreamstime.com; page 16 © (top) Expendiciones Sierra Norte; (bottom) Letloose78 | Dreamstime.com; page 17 © Holistik Temazcal & Masaje; page 18 © (bottom) Kobby Dagan | Dreamstime.com; page 22 © Xhico | Dreamstime.com; page 23 © (top) Mardzpe | Dreamstime.com; (middle) Amybbb | Dreamstime.com; (bottom) Marketa Novakova | Dreamstime.com; page 24 © Arkadij Schell | Dreamstime.com; page 26 © Leonid Andronov | Dreamstime.com; page 27 © (top) Restaurant Bar Terra Tipi; page 28 © Nailotl Mendez | Dreamstime.com; page 30 © (top) Matthew Bamberg | Dreamstime.com; (bottom) Aurora Esperanza Ángeles Flores | Dreamstime.com; page 33 © (top) Antwon Mcmullen | Dreamstime.com; (middle) © Xhico | Dreamstime.com; page 34 © Nailotl Mendez | Dreamstime.com; page 35 © (top) Jesus Eloy Ramos Lara | Dreamstime.com; page 36 © Holistik Temazcal & Masaje; page 38 © (bottom) Bernardo Ramonfaur | Dreamstime.com; page 41 © Kobby Dagan | Dreamstime.com; page 42 © (bottom) Aleksandar Todorovic | Dreamstime.com; page 43 © (top) William Perry | Dreamstime.com; page 44 © Elovkoff | Dreamstime.com; page 45 © (top right) William Perry | Dreamstime.com; page 57 © (top) Gerasimovvv | Dreamstime.com; (bottom) Enrique Gomez Tamez | Dreamstime.com; page 63 © (top left) Pedro Martínez; (top right) Mary Jane Gagnier; (bottom left) Fotografía Annemieke Buursink; (bottom right) Ervit Hernández Hernández; page 68 © William Perry | Dreamstime.com; page 82 © In Situ Mezcaleria; page 95 © Kmiragaya | Dreamstime.com; page 96 © (top left) Barna Tanko | Dreamstime.com; page 105 © (top) Kmiragaya | Dreamstime.com; page 110 © (bottom) Javarman | Dreamstime.com; page 113 © Ulita | Dreamstime.com; page 114 © Aurora Esperanza Ángeles Flores | Dreamstime.com; page 116 © Barna Tanko | Dreamstime.com; page 120 © (right middle) Brizardh | Dreamstime.com; (bottom) Albertoloyo | Dreamstime.com; page 124 © (bottom) Tra Hitt | Dreamstime.com; page 126 © Ulf Huebner | Dreamstime.com; page 130 © (top right) Centro Ecoturístico San Sebastián de las Grutas; (bottom left) 4 Seasons Tours and Travel Oaxaca; (bottom right) Aurora Esperanza Ángeles Flores | Dreamstime.com; page 133 © (top right) Yvette D. Hough; (bottom) Frida Libre; page 147 © (bottom) Roger Ramírez; page 153 © Hotel Papaya Surf; page 160 © (top) Letloose78 | Dreamstime.com; page 211 © (top left) Abimael Santiago Lopez; (top right) Ulf Huebner | Dreamstime.com; (bottom) Abimael Santiago Lopez; page 235 © Nelly Eblin Barrientos Gutierrez | Dreamstime.com; page 242 © (bottom left) Reinout Van Wagtendonk | Dreamstime.com; (bottom right) Expediciones Sierra Norte; page 267 © (bottom) Lifessunday | Dreamstime.com; page 274 © (bottom) Leonid Andronov | Dreamstime.com; page 278 © Robert Briggs | Dreamstime.com; page 317 © Rafal Kubiak | Dreamstime.com.

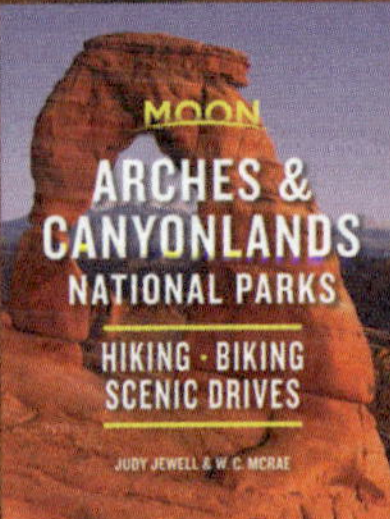

MOON
DEATH VALLEY
NATIONAL PARK
HIKING · SCENIC DRIVES
DESERT SPRINGS
JENNA BLOUGH

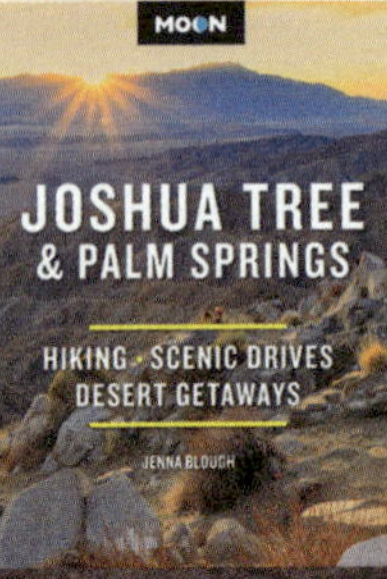

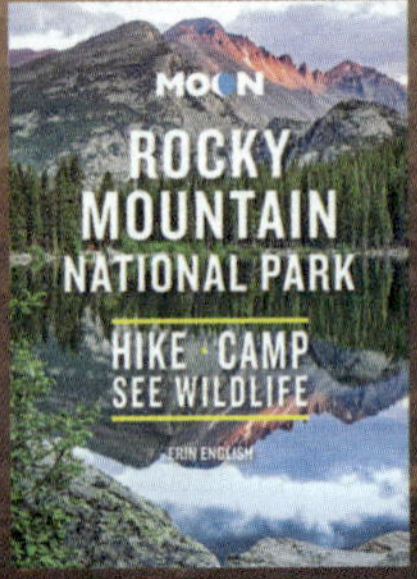

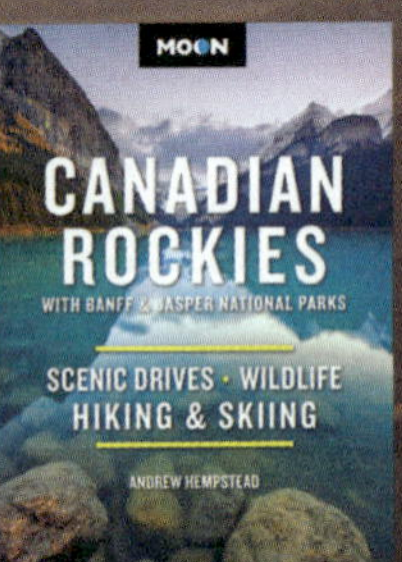

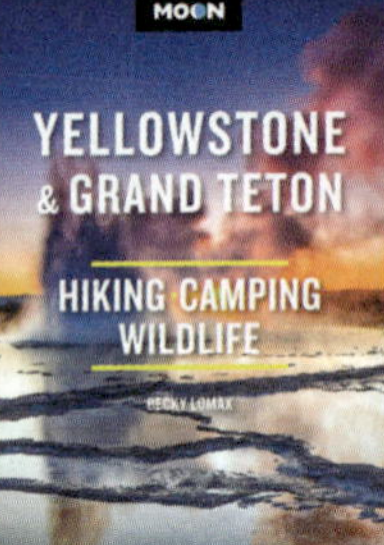

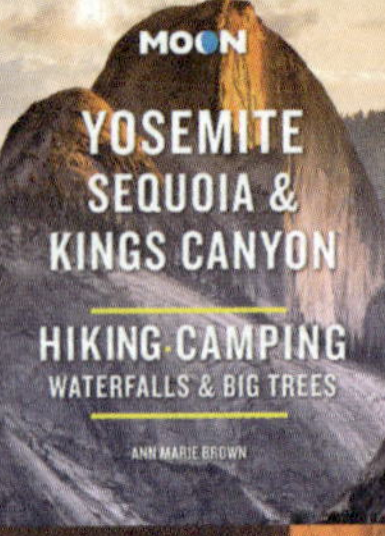

Spending only a few days in a park?

Try our Best Of guides.

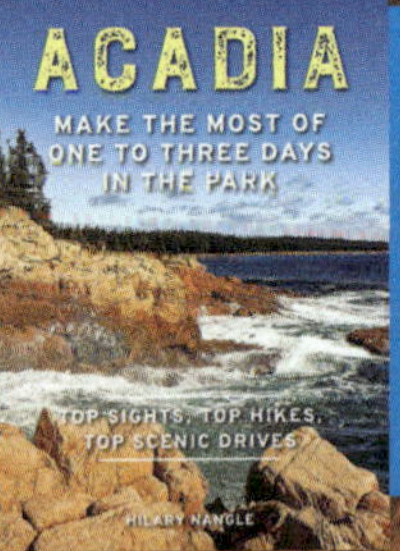

MOON
DRIVE & HIKE
APPALACHIAN TRAIL
Timothy Malcolm
THE BEST TRAIL TOWNS, DAY HIKES, AND ROAD TRIPS IN BETWEEN

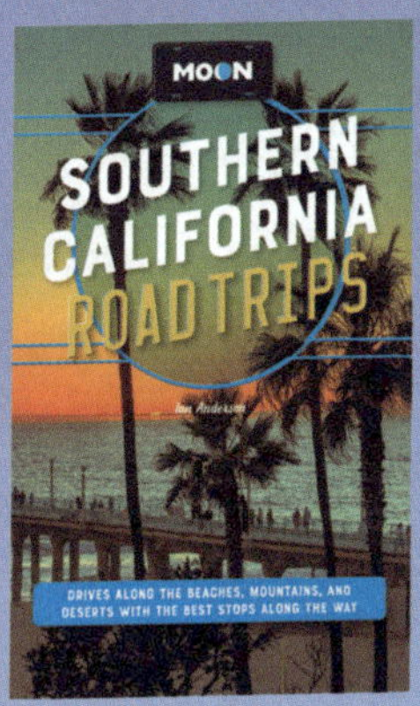
MOON
SOUTHERN CALIFORNIA
ROAD TRIPS
DRIVES ALONG THE BEACHES, MOUNTAINS, AND DESERTS WITH THE BEST STOPS ALONG THE WAY

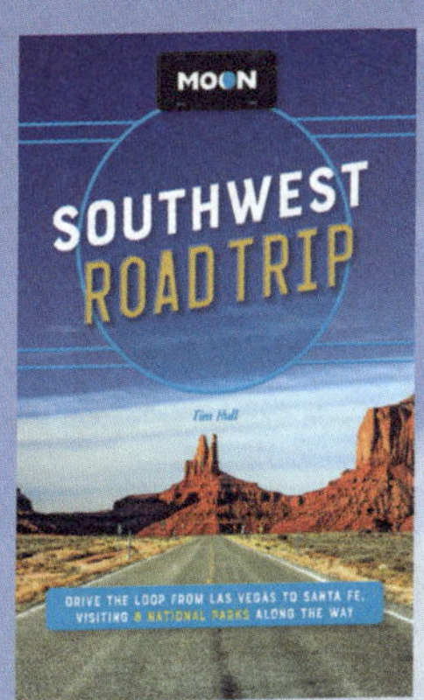
MOON
SOUTHWEST
ROAD TRIP
Tim Hull
DRIVE THE LOOP FROM LAS VEGAS TO SANTA FE, VISITING 8 NATIONAL PARKS ALONG THE WAY

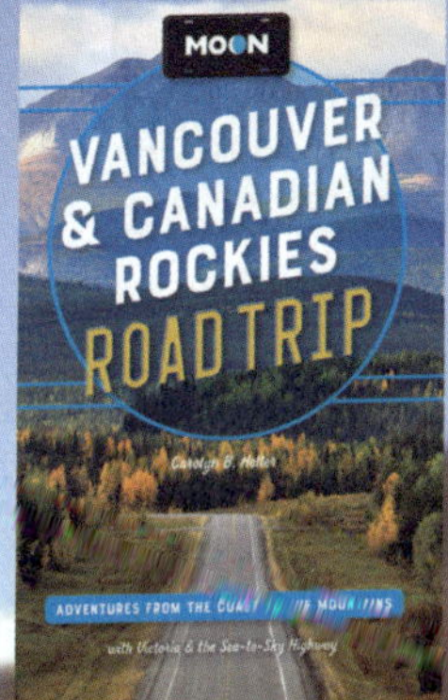
MOON
VANCOUVER & CANADIAN ROCKIES
ROAD TRIP

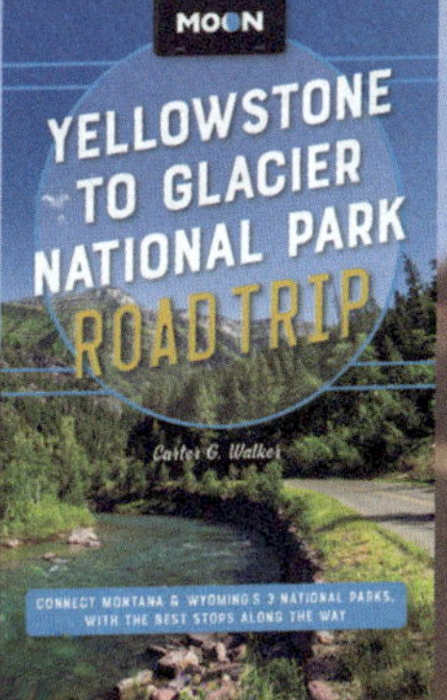
MOON
YELLOWSTONE TO GLACIER NATIONAL PARK
ROAD TRIP
Carter G. Walker
CONNECT MONTANA & WYOMING'S 3 NATIONAL PARKS, WITH THE BEST STOPS ALONG THE WAY

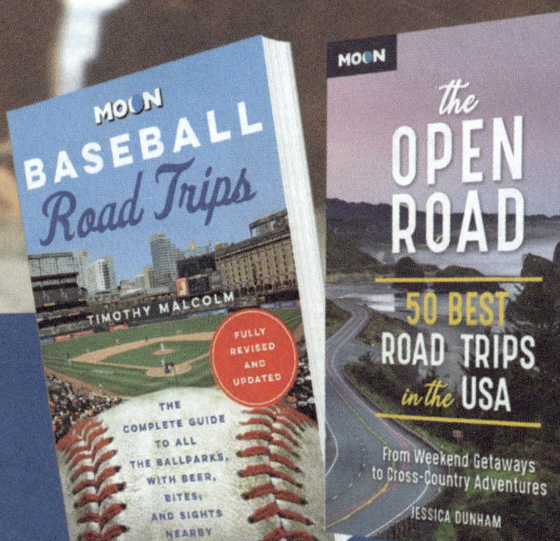
MOON
BASEBALL
Road Trips
TIMOTHY MALCOLM
FULLY REVISED AND UPDATED
THE COMPLETE GUIDE TO ALL THE BALLPARKS, WITH BEER, BITES, AND SIGHTS NEARBY
MOON
the OPEN ROAD
50 BEST ROAD TRIPS in the USA
From Weekend Getaways to Cross-Country Adventures
JESSICA DUNHAM

MOON
Road Trip USA
CROSS-COUNTRY ADVENTURES ON AMERICA'S TWO-LANE HIGHWAYS
Jamie Jensen

Latin America

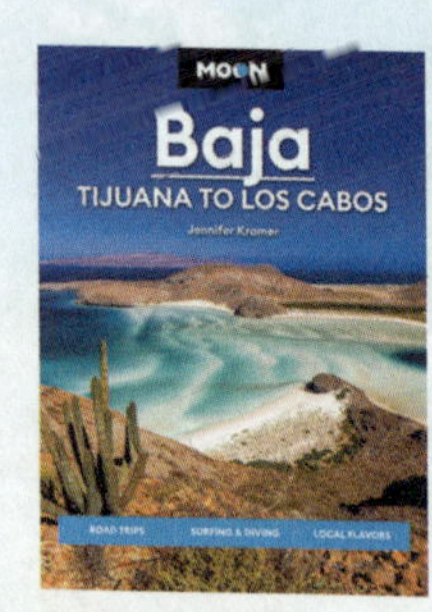

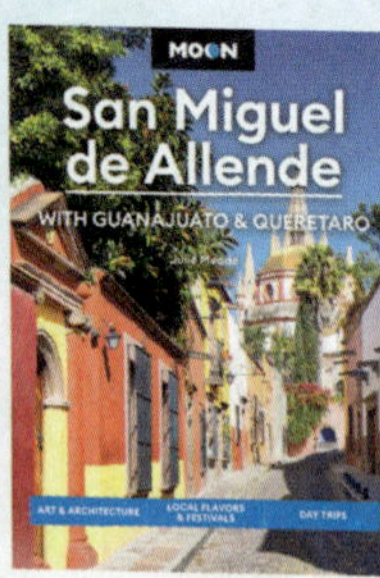

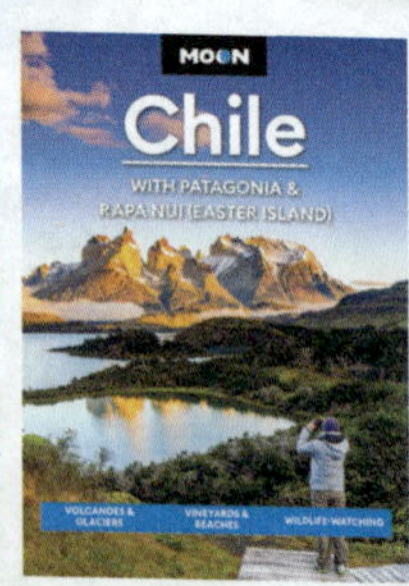

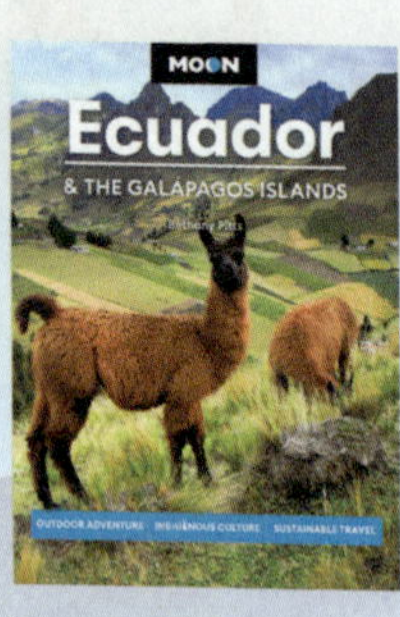

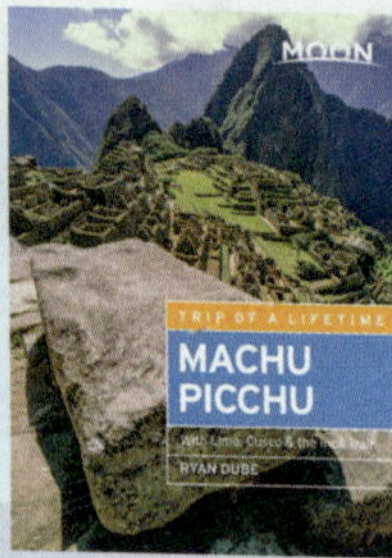

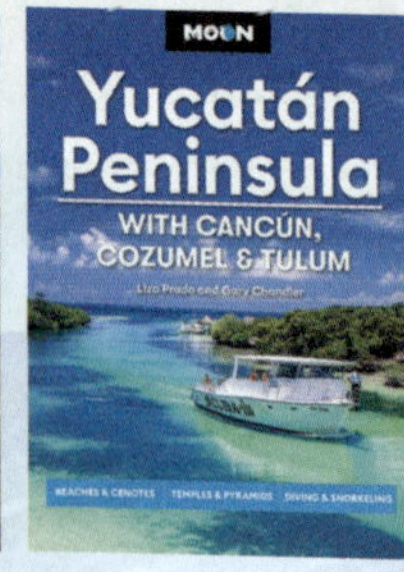

United States

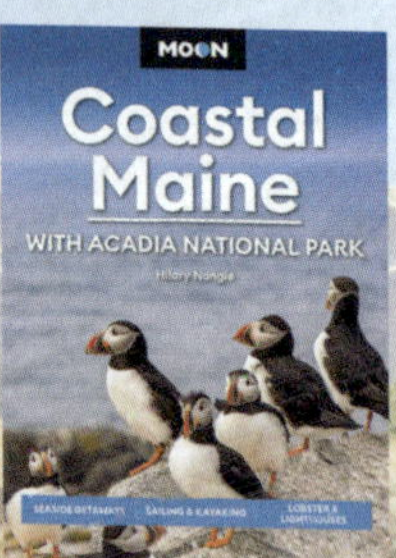

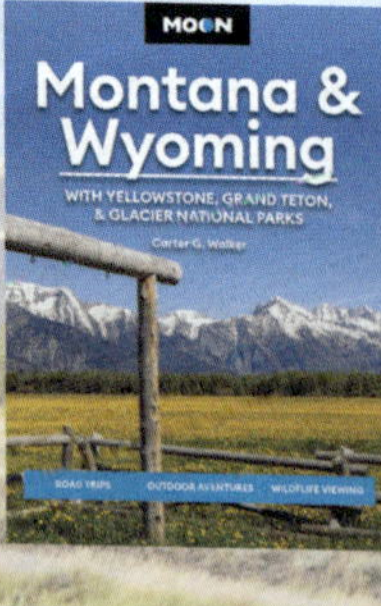

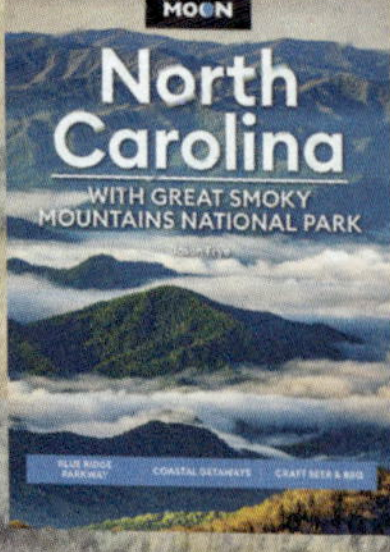

Cities

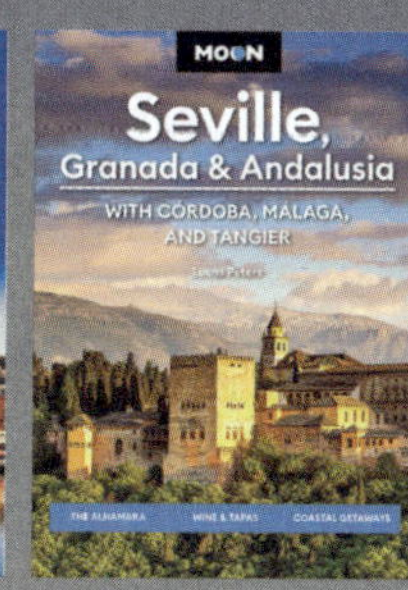

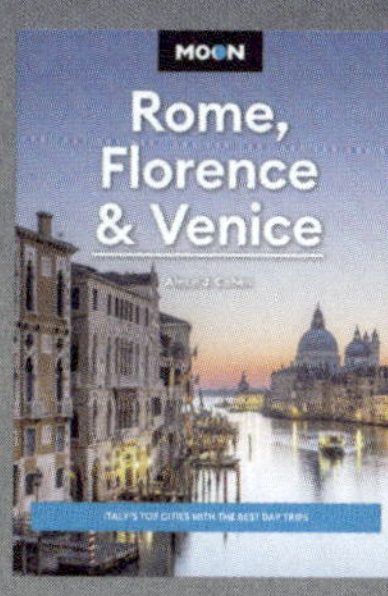

Europe, Middle East & Africa

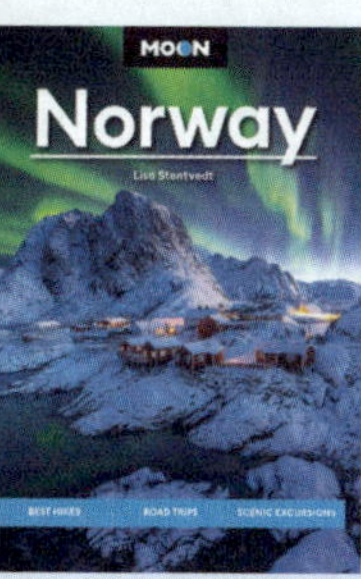

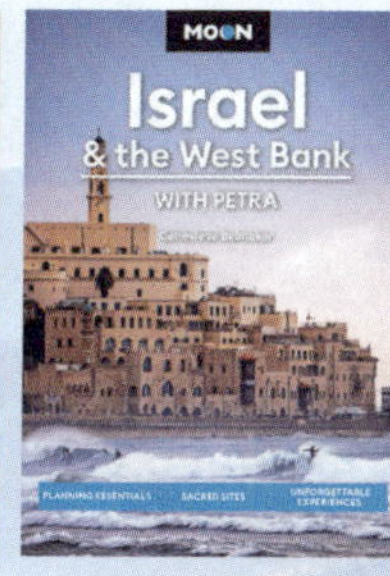

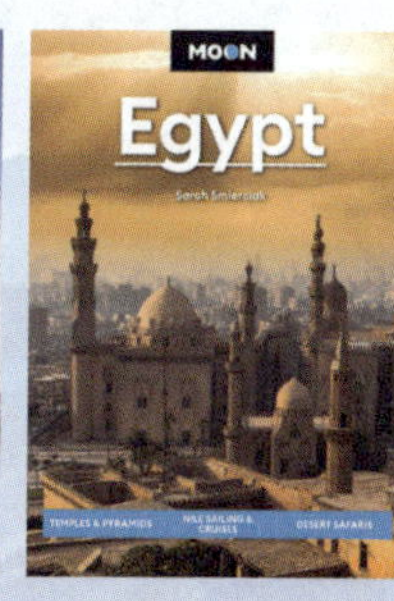

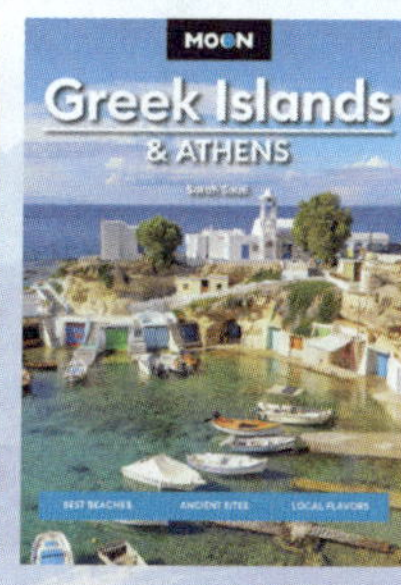

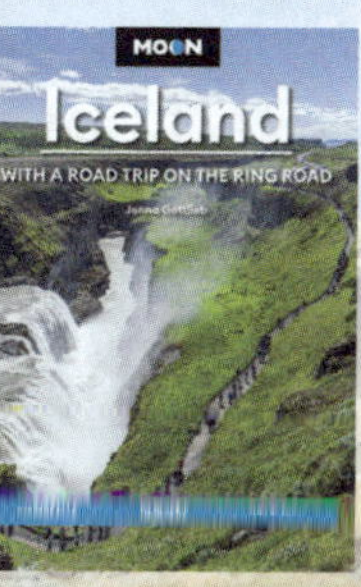

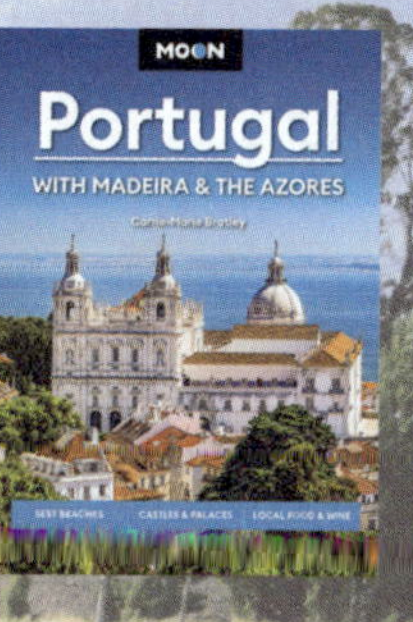

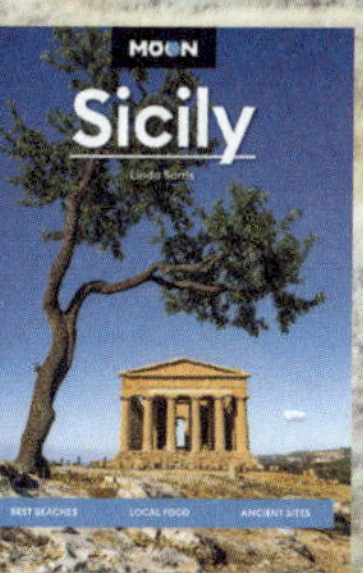

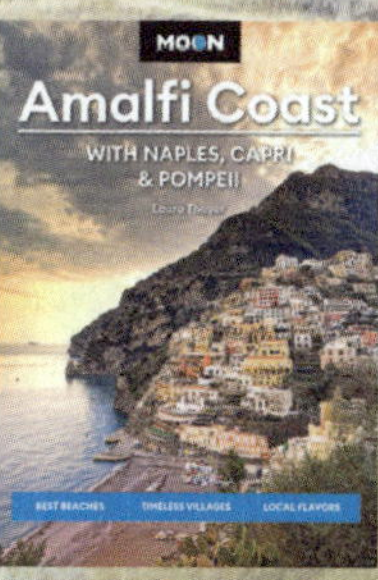

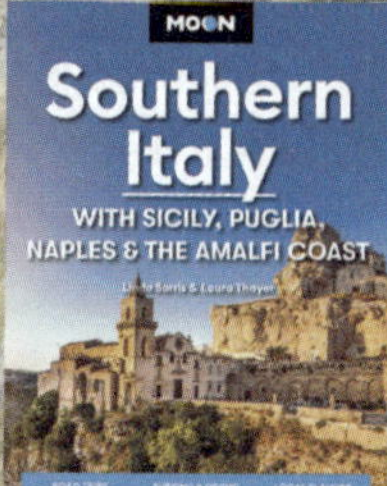

MAP SYMBOLS

	Expressway	○	City/Town		Information Center		Park
	Primary Road		State Capital		Parking Area		Golf Course
	Secondary Road		National Capital		Church		Unique Feature
	Unpaved Road		Highlight		Winery/Vineyard		Waterfall
	Trail		Point of Interest		Trailhead		Camping
	Ferry		Accommodation		Train Station		Mountain
	Railroad		Restaurant/Bar		Airport		Ski Area
	Pedestrian Walkway		Other Location		Airfield		Glacier
	Stairs						

CONVERSION TABLES

°C = (°F - 32) / 1.8
°F = (°C x 1.8) + 32
1 inch = 2.54 centimeters (cm)
1 foot = 0.304 meters (m)
1 yard = 0.914 meters
1 mile = 1.6093 kilometers (km)
1 km = 0.6214 miles
1 fathom = 1.8288 m
1 chain = 20.1168 m
1 furlong = 201.168 m
1 acre = 0.4047 hectares
1 sq km = 100 hectares
1 sq mile = 2.59 square km
1 ounce = 28.35 grams
1 pound = 0.4536 kilograms
1 short ton = 0.90718 metric ton
1 short ton = 2,000 pounds
1 long ton = 1.016 metric tons
1 long ton = 2,240 pounds
1 metric ton = 1,000 kilograms
1 quart = 0.94635 liters
1 US gallon = 3.7854 liters
1 Imperial gallon = 4.5459 liters
1 nautical mile = 1.852 km

MOON OAXACA

Avalon Travel
Hachette Book Group, Inc.
555 12th Street, Suite 1850
Oakland, CA 94607, USA
www.moon.com

Editor: Vy Tran
Managing Editor: Hannah Brezack
Copy Editor: Matthew Hoover
Graphics and Production Coordinator: Rue Flaherty
Cover Design: Toni Tajima
Interior Design: Avalon Travel
Map Editor: Karin Dahl
Cartographers: Erin Greb, Abby Whelan, John Culp, Brian Shotwell, Albert Angulo
Proofreader: Megan Anderluh

ISBN-13: 979-8-88647-124-3

Printing History
1st Edition — 2020
2nd Edition — August 2025
5 4 3 2 1

Front cover photo: Monte Albán, the Ancient City © Spacewalk / Getty Images
Back cover photo: Oaxacan handicrafts © William Perry | Dreamstime.com

Printed in China by RR Donnelley Dongguan